# SEXUALITY AND JEWISH LAW
IN SEARCH OF A BALANCED APPROACH IN TORAH
VOLUME ONE

## HALACHIC POSITIONS
WHAT JUDAISM REALLY SAYS
ABOUT PASSION IN THE MARITAL BED

AN OUTLINE, ANALYSIS AND CANDID DISCUSSION
YAAKOV SHAPIRO

EXPANDED EDITION

Copyright © 2015, 2016, 2017 by Jonathan Shapiro
All rights reserved

ISBN-13:
978-0692563236

ISBN-10:
0692563237

First Edition – November 24, 2015
Second Edition – January 7, 2016
Third Edition – January 22, 2017

SexualityandJewishLaw.com

Dedicated to our Creator,
Who fashioned husband and wife from the dust,
breathed into them of His own spirit,
and then commanded them to become one flesh
through the pleasure of sex

*Genesis 2:24; Sanhedrin 58b, Rashi: Shelo Cedarcah*

My Deepest Gratitude Goes To:

The Creator, for being 'my strength and the might of my hand'
– You know the intentions of my heart, and I ask Your
forgiveness for any inadvertent misrepresentations of Your will;

My wife, for her abundant patience
and unabashed support;

My children, who know not yet for what they have sacrificed
– you'll understand, and thank me, when you're older;

The rabbis who engaged me in serious discussion
and offered sage counsel;

My cover photographer, Meir Pliskin,
and cover designer, Sruli Leider,
for bringing the vision to life;

And all those who encouraged, and demanded,
the publication of this work.

The Talmudic sage, Rav Cahana, once hid under the bed of his master, Rav, and listened as he talked and laughed with his wife and performed his sexual needs.

Rav Cahana exclaimed: "Such talk? It sounds as if the master has never tasted sex in his life!"

Rav responded: "Cahana, get out of here! This is uncivilized!"

Rav Cahana answered back: "This, too, is part of Torah, and I need to learn it."

*Talmud, Tractates Brachos 62a, Hagigah 5b*

In all these matters [variety in sexual positions] it all follows the personal tastes of husband and wife.

And if a man has found a good wife who is of same mind with him in these matters, to him applies the verse in Proverbs (18:22): "He who has found a wife has found goodness, and has elicited favor from the Lord," and the verse in Ecclesiastes (9:7): "Go, eat your bread with joy and drink your wine with a merry heart, for G-d has already approved your deeds."

*Rabbi Yehudah the Pious, Sefer Chasidim 509*

# Preface to the Third Edition

The first edition of this book was released in November 2015, after eleven long years of research and writing. This third edition incorporates one additional year of study and discussion, before focus shall be turned to other important projects that beckon, including volume two of the *Sexuality and Jewish Law* series.

As noted in the original introduction, it was always in the plan to continue to refine and expand this work. Immediately after publishing the first edition, two revised editions were updated and made available in December 2015, followed by an official second edition in January 2016. All major revisions up to and including those in the second edition were made available to the public at SexualityandJewishLaw.com. This expanded, third edition includes additional elucidation and an index, both of which shall be made available for public reference at the said website as well. The original pagination has been maintained throughout all editions, so that the index is consistent with them all.

I would like to take this opportunity to recommend to readers two additional important Hebrew works that came to my attention over the past year, both by Orthodox rabbinic writers and both addressing the subject of marital harmony and sexual intimacy. They are *Es Lifrosh v'Es Le'ehov* by Rabbi Simcha Feuerman (Hadaf, 2016), and *Ladaat Le'ehov* by Rabbi Avraham Shmuel (second edition, 2015).

Most importantly, this past September the author of *Ladaat Le'ehov* brought to my attention two remarkable Hebrew halachic works about the laws of marital sexual intimacy, namely, *Simchat Habayit v'Birchato* by Rabbi Eliezer Melamed of Yeshivat Har Brachah in Israel (second edition, 2015), and *Harchavot l'Simchat Habayit v'Birchato*, written under Rabbi Melamed's guidance by a student of his, Rabbi Maor Kayam (2015). I believe these are quite literally the best practical halachic works out there on the subject that I am aware of to date, and it is my hope that they will soon be translated into English. Throughout this third edition, I've added references to corresponding discussions by Rabbi Melamed and Rabbi Kayam in these two works.* They are available for order in Israel on the

---

* One important correction brought to my attention by these two works relates to the identity of the medieval rabbinic authority referred to in *Shitah Mekubetzes, Nedarim 20b*, by the acronym, "Re'em." In previous editions, I mistakenly wrote that this referred to Rabbi Eliyahu Mizrachi (c.1455-c.1525). In the course of studying these two works, I was made aware that it refers to Rabbi Eliezer of Metz (12th century author of *Sefer Yeraim*).

Yeshivat Har Brachah website, and you can contact the online store manager, there, for overseas orders. In my humble opinion, both volumes are must haves for every Orthodox husband, wife and mature adult – in addition to the two Hebrew works I've already recommended to readers in previous editions of this book, namely, the anonymously authored online treatise, *Dvar Seser*, and Rabbi Yehuda Henkin's *Bnei Banim vol. 4*, responsa 16-17-18.**

It remains my sincere hope that this study will continue to contribute to a healthy reexploration of Torah sources, and to a positive – and immediate – reexamination of cultural norms, so that halachic individuals and couples may be granted "new eyes to see and new ears to hear" the realistic down-to-earth wisdom hidden between the lines of ancient sacred text, resulting in deeper understanding and acceptance of themselves, deeper vulnerability and bonding between spouses, and deeper appreciation of, and identification with, the Creator.

January 22, 2017
24 Tevet, 5777

---

** See below, pp. 210-212. I would also like to bring to readers' attention that in this edition correction has been made to an inadvertent misquote of Rabbi Henkin's discussion about the meaning of the term *"paam achas"* found in *Rabeinu Yeruchem, Nesiv 23*. The relevant correction has been made to endnotes 268 and 613, and the precise textual revision may be found at SexualityandJewishLaw.com.

# TABLE OF CONTENTS

## *Introduction*
Jews and Sex .................................................................................................. 1
Why I Wrote this Book .................................................................................. 2
Who this Book is For ..................................................................................... 5
A Note on Sources ........................................................................................ 10
Methodology and Format ........................................................................... 12
What this Book is and What it is Not ........................................................ 12
The Structure of Our Study ........................................................................ 15
Terminology – *Important!* ......................................................................... 16
Souls Lost in Translation ............................................................................. 18

## *Part One: First Impressions*
Shulchan Aruch, Orach Chaim 240, Laws of Modesty ........................... 22
Shulchan Aruch – Initial Analysis .............................................................. 26
Shulchan Aruch, Even Haezer 25, Laws of Marriage .............................. 28

## *Part Two: Deconstructing the Code*
Babylonian Talmud, Tractate Nedarim 20ab ........................................... 32
Nedarim 20ab – Summary .......................................................................... 39
Mesechtos Callah .......................................................................................... 40
    Tractate Callah ....................................................................................... 41
    Callah Rabti ............................................................................................ 44
Mesechtos Callah – Summary .................................................................... 50
Nedarim 20ab – Analysis ............................................................................ 52
Objections to Marital Sexual Exploration ................................................ 54
The Definition of "Sex-related Talk" ......................................................... 57
The Definition of "Overturning the Table" .............................................. 59
The Sages' Ruling: Anything a Couple Craves to do Together Sexually, They May Do .................................................................................................................. 62
The Sages' Reasoning .................................................................................. 66
Three Small Words Every Man and Woman Needs to Hear ................. 68

Babylonian Talmud, Tractate Hagigah 5b .................................................................. 69
Hagigah 5b – Summary .................................................................................................. 71
Hagigah 5b – Analysis ................................................................................................... 72
Sexy Talk, Vulgar Talk, Vain Talk ............................................................................... 73
Talk During Sex Analyzed ............................................................................................ 75

Babylonian Talmud, Tractate Sanhedrin 58b ............................................................. 84
Sanhedrin 58b – Summary ............................................................................................ 85
Sanhedrin 58b – Analysis .............................................................................................. 86

Babylonian Talmud, Tractate Yevamos 34b ............................................................... 89
Yevamos 34b – Summary and Analysis ...................................................................... 91

The Letter of the Law and its Spirit ............................................................................. 93
The Definition of "Sanctification" in Marital Sex .................................................... 93
The Spirit of Jewish Sex Summarized ....................................................................... 100
Permitted or Encouraged? .......................................................................................... 102
    Maimonides' *Commentary to the Mishnah* .......................................................... 103
    Maimonides' *Mishneh Torah* .................................................................................. 105
    Maimonides – Summary ......................................................................................... 106
"Good Sex" .................................................................................................................... 107
    Rabbi Yehudah Hachasid's *Sefer Chasidim 509* ................................................. 107

## Part Three: The Letter of the Law

And Now, the Letter of the Law ................................................................................. 110
Talk During Sex ............................................................................................................ 111
Gazing at the Female Genitals .................................................................................... 113
Cunnilingus ................................................................................................................... 114
Wife-on-Top ................................................................................................................... 115
Side-by-Side, Sitting, Standing, On the Floor .......................................................... 116
"Animal-style" ............................................................................................................... 117
Anal Sex .......................................................................................................................... 118
"Intercourse between limbs" (Outercourse and Fellatio) ....................................... 123

## Part Four: Halachah Mimics Kabbalah

So why wasn't I ever told all this? .................................................. 132
The Zohar .................................................................................. 134
Rabbi Yosef Caro ...................................................................... 135
    Rabbi Caro's Inspiration – Rabbi Yaakov ben Asher's *Tur* ............... 136
    Rabbi Caro's *Beis Yosef* – Legal Concerns .................................. 138
    Rabbi Caro's *Bedek Habayis* – Kabbalistic Concerns .................. 143
    Rabbi Caro's *Shulchan Aruch* ...................................................... 146
    Rabbi Caro's Bottom Line .............................................................. 148
    Halachah Mimics Kabbalah .......................................................... 150
The Safed School of Kabbalists
    Rabbi Yitzchak Luria – *Kisvei HaArizal* ....................................... 152
    Rabbi Eliyahu de Vidas – *Reishis Chochmah* ............................... 153
    Rabbi Elazar Azikri – *Sefer Charedim* ......................................... 157
    Rabbi Yeshayah Horowitz – *Shnei Luchos Habris* ....................... 159
"Torah is forgotten from the House of Israel" ................................ 161
Later Restrictive Codes
    Rabbi Avraham Danzig – *Chochmas Adam* ................................. 162
    Rabbi Shlomoh Ganzfried – *Kitzur Shulchan Aruch* .................... 162
    Rabbi Yisrael Meir Kagen – *Mishnah Berurah-Biur Halachah* ...... 162
    Rabbi Yaakov Chaim Sofer – *Kaf Hachaim* ................................. 163
Rabbi Moshe Isserles and Other Permissive Authorities ............... 164
    Misrepresentations of Rabbi Isserles ............................................ 166

## Part Five: Raavad III's Baalei HaNefesh

A Critical Look at Rabbi Caro's Source in *Shulchan Aruch*:
Raavad III's *Baalei HaNefesh, Shaar Hakedushah* ........................ 170
Raavad III's Interpretation of Nedarim 20ab .................................. 171
Non-sex-related talk and Hagigah 5b ............................................. 175
Gazing at the Female Genitals and Shamefacedness, Part One:
Equating Rabbi Shimon ben Lakish and Rabbi Yochanan ben Dahavai ...... 177
Gazing at the Female Genitals and Shamefacedness, Part Two:
Tractate Derech Eretz, Vayikra Rabah ........................................... 183

Mesechtos Derech Eretz, Perek Arayos 13 ............................................................. 184
Mesechtos Zeiros, Mesechta Arayos 21-22 ........................................................... 185
Vayikra Rabah 23:12-13 ........................................................................................... 186
Gazing at the Female Genitals and Shamefacedness, Part Three:
The Definition of "Shame" ....................................................................................... 187
Gazing at the Female Genitals and "Modesty" ..................................................... 189
Gazing at the Female Genitals and "Inciting the Evil Urge" ............................... 190
Kissing the Female Genitals and "Disgustingness" .............................................. 191
The Case Precedents of Rebbi and Rav ................................................................. 192
*Baalei HaNefesh, Shaar Hakedushah* – Letter or Spirit of the Law? ................. 193

## Part Six: Summary and Conclusion
The Sages ..................................................................................................................... 196
The Medieval Authorities ........................................................................................ 198
Rabbi Yosef Caro versus Rabbi Moshe Isserles .................................................... 199
The Post-Medieval Authorities ............................................................................... 199
Incomplete Presentations of Callah Rabti and/or Raavad III ............................. 202
Conclusion .................................................................................................................. 206

## Appendices
Vaginal Massage ........................................................................................................ 208
Jewish "Family Purity" and Marital Intimacy Guide Reviews ........................... 210
Sex Above the Covers ............................................................................................... 213
A Word about Rabbinic Fallibility .......................................................................... 222

Timeline of Rabbinic Authorities ........................................................................... 226
Endnotes ..................................................................................................................... 232
Glossary ...................................................................................................................... 443
Index ........................................................................................................................... 444
About the Author ...................................................................................................... 465

# Introduction

Jews and sex can appear to have a love-hate relationship.

Judaism generally gets better reviews than some other religions when it comes to sex, by virtue of the fact that it ascribes holiness to the act when performed lovingly between husband and wife, and because it obligates, rather than prohibits, its clergy to marry. This positive attitude is an extension of Judaism's overall view that this world and its pleasures are not intrinsically evil, but rather the physical is a neutral gift from G-d that can be used by man for curse or for blessing. That being said, delving into the actual rabbinic sources on the matter of Jewish marital intimacy, this seemingly positive approach can get obscure rather quickly.

On the one hand, there are authoritative sources that look approvingly upon sex as the opportunity for husband and wife to share complete vulnerability, to bare their whole selves to one another – psychologically, emotionally, spiritually, physically, erotically.[1] On the other hand, there are sources that see "G-dliness" in the conjugal act only if it is done for "noble" purposes, such as the wife's gratification or simple procreation. G-d forbid the husband should get carried away and enjoy it too much… G-d forbid things might get a little too…sexy.[2] And then there are those who display a combined approach, denigrating sexual indulgence philosophically, while acknowledging from a legal standpoint G-d's empathy and acceptance of human erotic nature as expressed within marriage.[3]

Such paradox is especially evident in rabbinic teaching in the area of sexual technique and positions within marriage, the main focus of this book. There are sources that can be understood to permit any sexual technique or position a couple might find curious or enjoyable, while other sources collectively predict physical or spiritual harm upon them, or their offspring, for anything more adventurous than "missionary style."

Since ancient times, then, Judaism has offered a wide range of approaches on the matter of sexual expression within marriage, reflecting a wide-range of interpretation and sensibility, and theoretically enabling each and every couple to tailor the law of this most intimate, private part of life to the unique physical and spiritual dimensions of their relationship.

But a study of the sources reveals a trend in the last few hundred years to downplay, or even deny, Torah's embrace of sexual exploration within marriage, generally revealing to the masses only its most puritanical approach – an approach that is today presented by many Ultra-Orthodox Chasidic-Charedi[1] rabbis in their

---

[1] The two titles, "Chasidic" (*those who are pious*) and "Charedi" (*those who tremble before the word of G-d*), are used in modern times to refer to the Ultra-Orthodox demographic within Jewish society. While this is not the place to explore their differences in history and etymology, for the purposes of our study the former refers specifically to those who ascribe to the spiritual teachings of the 18th century Chasidic movement, whereas the latter refers to wider groups that generally support the strictest interpretations and implementations of Jewish law and philosophy.

pre-marriage lessons and in their ritual "family purity"[II] or marital intimacy guides as the *only* Torah approach. The result is a widespread extremely pietistic, overly spiritualized attitude toward sex – and by sex, I mean marital sex – and a belief system that is not only false, but unhealthy.

## Why I Wrote this Book

When I attended Jewish "family purity" classes shortly before my own marriage, the sincere and well-meaning Chasidic teacher taught us a very one-sided ultra-pietistic approach to physical intimacy according to which anything other than husband-on-top/face-to-face/face above the "waist"[3] was forbidden and/or would result in the physical deformity of one's children.[III]

---

While the ancient texts and commentaries we shall be exploring are held sacred by the modern, or centrist, streams of Orthodoxy as well, such streams are already more open to acknowledging, and implementing, the liberal approaches within Jewish thought. For that reason, throughout this study we generally address the trends within Chasidi-Charedi literature and society specifically.

[II] The term "family purity" generally refers to Judaism's laws about abstinence from sex during the wife's menstrual cycle (see below, footnote to page 22). But many publications and classes dedicated to the subject discuss the laws of permitted marital sexual behaviors as well.

[III] Let it be noted from the outset that there will be certain elements of belief touched upon in this study that many in the Ultra-Orthodox community itself already – quietly – find questionable, even unhealthy. But healing will not come by covering up such beliefs from the outside world or pretending in one's own life they don't exist.

Healing in this respect requires identifying and clarifying confusing legal, philosophical and/or mystical notions about physical pleasure in general and sexual pleasure in particular, as well as related beliefs about reward, punishment and perfectionism. And enough is already known among non-Jewish circles, and has already been revealed in the media before the eyes of the entire world, about sexual difficulties in the Ultra-Orthodox community resulting from religious puritanism. The said community has thus already been cast into the spotlight.

Therefore now, its contributing role as a "light unto the nations" arguably includes leading the charge in reevaluating extreme beliefs in light of the new insight G-d reveals in each generation – as the Sanhedrin had power to do even in certain areas of Jewish law (see *Mishneh Torah, Sefer Shoftim, Memrim 2:1*, to be explored further in volume two of this series) – until G-d reveals His ultimate absolute truth to all in the Messianic Age. Indeed, judging by the direction of things, the eventual return of the Sanhedrin to Jewish life will not just be the realization of an ancient prophecy, but a simple necessity for achieving and sustaining a dynamic, balanced, holistic Judaism into the future. But the Ultra-Orthodox community need not, and arguably cannot afford to, wait until such a legal body is restored before it fundamentally reevaluates some of the extreme expressions found in its non-canonical literature with an eye toward providing greater psychological-emotional-physical-spiritual balance to its men, women and children.

And so I place this book before you, as one who has lived and breathed among you, as a contribution toward that healing.

# INTRODUCTION

Having done some rudimentary research of my own into the matter prior to the class, I asked our teacher to share with us one of the more permissive sources I already knew to exist.[4] But his response made it unclear if he were even aware of such a source. And when I pulled out the book and showed it to him, he pointed to the interpretation of one commentary[5] that minimizes that source's leniency – an interpretation considered erroneous by other equally weighty authorities (authorities which, perhaps, our teacher was unaware of at the time).[6]

Subsequently, in discussion with friends, I discovered that they, too, or their spouses, had been taught by their Chasidic pre-marriage mentors a similarly puritanical, and threatening, approach to sexual exploration within marriage, and that many, if not most, available Chasidic-Charedi "family purity" and marital intimacy guides do the same. Not only do the vast majority of these publications denigrate or forbid most sexual positions and techniques, they put forward the claim that most vile is the act of "wasting seed in vain" – which they interpret to mean ejaculation of the husband's seed anywhere outside the wife's vagina.[IV]

In broaching the topic with others, I also began to hear painful stories of marital discord resulting from one or both spouses' misinformation in this very sensitive area of domestic life, in at least one case exacerbated by an embarrassment to approach pious rabbinical authorities for further clarification.

And yet a healthy, balanced approach was right there, bouncing off the pages of Jewish law!

As for the few I met who had not only been taught a stringent approach, but a more "liberal" one as well, it was clear that even they had not actually been given the whole picture of what is permitted, nor had they been given to understand the underlying sources and reasoning behind the two approaches of "letter" versus

---

[IV] For a preliminary exploration into the subject of "wasting seed in vain" according to Jewish law, see *Encyclopedia Talmudis vol. 11, entry: Hashchatas Zera; Otzar HaPoskim Even Haezer 23* (volume 9 in the *Otzar HaPoskim* series); Rabbi Schneur Zalman of Lublin, *Shaalos uTeshuvos Toras Chesed*, vol. 2, Responsum 43; *Jewish Law and The New Reproductive Technologies* by Rabbi Dr. Emanuel Feldman and Rabbi Dr. Joel B. Wolowelsky (Ktav 1997), pp. 120-123 and endnotes thereon.

An in-depth analysis of the subject will be covered in volume two of this series. Of particular importance will be a serious reexploration of the heretofore rabbinical approach to masturbation - a matter that has historically caused, and continues to cause, untold sexual anxiety in Orthodox boys and men. In the meantime, see below, pp. 91-92, 118-122, 123-129, 132-168 (and footnotes to pages 134 and 144), 190, and endnotes 335, 343, 518, 524, 553, 563-565, 567, 569, 591-593, 594, 633, 718, 818.

And see the professional essay of Orthodox sex therapist Talli Rosenbaum, explaining how male masturbation anxiety, or, if we may, "wasting seed in vain anxiety," profoundly affects the sex lives of wives as well – available online at *http://tallirosenbaum.com/en/node/201*.

Volume two of our series will also explore rabbinic statements in regard to female masturbation.

"spirit" of the law.ᵛ This information is paramount for husbands and wives to learn not only what is "technically permitted" by G-d according to Torah, but also

---

ᵛ In fact, based on discussions with others, and as we shall see from the results of our analysis below, it appears that many pre-marriage classes and many "family purity" and marital intimacy guides are (knowingly or unknowingly) teaching the spirit or stringency of Jewish sex as baseline law, and its baseline law (if they teach it at all) as if it were leniency.

Some have said to me that in Chasidic-Charedi circles the pious spirit of the law is always strived for, so such classes and publications are justified in this approach even where it is intentional. But to borrow the teaching of *Ethics of our Fathers 2:5*: "Ignorance does not lead to piety" (*ein am haaretz chasid*).

Firstly, the ultimate purpose of the spirit of the law is that one should *choose* to follow it as a voluntary choice as part of one's individual spiritual maturing process. The value of having the spirit of the law forced upon an adult, without he or she even knowing it is spirit, is debatable.

Secondly, when people are not informed about the baseline law of Jewish marital sex, or when they are taught its spirit or stringency as if they were baseline law, this itself can lead people to question the wisdom of Torah – the wisdom of G-d – as being out of touch with the reality of human nature. This, as a matter of consequence, can breed doubt about Torah – and G-d – and thoughts and feelings and actions of rebellion in the bedroom. And when one cannot reconcile G-d in the bedroom, it is only a matter of time before one begins to push Him out of other areas of life as well. Thus, ignorance of the actual distinction between law versus spirit, or baseline law versus stringency, can not only keep people far from piety, it can ultimately distance them from the law itself (and see endnote 10).

[This is also the response to those who have said to me that "crass" people will do what they want anyway, they don't need such a book, so we should not spoil the innocent minds of those who want to do "the right thing" by revealing such information. But what right do we have to sacrifice the souls of the "crass," especially when they are no more than normal human beings among us? And why are we infantilizing the "innocent" – or continuing to pretend they are so innocent in the first place?

A related school of thought that has been argued to me goes like this: It is best to first give young couples as little information as possible about what is permitted in the marital bed, and when they later have "issues" in the bedroom they will go back to their rabbi or teacher and the rabbi or teacher will then permit for them more. The cruelty of such an approach needs no elaboration. And it is simply not acceptable in my book to wait until couples come crawling back to their rabbis or teachers in shame, anxiety and dysfunction before considering them worthy of receiving the "secret" of what G-d actually permitted them all along. Supporters of the said approach are also assuming couples will actually have the courage to come back to their pious rabbis or teachers with such questions. It is equally likely that they will simply begin to ignore (read: rebel against) what they were taught was law rather than suffer such embarrassment. And if they find out from other sources that there was more that was permitted them than these rabbis or teachers originally taught, why would they continue to trust these rabbis or teachers at all, about anything?]

Thirdly, the question of spirit or stringency in the area of sex is not equivalent to the question of spirit or stringency in other areas of Jewish life, such as Sabbath observance or kosher dietary laws (to name just two). In the case of sex, what one teaches people about what is allowed or not allowed (or "disgusting") in the eyes of G-d is not just a technical matter of "dos and don'ts," it has profound ramifications in how they will perceive themselves psychologically, emotionally, physically and spiritually.

compassion, understanding and acceptance of each other's differing needs when it comes to sex, as well as to approach the wider concept of physical intimacy in a more natural balanced manner, counteracting the messages in certain literature or by certain teachers that over-think and over-spiritualize it.

And so I continued to research deeper into the subject, sharing my findings with grateful friends, who insisted I share it with the wider public.

## Who this Book is For

Now let it be stated clearly from the outset that this research is about Jewish sexual law **within marriage**. Any application of its findings to any other form of relationship is solely the reader's interpretation and responsibility, and is inconsistent with the intention of this book.

That being said, the Jewish spiritual leadership in every generation is expected – nay, obligated – to address the unique needs of its time.[7]

Childish naiveté in matters of sex in general, and stringency in marital sex in particular, may have helped keep people of past centuries "in line" or "closer to G-d." But in present – and dare I say, future – generations, with sexual awareness at unprecedented heights, continuing to perpetuate such naiveté and impose such stringency can have the exact opposite effect.

With all the sexual awareness the world lays at their bedroom doorstep, a Jewish couple needs to know now more than ever that G-d understands, accepts and loves them even with their expanded sexual consciousness and curiosities. To give them any impression otherwise is to further stoke the flames of inner turmoil that are the challenge of many a 21st century Jew.

And even for curious teenagers who seek to understand Torah's views on marital sex earlier on, the strictest opinions are generally the only ones they will find their way to, they being the most widely circulated. These young adults are thus given the impression that a variety of natural sexual curiosities puberty arouses within them are, from the standpoint of Judaism, abnormal and sinful –

---

Finally, I have had some people say to me that their teachers did in fact teach them that "everything" is permitted between husband and wife in the marital bed. But even those who teach that all is permitted are not necessarily making clear that all is also medically safe and will not physically or spiritually harm the couple or their children. And what I have found is that when I proceed to ask such people to explain what "everything is permitted" means, they will then qualify it by saying that they were in fact taught that there are exceptions, such as oral sex or extra-vaginal ejaculation. Or they do not really know upon what halachic grounds such a statement is based. Therefore, I do not believe such will be convincing to one who is learned and who knows the many sources that contradict it. To the learned student such an approach will most likely appear to be nothing more than a teacher's inability to reconcile the actual sources with human nature and/or the condition of modern sexual awareness – in other words, a desperate attempt to curb adultery. It is therefore especially for such learned students that our present study will be of value.

even if controlled, locked away and saved for future exploration within marriage. Just as these young men and women's hormones are beginning to rage, they are left to grapple developing a meaningful adult relationship with a G-d who – as it appears from the Torah sources available to them – does not seem to understand the natural human sex drive He Himself fashioned.[8]

The conscientious, intelligent reader must therefore recognize that as "unholy" influences grow greater, more attractive, and more accessible in the outside world, reclaiming sexual exploration within marriage as something holy[9] may just prove a key factor in preserving Judaism into the next generation – and beyond.[10] Thus, I believe it is high time this material be made available to the public[11] – to enable married couples who respect and take Torah seriously to choose for themselves between basic law and strictest piety as appropriate to the unique spiritual and physical dimensions of their relationship, and to provide adolescents and single adults a more balanced, healthy view – according to Torah, G-d's view – of their individual sexuality.

Of course, I do not claim to be the first to "discover" all or any of the sources that follow, nor will I be the first to argue the critical need for shifting the Chasidic-Charedi world's sexual consciousness back to such sources in order to restore balance of mind, body and spirit. My utmost respect and admiration goes to those rabbis, teachers and mental health professionals who have already blazed such trails in their personal spheres of influence. But if there is a book that provides this critical information to the wider public,[12] and in English, I have yet to find it. And so I offer this work as a personal contribution.[VI]

I also cannot testify to having encountered and analyzed all the Torah sources out there on this very deep and sensitive subject, nor to having avoided all human error. As anyone who has ever studied Torah (or any other wisdom) knows, you can never really claim to know it all, and certainly not perfectly. I therefore beg my readers to bring to my attention any errors or omissions in source or logic they may find, which I shall consider for correction in future editions – and which, in

---

[VI] The basic findings of this study were delivered as a video lecture on January 25, 2015, entitled, *Halachic Positions Your Rabbi Never Told You: What Judaism Really Says about Passion in the Marital Bed*, and posted online to Youtube.com on February 20, 2015.

## INTRODUCTION

the meantime, I shall post online at SexualityandJewishLaw.com. I thus encourage my readers to periodically check this website for updates.[VII]

Finally, I cannot predict where the implications of this research and analysis will ultimately lead, either in the short or long term. I can only trust truth to lead us where it will – trusting also that truth is the ultimate concern and goal of my readers. But the halachic positions[VIII] you will find on the following pages stand upon sufficiently firm and holy ground to warrant the Ultra-Orthodox Chasidic-Charedi Jewish world's attention.

And if there be some modest, pious individuals out there, men or women, who do not openly approve of this information being made available to the public, I do hope they will be responsible enough, and scrupulous enough, to actually read the book in its entirety before passing judgment on its content, and that even they will be thankful in their heart of hearts... and perhaps even in the bedroom.

---

[VII] It has been said to me that were I to publish this study without rabbinical approbation, or were I to make even a single important unintentional omission in presentation or error in analysis, it would be rendered worthless in the eyes of the Chasidic-Charedi community. Perhaps. But I trust that the same community will then begin to apply the same standard of criticism to many, if not most, of the other works already out there on the subject, some authored by well-known rabbinic authorities and/or bearing eminent rabbinical endorsement, that feature important human errors or omissions which have most certainly led couples to implement unnecessary strictures in marital sexual life, and which have thereby engendered painful confusion, anxiety and marital discord. For in such a delicate matter as marital sex, erring on the side of stringency is just as damaging as erring on the side of leniency – if not more so. And see below, *Appendices: Jewish "Family Purity" and Marital Intimacy Guide Reviews.*

[VIII] Deriving from the Hebrew "*halachah*" – Jewish law.

I never wished to elaborate on such matters [of physical intimacy] at length, and it would have been better not to write about them at all. But because there are those who are mistakenly lenient or stringent, the result of which, G-d forbid, is the lack of [marital] peace and love that are so necessary, I said to myself: It is Torah, and I am required to write about it.

*Rabbi Moshe Feinstein*
*Igros Moshe, Even Haezer 4, Responsum 66*

Who am I to decide [between Torah giants of past generations]…

But if for the sake of establishing peace between husband and wife, G-d allows His own holy Name to be erased, certainly, then, the honor of earlier Torah giants – despite the fact that they were our great masters and world geniuses – cannot hold me back from writing that which appears correct in my own humble opinion according to practical Jewish law.

And may G-d protect us from erring in determining His will.

*Rabbi Moshe Feinstein*
*Igros Moshe, Even Haezer 1, Responsum 63, Paragraph 1*

# A Note on Sources

A study of this particular area of Jewish law forces us to face the fact that the original Talmudic sources themselves are to some degree limited in their ability to shed total light on the matter. Certain questions shall be raised in the course of our discussion that we shall not yet succeed in clarifying entirely.[13] And there is the issue of variant texts or traditions, whereby different ancient sources provide divergent versions or interpretations of the same teachings. In our case, at least one fundamental teaching has two mutually exclusive versions.[14]

Add to this the fact that the Talmud itself was never intended as a complete historical record of every conversation ever had by the prophets or sages on Jewish law. In other words: the Talmud does not contain, nor does it claim to contain, every single legal-moral discussion of every prophet or sage from Sinai until its time, a period spanning eighteen hundred years.[15] Rather, the goal of the Talmud's compilers-editors appears to have been to collect, record, analyze, authenticate, clarify, refine, distill, reconstruct and/or further apply the portion of the Oral Torah corpus that had been passed down, or survived, to their day. This they had received orally or in the form of rabbinic discussions, rulings and life-anecdotes that had been recorded in long or short hand and stored in (official and perhaps unofficial[16]) archives across the Jewish world. But the vast majority of detailed legal-moral discussions of the prophets and sages, especially the private ones between master and disciple, were for whatever reason[17] never recorded, never passed down to us, or lost.

In addition, the definitive identities of the Talmud's compilers-editors[IX] (including, and especially, that anonymous voice running through the Talmud like a commentary, which at times offers what can appear to be conjectural, even counter-intuitive, reconciliations for contradictory traditions that force them to fit together[18]) and the exact time period(s) when the text of the Talmud as we have it was written down, and by whom, remain matters of some debate.[19] [20]

But even accepting that the Talmud, in conjunction with other early rabbinic writings, preserves a comprehensive enough archive of records to construct, or reconstruct, a valid representation of G-d's will for humanity, and even if one takes it as a given that its compilers-editors were unimpeachable Torah scholars, guided in their work by divine inspiration, it is arguable that the more

---

[IX] The title "compilers-editors of the Talmud" which we use throughout our study is not meant to identify any one specific rabbi or group of rabbis nor to describe the manner of the Talmud's multi-generational, multi-layered construction. It is merely a way of referring to those who collectively contributed toward the formation and refinement of the Talmudic text as we have it today – whoever they might have been and however they might have done it.

The Talmud's history remains a matter of some mystery. Commonly taught rabbinic tradition places its compilation and/or editing in the 4th-5th centuries. And see the sources referenced in endnote 19.

information they would have passed on to us, the more clarity they would have passed on to us as well.[21]

In investigating our topic – G-d's attitude on marital sex technique and positions as understood by the ancient sages, custodians of His Oral Law – there are in essence only a handful of passages across the "sea of Talmud" that form the basis of organized Jewish teaching in this regard. These few passages, which include tersely, even cryptically, reported statements and anecdotes from hundreds of years before the Talmud as we know it was complete, are dissected, analyzed and interpreted – and in some cases not only based upon what they say, but also upon what they don't say.[22]

More importantly, we can be certain that over the course of the eighteen hundred years between Sinai and the Talmud, each prophet and sage in every generation held dozens, if not hundreds, if not thousands of discussions on the topic of marital intimacy with their followers and disciples who turned to them for personal and religious guidance (remember, according to rabbinic tradition no in-depth written manuals of Jewish Oral Law were permitted to be circulated to the public throughout this nearly two thousand year period). If there had been recordings of even a handful more of such discussions, the impact upon Jewish sexual attitude – historically and today – would have been extreme.

All that being said, our purpose in this work is not to investigate or debate the historical accuracy, comprehensiveness, or logical veracity of the Talmud,[23] but merely to reconstruct, based upon what Talmudic-era teachings have survived and reached us, a more original and genuine rabbinical approach to sex that was forced underground by later forces – a balanced approach that is surprisingly liberal, and liberating, on both a human and spiritual level.

## Methodology and Format

In this study, we assume a reverential approach to the classical Jewish commentaries on the Bible and Talmud. Nevertheless, we will not shy away from raising difficulties in their statements, nor from suggesting daring, perhaps revolutionary, re-interpretations of established assumptions, taking the stance that where people's psychological-emotional-physical-spiritual lives are at stake, no authority is beyond question and no reasonably-argued solution is too daring.

## What this Book is and What it is Not

But first a brief clarification of what this book is not:

This is not an advice book on marital harmony or how sex can be used to improve one's marriage.[24] It is a technical (at times, hyper-technical) presentation and clarification of Jewish sexual law, focusing on what precise practices are permitted in the marital bed. For those seeking deeper insight into sex as a fundamental part of a strong, loving marriage, or candid discussion about sexuality in the modern age in general, they might find what they are looking for in one book by Rabbi Shmuel Boteach, *Kosher Sex*,[25] and in the chapter on sex in Rabbi Adin Steinsaltz's *Simple Words*. For those seeking practical guidance on sex and sex-related matters from sources cognizant of Orthodox sensitivities, I would turn their attention to *The Newlywed's Guide to Physical Intimacy* (*Es Le'ehov*) by Jennie Rosenfeld, PhD and Rabbi David S. Ribner, DSW, and *Getting Closer: Understanding and Treating Issues in Marital Intimacy*, by Rabbi Daniel Schonbuch, MA. There are also many informative articles by Orthodox sex therapist Talli Rosenbaum available online at tallirosenbaum.com.

This book is not an attempt to whitewash, or apologetically justify, what are at times blunt, less-than-politically-correct manners of expression in regard to sex and the sexes found in rabbinic writing, nor to project 20th-21st century romantic and/or liberal notions onto the Talmudic or medieval scholars of old. In particular, it is abundantly clear from certain (though not all) such sources that while they acknowledged man's and woman's erotic inclinations, and they, of course, preferred there be passion between husband and wife during physical intimacy, and they demanded respect for individual sensitivities in the bedroom, these were not of ultimate "pietistic" concern to them. Higher priority in their minds from a pietistic perspective, as demonstrated by the infinitely more space and ink they devoted to the subject, were the couple's "purity" of thought, speech and action during sex in order to bear "unblemished children" and to deliver to G-d an "unblemished *mitzvah*" – even, according to some, if such piety meant rushing through, and thus sapping the joy and/or pleasure out of,[26] the conjugal act.

This book also does not comprehensively explore the evolution of Judaism's philosophical and psychological attitudes toward sex, though in the course of understanding its legal evolution on sexual positions and technique in particular

# INTRODUCTION

some fundamental aspects of its philosophical/psychological evolution will come to light as well.[x]

Nor does this book address every aspect of the "who, what, how, when, where and why" of Jewish sex. The main body of this volume addresses only the "what," and to some degree, the "how" – that is, the technical sexual behaviors permitted by Jewish law for husband and wife within marriage. The "who, when, where, and why" will be more fully explored in future volumes of this series.

So what, then, is this book?

Simply put: It is a reclamation of Torah's – G-d's – humane, realistic, sexy approach to marital sex.

In this spirit, the purpose of our study is to unmask and clarify the positive, permissive views on marital sexual practice within the Talmud itself and in its medieval and post-medieval commentaries, while readers seeking only pietistic guidelines can turn to any of the many "family purity" and/or marital intimacy guides already available in Jewish bookstores that focus on strictures.

In writing this book, enormous challenges arose regarding the method and style of presentation and the scaling and organization of content in order to achieve a result that would be clear and comprehensive, user-friendly to the novice and compelling to the scholar. In many ways it is written in the form of a Talmudic discourse, and as anyone familiar with Talmudic discourse knows, it is an exercise in establishing order in chaos: there is much cross-referencing and cross-fertilization between texts and topics, even those that at first glance appear unrelated; there is much analysis of divergent opinion, besides for multiple commentaries and translations of each text in and of itself; and one logical conclusion leads to another question, and one source leads to another, and another, and another…

For all these reasons, there is extensive cross-referencing[xi] and additional analysis in the endnotes for those interested in delving deeper into many of the key concepts touched upon in the book and some of their wider ramifications in Jewish law and belief, while the body of the book itself is kept as easy and focused a read as possible. We have strived for a swift, vibrant presentation and analysis of the sources – even where it meant resorting to bullet points or numbered lists – providing a clear story line, and bottom line, as well as a wealth of source-references for the interested reader to explore further. This, in fact, is one of the main goals of the book: to enable the reader to discover and understand the sources more thoroughly than the already available Jewish "family purity" and

---

[x] In endnote 595 we shall raise a sensitive, yet necessary, discussion about extreme attitudes about sexuality found in some Chasidic texts that we believe require serious and immediate rabbinical/professional attention and reevaluation.

[xi] In the 1st and 2nd editions of the book, the cross-referencing also served in lieu of Index.

marital intimacy guides allow, resulting in educated dialogue and confident personal decision making.[XII]

That being said, I strongly encourage the reader who is intent on penetrating the topic to its depths to read this book twice – once without any endnotes at all, to gain a broad perspective of the core sources and viewpoints, and then a second time with the endnotes, for an infinitely wider world of analysis.

[Another reason for suggesting this order: due to the challenges of organization described above, the endnote analyses are not always in complete chronological syncronization with the body of the book, and issues or opinions discussed later in the book will sometimes appear earlier in the endnotes. While I've attempted to minimize such instances, I must beg my readers' pardon that they were not avoidable entirely – though where they weren't we attempt to reference where to turn for immediate clarification.]

Admittedly, the finished product is not for casual reading, and is perhaps best geared for the Talmudic-trained reader who is familiar with Talmudic terms, methods, personalities and commentaries. And while clarity of the sources and their practical implications has been our paramount goal, in one or two (or three) places hair-splitting technical analysis simply could not be avoided.

Nevertheless, the study will provide any reader unprecedented entry into the fascinating world of Jewish sexual law. And it will offer deeper insight into the beliefs a halachic Jew must come to terms with in order to achieve psychological-emotional-physical-spiritual-sexual balance.

As stated, the work is far from done.

Additional volumes will address wider topics. Translation into other languages is in the plan. And an online resource, SexualityandJewishLaw.com, is already in the works.

In the meantime, to share a question, source, personal testimonial or correction, please contact us at: SexualityandJewishLaw@gmail.com.

We look forward to hearing from you!

---

[XII] While the hard sources we shall encounter speak for themselves, where we have utilized logic to suggest new interpretations, or to question pre-existing ones, I encourage readers to explore further to come to their own conclusions and then to confer with a halachically-competent rabbi. And even in regard to the hard sources, rabbinical guidance is advised.

[For a discussion on whether areas of Jewish law that were eventually categorized as matters of "*Orach Chaim*" ever required rabbinical ordination in order to rule upon them, and whether areas that were eventually categorized as matters of "*Even Haezer*" still do, see Rabbi Moshe Walter's *The Making of a Halachic Decision* (Menucha Publishers, 2013), Chapter 9, pp. 115-116.

See also Rabbi Yehudah Loew's *Nesivos Olam, Nesiv HaTorah*, Chapter 15 – below, p. 204.]

INTRODUCTION

## The Structure of Our Study

We shall begin our study with a basic understanding of what the average Chasidic-Charedi adolescent has traditionally been exposed to on the topic of sex within marriage in the post-medieval *Code of Jewish Law, Shulchan Aruch, Orach Chaim 240* of Rabbi Yosef Caro (16th century Safed, Israel).

I have not chosen this work because it offers a comprehensive, balanced presentation of Jewish legal-spiritual teaching and awareness on sex – as we shall see, its presentation is, in fact, quite one-sided. Rather, as stated, I've chosen it because it is what the average Chasidic-Charedi Jew has traditionally first been exposed to when it comes to Jewish sex law, providing them their "first impression" about G-d's own attitude toward sexuality. This is due to the universal authority and central place in Torah learning over the past few centuries of Rabbi Caro's *Code*, and because Rabbi Shlomoh Ganzfried's popular *Concise Code of Jewish Law* (*Kitzur Shulchan Aruch*), the halachic work many Chasidic-Charedi youth study in yeshivah as they enter into the age of puberty, quotes Rabbi Caro's rulings in this regard practically verbatim. Another popular legal work studied by Chasidic-Charedi youth, Rabbi Yisrael Meir Kagan's *Mishnah Berurah-Biur Halachah*, also seems to entirely endorse Rabbi Caro's rulings in *Shulchan Aruch* in this regard.

Once the reader has gained this frame of reference, this "first impression," we will trace Rabbi Caro's rulings back to their roots in the ancient Talmudic sources and medieval commentators and watch as a dramatically more varied picture of Jewish marital sex law emerges. In tracing these sources, we will explore four key texts of the *Babylonian Talmud*[XIII] – *Nedarim 20ab, Hagigah 5b, Sanhedrin 58b,* and *Yevamos 34b* – along with two pseudo-Talmudic texts – *Tractate Callah* and *Callah Rabti* – which together form the general basis for modern-day halachic Judaism's opinion on acceptable sexual practices in the marital bed. Each text will be accompanied by a summary and analysis of its key points.

After these original sources are clear, we will explore the views of various Jewish legal authorities down through the ages, first listing those who allow specific sexual techniques/positions within marriage, and then understanding from a historical/analytical perspective how the pietistic Chasidic-Charedi approach ever came to be in the first place.

The work will conclude with some supplementary essays in the *Appendices*.

---

[XIII] Wherever we refer to "the Talmud," we are referring to the *Babylonian Talmud*. Wherever we mean to reference the *Jerusalem Talmud*, we shall specify it.

## Terminology

*Now this is important, so please pay attention!*

The reader will find that the wording in this study is of an explicit – though never provocative – nature. When it comes to Jewish law one must speak clearly and unambiguously, even if the subject matter or terminology appear "unclean."[27]

As we shall see, much of the divergence of opinion in the realm of Jewish marital sex law, even among the medieval halachic authorities, was a direct result of the Talmud's own use of "clean" euphemistic language[28] – which may have been commonly understood in its day, but whose exact meaning became lost over time, resulting in extremely serious matters of halachic debate through the ages and until today (and undoubtedly contributing to sexual repressions, anxieties, marital strains, infidelities, etcetera). I have therefore chosen to use clear, clinical, but what some Chasidic-Charedi readers may consider "crude," modern terminology to refer to all things sexual (and such terms shall be repeated as often as necessary, even within single pages, paragraphs or sentences, so that absolute clarity to the reader shall be maintained).

Thus, for example, in translating the halachic sources, I intentionally avoid the use of vague, pristine renditions, such as "marital relations" or "unnatural intercourse," instead using the English terms that express exactly what they are referring to – in this case, "sex" and "anal sex" respectively.

And while we're on the topic of anal sex...

In Jewish law and ethics, face-to-face vaginal intercourse with the husband on top – the "missionary position" – is generally considered to be the most preferred method of sexual intimacy between husband and wife.[29] But in discussing what other positions may or may not be permitted, the most opposite extreme in Jewish law is considered to be anal intercourse, and more specifically, anal intercourse to the point of the husband's climax and ejaculation (an issue relating to the concept of "wasting seed in vain," to be discussed).

Thus, please note that while the halachic discussions we will encounter address a wide variety of sexual technique and positions within marriage, we will find an inordinate amount of discussion in the classical Talmudic-rabbinic sources themselves focusing on anal sex. And an important direct ramification of these discussions about anal sex will be the potential permissibility of other forms of extra-vaginal penile stimulation within marriage, including, but not limited to, a wife's manual or oral stimulation of her husband's sex organs – even to the point of his climax and ejaculation.

Another important technical point: There is a precise dialectic in Jewish law, the implications of which can be missed or confused by the uninformed reader. In our case, we will be exploring not only widely permissive halachic views, but also some opinions that reject certain sexual practices even within marriage. But a distinction must be made between that which they "forbid" and that which they merely "discourage." For example, when a halachic authority writes, "It is forbidden to..." the intention is generally a categorical prohibition. But in some cases when the same authority uses milder terminology, "Do not..." it is not prohibiting that action categorically,[30] and sometimes it is only discouraging it on moral, pious or health – not legal – grounds. As we investigate and analyze the actual sources, the precision and ramification of this critical distinction will be made clearer.

Finally, it was the style of the ancient sources to discuss Jewish marital sex law in terms of what is permitted or prohibited "for a husband to do with his wife." Although this might strike the modern reader as sexist, I urge you to set such knee-jerk reactions aside, for when it comes to the laws of sex the Talmud generally also only speaks in terms of the husband's obligations to his wife in the bedroom. And rest-assured, Jewish law does not allow a man "to do" anything with his wife's body against her wishes,[30*] nor does it play ignorant to the fact that women, not just men, have powerful sexual drives and needs. On the contrary, there is infinitely more discussion in Jewish law about a husband's obligation to fulfill his wife sexually than her obligation to fulfill him.

[**Important**: Concerning our use of the terms "pure" and "impure" in relation to a woman and her menstrual cycle, see below, footnote to page 22.]

## Souls Lost in Translation

Translators of Torah works hold in their hands the power to destroy or build souls.

A translator of Judaism's texts on sex, in particular, can either clarify or obscure the message largely depending on his or her own personal level of comfort with the subject. And in as delicate a subject as sex, even minor discomfort on the part of the translator can result in misrepresentations that engender profound confusion and anxiety in the hearts and minds of readers.[31] Therefore, we have strived in our translation and interpretation of Torah sources to reveal G-d's own humane side, the Creator's own comfort in discussing all things sexual, by not only conveying the authentic academic meaning of texts, but bringing to life the scenarios of natural human desire and frailty they originally came to address – already hundreds, even thousands, of years ago.

As mentioned, this sometimes results in our suggesting bold reinterpretations of commonly held assumptions. But where a suggested translation or interpretation significantly diverges from common assumption, we note it – and we justify it.[32] And in such translative and interpretive work we have allowed the instruction of Maimonides to guide us – indeed, the instruction he gave his own personal translator:

> One who wishes to translate from one language to another, and tries to translate word by word, maintaining the order of both the subject and the words, will find his work very difficult, and will ultimately end up with a translation that is highly questionable and confusing.
>
> Rather, one who translates from one language to another must first understand the concept. Then he should relate and explain the subject according to his understanding, providing a clear exposition in the language [into which he is translating]. This is impossible without transposing the order of words.
>
> Moreover, the translator will sometimes have to use many words to translate a single word, while at other times he will have to use a single word to translate many. He will have to add and delete words so that the concept may be clearly expressed in the language into which he is translating.[33]

Translations of Talmudic texts are generally based off the Soncino, Steinsaltz and/or Artscroll English editions – adapted into more direct, real-world modes of expression, which also, we believe, more faithfully conveys the pulse of the Sages' real-life discussions.

Translations of commentaries and halachic codes are our own.

Emphasis added to translated source-text is our own.

## INTRODUCTION

We use brackets to denote added supplementary explanation between the words and lines of translated source-text.

We use parentheses to provide English transliteration of original Hebrew/Aramaic phraseology, where such might add clarification to the reader or justification for a particular choice of translation.

Hebrew/Aramaic transliteration is italicized.

In line with accepted halachic convention, the English name for the Creator, "G-d," is not written out completely.

And now, we begin.

# PART ONE
# FIRST IMPRESSIONS

# HALACHIC POSITIONS

## Shulchan Aruch, Orach Chaim 240, Laws of Modesty (excerpts)

1. A husband should not excessively frequent his wife for sex beyond what Torah mandates him to do in order to satisfy her sexual needs.

Those who need not worry about earning a living or paying taxes are mandated to satisfy their wives every single day.

Laborers who work in a different city, but return home to sleep each night, are mandated to satisfy their wives once a week. And if they work in their home city, twice a week.

Donkey drivers, once a week.

Camel drivers, once in thirty days.

Sailors, once in six months.

And a Torah scholar is obligated to satisfy his wife every Friday night.

And every man is mandated to satisfy his wife on the night of her [post-menstrual] *mikveh* immersion,[XIV] and the night before he leaves on a trip abroad – if it is not a trip for the sake of a *mitzvah*.

And if his wife is nursing,[34] and he sees that she is actively trying to gain his affection and she is beautifying herself in order to attract his attention, he is mandated to satisfy her.

And even when he is with her, it should not be in his mind about satisfying his own desires, but rather about fulfilling his obligation to satisfy her sexual needs, and about fulfilling the commandment of his Creator to procreate and raise children who study Torah and live according to its commandments amongst the Jewish people.

Similarly, if his intention is to improve the fetus of their unborn child – for during the last six months of pregnancy passionate intercourse between father and mother helps make the child comely and vibrant[35] – this is considered worthy.

---

[XIV] According to Biblical law, husband and wife may not engage in sexual relations during the "impurity" of the wife's menstrual cycle, nor even after it is over until she immerses and "purifies" herself in a ritual *mikveh* bath.

While there are to be found in ancient rabbinic records some statements in regard to this impurity that are disturbing to modern sensibilities, it has also been explained that its fundamental nature has nothing to do with a woman being inferior in any way to a man. Rather, the impurity is said to stem from the loss of potential life when each potential for birth is evacuated from the wife's body – for in Jewish law, where there is loss of lifeforce spiritual impurity fills the void. This is perhaps also why a man is considered by Jewish law to harbor a certain (albeit lesser) degree of impurity after ejaculation.

In any case, we certainly mean no disrespect with our use of the terms "pure" or "impure" in relation to a wife and her menstrual cycle where such is necessary for clarity and analysis of the halachic sources throughout this book.

And if his intention is to guard himself from temptation to sin, because he senses within himself such temptation,[36] it would have been better had he ignored his sexual instinct and conquered it, for, as the Sages teach, "There is a small limb in the body of man – when you starve it, it feels satisfied; when you satisfy it, it feels starved."[37]

But if a husband doesn't need sex, and he intentionally arouses himself in order to indulge his pleasures, this is the work of the evil inclination, for from this permissible act he will be led to that which is forbidden...

4. It is forbidden to gaze at the female genitals,[XV] for one who gazes there displays no shamefacedness and transgresses the prophet's admonition to "walk modestly with the L-rd."[38] He diminishes whatever shamefacedness he does have, whereas one who has a sense of shame does not readily sin, as the verse states, "[Moses said to the people at Sinai: "Do not fear, for in order to elevate you has G-d come; and] so that awe of Him" – a sense of shame – "shall be upon your faces, so that you shall not sin."[39]

What is more, gazing at the female genitals incites the evil urge.[40]

And kissing the female genitals is even worse, for besides transgressing all the above, one also transgresses the biblical commandment, "Do not make yourselves disgusting."[41]

5. Intercourse with him-on-bottom and her-on-top is arrogant.

Intercourse side-by-side is obstinate.

7. Do not[42] have sex at the beginning of night or at the end of night – that way you will avoid hearing voices from the street and fantasizing about other women. Sex should be in the middle of the night.

8. And you should perform your sexual duty with awe and fear, as it is said[43] of the sage, Rabbi Eliezer, [about how he would perform sex with his wife,] that "he would uncover a hand's-breadth and cover over a hand's-breadth, and it was as if he were compelled by a demon" – meaning, with the kind of awe and fear (*b'eimah ub'yirah*) one would have if a demon were pressuring him.[44]

---

[XV] Regarding why the *female* genitals are singled out, here, see below, pages 33-34 and endnotes 72 and 75 thereon.

Alternatively, some interpret, "he would uncover a hand's-breadth and cover over a hand's-breadth" to mean that he would not thrust his penis very much during intercourse (*shelo hayah memarek ha'ever b'shaas tashmish*[XVI]), so as to minimize his pleasure. And the meaning of "it was as if he were compelled by a demon" is that it was as if he were forced to have sex against his will.

Alternatively, some interpret, "he would uncover a hand's-breadth and cover over a hand's-breadth" as referring to a hand's-breadth of the wife's genitals, meaning that just as he was uncovering his wife's body, it was as if he were already covering her back up, for he would not draw out sexual intercourse (*shelo hayah maarich b'oso maaseh*). It was as if he had a fear of a demon and he was terrified, and he would [complete the deed and] pull out – that's how fast he would engage in sexual intercourse (*col cach hayah mekatzer b'tashmish*).

And some interpret it to mean that "he would uncover a hand's-breadth" of her breechcloth, for even during intercourse (*af b'shaas tashmish*) he would require her to wear it,[45] and he would uncover only a hand's-breadth of it and then cover it over again immediately, in order to minimize his pleasure.

All these interpretations have truth to them,[46] and someone who is conscientious of his soul should live up to all of them (*v'tzarich baal nefesh lizaher bahem*).

9. Do not speak with her about anything non-sex-related – not during intercourse, nor immediately before it (*lo b'shaas tashmish v'lo kodem lachen*) – so that you will not fantasize about other women.

---

[XVI] The Hebrew term *"b'shaas tashmish"* shall be assumed throughout our study of Talmudic, medieval and later rabbinic texts to mean "during sexual intercourse" (as opposed to during sexual foreplay) – as Rabbi Caro clearly intends its use here and throughout his discussion in *Orach Chaim 240:8, 9, 10*. Similarly, the terms *"tashmish"* and *"hamaaseh"* shall be understood to mean "the act of intercourse," and *"b'shaas maasesh"* to mean "during the act of intercourse." Our use of the term "sex" (as in "had/have sex") shall also be equivalent to, or at least shall be meant to include, intercourse (as in "had/have intercourse").

The Hebrew term for "foreplay," on the other hand, would be something akin to Raavad III's phraseology in his *Baalei HaNefesh, Shaar Hakedushah* (pp. 175-176 in the Buchwald edition): *"m'shehuzkaku l'oso maaseh* – when they begin to embrace [with the intention] for intercourse" (but see below, endnote 683). In any case, when we wish to speak of foreplay, we shall refer to it specifically.

If you did converse with her [about other such matters], and then immediately had sex with her, it is of this behavior that they [sages[46*]] said the prophet was referring when he declared, "G-d recounts to man what his words were"[47] – [they explained that the prophet meant to caution that] "Even the light-headed talk between husband and wife will be recounted to him on the Day of Judgment."

10. If he displayed anger toward her it is forbidden for him to have sex with her until he appeases her. And he may speak words of appeasement to her immediately before having sex with her.

## Shulchan Aruch – Initial Analysis

If one were exposed only to the above excerpts of Jewish sexual law, as many young Chasidic-Charedi men and women are, one could not be blamed for walking away with the following impressions of G-d's will:

- During sex, a husband's focus must be entirely on his wife's sexual needs or benefits to their unborn child. His own sexual needs are unimportant and in fact deplorable.

- A husband's curiosity to explore his wife's genitals is un-Jewish. It is not only forbidden to do so, it is a kind of insult to G-d.

- Kissing the female genitals is disgusting and absolutely forbidden.

- Talking is restricted – it might lead the man to think of other women.

- Ideally, the husband should approach the sex act as a matter of obligation, performed hastily and in a state of awe and fear – not love, connection and passion.

- The "missionary" position is probably the only position considered acceptable by G-d.

    While other obvious positions such as rear-entry vaginal intercourse[48] and anal intercourse are left out of the discussion entirely, one might surmise from the fact that the her-on-top and side-by-side positions, while not categorically forbidden, are considered to expose serious character flaws in the couples who perform them, that any positions other than "face-to-face, husband-on-top" are at best deplorable.

    Indeed, the fact that rear-entry vaginal intercourse and anal intercourse are not discussed at all could leave a reader thinking that these two positions are not only forbidden, but they are so perverse that Rabbi Caro could not bring himself to even speak of them; or that he assumed a reader would know on his or her own not to even ask about them; or that he never imagined a Jew would ever entertain the thought of them.

- Although the only kissing discussed, and forbidden, is kissing of the female genitals, the fact that the man's instinctual desires are so deplored can easily leave the impression that he should not allow himself to indulge his instincts to kiss anywhere else too "sexy" either.

We will now turn our attention to a second section of Rabbi Caro's *Code of Jewish Law*, his *Even Haezer-Laws of Marriage*.

Mind you, many, if not most, Chasidic-Charedi Jews I have asked – learned and unlearned alike – are entirely unaware that the *Code of Jewish Law* has another (somewhat) detailed section dedicated to the laws of sexual conduct between husband and wife. Most turn to the *Laws of Modesty* in the *Orach Chaim-Laws of Daily Living* section of Rabbi Caro's code, quoted above, and innocently assume they have found all there is to know on the subject.

Although Rabbi Caro does not add much in the way of new perspectives in his *Even Haezer-Laws of Marriage*, an important gloss-note, there, by the foremost annotator of the *Code of Jewish Law*, Rabbi Moshe Isserles (1520-1572), will open the floodgates of an entirely refreshing, and widely forgotten, liberal Jewish approach to marital sexual intimacy.

## Shulchan Aruch, Even Haezer 25, Laws of Marriage (excerpts)

1. A person should habituate himself to extra holiness, purity of mind and proper focus, to save himself from stumbling into fornication...

2. He should not act light-headedly with his wife, nor make his mouth vulgar with vain talk[49] even when he is alone with her. Behold, the prophet states, "G-d recounts to man what his words were." Sages,[49*] of blessed memory, explained: "Even the light-headed talk between husband and wife will be accounted for on the Day of Judgment."

And he should not converse with her during intercourse, nor immediately before it, so as not to fantasize about other women.

And if he did converse with her and then immediately had intercourse with her, to him applies the verse, "G-d recounts to man what his words were."

But if it is sex-related, it is permitted for him to talk to her in order to increase his passion (*c'dei l'harbos taavaso*).

Or if he displayed anger toward her and he needs to appease her, he may speak to her in order to appease her.[50]

And he should not excessively frequent his wife for sex, for this is extremely deficient behavior, the behavior of a crass boor. Rather, minimizing sex as much as possible is to be praised, so long as he does not shirk his Torah mandate to satisfy his wife's sexual needs – at least not without her permission.

And even when he is having sex with her according to Torah's mandate, it should not be in his mind about satisfying his own desires, but rather about discharging an obligation, in this case his obligation to satisfy her needs, and about fulfilling the commandment of his Creator to procreate and raise children who study Torah and live according to its commandments amongst the Jewish people.

3. One should not have sex at the beginning or end of night, but in the middle of night.

As noted, Rabbi Caro does not add much, here, that we don't already know from his *Laws of Modesty* – though it is now expressly permitted for a husband to speak words that will increase his, and presumably also his wife's, erotic passion.

But here is the game-changing gloss by the foremost annotator on the *Code of Jewish Law*, Rabbi Moshe Isserles:

> 25:2. And he may do with his wife anything he desires: he may have intercourse with her any time he desires,[XVII] and he may kiss any part of her body he desires, and he may penetrate her vaginally or anally or between limbs [i.e. in, against or between any other parts of her body], so long as it does not lead to "wasting seed in vain" [i.e. ejaculation outside the vagina].
>
> And some are lenient and say that anal sex is permitted even to the point of [intra-anal] ejaculation if he desires it randomly [in the heat of passion] (*b'akrai*) but does not make a habit of it.
>
> And even though all these things are permitted, whoever sanctifies himself in that which is permitted shall be called 'holy.'[51]

According to Rabbi Moshe Isserles, then:

- G-d acknowledges, empathizes with and legitimizes *all* of a man's (and woman's) sexual desires and permits them within marriage.

- Husband and wife may have intercourse "any time" they mutually want – meaning, even in excess of Torah's mandate upon him to satisfy her (or, as we shall see, perhaps regardless of what kind of conversation they may be having or may have had just prior[52]).

- It is natural, and acceptable before G-d, for a man to desire to kiss every part of his wife's body, including her genitals, and to actually do so.

- Although he does not speak of the her-on-top or side-by-side positions, from the fact that Rabbi Isserles permits anal sex as well as penetration "between limbs" (i.e. in, against or between any other parts of his wife's body) we may surmise that the former two positions are not as categorically objectionable as one might have believed from Rabbi Caro's discouragement of them in *Orach Chaim*.

- And if anal intercourse is permissible, rear-entry vaginal intercourse is presumably permitted as well.

---

[XVII] Though certainly not during her impure menstrual state (see above, footnote to page 22). And according to generally accepted opinion, not with the lights on at night nor during the daytime unless the room is darkened or the couple covers themselves with a blanket. An in-depth analysis of Jewish law's approach to sex at night with the lights on or during the day in the daylight will be the topic of a dedicated essay in a future volume of this series. In the meantime, see below, pages 95-96 and endnotes 833, 844, 845.

- We are given a key distinction between that which is categorically "forbidden" or "permitted" versus that which one may choose to strive toward as voluntary "sanctification."

We must now address a few glaring questions:

How could such opposed approaches to marital sex – the approaches of Rabbi Caro and Rabbi Isserles – derive from one and the same Torah? Or are they perhaps not so mutually exclusive?

Rabbi Isserles presents an extremely permissive stance compared to Rabbi Caro on the matter of variety in sexual technique and positions. But why does he tell us of it only in the *Laws of Marriage,* where Rabbi Caro does not discuss technique or positions at all, and not in the *Laws of Modesty,* where Rabbi Caro does discuss them at least partially?

And why does Rabbi Caro, in his *Laws of Modesty,* entirely ignore the discussion of anal intercourse and intercourse between limbs? By virtue of their fundamental difference in form from any vaginal sex position they should have been afforded special mention apart from his discussion about the her-on-top or side-by-side positions?

We shall seek to clarify these questions, and more, as we embark on our journey into the original Talmudic sources and medieval commentaries from whence Rabbis Caro and Isserles derived their respective rulings.

# PART TWO
# DECONSTRUCTING THE CODE

# HALACHIC POSITIONS

## Babylonian Talmud, Tractate Nedarim 20ab

A Tanna[53] taught in a *braisa*[54]:

> Never accustom yourself to making vows, because you might ultimately transgress them.
>
> Do not frequent an ignorant person, because he might ultimately give you un-tithed produce to eat.
>
> Do not frequent an ignorant priest (*kohen*), because he might ultimately feed you sanctified food [permitted only to priests].
>
> And do not unlimit your conversation with a woman,[XVIII] for it will ultimately lead to adultery.

Rabbi Acha [Achi][55] son of Rabbi Yoshiyah[56] says:

> Whoever makes a habit[57] of looking around[58] at women [in order to sexually fantasize[59] about them] will ultimately come to [actual] sin, and whoever gazes[XIX] at the heel of a woman [in order to derive sexual satisfaction from it[60]] will ultimately have uncouth children.[61]

Rav Yosef[62] said:

> And this refers [even[63]] to [the heel of] one's own wife during her [forbidden] menstrual period.

Rabbi Shimon ben Lakish[64] said:

> 'Heel' refers to the private place,[65] which is opposite the heel.

It was taught in a *braisa*:

---

[XVIII] Literally: "*al tarbeh sichah im ha'ishah*" – One should not prolong-extend-protract conversation with a woman other than one's own wife.

However, this teaching is also brought in regard to conversation with one's own wife, such as in *Ethics of the Fathers 1:5* and in *Avos D'Rabbi Noson 7:2-3*. Being that the latter source gives a specific example of "*al tarbeh sichah*" within marriage, namely, that a husband should not inform his own wife of an episode that will diminish his respect in her eyes, we have chosen to translate the phrase as "do not unlimit conversation" – for the message in that context is clearly that even husband and wife should not feel the obligation to reveal all to one another in the name of "sharing everything" if such sharing will ultimately compromise their closeness. And how much more so with another member of the opposite sex, where unlimited conversation and familiarity can lead to illicit behavior.

The entire topic of "*al tarbeh sichah im ha'ishah*" will be explored more fully in a future volume of this series. And see below, endnote 695.

[XIX] The term "gaze" in all discussions in this book refers to **steady intent looking**, as opposed to simply seeing or glancing in passing. See also *Ezer Mekudash* to *Shulchan Aruch, Even Haezer 25:2:Hagaah*.

# DECONSTRUCTING THE CODE

[Moses said to the people at Sinai: "Do not fear, for in order to elevate you has G-d come; and so that awe of Him shall be upon your faces, so that you shall not sin."[66]

The *braisa* elucidates the verse:]

"So that awe of Him shall be upon your faces" – to instill a sense of shame [read: dignity[XX]].

"So that you shall not sin" – this teaches that a sense of shame fosters fear of sin.

Based on this [*braisa's* interpretation of the verse,] there are those who say that a sense of shame is a sign of good character.

Others say that anyone who has a sense of shame does not readily sin. And if someone has no shamefacedness, it can be assumed that his ancestors were not among those who stood at Sinai.[67]

[The anonymous compilers-editors of the Talmud bring a loosely related teaching on the subject of gazing at one's own wife's body]

Rabbi Yochanan ben Dahavai[68] [a sage known for his extreme piety[69]] said:

The ministering angels told four things to me:

1. Why are some [children[70]] lame?

Because they[XX*] [the fathers[70*]] "overturn the table"[71] [i.e., they do not engage in the normal sex position of "face-to-face, husband-on-top"].

2. Why are some [children] mute?

---

[XX] See below, pp. 187-188, where we argue that the intention, here, in extolling the virtues of "shame" and "shamefacedness" is not to glorify a sense of embarrassment, timidity or bashfulness, but a sense of *dignity* – which *manifests* as shame and shamefacedness when one has not lived up to one's own expectations of oneself and/or the respectable expectations of others, including, and first and foremost, the expectations of the Almighty.

[As for why, then, as the Talmud continues, only "some say" that dignity is a sign of good character, the intention appears not to be that others disagreed about the worthiness of dignity, but only that others expressed its worth in a different manner ("Others say that anyone who has a sense of shame does not readily sin..."). If, however, the Talmud did mean to say that others did not laud the trait of dignity, perhaps it was because dignity easily degenerates into ego.

In any case, those who would insist on the latter manner of reading the Talmud, and who would also insist on interpreting the term "shame" literally, would also have to contend with the implication that "others" did not consider "shame" to be a worthy or useful trait.]

[XX*] Ostensibly, "they" could refer to either father or mother. See endnote 70*, addressing this point.

> Because they [the fathers] kiss the [mothers'] genitals.[72]
>
> 3. Why are some [children] deaf[73]?
>
> Because they [the fathers] speak during sex[XXI] (*shemisaprin b'shaas tashmish*).[74]
>
> 4. Why are some [children] blind?
>
> Because they [the fathers] gaze at the [mothers'] genitals (*mistaclim b'oso makom*).[75]

[The compilers-editors of the Talmud ask:] Contrast this [caution of Rabbi Yochanan ben Dahavai against speaking during sex] with the following reported episode:

> They asked Ima Shalom, [sister of Raban Gamliel II of Yavneh and] wife of Rabbi Eliezer [ben Hyrcanus][76]: "How did your children all turn out to be so beautiful?"[77]
>
> She answered them: "My husband speaks[78] to me [that is, initiates sex with me through speaking] not at the beginning of night nor at the end of night, but only in the middle of night. And as he speaks, he uncovers a hand's-breadth and covers over a hand's-breadth [i.e., as he speaks he performs intercourse][79] and it's as if he were compelled by a demon.[80]
>
> "When I asked him the reason (*mah taam*) [for this behavior], he answered me: 'So that I will not [come to] set my [mind's] eye on [fantasies of] another woman (*c'dei shelo eten es einai b'ishah acheres*)[81] [82] and make our children tantamount to bastards.'"[83]

[The compilers-editors of the Talmud suggest a resolution to the contradiction between Rabbi Yochanan ben Dahavai's caution against speaking during sex and Rabbi Eliezer's behavior of speaking with his wife during sex[84]:]

> This need not be left as a contradiction: [Perhaps] here, [in the case of Rabbi Eliezer's talking,] it was sex-related talk (*mili d'tashmisha*), while there [in the case of Rabbi Yochanan ben Dahavai's caution] it was referring to non-sex-related talk (*mili achronaisa*).

[The compilers-editors of the Talmud now quote a majority opinion that rejected Rabbi Yochanan ben Dahavai's teaching:]

**Rabbi Yochanan [bar Napacha][85] said:**

> That was the view of Rabbi Yochanan ben Dahavai.
>
> **But the Sages (*chachamim*) said that the law does not follow Rabbi Yochanan ben Dahavai.**[86] [87]

---

[XXI] See above, footnote to page 24.

Rather, anything a man craves to do with his wife sexually, he may do – no less than the way a man is permitted to eat his [koshered] meat from the butcher in any way he likes: if he craves his meat salted, he may eat it salted; if he craves his meat roasted, he may eat it roasted; if he craves his meat cooked, he may eat it cooked; if he craves his meat stewed, he may eat it stewed.

Similarly, [a man may enjoy his wife any way he and she desire,] just like [he may enjoy] his [kosher] fish from the fish market [any way he desires].

Ameimar[88] said:

Who were these 'ministering angels' [that Rabbi Yochanan ben Dahavai had quoted]?

[The Sages and Rabbi Yochanan bar Napacha must have understood that] they were human rabbis (*rabanan*[89]) – for if you say [that the Sages and Rabbi Yochanan bar Napacha thought] he was quoting actual supernal angels, why would [the Sages and] Rabbi Yochanan [bar Napacha] have said that the law does not follow Rabbi Yochanan ben Dahavai? The angels know more about the science of fetal development (*tzuras havlad*)[XXII] [than any mere mortal]!

[So if Rabbi Yochanan ben Dahavai's 'ministering angels' were in fact actual supernal beings, the Sages and Rabbi Yochanan bar Napacha would certainly have trusted their knowledge and ruled Jewish law accordingly].

Why, then, did he [Rabbi Yochanan ben Dahavai] call them [these rabbis] 'ministering angels?' Because they were distinguished [from the common folk] like 'ministering angels.'[90]

[The compilers-editors of the Talmud conclude with case precedents proving that Jewish law followed the Sages (and Rabbi Yochanan bar Napacha) on this matter, both in the Land of Israel and in Babylonia:]

---

[XXII] **IMPORTANT NOTE:** It must immediately be noted that Ameimar's certainty about the ministering angels' proficiency in the *science* of fetal development (*tzuras havlad*) could be understood as referring to their knowledge of natural *physical* factors, natural *metaphysical* factors and/or supernatural *spiritual* factors. Similarly, his recognition of the rabbis' (*rabanan's*) **imperfect** knowledge could be referring to their perception of the physical, the metaphysical and/or the spiritual. Therefore, throughout our study we refer to the cautions of Rabbi Yochanan ben Dahavai and his "ministering angels" as "medical cautions," for regardless of what they had meant the nature of the causes to be – physical, metaphysical or spiritual – the effect they were cautioning about was medical. On this point, see also above, endnote 86, and below, endnote 155.

A certain woman came before Rebbi[91] [Rabbi Yehudah Hanassi, 2nd century leader of the sages in the Land of Israel] and said to him:

> My master, I laid out a 'set table' for my husband, and he "overturned it!" [i.e., she laid herself out for him to be on top, face-to-face with her, but instead he turned her over for a different position of intercourse][92]

Rebbi eased her concern:[93]

> My daughter, [as long as it's] with you, Torah permits it.[94] [95] [96]

A certain woman came before Rav [Abba Arikha, 2nd-3rd century leader of the sages in Babylonia][97] [98] and said to him:

> My master, I laid out a 'set table' for my husband, and he "overturned it!"

Rav eased her concern:[99]

> [A husband's predilections for how he likes his sex are] no more objectionable [in the eyes of G-d] than [how he likes his] fish.[100]

[Having quoted the legal ruling of Rebbi – the 6th generation Tanna – above, that a husband may have sex with his wife in any manner he (and she) desire, the compilers-editors of the Talmud mention one pious restriction which Rebbi himself may[101] have deduced based upon a biblical verse:]

[The verse states:] "And do not stray after your heart [and after your eyes, after which you whore.]"[102]

From here [from this verse], Rebbi said:

> "A man should not[103] drink from one cup and set his eyes upon another cup [that is, he should not intentionally[104] fantasize of another woman during sex with his own wife.]

[The compilers-editors of the Talmud quote an interpretation of Rebbi's statement given by a sage who lived and taught seven generations – roughly 175 years – later:]

Ravina[105] said:

> This [teaching of Rebbi] was only necessary to be taught in a case where [the woman he is having sex with and the woman he is intentionally fantasizing about] are both his own wives. [But there was no need to speak against intentional fantasies of a woman he is not married to, for one should know not to do that even without Rebbi's teaching.]

[Having quoted this teaching and interpretation of Rebbi and Ravina, the compilers-editors of the Talmud quote a related teaching of a sage who lived in the transitional period between the Tannaim and Amoraim – that is, a near contemporary of Rebbi:]

[The verse states:] "I will select from among you those who rebel and those who transgress against me."[106]

Rabbi Levi said:

> These [spiritually flawed rebels and transgressors] are the offspring [of parents[107] who conceive children in a state] of nine [or ten[XXIII] spiritually flawed] conditions of mind or circumstance (*bnei teisha midos*) [represented by the mnemonic] – "Children of A'SH'N'T M'Sh'G'T'Ch":
>
> 1. *Bnei Aimah; Bnei Anusah* – Children conceived in a state of fear[108]; Children conceived in a state of force[109]
>
> 2. *Bnei Snuah* – Children conceived in a state of hatred[110]
>
> 3. *Bnei Nidoi* – Children conceived in a state of excommunication[111]; [alternatively, *Bnei Nidah* – children conceived in a state of menstrual impurity[112]]
>
> 4. *Bnei Temurah* – Children of an exchanged woman"[113]
>
> 5. *Bnei Moredes* – Children conceived in a state of rebelliousness;[114] [alternatively, *Bnei Merivah* – Children conceived in a state of strife[115]]
>
> 6. *Bnei Shichrus* – Children conceived in a state of intoxication[116]
>
> 7. *Bnei Grushas Halev* – Children conceived in a state of pending divorce[117]
>
> 8. *Bnei Irbuvya* – Children conceived in a state of intentional illicit sexual fantasy[118]
>
> 9. *Bnei Chatzufah* - Children conceived in a state of brazenness [i.e., the wife asks her husband for sex][119]

[The compilers-editors of the Talmud challenge the last example of flawed condition listed in Rabbi Levi's teaching:]

Is this so [that Rabbi Levi is correct in designating a wife who asks her husband for sex as "brazen"]?

---

[XXIII] *Nedarim* 20b speaks of nine. *Tractate Callah* 10, to be discussed below, speaks of ten. We therefore refer to them throughout our study interchangeably as the "nine" or "nine-ten" flawed conditions.

But Rabbi Shmuel bar Nachmani[120] taught in the name of Rabbi Yonasan[121]:

> Any man whose wife asks him for sex (*tovaato*) will bear children the likes of whom even the generation of Moses did not merit.[122]

> [Here, Rabbi Shmuel bar Nachmani's logic is explained. His proof is from the episode of the matriarch Leah, who, as recounted in Genesis 30:16, verbally asked[123] that her husband, Jacob, come to her one night – the same night she conceived a son, Isachar, whose descendants later became intellectual leaders of the Jewish people.[124]

The compilers-editors of the Talmud resolve this challenge:]

> That [teaching of Rabbi Shmuel bar Nachmani] was referring to a wife whose intention is to arouse her husband (*d'meratzya artzuyei*).[XXIV] [125]

---

[XXIV] Traditionally, rabbinical commentaries have interpreted the conclusion of the compilers-editors of *Nedarim 20b*, here, as curtailing a wife from using any sexually explict terminology to make her mood known to her husband (or at least from using the actual word "sex," as in, "Let's have sex"). And some would seemingly have her not verbalize her wishes to her husband at all, but rather have her rely solely on non-verbal cues.

But the term "*d'meratzya artzuyei*" on *Nedarim 20b* is very similar to the term "*tzarich l'ratzuya*" found on *Hagigah 5b* (to be discussed at length below). This latter term is used to explain that the intention of the sage, Rav, in talking sexually to his own wife was in order to arouse her to the mood for lovemaking. Thus, it is perhaps possible to read the conclusion of *Nedarim 20b*, too, as teaching that it is perfectly acceptable for a wife to lovingly ask her husband for sex directly, or to even lovingly/playfully *demand* sex from him, so long as her intention is also to please and arouse him – knowing that he will find such strong/confident sexual expressions on her part to be pleasing and/or arousing. But if she knows that he will find such expressions offensive, either because they make him uncomfortable in general or because he is adamantly not in the mood on a particular occasion, then her persistence to express herself so assertively would be categorized as "chutzpah" (*chatzufah*). See endnote 125 for an in-depth analysis of the plausibility of this suggested interpretation.

In any case, the emphasis, here, appears to be in regard to a wife *initiating* such overt discussion. But where the husband initiates, or once they are passionately involved in the bedroom, we would not necessarily know from here any restriction upon the wife from verbally, and explicitly, expressing her passion and desires to her husband – especially since such expression could arguably be included under the category of sex-related talk (*mili d'tashmisha*). And see below, pp. 57-58.

## Nedarim 20ab – Summary

The compilers-editors of the Talmud on *Nedarim 20a* begin with a discussion in the names of various sages about the emotional-spiritual impact upon a man's children caused by his gazing at certain body parts of forbidden women – perhaps even of his own menstruating wife.

They follow this with a teaching extolling a sense of shame/shamefacedness – read: dignity – as a virtuous, Jewish character trait.

The discussion is then turned to the statement of one sage known for his extreme piety,[126] Rabbi Yochanan ben Dahavai.

Rabbi Yochanan ben Dahavai cautions in the name of certain "ministering angels" that four sexual behaviors even between husband and wife can, or perhaps will, physically harm a fetus, namely:

- "Overturning the table" causes congenital lameness

- Gazing at the female genitals causes congenital blindness

- Kissing the female genitals causes congenital muteness

- Non-sex-related talk during sex causes congenital deafness

On the next page, *Nedarim 20b*, another sage, Rabbi Yochanan bar Napacha, is quoted ruling in the name of the Sages (*chachamim*) against Rabbi Yochanan ben Dahavai, and declaring instead that, "Anything a husband craves to do with his wife sexually, he may do."

A late Babylonian Amora, Ameimar, is then quoted definitively asserting that the Sages (*chachamim*) not only rejected Rabbi Yochanan ben Dahavai and his "ministering angels" legally, but also medically. That is, they did not believe Rabbi Yochanan ben Dahavai to be invoking actual spiritual beings to whom the full mysteries of creation were revealed. Rather, they believed him to be quoting mortal human rabbis (*rabanan*). And because the Sages believed these human rabbis' cautions to be invalid medically, they therefore also believed them to be invalid halachically.

The compilers-editors of the Talmud conclude with stories of two Talmudic sages, Rebbi (Rabbi Yehudah Hanasi) of the Land of Israel and Rav (Abba Arikha) of Babylonia (Rabbi Yochanan bar Napacha's master and elder colleague, respectively), who each permitted "overturning the table" in line with this ruling of the Sages.[127]

The discussion then turns to nine spiritually flawed conditions of mind or circumstance during sex that one sage taught could have negative psychological-emotional-spiritual impact upon one's children.[128]

## Mesechtos Callah

Before delving any deeper into our analysis of *Nedarim 20ab*, we will briefly explore alternate versions of its Talmudic discussion as found in two early works of obscure origin,[129] both of which focus on the topics of marital sex law and ethics: *Tractate Callah* and *Callah Rabti*.

The two texts, *Tractate Callah* and *Callah Rabti*, form a kind of "Braisa-Talmud" synthesis, with the latter elucidating the former in pseudo-Talmudic style. Combined, they offer an alternate version of the entire Talmudic discussion on *Nedarim 20ab* from beginning to end, albeit in a different order and format.

That being said, there are numerous contradictions and textual variations to be found between these two works themselves, as there also are to be found between the two of them combined when compared to *Nedarim 20ab*.

We shall not analyze in depth the ramifications of all these discrepancies, although the summary, as well as the endnotes, will bring to attention some of the more important difficulties they raise.[130] But exploring key excerpts of these two works will provide the reader a clearer perspective on, and appreciation of, the gravity of the problem of contradictory textual traditions and/or interpretations that we touched upon in our Introduction. It will also introduce additional marital sex positions into the discussion.[131]

After exploring these two works we shall pick up again our analysis of *Nedarim 20ab*.

Note that chapter and passage references to *Tractate Callah* and *Callah Rabti* throughout this book correspond to the scholarly edition of Dr. M. Higger (*Mesechtos Callah*, New York, 1936).

## Tractate Callah (excerpts)

> 8. Whoever gazes at the heel of a woman will have maimed children.[132]

> What causes babies to be born lame, blind, mute, deaf?[133]

> Rabbi Eliezer said:
>
>> Because when the husband asked his wife for sex, she refused [and he nevertheless forced her[134]].
>
> Rabbi Yehoshua said:
>
>> Because in the midst of intercourse she says that she is being forced [and her husband nevertheless continues to force her].
>
> Rabbi Akiva said:
>
>> Because they quarrel for no reason[135] [*alt.* Because she tells him that she is menstrually impure when she is actually pure . . .[136]]
>
> . . . One who possesses the quality of shamefacedness does not readily sin, as the verse says, "[Moses said to the people at Sinai: "Do not fear, for in order to elevate you has G-d come; and] so that awe of Him shall be upon your faces, and so that you shall not sin."[137]
>
> [*According to some versions add here:*] And of anyone who does not possess the quality of shamefacedness it can be certain that he does not descend from those who stood at Sinai.

> 9. Rabbi Yochanan ben Dahavai said:
>
>> The ministering angels told four things to me, concerning the lame, the blind, the mute and the deaf:
>>
>>> Why are some [children[137*]] lame? Because they [the fathers[XXIV*]] overturn their table [*some versions add:* and have sex in the manner of animals (*maaseh beheimah*) – i.e., rear-entry vaginal intercourse].
>>>
>>> Why are some [children] blind? Because they [the fathers] gaze at the [mothers'] genitals.
>>>
>>> Why are some [children] mute? Because they [the fathers] kiss the [mothers'] genitals.
>>>
>>> Why are some [children] deaf? Because they [the fathers] talk during sex[XXV] (*b'shaas tashmish*).

> **And the Sages [*chachamim*] say:**

---

[XXIV*] See above, footnote XX* to page 33.

[XXV] See above, footnote to page 24.

**Anything a man craves to do with his wife sexually, he may do.**

It is no different than how he is permitted to enjoy his [koshered] meat from the butcher or his fish from the fisherman any way he craves – if he wants to eat it roasted, he may do so; if he wants to eat it salted, he may do so; if he wants to eat it cooked, he may do so; if he wants to eat it grilled, he may do so.[138]

10. Ima Shalom, wife of Rabbi Eliezer and sister of Raban Gamliel, was asked:

How did it come to be that all of your children are so beautiful [*according to one version add here:* and they have such alacrity in Torah], and how does he conduct himself with you during sex?"

She said:

He does not talk [i.e. initiate sex through talking] with me during the first third of night, nor during the last third, but only during the middle third.

He uncovers a hand's-breadth and covers over a hand's-breadth.

And it's as if he were being compelled by a demon.

I [once] said to him, "Why such extremes (*col cach lamah*)?"

He responded, "So that I will not [come to] set my focus on [fantasies of] another woman (*c'dei shelo taaleh al daati ishah acheres/c'dei shelo eten daati b'ishah acheres/c'dei shelo eten libi daas b'ishah acheres*), causing my children to be tantamount to bastards.'"

13. Intercourse standing causes convulsions…[139]

15. Intercourse sitting causes diarrhea…[140]

Intercourse with him-on-bottom and her-on-top causes convulsions…[141]

Him-on-top and her-on-bottom is the way of humans.

Intercourse side-by-side is obstinate.[142]

17. Rabbi Achi son of Rabbi Yoshiyah says:

Whoever looks around at women [*alt.* whoever empties his mind to fantasize of women] will eventually fall to sin. And whoever turns himself away from sin and does not go through with it,[143] even if he is an Israelite [not a Levite or Priest], he is worthy to bring a sacrifice upon the altar as if he were a High Priest, as the verse (Exodus 24:5) states, "And he [Moses] sent the youths of the children of Israel, and they offered up burnt offerings, [and they slaughtered peace offerings to the Lord, bulls]."[144]

And whoever makes himself slow [*lit.* lazy] to sin and does not go through with it, is nourished from the radiance of the Divine Presence like the ministering angels, as the verse (Exodus 24:11) states: "[And upon the nobles of the children of Israel He did not lay His hand,] and they perceived G-d, and they ate and drank."[145]

21. What should a man do in order to ensure that his children become wealthy [*alt.* survive]?

He should fulfill the wishes of Heaven and the wishes of his wife . . .

22. What is meant by "the wishes of his wife"?

Rabbi Eliezer says:

> He should speak seductively to her during sex[XXVI] (*yefateh osah b'shaas tashmish*).[146] [147]

Rabbi Yehudah says:

> He should [endeavor to] gladden her during sex as part of his fulfillment of the commandment, as the verse states, "He who keeps the commandment shall know no evil."[148]

---

[XXVI] See above, footnote to page 24.

## Callah Rabti (excerpts)

Chapter 1

11. Whoever gazes at the heel of a woman will have maimed children born from the womb.[149]

What causes babies to be born lame, blind, mute, deaf?

Rabbi Eliezer says:

> Because when the husband asked his wife for sex, she refused" [and he nevertheless forced her].

Rabbi Yehoshua says:

> Because in the midst of intercourse she says to him, "I am being forced" [and he nevertheless continues to force her.]

Rabbi Akiva says:

> Because they quarrel for no reason.

[*One textual version adds here*:

Rabbi Yochanan [bar Napacha] said:

> [Regarding the teaching that gazing at the 'heel' of a woman causes one to have maimed children from birth,] this was only needed to be taught to warn a husband from gazing even at his own [impure] menstruating wife.[150]
>
> And [when it says not to gaze at her] 'heel,' [it] means literally, [he should not even gaze at] her foot.

Reish Lakish[151] said:

> The term 'heel,' here, is a euphemism for the backside of her private parts (*makom hatoref*), which lies parallel to her heel [the backside of her foot], but [it is] not [cautioning against gazing at] the actual heel of her foot.[152] [153]

*Here the lone textual version ends*]

Rava said:

> [When it was taught that gazing at the 'heel' of a woman causes one to have maimed children from birth,] it was referring to one's own [pure] wife.[154]

They retorted to him [to Rava]:

> The master does not permit any creature to live! [– i.e., it is not possible to expect a husband not to gaze at his wife's private body parts when she is pure, and therefore, according to Rava, every child should be doomed to congenital illness.[155]]

Rather, this [interpretation of Rava, that gazing at the private body parts of one's own pure wife causes one to have maimed children from birth,] only applies when [such gazing is immediately] followed by sexual intercourse and conception of a child – as he [Rava] needed to say below [in *Callah Rabti 1:13*, in regard to the congenital illnesses cautioned against by Rabbi Yochanan ben Dahavai].

[*Callah Rabti* now clarifies the opinions of Rabbi Eliezer and Rabbi Yehoshua mentioned in *Tractate Callah* in regard to what allegedly causes children to be born lame, blind, mute or deaf:]

Rabbi Eliezer said:

> Because he asks her for sex [and she refuses, but he nevertheless forces her.

Rabbi Yehoshua says:

> Because in the midst of intercourse she says to him, "I am being forced" – and he nevertheless continues to force her.]

They are both dealing with force, so what is the difference between them?

One believes it is the forcefulness *before* intercourse that causes the illness [in their child], and the other believes it is the forcefulness *during* intercourse that causes the illness [in their child].[156]

13. Rabbi Yochanan ben Dahavai said:

> The ministering angels told four things to me, concerning the lame, the blind, the mute and the deaf:
>
> > Why are some [children[156*]] lame? Because they [the fathers[XXVI*]] "overturn their table."
> >
> > Why are some [children] blind? Because they [the fathers] gaze at the [mothers'] genitals.
> >
> > Why are some [children] mute? Because they [the fathers] kiss the [mothers'] genitals.
> >
> > Why are some [children] deaf? Because they [the fathers] talk during sex[XXVII] (*b'shaas tashmish*).

Rava said:

> All the ways of the Holy One, blessed be He, are measure for measure[157] [158] [and in these cases]:

---

[XXVI*] See above, footnote XX* to page 33.

[XXVII] See above, footnote to page 24.

He "overturned his table,"¹⁵⁹ therefore the legs of his children will be "overturned."¹⁶⁰

He gazed [with his eyes] at that which is hidden from all, therefore all will be hidden from [the eyes of] his children.

He abandoned the mouth [of his wife] that speaks and to which [the power to] kiss [in return] was given, and he kissed that which is closed up, therefore the mouths of his children will be closed up.¹⁶¹

He spoke at a time when he should have been silent, therefore the ears of his children will be silenced.

Why is the term *"cheresh"* used to describe deafness? Because it also connotes "silence" from speech,¹⁶² as the verse says, "And Jacob kept silent (*v'hichrish Yaakov*) until they came."¹⁶³

Rava said:

[Even according to Rabbi Yochanan ben Dahavai himself,] all these [four illnesses] only afflict a fetus that is conceived during the same sexual encounter [in which these four behaviors are performed. But if conception does not occur during that same sexual encounter, no such harm will result from any of these four behaviors to a fetus that was conceived prior or that will be conceived in the future].¹⁶⁴

14. And the Sages say:

The law does not follow Rabbi Yochanan ben Dahavai. Rather, anything a man craves to do with his wife sexually, he may do.¹⁶⁵

To what can they [these sexual preferences] be compared? To [koshered] meat bought from the butcher or fish from the fisherman: [as long as it is kosher] if he wants to eat it salted, he may do so; if he wants to eat it cooked, he may do so; if he wants to eat it roasted, he may do so; if he wants to eat it grilled, he may do so.

But still, Rabbi Yochanan ben Dahavai was not speaking in his own name [alt. from his own reasoning], [he was speaking in the name of 'ministering angels'], so why did the Rabbis (*rabanan*)¹⁶⁶ not concede to him?

Because Rabbi Yochanan [ben Dahavai] said that these behaviors were 'forbidden' (*asurim heim*¹⁶⁶*)¹⁶⁷ The Rabbis [therefore] said back to him:

It could be that you are speaking in the name of ministering angels, but there is no prohibition that forbids [them¹⁶⁷*] (*mihu asur ein isur*).¹⁶⁸ ¹⁶⁹

# DECONSTRUCTING THE CODE

Rabbi Yochanan [ben Dahavai] said back [to the Rabbis]:

> But at least admit to me that it is because of these [four behaviors, if performed during the same sexual encounter in which conception occurs, that these four congenital illnesses manifest].

Know [that the Rabbis must have admitted this to him], because [when] they responded [with the analogy of how a man likes to eat his kosher meat or fish,] they used the term "If he wants..."[170] [as if to say that it is not necessarily *healthy* for him to eat his meat or fish prepared in a certain manner, but so long as it is kosher it is not forbidden for him to eat it prepared in an unhealthy way "if he wants"[171]].

Why did they have to bring the [second] analogy of [how a man likes to eat his] fish from the fisherman?

[Because] when they [the Rabbis] first gave him [Rabbi Yochanan ben Dahavai] the analogy of the [koshered] meat from the butcher, he retorted back to them:

> But even with kosher meat, if he wants to eat it with milk, he is not allowed.

So the Rabbis responded with the second analogy of fish from the fisherman [which is permitted to be eaten with milk].[172]

15. Ima Shalom, wife of Rabbi Eliezer and sister of Raban Gamliel, was asked,

> How did it come to be that [all of] your children are so beautiful?
>
> How does he conduct himself with you during sex?[173]

She said:

> He never spoke[174] [i.e. initiated sex through speaking] with me during the first third of night, nor during the last third, but only during the middle third. And he would uncover a hand's-breadth and cover over a hand's-breadth. And it was as if he were being compelled by a demon.
>
> I [once] said to him, "Why such extremes (*col cach lamah*)?"
>
> He responded to me, "So that the thought of another woman does not enter my deliberate intention (*c'dei shelo taaleh al daati ishah acheres*), causing my children to be tantamount to bastards."

At first they said to her that her children were beautiful. She blushed and would not say anything in return.

So they said to her:

> There is a topic in Torah that we need to learn, but we are embarrassed to ask... How does he behave with you during sex?

When she saw this [that their question was purely motivated], she told them the whole story: Not during the first third of night or the last third of night [did he have sex with her], which are the normal times for sex, but only during the middle third of night, which is not the normal time for sex.

23. Intercourse sitting causes diarrhea...[175]

Intercourse with him-on-bottom and her-on-top is arrogant[176] and causes fickle-mindedness.[177] [178]

Her-on-bottom and him-on-top is the way of humans.

Both of them thrusting simultaneously is obstinate.

> What position is meant here [by 'both of them thrusting simultaneously']?
>
> For example, they are lying on their sides [during intercourse]. And because of this the child will come out with crooked posture.[179]

Rava said:

> If one asks for sex when his wife is fertile,[180] he should see to ejaculate in the most effective manner [i.e., sexual position], for all depends upon the ejaculation.

[*A second version here reads*:

Rava said:

> Just like the one sowing a field must plow well and sow the seed in a good place, and properly, and all at once, and then that sowing of seed will be successful and the field will give forth much more seed, so too, one who has sex must do it optimally, not tampering with the methods at all[181]].

Chapter 2

3. Rabbi Achai [Achi] son of Rabbi Yoshiyah says:

> Whoever looks around at women will eventually come to sin. And whoever turns himself away from sin and does not go through with it, even if he is an Israelite [not a Levite or Priest], he is worthy to bring a sacrifice upon the altar as if he were a High Priest, as the verse (Exodus 24:5) states, "And he [Moses] sent the youths of the children of Israel, and they offered up burnt offerings, [and they slaughtered peace offerings to the Lord, bulls]."

> And whoever makes himself slow [*lit.* lazy] to sin in this world and does not go through with it, is nourished in the World to Come from the radiance of the Divine Presence, as the verse (Exodus 24:11) states: "[And upon the nobles of the children of Israel He did not lay His hand,] and they perceived G-d, and they ate and drank."[182]

11. …What should a man do so that he will have offspring[183]?

Rabbi Eliezer says:

> He should distribute his money freely to the poor… or he should fulfill the wishes of his wife.

What are "the wishes of his wife"?

Rabbi Eliezer says:

> He should speak seductively to her during sex.[XXVIII]

Rabbi Yehudah says:

> He should [endeavor to] gladden her during sex as part of his fulfillment of the commandment, as the verse states, "He who keeps the commandment shall know no evil, and the heart of a wise man knows time and justice."[184]

And one who wants to have sons who will also grow to be men of wisdom, should refine his own actions.

What does it mean "to speak seductively"?

If you say it means to actually speak to her [during sex], this would contradict Rabbi Yochanan ben Dahavai [who warns that speaking during sex causes congenital deafness]?

Rather, it means to love her and have passion for her [so much so that she feels she is the object of your love and passion without the need for words].

---

[XXVIII] See above, footnote to page 24.

## Mesechtos Callah – Summary

While there are numerous discrepancies between *Tractate Callah* and *Callah Rabti* versus *Babylonian Talmud, Nedarim 20ab*, some of the most important ones are the following:

### Tractate Callah

1. *Tractate Callah 8* states that gazing at a forbidden woman's heel causes one's children to be physically maimed, while *Nedarim 20a* quotes certain sages saying only that it causes one's children to be spiritually uncouth.

2. *Tractate Callah 8* states that children are born blind, dumb, mute or deaf due to the father forcing the mother (i.e., his wife) into sex. *Nedarim 20b* says that such force results in spiritually rebellious children.

### Callah Rabti

1. *Callah Rabti 1:14* strongly implies that Rabbi Yochanan ben Dahavai's "ministering angels" were actual spiritual beings with perfect knowledge of the science of fetal development, whereas *Talmud, Nedarim 20b* definitely understands them as being pious human rabbis (*rabanan*) with imperfect knowledge of this science.

2. *Callah Rabti 1:14* definitely understands that the Rabbis (*rabanan*) admitted to Rabbi Yochanan ben Dahavai that the four behaviors he cautioned against, while not legally forbidden, do cause the four congenital illnesses he warned about, whereas *Talmud, Nedarim 20b* definitely understands that the Sages (*chachamim*) did not admit such a thing, but rather they considered the medical predictions of Rabbi Yochanan ben Dahavai and his rabbis (*rabanan*) to be invalid.

   According to Ameimar as quoted in the Talmud, it was specifically *because* these rabbis (*rabanan*) were mere mortals and thus not expert in the science of fetal development that the Sages (*chachamim*) ruled the law against them. In other words: because the Sages deemed these human rabbis' cautions to be invalid medically, they therefore also deemed them to be invalid halachically.

3. Notwithstanding the previous point, *Callah Rabti 1:13* explains that even Rabbi Yochanan ben Dahavai himself considered his own cautions to be valid only if a child is conceived during the same sexual encounter in which one of the four behaviors he cautioned against are performed. But if no child is, or can be, conceived during that sexual encounter, then there should be no fear of medical repercussion to anyone if a husband, with his wife's permission, were to "overturn the table," talk during sex (*Tractate Callah* and *Callah Rabti* make no distinction between sex-

related talk and non-sex-related talk, even regarding Rabbi Yochanan ben Dahavai's opinion), or gaze at or kiss the female genitals.[185]

4. *Callah Rabti 1:14* suggests that Rabbi Yochanan ben Dahavai considered the four sexual behaviors to also be legally forbidden, though it is unclear whether he believed them to be so at all times or only during sexual encounters in which conception could possibly occur – that is, only when he also considered them to be unsafe.

5. *Callah Rabti 2:11* takes it for granted that Rabbi Eliezer could not have encouraged "seductive talk" during marital sex, because of the caution against any talk during sex by Rabbi Yochanan ben Dahavai (Rabbi Eliezer's junior by at least two generations).

But this contradicts *Talmud, Nedarim 20b*, which maintains that Rabbi Yochanan ben Dahavai himself embraced "sex-related talk" during sex, as proven by the behavior of none other than Rabbi Eliezer himself, and which according to some commentaries we shall see[186] would logically include the kind of "seductive talk" spoken of in *Tractate Callah/Callah Rabti* in the name of the same Rabbi Eliezer.

It is possible, however, that when the authors of *Callah Rabti 2:11* stated, on account of Rabbi Yochanan ben Dahavai's teaching, that Rabbi Eliezer could not possibly have encouraged a husband to talk seductively with his wife *in order to succeed in conceiving a child* ("What should a man do so that he will have offspring"), it was not because they believed such talk to be *forbidden* by the Sages or Rabbi Eliezer, but because it believed such talk to still be *dangerous* to the child even according to the Sages and Rabbi Eliezer *if performed during the same sexual encounter in which conception occurs.*

[One difficulty with this last suggested approach would be that in Ima Shalom's account on *Nedarim 20b*, it is somewhat implied that her husband's intention *was* to conceive a child on the same nights that he would speak to her during sex.]

*Tractate Callah* and *Callah Rabti* also introduce four new sex positions into the discussion – sitting, standing, wife-on-top and side-by-side – which they denounce on pious or health, but not legal, grounds.

[*Babylonian Talmud, Tractate Gitin 70a* also discusses sex in the sitting and standing and wife-on-top positions, which it also cautions against only on health grounds.]

We will now return to our analysis of *Nedarim 20ab*, which shall also shed further light on what we've just seen from *Tractate Callah* and *Callah Rabti*.

## Nedarim 20ab – Analysis

We will be reminded that on *Nedarim 20a*, Rabbi Yochanan ben Dahavai is quoted, in the name of certain "ministering angels," cautioning against four sexual behaviors between husband and wife:

1. "Overturning the table"
2. Gazing at the female genitals
3. Kissing the female genitals
4. Talk during sex

On *Nedarim 20b*, the anonymous compilers-editors of the Talmud maintain that even Rabbi Yochanan ben Dahavai himself, and his "ministering angels" themselves, would have no objection at all to "sex-related-talk" (*mili d'tashmisha*) between husband and wife during sex, they were only cautioning against "non-sex-related talk" (*mili achronaisa*).[XXIX]

Rabbi Yochanan bar Napacha is then quoted, in the name of the Sages (*chachamim*), ruling against Rabbi Yochanan ben Dahavai and permitting "anything a husband craves to do with his wife sexually."

Finally, Rebbi and Rav (Rabbi Yochanan bar Napacha's master and elder colleague, respectively) are both invoked as having permitted "overturning the table" in practical cases of Jewish law.

There are now five fundamental questions that must be addressed in order for us to gain any practical halachic insight from this Talmudic discussion:

1. What exactly were the "ministering angels'" objections to each of these four behaviors?
2. What exactly is the definition of "sex-related talk" (*mili d'tashmisha*)?

   Whatever its definition, even Rabbi Yochanan ben Dahavai himself and his "ministering angels" would be understood as having no objection to this kind of talk during sex.

3. What exactly is the definition of "overturning the table"?

   Whatever the definition of this term is, the Sages, Rebbi, Rav and Rabbi Yochanan bar Napacha all permit it.

4. When the Sages ruled that, "Anything a husband craves to do with his wife sexually, he may do," were they in fact coming to allow all four of

---

[XXIX] Below, in analyzing the Talmudic passage of *Hagigah 5b*, further categories of talk during sex shall enter into the discussion.

the behaviors Rabbi Yochanan ben Dahavai and his "ministering angels" had cautioned against?

5. What was the Sages' reasoning in asserting their permissive stance?

## Objections to Marital Sexual Exploration

Not many commentaries give clear explanation as to what Rabbi Yochanan ben Dahavai's "ministering angels" found objectionable about the four behaviors they cautioned against.

While it is possible they were not actually asserting any spiritual fault in such behaviors, but merely stating their beliefs about the physical or metaphysical effects of certain behaviors upon a fetus (perhaps due to ancient beliefs, apparently even among non-Jews,[187] that the action and/or mindset of a parent during conception affects the formation of his or her child), there are commentaries that do interpret them as cautioning about punishments resulting from that which they considered to be innapropriate.

We've already seen, above, the teaching brought in *Callah Rabti 1:13* in the name of Rava that each of the four illnesses cautioned against by Rabbi Yochanan ben Dahavai's "ministering angels" resulted "measure for measure" from what they considered to be the father's innapropriate behavior. But we are only told, there, how the four illnesses supposedly correlate *in form* to the four behaviors, it is not clarified what is *fundamentally objectionable* about the behaviors in the first place nor why such extreme punishments are *commensurate* to them.[188]

In any case, here we will list the few comments found among the medieval commentators that shed light on how they at least interpreted such objections.

### *"Overturning the Table"*

    a) He treats his wife without regard for her dignity (*nahag bah minhag hefker*)[189] XXX

    b) It veers from the ideal marital sex position G-d intended[190]

    c) The husband causes his wife discomfort upon her knees[191]

### *Gazing at the Female Genitals*

    a) He treats his wife without regard for her dignity[192]

### *Kissing the Female Genitals*

    a) He treats his wife without regard for her dignity[193]

---

XXX See below, endnote 664, for an explanation of our choice of translation of the phrase "*nahag bah minhag hefker*" as "He treats his wife without regard for her dignity."

## Non-sex-related Talk

a) It might conjure thoughts of other women in the mind of the husband, leading him to intentionally focus his mind's eye upon illicit sexual fantasies[194]

b) It turns intimacy into an act of prostitution[195]

c) Other people might hear them,[196] which is immodest[197]

d) It might distract them and diminish their sexual arousal[198]

e) Other people might hear them, which might cause them to become distracted and lose their passion[199]

A few important observations:

1. The notion that the first three behaviors treat the wife without regard for her dignity is stated by one and the same medieval commentator, Rabbi Avraham ben Dovid of Posquières, "Raavad III," in his work on "family purity," *Baalei HaNefesh, Shaar Kedushah*.

2. According to the reasoning that these behaviors treat the wife without regard for her dignity, it is arguable that if the wife herself enjoys, requests, or even (lovingly) demands these behaviors from her husband (knowing that he enjoys them as well), they would no longer be deemed disrespectful toward her.

As we shall see, even Raavad III himself concedes that "overturning the table," if done with the wife's permission, is completely permitted by the Sages – which suggests that the question of a wife being disrespected by it depends entirely on her feelings on the matter.[200] The same would therefore reasonably apply to gazing at or kissing the female genitals – the problem of a spouse feeling disrespected by them is not intrinsic to these actions, but rather assumed by Rabbi Yochanan ben Dahavai as interpreted by Raavad III.

Similarly, in regard to "overturning the table," the logic that it causes the wife "discomfort upon her knees" would be of no consequence if she actually enjoys such a position.

3. While "overturning the table" carries a variety of interpretations vis-a-vis Rabbi Yochanan ben Dahavi's (and his "ministering angels'") own objections to it, it is actually the one behavior that all medieval commentaries (including Raavad III) agree the Sages to permit (as will be explained below[201]).

4. In regard to non-sex-related talk, it is not clear why reasons d) and e) would even be worthy of G-d's notice.

Rabbi Betzalel Ashkenazi, in his *Shitah Mekubetzes*, reports reason d) in the name of Rabbi Eliezer of Metz (Re'em), along with the explanation that the diminishment of passion is, in the mind of Rabbi Yochanan ben Dahavai, a transgression of sexual "sanctity"[202] – though he gives no explanation why this is so, nor why ignoring the spirit of the law in such a case might warrant such severe repercussion as congenital deafness.

5. According to reasons c) and e), that Rabbi Yochanan ben Dahavai's concern about talk during sex was about other people catching the couple in the act, there really should be no difference between "sex-related talk" or "non-sex-related talk" – for the issue is not about what they're saying, but who might hear them.[203]

6. In regard to gazing at or kissing the female genitals and non-sex-related talk, Raavad III brings additional reasons why he believed they should be forbidden – to be discussed below, in Part Five.

Finally, Maimonides,[204] Rabbi Menachem Meiri,[205] *Tosfos Yeshanim*,[206] Rabbi Eliezer of Metz (Re'em)[207] and *Tosfos* (to *Talmud, Nidah 17a*) all imply that Rabbi Yochanan ben Dahavai's concern about all four behaviors was a general one about lack of "sanctification" and/or "modesty" – matters of extra-halachic piety, not baseline obligatory law, also to be discussed below.

## The Definition of "Sex-Related Talk"

Unanimously acceptable "sex-related-talk" would obviously encompass any words necessary to facilitate the technicalities of the act of lovemaking.

But there are numerous other examples brought in rabbinic commentary[208] as to what would also be included in this category:

1. Talk required to make peace with one's spouse after an argument[209]
2. Talk required to help arouse one's spouse to the mood for sex[210]
3. Talk that increases the heat of the husband's passion[211]
4. Talk that increases the "joy" of the husband's climax[212]
5. Talk that increases the heat of the wife's passion, bringing her to climax more speedily[213]

Now, according to those whom we shall see below believed the Sages to permit all four behaviors cautioned against by Rabbi Yochanan ben Dahavai, both sex-related and non-sex-related talk would be permitted both during foreplay and actual intercourse. This is implied by the fact that Rabbi Yochanan ben Dahavai's own original caution was about talk during actual sexual intercourse (*shemisaprin b'shaas tashmish*[XXXI]), and thus the Sages' rejection of his caution would equal their permission of any talk during intercourse.

But even according to Rabbi Yochanan ben Dahavai's opinion, as interpreted by the compilers-editors of *Nedarim 20b*, it would appear that sex-related talk would be acceptable both during foreplay and actual intercourse as well. This is implied by Ima Shalom's own account – from which the Talmud's compilers-editors derived their interpretation of Rabbi Yochanan ben Dahavai's opinion – in which she described her husband, Rabbi Eliezer, as first initiating sex with her through speaking[214] and then continuing to speak to her "as he uncovered a hand's-breadth and covered over a hand's-breadth" – a euphemism understood by commentaries as referring to the actual act of penetration and intercourse.[215]

Rabbi Yosef Caro, in his *Beis Yosef* commentary to *Even Haezer 25:2b:V'al yesaper imah*, states clearly that when Ima Shalom described her husband as speaking to her "as he uncovered a hand's-breadth and covered over a hand's-breadth," she was referring to him literally speaking to her during intercourse. And Rabbi Caro goes on to say that the Talmud's compilers-editors did not resolve this with a distinction between speaking before intercourse versus during intercourse, but rather with a distinction between sex-related talk versus non-sex-related talk. Rabbi Caro therefore derives that non-sex-related talk must have been cautioned against by Rabbi Yochanan ben Dahavai both during intercourse and foreplay. But the reverse implication, which Rabbi Caro himself does not spell out, is that (according to the Talmudic compilers-editors' interpretation) sex-related

---

[XXXI] See above, footnote to page 24.

talk would be acceptable to Rabbi Yochanan ben Dahavai both during foreplay and intercourse.

Note also that according to *Tractate Callah* in the name of Rabbi Eliezer himself, "seductive talk" would also be permitted as a necessary component relating to the sex act, and would most likely be the kind of talk his own wife, Ima Shalom, was describing. Thus, while the compilers-editors of *Nedarim 20b* distinguish only between "sex-related talk" versus "non-sex-related talk," they do so as a direct result of Ima Shalom's account of her husband's manners of sexual intimacy, and thus it is reasonable to believe that they would have categorized the "seductive talk" encouraged by Rabbi Eliezer himself as a subcategory of "sex-related talk."[216]

[*Callah Rabti 2:11*, however, does not seem to accept that "seductive talk" could possibly be permitted according to Rabbi Yochanan ben Dahavai, presumably because *Callah Rabti* did not categorize "seductive talk" as "sex-related," or because it did not accept, or did not know, the Talmud's resolution on *Nedarim 20b* that Rabbi Yochanan ben Dahavai himself embraced "sex-related talk."[217] Alternatively, the authors of *Callah Rabti* may have merely been assuming that even Rabbi Eliezer himself would never have encouraged any talk at all during a sexual encounter in which the *specific intention* is to *conceive* a child.[XXXI*]

The matter of permitted talk during sex shall be clarified further below, in our analysis of *Babylonian Talmud, Hagigah 5b*.

---

[XXXI*] But see above, page 51, end of point 5.

## The Definition of "Overturning the Table"

Among the medieval commentaries there are four approaches on how to define the term "overturning the table."

Note, again, that whichever position a medieval commentator chose as the correct definition, that is the position he understood the Sages, Rebbi, Rav and Rabbi Yochanan bar Napacha as permitting:

### Rear-Entry Vaginal Intercourse[218]

1. *Tractate Callah 9* [218*]
2. Rabbi Avraham ben Dovid, *Raavad III, Baalei HaNefesh, Shaar Hakedushah*[219]
3. Rabbi Avraham of Montpellier (*Avraham min Hahar*), *Nedarim 20a*
4. Rabbi Yaakov ben Asher, *Tur, Orach Chaim 240:2-4, Even Haezer 25:8-10*
5. Rabbi Yaakov ben Yehudah Landau, *HaAgur, Hilchos Tefilas Arvis, 336*

### Anal Intercourse[220]

1. *Tosfos, Nedarim 20a*
2. *Tosfos, Sanhedrin 58b*
3. Rabeinu Yitzchak, *Tosfos, Yevamos 34b*
4. *Tosfos Yeshanim, Nedarim 20ab*
5. *Tosfos Yeshanim, Yevamos 34b*
6. *Tosfos Talmid Rabeinu Tam Al HaTorah, Manuscript, Genesis 38:9*[221]
7. Rabeinu Nissim of Gerona, *Peirush HaRan, Nedarim 20b; Chidushei HaRan, Sanhedrin 58b*
8. Rabeinu Yonah of Gerona, *Sanhedrin 58b*
9. Rabbi Yeshayah of Trani I, *Tosfos Rid, Yevamos 12b*
10. Rabbi Yeshayah of Trani II, *Riaz, Kuntres Harayos, Sanhedrin 58b*[222]
11. Rabbeinu Asher ben Yechiel, *Peirush HaRosh, Nedarim 20a*[223]; *Tosfos HaRosh, Nedarim 20b, Yevamos 34b*; Rabeinu Asher to *Yevamos 34b* (no longer extant, but preserved in *Hagahos Habach* to *Rosh, Yevamos 34b*, in *Yam Shel Shlomoh* to *Yevamos 34b*, and in *Beis Yosef* to *Tur, Orach 240:2-4:4*)
12. Rabbi Yaakov ben Asher, *Tur, Orach Chaim 240:2-4*

## HALACHIC POSITIONS

13. *Talmidei Rabeinu Peretz, Nedarim 20b*
14. Rabbi Yisrael Alnaqua, *Menoras Hamaor, Perek Nisuei Ishah*[223*]
15. Rabbi Betzalel Ashkenazi, *Shitah Mekubetzes, Nedarim 20b*[224]
16. Rabbi Avraham of Montpellier (*Avraham min Hahar*), *Nedarim 20b*
17. Rabbi Yeruchem ben Meshulam, *Rabeinu Yeruchem, Nesiv 32*
18. Rabbi Alexander Suslin, *Sefer HaAgudah, Nedarim 20a, Sanhedrin 58b, Yevamos 34b*
19. Rabbi Mordechai ben Hillel, *Mordechai, Hilchos Nidah 731-732*
20. Rabbi Menachem Ibn Zerach, *Tzeidah Laderech, Maamar 3, Clal 4, Chapter 14*[225]
21. Rabbi Yitzchak of Corbeil, *Sefer Mitzvos Katan, Positive Commandment 285*

## Wife-on-Top[226]

1. Maimonides, *Commentary to the Mishnah, Sanhedrin 7:4*
2. Rabbi Yom Tov ben Avraham Asevilli, *Ritva*[227]
3. *Tosfos Yeshanim, Nedarim 20a*
4. *Tosfos Talmid Rabeinu Tam Al HaTorah, Manuscript, Genesis 38:9*[228]
5. *Talmidei Rabeinu Peretz, Nedarim 20b*

## Rear-Entry Vaginal Intercourse with Wife-on-Top[229]

1. Rabeinu Peretz, *Nedarim 20a*[230]

## Mefaresh, *Nedarim 20a*

The foremost medieval commentator on the Talmud was Rabbi Shlomoh Yitzchaki (1040-1105), commonly known by the acronym of his name, "Rashi." However, it is today generally understood that the commentary traditionally printed on the Talmudic page of *Nedarim 20ab* as "Rashi" was not actually penned by him, but by an unknown writer, referred to in rabbinic literature as "*Mefaresh* – the Commentator."[230*]

The precise intention of the *Mefaresh* commentary, here, is somewhat obscure, for when it interprets the term "overturning the table" on *Nedarim 20a* it mentions three different positions in tandem, and in the following order:

> "Face-to-back" (*panim c'neged oref*) – which in rabbinic literature always refers to rear-entry vaginal intercourse (unless otherwise specified).

"Unnatural intercourse" (*shebaim al neshoseihem shelo cedarcan*) – which in rabbinic literature always refers to anal intercourse (unless otherwise specified).

"Her-on-top, him-on-bottom" (*hee l'maalah v'hu l'matah*).

When the *Mefaresh's* three comments are combined, the result is: rear-entry vaginal or anal intercourse, with the wife on top and her back to the husband.[231]

Alternatively, the *Mefaresh* may have been offering two separate, but equally valid, interpretations of the term "overturning the table": rear-entry anal intercourse[232] or wife-on-top.

Or, it may have simply meant to explain that "overturning the table" is a general all-inclusive term[233] that could refer to any position other than standard face-to-face, husband-on-top, vaginal intercourse.[234]

## Maimonides, *Commentary to the Mishnah; Mishneh Torah*

Maimonides, in his *Commentary to the Mishnah, Sanhedrin 7:4*, first defines "overturned laying" (*mishkav hafuch*) as "man-on-bottom, woman-on-top," but he later includes "anal intercourse" and "intercourse between limbs" (a term to be defined below, in Part Three) in the permissive ruling of Rebbi and/or Rav as quoted on *Nedarim 20b* in regard to "overturning the table."

And in his *Mishneh Torah, Sefer Kedushah, Isurei Biah 21:9*, he lists only anal intercourse and intercourse between limbs by name.

Thus, Maimonides, too, may have understood "overturning the table" as a collective term referring to any form of creative sexual congress, which is permitted for married couples.[234*]

## The Sages' Ruling: Anything a Couple Craves to do Together Sexually, They May Do

As noted, Rabbi Yochanan bar Napacha, in the name of the Sages, rejects the opinion of Rabbi Yochanan ben Dahavai and the "ministering angels," and instead rules that "Anything a husband craves to do with his wife sexually, he may do." But did the Sages really mean to permit all four of the behaviors Rabbi Yochanan ben Dahavai had cautioned against?

Not many medieval commentaries offer direct interpretation on this statement of the Sages, for what interpretation could possibly be needed? "Anything is permitted" means *anything* is permitted! Nevertheless, because one opinion, Raavad III, asserts that "anything is permitted" meant *only one* out of the four, we will list, here, other medieval scholars who do comment directly or indirectly on this passage regarding how many, and which, of the four behaviors the Sages intended to permit:

<u>*All four*</u>: *"Overturning the table," gazing at and kissing the female genitals, non-sex-related talk*

1. Rabbi Avraham ben Yitzchak of Narbonne, *Raavad II*, *Sefer HaEshkol, Hilchos Tznius*[235]
2. Rabbi Avraham Hayarchi, commentary to *Callah Rabti*[236]
3. Rabbi Yitzchak of Corbeil, *Sefer Mitzvos Katan, Positive Commandment 285*[237]

<u>*At least three*</u>: *"Overturning the table," gazing at the female genitals, non-sex-related talk*

1. Rabbi Avraham of Montpellier (*Avraham min Hahar*), *Nedarim 20b*
2. Rabbi Betzalel Ashkenazi, *Shitah Mekubetzes, Nedarim 20b*

<u>*At least two*</u>: *Sex any time*[238], *kissing the female genitals*

1. Rabbi Yisrael Alnaqua, *Menoras Hamaor, vol. 4, Perek Nisuei Ishah*[239]

<u>*Only one*</u>: *"Overturning the table"*

1. Rabbi Avraham ben Dovid of Posquières, *Raavad III, Baalei HaNefesh, Shaar Hakedushah*[240]
2. Rabbi Shmuel ben Meshulam Yerondi, *Ohel Moed, Shaar Isur V'heter, Derech 11, Nesiv 2*[241]

Raavad III, in his work on Jewish "family purity" law, *Baalei HaNefesh*, argues in chapter *Shaar Hakedushah* that when the Sages ruled, "Anything a husband craves to do with his wife sexually, he may do," they came only to reject *one* caution of Rabbi Yochanan ben Dahavai, namely, his caution against "overturning the table" – which Raavad III interprets as rear-entry vaginal intercourse.

In his words:

> Only "overturning the table" [did the Sages come to permit]. But concerning the others [non-sex-related talk and gazing at or kissing the female genitals], even though they do not warrant harsh punishment (*eino nidon aleihem din chamor*), they nevertheless carry a prohibition (*mikol makom isur yesh bahem*), like we discussed before, that it is forbidden to speak non-sex-related words (*dvarim acherim*) during sex, unless it is necessary for the sexual act (*tzarchei tashmish*)...[242]

Raavad III goes on to argue why he believed the other three behaviors to still be forbidden – and we will explore and analyze his arguments in Part Five of this book. But of immediate concern, and which we shall not succeed in offering definitive clarity on, is his intention with the statement that "they do not warrant harsh punishment." It would seem that with this he had meant to, at the very least, reject the harsh cautions of physical congenital illness spoken of by Rabbi Yochanan ben Dahavai as resulting from these sexual behaviors. But Raavad III's very next words pointing to an earlier discussion in his same chapter[243] about non-sex-related talk obscures his intent, for there, in his earlier discussion, he writes:

> Even from the moment they begin foreplay [that is, not just from the moment they begin intercourse], it is forbidden for them to speak anything but sex-related talk. And if they did speak [non-sex-related talk], what is his punishment[244] [in the next world]? ... And what is his punishment in this world?[245] So did our rabbis teach: "What causes deafness? Because they talk during sex – which refers to non-sex-related talk."

Perhaps Raavad III had changed his mind about this punishment by the time he wrote the later passage in *Shaar Hakedushah*. But if he intended to say that non-sex-related talk and gazing at or kissing the female genitals still result in one's children being deaf, blind or mute, respectively, then what else could he have possibly been excluding when he said "they do not warrant harsh punishment"?

Rabbi Yaakov ben Asher in his *Arbaah Turim*, "*Tur*," quotes Raavad III's opinion that these three behaviors are forbidden and are not included in the permissive ruling of the Sages on *Nedarim 20b*. But Rabbi Yaakov makes no mention that "they do not warrant harsh punishment." Perhaps he had a different manuscript version of *Baalei HaNefesh, Shaar Hakedushah*. But whatever the case may have been, his presentation of Raavad III's intent is the one perpetuated in later halachic works, such as *Levush*,[246] *Chochmas Adam*,[247] *Mishnah Berurah-Biur*

*Halachah*[248] and *Kaf Hachaim*,[249] all of which give the (potentially erroneous) impression that Raavad III himself definitively endorsed Rabbi Yochanan ben Dahavai's cautions about congenital illness resulting from these three behaviors.

Now, *Callah Rabti* 1:14 does maintain that while all four of these behaviors are permissible by law, they are all still dangerous to the health of a fetus. But it is difficult to point to *Callah Rabti* as the source of what these later authorities present as Raavad III's approach, for in addition to the fact that the Talmudic version of Ameimar should arguably take legal precedence over the version of *Callah Rabti*,

a) Nowhere does Raavad III mention *Callah Rabti* in this particular discussion;

b) *Callah Rabti* expressly states that all four of these sexual behaviors are simultaneously <u>permitted</u> and <u>dangerous</u>, while Raavad III in *Baalei HaNefesh, Shaar Hakedushah* teaches that one of them ("overturning the table") is both <u>permitted</u> and <u>safe</u>, and the other three are <u>forbidden</u>;

c) *Callah Rabti* believed these behaviors to be dangerous only to a fetus that is conceived during the same sexual encounter in which they are performed. Raavad III makes no such distinction (although he does make such a distinction in regard to children conceived in a state of one of the nine-ten flawed conditions[250]).

Note also that Raavad III and Rabbi Shmuel ben Meshulam Yerondi (who is endorsing Raavad III) are alone among the medieval commentators listed above in stating that only one of the four behaviors cautioned against by Rabbi Yochanan ben Dahavai was permitted by the Sages *to the exclusion of the other three*. Rabbis Avraham of Montpellier, Yisrael Alnaqua and Betzalel Ashkenazi, while listing only two or three of the four behaviors in their comments on the Sages' ruling, do not state that they meant to exclude the unmentioned one or two. It is quite possible they were just listing a few representative examples of that which the Sages permitted, and they left it to the reader to understand that all four were in fact allowed.[251]

The case of Rabbi Alnaqua is especially informative, for considering that according to all opinions, including Raavad III, "overturning the table" is included in the Sages' permission (as proven by *Nedarim 20b*'s subsequent report of Rebbi and Rav permitting it in practical cases of Jewish law), Rabbi Alnaqua's omission of it in his specific comment upon the Sages' ruling proves he was only giving one or two general, not exclusionary, examples of what the Sages came to permit against Rabbi Yochanan ben Dahavai.[252]

We will yet return to explore and analyze Raavad III's interpretation of the Sages' ruling.[253] For now, let us conclude this section listing a number of other early sources who, while not necessarily spelling it out clearly in commentary format, indicate through their presentations in practical Jewish law that they understood the Sages on *Nedarim 20b* as permitting all four of these behaviors (even if for no other reason than the fact that they do not exclude any one of the behaviors in their presentation of the Sages' blanket permissive ruling):

1. *Tractate Callah 9*
2. *Callah Rabti 1:13-14* (though *Callah Rabti* still warns that these four behaviors are dangerous to a fetus conceived during the same sexual encounter in which they are performed)
3. *Halachos Gedolos, Hilchos Nazir*[254]
4. Maimonides, *Commentary to the Mishnah, Sanhedrin 7:4*;[255] *Mishneh Torah, Sefer Kedushah, Isurei Biah 21:9*[256]
5. Rabbi Simchah ben Shmuel of Vitri, *Machzor Vitri 528*[257]
6. Rabbi Yitzchak Aboab, *Menoras Hamaor, Ner Shlishi, Clal 6, Part 5: B'derech Hachibur*[258]
7. Rabbi Menachem Meiri, *Beis Habechirah, Nedarim 20b*[259]

Note that other medieval authorities who rule according to Maimonides on the matter of sexual technique and positions within marriage, can all possibly be presumed to interpret the Sages' ruling on *Nedarim 20b* in kind.[259*]

Finally, the "statement" of Rabbi Yitzchak Alfasi (1013-1103), "Rif," author of one of the first medieval halachic compendiums of Jewish law, is informative: He does not bring the entire discussion of Rabbi Yochanan ben Dahavai and the Sages at all.

Rabbi Alfasi to *Nedarim 20ab* leaves out all discussion concerning forbidden sexual positions or techniques within marriage. He mentions only the earlier discussions, about gazing at a forbidden woman's "heel" and shame/shamefacedness – dignity – as a Jewish quality. At most, in a totally separate Talmudic Tractate, *Shavuos 18b*, when defining the concept of "sanctifying oneself during sex" (for the purpose of bearing male offspring), Rabbi Alfasi brings Rabbi Eliezer's behavior with Ima Shalom as an example of extra-halachic piety.

As known to those familiar with his methodology, Rabbi Alfasi's omission of a Talmudic passage is tantamount to his rejection of it as a legally binding one.[260] Thus, we can reasonably assume that he understood the entire debate on *Nedarim 20ab* about sexual positions and technique to be only of an extra-halachic, pious nature.[261]

And perhaps his silence on the matter was a factor influencing the approach of a later admirer of his, who was also the disciple of a disciple of his disciple: Maimonides.[262]

## The Sages' Reasoning

We've established what a majority of medieval commentators understood the Sages on *Nedarim 20b* as permitting in the realm of sexual exploration within marriage. But let us also understand the underlying reasoning *why* the Sages permitted it.

There are four general approaches among the medievals:

1. G-d did not establish His law on sex only for the pious few, but for the majority of normal human beings. Because G-d knows His creations, He permitted a husband and wife to do anything they crave sexually together. But this was only out of consideration for the animalistic side of their natures. Ideally, G-d would like to see man and woman (gradually) transcend the animal within themselves and learn to perceive the divine purpose in all things, including sex.[263]

2. The Sages' analogy of "kosher meat from the butcher" explained:

   Meat is forbidden to be eaten by Jews until it is prepared properly in a "kosher" manner according to Jewish law. But once it is prepared properly it becomes permissible to enjoy in any way a person may crave, without guilt.

   So too, sex is completely forbidden for Jews until the relationship between man and woman is properly prepared.[264] But once the relationship is established on "kosher" grounds, man and woman become completely permissible to one another, to enjoy each other sexually in any way they mutually agree.[265]

3. In what the Sages understood to be a biblical reference to the technical legal/spiritual mechanics of the binding of marriage, the verse in Deuteronomy 24:1 describes it as a form of "acquisition" in which the husband accepts upon himself the obligations to support, respect and protect her, and to provide her sexual fulfillment to the best of his abilities, and in which she grants him exclusive rights to enjoy an intimate spiritual-physical relationship with her.

   Accordingly, the couple is granted by G-d permission to enjoy each other sexually in any way they mutually agree.[266]

4. The biblical verses in Leviticus 18:22 and 20:13 speak of "*mishkevei ishah* – a woman's *places* of intercourse."

   The plural tense of "places" implies that, according to G-d, a woman has two recognized places of intercourse, the vagina and the anus, and intercourse in either of these two places is forbidden when the nature of the relationship is illicit.[267]

   However, when a proper relationship has been established, such as through marriage, the man is permitted, and perhaps even expected by nature to crave, penetration in both places.[268] [269]

Note that while the first three approaches could justify the enjoyment of all four behaviors cautioned against by Rabbi Yochanan ben Dahavai, the fourth approach only justifies "overturning the table," and only as defined to mean anal sex.

## Three Small Words Every Man and Woman Needs to Hear

We will conclude our analysis of *Nedarim 20ab* with three small, but revolutionary, words of commentary in two medieval sources – perhaps the three most important words that will be encountered in this book.

As we've just seen, the Sages' permissive approach to marital sexual exploration could be understood as coming only to pacify the animalistic sides of man and woman, but not to welcome human erotic nature as something "holy," even within marriage.

However, directly upon the Sages' ruling that a husband and wife may do anything they crave sexually together, *Tosfos Yeshanim* and Rabbi Eliezer of Metz (12th century author of *Sefer Yeraim*)[270] comment:

> ***V'ein chisaron kedushah*** **– And there is no lack of holiness.**[271]

We will now turn to our second Talmudic text: *Hagigah 5b*.

## Babylonian Talmud, Tractate Hagigah 5b

Rabbi Illa[272] was once ascending the stairs of the house of Rabah bar Shila,[273] when he heard a young child reciting the following verse: "For behold, He forms mountains and creates winds; He recounts to man what his words were."[274]

Rabbi Illa exclaimed:

A slave whose master can tell him what all his words were, is there any remedy for him?

[The compilers-editors of the Talmud ask:]

What is the meaning [in the verse] of "what his words were"?

[They suggest an interpretation of the verse based on a statement of a sage two generations Rabbi Illa's senior; alternatively, the following sage himself interpreted this very verse in the following way]:

Rav[275] said:

Even the excess light-headed talk[XXXII] between husband and wife is recounted to a person at the time of [his or her] death.[276]

[The compilers-editors of the Talmud ask:]

But is this so [that Rav believed one must be so careful about one's words even in the privacy of one's own spouse]?

What about the case when Rav Cahana hid under the bed of his master, [this very same] Rav, and heard how he spoke to his wife, laughed with her, and performed his [sexual] needs?

Rav Cahana called out from under the bed: "Rav sounds like one who has never tasted hot food [i.e., sex] in his life!"

Rav called back to him, "Cahana, get out of here! This is uncivilized!"

[Rav Cahana responded: This, too, is Torah and I need to learn it.][277]

[In any case, Rav's excessive "talk and laughter" with his wife in bed would seem to contradict his very own caution against "excess light-headed talk" with one's own spouse.

The compilers-editors of the Talmud suggest a solution:]

---

[XXXII] Alternate textual versions of the Talmud read: excess talk (*sichah yeseirah*), light-headed talk (*sichah kalah*) or excessive/excessively light-headed talk (*sichah kalah yeseirah*).

Being that a survey of the medieval commentaries does not yield any clear correlation between discrepancy in textual version to discrepancy in interpretation, we have rendered it generally as "excess light-headed talk."

> This need not be left a contradiction: [Perhaps] here, [in the case of Rav's behavior], such talk was ["mood-related" – that is, it was] needed to arouse her to the mood [for lovemaking] (*tzarich l'ratzuyah*), while there [in the case of Rav's caution against excess light-headed talk, he was speaking of a wife for whom] such talk is not needed to arouse her to the mood (*lo tzarich l'ratzuyah*).

This is where the late-19th century Vilna edition of the Talmud ends the discussion.

But there are two important manuscript variations[278] of the Talmud's conclusion:

*Version one:*

> [Perhaps] here [in the case of Rav's behavior] it was in lead up to intercourse, while there [in the case of Rav's caution] it was [referring to] after intercourse was complete.
>
> Or, if you want, you may answer that [perhaps] both were in lead up to intercourse. But here [in the case of Rav's behavior] such talk was ["mood-related" – that is, it was] needed to arouse her to the mood [for lovemaking], while there [in the case of Rav's caution, he was speaking of a wife for whom] such talk is not needed to arouse her to the mood.

*Version two:*

> [Perhaps] here [in the case of Rav's behavior], such talk was ["mood-related" – that is, it was] needed to arouse her to the mood [for lovemaking], while there [in the case of Rav's caution, he was speaking of a wife for whom] such talk is not needed to arouse her to the mood.
>
> Or, if you want, you may answer that [perhaps] here [in the case of Rav's behavior] it was in lead up to intercourse, while there [in the case of Rav's caution] it was [referring to] after intercourse was complete.

## Hagigah 5b – Summary

The compilers-editors of the Talmud quote a statement of Rav that G-d will call a person to task for "excess light-headed talk," even if such talk be between husband and wife.

They then highlight an episode in which Rav's own disciple, Rav Cahana, hid under Rav's bed and heard the shocking amount of talk and laughter in which Rav himself engaged with his own wife before sexual intercourse.

They conclude offering a possible resolution to the matter: Rav was not cautioning against "mood-related talk," that is, any kind of talk that is required to arouse one's spouse to the mood for sex – no matter how "excessive," no matter how "light-headed." Only in regard to "non-mood-related talk", that is, if one's spouse is already in the mood for sex and thus light-headed talk is entirely unecessary, did Rav issue his caution.

A second, less widely known textual version of the Talmud[279] offers an alternate, even more liberal explanation: *Any kind of talk during foreplay* in lead up to intercourse – no matter how "excessive," no matter how "light-headed," "mood-related" or not – is completely excused by G-d, presumably because He understands that husband and wife cannot be expected to monitor everything that comes out of their mouths during the throes of passion. But after intercourse – in other words, at any other time of daily life – such "excess light-headed talk" is assumed by the compilers-editors of the Talmud to be objectionable in Rav's (and G-d's) eyes.

## Hagigah 5b – Analysis

The main issues that require analysis on *Hagigah 5b* are the following:

1. Before mixing in the episode of Rav Cahana under Rav's marital bed, what was the context of Rav's original caution against "excess light-headed talk" – was he speaking of words spoken between husband and wife in a strictly sexual atmosphere, or even to general conversation during non-sexual moments of life?

2. If in a sexual atmosphere, what was the actual nature of such talk itself – strictly sexual-sexy talk or even general jokingness?

3. In their first answer, the compilers-editors of *Hagigah 5b* have Rav's caution against "excess light-headed talk" (*sichah yeseirah/sicha kalah/sichah kalah yeseirah*) referring to talk during sexual foreplay that is "non-mood-related." Is such "non-mood-related talk" synonymous with the "non-sex-related talk" (*mili achronaisa*) the compilers-editors of *Nedarim 20ab* understood Rabbi Yochanan ben Dahavai as cautioning against?

   Conversely, is *Hagigah 5b's* unanimously acceptable "mood-related talk" (*tzarich leratzuya*) synonymous with *Nedarim 20b's* unanimously acceptable "sex-related talk" (*mili d'tashmisha*)?

   And is the "seductive talk" (*yefateh osah*) that *Tractate Callah 22* encourages in the name of Rabbi Eliezer closer in form to the "sex-related-talk" of *Nedarim 20ab* (which is in fact discussed, there, in tandem with the behavior of Rabbi Eliezer himself) or to the "mood-related talk" of *Hagigah 5b*?

A more fundamental question to be explored in a future volume of this series is what could possibly have been the reasoning behind Rav's objection to "excess light-headed talk" between spouses in the first place.

# DECONSTRUCTING THE CODE

## Sexy Talk, Vulgar Talk, Vain Talk

The medieval scholars, Rabbis Shlomoh Yitzchaki (Rashi) and Avraham of Montpellier,[280] define Rav's original use of the term "excess talk" (*sichah yeseirah*) in a specifically sexual context as referring to "playful-joking talk before intercourse" (*divrei s'chok shelifnei hatashmish*), during foreplay.

Rabeinu Chananel has Rav originally speaking against "lightheaded talk" (*sicha kalah*) without any given sexual context at all. He says only that it referred to a husband who does not appropriately limit conversation with his wife. But the example Rabeinu Chananel then offers of "appropriate" talk (possibly based on the conclusion of the compilers-editors of *Hagigah 5b*) is that which is needed to appease her from upset – an example that later commentaries bring specifically in the context of appeasement for the sake of sex.[281][282]

Rabbi Ovadiah Bartenura, however, in his commentary to *Ethics of the Fathers 1:5*, compares the teaching, there, about a husband not "unlimiting conversation"[283] with his own wife in general to Rav's original caution against "excess light-headed talk" (*sichah kalah*).

Thus, the discouragement of "excess light-headed talk" in the original teaching of Rav can perhaps be understood according to varying commentaries as having been said in regard to either sexual or non-sexual moments of life.

But the compilers-editors of *Hagigah 5b* then challenge Rav's caution from a strictly sexual context, questioning his very own excessive "talk and laughter"[284] in the marital bed. And there it hints to the kind of talk that would shock the likes of Rav Cahana, that is, sexually charged talk – "sexy talk."[285]

[It remains to be explored if such sexy talk is being embraced by the compilers-editors of the Talmud only when it is intended to facilitate full sexual intimacy or if they would embrace such talk even when a husband simply wants to playfully restore peace and harmony in the home or give his wife a loving, humorous, sexy mood lift at any time of day.

To this point, it must be emphasized that the sage, Rav, never actually said that "excess light-headed talk" is "forbidden," but only that a couple may be called upon one day to justify it. So if a sincere loving husband believes his wife is in real need of a mood lift at any time of life, and, knowing her better than any other human being, he believes that the best, or only, way to achieve that mood lift is through sexy humor, we can reasonably trust that the Creator Himself would empathize with and forgive him for it – and perhaps even encourage him to do it.]

Let it, however, be noted that *Babylonian Talmud, Shabbos 33b* and *Kesubos 8b* designate a subcategory of sexual talk, "vulgar talk" (*nivul peh*), which they vehemently discourage.[286] But these same Talmudic passages both offer a clear example of what is meant by "vulgar talk" – namely, guests at a wedding whispering amongst themselves about what the bride will be up to after the festivities are over…

According to a simple and reasonable reading of the Talmud, then, talk is only considered by G-d to be "vulgar" when it involves a sexually *illicit* context relative to the speaker and/or listener.[287] But "light-headed" loving sexy talk spoken between husband and wife – such as one spouse describing the other's physical beauty, or how the other turns them on sexually, or what he or she wants "to do" to the other – does not appear to be intrinsically "vulgar" according to these sources in the Talmud.[XXXIII]

That being said, in the next section we shall see at least one major commentary, Maimonides, discouraging – but not forbidding – pious married couples from "making their mouths vulgar with vain talk" (*lo yenavel piv b'divrei havai*)[XXXIV] – "vain talk" referring to that which fixates on the beauty of bodily form.[288]

---

[XXXIII] As for whether such "light-headed talk" need be initiated by the husband rather than by the wife, see above, footnote to p. 38 and endnote 125 thereon.

[XXXIV] Although Maimonides describes "vain talk" as a manner of "making one's mouth vulgar," there is clearly a legal and moral distinction between loving "vain talk" between husband and wife about each other and illicit "vulgar talk" between anyone about another person's spouse.

And the Talmud in *Shabbos* and *Kesubos* could have simply defined "vulgar talk" as any talk of a sexual nature even between husband and wife – and we would have known *a fortiori* that illicit sexual talk was included – yet the Talmud did not do so.

Therefore, for the purposes of this study we will maintain the general distinction between (permitted, albeit unpious) "vain talk" and (presumably forbidden) "vulgar talk."

And see below, endnote 419 point 5.

**Added note to the third edition:** See also Rabbi Eliezer Melamed's *Simchat Habayit v'Birchato* (second edition, 2015), p. 54.

## Talk During Sex Analyzed

[*Note to the Reader: The following section is somewhat technical. Feel free to skip to the Summary on page 81*]<sup>289 290</sup>

### Raavad III

Raavad III explicitly distinguishes between "sex-related talk" (*mili d'tashmisha*) and "mood-related talk" (*c'dei l'ratzosa*).[291] Regarding the former, Raavad III is somewhat vague, and he could be read as permitting it even mid-intercourse.[292] The latter he deduces to be permitted only during foreplay, prior to intercourse, but including any (non-illicit) talk necessary to arouse her to the mood for sex, even "non-sex-related talk."

Two alternate textual versions of Raavad III[293] have him defining "mood-related talk" (*c'dei l'ratzosa*) as talk that is meant to make peace with one's wife after an argument and/or a husband's "seductive talk" to his wife, as encouraged by *Tractate Callah 22* in the name of Rabbi Eliezer.[294]

But Raavad III then goes on to equate the reverse terms "non-sex-related talk" (*mili achronaisa*) and "excess light-headed talk" (*sichah yeseirah*) to both equally refer to one and the same kind of talk: talk that is both non-sex-related and unnecessary to arouse the wife to the mood. Therefore, he applies the caution of Rabbi Yochanan ben Dahavai on *Nedarim 20a* about congenital deafness and the caution of *Hagigah 5b* about being called to task on Judgment Day to both "non-sex-related talk" and "excess light-headed talk" equally and interchangeably. In other words, because Raavad III understands "*mili achronaisa*" and "*sichah yeseirah*" to be synonymous, he also understands the warnings about each one of them, in each of their respective Talmudic passages, as applying equally to the other.

To summarize Raavad III's opinion in regard to the four types of talk:

1. Sex-related/mood-related talk – Permitted, perhaps even during intercourse

2. Sex-related/non-mood-related talk – Permitted, perhaps even during intercourse

3. Non-sex-related/mood-related talk – Permitted only during foreplay

4. Non-sex-related/non-mood-related talk – Forbidden even during foreplay

## Maimonides

Maimonides, in *Mishneh Torah, Sefer Kedushah, Isurei Biah 21:9*, after permitting practically all sexual techniques and positions to husband and wife (to be discussed below), notes that:

> It is, however, the way of the pious not to act light-headedly in matters of sex (*midas chasidus shelo yakel adam es rosho lekach*) and to sanctify oneself during sex as we explained in *Hilchos Deos*.

In *Sefer Hamada, Deos 5:4*, in discussing appropriate sexual piety for Torah scholars, we again find Maimonides discouraging "excessive lightheadedness" as well as "vain talk":

> And he should not act excessively light-headed (*lo yakel rosho beyoser*), and he should not make his mouth vulgar with vain talk (*lo yenavel piv b'divrei havai*), even just between he and his wife. On the verse, "G-d recounts to man what his words were," sages explained: "Even the excess light-headed talk between husband and wife one is called to account for on the Day of Judgment..."

Now, it is not entirely clear what Maimonides intended with the term "light-headedness" in these two places. His use of the term "light-headedness" in *Isurei Biah 21:9* doesn't seem to be in reference to sexual talk at all, but to sexual positions and technique – the topics of his immediately-preceding discussion there. And his reference in *Deos 5:4* to the verse in Amos and the caution of Rav can be read as connecting back only to the issue of "vain talk," not to general "light-headedness." But then in *Deos 5:4* he also encourages a husband to *always* "talk a little and joke with her a little, so that their souls [in the plural] become settled [aligned[295]]." [296] [297]

Thus, Maimonides seems to be combining the teachings of *Hagigah 5b* and *Tractate Callah 22* – the latter of which encourages a husband to always speak "seductively" to his wife during sex.[298]

Note, however, that some medieval commentaries define *Nedarim 20b*'s "sex-related talk" (*mili d'tashmisha*) as talk that increases sexual passion, and some therefore say that it is *always* good to speak such talk during sex.[299] It is possible, then, that Maimonides was echoing this as well in his instruction to always "talk a little and joke a little" (and see next section: *Rabbi Avraham de Boton - Lechem Mishneh*).

In any case, one thing is clear: Maimonides maintains a crucial distinction between the "letter of the law" and the "spirit of the law," for he relegates *Hagigah 5b*'s caution only to discussions about voluntary piety for Torah scholars.[300] [301] And in neither place – not in *Deos 5:4* nor in *Isurei Biah 21:9* – does he speak against "non-sex-related talk" (*mili achronaisa*) either before or during intercourse.

## Rabbi Avraham de Boton – *Lechem Mishneh*

Rabbi Avraham de Boton, in his *Lechem Mishneh* commentary to Maimonides' *Mishneh Torah, Deos 5:4*, insists that the universally acceptable "sex-related talk" of *Nedarim 20b* and the universally acceptable "mood-related talk" of *Hagigah 5b* are two entirely separate kinds of talk.

He suggests that the compilers-editors of the Talmud on *Nedarim 20b* chose "sex-related talk" versus "non-sex-related talk" to be at issue, because Ima Shalom described her husband as *always* speaking to her before sex, and it is unlikely that he had to arouse her with "mood-related talk" every single time they were together.

And he suggests that the compilers-editors of *Hagigah 5b* chose "mood-related talk" versus "non-mood-related talk" to be at issue, because they believed it unlikely that Rav's excessive "laughter" with his wife was "sex-related."

Legally speaking, Rabbi Avraham de Boton, like Raavad III, considers "sex-related talk" to be acceptable even if the wife *does not* need to be aroused to the mood; and he considers "mood-related talk" acceptable only if the wife *does* need to be aroused, but including even "non-sex-related talk" if it will help excite her. However, while Rabbi Avraham de Boton does consider the possibility that *Nedarim 20b* and *Hagigah 5b* would interchange each other's solutions on the matter of acceptable talk during sex, he only considers this as a means to explain the perplexing view of *Tur*, to be discussed below, and he ultimately rejects it as unlikely. Thus, we can deduce, unlike Raavad III, Rabbi Avraham de Boton would *not* apply *Hagigah 5b's* and *Nedarim 20a's* respective warnings of repurcussion interchangeably to each other's contexts.

But most importantly: Rabbi Avraham de Boton insists that Maimonides understood the Sages on *Nedarim 20b* as rejecting all four of Rabbi Yochanan ben Dahavai's cautions. Thus, according to the Sages and Rabbi Yochanan bar Napacha as understood by Maimonides according to Rabbi Avraham de Boton, a married couple is permitted by the letter of the law to speak any subject matter they wish both before and during sexual intercourse, even if it is entirely unrelated to the sex act itself.

That is why, Rabbi Avraham de Boton concludes, the only distinction Maimonides discusses in *Deos 5:4* is that of *Hagigah 5b*, where he (discourages, but does not forbid, "vain talk" and he) not only permits, but encourages, "speaking and joking a little to settle [align] their souls" – mood-related talk.[302] Nowhere is Maimonides concerned at all about non-sex-related talk.

## Rabeinu Yonah

Rabeinu Yonah, in *Sefer Hayirah,* writes:

> And if one has a wife, he should be modest with her and *be careful* not to talk vulgar with her (*v'yizaher m'ledaber imah neveilah*), because even for the empty talk (*sichah beteilah*) between husband and wife one is called to account."[303]

He does not distinguish between "sex-related talk" and "non-sex-related talk," nor between necessary "mood-related talk" and unnecessary "non-mood-related talk."

And while he does imply that "vulgar talk" is in a category of its own (lower than "empty talk"), he does not actually forbid it, nor does he define it (at least not here).

## Rabeinu Nissim

Rabeinu Nissim, "Ran," to *Nedarim 20b* succinctly equates "sex-related talk" with "mood-related talk."

In his words:

> "Sex-related talk – is permitted, to arouse her to the mood."[304]

## Rabbi Menachem Meiri

Meiri, in his *Beis Habechirah* to *Nedarim 20b,* strongly implies that the Sages permitted all four of the behaviors cautioned against by Rabbi Yochanan ben Dahavai, including non-sex-related-talk, which Meiri discourages, but does not forbid, among "other forms of light-headedness" (*she'ar minei kalus rosho*[305]). He certainly does not isolate non-sex-related talk as forbidden.

In *Beis Habechirah* to *Hagigah 5a,* Meiri prefaces in his commentary to that section that the Talmud will be speaking of a number of behaviors that are not actually sinful, but which are unbecoming of Torah sages and therefore make them – Torah scholars – worthy of divine punishment (*harbei devarim ain gufam aveirah, v'hein nimasos mitachsiseihen shel talmidei chachamim v'raoi li'anesh bahem*).

Although he is not yet speaking about the Talmud's discussion on *Hagigah 5b* about potential divine judgement for "excess light-headed talk," it is informative that Meiri understood the context of *Hagigah 5a,* which leads up to it, as being of pious, not legal, import, and as specifically addressed to Torah scholars, not common laymen.[306]

And when Meiri does reach *Hagigah 5b's* discussion on talk during sex, he says only that a person should always strive for refined character traits, including the minimizing of "private talk" with one's wife, "unless he needs to arouse her to the mood for sex, so that he not be like the ignorant masses who 'tear and eat like lions'[307] [i.e., like one who grabs his wife and has his way with her without regard for her sensitivities]."

Clearly, Meiri does not "forbid" any form of talk during foreplay or intercourse, he only demands respect for one's wife. And nowhere does he indicate any equivalence between the two kinds of talk discussed on *Nedarim 20ab* and *Hagigah 5b*.

### Rabbi Yaakov ben Asher

Rabbi Yaakov ben Asher, in his *Tur, Even Haezer 25:2b-3*, calls the talk discouraged by *Hagigah 5b* "empty talk" (*sicha beteilah*[308]) [or "unnecessary talk" (see *Prishah* there)] while in *Orach Chaim 240:7-10* he refers to it as "light-headed talk" (*sichah kalah*).

But in both places, Rabbi Yaakov says that the kind of talk that is acceptable is "sex-related-talk" (*inyonei tashmish* or *iskei tashmish*, Hebrew equivalents of the Aramaic, *mili d'tashmisha*) for the sake of increasing the husband's pleasure, as learned from the case of Rav Cahana under the bed of Rav, or "mood-related talk" for the sake of making up with one's wife after an argument (*c'dei l'ratzosah*).

On the surface, Rabbi Yaakov's interpretation is difficult threefold:[309]

a) The universal acceptance of "sex-related talk" (*mili d'tashmisha*) is learned not from Rav's behavior as reported on *Hagigah 5b* (or *Brachos 62a*), but from Rabbi Eliezer's behavior as reported on *Nedarim 20b*;

b) He says that Rav's purpose in speaking with his wife was to increase his *own* sexual pleasure, while the compilers-editors of the Talmud on *Hagigah 5b* expressly posit that his purpose was to help arouse **her** to the mood;[310]

c) He presents the concept of mood-related talk (*c'dei l'ratzosah*) as an alternate acceptable context of talk during sex in addition to talk intended to increase a husband's erotic passion.

One possible way to reconcile all three points would be to suggest that Rabbi Yaakov accepted the lesser-known textual version of the Talmud on *Hagigah 5b* that: a) accepts *any* kind of (non-illicit) light-headed talk before intercourse, during foreplay, which could include talk that is intended to increase the husband's own passion as well;[311] and b) also accepts talk that is required to arouse the wife to the mood (*c'dei l'ratzosah*).

The only problem with this solution is that Rabbi Yaakov presents talk that is intended to increase the husband's sexual passion as a definition of "sex-related talk" – the topic of *Nedarim 20b*, not *Hagigah 5b*. We would have to say, then, that

Rabbi Yaakov understood that the compilers-editors of *Hagigah 5b* took it as a given that passionate talk during foreplay is "sex-related" (*mili d'tashmisha*), even though they did not expressly call it such in the Talmudic text itself (and see next page: *Rabbi Betzalel Ashkenazi*).

It should also be noted that, like Raavad III, Rabbi Yaakov can possibly be read to imply that "sex-related talk" is perfectly acceptable even during sexual intercourse[312] – which would include talk that is intended to increase the husband's sexual passion even mid-intercourse (and we have no logical or halachic reason to believe it would not also include talk meant to increase the wife's sexual passion mid-intercourse). Indeed, following Raavad III's lead, he quotes the teaching of *Tractate Callah 22* in the name of Rabbi Eliezer encouraging husbands to talk seductively to their wives during sex.[313]

Finally, while Rabbi Yaakov discourages "non-sex-related talk" both before and during intercourse, he never does expressly "forbid" it.

### Rabbi Yosef Caro

Rabbi Yosef Caro, in his *Beis Yosef* commentary to *Tur, Orach Chaim 240:9-10*, says that both *Nedarim 20b* and *Hagigah 5b* speak of sex-related talk (*mili d'tashmish*).

Apparently, that is why in his *Shulchan Aruch, Orach Chaim 240:9-10*, he applies the caution of the verse quoted on *Hagigah 5b* to the "non-sex-related talk" (*dvarim she'einam me'inyonei tashmish*) cautioned about on *Nedarim 20b* – which Rabbi Caro discourages (but does not expressly "forbid") both before and during sexual intercourse.

He then goes on to accept a husband speaking to his wife before intercourse in order to appease her after an argument – which he calls "mood-related talk" (*c'dei l'ratzosa*).

*Shulchan Aruch, Even Haezer 25:2* combines Maimonides' presentation in *Deos 5:4* with that of *Tur, Even Haezer 25:2b-3* – though he changes Maimonides' discouragement of "excessive lightheadedness" (*lo yakel rosho beyoser*) into a discouragement (though not a prohibition) of "any lightheadedness" (*lo yakel rosho*).[314]

Rabbi Caro, too, like Raavad III and Rabbi Yaakov ben Asher before him, is somewhat vague in his *Shulchan Aruch* on whether "sex-related talk" is permitted even during intercourse. But as noted above,[315] his comments in *Beis Yosef* to *Even Haezer 25:2b:V'al yesaper imah* can be read to imply that he understood the compilers-editors of the Talmud as unanimously permitting sex-related talk not only during foreplay, but also during intercourse.

In any case, he states in *Even Haezer* that "sex-related-talk" encompasses talk intended to intensify the husband's sexual arousal – which logically encompasses talk intended to intensify the wife's arousal as well.

# DECONSTRUCTING THE CODE

### Rabbi Betzalel Ashkenazi

Rabbi Betzalel Ashkenazi, in his *Shitah Mekubetzes, Nedarim 20b*, differentiates between "sex-related talk" and "mood-related talk," permitting both, but describing the former as for the purpose of increasing the husband's passion, and the latter, as simply stated on *Hagigah 5b*, as for the purpose of arousing the wife to the mood for sex.

### Rabbi Yaakov Emden

Rabbi Yaakov Emden equates the talk of Rabbi Eliezer with his wife to the talk of Rav with his – namely, that both were for the sake of arousing the wife to the mood. But, Rabbi Emden suggests, Rav did so more excessively than Rabbi Eliezer, because due to the unfortunately difficult nature of Rav's overall relationship with his wife, she required extra appeasement.[316]

### Summary

While at first glance it might appear that the compilers-editors of *Nedarim 20b* (in regard to the teaching of Rabbi Yochanan ben Dahavai and the real-life episode of Rabbi Eliezer) and of *Hagigah 5b* (in regard to the teaching and real-life-episode of Rav) were coming to accept and discourage the same kinds of talk in both places, they were actually, according to fundamental commentaries, discussing two entirely different kinds of talk, reflecting two entirely different contexts and concerns.

Thus, it is entirely possible that even Rabbi Yochanan ben Dahavai himself, on *Nedarim 20b*, had absolutely no objection to the talk cautioned against by Rav on *Hagigah 5b*, and vice-versa.

Similarly, it is entirely possible that the Sages on *Nedarim 20b* rejected Rabbi Yochanan ben Dahavai's caution against "non-sex-related talk," while they accepted Rav's caution against "excess light-headed talk."

And even if the Sages accepted Rav's caution against "excess light-headed talk," it is possible they understood it only as a pious measure for Torah scholars, not as a baseline law for all couples. And even Rav himself may have only meant it as such.

Maimonides, for one, is said to have understood the Sages on *Nedarim 20b* as permitting even "non-sex-related talk" even during actual intercourse. And he relegated the caution of *Hagigah 5b* against "excess light-headed talk" only to the spirit of the law for pious Torah scholars, he did not state it as a legal "prohibition" binding upon all couples.

All these points will become crucial later on, in Part Five of our study.

## The Bottom Line

We noted earlier that the question of what could possibly have been any sage's, or the Creator's, objection to "excess light-headed talk" between loving husband and wife is an important question to address and it will be explored further in a future volume of this series. But in light of some of the above, let us at least note the possibility that perhaps such an objection originally had less to do with the nature of the talk itself among common married folk, and more to do with the concern among pious sages of attaining elevated levels of divine sensitivity, perception and/or insight – in line with the statement found in the *Mishnah, Ethics of the Fathers 6:6*: "Torah is acquired by way of forty eight manners . . . minimizing conversation, minimizing laughter (*miut sichah, miut sechok*)."

See also *Ethics of the Fathers 3:16*: "Laughter and lightheadedness accustom one to illicit sexuality" (*sechok v'kalus rosh margilin l'ervah*) – though the relevance of this to husband and wife between themselves is also debatable.

And see also *Ethics of the Fathers 1:5* and *Avos D'Rabbi Noson 7:2-3* (mentioned above, footnote to page 32; and see below, endnote 695).

In any case, while further research will certainly shed greater light on the matter, a reasonable coalescence of all the textual variations of the Talmudic page on *Hagigah 5b* with the teachings of *Nedarim 20b* and *Tractate Callah 22* (the latter two both derived from Rabbi Eliezer's behavior/teaching) and the realistic, liberal approaches among the commentaries, would yield this general (arguably non-obligatory) guiding principle:

**In general**, one should avoid excessive silliness, and especially excessive/excessively sexually charged talk (*sicha kalah yeseirah-divrei havai*), even with one's own spouse during non-sexual moments of life (unless, perhaps, such is needed to lighten a despondent mood or to make up after an argument – at any time, not just when it is intended to facilitate full sexual intimacy).

**During foreplay**, in immediate lead up to sexual intercourse, one should avoid "non-sex-related talk" (*mili achronaisa*) that might distract the build-up of intimacy or potentially call thoughts of other people to mind – unless (non-illicit) "non-sex-related talk" is necessary to clear any hard feelings that might (expectedly or unexpectedly) still be lingering from an earlier argument or if such is needed to help arouse one's spouse to the mood for lovemaking.

Silly talk, or even (non-illicit) sexually charged talk (*sichah kalah yeseirah*) is also universally acceptable during foreplay if necessary to arouse a spouse to the mood for lovemaking.

And according to some, all silly or (non-illicit) sexual talk is perfectly understandable and acceptable before G-d during foreplay, no matter whether it is "necessary" or not, especially if it is intended to intensify the sexual arousal of either spouse.

**During intercourse**, any sex-related talk required to facilitate the practical technicalities of the act is universally acceptable (*mili d'tashmisha*). According to some, (non-illicit) talk that is intended to increase the husband's or wife's sexual arousal is also considered "sex-related."

And according to those commentaries who take the Sages on *Nedarim 20b* at their word, that they rejected all four cautions of Rabbi Yochanan ben Dahavai on *Nedarim 20a*, even (non-illicit) "non-sex-related talk" is perfectly acceptable even mid-intercourse.

Now, let us turn to our third Talmudic text: *Sanhedrin 58b*.

## Babylonian Talmud, Tractate Sanhedrin 58b

Rabbi Elazar[317] said in the name of Rabbi Chanina[318]:

> If a non-Jewish man has anal sex with his own wife, he is liable [i.e., punished] – for G-d states [in regard to man]: "And he shall cling [to his wife],"[319] which implies that he should not engage in anal sex with her [for it does not create a bond of "clinging"[320]].

Rava[321] responded:

> Is there ever a case where a Jew is not liable (*lo mechayev*) [*an alternate version reads:* where a Jew is permitted (*shari*)] and a non-Jew is liable (*mechayev*)?
>
> [Meaning to say, if a Jewish man is permitted[322] to have anal sex with his own wife, why can't a non-Jewish man?]

Rather, Rava explained [the verse in Genesis as teaching a completely different law]:

> If a non-Jewish man has anal sex with another [non-Jewish] man's wife, he is exempt (*patur*) [from liability]. Why? Because the prohibition against [non-Jewish] adultery learned from that verse in Genesis only applies where there is a bond of "clinging," which is not the case with anal sex.[xxxv]

---

[xxxv] See Maimonides, *Mishneh Torah, Sefer Shoftim, Melachim 9:7*, perhaps implying that such an adulterous act is not "permitted" by Heaven, it is only that the court of man cannot punish one for it. In such a case, then, G-d Himself exacts justice. And see below, page 86 point 1, and endnote 327 thereon.

This understanding of Rava's intention could perhaps be said to be supported by the fact that there is no alternate textual version of the Talmud which has Rava saying that such infidelity is "permitted," only that one is "exempt" for it, whereas there is an alternate textual version earlier on the Talmudic page which has Rava saying that anal sex between husband and wife within marriage is not just "not liable," but "permitted" (*shari*).

But see *Peirush Rashi* and *Yad Ramah* to *Sanhedrin 58b*. And consider the perspective of Rabbi Moshe Weiner in his *Sheva Mitzvos Hashem*, vol. 2 (ANI 2009), pp. 451-452.

## Sanhedrin 58b - Summary

Rabbi Elazar reported in the name of another sage, Rabbi Chanina, that G-d's statement in Genesis, "And he shall cling to his wife," teaches that anal sex between husband and wife is forbidden to non-Jews.

Rava, who was probably a contemportary of Rabbi Elazar,[323] argues that being that we know anal sex is permitted to Jewish married couples, it must also be permitted to non-Jewish couples, for whom Torah's restrictions on sexual behavior are generally more lenient.[324] Thus, Rava explains,[325] the verse in Genesis was not meant to teach a prohibition about anal sex for anyone, but rather a leniency about anal sex for non-Jews (a leniency that does not extend to Jews), that anal sex between a married non-Jewish woman and another non-Jewish man is not liable for punishment (at least not in the human court).

## Sanhedrin 58b – Analysis

There are four key points to consider in analyzing *Sanhedrin 58b*:

1. The common Vilna edition of the Talmud does not actually have Rava stating that anal sex is "permitted" (*shari*) to Jewish couples, only that they are "not liable" (*lo mechayev*) for it. Ostensibly, it is conceivable that something could be forbidden by Jewish law for Jews even though one cannot be liable – i.e., punished – for it by the hand of the rabbinic court, only by the hand of Heaven.[326] [xxxv*]

Note, however, that numerous surrounding discussions, there, about the laws of Jews and non-Jews – including an immediately preceding discussion quoted in the name of the same Rabbi Elazar in the name of the same Rabbi Chanina – are clearly in the realm of justice meted out by the human court.[327]

And numerous medieval commentaries cite an alternate textual version that has Rava explicitly stating that anal sex is "permitted" (*shari*) to Jews within marriage, while yet others offer logical support for such a reading of the text.[328]

2. Rava, who permits anal sex between husband and wife in *Sanhedrin 58b*, is the same Rava quoted in *Callah Rabti 1:13* as explaining that according to Rabbi Yochanan ben Dahavai, "overturning the table" – which numerous textual versions of *Tractate Callah 9* define as rear-entry vaginal intercourse – can result in congenital lameness if performed during the same sexual encounter in which conception occurs. And *Callah Rabti 1:14* has the Sages agreeing to Rabbi Yochanan ben Dahavai about the dangers of such "overturning the table," even though it also has the Sages permitting it by law.

Thus, it must be stated for the record that it is possible Rava on *Sanhedrin 58b* would extend Rabbi Yochanan ben Dahavai's "risk" of congenital lameness to anal sex as well, if performed during the same sexual encounter in which conception occurs.[xxxvi] Still, Rava could permit it by law even when conception is expected to occur – just like, according to *Callah Rabti*, the Sages permitted by law all four of the behaviors cautioned against by Rabbi Yochanan ben Dahavai, including rear-entry vaginal intercourse, even during the same sexual encounter in which conception occurs.

3. There is an important point to consider from this Talmudic passage which has wide ramifications for our entire discussion – namely: while there are various interpretations among the medieval commentaries as to the meaning of Rabbi Yochanan ben Dahavai's euphemism on *Nedarim 20ab*, "overturning the table,"

---

[xxxv*] See above, footnote to page 84.

[xxxvi] As for how conception could occur during an encounter in which anal sex is performed, see below, pp. 156, 158.

for which he cautioned that children may be afflicted with lameness, *Sanhedrin 58b* is speaking about anal sex specifically.[329]

Thus, the argument among the commentaries over the definition of "overturning the table" on *Nedarim 20ab* is merely about which specific position Rabbi Yochanan ben Dahavai himself attributed childhood lameness to (and therefore perhaps forbade) and which position the Sages believed to be perfectly safe (and therefore they permitted). But it would be difficult for any commentary to deny that anal sex is legally permitted, in light of *Sanhedrin 58b*.

In fact, even Raavad III, who, in his *Baalei HaNefesh, Shaar Hakedushah*, maintains that "overturning the table" on *Nedarim 20ab* refers to rear-entry vaginal intercourse, is utterly silent in his critical notes to Maimonides' code of law, *Mishneh Torah, Sefer Kedushah, Isurei Biah 21:9*, where Maimonides permits anal sex.[330] It is reasonable to attribute Raavad III's silence, there, and hence his implied ultimate permission of anal sex, to his knowledge of *Sanhedrin 58b*.[331]

4. While all the medieval commentaries gave a straightforward reading of the passage in *Sanhedrin 58b* – that Rava took it as a given that anal sex is permitted to Jewish couples, and therefore he argued that it must also be permitted to non-Jewish couples – one much later commentary, Rabbi Elazar Azikri (1533-1600), in his legal-ethical-mystical work, *Sefer Charedim*, attempted to argue the exact opposite: that Rava understood anal sex to be forbidden, and not only for non-Jewish couples, but for Jewish ones as well.

Rabbi Azikri went so far as to say that Raavad III must have read *Sanhedrin 58b* in this way – for Rabbi Azikri assumed Raavad III could not possibly have permitted anal sex. But see the end of point 3 above, that Raavad III's view on anal sex cannot be assumed to be so clear and categorical.

Rabbi Eliyahu Spira (1660-1712), in his *Elyah Rabah* commentary to *Levush, Orach Chaim 240:10:4*, dismisses Rabbi Azikri's interpretation of *Sanhedrin 58b* (*gam shaarei dvarim shehe'erich lidchos raayas tosfos m'shas Sanhedrin eino l'maayein*).[332] But for those interested in understanding the main points of, and some possible difficulties in, Rabbi Azikri's argument, we present them below, in endnote 616.[333]

Let us now move on to one more fundamental question left to address:

If the medieval commentaries understood Rava on *Sanhedrin 58b* as permitting anal sex for married couples, and if a majority of medieval commentaries understood the Sages, Rebbi, Rav and Rabbi Yochanan bar Napacha on *Nedarim 20b* as permitting anal sex within marriage as the correct definition of "overturning the table,"[334] did they all understand all these sages as permitting only anal penetration without ejaculation, or even complete anal intercourse to the point of the husband's climax?

# HALACHIC POSITIONS

To clarify this, we must turn to one final Talmudic passage, on *Yevamos 34b*, after which an analysis of this question will be possible.

# DECONSTRUCTING THE CODE

## Babylonian Talmud, Tractate Yevamos 34b

> Er and Onan performed anal sex [with Tamar].<sup>XXXVII</sup> [335]

> But there is a *braisa* that contradicts this:

>> Throughout the twenty-four months [that a woman is nursing her baby, if her husband has sex with her] he should penetrate vaginally and pull out to ejaculate [i.e. coitus interruptus, so as not to impregnate his wife again and disrupt her milk flow]. This is the opinion of Rabbi Eliezer.[336]

>> The Sages said to him: "But this is nothing other than the act of Er and Onan [for which they were punished]?!"[337]

> [The compilers-editors of the Talmud suggest a resolution to the contradiction:

>> The Sages meant that] it resembles the act of Er and Onan [in one respect], but it was not the actual act of Er and Onan [in another respect].

>> It resembles the act of Er and Onan [insofar as it involves the ejaculation of seed outside the vagina], as the verse says [of Onan], "And when he would come upon his brother's wife, he would spill his seed to the ground."

---

[XXXVII] *The biblical story of Er and Onan is recounted in Genesis, Chapter 38 (translation by Judaica Press):*

1. Now it came about at that time that Judah was demoted by his brothers, and he turned away until [he came] to an Adullamite man, named Hirah.

2. And there Judah saw the daughter of a merchant named Shua, and he took her [i.e., he married her] and came to her.

3. And she conceived and bore a son, and he named him Er.

4. And she conceived again and bore a son, and she named him Onan.

5. Once again she bore a son, and she named him Shelah, and he (Judah) was in Chezib when she gave birth to him.

6. And Judah took a wife for Er, his firstborn, named Tamar.

7. Now Er, Judah's firstborn, was evil in the eyes of the Lord, and the Lord put him to death.

8. So Judah said to Onan, "Come to your brother's wife and perform the rite of the levirate, and raise up progeny for your brother."

9. Now Onan knew that the progeny would not be his, and it came about, when he came to his brother's wife, he wasted [his semen] on the ground, in order not to give seed to his brother.

10. Now what he did was evil in the eyes of the Lord, and He put him to death also.

But it does not resemble the act of Er and Onan insofar as there [by Er and Onan] it was anal intercourse, whereas here, [in the above-quoted *braisa* about a nursing mother,] it is vaginal intercourse [concluding with coitus interruptus].

[The compilers-editors of the Talmud ask:]

The verse clearly says that Onan spilled his seed to the ground, but how do we know that his older brother, Er, did the same before him?

[The compilers-editors of the Talmud answer:]

Rabbi Nachman bar Yitzchak[338] explained: It says about Onan, "And G-d killed him also." [The word "also" implies that] he died for the same reason [as his brother, Er, before him.]

[The compilers-editors of the Talmud ask further:]

The verse gives us a reason for Onan [wanting to avoid getting Tamar pregnant], because he did not want her to bear a child that the community would consider his brother's. But what reason did Er have [for not wanting to get Tamar pregnant]?

[The compilers-editors of the Talmud answer:]

So that her beauty would not be diminished by pregnancy.

# DECONSTRUCTING THE CODE

## Yevamos 34b – Summary and Analysis

The Talmud on *Yevamos 34b* states that the two biblical sons of Judah, Er and Onan, were both killed by the hand of Heaven for the "sin" of anal sex.

In the case of Er, it is suggested that he performed anal sex with his wife, Tamar, in order to prevent any change in her beauty as a result of pregnancy. For this, the Talmud tells us, Er died young.

A younger brother, Onan, was then given Tamar in levirate marriage to sire a son who would carry on Er's name. But Onan, too, performed anal sex with her, to avoid conceiving a child that would be considered his brother's in the eyes of the community.[339] For this, we are told, he, too, died young.

It is thus implied by *Yevamos 34b* that anal sex is sinful.

*Tosfos* on *Yevamos 34b* and on *Sanhedrin 58b* ask the obvious:

If *Sanhedrin 58b* and (according to most medieval interpretations of the term "overturning the table") *Nedarim 20b* both permit anal sex, how could it be stated on *Yevamos 34b* that anal sex was the "sin" of Er and Onan?

*Tosfos*, in the name of Rabeinu Yitzchak of Dampierre, "Ri" (1120-1200),[340] offers two explanations:

a) Anal sex is permitted only without intra-anal ejaculation. The sin of Er and Onan was that they went so far as to ejaculate intra-anally.

b) Anal sex is permitted even with intra-anal ejaculation from time to time, randomly in the heat of passion for the sake of the husband's (or couple's) sexual fulfillment (*b'akrai b'alma umisaveh lavo al ishto shelo cedarcah, shari*), just not as an intentional and constant means of halachically-unsanctioned birth control. The sin of Er and Onan was that they intentionally used anal sex as a regular means to avoid pregnancy.[XXXVIII][341]

The issue under discussion is that of "wasting seed in vain," perhaps one of the most misunderstood concepts in all of Jewish law. A full historical exploration and analysis of the concept will be the subject of volume two of this series.[XXXIX]

But as pertains to the matter of birth control, here, suffice it to say that according to certain commentaries, a man who falls within the biblical obligation to procreate by default also falls within the prohibition of "wasting seed in vain"[342]

---

[XXXVIII] Note that birth control is not categorically forbidden by Jewish law. Readers seeking practical guidance are encouraged to consult a halachically-competent rabbi. And see *Contraception in Contemporary Orthodox Judaism*, by Gedalia Meyer and Henoch Messner, available online at: *http://finkorswim.com/wp-content/uploads/2012/06/Contraception.pdf*.

[XXXIX] And see above, footnote to page 3.

– which, on the surface, implies a categorical prohibition against any and all extra-vaginal ejaculation (i.e., ejaculation outside the wife's vagina).[XL]

*Tosfos*, however, explains in the name of Rabeinu Yitzchak that intra-anal ejaculation is only problematic as "wasting seed in vain" if it is done constantly, betraying a specific intention for (unsanctioned) birth control. If, however, a man craves anal sex with his wife from time-to-time as a matter of sexual fulfillment within marriage, it is permitted for him even to ejaculate intra-anally.[343] [344]

As we shall see in Part Three, below, most medieval commentators who weigh in on the question of intra-anal ejaculation endorse this second approach of Rabeinu Yitzchak,[345] and they therefore permit anal sex within marriage even to the point of the husband's climax.

---

[XL] Note that as long as the husband's ejaculation occurs intra-vaginally (i.e., into his wife's vagina), it is not considered problematic even if she does not, or cannot, become pregnant by it. According to Jewish law, such intra-vaginal ejaculation is considered worthy in-and-of-itself, because it occurs naturally in the course of the husband providing his wife her need for physical intimacy and sexual fulfillment, and because it itself even enhances the wife's pleasure.

## The Letter of the Law and its Spirit

It is important before concluding this chapter to introduce a concept that is fundamental to our discussion, namely, that like much else in Judaism, when it comes to the laws of Jewish sexuality there is the "letter of the law" and its "spirit."

As pertains to our current topic, marital sex, there are two related concepts that must be explored[346]: the specific concept of "sanctifying oneself during marital sex" (*mekadesh atzmo beshaas tashmish*)[347] and the general concept of "sanctifying oneself in that which is permitted" (*kadesh atzmecha b'mutar lach*).[348]

## The Definition of "Sanctification" in Marital Sex

Now, the Hebrew term, "*kedushah*," generally translated as "sanctity" or "holiness," is a vague term that requires detailed analysis in each context in which it appears – an analysis that will have to wait for a future volume of this series. There, we will also explore in greater depth the above two concepts. But in order to at least dispel some widespread misconceptions, we will list, here, the Talmudic sources and medieval interpretations about the concept of "sanctity" within marital sex in particular.

### Babylonian Talmud, Tractate Nidah 71a:

> What should a man do in order to bear male offspring? He should marry a woman appropriate to him and sanctify himself during sex.

### Babylonian Talmud, Tractate Shavuos 18b:

> Rabbi Binyamin bar Yefes said in the name of Rabbi Elazar:
>> Whoever sanctifies himself during sex will bear male offspring, for the verse (Leviticus 11:44[349]) states, "And you shall sanctify yourselves, and you shall be sanctified," and not long afterwards the verse (Leviticus 12:1) states, "When a woman gives seed and gives birth to a son…"

Firstly, note that the Talmud in both places speaks of sanctity during sex as something one does in order to "merit" male offspring, not to "fulfill" the letter of the law.

But what does this "sanctity during sex" actually look like? Do the commentaries give any examples to help define it?

In fact, they do.

Rabbi Shlomoh Yitzchaki, in *Peirush Rashi*, defines "sanctity," here,[350] as "modesty"[351] – though he does not explain what this specifically means in this context.

Rabbi Yeshayah of Trani I (author of *Tosfos Rid*) explains that "sanctity," here, refers to the husband not intentionally fantasizing about other women. This would imply that sexual sanctity within marriage is not about "modesty," but about focus.[352]

Rabbi Yitzchak Alfasi, Rif, gives five specific examples of what "sanctity" in marital sex might look like[353]:

- Rabbi Eliezer's behavior with his wife, Ima Shalom. That is, he had sex with her only in the middle of night, he uncovered only a small portion of her nether region, and he penetrated her "as if he were compelled by a demon" – all, or in part, so that he would not come to intentionally fantasize of other women, because he believed such fantasies might cause spiritual harm to his children-to-be-conceived[354]

- The husband strives to give his wife her climax first, before allowing himself to have his own[355]

- Avoiding sexual intercourse during the daylight hours, as an expression of the Jewish people's "holiness"

- Waiting roughly ten minutes[356] after using the latrine before having sex, so that the "demon of the latrine" will not physically harm the child-to-be-conceived

- To abstain from sex on the day one's wife expects her period, as an added measure of rabbinic stringency

Let us now explore the implications of each of Rabbi Alfasi's examples.

## *Rabbi Eliezer's Behavior*

Rabbi Alfasi's first example alone, that of Rabbi Eliezer's behavior with Ima Shalom, encompasses both Rashi's and Rid's interpetations (modesty and focus, respectively).[357] But it must be noted that according to a simple reading of the story, Rabbi Eliezer's own concern was about the spiritual purity of his children, not purity of mind for its own sake, nor fulfilling his wife's sexual needs.[358] And Rabbi Eliezer's behavior is not considered by any authorities to be legally binding, but only a matter of extra-halachic piety.[358*]

## DECONSTRUCTING THE CODE

### Ladies First

Rabbi Alfasi's second example is that of a husband striving to give his wife her climax before allowing himself to enjoy his own. As seen above, this is the example of "sanctity" that the Talmud itself speaks of, the purpose of which is not fulfillment of the law nor even necessarily one's wife's happiness, but his (and/or her) desire for male offspring.

### Sex in the Night

The notion of not having sex during the day is a complex topic that will be more fully explored in a future volume of this series. But to offer a brief outline here:

The Talmud in *Tractate Nidah 16b-17a* quotes various explanations for such a stringency, from loose biblical inferences to a concern expressed by the third generation Babylonian Amoraic sage, Rav Chisda, that sex during the day would compromise a husband's ability to "love his wife like himself."[359] The fourth generation Babylonian Amoraic sage, Abayei, explains Rav Chisda's concern: a husband seeing his wife's body in the light might turn him off sexually – the apparent implication being that he might find something temporarily unhygienic,[359*] and that his loss of arousal would cause her to suffer humiliation, not to mention doubt about his love and/or her own beauty.

But the reason Rabbi Alfasi himself mentions for daytime abstinence is that of the second generation Babylonian Amora, Rav Huna, that "the Jews are a holy people and therefore they do not have sexual intercourse during the day" (*yisrael kedoshim heim, v'ein meshamshin mitoseihem bayom*). This teaching, repeated in the name of Rav Huna in *Talmud, Shabbos 86a, Kesubos 65b* and *Nidah 17a*, suggests that at some point in history the Jewish people accepted upon themselves not to have sex during the day – even though this was not prohibited by G-d Himself and it is unclear if the original ban was initiated by the rabbis.[360]

The compilers-editors of the Talmud, in fact, seem to have believed that the Jews as a people already took this custom upon themselves before the Giving of the Torah – though they present this as a given without specific evidence to support it.[361]

As for why the Jewish people might have taken on such a stringency, and even before the Giving of the Torah, perhaps one might posit that the general concern in ancient times, especially in a tent encampment, was that during the daytime the risk of being heard or observed by others, especially family members, was greater. At night, at least, people were out of the streets, and family members and neighbors were (hopefully) sound asleep.[362]

But on this passage of Rabbi Alfasi's, some commentaries explain that the Jewish men took upon themselves this stringency in order to avoid "fully satiating themselves" from the sight of their wive's faces[363] or bodies[364] (sic). And these same commentaries also put forth a second, somewhat contradictory (albeit rooted in the Talmud) explanation, that the Jewish husbands did not want to see anything on their wive's naked bodies that might turn them off from wanting to be intimate with them[365] and thus cause the sexual encounter to be loveless[366] [367] or cause them to intentionally fantasize about other women.[368] [369]

In any case, whatever the true original reason for this stringency might have been, sexual intercourse during the day is permitted by Jewish law when the room is darkened – as reported in the name of Abayei's colleague, Rava, on *Nidah 17a*. Rava adds that even in a lit room that cannot practically be darkened during the day, if the husband is a Torah scholar – which presumably means he can be trusted to act modestly – he and his wife may simply cover themselves head-to-toe by a blanket for intercourse.[370] And according to one latter-day opinion, they need only cover the actual genitalia and the immediately surrounding lower bodily regions for intercourse.[371]

Sexual foreplay prior to intercourse – including, according to those who permit it, oral sex – could perhaps be allowed for all couples at night even in a perfectly lit room, as well as during the day in a lit room (that can later be darkened), and in both cases perhaps even without a blanket covering, so long as the room is subsequently darkened for intercourse. And the same could perhaps apply for a Torah scholar during the day in a lit room that cannot practically be darkened, so long as he and his wife are subsequently appropriately covered for intercourse.

As stated, more on this topic in a future volume of this series.[XLI]

### Avoiding Demons

Rabbi Alfasi's example of waiting for sex until after a certain amount of time has elapsed after using the latrine was for the sake of avoiding the influence of "demons" upon the fetus of one's child.[372]

---

[XLI] In the meantime, see also endnotes 369, 845.

**Added note to the third edition:** See the ruling of Rabbi Yosef Messas (1892-1794) in his *Mayim Chaim, Responsum 97*, that with modern advances in matters of hygiene, it is permissible **on occasion, randomly in the heat of passion (*b'akrai*)**, for any husband and wife who desire the sight of each other's bodies during intercourse to have sex during the day or night in a perfectly lit room, even without covering themselves head to toe – on the logic that such is certainly no worse than intra-anal ejaculation, which, Rabbi Messas says, is also permitted within marriage on occasion, randomly in the heat of passion. Rabbi Messas does not specify if the genitals, or any other specific body parts, must be covered for foreplay or intercourse on such an occasion. To learn more about Rabbi Yosef Messas, see the online essay by Rabbi Dr. Marc Shapiro at www.jewishideas.org/article/rabbi-joseph-messas. Credit goes to Rabbi Eliezer Melamed for bringing this source in *Mayim Chaim* to my attention in his *Simchat Habayit v'Birchato* (second edition, 2015) p. 64, end of footnote 21. See also pp. 55-57, there, and footnote 16 thereon. And especially see Rabbi Maor Kayam's *Harchavot l'Simchat Habayit v'Birchato* (2015), pp. 155-162.

Again, this is a matter concerning the physical health of the child, not the purity of thought, speech or action of the parents, and in this case arguably the expression of an ancient pseudo-scientific frame of reference.[373] And even if this instruction had wisdom to it from a hygenic perspective, it would not necessarily apply to modern-day private indoor residential bathrooms, which are arguably more sanitary than the average kitchen was in biblical, Talmudic or medieval times. But this example further demonstrates that "sanctity" within sex need not carry a puritanical connotation at all; that it need not include any attempt to curb sexual enjoyment or curiosity.

### Rabbinic Decree

Finally, Rabbi Alfasi's example about abstaining from sex on the day one's wife expects her menses is simply a matter of rabbinic decree to avoid transgression of the biblical prohibition of intercourse during menstruation.

### Other Medieval Opinions

Rabbi Avraham of Narbonne, Raavad II, in his *Sefer HaEshkol, Hilchos Tznius*,[374] includes all five of Rabbi Alfasi's examples to define "sanctity" in marital sex, adding also not having sex with the lights on at night[375] and not having naked sex uncovered by a blanket.[376]

Rabbi Avraham Hayarchi adds, as examples of "sanctity," avoidance of the nine-ten flawed conditions of mind or circumstance during sex, as well as the avoidance of sex standing up, sitting down, side-by-side or with the lights on.[377] The analogy Rabbi Avraham Hayarchi offers of the ideal holy lover is that of a gentleman who does not gorge himself to the point of nausea from all the permissible delights of the dinner table, but who rather takes only that which he needs to satisfy his hunger pangs.[378]

*Igeres Hakodesh*, the mystical work of an anonymous medieval author or group of authors (attributed by some to Nachmanides, "Ramban"[379]), was composed with the express purpose of teaching sanctity in sex.[380] While the general thrust of the work is that focusing on G-dly intent during conception will guarantee[381] one's child turns out righteous, the author also mentions some practical steps he believed a person could take toward attaining this goal.

One example:

> The man should sanctify himself also by eating proper foods shortly before sex, so that his sperm will be clean and pure and balanced.[382]

The author of *Igeres Hakodesh* explains earlier in his discussion that proper food results in proper blood, which in turn results in proper sperm, and hence, proper children (physically and spiritually). He says that the quality of the food will determine whether the child will be wise or foolish, righteous or wicked (*hamazon hanilkach terem hachibur hu sibah l'havyas ha'adam hachanah lihiyos havlad chacham oe pesi oe tzadik oe rasha*) – and that choosing one's food properly is included in the principle of "sanctifying oneself during sex."

Another example:

> He should not think about sin or illicit sexuality, but only about holy things. And he should think about pure righteous men, men of knowledge and intellect and wisdom, for those thoughts during intercourse will affect his semen and cause it to be formed in their quality (*ci osan hamachshavos yacholu al hazera v'yitzairahu b'tzurasan*). And the same goes for his wife's thoughts.[383][384]

Rabbi Menachem Meiri, in his *Beis Habechirah* to *Shavuos 18b*, writes just general encouragement, that:

> It is appropriate (*raoi*) for a person to sanctify himself during sex and to behave with extra modesty, both in terms of the time for sex – only to engage in sex at times when everyone is asleep, not during the daytime at all and not at the beginning or end of night – and in terms of the quality and form of the behaviors (*b'eichus ha'inyanim utechunasam*)

In his commentary to *Nedarim 20b*, Meiri explains that the Sages permitted a couple to do anything they crave sexually together, because they understood that G-d simply does not expect it to be possible for all normal human beings to "sanctify" themselves in that which is permitted (*she'ee efshar l'chol bnei adam l'kadesh atzmam b'mutar lahem*). His implication, there, then, is that avoidance of those behaviors listed by Rabbi Yochanan ben Dahavai – non-sex-related talk during sex, gazing at or kissing the female genitals, and "overturning the table" – would also be considered a form of voluntary, idealistic "sanctification."

The same is implied by Maimonides in his *Commentary to the Mishnah, Sanhedrin 7:4* and *Mishneh Torah, Sefer Kedushah, Isurei Biah 21:9*.

[But recall *Tosfos Yeshanim*, as well as *Re'em* quoted in *Shitah Mekubetzes*, both to *Nedarim 20b*, that according to the Sages there is absolutely no lack of holiness (*ein chisaron kedushah*) in the behaviors listed by Rabbi Yochanan ben Dahavai.[385]]

In addition, twice in his *Mishneh Torah*, Maimonides encourages a man not to frequent his wife sexually "like a rooster" – in one place invoking the issue of "sanctification" specifically[386] (and in the other, calling such sexual addiction the behavior of "uncouth ignoramouses" (*maaseh borim*)[387]). [Note, however, that some men are obligated by Jewish law to satisfy their wives sexually every single night,[388] and that where conception is the goal, the Talmud recommends multiple climaxes for both husband and wife as a means of increasing the chances of conceiving male offspring.[389]]

Maimonides also speaks of relegating sex to the middle of the night as a manner of "sanctification" (though his reason is not because it helps the couple avoid hearing voices from the street, but because of issues relating to digestion).[390]

Another form of sanctification discussed by the medievals – although the actual word "sanctification" is not necessarily employed directly in its regard – is that of noble intention.

Maimonides, in describing not a halachic obligation but the ideal state of psychological-emotional-physical-spiritual balance that G-d intends mankind to strive for, writes[391]:

> In all areas of life, a person must direct his [or her] intentions only to more deeply appreciate [lit. know] G-d . . . How? . . . When he eats and drinks and has intercourse, he should not set his heart to do these things only for the pleasure of them alone until it comes to the point that he chooses what he eats only based on its flavor and he has sex only for its pleasure . . . He should have sex only for the sake of keeping his body healthy and to bear offspring. Therefore, he does not have sex every time he has an urge for it,[392] but rather every time he knows that his body needs to ejaculate, as medical wisdom would have him do (*c'derech harefuos*),[393] or to bear offspring.

In his *Commentary to the Mishnah*, too, Maimonides speaks of "sanctifying" the act of marital sex by focusing on the Creator's ultimate purpose in it: procreation.[394]

Maimonides' contemporary, Raavad III, addresses the matter of a husband's ideal sexual intentions as well, which he discusses in his *Baalei HaNefesh, Shaar Hakedusah* in the general context of "sanctifying oneself in that which is permitted." Raavad III enumerates four levels of intention for marital sex that are more elevated than simply satisfying one's own sexual appetite[395] (listed here from most elevated to least):

a) To fulfill G-d's command to procreate and/or satisfy one's wife's need for sex.

b) To benefit the health of the fetus – as a subcategory of the commandment to procreate, for the sages believed sex during certain stages of pregnancy would make the unborn child comely and vibrant.

c) To respond to one's wife's overtures showing that she needs sexual intimacy – as a subcategory to fulfill one's wife's sexual needs.

d) To have sex with one's own wife as soon as one feels sexual stirrings within, with the intention of preventing such impulses from leading to illicit sexual thoughts and/or actions.[396] This also includes having sex with the intention of maintaining one's health (presumably both physical and mental/emotional health).

## The Spirit of Jewish Sex – Summarized

To summarize, then, the examples of "sanctified" sex brought among the medieval commentaries, and their express purposes or the spiritual sensitivities they can perhaps be said to engender:

a) Avoidance of unnecessary nakedness (pious modesty)

b) Avoidance of that which may bring to intentional sexual fantasies of others (marital bonding; refinement of one's children)

c) The husband striving to give his wife her climax first (selflessness; male offspring)

d) Avoidance of sex immediately after using the bathroom (hygiene)

e) Avoidance of sex during the day (love over lust; preserving the husband's attraction and/or preserving the wife's self-image)

f) Abstinence from sex on the day the wife expects her menses (rabbinic decree)

g) Avoidance of unhealthy food or overeating before sex (refinement of one's children)

h) Avoidance of sex in a sitting, standing or side-by-side position (medical; mutual respect)

i) Avoidance of sex with the lights on at night (love over lust; preserving the husband's attraction and/or preserving the wife's self-image)

j) Avoidance of naked sex without a blanket covering (pious modesty)

k) Avoidance of hedonism (appreciation of the Creator's greater purpose)

l) Avoidance of non-sex-related talk during sex, gazing at or kissing the female genitals, and "overturning the table" (mutual respect;[397] pious modesty; appreciation of the Creator's greater purpose)

m) Minimizing frequency of sex (avoidance of addiction)

n) Relegating sex to the middle of the night (medical;[398] marital bonding; refinement of one's children)

o) Avoidance of the nine-ten flawed conditions of mind or circumstance (respect; mindfulness; refinement of one's children)

### Three important notes:

1. As mentioned in various places of our discussion until now, some of the above manners of "sanctification" – b), d), g), h) and i) – were/are believed to help avoid certain harmful physical repercussions to the couple or their offspring.

## DECONSTRUCTING THE CODE

Others – b), g), n) and o) – were/are believed to help avoid negative spiritual impacts upon one's children.

An in-depth discussion about such beliefs will be included in a future volume of this series.

2. Types e), f), i) and o) are generally presented in rabbinic writings as matters of obligatory law, not just voluntary piety. We shall reexamine this manner of presentation in a future volume of this series.[399]

3. In regard to j), see below, *Appendices: Sex Above the Covers.*

In any case, we may conclude from all the above that there is a broad range of manners by which a couple may choose to "sanctify" their sex life, and they need not jump to physical and/or spiritual extremes. But love, bonding and vulnerability between husband and wife, and the joy and sexual fulfillment of either one of them, should never be compromised unilaterally by one side "in the name of G-d." On the contrary, G-d Himself instructs that His own holy Name be erased in order to maintain or restore peace, love and sexual harmony within marriage.[400]

## Permitted or Encouraged?

We shall conclude our discussion about "sanctified sex" with what is perhaps the most eloquent and fundamental statement on the distinction between Jewish marital sex law versus spirit, penned by Maimonides in his *Commentary to the Mishnah, Sanhedrin 7:4* – possibly the first compendium ever written on the subject, which Maimonides found necessary to compile already in his day for the sake of popular consumption and clarity.[401]

We will turn to this passage now, followed by Maimonides' famous and succinct codification of Jewish marital sex law in his *Mishneh Torah*, which appears to reflect the more prevalent Jewish approach to sex among rabbinic authors[402] during the Middle Ages.

# DECONSTRUCTING THE CODE

## Maimonides, *Commentary to the Mishnah, Sanhedrin 7:4*[403]

> A man is permitted to have sexual intercourse with his wife even anally (*shelo cedarcah*) or between limbs[XLII] (*derech evarim*), or however he desires. And this was the response of one of the sages[404] to a wife who asked him about this subject. He ruled for her that all her husband's sexual desires were permissible if done with her.
>
> There was already one sage[405] who wanted to establish that it was unbecoming for a husband to engage in these sexual activities with his wife or to perform various sexual positions with her as the common folk do in order to fulfill their excessive sexual appetites – such as her-on-top,[406] kissing certain parts of the body, and other such things.

---

[XLII] That is, in, against or between any of her other body parts. See below, pages 123-129, and endnotes 511, 513.

There are those who claim that Maimonides, in his *Commentary to the Mishnah, Yevamos 6:1* and *Sanhedrin 7:4*, defined the term "intercourse between limbs" (*derech evarim*) only as partial penetration of the penile head (glans penis) into the vagina. But when both passages are read together, it becomes obvious that Maimonides was not saying that such partial penetration is the *sole* definition of "intercourse between limbs," but rather that it is *one* definition of it – that is, halachically speaking, *it falls under the category* of "intercourse between limbs" rather than actual vaginal intercourse – for in *Sanhedrin 7:4* Maimonides states clearly that "one who inserts only part of the head *is like one* who penetrates between limbs." Hebrew text from the Kapach edition:

**Commentary to the Mishnah, Yevamos 6:1**

> U'me'eis pegishas shnei ha'eivarim, v'hee shekorim neshikah, ad hachnasas atarah culah, nikra shimush derech evarim.

**Commentary to the Mishnah, Sanhedrin 7:4**

> Aval hachnasas miktzas ha'atarah **harei hu c'mee** sheba derech evarim.

And see further in his commentary to *Sanhedrin*, there, that Maimonides goes on to speak about "intercourse between limbs" in conjunction with other acts of non-penetrative sexual behavior against the limbs of the woman's body – clearly not restricting the term "limbs" to just the vulva or the vaginal opening:

> And one who has intercourse with a forbidden woman between limbs (*derech evarim*), or he kissed a forbidden woman, or he hugged her or touched one of her body parts (*ever me'evareha*) to derive [sexual] pleasure, whichever part of her body it might have been (*b'eizeh ever sheyaga mei'evrei gufah*), like those who rub [each other's genitals] with their hands or feet/legs – the manner of which is called by our sages, rest in peace, "adultery by hand or foot" . . . these are all forbidden [when done with a forbidden woman].

Note that Maimonides is not saying that intercourse between or against one's own wife's hand or leg is called "adultery by hand or foot" rather than "intercourse between limbs." It is obvious that such intercourse would certainly fall under the category of "intercourse between limbs" when done with one's own wife. It is only that it is *also* called "adultery by hand or foot" when done in an *adulterous* context – i.e., with a *forbidden* woman.

But those who opposed this view[407] stated the opinion of the Sages, that whatever a husband craves to do with his wife sexually, he may do.

And the Talmud rules according to the Sages.

But even though all these things are permitted, as we've explained, the modest pious ones distance themselves from all these animalistic behaviors, they denigrate these behaviors, and they denigrate those who fixate all their thoughts and yearnings upon them,[XLIII] for the ultimate purpose of sexual relations is the continuation of the species, not just erogenous pleasure; the pleasure was only created in order to stimulate living creatures to the main purpose: procreation. Proof of this is the fact that the male's sexual urge, as well as the male's erogenous pleasure, dissipate after ejaculation of the seed – for it was only for this purpose that sexual stimulation occurred.[408] If the purpose of sex were purely the pleasure of it, the pleasure would continue as long as the person wants it to, which is not the case.

Therefore, the intention of the pious is to fulfill the purpose of nature alone, and the Sages praise this approach and hold it precious. And they refer to someone who follows this intent as "one who sanctifies himself during sex," meaning that his intention is only to release the excess [sexual energy] (*liflot ha'odef*). And they said that this will increase the purity, refinement and good character of the children he conceives.

And they heaped praise upon one sage whose wife had obvious and noticeable physical blemishes, yet he was not conscious of them, because his mind was focused upon that which the pure pious are focused upon, and when he was needed to fulfill her sexual needs his sole intention was the G-dly intention within nature.

But this does not contradict the principle of the Sages that we opened with, that anything a husband craves to do with his wife sexually he may do, because the question of what is forbidden versus permissible (*ha'asur v'hamutar*) is not the same as the question of what is distasteful versus pleasing and beloved (*hamegunah v'haratzoi v'ha'ahuv*) and how one should strive for the path of modesty and extreme moderation[409] (*hatznius v'hahaflagah b'prishus*).

---

[XLIII] A possible reference to what is now recognized as "sexual addiction." It is unlikely that this is referring to involuntary sexual obsessions in adolescents or otherwise normal, healthy unmarried men, for whom sexual fixations are generally nothing more than a manifestation of the body's natural chemistry and/or the temporary lack of a halachically-sanctioned sexual outlet. In any case, the greater context of Maimonides' discussion, here, is clearly about married men.

And see the letter of Rabbi Yaakov Yisrael Kanievsky, the "Steipler Gaon," in his *Karyana d'Igarta vol. 1, Letter 166*, where he assures a young student that it is not abnormal for an adolescent to involuntarily imagine sexual imagery in all things around him (*mah she'micol davar katan ba lidei hirhur zehu ragil meod b'harbeh tze'irim*).

## Maimonides, *Mishneh Torah, Sefer Kedushah, Isurei Biah* 21:9

21:9. A man's wife is permitted to him. Therefore, whatever a husband craves to do with his wife sexually he may do: he may have sex with her any time he wants;[410] he may kiss any part of her body he wants; he may have intercourse with her vaginally (*cedarcah*), anally (*shelo cedarcah*) or between limbs (*derech evarim*) [*some textual versions add here*: as long as no seed is "wasted in vain"[411]].

Nevertheless, the way of the pious is to not act light-headedly in this area (*shelo yakel adam es rosho l'cach*), and to sanctify oneself during sex,[412] as we explain in *Hilchos Deos* (*Laws of Character Refinement*), and to not veer from the way of nature, for the ultimate purpose of sex is procreation.

## Maimonides, *Mishneh Torah, Sefer HaMada, Deos* 5:4-5

5:4. Even though a husband's wife is permitted to him at all times,[413] it is fitting for a *Torah scholar* to conduct himself with holiness, and not frequent her like a rooster [does a hen], but only every Sabbath night, if he is able.

And when he talks to her [to initiate sex], he should not initiate at the beginning of night, when his stomach is full, nor at the end of night, when he is famished, but in the middle of night, when his food has digested.[414]

And he should not act excessively light-headed, and he should not make his mouth vulgar with vain talk, even just between he and his wife. On the verse, "G-d recounts to man what his words were," sages explained (*amru chachamim*[414*]): even the excess light-headed talk between husband and wife one is called to account for on the Day of Judgment.

And neither of them should be intoxicated, or sluggish, or depressed, or asleep. And he should not force her against her will – rather it should be to both of their agreement and joy.[415] He should speak with her a little, and play with her a little, so that their souls become settled [read: aligned[416]], and he should penetrate her with shame [read: dignity[417]], not brazenous…

5:5. Whoever conducts himself in this manner, not only has he sanctified his soul, purified himself, and refined his character traits, but if they [he and his wife] conceive children, they [the children] will be pleasant and dignified,[418] receptive to wisdom and piety. And whoever conducts himself in the ways of the rest of the nation, who walk in darkness, will have children like them.

## Maimonides – Summary

From Maimonides' collective words we see that from a legal-halachic perspective[419] G-d understands, empathizes with, and accepts a man's and woman's erotic sexual natures – which He Himself fashioned. Thus, G-d permits husband and wife to enjoy together whatever sexual cravings they might have in the context of a loving, respectful, devoted relationship. Nevertheless, G-d's own craving is for man and woman to recognize that there are higher values and purposes for which he and she were created, and thus one should be mindful not to allow sexual fixations to become an impediment to more worthy, altruistic pursuits and elevations of the spirit.

But it is patently clear from Maimonides' words in his *Commentary to the Mishnah, Sanhedrin 7:4* and in his *Mishneh Torah, Isurei Biah 21:9* (as also pointed out by numerous later commentaries[420]) that he understood the Sages on *Nedarim 20b* as rejecting all four of Rabbi Yochanan ben Dahavai's cautions, for Maimonides expressly permits anal sex and wife-on-top ("overturning the table"), as well as kissing the female genitals (which both practically and halachically encompasses within it gazing at them).[421]

And in *Deos 5:5*, Maimonides warns that unrefined sexual behavior – perhaps including again "vain talk," if it is also non-mood-related and therefore falls under the category of the "excess light-headed talk" cautioned against on *Hagigah 5b*[422] – could result in the conception of spiritually insensitive children,[423] but nowhere does he speak against non-sex-related talk.

And nowhere does he predict that physical illness will befall one's children.[424]

## "Good Sex"

We have just now seen the halachic approach of Maimonides to marital sex, distinguishing between that which is "permitted" versus that which is "sanctified" and "beloved" by G-d.

We've already seen earlier (page 68) the statement of *Tosfos Yeshanim* and Rabbi Eliezer of Metz (Re'em), that according to the Sages on *Nedarim 20b* a husband and wife may do all they crave sexually together, "and there is no lack of holiness."

We will now conclude our chapter with one last fundamental nuanced approach of the medieval period, that of the ascetic Rabbi Yehudah Hachasid of Regensburg, "Rabbi Yehudah the Pious" (1150-1217).[425]

### Rabbi Yehudah the Pious, *Sefer Chasidim 509*

> Although the Sages teach that humans, fish and snakes have intercourse face-to-face because the Divine Presence spoke to them, nevertheless, the sage, Rav,[426] said that a man's wife is permitted to him however he desires.[XLIV]
>
> On the night of her ritual immersion, it is not appropriate other than with him on top and her on bottom, because the wife has no pleasure if he is on bottom (sic) . . . But on all other nights, he should do whatever gives him pleasure (*c'fi hanaaso*), so that he should not lust to do it with other women.[427] But it must be with his wife's permission . . .
>
> In all such matters, it all follows the personal tastes of husband and wife. And if a man has found a *good wife* who is of same mind with him in these matters, to him applies the verse in Proverbs (18:22): "[He who has found a wife has found goodness,[428]] and has elicited favor from the Lord," and the verse in Ecclesiastes (9:7): "[Go, eat your bread with joy and drink your wine with a merry heart, for] G-d has already approved your deeds."[429]

---

[XLIV] The clear implication is that Rabbi Yehudah the Pious understood Rav as permitting marital sex "face-to-back." It is not clear, however, if he understood this to mean only rear-entry *vaginal* intercourse or also rear-entry *anal* intercourse. In any case, he does go on to permit a husband to enjoy with his wife, with her permission, "*whatever* gives him pleasure."

# PART THREE
# THE LETTER OF THE LAW

## And Now, the Letter of the Law…

We have seen above that even some of the most permissive halachic approaches to marital sex do not disregard the concept of elevating the act, either by putting one's spouse's needs first or striving for more altruistic intentions.

As discussed, this is all part of the concept encouraged in the Talmud to "sanctify oneself during sex" and the more general Jewish principle to "sanctify yourself in that which is permitted to you."

However, being that most Jewish "family purity" and marital intimacy guides I have seen focus on the "sanctification" aspect and do not give due attention to "that which is permitted," we focus in this book, and particularly in the present section, on the latter, trusting that those seeking methods of higher sanctity have ample sources to turn to.

We will now outline the baseline permissive legal opinions on the matter of Jewish marital sex law according to categories of sexual behavior, technique and position.

Note that under each behavior, technique or position we will list those opinions who clearly and explicitly permit it, as well as those who can reasonably be believed to permit it by logical inference. In the case of the latter, we will succinctly explain how such deduction is made or refer back to an earlier discussion explaining it.[XLIV*]

---

[XLIV*] As noted above, page 59, whichever sexual position a medieval commentator chose as the correct definition of "overturning the table" on *Nedarim 20ab*, that is the position he understood the Sages, Rebbi, Rav and Rabbi Yochanan bar Napacha as permitting within marriage.

## Talk During Sex

The topic of talk during sex is discussed in *Babylonian Talmud, Nedarim 20ab* and *Hagigah 5b*.[430]

*Nedarim 20ab* distinguishes between "sex-related talk" (*mili d'tashmisha*) and "non-sex-related talk" (*mili achronaisa*). According to the compilers-editors of the Talmud, there, non-sex-related talk is cautioned against by one sage, Rabbi Yochanan ben Dahavai (in the name of certain "ministering angels") both immediately before or during intercourse, while sex-related talk is perfectly acceptable to Rabbi Yochanan ben Dahavai immediately prior to intercourse, and presumably even during intercourse. But the Sages quoted on *Nedarim 20b* reject Rabbi Yochanan ben Dahavai, and thus, according to key commentaries, even non-sex-related talk is perfectly acceptable by Jewish law both before and during intercourse.

On *Hagigah 5b*, the compilers-editors of the Talmud posit a distinction between "mood-related talk" (*tzarich leratzuyah*) that is necessary prior to intercourse (during foreplay) to arouse one's wife to the mood for lovemaking versus "excess light-headed talk" (*sichah yeseirah/sichah kalah/sichah kalah yeseirah*) that is "non-mood-related" because the wife is already in the mood for sex and therefore such light-headed talk is unneeded. The latter, they theorize, was cautioned against by the sage, Rav, in a statement recorded in his name that G-d will call a man on the Day of Judgment to justify the "excess light-headed talk" he had with his own wife. *Hagigah 5b* does not explain exactly what might be objectionable about such "excess light-headed talk" within marriage, nor do its medieval commentaries.

A second version of *Hagigah 5b* perfectly accepts any kind of "excess light-headed talk" between husband and wife *before* intercourse, during foreplay, mood-related or not – presumably because G-d understands human nature and that man and wife cannot be expected to be held responsible for everything that comes out of their mouths during the throes of passion. But "excess light-headed talk" *after* intercourse – i.e., during non-sexual moments of daily life – should be avoided.

## The Stringent Views

According to Raavad III, Rabbi Yaakov ben Asher and Rabbi Yosef Caro, all talk immediately before intercourse should only be "sex-related," unless "non-sex-related/mood-related talk" is necessary prior to intercourse to arouse the wife to the mood for lovemaking. But "sex-related talk" itself is understood to include even (non-illicit) talk that is intended to intensify the husband's or wife's sexual arousal.[431] And it is arguable that such "sex-related talk" would be permitted by these sources even mid-intercourse.[432]

# HALACHIC POSITIONS

## The Permissive Views

The following sources permit even "non-sex-related talk" both during foreplay and intercourse[433] [434](the topic of *Nedarim 20ab*):

1. *Tractate Callah 9*[434*]
2. *Callah Rabti 1:13-14*[435]
3. Rabbi Avraham ben Yitzchak of Narbonne (Raavad II), *Sefer HaEshkol, Hilchos Tznius*[436]
4. Maimonides, *Commentary to the Mishnah*, Sanhedrin 7:4; *Mishneh Torah, Sefer Kedushah, Isurei Biah 21:9*; *Mishneh Torah, Sefer HaMada, Deos 5:4*[437]
5. Rabbi Avraham Hayarchi, commentary to *Callah Rabti*[438]
6. Rabbi Avraham of Montpellier (*Avraham min Hahar*), *Nedarim 20b*
7. Rabbi Yitzchak ben Yosef of Corbeil, *Sefer Mitzvos Katan*, Positive Commandment 285[439]
8. Rabbi Betzalel Ashkenazi, *Shitah Mekubetzes, Nedarim 20b*

The following sources relegate restrictions on "excess light-headed talk" (the topic of *Hagigah 5b*) only to the *spirit* of the law:

1. Maimonides, *Mishneh Torah, Sefer Kedushah, Isurei Biah 21:9*; *Sefer HaMada, Deos 5:4*[440]
2. Rabbi Menachem Meiri, *Beis Habechirah, Hagigah 5ab*[441]

Note that those medieval commentators who reflect Maimonides' rulings in marital sex law could presumably agree with him on the matter of talk during sex as well.[441*]

## Gazing at the Female Genitals

Gazing at the naked genitals of one's wife is discussed on *Nedarim 20ab*.

It is permitted within marriage according to the following commentaries:

1. *Tractate Callah 9*[441**]
2. *Callah Rabti 1:13-14*[442]
3. Rabbi Avraham ben Yitzchak of Narbonne (Raavad II), *Sefer HaEshkol, Hilchos Tznius*[443]
4. Maimonides, *Commentary to the Mishnah, Sanhedrin 7:4*; *Mishneh Torah, Sefer Kedushah, Isurei Biah 21:9*[444]
5. Rabbi Avraham of Montpellier (*Avraham min Hahar*), *Nedarim 20b*
6. Rabbi Yitzchak ben Yosef of Corbeil, *Sefer Mitzvos Katan*, Positive Commandment 285[445]
7. Rabbi Betzalel Ashkenazi, *Shitah Mekubetzes, Nedarim 20b*
8. Rabbi Eliezer Melamed, *Simchat Habayit v'Birchato*[445*]

Gazing at the female genitals would possibly also be allowed by all those who allow cunnilingus (see next section). The logic for this is that Rabbi Avraham ben Dovid of Posquières, Raavad III, the original medieval source for all who forbid cunnilingus,[446] states that it is worse to kiss the female genitals than it is to gaze at them.[447] Thus, assuming this conviction is universally shared, all those who permit kissing the female genitals can be believed to permit gazing at them as well – especially since, practically speaking, the former often involves the latter.[XLIV**]

---

[XLIV**] **Added note to the third edition:** See Rabbi Eliezer Melamed's *Simchat Habayit v'Birchato* (second edition, 2015), bottom of page 63, asserting that there are no restrictions on a wife gazing at her husband's genitals.

## Cunnilingus

Discussed on *Babylonian Talmud, Nedarim 20ab* as "kissing that place," cunnilingus – oral sex performed on the vagina[XLV] – is expressly permitted within marriage by the following sources:

1. *Tractate Callah* 9[447*]
2. *Callah Rabti* 1:13-14[448]
3. Rabbi Avraham ben Yitzchak of Narbonne (Raavad II), *Sefer HaEshkol, Hilchos Tznius*[449]
4. Maimonides, *Commentary to the Mishnah, Sanhedrin* 7:4; *Mishneh Torah, Sefer Kedushah, Isurei Biah* 21:9
5. Rabbi Yisrael Alnaqua, *Menoras Hamaor*, vol. 4, *Perek Nisuei Ishah*[450]
6. Rabbi Yitzchak ben Yosef of Corbeil, *Sefer Mitzvos Katan*, Positive Commandment 285[451]
7. *Col Bo, Hilchos Ishus*, Siman 75[452]
8. Rabbi Menachem Ibn Zerach, *Tzeidah Laderech*, Maamar 3, Clal 4, Chapter 14[453]
9. Rabeinu Yaakov of London, *Etz Chaim, Hilchos Piryah Vrivyah*, Chapter 3[454]
10. Rabbi Aharon Hacohen of Lunil, *Orchos Chaim, Hilchos Kesubos*, Siman 7[455]
11. Rabbi Moshe Isserles, *Rema, Shulchan Aruch, Even Haezer* 25:2[456]
12. Rabbi Mordechai Yoffe, *Levush, Even Haezer* 25:2[457]
13. Rabbi Yechiel Michel Epstein, *Aruch Hashulchan, Even Haezer* 25:11[458]
14. Rabbi Eliezer Melamed, *Simchat Habayit v'Birchato*[458*]

Permission for cunnilingus quoted by:

1. Rabbi Yaakov ben Asher, *Tur, Even Haezer* 25:2[459]

---

[XLV] For the letter of the law about fellatio, oral sex performed on the penis, see below, this chapter, "Intercourse between limbs," pp. 123-129.

And about cunnilingus or "intercourse between limbs" performed in a lit room, see above, page 96, and endnotes 369, 845.

## Wife-on-Top

Referred to in rabbinic writing as "her-on-top, him-on-bottom" (*hee l'maalah, hu l'matah*), there are early sources that discourage the "wife-on-top" position on health or pious – but not legal – grounds.[460]

As far as the letter of the law is concerned, many commentaries specifically define "overturning the table" on *Nedarim 20ab* as "wife-on-top,"[461] which they would therefore understand the Sages, Rebbi, Rav and Rabbi Yochanan bar Napacha as permitting.

The following commentaries expressly permit "wife-on-top":

1. Maimonides, *Commentary to the Mishnah, Sanhedrin 7:4*
2. *Tosfos Yeshanim, Nedarim 20a*
3. *Mefaresh, Nedarim 20a*
4. *Tosfos Talmid Rabeinu Tam Al HaTorah*, Manuscript, Genesis 38:9[462]
5. Rabbi Yehudah HaChasid, *Sefer Chasidim 509* (but not on the wife's *mikveh* night[463])
6. Rabeinu Peretz, *Nedarim 20ab*[464]
7. *Talmidei Rabeinu Peretz, Nedarim 20b*
8. Rabbi Yom Tov ben Avraham Asevilli, *Ritva*, quoted by Rabbi Betzalel Ashkenazi in *Shitah Mekubetzes, Nedarim 20b*
9. Rabbi Alexander Suslin, *Sefer HaAgudah, Nedarim 20b*
10. Rabbi Yeruchem ben Meshulam, *Rabeinu Yeruchem, Nesiv 32*
11. Rabbi Mordechai ben Hillel, *Mordechai, Hilchos Nidah 731-732*
12. Rabbi Chaim Yosef Dovid Azulai, "Chida," *Kisei Rachamim, Tractate Callah 3:3*
13. Rabbi Elazar Azikri, *Sefer Charedim*, Chapter 64 (in the name of Rashi[464*])
14. Rabbi Yom Tov Lipman Heller, *Lechem Chamudos, Tractate Nidah*, Ch. 2, Comment 10
15. Rabbi Yechiel Michel Epstein, *Aruch Hashulchan, Even Haezer 25:10-11*[465]
16. Rabbi Eliezer Melamed, *Simchat Habayit v'Birchato*[465*]

Rabbi Avraham Hayarchi, in his commentary to *Callah Rabti*,[466] permits "overturning the table" in a manner that involves intra-vaginal penetration and ejaculation. He could thus be presumed to permit her-on-top under these conditions.[467]

## Side-by-Side, Sitting, Standing, On the Floor

Like the wife-on-top position, side-by-side intercourse – in rabbinic terminology, "both thrusting at once" – is also discouraged on health or pious, but not legal, grounds.[468]

Sitting and standing positions are also discussed by the Talmud, *Tractate Callah* and *Callah Rabti* as being unhealthy to the couple themselves.[469] But not one of them – not the Talmud, not *Tractate Callah* and not *Callah Rabti* – nor any of the commentaries I've seen on them,[470] ever label these positions as "forbidden."

Sex on the floor is cautioned against on health grounds, because it supposedly could cause a fetus's neck to become elongated.[471] But it, too, is not prohibited by any of the major codifiers – and is in fact not even mentioned by them at all.

And it is implied by Maimonides' all-inclusive permissive approach in his *Commentary to the Mishnah, Sanhedrin 7:4*, that all these would be perfectly allowable according to the letter of the law.

## "Animal-style"

Referred to in rabbinic writing as "face-to-back" (*panim c'neged oref*) or "animal style" (*maaseh b'heimah*), rear-entry vaginal intercourse[472] is permitted by the following sources[XLV*]:

1. *Tractate Callah 9*[473]
2. *Callah Rabti 1:13-14*[474][475]
3. Rabbi Avraham ben Dovid, Raavad III, *Baalei HaNefesh, Shaar Hakedushah*[476]
4. Rabbi Avraham of Montpellier (*Avraham min Hahar*), *Nedarim 20a*
5. Rabbi Yaakov be Asher, *Tur, Orach Chaim 240:2-4, Even Haezer 25:8-10*[477]
6. Rabbi Yaakov ben Yehudah Landau, *HaAgur, Hilchos Tefilas Arvis, 336*[478]
7. Rabbi Eliyahu de Vidas, *Reishis Chochmah, 16:29* (in the name of Rashi[478*] and Rabeinu Asher[478**])
8. Rabbi Elazar Azikri, *Sefer Charedim, Chapter 64* (in the name of Raavad III)
9. Rabbi Yitzchak Lampronti, *Pachad Yitzchak, Entry: Arbaah devarim amru li malachei hashares*
10. Rabbi Eliezer Melamed, *Simchat Habayit v'Birchato*[478***]

Rabbi Avraham Hayarchi, in his commentary to *Callah Rabti*,[479] permits "overturning the table" in a manner that involves intra-vaginal penetration and ejaculation. He could thus be presumed to permit "animal-style" intercourse under these conditions.

Rabbi Yehudah the Pious, in his *Sefer Chasidim 509*, says that marital sex that is not "face-to-face" is permitted. He does not specify if he meant only rear-entry vaginal intercourse or also rear-entry anal intercourse, but there can be little doubt that at the very least he meant the former.

Note also that the rear-entry vaginal position can reasonably be presumed to be permitted by all those who permit anal sex (to be discussed next), for anal sex is considered by Jewish law to be the more-strictly-dealt-with position of the two.

---

[XLV*] See above, footnote to page 110.

## Anal Sex

Referred to in rabbinic terminology as *"biah shelo cedarcah,"* generally translated as "unnatural intercourse."[XLV**]

A brief re-introduction and additional elaboration are in order here:

As mentioned earlier, the Talmud on *Nedarim 20ab* rules that a sexual position called "overturning the table" is permitted. Though the commentaries disagree on the exact definition of this term, a majority understands it to mean anal sex. The Talmud on *Sanhedrin 58b* clearly states that anal sex is permitted. However, the Talmud on *Yevamos 34b* maintains that the two biblical sons of Judah, Er and Onan, were both killed by the hand of Heaven for the "sin" of anal sex, for it involves "wasting seed in vain" through extra-vaginal ejaculation.[480]

*Tosfos* on *Yevamos 34b*, in the name of Rabeinu Yitzchak, offers two explanations to resolve the contradiction between *Nedarim* and *Sanhedrin* with *Yevamos*:

a) Anal sex is permitted only without intra-anal ejaculation. The sin of Er and Onan was that they went so far as to ejaculate intra-anally.

b) Anal sex is permitted even with intra-anal ejaculation from time to time, randomly in the heat of passion for the sake of the husband's sexual fulfillment (*b'akrai b'alma umisaveh lavo al ishto shelo cedarcah, shari*), just not as an intentional and constant means of halachically-unsanctioned birth control. The sin of Er and Onan was that they intentionally used anal sex as a regular means to avoid pregnancy.[XLVI]

As we shall see in a moment, most medieval commentators who weigh in on the question of intra-anal ejaculation endorse the *second* approach of Rabeinu Yitzchak, and they therefore permit anal sex for married couples even to the point of the husband's climax. As for those who permit it only *without* ejaculation, they all do so upon the authority of Maimonides, who, in his *Mishneh Torah, Sefer Kedushah, Isurei Biah 21:9*, permits "vaginal intercourse, anal intercourse and intercourse between limbs, as long as no seed is wasted in vain." According to this wording of Maimonides, his view would match that of Rabeinu Yitzchak's *first* approach: that anal intercourse is permitted only without intra-anal ejaculation.

It must be stressed again that all the other medieval authorities we find forbidding anal sex to the point of the husband's climax merely restate verbatim, or practically verbatim, the wording of Maimonides, and it is thus reasonable to

---

[XLV**] As for those latter day "family purity" or marital intimacy guides that suggest *"shelo cedarcah"* refers to rear-entry vaginal intercourse, see below, p. 166 and endnotes 645*, 647.

[XLVI] Note that birth control is not categorically forbidden by Jewish law. Readers seeking practical guidance are encouraged to consult a halachically-competent rabbi. And see *Contraception in Contemporary Orthodox Judaism*, by Gedalia Meyer and Henoch Messner, available online at: *http://finkorswim.com/wp-content/uploads/2012/06/Contraception.pdf*.

believe that they forbade it largely, if not entirely, relying upon the weight of his authority. This being the case, there is reason to believe that had Maimonides permitted anal sex to the point of the husband's climax, like Rabeinu Yitzchak's *second* approach, few, if any, of his halachic supporters would have argued otherwise.

In fact, there are modern scholars of Maimonides who do believe that the concluding restrictive phrase, "as long as there is no seed wasted in vain," was not penned by Maimonides himself, but rather by a copyist, for it is not found in most handwritten manuscripts of *Mishneh Torah*, including those universally acknowledged as among the most reliable, those preserved by the Yemenite Jewish community.[481]

Thus, Maimonides' opinion can be equally understood as matching that of Rabeinu Yitzchak's second approach, that anal sex to the point of ejaculation is permitted occasionally for the sake of sexual fulfillment between husband and wife. It is only forbidden even within marriage if performed constantly as an intentional means of unsanctioned birth control.[482]

This, in fact, is most certainly how Rabbi Meir ben Yekusiel Hacohen of Rothenburg (c.1260-1298), author of *Hagahos Maimonios,* understood Maimonides' opinion, for he comments on Maimonides' ruling in *Isurei Biah 21:9* permitting anal sex:

> This means only randomly in the heat of passion, not as a regular practice, as *Tosfos* explains on *Yevamos 34b.*

As we know, *Tosfos* on *Yevamos 34b* speaks of "random anal sex" only in the context of permitting intra-anal *ejaculation.*[482*]

[Parenthetically, two of Rabbi Meir Hacohen's contemporaries and fellow disciples under the famous Rabbi Meir "Maharam" of Rothenburg, namely, Rabeinu Asher ben Yechiel (Rosh) and Rabbi Mordechai ben Hillel, both permit occasional intra-anal ejaculation for married couples, and neither one references Maimonides as forbidding it.]

In fact, it is not only *equally* likely that Maimonides' true opinion matched that of Rabeinu Yitzchak's second approach, it is arguably *more* likely, for in his earlier parallel ruling in his *Commentary to the Mishnah, Sanhedrin 7:4*, where he also permitted anal intercourse, as well as intercourse between limbs, he did not add a single cautionary word or stipulation against ejaculation – not in regard to frequency and not even in regard to intention. Thus, it could actually be argued that Maimonides' opinion goes much farther than Rabeinu Yitzchak's second approach discussed above, and that it surpasses even the opinion of Rabbi Yeshayah of Trani I (listed below), who does not stipulate any limitation on the *frequency* of intra-anal ejaculation, only on the *intention* that it be for pleasure, not unsanctioned birth control.[483]

In any case, in light of Maimonides' presentation in *Commentary to the Mishnah*, even if we were to accept the authenticity of the restrictive phrase against "wasting seed in vain" in *Mishneh Torah*, it is perhaps possible to argue that the very *definition* of "wasting seed in vain," there, as Maimonides himself intended it, referred *only* to intra-anal ejaculation that is performed *as a means of constant and intentional unsanctioned birth control*. Thus, occasional intra-anal ejaculation with one's wife as a means of sexual fulfillment could perhaps still be permitted even according to the restrictive textual reading of *Mishneh Torah*.[484]

[Note also that later in the very same chapter of *Mishneh Torah*, in *Isurei Biah 21:18*, when Maimonides formally defines the concept of "wasting seed in vain" for the first time, he does not give intra-anal ejaculation or ejaculation between limbs as examples of "wasted seed," but only coitus interruptus – an undeniably intentional form of birth control.[485]]

But here is what the sources expressly permit[XLVI*]:

### Anal sex – without intra-anal ejaculation
(*Based on a questionable manuscript of Maimonides*)

1. Rabbi Avraham of Montpellier (*Avraham min Hahar*), Nedarim 20b[486]
2. R. Aharon Hacohen of Lunil, *Orchos Chaim, Hilchos Kesubos, Siman 7*[487]
3. *Col Bo, Hilchos Ishus, Siman 75*[488]
4. Rabbi Moshe of Trani, *Kiryas Sefer, Isurei Biah 21*
5. Rabbi Yaakov Emden, *Hagahos Yaavetz, Sanhedrin 58b*;[489] *Commentary to Siddur, Mitas Hakesef, chapter 7, section 2:2*
6. R. Yaakov Meshulam Orenstein, *Yeshuos Yaakov, Orach Chaim 240:5:4*

### Anal Sex – intra-anal ejaculation unspecified or undetermined[490]

1. Maimonides, *Commentary to the Mishnah, Sanhedrin 7:4*; *Mishneh Torah, Sefer Kedushah, Isurei Biah 21:9*
2. *Mefaresh, Nedarim 20a*[491]
3. *Tosfos, Nedarim 20a*
4. *Tosfos Yeshanim, Nedarim 20ab*
5. Rabeinu Nissim of Gerona, *Peirush HaRan, Nedarim 20b*;[492] *Chidushei HaRan, Sanhedrin 58b*[493]
6. Rabeinu Yonah of Gerona, *Sanhedrin 58b*[494]

---

[XLVI*] See above, footnote to page 110.

7. Rabbi Alexander Suslin, *Sefer HaAgudah, Nedarim 20b*
8. Rabeinu Yaakov of London, *Etz Chaim, Hilchos Piryah Vrivyah, Ch. 3*[495]
9. Rabbi Menachem Meiri, *Beis Habechirah, Nedarim 20b*
10. Rabbi Netanel ben Yeshaya of Yemen, *Maor Ha'afelah, Parshas Acharei;*[496] *Parshas Kedoshim*[497]
11. Rabbi Yitzchak of Corbeil, *Sefer Mitzvos Katan, Positive Command 285*[498]

## Anal Sex – with intra-anal ejaculation; no limit mentioned on intention or frequency

1. Rabeinu Meyuchas ben Eliyahu, *Commentary to Genesis*[499]
2. Rabbi Yisrael Alnaqua, *Menoras Hamaor, Perek Nisuei Ishah*[499*]

## Anal Sex – with intra-anal ejaculation, as long as it is for sexual fulfillment (not intentional unsanctioned birth control); no limit mentioned on frequency

1. Rabbi Yeshayah of Trani I, *Tosfos Rid, Yevamos 12b*[500]
2. Rabbi Yeshayah of Trani II, *Riaz, Kuntres Harayos, Sanhedrin 58b*[501]

## Anal sex – with intra-anal ejaculation, as long as it is for sexual fulfillment (not intentional unsanctioned birth control) and the majority of ejaculations are intra-vaginal

1. *Tosfos, Sanhedrin 58b*

## Anal sex – with intra-anal ejaculation, as long as it is for sexual fulfillment (not intentional unsanctioned birth control) and it occurs "randomly" in the heat of passion (*b'akrai*), not as a regular habit

1. Rabeinu Yitzchak, *Tosfos, Yevamos 34b*
2. Rabeinu Asher ben Yechiel, *Peirush HaRosh, Nedarim 20a;*[502] *Tosfos HaRosh, Nedarim 20b, Yevamos 34b; Rabeinu Asher, Yevamos 34b* (no longer extant but preserved in *Hagahos Habach to Rosh*, in *Yam Shel Shlomoh to Yevamos 34b*, and in *Beis Yosef to Tur, Orach 240:2-4:4*[503])
3. *Tosfos Yeshanim, Yevamos 34b*
4. *Tosfos Talmid Rabeinu Tam Al HaTorah, Manuscript, Genesis 38:9*[504]
5. *Talmidei Rabeinu Peretz, Nedarim 20b*
6. Rabeinu Yeruchem ben Meshulam, *Rabeinu Yeruchem, Nesiv 32*

7. R. Menachem Ibn Zerach, *Tzeidah Laderech, Maamar 3, Clal 4, Ch. 14*[505]

8. Rabbi Alexander Suslin, *Sefer HaAgudah, Sanhedrin 58b; Yevamos 34b*

9. Rabbi Mordechai ben Hillel, *Mordechai, Hilchos Nidah 731-732*

10. Rabbi Yaakov ben Asher, *Tur, Orach Chaim 240:4; Even Haezer 25:2*[505*]

11. Rabbi Shlomoh Luria, *Yam Shel Shlomoh, Yevamos 34b*

12. Rabbi Moshe Isserles, *Rema, Shulchan Aruch, Even Haezer 25:2*

13. Rabbi Mordechai Yoffe, *Levush, Orach Chaim 240:4; Even Haezer 25:2*

14. Rabbi Yom Tov Lipman Heller, *Lechem Chamudos, Tractate Nidah, Chapter 2, Comment 10*[506]

15. Rabbi Meir Eisenstadt, *Panim Meiros vol. 2, Responsum 158*[507]

**Anal sex – with intra-anal ejaculation, as long as it is for sexual fulfillment (not intentional unsanctioned birth control) and it occurs "occasionally" (*l'paamim*), not as a regular habit**

1. Rabbi Betzalel Ashkenazi, *Shitah Mekubetzes, Nedarim 20b*[508]

The following post-medieval authorities, while mentioning that one should consider avoiding intra-anal ejaculation for halachic and/or kabbalistic reasons (to be discussed at length in Part Four of our study), do not categorically "prohibit" it if it is done occasionally for the sake of a couple's sexual fulfillment within marriage. And they certainly do not prohibit anal penetration in-and-of-itself.[XLVI**]

1. Rabbi Yosef Caro, *Beis Yosef, Tur, Even Haezer 25:2*[509]

2. Rabbi Yehoshua Falk, *Drishah, Tur, Even Haezer 25:2*[510]

3. Rabbi Eliyahu Spira, *Elyah Rabah, Levush, Orach Chaim 240:4:10*

4. Rabbi Yechiel Michel Epstein, *Aruch Hashulchan, Even Haezer 25:11*

5. Rabbi Moshe Leima, *Chelkas Mechokek, Tur, Even Haezer 25:2*

6. Rabbi Gur Aryeh HaLevi, *Gur Aryeh, Tur, Even Haezer 25:2*

7. Rabbi Yehudah Ashkenazi, *Be'er Heitev, Tur, Even Haezer 25:2*

8. Rabbi Yaakov Meshulam, *Yeshuos Yaakov, Even Haezer 25:2:2*

---

[XLVI**] **Added note to the third edition:** Additional post-medieval authorities who permit occasional intra-anal ejaculation include R. Yosef Messas in *Mayim Chaim, Resp. 97*, R. Avraham Yitzchak Kook in *Ezrat Cohen 35, 37* (in *Shmoneh Kovtzim 6:99* he permits at least anal penetration), and R. Eliezer Melamed in *Simchat Habayit v'Birchato*, page 60. Credit goes to R. Eliezer Melamed and R. Maor Kayam for bringing these sources in Rav Kook's works to my attention – see below, endnote 555.

## "Intercourse Between Limbs" (Outercourse and Fellatio)

Here, too, brief introduction and analysis are in order:

The term "intercourse between limbs" is generally understood as referring to stimulation of the husband's penis in, against or between any part of the wife's body other than inside her vagina or anus.[511] This would include the wife's oral[512] or manual[513] stimulation of the husband's sex organs.[514]

The question of whether or not this is permitted even to the point of *ejaculation* between limbs is an important one.

A number of medieval commentaries that discuss and permit "intercourse between limbs" stipulate that it must not result in "wasted seed." It must be noted, however, that, just like in the case of intra-anal ejaculation (discussed in our previous section), the medieval sources who forbid ejaculation between limbs all merely restate the wording of Maimonides in *Mishneh Torah, Isurei Biah 21:9* – who, as we saw before, permits "vaginal intercourse, anal intercourse, or intercourse between limbs, as long as no seed is wasted in vain."

But again, as explained above, there are modern scholars of Maimonides who believe that the concluding restrictive phrase, "as long as no seed is wasted in vain," was not penned by Maimonides himself, but rather by a copyist, for it is not found in most handwritten manuscripts of *Mishneh Torah*, including those universally acknowledged as among the most reliable, those preserved by the Yemenite Jewish community.[515] Thus, as we said, on the matter of anal sex it is arguably most reasonable and most likely that Maimonides held the same approach as his European contemporary, Rabeinu Yitzchak, that anal sex is permitted even to the point of ejaculation if done for the sake of the husband's (or couple's) sexual fulfillment – just not as a means of constant intentional unsanctioned birth control. And Maimonides brought the case of intercourse between limbs in conjunction with anal intercourse in order to permit *both* to husband and wife even to the point of ejaculation.[516]

Support for this reading of *Mishneh Torah* can again be brought from Maimonides' own *Commentary to the Mishneh, Sanhedrin 7:4*, where he also discusses marital anal intercourse and intercourse between limbs in tandem, yet nowhere does he caution against ejaculation resulting from either one of them. In fact, Maimonides, there, states that anal intercourse and intercourse between limbs were *both* included in the permissive ruling of Rebbi and/or Rav for "overturning the table" as quoted on *Nedarim 20b*. And the implication of the Talmud, there, is that Rebbi and Rav were both invoking the ruling of the Sages quoted earlier on the very same Talmudic page,[516*] that "Anything a husband craves to do with his wife sexually, he may do" – the very principle which Rabeinu Yitzchak invokes as his basis for permitting intra-anal ejaculation for couples.

In Rabeinu Yitzchak's own words (*Tosfos, Yevamos 34b*):

> It [intra-anal ejaculation] is not considered similar to the act of Er and Onan unless his [the husband's] intention is to destroy seed [by preventing pregnancy] and he [therefore] accustoms himself to do it constantly.
>
> But if it is merely done randomly [in the heat of passion] (*b'akrai b'alma*) and he desires to come upon his wife anally (*umisaveh lavo al ishto shelo cedarcah*), it is permitted, as we are taught in *Nedarim*: "Anything a man craves to do with his wife sexually, he may do..."

Therefore, if Maimonides' true opinion did match the second approach of Rabeinu Yitzchak, and he equated anal intercourse and intercourse between limbs as *both* being included in the permissive ruling of Rebbi and/or Rav (and the Sages) on *Nedarim 20b*, then it is perfectly understandable, and expected, that he would permit *both* to the point of ejaculation.[517] And being that Maimonides in his *Commentary to the Mishnah* issues no warning or stipulation whatsoever against intra-anal ejaculation or ejaculation between limbs for married couples – not in regard to frequency, and not even in regard to intention – Maimonides' view could be said to surpass that of Rabeinu Yitzchak and even that of Rabbi Yeshayah of Trani I (who gives no limit on *frequency* of intra-anal ejaculation, only on *intention*) not only in regard to intra-anal ejaculation, but even in regard to ejaculation between limbs.

But assuming Maimonides would at least stipulate that a couple's intentions and actions in these cases be only for occasional sexual fulfillment, not constant intentional unsanctioned birth control, both in regard to intra-anal ejaculation and ejaculation between limbs, still, logically speaking, both could potentially be permitted by him in every instance where avoidance of conception is not an issue – such as when the wife is pregnant, post-menopause, or where birth control is sanctioned.[518]

Now, as far as Rabeinu Yitzchak's or Rabbi Yeshayah of Trani I's own personal opinons about intercourse and ejaculation between limbs, they themselves do not spell it out for us. But in not one, but two, places in his *Drishah* commentary to *Tur, Even Haezer*,[519] Rabbi Yehoshua Falk (a disciple of Rabbis Moshe Isserles and Shlomoh Luria) unequivocally states that Rabeinu Yitzchak permitted ejaculation between limbs as a logical extension of intra-anal ejaculation – and he possibly implies that this is how Rabbi Yaakov ben Asher himself understood Rabeinu Yitzchak's opinion as well.[520] [521]

How Rabbi Falk himself decided the law in regard to intra-anal ejaculation and ejaculation between limbs is unclear, as he seems to be assuming the role, here, of interpreter, not decisor.[522] He does quote a halachic caution (though not prohibition) of Rabbi Yosef Caro against intra-anal ejaculation – to be discussed below, in Part Four – though he does not clearly endorse it.[523] But Rabbi Falk is confident in his logic that Rabeinu Yitzchak himself would permit occasional ejaculation between limbs for the sake of sexual fulfillment within marriage –

which would, by definition, include a wife's oral or manual stimulation of her husband's sex organs, or his stimulation in, against or between any other part of her outer body (as discussed above, page 123, and endnotes 511-514 thereon).

[It should make no difference in the eyes of halachah whether such stimulation occurs through his thrusting against her body or her moving her body against him, for in the case of the permitted wife-on-top sex position the husband's body is generally more-or-less stationary while she stimulates him through her movements.

But whether or not it would be permitted for a husband to self-masturbate in the presence of his wife so long as the final stimulation that results in ejaculation is caused by a part of her body requires further investigation.[524]]

That being said, the same stipulation Rabeinu Yitzchak applies to intra-anal ejaculation would apply to ejaculation between limbs as well, namely, that it is only permitted occasionally – "randomly" in the heat of passion (*b'akrai*) – for the sake of the couple's sexual fulfillment, but not as a regular means of intentional unsanctioned birth control[525] (which, again, logically speaking, could potentially not be of any concern during the nine months of pregnancy, post-menopause, or where birth control is in fact sanctioned).

[Along this line of reasoning, according to *Tosfos, Sanhedrin 58b*, the husband would need to ejaculate intra-vaginally only a *majority* of the time – even in regard to intercourse between limbs.]

See also Rabbi Yechiel Michel Epstein, in his *Aruch Hashulchan, Even Haezer 25:11*, whose wording applies Rabeinu Yitzchak's permission of occasional intra-anal ejaculation for couples to occasional ejaculation between limbs as well – though Rabbi Epstein, too, mentions, and even appears to endorse, Rabbi Yosef Caro's halachic caution (though not prohibition) against intra-anal ejaculation (to be discussed below, in Part Four).[525*]

[Note, however, that in regard to Rabbi Yaakov ben Asher in *Tur, Even Haezer 25:2*, Rabbi Moshe Isserless in *Shulchan Aruch, Even Haezer 25:2*, and Rabbi Mordechai Yoffe in *Levush, Even Haezer 25:2*, it is not objectively clear that they understood Rabeinu Yitzchak as halachically equating intra-anal ejaculation and ejaculation between limbs. In all three of their presentations on the subject, they first quote (the version available to them of) Maimonides' ruling in *Mishneh Torah, Isurei Biah 21:9*, permitting anal intercourse and intercourse between limbs only without extra-vaginal ejaculation, followed by Rabeinu Yitzchak's ruling permitting occasional intra-anal ejaculation. Whether or not they agreed with Rabbi Yehoshua Falk's assertion in *Drishah* that Rabeinu Yitzchak's permission of occasional intra-anal ejaculation encompassed a permission of occasional ejaculation between limbs remains undetermined.]

Now, there is, in fact, a medieval source that explicitly reflects this attitude of legal permission of ejaculation between limbs alongside pious denigration of it:

Rabeinu Meyuchas ben Eliyahu was a medieval scholar about whom little is known – even when and where he lived is a matter of conjecture among academics. The consensus assumption is that he lived in Greece. But some place him as early as the 12th century, as a contemporary of Maimonides, while others place him as late as the 15th century, as a near-contemporary of Rabbi Eliyahu Mizrachi (Re'em).[526]

His biblical commentary style is said to be unique in its manner of blending literal and halachic interpretation. On pages 8-9 of his commentary on Genesis, published by A. W. Greenup, Rabeinu Meyuchas writes:

> And He [G-d] said: "Be fruitful and multiply."
>
> The literal connotation is that this is a blessing [not a command] . . .
>
> And our rabbis expounded in the *Mishnah* that it connotes an actual command and obligation, implying that one should engage in [sex in a manner that is conducive to] fulfilling the commandment of procreation, not for other purposes (*lo l'inyan acher*).
>
> This teaches us that it is forbidden to ejaculate seed in vain (*l'hotzi tipas zera l'vatalah*), but rather [one should ejaculate] only for the sake of procreation.
>
> And even though one who has sex with his wife at a time that she cannot get pregnant is "wasting his seed" (sic), [G-d in His] Torah permits him to do so for the sake of [fulfilling his obligation to provide his wife] her joy of sexual fulfillment.
>
> But a husband who has anal sex with his wife . . . and she does not derive the joy of sexual fulfillment from it, he certainly "destroys his seed" (*vadai mashchis zaro*) and Torah's spirit is not at ease with him (*v'ein ruach haTorah noach heimenu*).
>
> Similarly, one who rubs [his penis] against his wife's [other] body parts (*derech eivarim*), and one who fondles her (*maaseh chidudim*) and becomes erect but does not have intercourse, causes himself to "waste seed," and it is "evil in G-d's eyes" [a reference to the biblical story of Er and Onan – see above, footnote to page 89; but see endnote 335].
>
> Rather, a man should only cause himself to become erect for the sake of intercourse for the purpose of procreation or the joy of his wife's sexual fulfillment – and this fulfills the commandment of the Torah and is the way of the pious (*midah chasidus*), and his children will be holy.
>
> **And even though a man's wife is permitted to him in all ways** (*v'af al pi she'ishto muteres lo b'chol inyan*), nevertheless, the spirit of the rabbinic court is not at ease with him (*ein ruach beis din nochah heimenu*). It can be compared to one who eats kosher-slaughtered meat – even though it is permitted to be eaten in any manner [*lit*. with any food

– *bchol maachal*], still, the Sages' spirit is not at ease with one who eats it in an unrefined manner [*lit.* abnormal manner] (*shelo c'derech eretz*).

The four illuminating points we take from Rabeinu Meyuchas's words:

1. He implies that even intra-vaginal ejaculation with one's own wife during pregnancy is considered "wasted seed," it is only that G-d permits it.

2. He first implies that Torah *commands* a husband to only ejaculate for the sake of procreation or his wife's sexual fulfillment, but he then later calls this a matter of *piety*, and he concedes that baseline Jewish marital sex law permits to husband and wife intra-anal ejaculation, ejaculation between limbs, and "heavy petting" without intercourse.[527]

3. When he speaks against intra-anal ejaculation, he does so on the assumption that the wife does not derive pleasure from it. The implication of this would be that if a wife *were* to enjoy it, it would be perfectly acceptable even for a "pious" couple despite the issue of "wasting seed in vain" – just like he says it is permitted to "waste seed in vain" with one's wife through intra-vaginal intercourse for the sake of her pleasure even at times when they know she will not become pregnant. And from the flow of his argument it would seem that the same would hold true in regard to ejaculation between limbs or "heavy petting" if the wife derives personal pleasure from them.

4. His presentation echoes that of Maimonides' in *Commentary to the Mishnah, Sanhedrin* 7:4 in two ways:

    a. He distinguishes between that which is permitted and that which sets G-d (and the rabbis) at ease.

    b. He sets no actual legal limit on the frequency or intention of intra-anal ejaculation or ejaculation between limbs within marriage.

It also must be noted that Rabeinu Meyuchas's emphatic concern about the Torah's (i.e., G-d's), rabbinic court's and/or Sages' lack of ease caused by such sexual behavior within marriage must be reevaluated according to the circumstances of the times, for what may have caused such "lack of ease" in one generation cannot be assumed to do so in all others.

Case in point: In the 21st century, and dare I say in future generations, with sexual awareness at unprecedented heights and growing – even within Orthodox and Chasidic-Charedi Ultra-Orthodox communities – it is reasonable to believe that a husband and wife expressing all their sexual needs and desires with one another in a loving, devoted marriage would most certainly bring rabbinic courts and/or sages, and most of all, G-d Himself, infinitely more "ease of mind and spirit" than perpetuating restrictions that were possibly based on ancient assumptions (see above, point 3) and that arguably increase the risk of couples today, and in the future, fantasizing about, and G-d forbid seeking, sexual fulfillment outside the home.

This is without even getting into the argument that modern understandings of human sexuality must also be brought into the Jewish halachic-philosophical dialogue in order to help individuals, and communities, achieve more healthy balance, physically and spiritually.

Thus, while this is not the place for a lengthy discourse on this angle of the Jewish sexual discussion, let it be noted that the same conscientiousness we have just touched upon in regard to Rabeinu Meyuchas's view must arguably be applied as well to any strong philosophical and/or halachic attitude expressed by any other rabbinic thinker, old or new.

But I digress...

Getting back to the legal view of Maimonides, let it be added that, as we suggested above (pp. 119-120) in regard to intra-anal ejaculation, in light of Maimonides' presentation in *Commentary to the Mishnah*, even if we were to accept the authenticity of the restrictive phrase historically printed in *Mishneh Torah, Isurei Biah 21:9* against "wasting seed in vain," it is perhaps possible to argue that the very *definition* of "wasting seed in vain," there, as Maimonides himself intended it, referred *only* to intra-anal ejaculation and/or ejaculation between limbs that are done *as a constant means of intentional unsanctioned birth control*. Thus, occasional ejaculation between one's wife's limbs as a means of sexual fulfillment within marriage could perhaps still be permitted even according to the restrictive textual version of *Mishneh Torah*.[528]

In any case, in light of the strong evidence that Maimonides himself meant to permit ejaculation between limbs, we must reevaluate the views of those commentators who merely quoted verbatim the prohibition of it disseminated in his name.

And let it be noted that in the 1574-1576 Venice edition of *Mishneh Torah*, as well as in subsequent editions, Maimonides' permission of intercourse between limbs for married couples in *Isurei Biah 21:9* was censored completely.[529] The impact of this omission upon rabbinic attitudes and/or silence on the matter over the following four centuries cannot be underestimated.

But here are the actual sources and what they legally permit as baseline law:

### Intercourse between limbs – without ejaculation
(*Based on a questionable manuscript of Maimonides*)

1. Rabeinu Yaakov of London, *Etz Chaim, Hilchos Piryah Vrivyah*, Chapter 3[530]

2. *Col Bo, Hilchos Ishus, Siman 75*[531]

3. Rabbi Aharon Hacohen of Lunil, *Orchos Chaim, Hilchos Kesubos Siman 7*[532]

4. Rabbi Yehuda Henkin, *Bnei Banim, vol. 4, Responsum 18*[533]

### Intercourse between limbs – ejaculation unspecified/undetermined[534]

1. Maimonides, *Commentary to the Mishnah, Sanhedrin 7:4; Mishneh Torah, Sefer Kedushah, Isurei Biah 21:9*

2. Rabbi Yaakov ben Asher, *Tur, Even Haezer 25:2*

3. Rabbi Moshe Isserles, *Rema, Shulchan Aruch, Even Haezer 25:2*

4. Rabbi Mordechai Yoffe, *Levush, Even Haezer 25:2*

### Intercourse between limbs – with ejaculation

1. Rabeinu Meyuchas ben Eliayhu, *Commentary to Genesis*[535] (though, according to the spirit of the law, he discourages any extra-vaginal ejaculation even within marriage)

2. Rabbi Yehoshua Falk, *Drishah, Tur, Even Haezer 23:1:1, Even Haezer 25:2:5-6* (interpreting the view of Rabeinu Yitzchak – though Rabbi Falk also references Rabbi Yosef Caro's halachic caution in *Beis Yosef, Even Haezer 25:2*, against any extra-vaginal ejaculation even within marriage)

3. Rabbi Yechiel Michel Epstein, *Aruch Hashulchan, Even Haezer 25:11* (though Rabbi Epstein also endorses Rabbi Yosef Caro's halachic caution in *Beis Yosef, Even Haezer 25:2*, against any extra-vaginal ejaculation even within marriage)

Note that nearly all the opinions that speak of intercourse between limbs being permitted speak of cunnilingus being permitted as well.[536] Thus, they would presumably also all permit the two techniques being performed in tandem – such as a husband and wife simultaneously stimulating each other's genitals orally or manually.[537] [XLVII]

---

[XLVII] About cunnilingus or "intercourse between limbs" performed in a lit room, see above, page 96, and endnotes 369, 845.

**Added note to the third edition:** See Rabbi Eliezer Melamed's *Simchat Habayit v'Birchato* (second edition, 2015), bottom of page 63, asserting that there are no restrictions on a wife kissing her husband's genitals – though it is not specified if fellatio is permitted to the point of ejaculation. And see Rabbi Maor Kayam's *Harchavot l'Simchat Habayit v'Birchato* (2015), pages 183-184, discussing ejaculation between limbs for married couples.

# PART FOUR
# HALACHAH MIMICS KABBALAH

## So why wasn't I ever told all this?

The obvious question at this point is: If so many medieval authorities, as well as key post-medieval authorities, collectively permitted gazing at and kissing the female genitals, along with any type of sex position, including anal sex even to the point of intra-anal ejaculation, and there is solid logic and medieval basis in Maimonides to permit even ejaculation between limbs, with two post-medieval sources suggesting that Rabeinu Yitzchak himself permitted it, why, then, do practically no Chasidic-Charedi publications on "family purity" or marital intimacy[538] report any of this?

To be sure, the fact that the restrictive and/or censored versions of Maimonides' ruling in *Mishneh Torah, Isurei Biah 21:9* were the sole versions disseminated in many circles for centuries played a major role in the perceived prohibition of intra-anal ejaculation and/or ejaculation between limbs. But that does not explain the widespread obfuscation of what was still a majority view among medieval commentators permitting intra-anal ejaculation to married couples (unless we argue that the true majority opinion was unknown until only recently due to a scarcity of written manuscripts and/or printed works[538*]), and it certainly does not account for the widespread Chasidic-Charedi belief that oral sex – at least that of husband to wife – is absolutely forbidden and "disgusting."

Now, it has been hypothesized that certain Greek and/or Catholic philosophies were to blame for Judaism's shift toward marital-sexual puritanism at some point in the last two millennia. But while evidence might possibly be brought in support of this in the realm of Jewish philosophy, the trail of Jewish *legal* records arguably tells a different story. For even though in Talmudic times there were already sages who held puritanical notions about sex even within marriage, and even whilst many medieval Jewish authorities did not speak positively about the sexual impluse from a philosophical standpoint,[539] the bottom line practical legal-halachic approach of the majority of written rabbinical opinion throughout both these periods was extremely permissive on the matter of sexual positions and technique, in accordance with the Sages' ruling reported on *Nedarim 20b* that: "Anything a husband craves to do with his wife sexually, he may do."

It was not until the 16th century that a sudden shift in Jewish law's attitude toward sexual exploration within marriage came about – with the publication of two monumental works: Rabbi Yosef Caro's *Code of Jewish Law-Shulchan Aruch* and the *Book of Zohar*.

To summarize the argument we shall present on the following pages:

# HALACHAH MIMICS KABBALAH

## The Shulchan Aruch

During the medieval period, Raavad III's interpretation of the Sages on *Nedarim 20b*, by which he excluded gazing at or kissing the female genitals from their permissive ruling, was virtually a lone voice among halachic writers.[540]

But in his *Shulchan Aruch, Orach Chaim 240*, published in 1565, Rabbi Yosef Caro presented Raavad III as the *only* Jewish voice – essentially writing the permissive approach to cunnilingus shared by a majority of his medieval forebears out of common Jewish law and out of common Jewish consciousness.

Rabbi Caro also categorically denigrated the wife-on-top and side-by-side marital sex positions, without noting that they are, at the end of the day, permissible by law.

And in regard to anal sex/intra-anal ejaculation, from which stem any possible discussion on permitting intercourse/ejaculation between limbs, Rabbi Caro remained perfectly silent in *Shulchan Aruch*. In so doing, and combined with comments of his in an earlier halachic work, he (intentionally or unintentionally) created the impression that anal sex is categorically forbidden – an impression that arguably precluded the development of any subsequent mature halachic dialogue about intercourse/ejaculation between limbs. This it appears he did due to the rising influence of the *Book of Zohar*.

## The Book of Zohar

Rabbi Caro was not the only one in his time to write anal sex out of accepted Jewish practice. A number of pious Jewish scholars, kabbalistic mystics of 16th century Safed – all living in Rabbi Caro's lifetime and in his own city – collectively erased any trace of halachah's acceptance of anal sex from the common Jewish mindset.

What was it that sparked this sudden campaign?

The evidence suggests that it was the appearance and gradual rise to popularity of manuscripts of the *Zohar* through the 14th and 15th centuries, reaching a zenith with their publication in book form in 1558 – seven years prior to Rabbi Caro's publication of the *Shulchan Aruch*.

What follows is a brief timeline and synopsis of arguably how and why Rabbi Caro and his colleagues fundamentally changed Jewish marital sexual law and psychology in the 16th century and for centuries after.

## The Zohar

Toward the end of the 13th century, a respected Spanish kabbalist, Rabbi Moshe de Leon, began circulating handwritten copies of an ancient mystical midrashic manuscript he said was in his possession. He claimed that the work, which came to be known as the *Zohar*, was an enormous repository of secret teachings originating from the school of the 1st century Talmudic sage, Rabbi Shimon ben Yochai.

Although it is not known for certain if anyone other than Rabbi Moshe de Leon ever saw this manuscript, and despite the fact that many in his own day questioned his claims about the *Zohar's* antiquity and authenticity, its teachings were eventually accepted by key kabbalistic scholars as legitimate.[541] But more importantly, it slowly came to be granted a level of authority approaching, and even on par with, that of the Talmud.

First printed only two hundred and sixty years later,[542] in 1558, the *Zohar* takes an exceedingly harsh stance against "wasting seed in vain."[XLVIII] In one place,[543] it specifically lists intra-anal ejaculation among various forms of "wasting seed in vain" for which it claims there is a special place in Purgatory – though it does not specify whether the intra-anal ejaculation it speaks against includes even that which is done occasionally between loving husband and wife for the sake of sexual fulfillment within marriage or only that which is done constantly as an intentional means of unsanctioned birth control.

In the wake of the *Zohar's* growing popularity and authority, a number of important Jewish legal-ethical-mystical works coming out of 16th century Safed, the seat of the kabbalah movement of the day, created an atmosphere in which it came to be assumed that the *Zohar* forbade anal sex of any kind even within marriage, and that the Talmud itself did so as well.

---

[XLVIII] It is not practical to quote here the extensive relevant passages from the *Zohar* without diverting the reader's attention too far afield from the topic of marital intimacy. Such quotations would also be highly distracting on account of their astonishing severity. But for a collection of the *Zohar's* teachings on this topic, see Rabbi Eliyahu de Vidas's *Reishis Chochmah, Shaar Hakedushah*, Chapter 17. And see below, pages 143-144 and footnotes and endnotes thereon.

The *Zohar's* approach to "wasting seed in vain" will also be addressed in-depth in volume two of this series. And see above, footnote to page 3.

## Rabbi Yosef Caro

Rabbi Yosef Caro (1488-1575) is perhaps the most celebrated halachic authority of the 16th century.

Widely known for his famous *Code of Jewish Law*, the *"Shulchan Aruch,"* the work was not actually his most important. Rabbi Caro's main contribution to halachic thought was his commentary to an earlier code of law, that of Rabbi Yaakov ben Asher (c.1269-c.1343), entitled *"Arbaah Turim."*

Rabbi Yaakov ben Asher's *Arbaah Turim* (literally, *"Four Columns"*), nicknamed "the *Tur*," was the most comprehensive code of Jewish law organized according to topic after Maimonides' *Mishneh Torah*. It was he who divided Jewish law into the four famous categories, or volumes, of *Orach Chaim* (daily law), *Yoreh Deah* (ritual law), *Even Haezer* (marital law) and *Choshen Mishpat* (civil law). Authored over a hundred years after Maimonides' *Mishneh Torah*, the *Tur's* significance was its inclusion of a variety of medieval halachic opinion.

Rabbi Caro's commentary to the *Tur*, which he called after his own name, *"Beis Yosef,"* tracked more deeply the Talmudic and medieval sources and reasonings upon which the *Tur's* presentations were based, and was meant to spare the average rabbi the time and effort of analyzing a multitude of other works[544] – many of which were perhaps difficult to even obtain.

Rabbi Caro's *Shulchan Aruch*, on the other hand, was intended merely as a memorization device to help scholars and laymen, perhaps even children,[545] remember the final rulings of his *Beis Yosef* commentary. A halachic "Cliffs-notes" of sorts, organized in corresponding order to the four volumes of *Tur*, the terse *Shulchan Aruch* was never intended as a legal reference manual independent of the in-depth *Beis Yosef*.[546] But before long, that is exactly what the *Shulchan Aruch* became in the eyes of the masses.

As pertains to our discussion, how Rabbi Caro (intentionally or unintentionally) narrowed Jewish consciousness of Jewish marital sex law through his *Shulchan Aruch*, we must first understand how Rabbi Yaakov ben Asher presented these laws in his *Tur*, how Rabbi Caro elaborated on them in his *Beis Yosef* commentary to the *Tur*, and how he finally "codified" them in his "Cliffs-notes," the *Shulchan Aruch*.

## Rabbi Caro's Inspiration – Rabbi Yaakov ben Asher's *Tur*

Rabbi Yaakov ben Asher discusses Jewish marital sex law in two chapters of his *Tur*, in *Orach Chaim 240* and in *Even Haezer 25* – the same two chapters in which Rabbi Caro later included these laws in his own *Shulchan Aruch*.

As we've seen above, a majority of medieval halachic writers ruled according to, or in similar fashion to, Maimonides to permit anal sex and (gazing at or) kissing the female genitals. Additionally, the majority of medieval scholars who weigh in on the question of intra-anal ejaculation – including Rabbi Yaakov ben Asher's own father, Rabeinu Asher – expressly rule in accord with Rabeinu Yitzchak's *second* approach in *Tosfos* to *Yevamos 34b*, permitting occasional intra-anal ejaculation for the sake of a husband's sexual fulfillment.

And although Raavad III negates, or forbids, these behaviors in his *Baalei HaNefesh, Shaar Hakedushah*, we find only one other medieval scholar, Rabbi Shmuel ben Meshulam Yerondi (14th century),[547] lending Raavad III clear and unequivocal support. And even Raavad III himself remains perfectly silent in his gloss-notes to Maimonides' *Mishneh Torah, Isurei Biah 21:9*, where the latter permits anal intercourse and (gazing at or) kissing the female genitals.

Now, in his *Tur*, both in *Orach Chaim 240* and *Even Haezer 25*, Rabbi Yaakov quotes copiously from Raavad III's *Baalei HaNefesh, Shaar Hakedushah* about the proper approach to "sanctified" sex, including, in both places, Raavad III's restrictions against gazing at or kissing the female genitals and his seeming discouragement of anal sex of any kind. It thus appears that it was Rabbi Yaakov ben Asher, through the success of his *Tur*, who pushed Raavad III's views onto center-stage of the practical halachic world for the first time.

But it is not at all clear that Rabbi Yaakov himself actually meant to rule the law according to Raavad III concerning these sexual behaviors,[548] for in both places he also quotes the permissive approaches of Maimonides and/or Rabeinu Yitzchak.

In *Orach Chaim 240:2-4*,[XLIX] he quotes Raavad III's prohibition against gazing at or kissing the female genitals without quoting Maimonides' permissive view about them. But then he quotes Raavad III's definition of "overturning the table" as rear-entry vaginal intercourse directly followed by Rabeinu Yitzchak's definition of the term as anal intercourse even to the point of intra-anal ejaculation.

In *Even Haezer 25:2*, on the other hand, he first quotes the ruling of Maimonides, at least the version available to him, permitting anything a man

---

[XLIX] The *Tur* itself was not broken down by Rabbi Yaakov ben Asher into sub-laws, only into chapters. When sub-laws of the *Tur* are referenced in this book, they are presented according to the breakdown in the modern typeset edition by Mosdos Shiras Devorah, generally corresponding to the division of Rabbi Caro's sub-laws in his *Shulchan Aruch*.

craves to do with his wife sexually, including kissing her genitals as well as anal intercourse or intercourse between limbs without ejaculation. This is immediately followed by his quoting the ruling of Rabeinu Yitzchak permitting even intra-anal ejaculation. Only pages later does he mention Raavad III's view in *Baalei HaNefesh, Shaar Hakedushah* that gazing at or kissing the female genitals are still forbidden (for other reasons to be discussed below, in Part Five), along with Raavad III's definition of the term "overturning the table" as rear-entry vaginal intercourse ("animal style" – *maaseh beheimah*).

These discrepancies arguably make it impossible to say with certainty which opinion Rabbi Yaakov ben Asher actually endorsed. We cannot determine with whom he agreed purely based on the order in which he presented them, for he switched the order from one place to the other. It could be reasonably argued that in *Even Haezer* he intended to open the chapter ruling the succinct baseline letter of the law according to Maimonides and Rabeinu Yitzchak, permitting everything a husband and wife may wish to do together, followed by a lengthy discussion about sexual *sanctification*, the *spirit* of the law – beginning, actually, with Maimonides' views on the matter of sanctification, followed by Raavad's. And the fact that he did not quote Maimonides' permission to kiss the female genitals in *Orach Chaim* can hardly be used as definitive proof that he meant to prohibit it, for why would he have then bothered to bring it down in *Even Haezer* at all, especially in conjunction with Rabeinu Yitzchak, whom he brought as the *second* opinion in *Orach Chaim* in regard to anal sex/intra-anal ejaculation?[549]

In any case, whatever Rabbi Yaakov ben Asher's final rulings can be understood to have be, it is Rabbi Caro's comments on these chapters of the *Tur* in his own *Beis Yosef* commentary to which we will now turn our attention.

## Rabbi Caro's *Beis Yosef* – Legal Concerns

In his *Beis Yosef* commentary to *Tur, Orach Chaim 240:2-4*, Rabbi Caro points to *Tosfos* and to Rabbi Yaakov ben Asher's own father, Rabeinu Asher, as the source and support, respectively, of Rabeinu Yitzchak's opinion permitting intra-anal ejaculation for a husband's pleasure – though he notes that according to (the version of) *Mishneh Torah* (available to him) Maimonides permitted anal sex only without intra-anal ejaculation.

In *Tur, Even Haezer 25:2*, however, after pointing again to *Tosfos* and Rabeinu Asher as the source and support of Rabeinu Yitzchak, Rabbi Caro adds a note of caution:

> And it is difficult to permit one to stumble in "wasting seed in vain," even randomly, and one who is conscientious of his soul will distance himself from it and the like.[550] And I already wrote about this.

His comment, "And I already wrote about this," appears to be referring back to an explanation he gave just one passage earlier in regard to Maimonides – whom, again, *Tur* quotes as permitting anal sex only without intra-anal ejaculation. Rabbi Caro explains, there, that Maimonides (allegedly) forbade intra-anal ejaculation because the teaching of Rabbi Yochanan bar Napacha on *Nedarim 20b* permitting anal sex cannot contradict another teaching of Rabbi Yochanan bar Napacha himself elsewhere, on *Nidah 13a*, where he speaks harshly against "wasting seed in vain." This is the reason, Rabbi Caro says, that Maimonides permitted anal sex to couples only without intra-anal ejaculation.

In fact, Rabbi Caro was not the first to put forth such reasoning to explain Maimonides' alleged view. The medieval Rabbi Avraham of Montpellier (*Peirush R. Avraham min Hahar*) argued the same logic two centuries prior.[551]

But even without resorting to the argument that their textual version of Maimonides was presumably flawed (as discussed above at length[552]), there are a number of simple responses to their logic:

Firstly, Rabbi Yochanan's permission for "overturning the table" (defined as anal sex) on *Nedarim 20b* is brought in the context of marital intimacy between husband and wife, whereas Rabbi Yochanan's harsh words against "wasting seed in vain" on *Nidah 13a* are brought in (what is generally understood to be) a context of male self-masturbation – two very different halachic issues which even Rabeinu Yitzchak, who clearly permits intra-anal ejaculation to couples, does not give us explicit sanction to compare.[553]

Secondly, Rabbi Yochanan's words on *Nidah 13a* are only brought to explain the teaching of an earlier sage, Rabbi Eliezer ben Hyrcanus, in (what is generally understood to be) a context of masturbation, while Rabbi Eliezer himself, on *Yevamos 34b*, permits in a certain scenario the most severe form of extra-vaginal "wasting of seed" within the context of marital intimacy: coitus interruptus.

Rabbi Eliezer on *Yevamos 34b* permits, and perhaps even orders, coitus interruptus for a married couple when the wife is a nursing mother whose milk flow might be disrupted if she becomes pregnant again, putting her current baby at risk. Rabbi Moshe Feinstein explains[554] that according to Rabbi Eliezer if there is a holy purpose for the spilling of seed to the ground – in this case, for the sake of the husband continuing to fulfill his biblical obligation to give his wife sexual satisfaction even while she is nursing – then even deliberate coitus interruptus in order to intentionally prevent pregnancy *does not fall under the category* of "wasting seed in vain."

Rabbi Feinstein then extends this same logic[555] to explain the view of Rabeinu Yitzchak's second approach in *Tosfos* to *Yevamos 34b*, which allows intra-anal ejaculation for couples despite the "sin" of Er and Onan. He explains that according to Rabeinu Yitzchak since this ejaculation is for the sake of the husband's sexual fulfillment within marriage it is not "wasted" or "without purpose," for Torah grants a man the right to have pleasure from his wife's body in any way he and she mutually agree.[556]

Therefore, the reasoning Rabbi Feinstein uses to reconcile Rabbi Eliezer's and Rabbi Yochanan's teachings on *Nidah 13a* with Rabbi Eliezer's teaching on *Yevamos 34b*, which is the same reasoning, according to Rabbi Feinstein, used by Rabeinu Yitzchak to reconcile the teaching of the Sages on *Yevamos 34b* with the teaching of the Sages and Rabbi Yochanan on *Nedarim 20b*, could also be used to reconcile the two teachings of Rabbi Yochanan himself on *Nidah 13a* and *Nedarim 20b* – especially considering that Rabbi Yochanan on *Nidah 13a* actually invokes the episode of Er and Onan itself (the context of *Yevamos 34b*) as the basis of his teaching there.

[Rabbi Yochanan's actual statement on *Nidah 13a* is that "wasting seed in vain" is deserving of death by the hand of Heaven. But while the context of the discussion on *Nidah 13a* is generally understood to be about masturbation, Rabbi Yochanan himself bases his statement on the episode of Er and Onan, in which, the Talmud in *Yevamos 34b* tells us, both lost their lives on account of "wasting seed in vain" (not by masturbation, but) through their continuous intentional refusal to get their wife pregnant during marital sex.

Furthermore, in another responsum[557] Rabbi Moshe Feinstein notes that according to rabbinic tradition Er and Onan died while they were yet under the age of thirteen – that is, under the age of liability in either the human or Heavenly court. Therefore, Rabbi Feinstein argues, the message of their story cannot be that according to Jewish law a person is legally deserving of death by the hand of Heaven *across the board* for "wasting seed in vain," but only that *sometimes* G-d *might* take a person's life for it *for reasons known only to Him*. Rabbi Feinstein asserts that this must have been the meaning of Rabbi Yochanan's own statement on *Nidah 13a* as well, and that this was also the understanding of Maimonides, Rabbi Yaakov ben Asher and Rabbi Yosef Caro in their respective codes of law.

Accordingly, one could argue all the more that the statement of Rabbi Yochanan reported on *Nidah 13a* (regarding the *unusual* death of Er and Onan on account of their *constant intentional unsanctioned birth control*) was not in Rabbi Yochanan's own mind in any way relevant to his statement reported on *Nedarim 20b* (as understood by Rabeinu Yitzchak to be) legally permitting *occasional* intra-anal ejaculation for the sake of *sexual fulfillment within marriage*.[557*]]

Finally, Rabbi Yehoshua Falk, in his *Drishah* commentary to *Tur, Even Haezer 25:2:5-6*, states clearly that according to Rabeinu Yitzchak, Rabbi Yochanan's teaching on *Nidah 13a* against "wasting seed in vain" does not apply to intra-anal ejaculation or ejaculation between limbs performed occasionally as a matter of sexual fulfillment within marriage.[558]

In any case, Rabeinu Yitzchak was surely aware of Rabbi Yochanan's teaching on *Nidah 13a*, and still he gave his second answer – the answer that more medieval writers endorse – that intra-anal ejaculation is permitted by Rabbi Yochanan himself for the sake of a husband's sexual fulfillment within marriage.

Thus, Rabbi Caro's (and Rabbi Avraham of Montpellier's) legal concern based on the teaching of Rabbi Yochanan on *Nidah 13a* is surmountable.

What is more, it can be argued that the fundamental principle Rabeinu Yitzchak was getting at was that intra-anal ejaculation performed for the sake of a husband's sexual fulfillment *does not fall under the category of "wasting seed in vain" to begin with.*

As noted above, Rabbi Moshe Feinstein clearly states this to be Rabeinu Yitzchak's intention. In Rabbi Feinstein's own words (*Igros Moshe, Even Haezer 1, Responsum 63*, p. 156, paragraphs 2-3):

> The definition of "wasted [seed]" is literal waste (*l'vatalah mamash*), where there is no need in it [the ejaculation] at all . . .
>
> . . . That is why Rabeinu Yitzchak and Rabeinu Asher believed – on account of the Talmud on *Nedarim 20b* and the verse [Deuteronomy 24:1], 'When a man acquires a wife' – that a man's wife is 'acquired' to him to perform with her all their sexual desires,[558*] which is why Rebbi said [to the wife who informed him that her husband had performed anal sex with her], "Torah permits you."
>
> See there [*Nedarim 20b*], in [the commentary of] Rabeinu Nissim, [who implies] that in the context of marriage of husband and wife, Torah permits and considers even the husband's desire for anal sex as a "need" (*tzorech*).[559] And therefore, [according to Rabeinu Yitzchak and Rabeinu Asher] it [intra-anal ejaculation] is not "wasted" (*eino l'vatalah*) and it is permitted (*mutar*) . . .

> ... If he has this desire [for intra-anal ejaculation] randomly in the heat of passion, it is permitted [according to Rabeinu Yitzchak and Rabeinu Asher] even if it is not for the sake of the commandment [to satisfy his wife sexually], because the very fact that *he* desires it is also considered a "need" in the context of marriage of husband and wife, as revealed by the verse.

And if this is not spelled out clearly in Rabeinu Yitzchak's own words as quoted in *Tosfos* to *Yevamos 34b* (or by *Tosfos* to *Sanhedrin 58b*), it is most certainly unequivocal in the words of his contemporary, Rabbi Yeshayah of Trani I (c.1180-c.1250), who writes in his *Tosfos Rid* commentary to *Yevamos 12b*:

> If his [the husband's] intention is [to satisfy] his erotic sexual desires, not to prevent her from getting pregnant, it [intra-anal ejaculation] is permitted, like we said ... [in *Nedarim 20b*] ... that there was a wife who came before Rebbi and she said to him, "I prepared a table for my husband and he overturned it" – and he [Rebbi] permitted it ...

> They [Er and Onan], whose intention was to prevent her [Tamar] from becoming pregnant, sinned. But if his [a husband's] intention is [merely] his own sexual fulfillment (*l'hashlim taavas yitzro*), he does not sin, for "Anything a husband craves to do with his wife sexually, he may do" – and it is not called "destruction of seed" (*v'lo yikarei mashchis zaro*).

In any case, while Rabbi Caro himself might not have had access to Rabbi Yeshayah of Trani I's *Tosfos Rid* commentary,[560] the same approach is arguably implied by the over-arching message of Rabeinu Yitzchak.

[Recall also *Tosfos Yeshanim* to *Nedarim 20ab*, which interprets "overturning the table" as anal intercourse, and which comments on the ruling of the Sages' there: "Anything a husband craves to do with his wife sexually, he may do – *and there is no lack of holiness.*" While it is possible *Tosfos Yeshanim* were referring only to anal penetration without ejaculation, it is arguably unlikely, considering that it does not state such a stipulation, and that the majority of medieval commentaries who weigh in on the question of intra-anal ejaculation follow Rabeinu Yitzchak's *second* approach that it is permissible.]

Even the choice of wording of Rabbi Yaakov ben Asher himself in his *Tur*, and both in *Orach Chaim* and *Even Haezer*, somewhat implies that according to Rabeinu Yitzchak intra-anal ejaculation for the sake of sexual fulfillment within marriage does not fall under the category of "wasted seed":

### Tur, Orach Chaim 240:2-4

> And *Tosfos* explains that "overturning the table" means he penetrates her anally. And only if it is done in the heat of passion, because he craves it, is it permitted.
>
> But if he does it constantly it is forbidden, because it is "destroying seed" (*hashchatas zera*).

### Tur, Even Haezer 25:2

> ... And he can have intercourse with her vaginally, anally or between limbs, as long as he does not "waste seed in vain" (*ubilvad shelo yotzi zera l'vatalah*).
>
> And Rabeinu Yitzchak explains that it is permitted to have anal intercourse even to the point of [intra-anal] ejaculation (*afilu b'hotzaas shichvas zera*), as long as he does not do it constantly, but only randomly [in the heat of passion] because he desires to penetrate her anally. But to do so constantly is forbidden.

In both places, Rabbi Yaakov ben Asher refrains from categorizing *permissible* intra-anal ejaculation as "permissible destruction of seed" or "permissible wasting of seed in vain." He only employs the terms "destruction" or "waste in vain" when discussing *forbidden* contexts of ejaculation.

See also Rabbi Eliyahu Spira's *Elyah Rabah* commentary to *Levush, Orach Chaim 240:4:10*:

> According to what I've explained it all makes sense, for in truth it [intra-anal ejaculation performed randomly in the heat of passion for the sake of the husband's sexual fulfillment] is not "wasted seed."

And Rabbi Menachem Mendel of Lubavitch,[561] in his responsum, *Tzemach Tzedek, Even Haezer, 89:2*, asserts that Rabeinu Yitzchak and Rabeinu Asher – both quoted by Rabbi Yosef Caro in his *Beis Yosef* to *Orach Chaim 240* and *Even Haezer 25* – clearly believed that occasional intra-anal ejaculation for the sake of sexual fulfillment within marriage does not fall under the category of "spilling seed upon trees and rocks."[562]

We have thus addressed, and resolved, Rabbi Caro's legal concerns.

## Rabbi Caro's *Bedek Habayis* – Kabbalistic Concerns

But Rabbi Caro then goes further, beyond the "four cubits of Jewish law."

You see, after the printing of his *Beis Yosef* commentary during the 1550s, Rabbi Caro continued to review and revise the work, intending to publish addendum-notes, which he entitled, "*Bedek Habayis*." And we find in his *Bedek Habayis* notes to *Even Haezer 25:2* this additional later caution:

> And if Rabeinu Yitzchak had seen the punishment the *Zohar* forewarns for the "wasting of seed in vain," that it is greater than that of any other sin in the Torah, he would not have written what he did.

Rabbi Caro, here, is clearly referring to two passages in the Zohar, one in the Biblical portion of *Vayeshev*,[563] the other in the portion of *Vayechi*,[564] which state that the punishment for masturbation is worse than that of any other sin.[565]

But Rabbi Caro's assertion here is problematic on many levels:

Firstly, it assumes that not one, but over a dozen medieval scholars, some of whom lived centuries before him, would have changed their views of Talmudic law based upon a newly discovered, never-before-heard-of, kabbalistic midrash, the original manuscript of which was never found, and the origins, authenticity and authority of which were questioned by Torah scholars alive when copies of it first circulated. And even if Rabbi Caro himself did not have access to, and therefore was unaware of, many of the medieval commentaries who endorsed Rabeinu Yitzchak's second approach, we today do know of them.[566]

Secondly, as already seen above, the *Zohar* was not the first to speak against "wasting seed in vain" in the form of masturbation, for *Babylonian Talmud, Nidah 13ab* already quotes none other than Rabbi Yochanan himself speaking against it.[L] And yet, Rabeinu Yitzchak, based on the ruling of Rabbi Yochanan on *Nedarim 20b* permitting a husband to enjoy his wife sexually in any way he and she may desire, permits occasional intra-anal ejaculation to married couples (which, according to Rabbi Falk's understanding in *Drishah*, was meant to permit occasional ejaculation between limbs within marriage as well).

And Rabeinu Yitzchak said this despite the fact that *Nidah 13ab* itself already spoke against "wasting seed in vain" (in what is generally understood to be a context of masturbation) in the harshest of terms, calling it worthy of death by the hand of Heaven (in the name of Rabbi Yochanan himself), and, among other

---

[L.] See above, pp. 138-140.

severe statements, comparing it to the three cardinal sins of murder, idol worship and adultery.[LI]

In other words: In the eyes of Jewish law, or at least in the eyes of Rabeinu Yitzchak and the dozen medieval scholars who follow his approach, occasional intra-anal ejaculation (and according to *Drishah*, occasional ejaculation between limbs) caused by friction - "bonding" - against one's wife's body during lovemaking is not in any way to be compared with male self-masturbation. The only forms of extra-vaginal ejaculation caused by friction against one's wife's body that are possibly to be objected to, alongside male self-masturbation, are coitus interruptus, *constant* intra-anal ejaculation or *constant* ejaculation between limbs [though the latter three betray (in the eyes of halachah) an unequivocal motive for birth control, whereas male self-masturbation does not].[567]

And if this simple logic weren't enough, there is actually a commentator who already says something nearly identical to it:

Rabbi Shlomoh Yehudah Tabak (1830-1907), a rabbinical judge in the Chasidic city of Sighet and author of the halachic work *Erech Shai*, writes that Rabbi Yosef Caro's assertion in *Bedek Habayis*, that Rabeinu Yitzchak would have retracted had he seen (and believed in) the *Zohar*, is debatable:

> Because it is obvious from the context of the *Zohar* that this great severity [of punishment] applies only to one whose intention is to avoid pregnancy or he does it constantly, and specifically if he ejaculates by hand [through self-masturbation.][568] [569]

Thus, being that Rabeinu Yitzchak permits intra-anal ejaculation, and possibly even ejaculation between limbs, only when done occasionally for the sake of sexual fulfillment within marriage, not when done constantly for the sake of unsanctioned birth control, and only when the ejaculation results from the

---

[LI] The approach of the Talmud to masturbation will be addressed in volume two of this series. And see above, footnote to page 3 and endnote 524. In the meantime, note the halachic assertion of Rabbi Yehoshua Heschel ben Yosef of Cracow (c.1578-1648) in his *Shaalos uTeshuvos Pnei Yehoshuah vol. 2, Even Haezer 44* (page 22, middle of column 2, in the Lvov edition), that the Talmud's comparison of masturbation to the three cardinal sins was hyperbolic.

[This Rabbi Yehoshua Heschel is not to be confused with Rabbi Yaakov Yehoshua Falk (1680-1756), author of the *Pnei Yehoshua* commentary on the Talmud. He was, however, a student of Rabbi Yehoshua Falk (1555-1614), author of the *Drishah* and *Prishah* commentaries to the *Tur* that we have been discussing in our study.]

See also *Shaalos uTeshuvos Rivash, Responsum 171*, for the acknowledgment by Rabbi Yitzchak ben Sheshes (1326-1408) that the Sages' exaggerated when they compared the severity of certain sins to idolatry, adultery and/or murder, as a means of deterrence. Credit goes to Rabbi Dr. Marc Shapiro for bringing this source in *Rivash* to my attention, in his *Changing the Immutable: How Orthodox Judaism Rewrites its History* (The Littman Library of Jewish Civilization, 2015), chapter 8, page 242, footnote 15.

husband's friction – "bonding" – against his wife's body, not through his own hand, there is no contextual equivalence between the teachings of the *Zohar* and the ruling of Rabeinu Yitzchak.

This is all besides the logic put forth earlier, that Rabeinu Yitzchak, like Rabbi Yeshayah of Trani I, quite possibly did not consider intra-anal ejaculation for the sake of sexual fulfillment within marriage to fall under the category of "wasting seed" to begin with.

To summarize and simplify:

*Zohar Vayeshev, Zohar Vayechi* and *Nidah 13ab* are all similar in context to *Yevamos 34b*, which calls intra-anal ejaculation "sinful." But Rabeinu Yitzchak's approach, shared by over a dozen medieval scholars, reconciled *Yevamos 34b* with *Nedarim 20b* and *Sanhedrin 58b*, and therefore their approach would also reconcile both passages of *Zohar* and *Nidah 13ab* with *Nedarim 20b* and *Sanhedrin 58b* as well. Thus, the harsh statements of the *Zohar* against "wasting seed in vain" need not be understood as any obstacle whatsoever, halachically or kabbalistically, to permitting occasional intra-anal ejaculation, or even occasional ejaculation between limbs, when such is done solely for the sake of sexual fulfillment and bonding between loving husband and wife within marriage.

Having reconciled Rabbi Caro's halachic and kabbalistic concerns as expressed in his *Beis Yosef* and *Bedek Habayis* commentaries to *Tur*, we will now turn to the presentation offered in his concise code, the *Shulchan Aruch*.

## Rabbi Caro's *Shulchan Aruch*

Let us recall what we saw above, in the opening chapter to our book, what Rabbi Caro tells us – or doesn't tell us – in his *Orach Chaim 240* about permitted marital sex techniques and positions:

> 4. It is forbidden to gaze at the female genitals, for one who gazes there displays no shamefacedness and transgresses the prophet's admonition to "walk modestly with the L-rd." He diminishes whatever shamefacedness he does have, whereas one who has a sense of shame does not readily sin, as the verse states, "[Moses said to the people at Sinai: "Do not fear, for in order to elevate you has G-d come; and] so that awe of Him" – a sense of shame – "shall be upon your faces, so that you shall not sin."
>
> What is more, gazing at the female genitals incites the evil urge.
>
> And kissing the female genitals is even worse, for besides transgressing all the above, one also transgresses the biblical commandment, "Do not make yourselves disgusting."
>
> 5. Intercourse with him-on-bottom and her-on-top is arrogant.
>
> Intercourse side-by-side is obstinate.

Firstly, besides for not disclosing Maimonides' permission of (gazing at and) kissing the female genitals, Rabbi Caro leaves out entirely Maimonides' permissive view on anal sex and intercourse between limbs – with or without ejaculation. Secondly, he does not tell us Rabeinu Yitzchak's permissive view about anal sex either – with or without intra-anal ejaculation. Thirdly, with all his copious quotes from Raavad III, Rabbi Caro does not even disclose Raavad III's own permission for rear-entry vaginal intercourse. All we are told by Rabbi Caro on the topic of marital sex techniques and positions is that cunnilingus is forbidden (along with even gazing at the female genitals), and that sex with her-on-top or side-by-side is deplorable.

Now, we could perhaps say that Rabbi Caro assumed people would be studying his in-depth *Beis Yosef* commentary as a prelude to his succinct *Shulchan Aruch* and that they would therefore find their way to the permissive opinions in regard to other sexual practices within marriage there.[570] This answer is certainly plausible, but it is hardly sufficient, for when all is said and done, Rabbi Caro arguably should have stated *something* in his *Shulchan Aruch* on the matter of these sexual behaviors, even if only as part of the view of Raavad III himself, who permits rear-entry vaginal intercourse. After all, if Rabbi Caro deemed it appropriate, and necessary, to address cunnilingus in his *Shulchan Aruch*, alongside the wife-on-top and side-by-side sex positions, why wouldn't he address the other few basic and common sex positions that are discussed extensively in Talmudic and medieval writings?

Rabbi Caro's silence in *Shulchan Aruch* in regard to rear-entry vaginal intercourse remains an enigma.

But in regard to anal sex, perhaps Rabbi Caro left out any discussion of it because despite what he wrote in his *Beis Yosef* (and *Bedek Habayis*[571]) to *Tur, Even Haezer 25*, he himself did not actually come to a final conclusion on the matter.

With a clear ruling in *Talmud, Sanhedrin 58b* permitting anal sex, with so many medieval authorities permitting anal sex even to the point of intra-anal ejaculation, with even Raavad III himself remaining silent in his gloss-notes to *Mishneh Torah* about Maimonides' permission of anal sex in *Isurei Biah 21:9*,[571*] and with Rabbi Yaakov ben Asher in his *Tur* ultimately unclear as to which way he himself ruled on the matter, perhaps Rabbi Caro simply could not bring himself to "forbid" anal intercourse or even intra-anal ejaculation. But with the severe teachings of the *Zohar* against "wasting seed in vain" gaining wider popularity and authority, perhaps he did not feel comfortable outright permitting them either, so he chose to remain silent about them in *Shulchan Aruch* and rely on what he had already stated for the record in *Beis Yosef* (and *Bedek Habayis*).

## Rabbi Caro's Bottom Line

And here, after all the analysis of *Beis Yosef*, *Bedek Habayis* and *Shulchan Aruch*, is where the most important point must be made:

**Nowhere in any of these three major halachic works does Rabbi Caro actually "forbid" anal sex or occasional intra-anal ejaculation for the sake of sexual fulfillment within marriage.**

Yes, Rabbi Caro does caution twice against the latter – in *Beis Yosef* and in *Bedek Habayis*. Yes, he does twice leave out discussion of either of them – in *Shulchan Aruch, Orach Chaim 240* and *Even Haezer 25*. But never does he ever *forbid* them.

Let us remind ourselves what Rabbi Caro wrote in both of his comments upon the *Tur*:

### *Beis Yosef, Even Haezer 25:2*

> And it is difficult to permit one to stumble in "wasting seed in vain" even randomly, and *one who is conscientious of his soul* will *distance* himself from it and the like.

### *Bedek Habayis, Even Haezer 25:2*

> And if Rabeinu Yitzchak had seen the punishment the *Zohar* forewarns for the "wasting of seed in vain," that it is greater than that of any other sin in the Torah, *he would not have written what he did.*

Very strong language. But in both places Rabbi Caro stops short of issuing a simple clear-cut prohibition.

No less an authority than Rabbi Moshe Feinstein (1895-1986) acknowledges that the wording of Rabbi Caro's cautions in both places is reserved and is not equal to a full-fledged prohibition.[572]

And Rabbi Feinstein was not the first to point this out.

Rabbi Avraham Dovid Wahrman of Buczacz (1770-1840), in his *Ezer Mekudash* commentary to *Shulchan Aruch, Even Haezer,* also notes in regard to Rabbi Caro's caution in *Beis Yosef*:

> The wording of *Beis Yosef* implies somewhat that in actuality it [intra-anal ejaculation] is permitted, only that it is fitting for one to scrupulously guard oneself against it.[573]

This would explain, then, why in his *Shulchan Aruch* Rabbi Caro never categorically forbade anal sex of any kind, not even to the point of intra-anal ejaculation.[573*]

[And note that when Rabbi Caro cautioned against intra-anal ejaculation in his *Beis Yosef*, he ended off: "And one who is conscientious of his soul will distance himself from it *and the like*" – an apparent reference to ejaculation between limbs, which he thus also perhaps discouraged, but possibly never legally forbade.]

**Thus, we may reasonably conclude that concerning the practical letter of the law regarding anal sex and intra-anal ejaculation, not even Rabbi Caro and Rabbi Isserles are at odds!**[574]

Accordingly, the only real difference of opinion between Rabbis Caro and Isserles on this matter was whether or not the permittedness of anal sex and/or intra-anal ejaculation for married couples had an appropriate place in *Shulchan Aruch*, a halachic memorization device for the masses.[LI*]

In this light, we must call attention to the fact that Rabbi Moshe Leima in his *Chelkas Mechokek* commentary and Rabbi Yehudah Ashkenazi in his *Be'er Heitev* commentary, both to *Shulchan Aruch, Even Haezer 25:2*, as well as Rabbi Yechiel Michel Epstein in his code of Jewish law, *Aruch Hashulchan, Even Haezer 25:11*, all mention Rabbi Caro's halachic caution in *Beis Yosef* – and Rabbis Ashkenazi and Epstein don't just quote it, they appear to endorse it – but not one of them goes so far as to issue a clear-cut prohibition. And of the three, only Rabbi Ashkenazi quotes Rabbi Caro's kabbalistic caution from *Bedek Habayis* (the more strongly worded caution of the two).[575] Rabbis Leima and Epstein do not.

Nor does Rabbi Yehoshua Falk in his *Drishah* commentary to *Tur, Even Haezer 25:2:5-6*. Instead, immediately after quoting Rabbi Caro's halachic caution from *Beis Yosef* (the caution Rabbi Falk's own master, Rabbi Isserles, most certainly was aware of – yet disregarded as a matter of baseline law), he goes on to insist that Rabeinu Yitzchak permits for married couples even occasional ejaculation between limbs.[576]

---

[LI*] **Added note to the third edition:** See Rabbi Eliezer Melamed's *Simchat Habayit v'Birchato* (second edition, 2015), page 64, paragraph four of footnote 21, suggesting that Rabbi Caro may have in fact permitted cunnilingus – that Rabbi Caro's "prohibition" of cunnilingus in *Shulchan Aruch, Orach Chaim 240*, may have only been in the realm of holiness and modesty (*kedushah utznius*), whereas because he knew that baseline law ultimately permits it, he did not include a legal prohibition against it in *Shulchan Aruch, Even Haezer 25*.

According to this line of reasoning, then, Rabbi Caro and Rabbi Isserles did not differ either about a husband being permitted to kiss (or gaze at) his wife's genitals.

## Halachah Mimics Kabbalah

As for which of Rabbi Caro's concerns about intra-anal ejaculation – the halachic or the kabbalistic – played a greater role in influencing his silence in *Shulchan Aruch*, we may never know for certain. Perhaps they played equal parts.

His halachic concern expressed in *Beis Yosef* to *Even Haezer* certainly preceded his composition and printing of *Shulchan Aruch*. But did his kabbalistic concern expressed in *Bedek Habayis* also precede his *Shulchan Aruch*?

In his brief introduction to *Bedek Habayis*, published posthumously in 1605,[577] Rabbi Caro wrote:

> It was my intention to publish these novel addenda in the second edition [of *Beis Yosef*], but my plan did not come to fruition, because the printers rushed to put out the second edition[578] before my manuscript reached them.

As noted, the complete *Beis Yosef* was first published in the 1550s[579] – *Orach Chaim* and *Yoreh Deah* between 1550-1551, *Even Haezer* in 1553, and *Choshen Mishpat* in 1559.[580] We find second editions of parts of the *Beis Yosef* published already in 1564,[581] a year before the publication of *Shulchan Aruch* in 1565. This might suggest that Rabbi Caro had already authored his *Bedek Habayis* addendum notes prior to the *Shulchan Aruch's* printing. But considering that Rabbi Caro began to compose drafts of *Shulchan Aruch* as early as 1555,[582] before even the first edition of his *Beis Yosef* was complete, we cannot determine with any degree of certainty whether this specific kabbalistic cautionary note in *Bedek Habayis* came before or after his composition of *Shulchan Aruch Orach Chaim 240* and/or *Even Haezer 25* and his delivery of them to the printer for pre-publication preparation.[583] And being that his *Bedek Habayis* remained unpublished in his lifetime, it is possible Rabbi Caro expanded it at some later point in life.

In any case, it is extremely difficult to understand Rabbi Caro's utter and complete omission of both Maimonides and Rabeinu Yitzchak from *Shulchan Aruch*, here, on legal grounds alone, especially considering the weight of other medieval legal authorities who rule in their favor, many of whose writings we know Rabbi Caro had access to.[584] [585]

But regardless of what Rabbi Caro's motivations might have been, and whether it was his intention or not,[586] his omission in *Shulchan Aruch* of all permissive halachic approaches to marital sex arguably resulted in a major paradigm shift in the Jewish people's psychological and emotional approach to physical intimacy:

- He omitted Rabeinu Yitzchak's permission for occasional intra-anal ejaculation (which, by extension, could also be said to include occasional ejaculation between limbs)

- He omitted Maimonides' permissions for anal intercourse, intercourse between limbs and (gazing at or) kissing the female genitals
- And he omitted the crucial humane statement of the Sages on *Nedarim 20b*,[587] reworded by Maimonides,[588] validating a man's sexual needs[589]

Arguably, then, Rabbi Caro's manner of presentation in *Shulchan Aruch* was the foremost historical cause of Torah's – G-d's – permissive approach to marital sex being largely "forgotten from the House of Israel" for centuries after him and until this very day.

But this was not the only cause.

Rabbi Caro's colleagues, his fellow mystics of 16th century Safed, played a crucial part as well.

## Rabbi Yitzchak Luria – *Kisvei HaArizal*

Rabbi Yitzchak Luria (1534–1572), famously known as the "Arizal," was the most important kabbalist of the 16th century, despite his short two-year leadership of the Safed school of mystics.[590] His teachings were mainly preserved in the writings of his foremost disciple, Rabbi Chaim Vital (1542-1620).

According to Rabbi Vital, the concept of "wasting seed in vain" is to be expanded to include even the drips of pre-ejaculate that accumulate at the head of the penis during foreplay (outside the wife's vagina),[591] as well as any drips of seed that may emerge after climax has subsided[592] (after the husband has pulled out of his wife) – even in the context of regular vaginal intercourse. Yet we are given no logical or source-derived proof for such extreme claims.[593] At the same time, he prescribed no less than 84 fast days as penitence for "wasting seed in vain."[594][LII]

Additionally, Rabbi Vital offers a radical definition of the concept of "sanctifying oneself during sex" – namely, that sex for the man should be "without pleasure" (*gam yekadesh es atzmo b'tashmish hamitah shelo yehaneh*).[595] If sex, then, according to Rabbi Luria's foremost expositor, is ideally to be without pleasure to the husband, then how could one ever justify intra-anal ejaculation or ejaculation between limbs if the main halachic justification for these behaviors is that they are for the husband's sexual fulfillment?!

[Indeed, for that matter, how could one justify *any* sexual exploratory behaviors within marriage, even those that do not result in extra-vaginal ejaculation, unless such are solely intended to satisfy the wife?]

Rabbi Chaim Vital passed away in 1620, and his records of Rabbi Luria's teachings, which came to be known as *Kisvei HaArizal*, were not published in an organized fashion until after his death. But ever since, they have been the cornerstone of most creative kabbalistic thought, and the bedrock of pious mystical outlook and lifestyle – most notably that of the 18th century Chasidic movement.

---

[LII] The approach of Rabbis Luria and Vital to "wasting seed in vain" will be addressed in volume two of this series. And see above, footnote to page 3.

## Rabbi Eliyahu de Vidas – *Reishis Chochmah*

Rabbi Eliyahu de Vidas (1518-1592) was a prominent member of the Safed school of kabbalists. His work, *Reishis Chochmah* (which translates literally as, "*The Beginning of Wisdom*"), has been described as the first to fully integrate and present teachings of the *Zohar* as part of the rabbinical legal/ethical worldview.[596]

Rabbi Eliyahu devotes an entire chapter, Chapter 17, of *Reishis Chochmah, Shaar Hakedushah*, to awareness of the *Zohar's* harsh condemnations of "wasting seed in vain."

One chapter earlier, Chapter 16, is devoted to prescriptions for sexual sanctity within marriage based upon teachings of the *Zohar*.[597]

The chapter opens with Rabbi Eliyahu endorsing the halachic views on marital sex of Rabbi Yitzchak Aboab's *Menoras Hamaor*.[598] As noted above,[599] Rabbi Aboab implies that the Sages legally permitted all four of the behaviors cautioned against by Rabbi Yochanan ben Dahavai, including non-sex-related talk during sex, gazing at or kissing the female genitals, and "overturning the table" (though Rabbi Aboab does not tell us how he himself defined this last term).[600]

Twenty-eight sections into the discussion,[601] Rabbi Eliyahu quotes the *Zohar's* discouragement – though not prohibition – of sex that is not performed face-to-face with one's spouse, but rather from behind her (*achorei ishto*), invoking the same biblical chapter and verse as *Sanhedrin 58b* – Genesis 2:24: "And he shall cling to his wife." However, whereas *Sanhedrin 58b* makes clear that it is speaking about anal intercourse specifically, Rabbi Eliyahu does not clarify if he understood the *Zohar* – which emphasizes the issue of being 'face-to-face' – to be discouraging anal intercourse or rear-entry vaginal intercourse.

But Rabbi Eliyahu then continues in sections twenty-nine and thirty (note our bold-type emphases, to be explained following the source quote):[602]

> 29. The meaning of [the term] "behind the wife" (*achorei ishto*) is [equivalent to the term] "overturning the table" (*hafichas shulchan*) about which they [Rabbi Yochanan ben Dahavai and his "ministering angels"] said [on *Nedarim 20a*]:
>
>> Why are some [children] lame? Because they [the fathers] 'overturn their table.'
>
> Rabbi Shlomoh Yitzchaki [Rashi – i.e, the *Mefaresh*[602*]] interprets:
>
>> They "overturn [their table" to perform intercourse] **face-to-back**, for they engage with their wives in **rear-entry vaginal intercourse** (*shehofchim panim c'neged oref, sheba'in al neshoseihem l'shamesh shelo cedarcan*).
>
> Rabeinu Asher [Rosh], too, interprets:

Because they "overturn their table" to have **rear-entry vaginal intercourse** (*shehofchim es shulchanam l'shamesh **shelo cedarcah***) – and it [the congenital illness] is measure-for-measure: he caused his wife inconvenience upon her knees (*shematriach osah al arkevosehah*), therefore the children will be afflicted in their legs.

30. And everything we find in [the continuation of] the Talmudic discussion after that about "overturning the table," where the Talmud permits it – as they reported that a wife came before Rav to inform him that her husband had "overturned her," and he responded, "[A husband's predilections for how he likes his sex are] no more objectionable [in the eyes of G-d] than how he likes his fish" – **this is certainly the context** [that it refers only to **rear-entry vaginal intercourse**].

And I write this to **dispel** [the interpretation of] those who eliminate from themselves fear [of G-d] and shame and they ejaculate seed "in vain" through **intercourse in the impure hole**, the place where feces are excreted [the anus] – for intercourse in that place cannot result in conception, whereas they [Rabbi Yochanan ben Dahavai and his 'ministering angels'] said that [congenital] lameness results from [the fathers] "overturning their table" [during the same sexual encounter in which conception occurs].

And Maimonides, rest in peace, wrote that one must not "waste seed in vain" – and if intercourse is performed there [in the anus] it [the seed] is "wasted."

And so appears [to be corroborated] from the words of Raavad III, rest in peace, [in *Baalei HaNefesh, Shaar Hakedushah,*] that the intention of the term we have been discussing, "overturning the table," is *only* that they are **"face-to-back" [performing rear-entry vaginal intercourse]** (*she'ein hacavanah b'inyan hafichas shulchan ha'amur ele **panim c'neged achor***), and [the concern of Rabbi Yochanan ben Dahavai and his "ministering angels" was that] it results in conception, as we interpreted it.

Rabbi Eliyahu's line of reasoning, here, is extremely difficult:

Firstly, his quote from the *Zohar* appears to be stressing that sex must be "face-to-face" with one's wife, not "from behind her" (*achorei ishto*), implying that at issue is *front-entry vaginal* intercourse versus *rear-entry vaginal* intercourse – not *vaginal* intercourse versus *anal* intercourse. But then Rabbi Eliyahu equates the *Zohar's* term "from behind her" with the term on *Nedarim 20a*, "overturning the table" – as interpreted by the *Mefaresh* and Rabeinu Asher, both of whom expressly define it as "*shelo cedarcah*" – *anal* intercourse.

Now, you might have noticed that for the sake of presenting Rabbi Eliyahu's flow of logic, we translated (in bold) his quotations of the *Mefaresh* and Rabeinu Asher's use of the term "*shelo cedarcah*" as "rear-entry vaginal intercourse" rather than "anal intercourse." This was clearly Rabbi Eliyahu's intent, for he goes on to say that the rest of the Talmudic discussion on *Nedarim 20b*, which *permits* "overturning the table," could not possibly have been referring to anal intercourse; and he maintains that the caution found on *Nedarim 20a* against "overturning the table" had to do with concerns about conception[603] – and anal sex does not result in conception.

But the fact of the matter is that it is extremely difficult to force such a meaning into the term "*shelo cedarcah*,"[604] and Rabbi Eliyahu's attempt to do so in interpreting the words of the *Mefaresh* and Rabeinu Asher fundamentally undermines the rest of his argument.[605] [606]

This attempt is particularly problematic in regard to Rabeinu Asher, for in his *Tosfos HaRosh* to both *Nedarim 20b* and *Yevamos 34b*, Rabeinu Asher defines the term "overturning the table" as "*shelo cedarcah*," and he makes perfectly clear that he meant this as referring to anal sex.[606*]

Secondly, Rabbi Eliyahu invokes Maimonides to prove that anal intercourse is forbidden because it could lead to "wasted seed." But according to all readings and intepretations of Maimonides, anal *penetration* in-and-of-itself is permitted, even according to those whose textual versions of *Mishneh Torah* have him permitting it only without intra-anal ejaculation.

Thirdly, as "definitive" support of his interpretation, Rabbi Eliyahu invokes Raavad III's *Baalei HaNefesh, Shaar Hakedushah*, that the definition of "overturning the table" is exclusively rear-entry vaginal intercourse. But Raavad III, himself, in his glosses to *Mishneh Torah*, does not argue with Maimonides' permission of anal sex in *Isurei Biah 21:9*, presumably on account of *Sanhedrin 58b's* express permission of it.

A few additional points:

1. One might be tempted to reconcile some of these inconsistencies by saying that Rabbi Eliyahu meant to forbid only intra-anal *ejaculation*, but not anal *penetration* followed by *intra-vaginal* ejaculation. But then his "proof" from Raavad III in *Baalei HaNefesh* would fall away completely, for by his own admission, Raavad III writes, there, that the term "overturning the table" means *only* rear-entry vaginal intercourse.[607]

In any case, such a reading would be somewhat forced in Rabbi Eliyahu's wording and train of thought. And if this were his intention, he could have easily made it clear.

2. Rabbi Eliyahu's suggestion that those who rely on the well-established viewpoint of Rabeinu Yitzchak as quoted in *Tosfos* to *Yevamos 34b* (which permits occasional intra-anal ejaculation for married couples) are somehow deliberately uprooting from within themselves "fear of heaven and shame," is difficult to fathom.

[Although Rabbi Eliyahu doesn't actually mention Rabeinu Yitzchak by name, it's hard to believe he was unaware of Rabeinu Yitzchak's view as quoted in *Tosfos*. And if he were unaware of it, that itself would further undermine his entire presentation.[607*]]

That being said, it is possible that at the time of his writing this, Rabbi Eliyahu did not know of Rabbi Moshe Isserles's endorsement of Rabeinu Yitzchak, as found in *Shulchan Aruch, Even Haezer 25:2*, for *Reishis Chochmah* was printed in 1578, the same year Rabbi Isserles's gloss-notes to *Even Haezer* first began to appear in print.

3. The very premise that the term "overturning the table" could not possibly mean anal intercourse merely because intra-anal ejaculation does not result in conception is easily refuted by the approach of Rabbi Yisrael Alnaqua in his *Menoras Hamaor*[608] – excerpts of which were, incidentally, first published by none other than Rabbi Eliyahu de Vidas himself, in none other than his *Reishis Chochmah* itself. Rabbi Alnaqua explains that "overturning the table" on *Nedarim 20ab does* refer to anal sex (and intra-anal ejaculation), and that in the case of anal sex, Rabbi Yochanan ben Dahavai believed it could harm a fetus *already* growing inside the mother.

An even simpler response is that just like gazing at or kissing the female genitals do not – in-and-of-themselves – result in conception, and nevertheless Rabbi Yochanan ben Dahavai believed them to cause congenital illness if they are performed and immediately followed within the same sexual encounter by intercourse and conception, so too, "overturning the table" could have referred in Rabbi Yochanan ben Dahavai's mind to anal penetration immediately followed by vaginal intercourse, intra-vaginal ejaculation and conception.

4. In regard to Rabbi Eliyahu's seeming misrepresentation of Maimonides, perhaps he was in possession of a censored version of *Mishneh Torah* in which Maimonides' permission of anal sex in *Sefer Kedushah, Isurei Biah 21:9* had been omitted entirely.[609] But we can be certain Rabbi Eliyahu would never have put forth this argument had he known, as we do, that Maimonides in fact permits not only anal intercourse, but also intercourse between limbs – and that according to most manuscript versions Maimonides never spoke, there, against "wasting seed" at all.[610]

*Reishis Chochmah* was first published in Venice, in 1578 (still in the lifetime of its author). There can thus be little doubt that the author's categorical "halachic" prohibition against anal sex – which we have every reason to believe was influenced by his faithful endorsement of the *Zohar's* kabbalistic attitude toward "wasting seed in vain"[611] – was an important contributing factor to the subsequent widespread lack of awareness of G-d's potential permission of intra-anal-ejaculation for married couples, and, by extension, His potential permission for their ejaculation between limbs.

## Rabbi Elazar Azikri – *Sefer Charedim*

Rabbi Elazar Azikri (1522-1600), another member of the Safed school of kabbalists, authored a famous work on Jewish law and ethics, *Sefer Charedim – Book of Those who Tremble [before G-d's Word]*.

Chapter 64 of the book is entitled, *The Severity of the Sin of Anal Sex*.

The chapter opens with a quote from the *Zohar* describing a special place in Purgatory for those who "waste their seed by spilling it to the ground [coitus interuptus] or who ejaculate seed through anal sex..." After quoting this kabbalistic passage, Rabbi Azikri discusses *Sanhedrin 58b* – which, according to all medieval writers I've seen on the subject, categorically permits at least anal *penetration* to husband and wife – and Rabbi Azikri offers a complex reinterpretation of it in an attempt to prove that anal sex of any kind is absolutely forbidden, not only from a kabbalistic standpoint, but from a Talmudic one as well. Rabbi Azikri expressly states that part of his motivation in forcing this interpretation is his assumption that Raavad III categorically forbade anal sex – even simple *penetration* without intra-anal ejaculation – and thus it cannot be that Raavad III understood *Sanhedrin 58b* as permitting it. He concludes his chapter with a story about Rabbi Yosef Caro and the sages of Safed banishing a man from the Land of Israel for engaging in anal sex with his wife.

The problems with Rabbi Azikri's arguments are just as fundamental as those with Rabbi Eliyahu de Vidas's, a number of which are already raised by Rabbi Eliyahu Spira of Prague (1660-1712) in his *Elyah Rabah* commentary to *Levush*.[612]

To summarize these problems:

1. Like Rabbi Caro, he does not prove that when the *Zohar* speaks against intra-anal ejaculation it was in the context of occasional sexual fulfillment between husband and wife within marriage. Rather, the *Zohar* is just as likely as *Yevamos 34b* (as understood by Rabeinu Yitzchak and most other medieval writers) to be speaking *only* against intra-anal ejaculation as a form of constant intentional unsanctioned birth control.[613]

2. Like Rabbi Eliyahu de Vidas in *Reishis Chochmah*, in the course of his argument to forbid anal sex even from a Talmudic standpoint, there are innacuracies in Rabbi Azikri's reporting of sources. Here, too, the innacuracies relate to quotations of Rabeinu Asher (Rosh)[614] and Rashi (presumably the *Mefaresh* commentary)[615] – though here the innacuracies could perhaps be attributed to alternate textual versions of both.[615*]

3. His re-interpretation of *Sanhedrin 58b* is problematic.[616]

4. Similar to Rabbi Eliyahu de Vidas, in reference to those who permit intra-anal ejaculation Rabbi Azikri writes that they "lack fear of heaven." He thus seems to be unaware that the original source permitting it, Rabeinu Yitzchak of Dampierre (1120-1200), was one of the greatest and most pious medieval Jewish masters, who, apart from being one of the most prominent and widely quoted

Tosafists, was also a kabbalist who reportedly prayed at great length, lived an ascetic life, fasted constantly, and observed two days of Yom Kippur. Perhaps that is why he was also referred to by some of his disciples as "*HaKadosh* – The Saint."[617]

Additionally, if prior to his writing of this chapter Rabbi Azikri had access to the *Shulchan Aruch, Even Haezer* with Rabbi Moshe Isserles's glosses (printed between 1578 and 1580), he would also then seem to be accusing Rabbi Isserles of lacking fear of Heaven.[618]

5. Like Rabbi Eliyahu de Vidas in *Reishis Chochmah*, Rabbi Azikri argues that "overturning the table" on *Nedarim 20a* could not possibly refer to anal sex, for no child could be conceived from such a sexual encounter.

But see our responses to this same point above,[619] as well as the response of Rabbi Eliyahu Spira in *Elyah Rabah* in direct rebuttal of Rabbi Azikri.[620]

6. The episode reported by Rabbi Azikri in which the rabbis of Safed, including Rabbi Yosef Caro, exiled a husband for performing anal sex with his wife may well have been a case of *constant* intra-anal ejaculation, where it betrayed the husband's intentions for unsanctioned birth control. Rabbi Aharon Alfandri (1700-1774), in his *Yad Aharon* commentary to *Tur, Even Haezer*, in fact argues that this must have been the context of the case.[621]

*Sefer Charedim* was published for the first time in Venice, in 1601, one year after the author's passing. It is considered a legal-ethical classic.

## Rabbi Yeshayah Horowitz – *Shnei Luchos Habris*

Despite the manifold difficulties in the arguments of Rabbi Eliyahu de Vidas in *Reishis Chochmah* and Rabbi Elazar Azikri in *Sefer Charedim*, their views were wholeheartedly endorsed by a prominent legal and mystical authority of the subsequent generation, Rabbi Yeshayah Horowitz (c.1565-1630).

Born in Prague, *circa* 1565, Rabbi Horowitz moved to Safed in the last years of his life, in 1626.

In his famous legal-ethical-mystical work, *Shnei Luchos Habris*, he devotes a lengthy section to the topic of "sanctified sex" in *Shaar Haosios, Kedushas Hazivug*, comprised of 89 "paragraphs."

In paragraphs 41-48, Rabbi Horowitz categorically endorses Rabbi Azikri's prohibition of anal sex, going so far as to quote the entire Chapter 64 of *Sefer Charedim* verbatim.[622] Later, in paragraph 77, when moving from the question of "sanctity" to the question of "law,"[623] he instructs his readers, and especially his descendants, as well as all those who consider themselves his disciples, to follow (and even memorize) the entire Chapter 16 of *Reishis Chochmah, Shaar Hakedushah*.[624] Rabbi Horowitz also instructs his readers, there, to memorize both sections of *Tur's* presentation of marital sex law, both *Orach Chaim 240* and *Even Haezer 25*, implying for a moment that, according to the letter of the law, he ultimately accepted Maimonides' permission of anal penetration, and even Rabeinu Yitzchak's permission of intra-anal ejaculation (the latter of which is quoted by Rabbi Yaakov ben Asher in both sections). But he immediately reminds his readers to disregard (the medieval) Maimonides and Rabeinu Yitzchak on the matter of anal sex in favor of (the post-medieval) Rabbi Azikri.[625]

Thus, Rabbi Horowitz's view on anal sex is unquestionably negative.

[His view is also referenced in *Nachlas Tzvi* and *Be'er HaGolah*[626] to *Shulchan Aruch, Even Haezer 25:2*.]

But what were Rabbi Horowitz's views on (gazing at or) kissing the female genitals?

One might think it implied by his own words that he came only to reject *Tur's* inclusion of Maimonides' and Rabeinu Yitzchak's permission for anal sex, but not to reject *Tur's* inclusion of Maimonides' permission for kissing the female genitals – as he writes:

> One must study, guard, implement and carry out all the words of the *Tur* in *Orach Chaim 240* and in *Even Haezer 25*. Do not let a single point fall to the wayside from all that is presented there.
>
> And one must know by heart absolutely every single word that is written there – except for the discussion about the law of "overturning the table." I already quoted earlier what [the author of] *Sefer Charedim* wrote in this regard – and to him you should hearken.

Rabbi Horowitz only expresses an explicit rejection of anal sex, he doesn't explicitly reject cunnilingus. Thus, even though *Tur*, both in *Orach Chaim 240* and in *Even Haezer 25*, also quotes Raavad III's prohibition of kissing the female genitals, it could seem that Rabbi Horowitz, himself, did not feel as strongly as Raavad III on this matter.

Such an interpretation of Rabbi Horowitz could perhaps be supported by the fact that, as mentioned, he also endorses the approach of Rabbi Eliyahu de Vidas in *Reishis Chochmah* – and we've already seen above that Rabbi Eliyahu himself endorsed the approach of Rabbi Yitzchak Aboab in *Menoras Hamaor*. As discussed, Rabbi Aboab implies in *Menoras Hamaor* that he understood the Sages on *Nedarim 20b* as rejecting all four of Rabbi Yochanan ben Dahavai's cautions, including the one against kissing the female genitals.[627] [Rabbi Eliyahu, himself, mentions no prohibition against cunnilingus, even though he does address the issue of anal sex – which he, like Rabbi Azikri, forbids.]

Thus, Rabbi Horowitz could appear to be precise in his wording, and consistent with Rabbis Eliyahu de Vidas and Yitzchak Aboab, in permitting, or at least not expressly forbidding, the kissing of the female genitals.

However, it is equally possible that he assumed it to be self-evident that Rabbi Yaakov ben Asher himself, in his *Tur*, rejected Maimonides' permission of cunnilingus – much like Rabbi Moshe Isserles (*Darchei Moshe*) seems to have assumed it to be self-evident in Rabbi Yaakov ben Asher's manner of presentation.[628] If so, Rabbi Horowitz's admonition to follow every word of the *Tur* may have been, in his own mind, equal to a warning against the kissing of the female genitals as well.

And so, in the end, his views on the matter of cunnilingus remain inconclusive.

*Shnei Luchos Habris* was published posthumously by Rabbi Horowitz's son, in 1648-1649. The work, along with his commentary on the prayer book, had profound influences upon the world of rabbinic scholarship and piety in general, and especially upon the soon-to-emerge 18th century Chasidic movement (the Chabad-Chasidic movement in particular[629]).

## "Torah is Forgotten from the House of Israel"

Considering the views of these venerated halachic-kabbalistic authorities of 16th-17th century Safed – the authors of *Shulchan Aruch, Kisvei HaArizal, Reishis Chochmah, Sefer Charedim* and *Shnei Luchos Habris* – who all lived and taught in the aftermath of the *Zohar's* appearance and rise to near-canon status, whose collective teachings profoundly influenced the course of rabbinic scholarship and piety in general, and who were all considered to one degree or another to be spiritual-theological forebears of the soon-to-emerge 18th century Chasidic movement, it is this author's belief that their combined negativity and/or ambiguity on matters of sexual exploration within marriage is what caused a drastic paradigm shift in the mystically-inclined Jewish world of the time, ultimately resulting in the hyper-pietistic approach to sex which the Chasidic-Charedi movement has perpetuated to this day.

In the generation after Rabbi Yeshayah Horowitz, we find Rabbi Yaakov Emden (1697-1776), in the guide to Jewish marital sex he included in his commentary to the prayer book,[630] categorically forbidding gazing at or kissing the female genitals – though he permits anal intercourse without intra-anal ejaculation.

We find Rabbi Yitzchak Lampronti (1679-1756), in his halachic encyclopedia, *Pachad Yitzchak*,[631] quoting only Raavad III's interpretation of *Nedarim 20b* that gazing at or kissing the female genitals are still forbidden despite the Sages' permissive ruling, and quoting only Raavad III's and Rabbi Yaakov ben Yehudah Landau's[632] definition of "overturning the table" as rear-entry vaginal intercourse.

And in numerous halachic codes authored since[633] – such as *Chochmas Adam* (Rabbi Avraham Danzig, 1748-1820), *Kitzur Shulchan Aruch* (Rabbi Shlomoh Ganzfried, 1804-1886), *Mishnah Berurah-Biur Halachah* (Rabbi Yisrael Meir Kagan, 1838-1933) and *Kaf Hachaim* (Rabbi Yaakov Chaim Sofer, 1870-1939) – the liberal approaches to sex of Maimonides and Rabeinu Yitzchak and the dozen-plus medieval scholars who endorsed them are omitted completely.

# Later Restrictive Codes

### Rabbi Avraham Danzig – *Chochmas Adam*

Rabbi Avraham Danzig addresses the topic of marital sexual behavior in his *Chochmas Adam, Clal 128*.

In 128:2, he restricts talk during sex.

In 128:3, he states that "a man is permitted to do anything he craves sexually with his wife," but he forbids him to kiss her vagina (see our discussion below, pages 167-168).

In 128:7, he again forbids kissing the vagina, as well as gazing at it, for which he predicts congenital muteness and blindness, respectively. And he concludes, there, not forbidding, but predicting congenital lameness as a result of, sex with her-on-top – which he seems to have understood as the definition of the term "overturning the table" on *Nedarim 20ab*.

Now, Rabbi Danzig could not have been basing his presentation of these laws on Raavad III in *Baalei HaNefesh, Shaar Hakedushah*, for while Raavad III, there, does forbid, and possibly predicts blindness and muteness for, gazing at and kissing the female genitals, he also predicts deafness for non-sex-related talk, while Rabbi Danzig doesn't, and Raavad III does not predict lameness for "overturning the table," while Rabbi Danzig does.

Nor could Rabbi Danzig be basing himself on *Callah Rabti*, for while *Callah Rabti 1:13-14* does predict that congenital illness can result from all four behaviors cautioned against by Rabbi Yochanan ben Dahavai, including "overturning the table," it only predicts such if these behaviors are performed during the same sexual encounter in which conception occurs – and even then, *Callah Rabti* categorically permits all four behaviors halachically.[634]

[Rabbi Danzig also defines "overturning the table" as her-on-top, while versions of *Tractate Callah 9*, upon which *Callah Rabti* is based, define it as rear-entry vaginal intercourse – as does Raavad III in *Baalei HaNefesh, Shaar Hakedushah*.]

### Rabbi Shlomoh Ganzfried – *Kitzur Shulchan Aruch*

For the most part, Rabbi Shlomoh Ganzfried, in his *Concise Code of Jewish Law-Kitzur Shulchan Aruch 150:5, Laws of Modesty*, restates or paraphrases Rabbi Caro's *Shulchan Aruch, Orach Chaim 240* and *Even Haezer 25*.

### Rabbi Yisrael Meir Kagen – *Mishnah Berurah-Biur Halachah*

In his *Biur Halachah* to *Shulchan Aruch, Orach Chaim 240:4*, Rabbi Yisrael Meir Kagan points to the Talmud, warning husbands that gazing at their wives' genitals will cause blindness in their children and that kissing their wives' genitals will cause their children to be mute. He thus presents the congenital illnesses cautioned about by Rabbi Yochanan ben Dahavai on *Talmud, Nedarim 20a* as if they were cautioned by practical Jewish law – a notion it is not entirely clear even Raavad III himself agrees with (see above, p. 63) and which Rabbi Caro, in his own *Shulchan Aruch*, there, refrains from predicting in Raavad III's name.[635]

Alternatively, Rabbi Kagan's source could have been *Callah Rabti 1:14*, which states that the Sages admitted to Rabbi Yochanan ben Dahavai that all four of the behaviors he cautioned against do cause the four congenital illnesses he described. But if that were case, Rabbi Kagan presumably would have referenced *Callah Rabti*, not the Talmud. And he presumably would have made clear that *Callah Rabti 1:13-14* has these behaviors only being dangerous to a fetus if performed during the same sexual encounter in which conception occurs, and that even then it has the Sages permitting all four by law.[636]

### Rabbi Yaakov Chaim Sofer – *Kaf Hachaim*

Rabbi Yaakov Chaim Sofer, in his *Kaf Hachaim, Shulchan Aruch, Orach Chaim 240:4:40*, quotes all four of Rabbi Yochanan ben Dahavai's cautions about congenital illness resulting from the four marital-sexual behaviors, in an implied legal context, under the heading: "It is forbidden to gaze at the female genitals."

He gives his sources as *Nedarim 20a* and *Tur*.

This presentation is problematic for the same reasons we've explained above in regard to *Chochmas Adam* and *Mishnah Berurah-Biur Halachah*.

In any case, not one of these four later halachic works inform their readers that a majority of medieval scholars, as well as numerous major post-medieval authorities, including Rabbi Moshe Isserles himself, considered all four of these behaviors to be both legally permitted and medically safe at all times. Perhaps they simply did not have access to many of the sources and thus did not know the extent to which the permissive approach was historically endorsed.[637]

## Rabbi Moshe Isserles and Other Permissive Authorities

Rabbi Moshe Isserles (1520-1572) is widely recognized as having been Rabbi Yosef Caro's European counterpart and halachic equal, and he was the foremost annotator of Rabbi Caro's *Shulchan Aruch*.[LIII] Despite the "new kabbalah" of the *Zohar*, Rabbi Isserles held fast to the full permissive legal approach to marital sex of the majority of medieval writers, ruling in his gloss to *Shulchan Aruch, Even Haezer 25:2* according to both Maimonides' and Rabeinu Yitzchak's liberal legal views, while gently encouraging the striving for sanctity.[638] [639]

As for why he brought this liberal approach only in *Even Haezer* and not in *Orach Chaim*, perhaps it was because Rabbi Caro had changed the name of *Orach Chaim 240* from "Laws of the Nighttime and the Husband's obligation to Sexually Please his Wife," as it had been named by Rabbi Yaakov ben Asher in the *Tur*, to "Laws of Modesty." Perhaps Rabbi Isserles did not append his ruling to Rabbi Caro's version of *Orach Chaim 240* out of recognition of Maimonides' fundamental principle that the permissive *letter* of Jewish marital sex law is not necessarily equivalent to its modest *spirit*.

In any case, a disciple of Rabbi Isserles, Rabbi Mordechai Yoffe (1530-1612), in his halachic code, *Levush*,[640] as well as a later codifier, Rabbi Yechiel Michel Epstein (1829-1908), in his *Aruch Hashulchan*,[641] quote and rule the letter of the law as Rabbi Isserles does – according to Maimonides and Rabeinu Yitzchak, permitting anal sex, intra-anal ejaculation and the (gazing at or) kissing of the female genitals for married couples.

Rabbi Epstein's wording in fact applies the permissive ruling of Rabeinu Yitzchak also to ejaculation between limbs within marriage. And although Rabbi Epstein quotes, and appears to even endorse, Rabbi Caro's halachic caution against intra-anal ejaculation (and therefore also against ejaculation between limbs), he stops short of forbidding it. Nor does he mention Rabbi Caro's kabbalistic caution against it.

The distinguished contemporary of Rabbi Isserles (and Rabbi Caro), Rabbi Shlomoh Luria (1510-1573), ruled the letter of the law according to Rabeinu Asher, permitting occasional intra-anal ejaculation for married couples,[642] as did a major 17th century authority, Rabbi Yom Tov Lipman Heller (c.1579-1654), in his *Lechem Chamudos* super-commentary to Rabeinu Asher's halachic summary of the Talmud.[643]

And as already discussed at length, Rabbi Yehoshua Falk (1555-1614), a disciple of both Rabbi Moshe Isserles and Rabbi Shlomoh Luria, in his *Drishah* commentary to *Tur*, significantly expanded the liberal approach of Rabeinu Yitzchak as permitting not only occasional intra-anal ejaculation for married couples, but occasional ejaculation between limbs as well.

---

[LIII] To generalize, Sefardic Jews may be more likely to defer to Rabbi Caro's opinions, while Ashkenazic Jews may be more likely to defer to Rabbi Isserles.

Rabbi Falk, too, quotes Rabbi Caro's halachic caution against intra-anal ejaculation. But not only does he not personally forbid it, he immediately goes on there to expand Rabeinu Yitzchak permissive view, as stated. And he, too, makes no mention of Rabbi Caro's kabbalistic caution.

But these opinions of Rabbis Luria, Isserles, Yoffe, Falk, Heller and Epstein are for the most part unrepresented in Chasidic-Charedi guides to "family purity" and/or marital intimacy.

## Misrepresentations of Rabbi Isserles

The first edition of *Shulchan Aruch* to feature the glosses of Rabbi Moshe Isserles was printed in Cracow in 1578, six years after the author's demise.

For clarity's sake, let us again see the full quote of Rabbi Isserles's gloss to *Even Haezer 25:2*, knowing what we know now, that he is quoting the opinions of Maimonides and Rabeinu Yitzchak:

> 25:2. And he may do with his wife anything he desires: he may have intercourse with her any time he desires, and he may kiss any part of her body he desires, and he may penetrate her vaginally or anally (*shelo cedarcah*) or between limbs (*derech evarim*), as long as it does not lead to "wasting seed in vain."
>
> And some are lenient and say that anal sex is permitted even to the point of [intra-anal] ejaculation, if he desires it randomly [in the heat of passion] but does not make a habit of it [as an intentional means of unsanctioned birth control].
>
> And even though all these things are permitted, whoever sanctifies himself in that which is permitted shall be called 'holy.'[644]

Barely a generation passed before attempts were made to censor or alter Rabbi Isserles's views here – some of which, it must be noted, may have been under pressure of non-Jewish censors.

The 1594, 1619 and 1632 Venice editions of *Shulchan Aruch* included an erroneous marginal note by an unknown author, stating that Rabbi Isserles's use of the term "*shelo cedarcah*," here, was not meant to refer to anal sex, but only to rear-entry vaginal intercourse.[645] This claim ignored the fact that the term "*shelo cedarcah*" in every other place in Talmudic-rabbinic literature refers exclusively to anal intercourse (unless otherwise specified), and that Rabbi Isserles was merely restating the wording of Maimonides (whom all understand as permitting anal sex). And to say that Rabbi Isserles understood his other source, Rabeinu Yitzchak in *Tosfos* to *Yevamos 34b*, as permitting only rear-entry vaginal intercourse, would be to imply that he also understood Rabeinu Yitzchak as presenting the sin of Er and Onan itself as rear-entry vaginal intercourse – an extremely difficult notion.[645*]

This marginal note, which was actually quoted by at least one major commentary[646] to *Shulchan Aruch, Even Haezer 25:2*, was ultimately definitively disproven by Rabbi Meir Eisenstadt in his *Shaalos uTeshuvos Panim Meiros*,[647] referenced in *Pischei Teshuvah* to *Shulchan Aruch* there.

A 1754 edition cut out the phrase "intercourse between limbs," as well as Rabbi Isserles's final ruling, "And even though all these things are permitted, whoever sanctifies himself in that which is permitted shall be called 'holy.'"[648]

Finally, on Rabbi Isserles's ruling permitting the kissing of "any part of her body," Rabbi Shmuel ben Uri Shraga Feivush (1640-1700), in his *Beis Shmuel* commentary to *Shulchan Aruch, Even Haezer 25:2*, comments that it is permitted for a husband to kiss any part of his wife's body *other than the vagina*. Rabbi Feivush points to the Talmud (*Nedarim*) and Raavad III (*Baalei HaNefesh*), to prove his point.

[Other commentaries to *Shulchan Aruch, Even Haezer 25:2* quote Rabbi Feivush, such as *Be'er HaGolah* and *Be'er Heitev*.]

Now, it is possible that Rabbi Feivush was merely stating his own personal opinion on the matter – and he is certainly entitled to such an opinion.

[Subsequently in his *Beis Shmuel* commentary to *Even Haezer 25:2*, Rabbi Feivush clearly understood Rabbi Isserles as quoting the ruling of *Tosfos* permitting anal sex – even though, until now, it has generally been believed among halachic commentaries that Raavad III forbade anal sex, based on his interpretation in *Baalei HaNefesh* of the term "overturning the table" as rear-entry vaginal intercourse.[649] Therefore, if Rabbi Feivush had understood Rabbi Isserles as rejecting Raavad III's perceived restriction on anal sex, why, then, would he have insisted on Rabbi Isserles accepting Raavad III's restriction on cunnilingus? This perhaps supports the notion that Rabbi Feivush was not coming to interpret Rabbi Isserles's opinion on cunnilingus, but merely to express his own.]

But if, as some commentaries have understood, he was coming to *interpret* Rabbi Isserles, such an interpretation would be highly questionable, for Rabbi Isserles was merely restating the view of Maimonides, and nobody interprets Maimonides the way *Beis Shmuel* would then have been interpreting Rabbi Isserles.[650]

*Bayis Chadash*[651] and *Lechem Mishneh*[652] both state clearly that Maimonides believed the Sages on *Nedarim 20b* to have permitted all four of the behaviors cautioned against by Rabbi Yochanan ben Dahavai, including the kissing of the actual female genitals – and *Biur HaGra*[653] comments that this is how Rabbi Isserles himself understood the Sages as well.

*Beis Yosef*[654] and *Darchei Moshe*[655] also understood Maimonides as permitting the kissing of the female genitals, as evident from the fact that they contrast Maimonides' view in *Mishneh Torah, Isurei Biah 21:9* with that of Raavad III in *Baalei HaNefesh, Shaar Hakedushah*.

And *Rosh Pinah-Ikvei Habayis*[656] and *Atzei Arazim*[657] call out *Beis Shmuel* directly on what they understood to be an erroneous interpretation of Rabbi Isserles's words.[658] [659]

If any further proof were needed, see Maimonides' own words in his *Commentary to the Mishnah, Sanhedrin 7:4*:

> There was already one sage [Rabbi Yochanan ben Dahavai] who wanted to establish that it was unbecoming for a husband to engage in these sexual activities with his wife or to perform various sexual positions with her as the common folk do in order to fulfill their excessive sexual appetites – such as her-on-top, *kissing certain parts of the body*, and other such things.
>
> But those who opposed *this view* stated the opinion of the Sages, that whatever a husband craves to do with his wife sexually, he may do.
>
> And the Talmud rules according to the Sages.

Clearly, Maimonides understood the Sages on *Nedarim 20b* as permitting the kissing of the actual female genitals (i.e., the part of the body that Rabbi Yochanan ben Dahavai himself had cautioned against), and we have no reason to question that this was his intent in *Mishneh Torah, Isurei Biah 21:9* as well. Consequently, there is no reason to believe that Rabbi Isserles, in quoting Maimonides' ruling in *Mishneh Torah* verbatim, meant anything else.

Nevertheless, there are Chasidic-Charedi pre-marriage teachers and publications that continue to point to this comment of *Beis Shmuel* to silence those who might invoke Rabbi Isserles's permissive view about cunnilingus.

# PART FIVE
# RAAVAD III'S *BAALEI HANEFESH*

## A Critical Look at Rabbi Caro's Source in *Shulchan Aruch*: Raavad III's *Baalei HaNefesh, Shaar Hakedushah*

As discussed in our previous chapter, the virtually lone medieval view[660] of Rabbi Avraham ben Dovid of Posquières, Raavad III, as set forth in his *Baalei HaNefesh, Shaar Hakedushah*, is quoted copiously by Rabbi Yaakov ben Asher in his *Tur*, and exclusively by Rabbi Yosef Caro in his *Shulchan Aruch*.

It is because of Rabbi Caro's exclusive endorsement of Raavad III in *Shulchan Aruch*, coupled with a deep-seated veneration of the *Zohar*, that Chasidic-Charedi "family purity" and marital intimacy guides do not inform couples of Maimonides' and Rabeinu Yitzchak's (and Rabbi Isserles's, etc.) permissive approaches to anal sex and intercourse between limbs. It is also because of Rabbi Caro's endorsement of Raavad III that Chasidic-Charedi couples are told that non-sex-related talk must be restricted during sex, that gazing at the female genitals is absolutely forbidden, and that kissing the female genitals is not only forbidden, but disgusting.

But what about the medieval writers who permitted these things? Obviously they knew the same biblical and Talmudic sources as Raavad III – so how might they have responded to his lines of reasoning?

In the following section we shall suggest what other medieval authorities may have deemed to be shortcomings in Raavad III's logic as set forth in his *Baalei HaNefesh, Shaar Hakedushah*.

## Raavad III's Interpretation of Nedarim 20ab

Let us first be reminded of Raavad III's interpretation of *Nedarim 20ab*.

On *Nedarim 20a*, Rabbi Yochanan ben Dahavai is quoted as cautioning that four sexual behaviors between husband and wife can (G-d forbid) cause four congenital illnesses in their children-to-be:

1. Non-sex-related talk during sex can cause deafness
2. Gazing at the female genitals can cause blindness
3. Kissing the female genitals can cause muteness
4. "Overturning the table" can cause lameness

On *Nedarim 20b*, the Sages, (Rebbi, Rav) and Rabbi Yochanan bar Napacha are quoted as rejecting Rabbi Yochanan ben Dahavai, and instead ruling that, "Anything a husband craves to do with his wife sexually, he may do."

Raavad III argues[661] that when the Sages ruled, "Anything a husband craves to do with his wife sexually, he may do," they came to permit *only one* out of the four behaviors cautioned against by Rabbi Yochanan ben Dahavai – namely, "overturning the table," which Raavad III interprets as rear-entry vaginal intercourse. Although he concedes that according to the final ruling of the Talmud, the other three behaviors (non-sex-related talk and gazing at or kissing the female genitals) do not warrant "harsh punishment" – presumably negating the cautions about congenital illness by Rabbi Yochanan ben Dahavai[662] – he maintains that the Sages still forbade them for other reasons.

In Raavad III's own words:

> ...There are other additional factors [besides the nine-ten flawed conditions] that blemish the act [of marital intimacy], and ruin it, and cause its reward to be lost – namely, those behaviors enumerated in *Nedarim [20ab]*:
>
>> Rabbi Yochanan ben Dahavai said, "The ministering angels told four things to me:
>>
>>> Why are some [children] lame? Because they [the fathers[LIII*]] 'overturn their table.'
>>>
>>> Meaning, they have sex in the position of animals (*maaseh beheimah*) [rear-entry vaginal intercourse].
>>>
>>> Why are some [children] blind? Because they [the fathers] gaze at the [mothers'] genitals.

---

[LIII*] See above, footnote XX* to page 33.

> And others explain this to mean (*v'yesh mefarshim*) that they gaze at the female genitals when they want to have sex,[663] even though during actual intercourse the husband makes things modest – that is, by day he darkens things by covering themselves with his robes, or by night he puts out the candle – still, since he did this just before intercourse he degraded himself, and he treated her without regard for her dignity (*nahag bah minhag hefker*[664]).
>
> And how much more so (*col shekein*) is he acting without regard for dignity if he gazes there during non-sexually-intimate moments, which also means the husband voluntarily incites his "evil urge," as we discussed in *Shaar Haprishah*.
>
> Why are some [children] mute? Because they [the fathers] kiss the [mothers'] genitals.
>
> Why are some [children] deaf? Because they [the fathers] talk during sex.

Raavad III continues:

> The first three [of these sexual behaviors – "overturning the table" and gazing at or kissing the female genitals – blemish the act according to Rabbi Yochanan ben Dahavai] because he [the husband] treats her without regard for her dignity;[665] the fourth [talking during sex], because he focuses his intentions on [fantasies of] another woman OR because he makes the act tantamount to an act of prostitution, for he does it without any [loving] intention.[666]
>
> And although the Talmud [on *Nedarim 20b*] quotes Rabbi Yochanan [bar Napacha] that "the law does not follow Rabbi Yochanan ben Dahavai, but rather anything a man craves to do with his wife sexually he may do, just as he may enjoy his fish from the fisherman, etc…" – which implies that all these [four behaviors] are perfectly permissible (*shemutar la'asos kein l'chatchilah*) – it appears to me (*nireh li*) that this is only true in regard to 'overturning the table,' for [only in regard to 'overturning the table' do we see that] the Talmud goes on to report that a woman once came before Rav[667] and informed him, 'Master, I set out a table for my husband and he overturned it!' And Rav replied to her: 'It is no different than how he likes his fish' – further implying that 'overturning the table' is not forbidden [at all].
>
> But this is only true of 'overturning the table.'

Concerning the others [non-sex-related talk and gazing at or kissing the female genitals], even though they do not warrant harsh punishment (*eino nidon aleihem din chamor*), they nevertheless carry a prohibition (*mikol makom isur yesh bahen*), like we discussed before, that it is forbidden to speak non-sex-related words (*dvarim acherim*) during sex unless it is necessary for the sexual act (*tzarchei tashmish*) or to arouse the wife to the mood (*tzarich l'ratzosa*).

And in *Tractate Hagigah 5b*, they explained [the verse], "'He [G-d] recounts to man what his words were' – even the "excess light-headed talk" (*sichah yeseirah*) he has with his own wife is recounted to him at the Time of Judgment.

Similarly, one who gazes at the female genitals transgresses the verse, "Walk modestly with your G-d," and he removes the sense of "shame" (*bushah*) from upon his face; behold, the verse states, "[Moses said to the people at Sinai: 'Do not fear, for in order to elevate you has G-d come; and] so that awe of Him' – a sense of shame – 'shall be upon your faces, so that you shall not sin,'" for one who has a sense of shame does not sin.[668]

How much more so does one who kisses the female genitals transgress all this. And what is more, he transgresses the prohibition, "Do not make yourselves disgusting" – as our Sages of blessed memory said [*Babylonian Talmud, Tractate Makos 16b*]:

> One who drinks water from a blood-letter's bowl transgresses the prohibition, 'Do not make yourselves disgusting.'

And [*Babylonian Talmud, Tractate Shabbos 90b* relates:]

> Rav Cahana once touched a locust to his lips, and Rav[668*] said to him, "Take it away lest people think you ate it and transgressed the prohibition, 'Do not make yourselves disgusting.'"

How much more so, [then, does the prohibition not to make oneself 'disgusting' apply] here [to kissing the female genitals].

And regarding this "overturning the table" which they [the Sages] do permit, I maintain that it is only allowed if he does not force her to do it – in other words, she must be in full agreement about it, because he makes it agreeable to her first. But if he forces her to do it [against her will], he certainly has not saved himself from sin, and to him I apply the verse [in Proverbs 19:2]: "It is also not good that a soul be without knowledge, [and he who hastens with his legs sins]."[669]

To summarize Raavad III's arguments:

a) <u>Non-sex-related talk during sex</u> must still be forbidden by the Sages, Rebbi, Rav and Rabbi Yochanan bar Napacha on *Nedarim 20b*, because in *Babylonian Talmud, Hagigah 5b* the compilers-editors of the Talmud interpret Rav as suggesting that a couple will be called to task for "excess light-headed talk" during foreplay.

b) <u>Gazing at the female genitals</u> must still be forbidden by the Sages, Rebbi, Rav and Rabbi Yochanan bar Napacha on *Nedarim 20b*, because it shows a lack of "shamefacedness," and immediately before quoting Rabbi Yochanan ben Dahavai on *Nedarim 20a*, the compilers-editors of the Talmud chose to juxtapose a teaching that shamefacedness is a virtuous Jewish quality.

It also transgresses the verse, "Walk modestly with your G-d."

[Though Raavad III does not mention it in discussing the Sages' view, in regard to Rabbi Yochanan ben Dahavai's view he adds that it incites the "evil urge" – a notion we shall address as well.]

c) <u>Kissing the female genitals</u> must still be forbidden by the Sages, Rebbi, Rav and Rabbi Yochanan bar Napacha on *Nedarim 20b*, because it not only shows a lack of "shame" and "modesty" (like gazing at the female genitals), it also transgresses the biblical commandment of *"Bal Teshaktzu* – Do not make yourselves disgusting."

d) Raavad III also mentions in passing the fact that the Talmud on *Nedarim 20b* only brings actual "case precedent" of (Rebbi and) Rav permitting "overturning the table." His implication is that since no case precedents are brought permitting non-sex-related talk during sex or gazing at or kissing the female genitals, these three behaviors must never have been permitted by the Sages in actual Jewish practice.

We will now suggest what other medieval writers may have considered to be difficulties in each of these four arguments.

## Non-sex-related Talk and Hagigah 5b

Raavad III does not specifically point it out, but his "proof" from the teaching of Rav on *Hagigah 5b* is more significant than he stated, for Rav himself is one of those quoted (indeed, the one Raavad III himself quotes) on *Nedarim 20b* invoking the leniency of the Sages for a husband to do anything he craves sexually with his wife (just like a man may enjoy his fish from the fisherman any way he craves). So how could Rav permit non-sex-related talk on *Nedarim 20b* while he forbids it on *Hagigah 5b*?

But as we discussed and analyzed at length above,[670] there is a critical distinction between the two Talmudic discussions: Rabbi Yochanan ben Dahavai, according to the compilers-editors of the Talmud on *Nedarim 20b*, was warning against "non-sex-related talk" (*mili achronaisa*) before and/or during intercourse, while Rav, according to the compilers-editors of *Hagigah 5b*, was warning against "excess light-headed talk" (*sichah yeseirah/sichah kalah/sichah kalah yeseirah*) that is unnecessary to help arouse one's spouse to the mood for lovemaking during foreplay. Thus, it is entirely possible that the Sages on *Nedarim 20b rejected* Rabbi Yochanan ben Dahavai's caution against "non-sex-related talk," while they *accepted* Rav's caution against "excess light-headed talk."[671] [672]

And even if the Sages accepted Rav's caution against "excess light-headed talk," it is entirely possible that they accepted it only as a pious measure for Torah scholars, not as a baseline law for all couples. Even more so, it is possible that Rav himself intended his statement as quoted on *Nedarim 20b* to be his opinion on the letter of the law, while his teaching as quoted on *Hagigah 5b* was meant only to address the law's spirit.

Maimonides, for one, does not rule against "non-sex-related talk" (the topic of *Nedarim 20b*) at all, not even during actual intercourse. And he relegates the caution (of *Hagigah 5b*) against "excess light-headed talk" only to the spirit of the law for pious Torah scholars, he does not present it as a legal "prohibition" binding upon all couples.[673]

And this is all besides the fact that this call to "judgement" that Rav cautioned about would certainly be judged by the Creator according to the unique circumstances of each and every individual couple during each and every individual intimate encounter. That is, what G-d might deem "excessive" for one couple one night, He might consider entirely appropriate for the same couple another night, and for another couple any time.

In any case, we are not compelled to believe that the Sages, Rebbi or Rabbi Yochanan bar Napacha (or even Rabbi Yochanan ben Dahavai himself) would have accepted the Talmudic compilers'-editors' interpretation of Rav's teaching on *Hagigah 5b* as applying to talk during sexual intimacy specifically. And even if they did agree that Rav as quoted on *Hagigah 5b* was referring to talk during sexual intimacy, there is no proof they actually agreed with Rav's opinion about this.

Furthermore, even if Rav himself did equate "excess light-headed talk" with "non-sex-related talk," as Raavad III seems to have believed he did, there is no evidence that the Sages, Rebbi or Rabbi Yochanan bar Napacha agreed with this equation of the two. And if they did, then a simple reading of the Sages' and Rabbi Yochanan bar Napacha's ruling rejecting all four cautions of Rabbi Yochanan ben Dahavai, including his caution against non-sex-related talk, would be the virtual equivalent of a legal rejection of Rav's caution against "excess light-headed talk."

And if there were in fact any argument in any of this between Rav and Rabbi Yochanan bar Napacha, the general rule in Jewish law is that in arguments between Rav and Rabbi Yochanan bar Napacha the practical law follows the latter.[674]

Finally, we already know the alternate textual version on *Hagigah 5b*, perhaps unknown to Raavad III, according to which Rav was understood by the compilers-editors of the Talmud themselves as accepting any and all "excess light-headed talk" during foreplay.[675] According to this version, Rav on *Hagigah 5b* perfectly complements Rav on *Nedarim 20b*.

## Gazing at the Female Genitals and "Shamefacedness" – Part One: Equating Rabbi Shimon ben Lakish and Rabbi Yochanan ben Dahavai

The extollation of "shamefacedness" discussed by the compilers-editors of the Talmud on *Nedarim 20a* was not brought by them in relation to the teaching *after* it, of Rabbi Yochanan ben Dahavai about gazing at one's own pure wife's naked genitals in privacy during physical intimacy, but in relation to the discussion *before* it,[676] of Rabbi Achi son of Rabbi Yoshiyah about gazing at a forbidden woman's "heel."

Let us recall the exact teaching of Rabbi Achi and the Talmudic discussion upon it[677]:

> Rabbi Achi son of Rabbi Yoshiyah says:
>> Whoever makes a habit of looking around at women [in order to sexually fantasize about them] will ultimately come to actual sin, and whoever gazes at the heel of a woman [in order to derive sexual satisfaction from it] will ultimately have uncouth children.
>
> Rav Yosef said:
>> This refers [even] to [the heel of] one's own wife during her impure menstrual period.
>
> Rabbi Shimon ben Lakish said:
>> 'Heel' refers to the private place, which is opposite the heel.
>
> It was taught in a *braisa*:
>> [Moses said to the people at Sinai: "Do not fear, for in order to elevate you has G-d come; and so that awe of Him shall be upon your faces, so that you shall not sin."
>>
>> The *braisa* elucidates the verse:]
>>> "So that awe of Him shall be upon your faces" – to instill a sense of shame.
>>>
>>> "So that you shall not sin" – this teaches that a sense of shame fosters fear of sin.
>
> Based on this [*braisa*'s interpretation of the verse,] there are those who say that a sense of shame is a sign of good character.
>
> Others say that anyone who has a sense of shame does not readily sin. And if someone has no shamefacedness, it can be assumed that his ancestors were not among those who stood at Sinai.

Now, it is apparent that the exact context of Rabbi Achi's original caution against gazing at the "heels" of women is unclear. This ambiguity existed already in the Talmud itself, and it extends into the medieval and later commentaries, and beyond, raising the following fundamental questions:

- Was Rabbi Achi referring to women *other* than one's own wife, *even* to one's own wife, or *only* to one's own wife?[677*]

- If even, or only, one's own wife, then only when she is impure, or even when she is pure?

- Only her buttocks and genital region, or even any part of her body that is normally covered, even down to her heel?

- Only naked skin or even clothed parts?

- Only in public or even in private?

- In private, only when not engaged in physical intimacy or even immediately prior to, or during, physical intimacy?

- Any time of physical intimacy or only when conception occurs as well?

According to Meiri, Rabbi Achi was mainly describing the all-too-familiar scene of a man "checking out" a woman passerby from behind, head-to-heel, with the term "heel" a clean way of saying her backside (buttocks).[678] We might extrapolate, then, that lack of "shamefacedness" in this context simply refers to such a man's lack of caring if other people (in the room or in the street), or even the woman herself, notice his crass sexual fixations and utter lack of sensitivity. And if such a man's own children observe such behavior we can assume some of it would rub off on them as well – they would grow to be "uncouth" not as a matter of mystical repercussion, but of simple behavioral science.

That Rabbi Achi's caution, here, was not a mystical warning, but an observation of behavioral science, is also supported by the fact that his immediately-preceding caution – that habitually looking around at other women for sexual satisfaction leads to sin – is certainly not a matter of "prophecy," but an observation about human nature.[678*]

And in this light, Rabbi Achi's second caution, against "checking out a woman's backside," can understandably be said to include one's own wife (menstruating or not) – and it is in fact a father's gazing at *his own wife's* body in particular that his children are most likely to notice on a regular basis and thereby grow to emulate.

[It is therefore reasonable to say that Rabbi Achi's first caution would apply equally to a woman who habitually looks around at men for sexual satisfaction, and his second caution would hold true for a woman who gawks at men's bodies, and even her own husband's, in the presence of her children.]

In any case, the fact of the matter is that it's impossible for us today, as it was arguably impossible for the compilers-editors of the Talmud already in their day, to determine with absolute certainty what Rabbi Achi's original intention was.

What we can be certain of, however, is that Raavad III, in another section of his *Baalei HaNefesh*, in *Shaar Haprishah*,[679] attributes to Rabbi Shimon ben Lakish an interpretation of Rabbi Achi's teaching that he was warning husbands not to gaze even at their own *pure* wives' genitals, even *in privacy*.

Raavad III writes:

> ... Some read Reish Lakish [Rabbi Shimon ben Lakish] as *responding* to Rav Yosef['s interpretation of Rabbi Achi] - that is, he was coming to be more lenient [than Rav Yosef], that even if a man's wife is menstrually impure [when he gazes at her] there will be no punishment of uncouth children unless he gazes at her genitals specifically [but not if he gazes at her heel].[680]
>
> And some read Reish Lakish as a separate interpretation [of Rabbi Achi] - that is, the two intepretations [of Rabbi Achi] given by Rav Yosef and Reish Lakish are entirely independent of each other [and are addressing two entirely different contexts, namely]:
>
> Rav Yosef was speaking against gazing [even] at the *heel* of one's own *menstrually impure wife* - which accords with the simple reading [of Rav Yosef's words in the Talmudic text].
>
> And Reish Lakish was speaking against gazing at one's own *pure* wife, but only against gazing at her *genitals*.
>
> Still, Rav Yosef and Reish Lakish are not [necessarily] fundamentally "arguing," [it is possible] they only differ in how to interpret the context of the original *braisa* [of Rabbi Achi] - one master [Rav Yosef] believed it to be cautioning against gazing even at the actual heel of one's own menstrually impure wife, while the other master [Reish Lakish] believed it to be cautioning against gazing at one's own wife at any time, whether she is menstrually impure or not, but only against gazing at her genitals.
>
> And it is not for us to decide between the two, for this [punishment of one's children growing to be uncouth] is a matter of Heaven [which only Heaven can decide the "science" of].
>
> Nevertheless, we cannot ignore the [implied] prohibition (*isura*),[681] and we follow both interpretations, erring on the side of stringency - that is, it is forbidden to gaze [even] at the heel of one's own menstrually impure wife; and from the [caution against gazing at her] heel we extrapolate [the caution] to every other normally-covered part of her body, lest it [gazing] breed [too much] familiarity [which could lead to sexual intimacy during the forbidden menstrual period].

And it is forbidden to gaze at her genitals even when she is pure.

What is more, it is also possible to say that one master was simply teaching one caution and the other master was simply teaching another, but each would agree with the other in their respective contexts.

In addition [we are told on *Nedarim 20a*]:

> It was taught in a *braisa*:
>
>> [Moses said to the people at Sinai: "Do not fear, for in order to elevate you has G-d come;] and so that awe of Him shall be upon your faces, so that you shall not sin."
>
> [The *braisa* elucidates the verse:]
>
>> "So that awe of Him shall be upon your faces" – to instill a sense of shame.
>>
>> "So that you shall not sin" – this teaches that a sense of shame fosters fear of sin.
>
> Based on this [*braisa's* interpretation of the verse,] there are those who say that a sense of shame is a sign of good character.
>
> Others say that anyone who has a sense of shame does not readily sin.

In any case, we have taken from this that it is forbidden to gaze at the female genitals at all, for whoever gazes at them has no "shamefacedness." And besides that, it incites the "evil urge" upon oneself,[682] as we shall explain later in *Shaar Hakedushah*, with G-d's help.

Now, for the purpose of our present analysis, we will not go into the question of whether or not the risk of one's children growing to be uncouth, here, is a matter of Heavenly "science" and/or punishment rather than a mere natural consequence of a father showing his children an uncouth example. We will also not question Raavad III's assertion that we should err on the side of stringency, even though logic could equally, if not more strongly, dictate that we err on the side of leniency considering all the ambiguity surrounding this rabbinic – not biblical – caution. We shall put aside, as well, the curiosity that in his gloss-notes to Maimonides' *Mishneh Torah, Isurei Biah 21:4*, Raavad III himself invokes this teaching only in the context of a husband gazing at the normally covered body parts of his *menstrually impure* wife. And we shall temporarily ignore the fact that just five passages later in *Mishneh Torah, Isurei Biah 21:9*, Raavad III remains silent on Maimonides' permission of (gazing at and) kissing the female genitals in the context of loving marital sexual intimacy.

Without getting into all that, let us analyze the contexts of Raavad III's comments in *Shaar Haprishah* versus *Shaar Hakedushah*:

In *Shaar Haprishah*, in regard to Rabbi Shimon ben Lakish's possible interpretation of Rabbi Achi's caution as being against gazing at one's own pure wife's genitals, Raavad III does not address the distinction of gazing at them (clothed) when other people are around – such as in public or in the company of one's children – versus gazing at them (clothed or naked) in privacy during non-sexual moments or (naked) during sexual moments. Indeed, part of his wording in *Shaar Haprishah* implies a blanket prohibition: "We have taken from this that it is forbidden to gaze at the female genitals *at all.*"

But we find in *Shaar Hakedushah* that Raavad III implies two or three interpretations of the context of Rabbi Yochanan ben Dahavai's caution against gazing at one's own pure wife's (naked) genitals: one interpretation, that it refers to gazing at them *during intercourse*;[683] a second interpretation (*v'yesh meforshim*), that it refers to gazing at them *during foreplay*, even if not during intercourse itself; and "how much more so" *during non-sexual moments.*[684]

And in conjunction with his third interpretation, that it refers to gazing during non-sexual moments because it "incites the evil urge," Raavad III cross-references his interpretation of Rabbi Shimon ben Lakish in *Shaar Haprishah*, implying that his interpretation, there, too, was in the context of gazing at her (naked) genitals during non-sexual moments.

Thus, Raavad III's *third* interpretation in *Shaar Hakedushah* equates Rabbi Yochanan ben Dahavai with Rabbi Shimon ben Lakish – that is, he has both of them cautioning against gazing at one's own pure wife's naked genitals during non-sexual moments.[684*]

And while his first and second interpretations of Rabbi Yochanan ben Dahavai's caution, that it was referring to gazing during sexually intimate moments, do not necessarily equate the two sages, they have Rabbi Yochanan ben Dahavai's caution implying Rabbi Shimon ben Lakish's by a greater force of logic (an *a fortiori* argument – "*col shekein*") – In Raavad III's words:

> ... *And how much more so* (*col shekein*) is it treating a wife without regard for her dignity if he gazes there during non-sexually-intimate moments...

A fuller analysis of Raavad III's interpretations of, and assertions from, Rabbi Achi, Rav Yosef and Rabbi Shimon ben Lakish on *Nedarim 20a* is already in preparation as the subject of an extended essay in a future volume of this series. But as pertains to our original discussion – Raavad III's assertion that the Sages on *Nedarim 20b* themselves still forbade a husband from gazing at or kissing his wife's genitals on account of the extollation of the virtues of "shame" and "shamefacedness" quoted by the compilers-editors of the Talmud on *Nedarim 20a* in conjunction with the cautions of Rav Achi, Rav Yosef and Rabbi Shimon ben Lakish – the bottom line is this:

1. If Rabbi Shimon ben Lakish and Rabbi Yochanan ben Dahavai were both speaking against gazing at the female genitals *during sexual moments*, then Rabbi

Yochanan bar Napacha's and the Sage's rejection of Rabbi Yochanan ben Dahavai would equal a rejection of Rabbi Shimon ben Lakish as well – and the general rule in Talmudic method is that in most arguments between Rabbi Shimon ben Lakish and Rabbi Yochanan bar Napacha the practical law follows the latter.[685]

2. If Rabbi Shimon ben Lakish and Rabbi Yochanan ben Dahavai were both speaking against gazing at the female genitals *during non-sexual moments*, then we do not even need Rabbi Yochanan bar Napacha[686] or the Sages to reject either one of them in order to permit gazing *during sexual moments* – for then neither Rabbi Shimon ben Lakish nor Rabbi Yochanan ben Dahavai can be assumed to have been including the latter context in their caution. Behold, by Raavad III's own logic, gazing during sexual moments is *less* objectionable than gazing during non-sexual moments.[687]

In other words, it would mean that there was never any caution at all against gazing *during sexual moments* – not from Rabbi Shimon ben Lakish nor from Rabbi Yochanan ben Dahavai.

3. If Rabbi Shimon ben Lakish was speaking against gazing during *non-sexual moments*, and Rabbi Yochanan ben Dahavai was speaking against gazing during *sexual moments*, then Rabbi Yochanan bar Napacha's and the Sages' rejection of Rabbi Yochanan ben Dahavai would not equal a rejection of Rabbi Shimon ben Lakish. But then, again, Rabbi Shimon ben Lakish would not be assumed to have had anything against gazing during sexual moments at all (see previous point).

Consequently, we have no reason to believe that the teaching (cited by the compilers-editors of the Talmud in conjunction with Rav Achi, Rav Yosef and Rabbi Shimon ben Lakish) extolling the virtues of "shame" and "shamefacedness" would have been accepted by the Sages or Rabbi Yochanan bar Napacha as legally binding upon, or even in any way applying to, a husband lovingly gazing upon or kissing his wife's genitals during sex (with her consent).[688] If we take them at their word, according to the legal view of the Sages and Rabbi Yochanan bar Napacha (and Rebbi and Rav) no sense of sexual "shame" need ever come between loving husband and wife during consensual marital intimacy.[689]

And see the commentary of Rabbi Elazar of Worms (c.1176-1238) to Genesis 2:25:

> "And both of them, the man and his wife, were naked and they were not ashamed" – [for] "Anything a husband craves to do with his wife sexually, he may do," in order to settle his soul.[690]

## Gazing at the Female Genitals and "Shamefacedness" – Part Two: Tractate Derech Eretz, Vayikra Rabah

There is also textual support for the argument that the teaching about "shamefacedness" on *Nedarim 20a* was brought solely in support of the teaching *before* it, of Rabbi Achi (and Rav Yosef and Rabbi Shimon ben Lakish) in regard to gazing at forbidden women's "heels," not the teaching *after* it, of Rabbi Yochanan ben Dahavai in regard to gazing at one's own pure wife's genitals during physical intimacy, from another version of Rabbi Achi's teaching as appears in another Talmudic-era work, possibly pre-dating the Talmud itself: *Derech Eretz Rabah, Perek Arayos–Chapter on Illicit Sexual Relationships*.

*Derech Eretz Rabah–Perek Arayos 13* offers an important alternate textual version, and crucial missing context, to Rabbi Achi's teaching. In fact, *Derech Eretz Rabah-Perek Arayos 13* first mentions the other cautions listed on *Nedarim 20a* as well, about avoiding casual vows, the company of ignorant priests (*cohanim*) and unlimited conversation with women – cautions which *Derech Eretz Rabah* puts in the mouth of the sage, Chilfa son of Igra. Second, it has Rabbi Achi cautioning that looking around at women in general can lead to actual sin. Third, it has the *Sages* (*chachamim*[691]), rather than Rabbi Achi, cautioning that gazing at women's "heels" can cause congenital illness (rather than uncouthness) in one's children. And in conjunction with this last caution, it has the *Sages* quoting the same teaching as *Nedarim 20a* about "shamefacedness."

Nowhere in this text is the caution against gazing at women's heels applied to gazing at one's own wife – menstrually impure or not. And Rabbi Yochanan ben Dahavai's teaching is nowhere to be found either. Instead, we find the teachings of Rabbi Achi and the Sages immediately followed by a teaching of Rabbi Miasha[692] grandson of Rabbi Yehoshua ben Levi[693] extolling a person who does not "feast their eyes" when they happen upon a scene of *illicit* sexuality. There is thus no indication that the compilers-editors of *Derech Eretz Rabah-Perek Arayos* understood this concept of "shamefacedness" as applying to married couples at all, and certainly not during (consensual) marital sexual intimacy.

Note that the chapter and passage breakdown of *Derech Eretz Rabah-Perek Arayos* that we present below is according to two scholarly editions by Dr. M. Higger (*Mesechtos Derech Eretz*, New York, 1935; *Mesechtos Zeiros*, New York, 1929).

And insofar as the midrashic work, *Vayikra Rabah*, quotes the teaching of Rabbi Yehoshua ben Levi's grandson, with perhaps even further clarification of context, we shall include it below as well.

## Mesechtos Derech Eretz, Perek Arayos 13

13. Aba Chalfi [Chilfa bar Igra][694] says [three teachings] in the name of his father, Aba Chigra:

Do not be casual about making vows (*al t'hi parutz b'nedarim*) lest you come to take lightly the taking of oaths (*shelo timol b'shvuos*);

and do not accept hospitality from a priest who is an ignoramous (*kohen am haaretz*) lest he feed you sanctified food;

[and] do not unlimit conversation with the woman, because a woman's conversation is only with the intention of adultery (*divrei niufim*). [*An alternate textual version*: Do not unlimit conversation with the woman, because the intention of one who unlimits conversation with a woman is only for adultery.][695]

Rabbi Achi son of Rabbi Yoshiyah says:

Whoever [makes it a habit that he] looks around at women, will in the end come to sin (*ba lidei aveirah*).

And the Sages say:

Whoever gazes at the heel of a woman, it is decreed upon him that he will have children with physical illness;[696] and anyone who does not have [the quality of] shamefacedness, readily sins, as the verse (Isaiah 3:9) states, "The recognition of their faces testified against them,[697] [and their sin, like Sodom they told, they did not deny; woe is to their soul, for they have paid themselves (with) evil."]

And anyone who has [the quality of] shamefacedness does not readily sin, as the verse states, [Moses said to the people at Sinai: "Do not fear, for in order to elevate you has G-d come;] and so that awe of Him shall be upon your faces, so that you shall not sin."

Rabbi Miasha grandson of Rabbi Yehoshua ben Levi says:

Whoever beholds illicit sexuality (*dvar ervah*[698]) and he does not feast his eyes (*zan es eino*) upon it, will merit to receive the Divine Presence, as the verse (Isaiah 33:15) states, "[He who walks righteously, and speaks honestly, who contemns gain of oppression, who shakes his hands from taking hold of bribe, closes his ear from hearing of blood,] and closes his eyes from seeing evil."

What is written next [in the verses]?

[Isaiah 33:16 promises:] "He shall dwell on high; [rocky fortresses shall be his defense; his bread shall be given (him), his water sure.]

[And Isaiah 33:17 promises:] "The King in His beauty shall your eyes behold; [they shall see [from] a distant land.]"

## Mesechtos Zeiros, Mesechta Arayos 21-22

21. Aba Chalufa [Chilfa bar Igra] said [three teachings] in the name of his father, Aba Gara:

> Do not be casual about making vows (*al t'hi poretz b'nedarim*) lest you come to take lightly the taking of oaths (*shema timol b'shvuos*);
>
> and do not accept hospitality from a priest who is an ignoramous (*kohen am haaretz*) lest he feed you from food sanctified to heaven [*mikodshei shamayaim*];
>
> and do not unlimit conversation with the woman, lest you commit adultery (*shema tinaef*), for women's conversation is only with the intention of adultery.

22. Rabbi Achi son of Yoshiyah said:

> Do not gaze at women, so that you do not come to illicit sexuality (*shelo tavo l'dvar ervah*).

And the Sages said:

> Anyone who has [the quality of] shamefacedness does not readily sin, as the verse states, [Moses said to the people at Sinai: "Do not fear, for in order to elevate you has G-d come;] and so that awe of Him shall be upon your faces, so that you shall not sin."
>
> And anyone who does not have [the quality of] shamefacedness readily sins, as the verse (Isaiah 3:9) states, "The recognition of their faces testified against them, and their sin, like Sodom they told," etcetera.
>
> And whoever gazes at the heel of a woman, causes that he will have children with physical illness.[699]

Rabbi Miasha grandson of Rabbi Yehoshua ben Levi says:

> Whoever beholds illicit sexuality (*dvar ervah*) and does not feast his eyes (*zan es einav*) upon it, will merit the radiance of the Divine Presence, as the verse (Isaiah 33:15-16) states, "He who walks righteously, and speaks honestly, who contemns gain of oppression, who shakes his hands from taking hold of bribe, closes his ear from hearing of blood, and closes his eyes from seeing evil; he shall dwell on high; rocky fortresses shall be his defense; his bread shall be given (him), his water sure."
>
> And what is written next [in the verses]?
>
> [Isaiah 33:17 promises:] "The King in His beauty shall your eyes behold; they shall see [from] a distant land."

## Vayikra Rabah 23:12-13 (excerpts)[700]

12. ... One who commits adultery[701] with his eyes is called an "adulterer" (*noef b'einav nikra noef*) ... [702]

13. Rabbi Menashya [Miasha] grandson of Rabbi Yehoshua ben Levi said:

We find that anyone who beholds illicit sexuality (*dvar ervah*) and does not feast his eyes (*zan einav*) upon it merits to receive the face of the Divine Presence.

Where?

The verse (Isaiah 33:15) states, "... And closes his eyes from seeing evil ..."

What is written next?

[Isaiah 33:17 promises:] "The King in His beauty shall your eyes behold; they shall see [from] a distant land."

## Gazing at the Female Genitals and "Shamefacedness" – Part Three: The Definition of Shame

Let us take this argument yet further.

This teaching on *Nedarim 20a* and in *Derech Eretz Rabah-Perek Arayos 13* about "shame" and "shamefacedness" would not, on its own, indicate any special connotation of sexual context if not for its juxtaposition by the compilers-editors of *Nedarim 20a* and by the Sages in *Derech Eretz Rabah* to cautions against innapropriate sexual gazing. On its own, however, it merely speaks of "shame" and "shamefacedness" as deterrents to sin in general.[703] In fact, this very same teaching extolling "shame" as a Jewish virtue is brought elsewhere in Talmudic literature without any surrounding sexual context at all.[704] And many other teachings addressing the qualities of "shame" and "shamefacedness" are asexual as well.[705]

The only source I have found in Talmudic-era literature[706] that speaks of "shame" or "shamefacedness" in a strictly sexual context, and more specifically, a sexual context *within marriage and during marital sexual intimacy*, is *Babylonian Talmud, Tractate Pesachim 49b*.

### *Babylonian Talmud, Tractate Pesachim 49b*

Rabbi Meir used to say:

> Whoever marries off his daughter to an uncouth ignoramus (*am haaretz*[707]) virtually binds and places her before a lion – just like a lion tears [its prey] and eats and has no 'shamefacedness,' so too, an uncouth ignoramus strikes [his wife] and rapes her[708] and has no 'shamefacedness.'

According to this Talmudic statement, the "virtue" of "shame" or "shamefacedness" in a purely sexual context within marriage is merely synonymous with virtues of "respect and sensitivity" (indeed, a husband who lacks such respect and sensitivity to his own wife, who is un-embarrassed to look her in the face as he attacks her, lacks much more than "shame"...[709])

And insofar as respect and sensitivity in this context have to do not only with a husband possessing these qualities inwardly, but with his sense of other's perception that he possesses them (including G-d's perception, and more specifically in this case, his own wife's perception), and his sense of disgrace, his sense of "shame" – manifesting in "shamefacedness" – in knowing that they perceive him to be lacking thereof, we have posited earlier[710] that a more proper English translation of the term "*bushah*" in this context is: dignity.

For to possess dignity is: a) to possess enough self-respect as to be concerned that others, and especially the Creator of all things, should hold you in high regard; and b) to possess enough respect of others as to be concerned that they feel respected, and safe, around you.

In other words: shame is merely a *manifestation* of dignity – and someone who has no dignity has no shame.

Thus, when G-d revealed Himself to the Jews at Sinai, it was arguably not to instill in them a sense of "shame-embarrassment," but a sense of dignity as the people who beheld the Almighty with their own eyes and heard His voice with their own ears, and who are therefore constantly aware of His omnipresence and cognizant and sensitive to what *He* thinks of them.

A person with no dignity, no "shame," however, has no concern as to whether or not others think highly of him or whether people feel respected or safe in his presence – the classic example being that described by Rabbi Achi bar Yoshiyah of the man who stands on the street checking out women passersby "head to heel."[711]

Therefore, if Raavad III expected such "shame" to preclude a husband from gazing at (or kissing) his own pure wife's genitals, even in private, even during intimacy, it would seem that Raavad III must have assumed that a wife would never approve or enjoy her husband doing such things and therefore they were always in his eyes a type of insensitive and undignified objectification of her body.[712] But the Sages, Rebbi, Rav and Rabbi Yochanan bar Napacha reject this stance, presumably upon the logic that such erotic behaviors cannot be deemed intrinsically "insensitive," "disrespectful," or "undignified" – i.e., "shameful" – especially if done with one's wife's own permission or encouragement or enjoyment. It all depends on the nature of the individual couple.

In this vein, let us borrow a principle of the Talmud elsewhere,[713] that in the context of Jewish tort law the degree of monetary compensation for "shame" (*boshes*) is determined in commensuration to the social status of the "shamer" and the "shamed" – to "estimate" the amount of dignity lost. In the case of a husband and wife, then, who are totally vulnerable, totally accepting and totally loving of one another in the marital bed, there is arguably no "shamer" and there is no "shamed," and therefore, by definition, there is no "shame."

That is: There is no lack of sensitivity. There is no disrespect. There is no loss of dignity.

Or in the words of Rabbi Yehudah the Pious, quoted above,[714] in regard to variety in sexual positions:

> In all such matters, it all follows *the personal tastes of husband and wife.* And if a man has found *a good wife* who is of same mind with him in these matters, to him applies the verse in Proverbs (18:22): "He who has found a wife has found goodness, and has elicited favor from the Lord," and the verse in Ecclesiastes (9:7): "[Go, eat your bread with joy and drink your wine with a merry heart, for] G-d has already approved your deeds."

## Gazing at the Female Genitals and "Modesty"

Raavad III gives an additional reason for not gazing at (or kissing) the female genitals, that is, that it transgresses the verse in Micah 6:8, "Walk modestly with your L-rd (*hatznea leches im Elokecha*)." But he offers no explanation as to why he understood this verse as having any relevance to the topic at hand. A simple reading of the verse and its surrounding context reveals not even a hint to such a meaning – at all. Taken at face value, the chapter and verse are admonishing a person to be humble, not haughty, before the Almighty.

Of course, Raavad III may have believed that the term "*tznius*," which is customarily translated as "modesty," must preclude such sexual exploration even in an unrelated verse, and even between loving and vulnerable husband and wife. But we would not necessarily be forced by Jewish law to accept such an interpretation. And while the term "*tznius* – modesty" is in fact brought by some other medieval commentaries in the context of "sanctifying" the marital sex act, even in regard to the four behaviors discussed by Rabbi Yochanan ben Dahavai,[715] those commentaries do not assert such modesty as a matter of binding law (as Raavad III appears to in *Baalei HaNefesh, Shaar Hakedushah*).

[The search for a precise definition of the term "*tznius*," especially in the context of physical intimacy within marriage – when, by the very nature of the sexual act itself, general notions of "modesty" are suspended by the letter of the law – will be the subject of an essay in a future volume of this series.]

The only hint of an explanation I have found as to Raavad III's source is that offered by Rabbi Eliyahu Kramer (the "Vilna Gaon – Genius of Vilna") in his *Biur HaGra* commentary to *Shulchan Aruch, Orach Chaim 240:4:12*, where he points us to his own earlier comments in *Orach Chaim 1:1:Hagaah:13*. There, in a completely non-sexual context, Rabbi Kramer references an elucidation of Micah 6:8 in *Babylonian Talmud, Tractate Sukkah 49b* (which is also found in *Tractate Makot 24a*).

But even the Talmud itself, there, according to all other medieval commentaries, understands the verse at face value as a caution against material or spiritual *ostentation*,[716] not as a promotion of sexual inhibition. The verse is given no sexual connotation, there, at all.[717]

## Gazing at the Female Genitals and "Inciting the Evil Urge"

As far as "inciting the evil urge," the source of this concern is *Babylonian Talmud, Tractate Nidah 13b,* which discusses the concept only in regard to a man who deliberately brings himself to erection (*maksheh atzmo ladaas*) for the sake of excess sexual indulgence, not to one whose bodily chemistry naturally causes him to become aroused – like any normal teenage or adult male (married or unmarried) with a healthy libido.[718]

While the actual scenario of *Nidah 13b* is somewhat obscure, it is generally assumed to refer to concerns about masturbation. Raavad III, however, earlier in *Shaar Hakedushah,*[719] explains that *Nidah 13b* is referring to a husband who deliberately arouses himself *to have sex with his own wife* even though he doesn't actually feel the "need" for it, which Raavad III says is not forbidden, it is merely a sexual "gateway drug" to potentially other illicit sexual compulsions (*vadai hu haderech la'atzas yetzer hora v'hasasaso. . .umin ha'heter y'vieno el ha'isur*) – perhaps a reference to what is now recognized as sexual addiction.

Therefore, let it be noted that Raavad III, here, is not calling the "sexual urge" in-and-of-itself "evil," but rather he is referring back to his earlier discussion that the act of voluntarily arousing the sexual urge *in turn* "incites the evil urge" to take matters yet further into the realm of sin.[LIV] [720]

But according to Raavad III's own admitted understanding of the concept, "inciting the evil urge" has no relevance to the scenario of a husband who is already sexually aroused and already has, or is already well on the way toward having, a natural erection.

Perhaps that is why Raavad III in *Shaar Hakedushah* mentions the concern about "inciting the evil urge" only (earlier in his discussion, in explaining the original concerns of Rabbi Yochanan ben Dahavai, not later, in regard to the view of the Sages,[721] and only) in regard to gazing at one's wife's genitals during non-sexual moments, for this particular concern should not even begin when husband and wife are already in the mood for lovemaking.

And the fact is, even in the non-sexual moments of life, the healthy urge for intimacy can stir itself suddenly without apparent cause and immediately compel one spouse to feast their eyes upon the other. Thus, there really is no way of telling what came first in that split-second moment – the arousal or the gazing. But even in a case where the gazing came first, by Raavad III's own admission earlier in his chapter, there really is no legal "prohibition" against a husband intentionally arousing himself to be sexually intimate with his own wife.

---

[LIV] See also above, page 23, the wording of Rabbi Yosef Caro in *Shulchan Aruch, Orach Chaim, 240:1*: "But if a husband doesn't need sex, and he intentionally arouses himself in order to indulge his pleasures, this is the work of the evil inclination, for from this **permissible** act he will be led to that which is forbidden..."

## Kissing the Female Genitals and "Disgustingness"

In regard to the kissing of the female genitals and the biblical commandment of *Bal Teshaktzu* (not to make oneself disgusted/disgusting), the examples of forbidden "disgustingness" which Raavad III points to in the Talmud in support of his argument – drinking out of a cupping horn[722] and passing an insect across one's lips[723] – have no sexual context at all.[724] [725]

More importantly, there are two approaches in Jewish law as to what defines "disgustingness" – one that it is determined by the sensibilities of the majority of humanity, the other that it is determined by the sensibility of each individual human being. According to the first approach, the rule regarding *Bal Teshaktzu* is that anything other than what the Talmud itself explicitly categorizes as "disgusting" cannot be prohibited by anyone else unless the majority of the world finds it repugnant.[726] According to the second approach, if even a minority of people finds it appealing, it cannot be categorically forbidden after the Talmud itself did not make it so.[727]

As pertains to the question of cunnilingus, then, if one were to take the first approach, one would be hard-pressed to prove that a majority of humans finds it unappealing. And if one were to take the second approach, then it is only the individual couple's personal desires that matter.

And where there are extenuating circumstances, the concept of *Bal Teshaktzu* can be suspended entirely[728] – and what could be more extenuating than keeping peace in the home and maintaining love and harmony and fidelity within marriage.

Finally, and most significantly, even Raavad III himself, in his gloss-notes to *Mishneh Torah*, does not argue against Maimonides' permission of kissing the female genitals in *Sefer Kedushah, Isurei Biah 21:9*.[729]

## The Case Precedents of Rebbi and Rav

As far as the Talmud only bringing case precedents in which "overturning the table" was permitted by various sages, the reason why cases permitting the other three behaviors were not brought could potentially be explained rather simply:

The case precedents of Rebbi and Rav were of women coming to them to complain that their husbands had "overturned" them for sexual intercourse. According to many commentaries, their complaint was that such a position was *uncomfortable*, and some medieval commentaries[730] use this to prove that the definition of "overturning the table" must be anal sex,[731] not her-on-top, because "a wife would never complain about being on top, for it is not uncomfortable."[732]

So, too, in regard to the other three practices: the fact that no real life cases were recorded of sages permitting to women non-sex-related talk during intercourse or the gazing at or kissing of the female genitals is perhaps simply because the sages never had to. Perhaps no wives ever came to complain about such behaviors for they do not generally cause the average woman discomfort. On the contrary, for many wives these can bring increased comfort, self-confidence, physical pleasure and/or emotional joy.[732*]

## *Baalei HaNefesh, Shaar Hakedushah* – Letter or Spirit of the Law?

Finally, it must be noted that in the opening paragraphs of his *Baalei HaNefesh, Shaar Hakedushah*, Raavad III explains at length that his purpose in writing the chapter was to clarify the way one should "sanctify oneself" during intimacy, and that part of the path of sanctity is to deny oneself that which is permitted.[733]

Even when introducing the four cautions of Rabbi Yochanan ben Dahavai, Raavad III writes only that, "There are other behaviors which blemish the act, degrade it, and cause it to lose its reward" – but not that these behaviors are "forbidden."[734] And when, in the course of that discussion,[735] he goes on to say that gazing at or kissing the female genitals, and non-sex-related talk during sex, "are not judged a harsh punishment, but they still carry a prohibition (*issur*)" it is not at all clear what the actual legal classification of this "prohibition" was even in Raavad III's own mind. He could not have been unaware of the potential difficulties others might find in his arguments, as discussed above. If he did understand the Sages as rejecting Rabbi Yochanan ben Dahavai's medical cautions about congenital illness – "harsh punishment" – then he must have been aware that according to Ameimar's clear statement on *Nedarim 20b* this would equal the Sages' permission of them halachically. And unless he had a different textual version of *Callah Rabti*, it is unlikely to have escaped him that *Callah Rabti 1:14* has the Rabbis responding to Rabbi Yochanan ben Dahavai *in regard to all four behaviors* that "There is no prohibition that forbids them."[736]

Thus, as unconventional an argument as it may be, it might just be possible that Raavad III was stretching the meaning of "prohibition," here, to include that which he personally felt was not in the *spirit* of ideal sanctity;[736*] but that when all was said and done, he really did concede to Maimonides and Rabeinu Yitzchak collectively according to the *letter* of the law, allowing these sexual behaviors between loving husband and wife.

Again, this would explain why in his glosses to Maimonides' *Mishneh Torah*, Raavad III does not argue with Maimonides' permission of kissing the female genitals and anal intercourse (and intercourse between limbs – the latter two possibly even to the point of ejaculation) in *Sefer Kedushah, Isurei Biah 21:9*.[737] As noted above, Raavad III was perhaps forced to concede that anal sex is permitted due to the Talmudic ruling of Rava on *Sanhedrin 58b*.[738] But the significance of his silence on Maimonides' permission of cunnilingus cannot be overstated, for there is no Talmudic passage other than the Sages' ruling reported on *Nedarim 20b* forcing Raavad III to permit it. And being that Raavad III believed kissing of the female genitals to be worse than gazing at them, his silent legal permission of kissing would equal a silent legal permission of gazing as well.

[See also the comment of Raavad III's colleague and "sparring partner," Rabbi Zerachiah HaLevi, to the opening line of *Baalei HaNefesh, Shaar Hakedushah*. To paraphrase his poetic words, there, he says that the chapter is "all beautiful and pleasant, with unblemished wisdom, to banish childish foolishness, and straighten the ways of the people. But we only expose *teachings of modesty* to those who are already modest."[739]]

All this suggests that perhaps Raavad III's ultimate concern in the *Shaar Hakedushah* chapter of *Baalei HaNefesh* was not the letter of the law, but its spirit. In regard to the letter of the law, it seems Raavad III may have been much more permissive than has until now been assumed by rabbinic literature; that he was in fact aware of, and empathetic to, the unique psychological, emotional, physical and spiritual dimensions of each and every individual marriage relationship.

And this would also resolve another significant point: the fact that Raavad III's own father-in-law and mentor, Rabbi Avraham of Narbonne, Raavad II, in his *Sefer HaEshkol, Hilchos Tznius*,[740] expressly holds that the Sages and Rabbi Yochanan bar Napacha on *Nedarim 20b* did in fact permit all four of the sexual behaviors cautioned against by Rabbi Yochanan ben Dahavai. Thus, the views of father-in-law and son-in-law, master and disciple, could be reconciled.

# PART SIX
# SUMMARY AND CONCLUSION

## Summary

The key points that emerge from the critical research are as follows:

### The Sages

In *Babylonian Talmud, Nedarim 20a*, Rabbi Yochanan ben Dahavai warns that four sexual behaviors between husband and wife can cause congenital illness in children: "overturning the table" can cause lameness, non-sex-related talk during sex can cause deafness, gazing at the female genitals can cause blindness, kissing the female genitals can cause muteness.

On *Nedarim 20b*, the Sages are quoted rejecting Rabbi Yochanan ben Dahavai, ruling instead that "Anything a husband craves to do with his wife sexually, he may do."

There are four approaches among the legal authorities as to how to understand and apply this ruling of the Sages:

- According to Ameimar as quoted on *Nedarim 20b*, as understood by Maimonides and most medieval commentaries,[741] the Sages rule that all four sexual behaviors cautioned against by Rabbi Yochanan ben Dahavai are not only legally permitted, they are also medically safe for the unborn child, even if performed during the same sexual encounter in which conception occurs.[742]

  A variety of interpretations are given for the permitted position called "overturning the table," including anal intercourse, rear-entry vaginal intercourse, her-on-top, or possibly any combination of the three.

- According to Ameimar as quoted on *Nedarim 20b*, as understood by Raavad III in his *Baalei HaNefesh, Shaar Hakedushah*, the Sages ruled only that one of these four sexual behaviors, "overturning the table," is both legally permitted and medically safe. And Raavad III interprets "overturning the table" as rear-entry vaginal intercourse.

  According to Raavad III in *Baalei HaNefesh, Shaar Hakedushah*, the other three behaviors – non-sex-related talk during sex and gazing at or kissing the female genitals – are still forbidden on some level by the Sages. But it is unclear if Raavad III still believed them (all) to be medically dangerous to the fetus. And even if he did still consider these behaviors to be dangerous, it is unclear if he understood them as being dangerous if performed *any* time or *only* if performed during the same sexual encounter in which conception occurs.[743]

## SUMMARY AND CONCLUSION

However, Raavad III remains silent in his glosses to *Mishneh Torah*, where Maimonides permits both anal sex and the kissing of the female genitals in *Sefer Kedushah, Isurei Biah 21:9*. He probably had to concede that anal sex is permitted based upon the ruling of Rava in *Sanhedrin 58b*. But his silence, there, about the kissing of the female genitals suggests he ultimately conceded to Maimonides that according to a straightforward reading of the Sages' ruling on *Nedarim 20b*, the kissing of the female genitals is also permitted by the letter of the law[744] – which would, in turn, suggest that gazing at the female genitals would be permitted by him as well.[745]

- According to *Tractate Callah 9*, the Sages legally permitted all four of the behaviors cautioned against by Rabbi Yochanan ben Dahavai. It does not comment on the Sages' view about their safety.[746]

  Some versions of *Tractate Callah 9* interpret "overturning the table" as rear-entry vaginal intercourse specifically.

- According to Rava as quoted by *Callah Rabti 1:13*, Rabbi Yochanan ben Dahavai himself only warned about congenital illnesses resulting from these four behaviors if they are performed during the same sexual encounter in which conception occurs. At any other time, however, even Rabbi Yochanan ben Dahavai himself would consider them to be medically safe.

  According to *Callah Rabti 1:14*, Rabbi Yochanan ben Dahavai also considered these four behaviors to be legally forbidden – though it is not clear if he considered them to be forbidden at all times or only during a sexual encounter in which conception is possible to occur (that is, when he also considered them to be medically dangerous for a potential child).

  According to *Callah Rabti 1:14*, the Sages conceded to Rabbi Yochanan ben Dahavai that all four behaviors are medically dangerous to a child conceived during the same sexual encounter in which they are performed. But the Sages rejected Rabbi Yochanan ben Dahavai's legal prohibition in regard to all four, and thus the Sages permit all four at all times – even if performed during the same sexual encounter in which conception is possible to occur.[746*] And where conception cannot occur, the Sages would consider all four behaviors to be both legally permitted and medically safe.

  Some versions of *Tractate Callah 9* interpret "overturning the table" as rear-entry vaginal intercourse. Rava himself, in *Talmud, Sanhedrin 58b*, permits even anal intercourse – though he may have considered that, too, to be dangerous to a fetus if performed during the same sexual encounter in which conception occurs.

## The Medieval Authorities

- Among the medieval authorities we have found, there is a majority who reflect the opinion of Maimonides in *Mishneh Torah, Sefer Kedushah, Isurei Biah 21:9*, permitting a man to do anything he craves sexually with his wife, including (gazing at or) kissing the female genitals, vaginal intercourse, anal intercourse, and intercourse between limbs.[747]

- There are a number of medieval authorities who permit anal intercourse, but do not clearly express their opinion in regard to intra-anal ejaculation.

- The majority of medieval authorities we have found who do weigh in on the question of intra-anal ejaculation endorse Rabeinu Yitzchak's second approach quoted in *Tosfos* to *Yevamos 34b*, that it is permissible as long as it's intended to satisfy the couple's occasional sexual fulfillment, not as a constant means of intentional unsanctioned birth control.[748]

    Rabeinu Yitzchak is understood by two post-medieval authorities – Rabbis Yehoshua Falk and Yechiel Michel Epstein (see below: *The Post-Medieval Authorities*) – as permitting not only occasional intra-anal ejaculation for couples, but occasional ejaculation between limbs as well.[749]

- Rabbi Yeshayah of Trani I, and his grandson, Rabbi Yeshayah of Trani II, both permit intra-anal ejaculation for married couples as long as the intention is for sexual fulfillment, not birth control. They mention no restriction on frequency of such ejaculation.

- *Tosfos, Sanhedrin 58b* permits intra-anal ejaculation for married couples as long as the majority of intercourses (or at least the majority of ejaculations) are intra-vaginal – for this adequately demonstrates that the couple is not intentionally avoiding pregnancy (where such avoidance is unsanctioned).

- Most ancient manuscripts of Maimonides' *Mishneh Torah, Isurei Biah 21:9*, including those among the Yemenite Jewish community (which are universally considered to be among the most precise), make no mention of any restriction on intra-anal ejaculation or ejaculation between limbs for married couples – not even in regard to intention or frequency of such ejaculation.

    In Maimonides' *Commentary to the Mishneh, Sanhedrin 7:4*, as well, no restriction is given on intra-anal ejaculation or ejaculation between limbs for married couples – not even in regard to intention or frequency of such ejaculation.

- One medieval source (perhaps unknown to many others), Rabeinu Meyuchas, in his commentary on Genesis, explicitly permits intra-anal ejaculation and ejaculation between limbs for married couples according to the baseline letter of the law. And he, like Maimonides in *Commentary to the Mishnah*, issues no legal restrictions upon them in terms of intention or frequency.[750]

- The minority of medieval authorities we have found who expressly permit anal intercourse only *without* intra-anal ejaculation base their stringency on a questionable manuscript version of Maimonides' *Mishneh Torah, Sefer Kedushah, Isurei Biah 21:9*, featuring a potentially forged restriction against intra-anal ejaculation for couples.[751]

- The medieval authorities we have found who expressly permit intercourse between limbs only *without* ejaculation base their stringency on a questionable manuscript version of Maimonides' *Mishneh Torah, Sefer Kedushah, Isurei Biah 21:9*, featuring a potentially forged restriction against ejaculation between limbs for couples.[751*]

## Rabbi Yosef Caro versus Rabbi Moshe Isserles

- Rabbi Yosef Caro, in *Shulchan Aruch, Orach Chaim 240* and *Even Haezer 25*, quotes only the view of Raavad III from *Baalei HaNefesh, Shaar Hakedushah* against non-sex-related talk during sex and gazing at or kissing the female genitals. He denigrates, but does not forbid, sex with the wife on top or side-by-side with her husband. And he does not rule for or against anal sex, intercourse between limbs or rear-entry vaginal intercourse.

- Rabbi Moshe Isserles, in *Shulchan Aruch, Even Haezer 25:2*, rules according to the combined views of Maimonides in *Mishneh Torah, Sefer Kedushah, Isurei Biah 21:9* and the second approach of Rabeinu Yitzchak in *Tosfos, Yevamos 34b*,[752] thus permitting by the letter of the law (gazing at or) kissing the female genitals, anal intercourse, intercourse between limbs and occasional intra-anal ejaculation.

## The Post-Medieval Authorities

- Rabbi Mordechai Yoffe in his *Levush, Even Haezer 25:2* and Rabbi Yechiel Michel Epstein in his *Aruch Hashulchan, Even Haezer 25:11* rule the letter of the law according to (Maimonides and Rabeinu Yitzchak and) Rabbi Isserles. And although Rabbi Epstein quotes, and endorses, Rabbi Caro's halachic caution against even occasional intra-anal ejaculation within marriage, he nevertheless does not actually forbid it.[753]

- Rabbi Shlomoh Luria in his *Yam Shel Shlomoh, Yevamos 34b* and Rabbi Yom Tov Lipman Heller in his *Lechem Chamudos, Tractate Nidah,*

*Chapter 2, Comment 10*, rule according to Rabeinu Asher, permitting occasional intra-anal ejaculation for married couples.

- Those post-medieval authorities who rule against Maimonides' permission for anal intercourse (even without intra-anal ejaculation) apparently base themselves on:
  - The <u>virtually lone opinion among the medieval scholars</u> of Raavad III in *Baalei HaNefesh, Shaar Hakedushah*, which is contradicted by Raavad III's own silence in his glosses to Maimonides' *Mishneh Torah, Isurei Biah 21:9*.[754]
  - The 1574-1576 <u>censored</u> Venice edition of *Mishneh Torah, Sefer Kedushah, Isurei Biah 21:9* in which Maimonides' permission of anal intercourse was omitted entirely.[755]
  - The 1598, 1617 and 1632 Venice editions of *Shulchan Aruch*, which included an <u>erroneous marginal note by an unknown author</u> stating that Rabbi Isserles's use of the term *"shelo cedarcah"* in *Even Haezer 25:2* was not meant to refer to anal intercourse, but only to rear-entry vaginal intercourse.

- Those post-medieval authorities who rule against Rabeinu Yitzchak's permission of occasional intra-anal ejaculation within marriage (and who thus also rule against the permission of it by Rabeinu Asher, Rabbi Yaakov ben Asher and the majority of other medieval authorities who weigh in on the question of intra-anal ejaculation), do so as a result of:
  - A <u>questionable</u> manuscript-version of Maimonides' *Mishneh Torah, Sefer Kedushah, Isurei Biah 21:9*, featuring a <u>potentially forged</u> restriction against intra-anal ejaculation for couples.
  - The <u>halachic caution – but not prohibition</u> – of Rabbi Yosef Caro based on *Nidah 13a* – though it is unclear if *Nidah 13a*'s context was ever meant to apply to occasional intra-anal ejaculation performed between husband and wife for the sake of sexual fulfillment within marriage.[756]
  - The <u>kabbalistic caution – but not prohibition</u> – of Rabbi Yosef Caro based on the *Zohar* – though it is unclear if the *Zohar*'s context was ever meant to apply to occasional intra-anal ejaculation performed between husband and wife for the sake of sexual fulfillment within marriage.[757]
  - Rabbi Yosef Caro's <u>omission</u> of any discussion about anal sex in his *Shulchan Aruch, Orach Chaim 240* and *Even Haezer 25* – <u>which does not prove his opinion on the matter either way</u>.

## SUMMARY AND CONCLUSION

- o The kabbalistic teachings of Rabbi Yitzchak Luria in regard to "wasting seed in vain," which are, in turn, based on the teachings of the *Zohar* (see point above).

- o The difficult Talmudic arguments of Rabbi Eliyahu de Vidas in *Reishis Chochmah* and of Rabbi Elazar Azikri in *Sefer Charedim*.[758]

- o Rabbi Yeshayah Horowitz's endorsement in *Shnei Luchos Habris* of *Reishis Chochmah* and *Sefer Charedim*.[759]

- o The 1594, 1619 and 1632 Venice editions of *Shulchan Aruch*, which included an erroneous marginal note by an unknown author stating that Rabbi Isserles's use of the term "*shelo cedarcah*" in *Even Haezer 25:2* was not meant to refer to anal intercourse, but only to rear-entry vaginal intercourse.[760]

• Rabbi Yehoshua Falk, in his *Drishah* commentary to *Tur, Even Haezer 23:1:1* and *25:2:5-6*, insists that Rabeinu Yitzchak's permission of occasional intra-anal ejaculation for couples encompasses also occasional ejaculation between limbs – and he possibly implies that this is how Rabbi Yaakov ben Asher himself, in the *Tur*, understood Rabeinu Yitzchak.[761]

Rabbi Yechiel Michel Epstein, too, in his wording of *Aruch Hashulchan, Even Haezer 25:11*, appears to apply the permissive ruling of Rabeinu Yitzchak about occasional intra-anal ejaculation for couples to occasional ejaculation between limbs as well.

But, arguably, no mature halachic discussion was ever allowed to develop among the post-medieval authorities about the permissibility of ejaculation between limbs due to:

- o The 16th-17th century rabbinic forces against anal sex and intra-anal ejaculation (listed above).

- o A questionable manuscript-version of Maimonides' *Mishneh Torah, Sefer Kedushah, Isurei Biah 21:9*, featuring a potentially forged restriction against ejaculation between limbs for couples.

- o The 1574-1576 censored Venice edition of *Mishneh Torah, Sefer Kedushah, Isurei Biah 21:9*, as well as subsequent censored editions, in which Maimonides' permission of intercourse between limbs was omitted entirely.[762]

- o A 1754 censored edition of *Shulchan Aruch, Even Haezer 25:2* in which Rabbi Isserles's permission of intercourse between limbs was omitted entirely.[763]

- - The obvious possibility that many rabbinic authorities since the time of Rabbi Falk were simply unaware of his interpretation of Rabeinu Yitzchak.
  - The probability that most rabbinic authorities were simply unaware of Rabeinu Meyuchas's view on the matter.[764]
- Those post-medieval authorities who rule against Maimonides' permission for cunnilingus, base themselves on:
  - The <u>virtually lone opinion among the medieval scholars</u> of Raavad III in *Baalei HaNefesh, Shaar Hakedushah*, whose Talmudic arguments, there, are debatable, and who ultimately remained silent in his glosses to Maimonides' *Mishneh Torah, Isurei Biah 21:9*, where Maimonides permits cunnilingus.[765]
  - The <u>ambiguous view of Rabbi Yaakov ben Asher in his *Tur*</u>, where he never makes his final ruling on the matter clear.[766]
  - Rabbi Yosef Caro in *Shulchan Aruch, Orach Chaim 240*, relying upon Raavad III and Rabbi Yaakov ben Asher.[767]
  - Rabbi Shmuel Feivush's comment in his *Beis Shmuel* commentary to *Shulchan Aruch, Even Haezer 25:2* – which is either <u>his own personal opinion</u> or a <u>disproven</u> interpretation of Rabbi Isserles's words.[768]
  - *Callah Rabti 1:14*, which, <u>in direct contradiction of Ameimar on Talmud, Nedarim 20b</u>, has the Sages believing that the four congenital illnesses *do* result from the four sexual behaviors cautioned against by Rabbi Yochanan ben Dahavai, including cunnilingus.

    But *Callah Rabti 1:14* also has the Sages *legally permitting all four* according to the letter of the law.

    And *Callah Rabti 1:13* insists that even according to Rabbi Yochanan ben Dahavai himself, the four congenital illnesses are only a risk if the four behaviors are performed during the same sexual encounter in which conception occurs. Therefore, where conception is not possible, *Callah Rabti* would understand the Sages as considering all four behaviors, including the kissing of the female genitals, to be both legally permitted and medically safe.

## Incomplete Presentations of *Callah Rabti* and/or Raavad III

- One medieval authority, Rabbi Yitzchak of Corbeil, in his *Sefer Mitzvos Katan, Positive Commandment 285*, appears to rule according to *Callah*

# SUMMARY AND CONCLUSION

*Rabti*, legally permitting all four behaviors cautioned against by Rabbi Yochanan ben Dahavai, but still mentioning the risk of danger to a fetus in regard to all four.

But he leaves out *Callah Rabti's* qualification that the risk of danger is only if these behaviors are performed during the same sexual encounter in which conception occurs. At any other time, all four behaviors would be perfectly permissible and perfectly safe even according to *Callah Rabti*.

- Important post-medieval authorities, such as the authors of *Chochmas Adam, Kitzur Shulchan Aruch, Mishnah Berurah-Biur Halachah* and *Kaf Hachaim*, offer varying presentations of Jewish sex law that endorse and/or combine the views of *Callah Rabti* and/or Raavad III, without clarifying the complexities of these two sources nor reflecting the majority of medieval written opinion we (now) know of – thereby (unintentionally or intentionally) leaving their readers with varying degrees of erroneously harsh impressions of the law.[769]

In light of all the above, even if one were to tally a majority of latter-day rabbinical authorities or modern-day family purity/marital intimacy guide authors who categorically forbid anal sex or intra-anal ejaculation, or intercourse between limbs or ejaculation between limbs, or gazing at the female genitals or kissing the female genitals, the argument that one should follow the majority of latest rabbinic opinion *even in post-Talmudic times*[770] would arguably not apply, for the grounds upon which they are based in this regard are extremely debatable, and the widespread acceptance among the masses of these rulings until now can be attributed to an equally widespread (perhaps unintentional) lack of education about the complexities of these points of debate.[771]

Behold: Even G-d Himself allows – nay, demands – that His own Holy Name be erased for the sake of restoring peace and harmony and sexual intimate life between husband and wife.[772] Do we not, then, have the obligation to clarify and correct incomplete (and arguably unhealthy) understandings about marital sex promulgated in His Name – however venerated their sources may be?

And concerning the opinion of the *Zohar* in particular, Rabeinu Yitzchak's dismissal of the problem of "wasting seed in vain" in regard to occasional intra-anal ejaculation within marriage – which encompassed, according to Rabbi Yehoshua Falk, a dismissal of the problem of "wasting seed in vain" in regard to occasional ejaculation between limbs within marriage as well – could apply equally to every discussion in the *Zohar* on the topic.[773] Consequently, there would be no halachic or kabbalistic problem of "wasting seed" at all where sexual fulfillment and bonding are the main intentions of loving and vulnerable husband and wife.[774]

If the codifiers [of Jewish law] had thought that their works would cause the masses to abandon the Talmud entirely and instead rule straight out of their codes [of Jewish law], they would never have written them in the first place.

For it is more worthy and appropriate to rule Jewish law from the Talmud itself. And even though this carries the risk that one might not discern the path of truth, and one might not rule the law according to its truth to instruct others according to its truth, nevertheless a wise person is only expected to discern what his [G-d-given] intellect gives him to understand from the Talmud.

And if his understanding and wisdom mislead him, he is nevertheless beloved by G-d, may He be blessed, by the very fact that he rules according to how his [G-d-given] intellect sees true.

For "a judge must only judge according to what his own eyes see" – and he is better than one who rules straight out of a code [of Jewish law] without knowing the underlying premises at all, for the latter is like a blind man walking the road.

*Rabbi Yehudah Loew, Nesivos Olam*
*Nesiv HaTorah, Chapter 15*

Those who walked in darkness now see a great light.

*Isaiah 9:1*

This refers to those who delved into the Talmud and saw great light, for G-d enlightens their eyes in that which is forbidden and that which is permitted.

*Midrash Tanchuma*

## Conclusion

As you can now see, there are long lists of compelling sources – and where needed, solid logic – to permit much more in the marital bed than your family purity/marital intimacy guide or pre-marriage teacher might have told you.

I hope you've enjoyed this brief journey, and that despite some unresolved (and even disturbing) questions and concepts we've encountered along the way, it has given you new faith in Torah as a revealed (and yet-further-to-be revealed) source of compassionate, realistic, down-to-earth divine wisdom for the human condition.

Of course, I have not come to argue that Judaism does not extol constant spiritual growth and refined sensitivity, including in matters of sex. As we've seen, most permissive liberal approaches that accept from a legal standpoint all of a man's or woman's sexual desires within the covenant of marriage immediately add that there is also the path of the pious, the spirit of the law, which seeks to focus on giving pleasure rather than on receiving it, and on fulfilling the Creator's own higher purposes.[LV]

Thus, in short, G-d's message concerning marital sex is this: Do not be afraid to express all your sexual vulnerabilities and to fulfill all your sexual curiosities and desires and needs together with your loving spouse. But do not resist either how your approach to sex will naturally change and refine itself as you mature spiritually.

---

[LV] For more on Judaism's approach to psychological-emotional-physical-spiritual balance in general, see Maimonides' *Introduction to Ethics of the Fathers, Shmoneh Perakim,* Chapters 4-5.

# APPENDICES

## Vaginal Massage

A personal friend of mine was told by his Chasidic pre-marriage teacher that it is forbidden for a husband to insert his finger(s) into his wife's vagina.

Referred to by some as "vaginal massage," the technique can be beneficial during foreplay to arouse both husband and wife, and it can even be used to satisfy the wife's need for climax when, for whatever reason, the husband is unable to perform intercourse.

And such massage is not only effective inside the vagina, but on the outer vulva as well.

Such a "prohibition" against vaginal massage does not feature in any biblical, Talmudic or medieval sources I have found, and it appears to trace mainly to a passage in the *Lechem Mishneh* commentary of Rabbi Avraham de Boton (c.1560-c.1605).

I was first made aware of this passage in *Lechem Mishneh* in reviewing the modern-day marital intimacy guide, *Ufakadata Navecha*, by Rabbi B. Fink.[775] Rabbi Fink offers a brilliant proof that it is permitted to touch one's wife's genitals from a story told in *Babylonian Talmud, Shabbos 140b*. The Talmud, there, relates that the sage, Rav Chisda, advised his daughters to increase their husbands' sexual arousals by first allowing them only to play with their breasts, and only after teasing them in this way to allow them to play with their vaginas (see the interpretation of Rabbi Shlomoh Yitzchaki, Rashi, there).

This clearly implies that a husband's touching of his wife's genitals – not only for the sake of her arousal, but even for the sake of his own – is perfectly permitted (and, if we may be so bold, not only permitted, but encouraged).

Rabbi Fink notes that *Lechem Mishneh* to *Mishneh Torah, Sefer Nashim, Ishus 15:18* reads an interpretation into this Talmudic passage that *assumes* vaginal touching by the husband to be forbidden. And while *Lechem Mishneh* does not distinguish between touching the inside or outside of the female sex organ, Rabbi Fink in any case references Rabbi Chaim Yosef Dovid Azulai (Chida) in *Birchei Yosef, Even Haezer 25:3*, who dismisses *Lechem Mishneh's* interpretation entirely.

Thus, we have a solid Talmudic source permitting vaginal massage – certainly the outside vulva, and there is no reason whatsoever to believe that massaging the inside should be any different.

Now, the only source I personally stumbled across asserting this "prohibition" (which Rabbi Fink discusses as well) is a 1913 book on "family purity" and piety by a certain Rabbi Yisrael Yitzchak Yanofsky, entitled *Taharas Yisroel*.

Rabbi Yanofsky writes:

> Putting one's hand on the private parts of a woman is a great perversion and it carries a prohibition.[776]

Note that Rabbi Yanofsky, too, does not differentiate between touching the outside vulva or the inside vagina.

But in his source-notes, there, he points to the medieval work, *Rabeinu Yeruchem Nesiv 32* – which, in actuality, states this "prohibition" in regard to fondling not one's own wife, but *another married woman!*[777]

Now, we must certainly give Rabbi Yanofsky the benefit of the doubt and attribute his wording, here, to a mere typographical oversight or error. But this is still a telling example of how erroneous reporting of sources – unintentional or otherwise – can cause innocent, trusting grooms and brides to endure not just sexual unfulfillment, but needless inhibition, anxiety, guilt or shame (if not straight out infidelity[778]), possibly over an entire lifetime.

## Jewish "Family Purity" and Marital Intimacy Guide Reviews

"Who can perceive all mistakes; cleanse me of hidden error" (Psalms 19:13).

The partial or mistaken reporting of sources on our subject in nearly every Jewish "family purity" and marital intimacy guide I have seen, innocent as such may have been, has undoubtedly caused untold pain to individuals, couples and families.[779]

However, I will refrain from impugning the intentions of the writers who have come before me, for they were certainly well meaning and may have deliberately structured/limited their presentations based upon considerations unknown to me; or such errors or omissions may have simply been unintentional. I myself in the course of researching and writing on this topic became acutely aware of how easy it is to miss a source, miss a point within a source, miss the implication of a source, or simply mistype a source. It is truly only by the good grace of G-d that numerous errors were caught even in the eleventh hour prior to publication – and I harbor no illusions as to the perfection of the final product (as indicated in our introduction).

But below I will list the family purity/marital intimacy guides and other modern-day rabbinical literature that were reviewed in the course of surveying the prevalent Orthodox and Ultra-Orthodox legal teachings on the subject – and we will leave it to readers to compare the scope and findings of this study to other presentations out there.

Note that some books listed do not actually address sexual technique or positions within marriage at all, even though they are devoted to, or at least have dedicated chapters on, the laws of marital sexual behavior.

And I would like to draw my readers' attention to two excellent (Hebrew) halachic works listed below, *Bnei Banim vol. 4*, by Rabbi Yehuda Henkin, and *Dvar Seser*, by an author who remains anonymous in his publication, as suggested reading for every Orthodox and Ultra-Orthodox husband and wife, groom and bride, single adult and mature teenager.[LVI*]

As of the publication of this book, the following family purity/marital intimacy guides and other related modern-day rabbinical literature were reviewed on the topic of sexual technique and positions within marriage (listed in order of publication):

---

[LVI*] See also above, our preface to the Third Edition of this study, where we **most highly** recommend the Hebrew work, *Simchat HaBayit v'Birchato* (Second Edition, 2015), by Rabbi Eliezer Melamed of Yeshivat Har Brachah, and *Harchavot l'Simchat Habayit v'Birchato* (2015), written under Rabbi Melamed's guidance by Rabbi Maor Kayam.

For those seeking practical guidance on sex and sex-related matters from sources cognizant of Orthodox sensitivities, see the sources recommended above in our Introduction, page 12.

## APPENDICES

Guides on Family Purity or Marital Intimacy

Rabbi Yisrael Yitzchak Yanofsky, *Taharas Yisrael*, vol. 2 (1913, Hebrew)[780]

Rabbi Shmuel Hominer, *Sefer Kedushah* (1947, Hebrew)[781]

Rabbi Kalman Cahana, *Taharas Bas Yisrael* (1954, Hebrew, English)[782]

Rabbi Chaim Dovid HaLevi, *Mekor Chaim* (1979, Hebrew)[783]

Rabbi Mordechai Eliahu, *The Paths of Purity* (1986, English)[784]

Rabbi Daniel Frisch, *Kedushah Utznius* (1994, Hebrew)[785]

Rabbi Moshe Sternbuch, *Orchos HaBayis* (1995, Hebrew)[786]

Rabbi Avraham Peretz Friedman, *Marital Intimacy: A Traditional Approach* (1996, English)[787]

Rabbi Shmuel Boteach, *Kosher Sex* (1999, 2000, English)[788]

Rabbi Fishel Jacobs, *Family Purity* (2000, English)[789]

Rabbi B. Fink, *Ufakadata Navecha* (2000, 2006, 2010, Hebrew)[790]

Mrs. T. Hendel, *Kedoshim Tihiyu* (2001, Hebrew)[791]

Rabbi Shaul Wagschal, *Taharas Am Yisrael* (2002, Hebrew, English)[792]

Rabbi Noson Stinetzki, *Naveh L'nesivosai* (2004, Hebrew)[793]

Deena R. Zimmerman, *A Lifetime Companion to the Laws of Jewish Family Life* (2005, English)[794]

Rabbi Simchah Rabinowitz, *Piskei Teshuvos, Orach Chaim 240* (2006, Hebrew)[795]

Rabbi Shalom Arosh, *B'Gan Eden Mikedem* (2008, Hebrew)[796]

Rabbi Elyashiv Knohl, *Es Dodim – A Guide to Marital Relations from a Torah Perspective* (2008, English)[797]

Rabbi Avraham Tzvi Friedman, *Otzar Halachos, Hilchos Tznius* (2009, Hebrew)[798]

Rabbi Yosef Chaim, *Compendium of Baalei HaNefesh Shaar Hakedushah, Likut Midivrei HaRambam, Igeres Hakodesh, Shulchan Aruch 240* (2010, Hebrew)[799]

Rabbi Rafael Shlanger, *Mishkan Yisrael Part 2* (2010, Hebrew)[800]

Rabbi Mordechai Eliahu, *Darchei Taharah HaShalem* (2011, Hebrew)[801]

Anonymous, *Dvar Seser* (2011-2013, Hebrew)[802]

Rabbi Yosef Yafeh, *Ashreichem Yisrael* (2013, Hebrew)[803]

Rabbi Ezra Batzri, *Dinei Ishus*, vol. 1 (2013, Hebrew)[804]

Rabbi Even-Shoshan, *Rabbi, My Husband wants a Blowjob* (2015, English)

Rabbi Even-Shoshan, *Rabbi, My Husband wants Anal Sex* (2015, English)

Rabbi Yehudah Leib Nachmanson, *Sheyekadesh Atzmo* (2015, Hebrew)[805]

# HALACHIC POSITIONS

Halachic Responsa and Other Commentary

*Otzar Haposkim, Even Haezer 25* (1965, 1971, 1982, Hebrew)

Rabbi Yehoshua Moshe Ahronson, *Yeshuos Moshe vol. 2, pp. 431-433* (1971, Hebrew)

Rabbi Moshe Feinstein, *Igros Moshe, Even Haezer vol. 1, Responsa 63-64* (1961, Hebrew)

Rabbi Moshe Feinstein, *Igros Moshe, Even Haezer vol. 3, Responsum 28* (1973, Hebrew)

Rabbi Moshe Stern, *Be'er Moshe, vol. 3, Responsa 152-153* (1973, 1984, Hebrew)

Rabbi Yitzchak Ratzabi, *Shulchan Aruch Mekutzar, 240:10* (2002, Hebrew)[806]

Rabbi Eliyahu Tauger, *Mishneh Torah, Sefer Kedushah: A new translation with commentary and notes, Isurei Biah 21:9* (2002, English)

Rabbi Yehudah Henkin, *Bnei Banim, vol. 4, Responsa 16-17-18* (2005, Hebrew)

Rabbi Yitzchak Abadi, *Or Yitzchak, vol. 2, Orach Chaim, Responsum 95* (2010, Hebrew)[807]

*Talmud – Halachah Berurah, Yevamos 34b* (Hebrew)


Studies by Orthodox-trained Rabbis (Non-Orthodox Affiliation)

Rabbi Dr. Louis Epstein, *Marriage Laws in the Bible and the Talmud* (1942, English)

Rabbi Dr. Louis Epstein, *Sex Laws and Customs in Judaism* (1948, English)

Rabbi Dr. David Feldman, *Marital Relations, Birth Control and Abortion in Jewish Law*, later renamed *Birth Control in Jewish Law* (1968, 1974, 1998, English)

Rabbi Dr. Louis Jacobs, *What Does Judaism Say About...?* (1973, English)

Rabbi Gershon Winkler, *Sacred Secrets: The Sanctity of Sex in Jewish Law and Lore* (1998, English)

APPENDICES

## Sex Above the Covers

It is commonly taught that sexual intercourse if done naked must only be performed under the covers – ideally up to the neck, but at least from the waist down.

But this "law" is not stated in any medieval works I have seen, save one, nor in any of the major codifiers.

One medieval authority calls it an act of "sanctification."[808]

Another considers it unhealthy.[809]

And one modern-day "family purity" guide refers to it as a "custom."[810]

I first had my doubts about this "legal requirement" in researching the various definitions of the term "overturning the table" on *Nedarim 20ab* (*hafichas shulchan*).

As we've seen above, in addition to the Talmud's clear ruling on *Sanhedrin 58b* permitting anal sex, according to most medieval commentaries[811] "overturning the table" also refers to anal sex – implying rear-entry anal intercourse specifically (in contrast to anal intercourse with the wife on her back, facing her husband). Rear-entry vaginal intercourse is certainly permitted even by the most stringent medieval view, Raavad III in *Baalei HaNefesh, Shaar Hakedushah*,[812] while others permit wife-on-top.[813] One opinion, Rabeinu Peretz, defines "overturning the table" as vaginal intercourse with the wife on top and facing away from her husband. The *Mefaresh* commentary to *Nedarim 20a* may be describing the same position as Rabeinu Peretz, extending it to include anal penetration.[814] And then there are the sitting and standing positions, both permitted by the letter of the law.[815]

Thus, the obvious question: Can all these positions honestly be done with the covers on? Even half on? Can we honestly believe the commentaries imagined them to be done so? Is that really even the pleasure the husband craves in all this – the position without the "view"?

Even in the case of rear-entry anal intercourse, where it is possible for the wife to lie flat down with both her and her husband completely under the covers, Rabeinu Asher in his *Peirush HaRosh* to *Nedarim 20a* – who himself interprets "overturning the table" as anal intercourse – clearly describes the position as causing the woman "inconvenience upon her knees" (*shematriach osah al arkevosehah*). Obviously he understood her to be up on all fours, which is not conducive to covering by a blanket.

So I started researching the sources, and this is what was found:

As is commonly known, the original source of the notion that naked sex should be performed under the covers is from the midrash, *Vayikra Rabah 21:8*:

# HALACHIC POSITIONS

> Rabbi Shimon ben Yochai said:
>
> There are four whom G-d abhors, and even I do not love them:
>
> 1. One who grasps hold of his shaft while urinating;[816]
> 2. One who has naked uncovered sexual intercourse (*meshamesh mitaso arum*);
> 3. One who divulges to others the private [sex] talk he had with his own wife;
> 4. One who enters a house, even his own, entirely unannounced.

Let it be noted immediately that G-d's alleged "abhorrence" of something in no way implies His "prohibition" of it, as Maimonides states unequivocally in his *Commentary to the Mishnah, Sanhedrin 7:4*, in the very context of sexual conduct within marriage.[817] Indeed, if Rabbi Shimon ben Yochai had intended these behaviors to be "forbidden" by Torah law, he could have easily made his intentions perfectly clear.[818] And if he were merely adding extra measure of "abhorrence" upon actual prohibitions, there are certainly much more heinous and "abhorrent" halachic crimes that could have been listed – first and foremost, the three cardinal sins of idolatry, murder and adultery?

Let it also be noted that all commentaries understand the phrase "naked uncovered sexual intercourse" as referring to sex *without the blankets on*, not sex without clothes on, for it is actually considered appropriate for husband and wife to make love skin-to-skin. In fact, if a husband insists against his wife's will on having sex only with clothes on, it is deemed as justifiable grounds for her to demand divorce.[819]

And Rabbi Shimon ben Yochai speaks specifically about naked uncovered sexual *intercourse*, which would not necessarily include naked uncovered *oral* sex.

Now, an alternate version of this teaching is found in the Talmud, in *Babylonian Talmud, Tractate Nidah 16b*:

> It is written in the *Book of Ben Sira*:[820]
>
> There are three I abhor, and four I do not love:
>
> 1. An official who frequents the pubs – and some say one with a loose tongue; and some say one who loses his temper
> 2. A Torah scholar who [haughtily] sets up his lessons in a place where all passersby will notice him
> 3. One who grasps hold of his shaft while urinating
> 4. One who enters the house of his friend unannounced; Rabbi Yochanan said, 'This includes entering even one's own house'"

Rabbi Shimon ben Yochai said:

> There are four behaviors which G-d abhors, and I do not love them:[821]
>
> 1. One who enters his house unannounced, and it goes without saying the house of his friend
> 2. One who grasps hold of his shaft while urinating
> 3. One who urinates naked next to his bed
> 4. One who has sex in front of others

The first thing the reader should take note of, here, is how similar the teachings of Ben Sira and Rabbi Shimon ben Yochai are. While it is possible that the two merely disagreed on the matter, it is also perhaps possible that one original teaching had evolved into two divergent versions over time.[822] This point becomes even more stark considering that Rabbi Shimon ben Yochai himself, in both places, in *Midrash Rabah* and in *Tractate Nidah*, is not only quoted as listing things he didn't like, but as listing a precise number of them. This further suggests that these two sets of teachings in the name of Rabbi Shimon ben Yochai were originally one and the same and had somehow become divergent, or that Rabbi Shimon ben Yochai himself had changed his mind on the matter at some point. Not to mention that the Talmud elsewhere, on *Pesachim 113b*, lists three entirely different behaviors that G-d is said to abhor. Clearly there was much disagreement or ambiguity about how many, and which specific, activities G-d "abhors," yet does not "forbid."

Thus, our first reaction should arguably be circumspect about implementing restrictions on behaviors that do not appear in both versions of Rabbi Shimon ben Yochai's teaching and about which we have no innate moral instinct to abhor ourselves. For while any sensitive individual would presumably abhor, or at least "not love," someone who reveals the private discussions he or she held in confidence with their spouse, or someone who urinates right next to their own bed, we have no reason to abhor or denigrate sex done naked and uncovered when such is done consensually and lovingly within marriage in complete privacy behind closed doors.[823] Therefore, even if this teaching were meant to reveal some sort of "prohibition," it could be classified as a *suspect rabbinic prohibition*, and when there is doubt concerning a rabbinic prohibition there is precedent to rule leniently (in the spirit of *safek d'rabanan l'kulah*).

In any case, *Tosfos* to *Nidah 17a* comments:

> Some versions of the Talmud, here, include "naked uncovered sexual intercourse" [in place of "urinating naked next to the bed"].

This is also the version in *Vayikra Rabah* [21:8].

And the reasoning behind it is that one should conduct oneself modestly during sex, as discussed in *Nedarim [20a]*.

In light of *Tosfos'* comment, our argument, above, to be circumspect about accepting the authenticity of the caution against "uncovered naked sexual intercourse" is possibly weaker, because it is, according to some textual versions, actually included in both places where Rabbi Shimon ben Yochai's teaching is reported – both in *Vayikra Rabah* and in *Talmud, Tractate Nidah*.

But nevertheless, according to *Tosfos*, Rabbi Shimon ben Yochai's teaching about G-d's "abhorrence" of naked uncovered sex is equivalent to Rabbi Yochanan ben Dahavai's implication about G-d's lack of love for "overturning the table," gazing at or kissing the female genitals, and non-sex-related talk during sex. In that case, being that the Sages, Rebbi, Rav and Rabbi Yochanan bar Napacha on *Nedarim 20b* all rule against Rabbi Yochanan ben Dahavai, saying instead that G-d Himself ultimately allows a couple to engage in any sexual activity they crave to explore together, and that such exploration is not considered "immodest" according to the letter of G-d's law, perhaps only according to its spirit, then Rabbi Shimon ben Yochai's teaching, too, must arguably be relegated only to the spirit of the law.

Accordingly, naked uncovered sex should be legally permitted.

And indeed it appears to be.

A perusal of Maimonides' *Mishneh Torah*, Rabbi Yaakov ben Asher's *Arbaah Turim*, and Rabbi Yosef Caro's *Shulchan Aruch* will reveal that not one of them forbade naked uncovered sex in their chapters on Jewish marital sex law.[824]

Only one medieval authority I have found, Rabbi Yisrael Alnaqua (d. 1391), in his *Menoras Hamaor*, used the word "forbidden" (*asur*) in conjunction with it.[825]

Two centuries earlier, Rabbi Avraham ben Issac of Narbonne, Raavad II (1110-1179), in his *Sefer HaEshkol, Hilchos Tznius*, categorized it as a matter of "sanctification."[826]

And the medieval author of *Likutei HaPardes* suggested it is unhealthy.[827]

The post-medieval Rabbi Eliyahu de Vidas (1518-1592), in his *Reishis Chochmah*, calls it a matter of "sanctification"[828] as well as a matter of avoiding "chutzpah."[829]

Rabbi Yaakov Emden (1697-1776), in his commentary to the prayer book, insists that a naked couple be covered with a blanket during intercourse even at night in the dark. But he does not say that to do otherwise is "forbidden" – a term he does use in seven subsequent laws there.[830]

Rabbi Chaim Yosef Dovid Azulai (Chida, 1724-1806), in his *Midbar Kedemos, Zayin:11:Zivug*, mentions that because even permitted marital sex can be prone to unholiness, one should "sanctify oneself very much, with trembling and sweat, and to cover oneself."

Rabbi Yisrael Meir Kagen (1839-1933), in his *Mishnah Berurah, Orach Chaim 240:8:36* echoes *Tosfos* that it is an issue of "modesty," but does not specify if it is obligatory.

And as mentioned, one modern-day "family purity" guide calls it just a "custom."[831]

Again, even if we are to accept Rabbi Shimon ben Yochai's teaching about that which G-d abhors, we need only look back to Maimonides' *Commentary on the Mishnah, Sanhedrin 7:4*, where, in discussing the Sages' definite preference for "sanctified" sexual behavior within marriage, he still maintains that:

> This does not contradict the principle of the Sages that we opened with, that anything a husband craves to do with his wife sexually he may do, because the question of what is forbidden versus permissible is not the same as the question of what is distasteful versus pleasing and beloved and how one should strive for the path of modesty and extreme moderation.[832]

See also Rabbi Yehuda Henkin's *Bnei Banim, vol. 4, Responsum 17:5*, that based on the *Hakdamas HaZohar* even Rabbi Shimon ben Yochai himself could be said to permit naked sex completely uncovered so long as it's performed in a dark room.[833]

Now, there are those who will counter that according to another teaching brought in Jewish law, we are told not even to dress or undress at any time outside the covers, so as not to reveal any normally covered skin. How, then, they might argue, could it possibly be permitted to have sex entirely naked without any blanket on at all?

The answer:

Firstly, as discussed at length above, there are many things that are permitted during physical intimacy of husband and wife that may not be permitted, or at least not encouraged, at other times, such as "excess light-headed talk" needed to arouse a spouse to the mood, all kinds of arousing behaviors for both husband and wife, and even certain cases of extra-vaginal ejaculation.

But quite aside from all that, the notion of not dressing or undressing outside the covers is, again, not a matter of law, but of piety.

We can actually deduce this from Rabbi Shimon ben Yochai's own teaching above – for if nakedness in general were in fact "legally forbidden," there would have been no need for him to tell us about G-d's alleged "abhorrence" of naked uncovered sex specifically.

But logical deductions aside, the actual source for this notion is *Babylonian Talmud, Tractate Shabbos 118b*, where Rabbi Yossi is quoted saying: "My entire life, the walls of my house did not see the seams of my shirt." Rabbi Shlomoh Yitzchaki, Rashi, explains this to mean that he would cover himself with his blanket when removing his shirt so as not to expose any normally covered skin – this, Rashi tells us, as a matter of "modesty."

Now, before examining how this teaching is discussed among the later legal authorities, we must first be clear about its context in the Talmud itself, for it is brought back-to-back with another quote of Rabbi Yossi: "My entire life I never gazed at my membrum." Rashi, on this quote of Rabbi Yossi, says clearly that this was an expression of his "extreme modesty," and Maimonides presents the quote in similar context when he writes:

> *One of the great sages and original pious ones* prided himself in having never gazed at his own membrum.[834]

Rabbi Yosef Caro, in his *Shulchan Aruch*,[835] repeats Maimonides' wording.[836]

And Maimonides maintains this context of piety even in regard to Rabbi Yossi's comment about dressing or undressing under the covers, for he writes:

> *Torah sages* accustom themselves to *extreme modesty . . .* they do not uncover their heads or bodies.[837]

Maimonides clearly does not expect such modesty from the average individual.

Even in the *Tur*[838] and *Shulchan Aruch*[839] where Rabbi Yossi's comment about dressing or undressing under the covers is brought, it is never stated as an obligation. It is apparently one of those cases we described in our introduction[840] where the legal codifiers carefully chose their words, precisely saying "*Do not* get dressed in a sitting position..." rather than "*It is forbidden* to get dressed in a sitting position..."

Thus, the reader must be aware that Rabbi Yossi's teaching about not dressing or undressing outside the covers is coming from a pietistic, individualistic source, not a baseline legal one for the masses.

Rabbi Schneur Zalman of Liadi, in his revised *Code of Jewish Law* known as *Shulchan Aruch HaRav*, provides two editions of this law.

Chapter 2 of his first edition reads:

> 1. Because a person is obligated to have the awe of his Creator upon himself at all times, he should be modest in all his ways, for modesty and shame (*boshes*) foster submission before G-d.
>
> Therefore, if someone sleeps naked without an undershirt, when he arises *it is good to be careful* (*tov lizaher*) not to first sit and then put on his undershirt...[841]

## APPENDICES

Rabbi Schneur Zalman says, here, only that avoiding uncovered nakedness is "good," not that it is "obligatory" – and this in spite of his extollation of both "modesty" and "shame," and what he calls an "obligation" to keep the awe of the Creator upon oneself at all times.

In Chapter 2 of his second edition, Rabbi Schneur Zalman writes:

> 1. The trait of modesty is praised in Scripture in many places, and the Sages *instructed* all people to be modest in all their ways (*vachachamim tzivu l'chol adam lihiyos tzanua b'chol orchosav*) . . .
>
> Therefore, one should not reveal even a little skin that is normally always covered in clothing, and even when he is sleeping in bed at night all his [normally covered] skin should be covered by a sheet (*lachen, lo yegaleh es bsaro, va'afilu me'at col mah shedarco lihiyos mechuseh b'begadim l'olam, va'afilu c'sheyashen al mitaso balailah yechaseh col besaro basadin*) . . .
>
> 2. Similarly, when he removes his clothes and undershirt to sleep naked in bed, he should be careful (*yizaher*) to cover each part of his skin with the sheet before he undresses it, such that once he does undress that part it is already covered by the sheet, and thus not even a single part of his [normally covered] skin will be revealed *for no reason* (*shelo letzorech*) even for a single moment.
>
> (So too, one who does not sleep naked, but only without pants (sic), he should first cover his legs with the sheet and then remove his pants under the sheet.)
>
> And similarly, when he gets up in the morning, he should put on his undershirt little by little underneath the sheet while he is still laying down, such that even a small amount of his [normally covered] skin will not be revealed even for a single moment *for no reason* . . .
>
> (So, too, with our pants: he should put them on little by little underneath the sheet in order not to reveal his legs – for in these countries [i.e., 18th-19th century Eastern Europe] it is customary that they are always covered, for people do not go barelegged ever, even in summer.)[842]

In this edition, Rabbi Schneur Zalman no longer writes that it is only "good to be careful" not to reveal normally covered skin. But now his preliminary statement in regard to nakedness in general, that "the Sages instructed all people to be modest in all their ways," does not appear to have a known source:

The footnotes added in by later publishers, which point to *Babylonian Talmud, Tractate Brachos 8b* and *62a* appear to be unclear, for no such rabbinic "commandment" is found on those pages, only more stories of the *personal* extreme modesty of the Sages themselves. *Brachos 8b* does not even discuss the

Sages' own acts of modesty, but rather only one particular sage's predilection for certain "modest" customs of the *Persians*.

[And see *Talmud, Kesubos 48a*, mentioning the Persian custom to only have sex while fully clothed, and denigrating it as a practice that is contrary to Torah's – G-d's – way for the average couple.]

In both editions, the footnotes to this law that were penned by Rabbi Schneur Zalman himself, or by his scholarly brother, Rabbi Yehudah Leib, make reference only to *Talmud, Tractate Shabbos 118* and *Tur, Orach Chaim 139*, which we already know are both in the context of Rabbi Yossi's extreme level of modesty beyond that of the average person.

And even where Rabbi Schneur Zalman explains in detail how to avoid revealing even the minutest amount of skin for even a single moment, he adds that one should not reveal such skin *"for no reason."* But in the case of sexual intimacy between husband and wife, there are behaviors that are not always conducive to being covered by a blanket – such as oral sex and a variety of sex positions – that are permitted by G-d to accommodate the natural human sex drive He Himself created. In other words, this temporary nakedness IS for a reason: to provide both husband and wife their sexual needs and fulfillment, and their resulting vulnerability and bonding, within the context of a loving devoted marriage.

Finally, and most importantly, see Rabbi Yosef Teomim, in his *Pri Megadim, Mishbetzos Zahav*, to *Shulchan Aruch, Orach Chaim 2:1*, who states clearly that this entire teaching about dressing or undressing under the covers applies only to Torah scholars, who practice extreme modesty, but not to average human beings, who are not careful about nakedness in general and for whom **"there is no such prohibition"** (*mashma she'ar adam misgalim gufam . . . mashma gam kein lachasidus, u'she'ar col adam ein isur*).

See also Rabbi Moshe Feinstein, *Igros Moshe, Yoreh Deah 3, Responsum 68:4*, page 316:

> The concept of modesty for men, to go out in public [only] with their bodies fully covered, does not stem from a matter of legal prohibition, but from a [pious] ideal and care (*eino mei'isurim eleh maaleh u'zehirus*) to be fully dressed even in private stemming from an awareness that one is always in the presence of G-d . . .
>
> For the same reason, when they were accustomed to sleeping naked at night, covered only by a sheet, this ideal would necessitate removing one's shirt under the sheet . . . and putting one's shirt back on under the sheet . . . And so must one take care to do if he is able to.
>
> But [in public,] the rule of [halachically required] dress [for men] follows the local accepted norms . . .

But it is forbidden [for a man] to go with genitals exposed [in front of other men at times other than when he is bathing], for even when bathing in the river it is good to cover [one's genitals outside the water] when he is facing others, in a manner that he does not actually touch them [his genitals] with his hands, as discussed in *Talmud, Shabbos 44*. And in his bedroom, even with no one else around, he must cover them, such as to go around with underwear. And there is also a prohibition [to go with them uncovered even in private] because then one cannot dwell on thoughts of Torah. But for medical purposes even this [to go completely naked in private] is permitted.[843]

According to Rabbi Feinstein, then, when one is in private there is no prohibition to change one's clothing outside the covers; the only possible legal prohibition would be to sit or walk around with one's genitals exposed. But even this prohibition is only on account of concerns about Torah study – which arguably does not apply to a woman most of the time, and arguably does not apply to either husband or wife during sexual intimacy ever. And in any case, for the sake of health – which, if we may be realistic about human nature and frailty, should include psychological-emotional-physical-spiritual balance resulting from the sexual fulfillment of either spouse, and the resultant health of their marriage and general family life as a whole – complete nakedness during sexual intimacy should arguably be permitted for those who feel the honest need for it.

However, this entire discussion about naked sexual intercourse above the covers is presuming it is done in the darkness of night or in a darkened room during the day.[844] But if the room is lit up at night or by day, a couple would perhaps be required to darken it or keep their bodies partially or entirely covered, or perhaps avoid sexual intercourse altogether.[845] [LVI**]

Look for our future study on that topic, and additional topics, in upcoming volumes of this series.

---

[LVI**] **Added note to the third edition:** See the ruling of Rabbi Yosef Messas (1892-1794) in his *Mayim Chaim, Responsum 97*, that with modern advances in matters of hygiene, it is permissible **on occasion, randomly in the heat of passion (*b'akrai*)**, for any husband and wife who desire the sight of each other's bodies during intercourse to have sex during the day or night in a perfectly lit room, even without covering themselves head to toe – on the logic that such is certainly no worse than intra-anal ejaculation, which, Rabbi Messas says, is also permitted within marriage on occasion, randomly in the heat of passion. Rabbi Messas does not specify if the genitals, or any other specific body parts, must be covered for foreplay or intercourse on such an occasion. Credit goes to Rabbi Eliezer Melamed for bringing this source to my attention in his *Simchat Habayit v'Birchato* (second edition, 2015), page 64, end of footnote 21. See also pp. 55-57, there, and footnote 16 thereon.

And see Rabbi Maor Kayam's *Harchavot l'Simchat Habayit v'Birchato* (2015), page 148, concluding as well that a blanket covering during intercourse, at least in a dark room, is a pious custom rather than a legal obligation.

## A Word about Rabbinic Fallibility

In the course of our study, we have seen predictions, or cautions, reported in the names of certain ancient sages attributing severe congenital illnesses in children to common sexual behaviors between loving spouses within marriage.

My sincere apologies go to my readers for having had to endure reference to such predictions/cautions repeatedly in the course of our study – and especially to parents who have valiantly raised children suffering such conditions, and most of all to those who have courageously and heroically lived with such conditions themselves.

As we have seen, most of the Talmudic and medieval sages did not believe in these predictions/cautions.

At the same time, I do not believe that rabbinic fallibility in matters of science in particular need create any fundamental crisis of faith in Torah. There are ample sources in medieval rabbinic writing that admit the Talmudic sages did not possess perfect scientific knowledge, but rather, much like rabbis today, they sometimes consulted the science of the day in their conception of the natural universe and its interface with Jewish law and philosophy.[LVI]

On this topic, I would recommend all readers explore the erudite studies of Rabbi Nathan Slifkin available online at RationalistJudaism.com, and especially the *Introduction* and *Chapter 16: The Spontaneous Sweat Louse* of his *Sacred Monsters* (Zoo Torah, 2007-2011). See also his essay, *The Sun's Path at Night*, which he has made available for viewing online.[846]

And see Rabbi Yehudah Levi's *The Science in Torah: The Scientific Knowledge of the Talmudic Sages* (Feldheim 2004).

To add some possible additional angles **for further research and discussion**, let us borrow an analogy from civil law:

If a rabbinic judge makes a ruling in a legal case based upon the evidence and testimony before him, and then the next day new evidence comes to light, or a flaw is found in the prior evidence, or one of the witnesses is suddenly found to be false, the judge would presumably change his ruling – and his doing so would create no fundamental crisis of faith in the truth of Torah. On the contrary, the fact that Torah – G-d – would obligate him to do justice and alter his previous ruling is a confirmation of Torah's – G-d's – interest in truth at all costs, even if it means the judge having to exhibit the humility to recognize that, for whatever reason, G-d in His great mysterious wisdom chose to withhold all the facts from him in the past.

---

[LVI] And who is to say that the science of today, which has been applied to modern questions of Jewish law and philosophy, and even mysticism, will not be found to be incomplete tomorrow.

Still, the judge himself did everything correctly in line with G-d's, and our, expectations of him: he issued his original ruling based on a faithful analysis of the evidence before him at the time. But when all is said and done, by Torah's – G-d's – own acknowledgment, a proper analysis of the available information, and a valid conclusion issued based upon it, does not always equal an **absolutely true** ruling – at least not when new evidence comes to light, when evidence is subsequently disqualified, or when witnesses are subsequently proven false. In such cases, once the facts come to light the ruling must be changed.

Similarly, if we may be so bold, Torah sages throughout history sought the testimony of science – the science of their day – to help them apply Torah's wisdom in all its facets – legal, ethical and/or mystical. Thus, as science refines its "testimony" – proving that its past evidence was incomplete, incorrect, or that it was provided by "false witnesses" – G-d arguably expects Torah scholars to take that new testimony into account, evaluate it, and, if truth be their goal, revise the law or philosophy that was built upon it.[LVII]

---

[LVII] Perhaps another way of expressing this: In the way G-d has interacted with His creation throughout history, it is evident that He Himself chooses to make a distinction between that which might be the **absolute truth (that is, the absolute comprehension) of reality and Torah** and that which might be His interim will for an individual, a community, the Jewish nation, or the world as a whole **to believe in and/or obey for a given time and in a given place**. G-d manifests this interim will by means of limiting or expanding the amount of information He makes available to the living Torah scholars of each generation and the degree of insight He bestows upon them (as well as the practical ability He grants them to articulate, communicate and/or disseminate that information/insight). This cycle continues until G-d is ready to reveal His absolute truth of reality and Torah to the whole of humanity in the Messianic Age (see below, endnotes 847, 848; and see our next point in regard to the prophets).

As for why G-d would do such a thing, to allow absolute truth to go unknown for so long, and even among the keepers and teachers of His Torah, such a question would be no different than any of the other great mysteries of the human condition. Indeed, the same question would have to be asked as to why G-d allowed the whole world to go without Torah itself for over two thousand years between Adam and Moses.

And to expand the question into other areas of Jewish law:

The one commandment in the Torah that supersedes all others is the saving of human life. Yet for the vast majority of human history, G-d, in His mysterious ways, chose to keep scholars of all nations, including those of the Jews, unaware of the medical secrets that would have allowed them to perform this commandment effectively. And with all the medical intelligence He has bestowed upon mankind today, He still withholds more.

In regard to the fallibility of the Sanhedrin itself, see *Talmud, Tractate Horayot*. And see *Rabbinical Authority and Personal Autonomy* (Rabbi Isaac Elchanan Theological Seminary, 1992), Chapter One by Lawrence Kaplan, *Daas Torah: A Modern Conception of Rabbinic Authority*, pp. 28-46.

And note that the Talmud does not hide the fact that not every Talmudic sage had access even to the entire gamut of the Oral Torah tradition before being authorized to teach it. See, for example, *Zevachim 96b*, the episode of Rabbi Yitzchak bar Yehudah and Rami bar Chama.

But let us take this argument yet further.

Even if the Talmudic sages' statements on science were spoken out of some learned derivation from Torah or some direct divine revelation by angels or the Creator Itself, by no means would this necessarily make their statements on such matters clear articulations of absolute truth either.

Maimonides writes that when the Sanhedrin derives the details of Jewish law by way of *interpreting* biblical verse, their derivations are not absolute and can be superseded by the understanding and interpretation of a later Sanhedrin (see *Mishneh Torah, Sefer Shoftim, Memrim 2:1* – to be explored further in volume two of this series). If such is the case in regard to the Sanhedrin's interpretations in matters of practical Jewish law – i.e., G-d's will – it should arguably also be the case, and even more so, in regard to statements of the Talmudic sages about science or metaphysics (or philosophy or psychology or history, etcetera) that they based on biblical interpretation.

As far as divine revelation is concerned, Maimonides explains that, other than Moses himself, the prophets did not necessarily see their prophecies with perfect clarity, but rather they experienced dreams or visions of parables requiring interpretation – and such prophecies included not just predictions of the future, but knowledge of the science of creation as well (see *Mishneh Torah, Sefer Hamada, Yesodei HaTorah 7*). Although Maimonides states that G-d helped the prophets interpret the messages of their visions, it is not clear at all that this meant they understood all the detailed historical facets that would unfold in their predictions or that they fathomed the absolute profundity of all the math, biology, chemistry or physics (or metaphysics) underlying their elevated perceptions of reality.[846'] This is especially so considering that whatever G-d might have revealed to any given prophet in matters of the natural world would have been comprehended by him or her, and expressed by them, according to the limits of their own frames of reference and vocabulary.[LVIII]

---

[LVIII] See Rashi's commentary to Numbers 30:2, quoting *Sifri 153*, acknowledging the difference in perception/articulation between Moses' prophecies and those of all other prophets (see the explanation of Rabbi Eliyahu Mizrachi on this, referenced in the Mosad HaRav Kook *Toras Chaim* edition of Numbers 30:2, Rashi, footnote 6).

Add to this the rabbinic principle that "G-d speaks in language that man relates to" (*dibrah Torah c'lashon bnei adam*) – that even G-d's own choice of wording is tailored to be meaningful to each prophet in his or her time and place.

And see *Mishneh Torah, Sefer Shoftim, Melachim 12:1* for a further angle relevant to this point.

**Added note to the third edition:** See also the medieval commentary of Rabbi Levi ben Gershon ("Ralbag," 1288-1384) to the Book of Job, beginning of Chapter 40, *Biur divrei hamaaneh*, where in the midst of a long discussion Ralbag asserts that if a prophet has a preconceived false belief about the nature of reality, that false belief is liable to color his prophetic vision:

Additionally, the fact that a certain specific prophecy might have elevated a certain individual prophet's perception of the natural universe in no way means that in that one revelation G-d had communicated to him or her the totality of the secrets of creation or even the totality of one field of science.

The implication of all this is that neither the predictions nor the scientific (or metaphysical) outlooks of the prophets were necessarily perfectly perceived or articulated by them – and how much more so the predictions or scientific (or metaphysical) outlooks of the Talmudic sages (and Torah scholars thereafter), whom we have no reason to believe ever attained the level of divine perception of the prophets. Rather, just as we must rely on the unfolding of human history, including non-Jewish history in all its facets, for us to properly unravel the complete meaning of G-d's messages to the prophets and Talmudic sages in the realm of prediction, so too must we rely on the unfolding of human inquiry, including non-Jewish scientific discovery, to come to a complete understanding of G-d's revelation to the prophets and Talmudic sages in the realm of the nature of reality.

We might say, then, that G-d intentionally gave the keys of scientific wisdom into the hands of the non-Jewish nations (*chochmah bagoyim taamin*) while He entrusted the principles of divine wisdom into the hands of the Jewish people, so that they would all one day come to realize their need for, and dependence upon, one another – and most importantly, they would actualize their united mission and purpose within creation: to marry their G-d-given wisdoms together in the pursuit of truth, the knowledge of G-d,[847] the new Torah revelations of the Messianic Age.[848]

---

...*V'yoser zar mizeh, shecvar yagia l'navi davar cozeiv b'eis hanevuah b'mah she'ein lo mitzad shehu navi, mitzad hadeos asher lo b'inyonim hahem, c'mo ha'inyan b'Yechezkel, shehigiya lo b'nevuah c'ilu hagalgalim mechadshim kolos b'tnuasam, mipnei shehaya maamin shehagalgalim yechadshu kolos b'tnuoseihem, c'mo shezachar haRav haMoreh...*

Credit goes to Rabbi Simcha Feuerman for bringing this source in Ralbag's commentary to my attention.

# Timeline of Rabbinic Authorities

*In lieu of bibliography, we present here a chronological list of the medieval and post-medieval rabbinic authorities referenced in this book, as well as the works they authored that are referenced and/or the acronyms by which they are commonly known*

## Medieval

R. Saadiah Gaon (*Arabic Commentary on the Bible*) – 882-942

R. Sherira Gaon (*Igeres Rav Sherira Gaon*) – 906-1006

R. Chananel (*Rabeinu Chananel*) – 990-1053

R. Yitzchak Alfasi (*Rif*) – 1013-1103

R. Shlomoh Yitzchaki (*Rashi*) – 1040-1105

R. Shmuel ben Meir (*Rashbam*) c.1085-c.1158

R. Avraham ben Meir Ibn Ezra (*Ibn Ezra*) 1089-c.1167

R. Simchah ben Shmuel of Vitri (*Machzor Vitri*) – died 1105

R. Yaakov ben Meir (*Rabeinu Tam*) – 1100-1171

R. Eliezer of Metz (*Re'em, Sefer Yeraim*) – died 1175

R. Avraham ben Yitzchak (*Raavad II, Sefer HaEshkol*) – 1110-1179

R. Zerachiah Halevi of Gerona (*Hasagos al Baalei HaNefesh*) – 1115-1186

R. Avraham ben Dovid, (*Raavad III, Baalei HaNefesh*) – 1120-1197

R. Yitzchak of Dampierre (*Rabeinu Yitzchak, Ri, Tosfos*) – 1120-1200

R. Moshe ben Maimon (*Maimonides, Rambam, Commentary to the Mishnah, Mishneh Torah, Moreh HaNevuchim*) – 1135-1204

R. Yehudah bar Kalonymous of Speyer (*Erchei Tannaim v'Amoriam*) – 12th century

R. Eliezer of Beaugency (*Peirush Rabbi Eliezer Mibalganzi*) – 12th century

R. Yosef Bechor Shor of Orleans (*Peirush al HaTorah*) – 12th century

[R. Meyuchas ben Eliyahu (*Peirush Rabeinu Meyuchas*) – 12th/15th century]

R. Yehudah the Pious (*Rabbi Yehudah Hachasid, Sefer Chasidim*) – 1150-1217

R. David Kimchi (*Radak*) – 1160-1235

R. Avraham Hayarchi (*Commentary to Callah Rabti*) – 1155-1215

R. Meir Abulafia (*Yad Ramah*) – 1170-1240

## APPENDICES

R. Elazar of Worms (*Sefer HaRokeach, Peirush HaRokeach al HaTorah*) – c.1176-1238

R. Yeshayah of Trani I (*Rid*) 1180-1250

R. Yonah ben Avraham of Gerona (*Rabeinu Yonah, Sefer Hayirah*) – 1180-1263

R. Yitzchak ben Moshe of Vienna (*Or Zarua*) – c.1185-c.1260

R. Moshe ben Nachman (*Ramban, Peirush Ramban al HaTorah, Kisvei Ramban*) – 1194-1270

R. Netanel ben Yeshaya of Yemen (*Maor Ha'afelah*) – c. early 13th century

R. Yitzchak of Carcassonne (*Peirush R. Yitzchak Karkosha al HaRif*) – 13th century

R. Tanchum Hayerushalmi (*Sefer Hamaspik*) – 13th century

R. Peretz ben Eliyahu of Corbeil (*Rabeinu Peretz*) – died c. 1295

R. Yeshayah of Trani II (*Riaz*) – 1235-1300

R. Menachem Hameiri (*Beis HaBechirah*) – 1249-1306

R. Mordechai ben Hillel Hakohen (*Mordechai*) – 1250-1298

R. Yitzchak ben Yosef of Corbeil (*Sefer Mitzvot Katan*) – 13th century

R. Avigdor of France (*Rabeinu Avigdor Tzarfati, Peirushim uPsakim al HaTorah*) – 13th century

R. Moshe de Leon (the first to circulate copies of the *Zohar*) – 1250-1305

R. Avraham ben Yitzchak of Montpellier (*Peirush R. Avraham min Hahar*) – d.1315

R. Asher ben Yechiel (*Rabeinu Asher, Rosh*) – c.1250-1327

R. Meir Hacohen of Rothenburg (*Hagahos Maimonios*) – c.1260-1298

R. Aharon Hacohen of Lunil (*Orchos Chaim*) – 13th-14th century

R. Yaakov ben Asher (*Arbaah Turim, Tur*) – c. 1269-c. 1343

R. Alexander Suslin Hakohen (*HaAgudah*) – died 1349

R. Yeruchem ben Meshulam (*Rabeinu Yeruchem*) – c.1280-c.1350

R. Levi ben Gershon (*Ralbag*) – 1288-1344

R. Menachem Ibn Zerach (*Tzeidah Laderech*) – 1310-1385

R. Nissim ben Reuven of Gerona (*Rabeinu Nissim, Ran*) – 1320-1376

R. Yom Tov ibn Asevilli (*Ritva*) – c.1320

R. Yisrael Alnaqua (*Menoras Hamaor*) – died c. 1390

R. Yitzchak Aboab (*Menoras Hamaor*) – 14th century

## HALACHIC POSITIONS

R. Shmuel ben Meshulam Yerondi (*Ohel Moed*) – 14th century

R. Yitzchak ben Sheshes (*Shaalos uTeshuvos Rivash*) – 1326-1408

R. Shimon ben Tzemach Duran (*Tashbatz, Ohev Mishpat*) – 1361-1444

R. Yitzchak ben Yehudah Abravanel – 1437-1508

R. Yaakov ben Yehudah Landau (*HaAgur*) – died 1493

[R. Meyuchas ben Eliyahu (*Peirush Rabeinu Meyuchas*) – 12th/15th century]

R. Ovadiah ben Avraham Bartenura (*Peirush R. Ovadia Bartenura*) c.1445-c.1515

R. Eliyahu Mizrachi (*Re'em*) – c.1455-c.1525

Post-Medieval to Present

R. Yosef Caro (*Kesef Mishneh, Beis Yosef, Bedek Habayis, Shulchan Aruch*) – 1488-1575

R. Moshe of Trani (*Kiryas Sefer*) – 1505-1585

R. Shlomoh Luria (*Yam Shel Shlomoh*) – 1510-1573

R. Eliyahu de Vidas (*Reishis Chochmah*) – 1518-1592

R. Moshe Isserles (*Rema*)– 1520-1572

R. Betzalel Ashkenazi (*Shitah Mekubetzes*) – c.1520-c.1592

R. Yehudah Loew (*Maharal, Nesivos Olam*) – c.1520-1609

R. Mordechai Yoffe (*Levush*) – c.1530-1612

R. Elazar Azikri (*Sefer Charedim*) – 1533-1600

R. Yitzchak Luria (*Kisvei HaArizal*) – 1534-1572

R. Yehoshua Falk (*Drishah, Prishah*) – 1555-1614

R. Avraham de Boton (*Lechem Mishneh*) – c.1560-c.1605

R. Yoel Sirkis (*Bayis Chadash, Bach*) – 1561-1640

R. Yeshayah Horowitz (*Shnei Luchos Habris*) – 1565-1630

R. Yosef Yuspa Hahn Nordlinger (*Yosef Ometz*) – d. 1637

R. Yom Tov Lipman Heller (*Lechem Chamudos*) – c.1579-1654

R. Moshe Rivkash (*Be'er Hagolah*) – 1591-1671

R. Moshe Leima (*Chelkas Mechokek*) – 1604-1658

R. Shlomoh Algazi (*Gufei Halachos*) – 1610-1683

R. Aharon Shmuel Kaidanover (*Maharshak*) – 1614-1676

## APPENDICES

R. Gur Aryeh HaLevi Finzi (*Gur Aryeh*) – 17th century

R. Tzvi Hakohen Katz (*Nachlas Tzvi*) – 17th century

R. Shmuel Feivush (*Beis Shmuel*) – 1640-1700

R. Eliyahu Hacohen (*Midrash Talpios*) - c.1659-1729

R. Eliyahu Spira (*Elyah Rabah*) - 1660-1712

R. Yaakov Reischer (*Iyun Yaakov*) – 1661-1733

R. Elazar Rokeach of Amsterdam (*Arbaah Turei Even*) – c.1665-1742

R. Meir Eisenstadt (*Panim Meiros*) – 1670-1744

R. Yitzchak Lampronti (*Pachad Yitzchak*) – 1679-1756

R. Yisrael Baal Shem Tov – c.1698-1760

R. David Altschuler (*Metzudas David, Metzudas Tzion*) - 1687-1769

R. Yaakov Emden (*Yaavetz*) – 1697-1776

R. Malachi ben Yaakov Hacohen (*Yad Malachi*) – 1700-1771

R. Dovber of Mezritch (*Maggid of Mezritch, Or HaEmes*) – d.1772

R. Aharon Alfandri (*Yad Aharon*) – 1700-1774

R. Moshe Chaim Luzzato (*Mesilas Yesharim, Derech Hashem*) – 1707-1746

R. Elimelech of Lizhensk (*Noam Elimelech*) – 1717-1787

R. Eliyahu Kramer (*Vilna Gaon, Biur HaGra*) 1720-1797

R. Chaim Yosef David Azulai (*Chida, Kisei Rachamim, Birchei Yosef, Pesach Einaim, Pnei David*) – 1724-1806

R. Yosef Teomim (*Pri Megadim*) – 1727–1792

R. Yehudah Ashkenazi (*Be'er Heitev*) – 1730-1770

R. Noach Chaim Tzvi Berlin (*Atzei Arazim*) – 1734-1802

R. Levi Yitzchak of Berditchev (*Or HaEmes*) – 1740-1809

R. Avraham "HaMalach" – 1740-1777

R. Schneur Zalman of Liadi (*Shulchan Aruch HaRav, Tanya, Igeres Hateshuvah, Igeres Hakodesh*) – 1745-1812

R. Yaakov Yitzchak Horowitz (*Chozeh-Seer of Lublin*) – 1745-1815

R. Avraham Danzig (*Chochmas Adam*) – 1748-1820

R. Avraham Yehoshua Heschel of Apta (*Oheiv Yisrael*) – 1748-1825

R. Moshe Sofer (*Chasam Sofer*) – 1762-1839

## HALACHIC POSITIONS

R. Tzvi Hirsch of Ziditchev (*Sur Mera*) – 1763-1831

R. Avraham Dovid Wahrman of Buczacz (*Eshel Avraham, Ezer Mekudash, Mili d'Chasidusa, Birchas David*) – 1770-1840

R. Dovber Schneuri (*Pokeach Ivrim*) – 1773-1827

R. Yaakov Meshulam Orenstein (*Yeshuos Yaakov*) – 1775-1839

R. Nosson of Breslov (*Likutei Eitzot*) – 1780-1844

R. Tzvi Elimelech Shapiro of Dinov (*Derech Pikudecha*) – 1783-1841

R. Shmaryahu Brandeis (*Rosh Pinah-Ikvei Habayis*) – 19th century

R. Ze'ev Wolf Einhorn of Grodno/Vilna (*Maharzu*) – d.1862

R. Menachem Mendel Schneersohn (*Tzemach Tzedek, Derech Mitzvosecha*) – 1789-1866

R. Chaim Halberstam of Sanz (*Divrei Chaim*) – 1793-1876

R. David Luria (*Radal*) – 1798-1855

R. Shlomoh Ganzfried (*Kitzur Shulchan Aruch*) – 1804-1886

R. Meir Leibush (*Malbim*) – 1809-1879

R. Avraham Tzvi Hirsch Eisenstadt (*Pischei Teshuvah*) – 1812-1868

R. Naftali Tzvi Yehudah Berlin (*Netziv, Meromei Sadeh, Meishiv Davar*) – 1816-1893

Rabbi Elazar Moshe Horowitz (Chief Rabbi of Pinsk) – 1817-1890

R. Yechiel Michel Epstein (*Aruch Hashulchan*) – 1829-1908

R. Schneur Zalman Fradkin (*Toras Chesed*) – 1830-1902

R. Shlomoh Yehudah Tabak (*Erech Shai*) – 1830-1907

R. Chaim Chizkiyahu Medini (*Sdei Chemed*) – 1833-1905

R. Yosef Chaim (*Ben Ish Chai*) – 1835-1909

R. Yisrael Meir Kagan (*Mishnah Berurah-Biur Halachah*) – 1838-1933

R. Eliyahu David Rabinowitz-Teomim (*Aderes, Machshirei Mitzvah*) – 1843-1905

R. Yaakov Chaim Sofer (*Kaf Hachaim*) – 1870-1939

R. Elchanan Bunim Wasserman (*Kovetz Shiurim*) – 1874-1941

R. Yosef Messas (*Mayim Chaim*) – 1892-1974

R. Avraham Yitzchak Kook (*Ezras Cohen, Shmoneh Kovtzim*) – 1865-1935

R. Yosef Yitzchak Schneersohn (*Sefer HaSichos, Igros Kodesh*) – 1880-1950

R. Yosef Eliyahu Henkin – 1881-1973

## APPENDICES

R. Avraham Shimon Engel-Horowitz of Zelichov (*Naharei Eish*) – 1886-1943

R. Reuven Margolis (*Mekor Chesed, Nitzutzei Ohr*) – 1889-1971

R. Moshe Feinstein (*Igrot Moshe*) – 1895-1986

R. Yisrael Yaakov Kanievsky (*Steipler Gaon; Karyana d'Igarta*) – 1899-1985

R. Yechiel Michel Gold (*M'aseif l'Chol Hamachanos*) – 1899-1944

R. Menachem Mendel Schneerson (*Likutei Sichos, Teshuvos uBiurim, Igros Kodesh, Hadranim al HaRambam*) – 1902-1994

R. Moshe Stern (*Be'er Moshe*) – 1914-1997

R. Yosef Kapach – 1917-2000

R. Ovadia Yosef (*Yabia Omer*) – 1920-2013

R. Shmaryahu Yosef Chaim Kanievsky (*Biur to Callah Rabti*) – b.1928

R. Mordechai Eliyahu (*Darchei Taharah*) – 1929-2010

R. Yitzchak Abadi (*Ohr Yitzchak*) – b.1933

R. Adin Steinsaltz – (*Steinsaltz Edition of the Talmud*) – b.1937

R. Yehuda Henkin (*Bnei Banim*) – b.1945

R. Yitzchak Ratzabi (*Shulchan Aruch Hamekutzar*) – b.1953

R. Eliezer Melamed (*Simchat Habayit v'Birchato*) – b. 1961

R. Chaim Rapoport (*Judaism and Homosexuality*) – b. 1963

# Endnotes

[1] See, for example, *Tosfos Yeshanim* and Rabbi Eliezer of Metz (Re'em) to *Babylonian Talmud, Nedarim 20b*, quoted below, p. 68.

[2] See, for example, the views of *Raavad III* in *Baalei HaNefesh, Shaar Hakedushah* and of the anonymous author of *Igeres Hakodesh* (attributed by some to Nachmanides). See below, endnotes 10, 429. See also below, page 152 and endnote 595.

[3] See, for example, the view of Maimonides expressed in his *Commentary to the Mishnah, Sanhedrin 7:4* and in his *Mishneh Torah, Sefer Kedushah, Isurei Biah 21:9*, and contrast these with his words in *Mishneh Torah, Sefer Hamada, Deos 5:4-5*. And contrast all these with his philosophical views in *Guide for the Perplexed* (see below, endnote 419).

[3*] I am referring here, of course, to the vagina specifically, not the actual waist or legs or feet.

[4] Rabbi Moshe Isserles, *Rema*, in *Shulchan Aruch, Even Haezer, 25:2*.

[5] *Beis Shmuel* to *Shulchan Aruch, Even Haezer, 25:2*.

[6] See our discussion below, pp. 167-168.

[7] See Rabbi Elazar of Worms in his *Rokeach, Hilchos Chasidus* (quoted also in *Kovetz Shitos Kamai, Shabbos 118b*, p. 602), where, in discussing the concept of "sanctifying oneself in that which is permitted," he recalls the example of the House of Raban Gamliel. *Babylonian Talmud, Tractate Beitzah 21b* tells us that the members of the House of Raban Gamliel were stringent upon themselves in Jewish law, but lenient upon the rest of the Jewish people. Rabbi Elazar also emphasizes that an "important person" (*adam chashuv*) is in a different category than the masses.

Of course, his intention, there, is to identify what kind of person should choose to be extra pious. But the reverse implication is that what might be appropriate for a leader of the people is not necessarily appropriate for anyone else.

[8] As far as concerns that this material might fall into the hands of teenagers, let it be noted that the Talmud and midrashim themselves are full of sexual passages, involving both the permitted and the forbidden, the normal and the perverse. And in the case of the Talmud, these passages have by now all been translated into English and other languages by the Soncino, Steinsaltz and Artscroll Talmud series – which means they are also all perfectly accessible to your teenage son or daughter. But teenagers will not necessarily know how to coalesce them.

And curious teenagers will generally find their way only to the harsh, threatening, pietistic approaches to marital sex that are disseminated in some famous post-medieval halachic works and in nearly all "family purity" and marital intimacy guides in print, which can easily result in the development of sexual anxieties.

Note also that none other than Maimonides, in his *Commentary to the Mishnah, Sanhedrin 7:4*, composed one of the most important "halachic sex essays" ever written – in Arabic, knowingly making it accessible to young and old, simpleton and scholar, alike.

[For those who would acknowledge the reality that teenage children are no longer so innocent or naïve in matters of sex, with all the sexual content they are exposed to in media, print and online, the possibility of this book falling into their teenagers' hands would perhaps bring them more comfort than concern. And a word to the wise is sufficient.]

[9] See below, p. 68.

[10] One authority, Raavad III, in his *Baalei HaNefesh, Shaar Hakedushah* (Buchwald edition, p. 171) believed that if a man indulges all his sexual desires with his wife, he will eventually search for forbidden pleasures, and one thing will lead to another until he ultimately denies G-d and His judgement…

But while anything can be taken to extremes, the exact opposite is arguably just as likely, if not more so: When one is taught that certain natural sexual urges are forbidden even when expressed with one's own spouse – even according to the letter of the law, not just as a pious stringency – it is *that* which plants the seeds of disbelief in G-d and His judgement, for how can one believe in a Creator who does not seem to understand the natural human sex drive He Himself created?

So on the contrary: It is G-d's *permission* of sexual exploration, expression and vulnerability within marriage that will prove to many His great wisdom and empathy and understanding. And it is *this* that will keep people close to Him and believing in His judgment.

[11] *Babylonian Talmud, Tractate Hagigah 11b* cautions that one should not teach Jewish sex law to more than two initiates at a time. But the Talmud itself explains the reason why: because while one student is asking the teacher a question, the other two might converse amongst themselves and not pay attention to the teacher's clarification. This may result in the other two mistakenly permitting something that is forbidden, especially considering man's proclivity to seek (or invent) leniencies in the realm of sex. However, it is perfectly clear that the Talmud is referring, there, only to the risk of someone permitting *forbidden incestuous relationships*. [For a synopsis of the Talmud's intention, see the Steinsaltz and Artscroll editions of *Hagigah 11b* and their respective footnotes thereon. See also *Sefer Chasidim 510*.] The Talmud is not referring at all to instruction in sexual positions and technique between husband and wife – if it were, it would call into question all the Orthodox marital intimacy classes that take place on a daily basis for groups of brides or grooms in excess of two students, as well as all the numerous marital intimacy guides that have already been disseminated in print.

[I am also aware that Rabbi Moshe Feinstein extended the spirit of *Hagigah 11b's* teaching to discourage lay publications about the laws of birth control (*Igros Moshe, Even Haezer vol. 1, Responsum 64*, page 163). We do not tackle the issue of birth control in depth in our study. And to the extent that we touch upon it as it relates to the question of extra-vaginal ejaculation during marital sex, it can hardly be denied that we are living in very different times than Rabbi Feinstein, with different sexual sensibilities gaining momentum in the Chasidic-Charedi community (that must be addressed, not ignored), and with greater access to information – as well as misinformation and disinformation – through the internet and infinitely more English translations of Talmudic and rabbinic texts. In any case, the definition of what constitutes a "lay" versus a "scholarly" publication is also a point to consider.]

[12] In the course of the final stages of preparation of this book for print, an excellent Hebrew work by an anonymous author, *Dvar Seser*, was brought to my attention by Orthodox sex therapist Talli Rosenbaum. While I have not had the opportunity to review its contents in entirety, its value is obvious even after just initial perusal. Its author has made it available at http://www.files.org.il/BRPortalStorage/a/79/28/48-1Dk33JHjhg.pdf

[13] See, for example, below, endnote 86.

[14] *Nedarim 20b* and *Callah Rabti 1:14*. See below, p. 50-51.

[15] For evidence of this based on the Talmud itself, see Rabbi Dr. Shlomoh Zalman Havlin, *Mesores HaTorah Shebaal Peh*, 2012, p. 423-424 – including evidence raised by Rabbi

Schneur Zalman of Liadi in his *Shulchan Aruch HaRav, Hilchos Talmud Torah, Chapter 3, Kuntres Achron 1.*

See also *Eruvin 13b*, evidence of lost halachic deliberations of Rabbi Meir and of his disciple, Sumchos.

And although additional Talmudic-era halachic and midrashic works fill in gaps left by the Talmud, it is a well-known fact that certain other Talmudic-era works were entirely lost to us, not to mention Biblical-era writings that disappeared. See, for example, *Daas Doros* (Feldheim, 2006) pp. 79-89 and Rabbi Meir Zvi Bergman, *Mevo She'arim-Gateway to the Talmud* (Artscroll-Mesorah Publication, 1985, 1986), Chapter 11.

[16] Rabbinic tradition reports that the disciples of the sages would keep personal notes of Talmudic lectures they attended, which they would later review privately before delivering lectures of their own (see Maimonides' *Introduction to Mishneh Torah*). These unofficial records may have been incorporated into the Talmud by its compilers-editors alongside the official records stored in the great yeshivos of Israel and Babylonia.

[17] Of course, in every generation certain legal, moral or philosophical discussions of the prophets or sages may have been consciously deemed unecessary, or impractical, to be recorded for posterity. But this doesn't change the fact that such records would have shed greater light on the attitudes, opinions and/or intellectual processes that contributed toward the form of the Talmud's teachings as we have them today.

[18] For one example relevant to our subject, see *Talmud, Nidah 17a*, whose anonymous compilers-editors appear to rewrite no less than three rabbinic statements under the preconceived notion that sexual intercourse in the light of day or to candlelight is to be restricted.

[19] To be explored at length in a future essay. In the meantime, for a glimpse into some of the complexities of these topics, see *Igeres Rav Sherirah Gaon*, English edition by Rabbi Nosson Dovid Rabinovich (Moznaim 1988), particularly pages 79, 82-83, 116, 118-119 and footnotes thereon; Maimonides' *Introduction to Mishneh Torah*; Rabbi Dr. Shlomoh Zalman Havlin, *Mesores HaTorah Shebaal Peh* (Michalalat Orot Yisrael, 2012), Chapter 11; Rabbi Dr. David Weiss-Halivni, *The Formation of the Babylonian Talmud* (Oxford University Press, 2013), Part II: The Editing of the Talmud (I will note, only because of the reality that some Chasidic-Charedi readers will deem it important, that while Professor Halivni is Orthodox-ordained, he is associated with the Union for Traditional Judaism, formerly a branch of the Conservative Movement; but see below, endnote 335 point 3); Rabbi Matis Kantor, *The Jewish Timeline* (Aronson Press, 1992) years 4235/475, 4236/476, 4519/759; the essay of Rabbi Dr. Meir Triebitz, accessible online at http://www.hashkafacircle.com/journal/R3_RMT_Talmud.pdf (accessed May 6, 2015); the lecture series of Rabbi Meir Triebitz, *The History and Development of the Talmud*, Lecture 20 in particular, accessible online at http://www.hashkafacircle.com/category/history-development-of-the-talmud (accessed May 6, 2015).

[20] Even the precise halachic grounds upon which the Talmud's canonical status was/is based is debated.

And see Rabbi Dr. Shlomoh Zalman Havlin, *Mesores HaTorah Shebaal Peh*, 2012, pp. 428-429, discussing the implication of the view of Rabbi Elchanan Wasserman (1874-1941) in his *Kuntres Divrei Sofrim* (printed in *Kovetz Shiurim vol. 2*) that the basis for the Talmud's canonical authority derived from a majority of leading Torah scholars at some point in history ruling together to make it legally binding – implying that, halachically speaking, a majority of leading scholars in a future Sanhedrin could perhaps potentially supersede that ruling.

# ENDNOTES

[21] To be sure, too much information can add confusion. But as I believe shall become clear in our study, such was/is not the case in the area of Jewish marital sex law.

[22] See, for example, Raavad III in *Baalei HaNefesh, Shaar Hakedushah* (page 179 in the Buchwald edition), interpreting *Talmud, Nedarim 20ab* and the Sages' rejection of Rabbi Yochanan ben Dahavai's cautions against a couple's non-sex-related talk during sex, "overturning the table," and gazing at or kissing the female genitals. Raavad III implies that the fact that case precedents were only brought on *Nedarim 20b* of Rebbi and Rav permitting "overturning the table" suggests that the sages never permitted the other three.

And see *Hagahos HaBach* to *Rosh, Yevamos 34b* and *Yam Shel Shlomoh* to *Yevamos 34b*, as well as *Beis Yosef* to *Tur, Orach 240:2-4:4*, all quoting Rabeinu Asher as deducing from the same case precedents in which Rebbi and Rav permitted "overturning the table" that the fact that Rebbi and Rav did not warn against "wasting seed in vain" suggests that occasional intra-anal ejaculation is permitted to married couples.

[23] For critical studies by Orthodox Jewish scholars on the roots and historical evolution of the Oral Torah in general, see Rabbi Dr. Shlomoh Zalman Havlin's *Mesores HaTorah Shebaal Peh* (Michalalat Orot Yisrael, 2012) and Rabbi Yehoshua Enbel's *Torah Shebaal Peh: Samchusah u'Drachehah* (Mosad HaRav Kook, 2015). Both are in Hebrew.

[24] Nor is this book a case study of Chasidic-Charedi couples and their personal horror stories in the bedroom – though such a study would perhaps be a valuable wake up call to some about the grave repercussions of extreme sexual stringency and/or naivete within marriage.

[25] Despite its name, I found *Kosher Sex* by Rabbi Shmuel Boteach to be less a study on halachic sex positions and technique than an eloquent discourse on sex as a critical ingredient for a passionate and lasting marriage, and a guide to marital harmony in general. If one is looking for a sensitive, yet modern and candid, discussion on the importance, and limits, of sexual activity within marriage, this is a book to consider.

Page 71 of the book addresses creative marital sex positions in general, and pages 80-84 discuss oral sex. Rabbi Boteach offers sound logic for permitting such behaviors between husband and wife – logic which does in fact have halachic basis to back it up, though he does not discuss the sources. But again, halachic analysis is not the main focus of the book.

[I have not read Rabbi Boteach's other books on related subject.]

[26] See, for example, *Raavad III, Baalei HaNefesh, Shaar Hakedushah* (pp. 176-177 in the Buchwald edition) and *Rabeinu Asher, Peirush HaRosh, Nedarim 20b*, interpreting Rabbi Eliezer's customary sexual behaviors with his wife, Ima Shalom. Their interpretations are quoted, in turn, by *Tur, Orach Chaim 240* and *Even Haezer 25*, by *Shulchan Aruch, Orach Chaim 240*, and by numerous other halachic works on the subject.

See also *Chasam Sofer* to *Nidah 17a*: *Yisrael kedoshim heim v'ein meshamshim mitoseihem bayom*, suggesting that it is an act of "sanctification" to have sex at night even when one is tired so that it will prevent one from having sex during the day (when one is alert). This interpretation is somewhat surprising, considering that the Talmud itself, there, praises a certain King Munbaz for having sex during the day rather than at night, because for him to have had sex with his wife when he was tired at night could have – would have – compromised the affection and intimacy that are meant to be fostered by the sexual act. And see below, pp. 95-96 and endnotes thereon.

[27] See *Likutei Sichos* of Rabbi Menachem M. Schneerson, the Lubavitcher Rebbe, *vol. 10, Parshas Noach #2, Section 6*, pp. 26-27.

See also Rabbi Schneerson's letter dated 26 Nissan, 5715 (1955) printed in his *Igros Kodesh*, vol. 11, page 38.

[28] We are, of course, referring to the term "overturning the table" found on *Nedarim 20ab*, the precise definition of which carries far-reaching halachic ramifications, to be discussed below.

[29] *Babylonian Talmud, Tractate Bechoros 8a* and *Breishis Rabah 20:3*:

> All creatures have sex face-to-back, besides three, who have sex face-to-face: fish, humans and snakes.
>
> Why are these three different? When Rav Dimi came [to Babylonia], he said, "They say in the West [in the Land of Israel] that it is because the Divine Presence spoke with them.

We will not go into the question, here, of whether from a zoological perspective fish and snakes do in fact procreate in such a manner. But one must note that while the Bible records G-d communicating with man from the beginning of his creation, as well as with the primordial snake in the Garden of Eden, there is no such communication recorded between the Creator and His primordial fish.

Rashi to *Bechoros 8a* points to the verse in Jonah 2:11 where G-d commands the fish to spit Jonah out of its belly. But fish had been procreating for thousands of years before Jonah walked the earth.

[See also *Chupat Eliyahu, Pirkei Rabeinu Hakadosh 3:114* (*Yalkut Midrashim vol. 1*, Eden Deshe, 2009). See also below, p. 107, *Sefer Chasidim 509*.]

Note that Rav Dimi was a 3rd-4th generation Babylonian Amora. If the teaching he reported had early origins, it is somewhat perplexing that it was unknown for so long in the Babylonian academies – unless it had not even been taught in the Land of Israel until so late.

Note also that it is not clear the teaching was ever meant to restrict human sex to the face-to-face position, but merely to explain why, physically speaking, humans are formed in a way that they are capable of it.

[See also *Nidah 31b*, the curious explanation of Rabbi Dostai son of Rabbi Yanai (a 2nd generation Israeli Amora) as to why men generally face down during sex and women face up, and compare it to what is possibly an alternate, yet equally curious, version of the teaching quoted in *Breishis Rabah 17:8* in the name of Rabbi Yehoshua, having nothing to do with male versus female sex positions, but with their (supposed) positions during birth.]

[30] See *Yad Malachi, Clalei Shaar Haposkim, Clal 6*.

[30*] See *Talmud, Nedarim 20b*, which warns either spouse from ever coercing the other in matters of sex (discussed below, pp. 37-38, footnote to page 38, and endnote 125; see also *Eruvin 100b*, referenced in endnote 125). See below, page 107, for a clear statement in this regard by Rabbi Yehudah HaChasid in *Sefer Chasidim 509*. And see below, endnote 476, for a reference to a similar statement in Raavad III's *Baalei HaNefesh*.

[31] Compare, for example, passages from the original Hebrew of Rabbi Noson of Breslov's *Likutei Etzot*, chapter on "*Bris: P'gamo v'tikuno*," to the English translation, *Advice*, by the Breslov Research Institute (1983), chapter on "The Covenant."

Over and over again, where Rabbi Noson speaks in *Likutei Eitzot* against "*arayn*" (illicit sexual relations) or "*taavas niuf*" (the desire for adultery; or, perhaps in this particular author's context, the desire for masturbation), the English translation speaks against "sexual appetite" or "sexual desire" in general – which to the innocent, and especially the young, reader could easily be taken to mean even normal, healthy sexual desire in-and-of-itself:

*Bris: P'gamo v'tikuno, Entry 2*: "*Ikra d'yitzra bisha hu al **arayn** v'hee ikra d'm'saavusa.*"

*The Covenant, Entry 2*: "The **sexual appetite** is the root of the evil inclination. It is the source of all impurity."

*Bris: P'gamo v'tikuno, Entry 10*: "***Taavas niuf*** *hu ra hacolel, shecol haraos shel col hashivim umos clulin bo . . . utzrichim anachnu lihiyos prushim micol rayoseihem, d'haynu micol hataivos she'einam shaychim lanu clal, ubifrat **mitaavas niuf** shehu hara hacolel shel col ha'umos, cn"l. Ci zeh ikar hahevdel v'hahefresh sheyesh beineinu l'vein hagoyim mah she'anu porshim atzmeinu **miniuf**, ci zeh ikar kedushas yisrael. Ci yesh co'ach ba'adam l'hasiach daato mitaavah zos ul'shavrah. V'zeh ikar kedushaseinu, cn"l.*"

*The Covenant, Entry 10*: "**Sexual desire** is the comprehensive evil. It is the root of all the different kings of evil found in the seventy nations of the world . . . We are therefore obliged to keep apart from all the different kinds of evil which are found among them. Their desires are totally worthless to us. More than anything we must guard ourselves against **sexual desire** which is the sum of all evil. The fact that we keep ourselves apart from **this** is the essential difference between ourselves and the other nations. It is the foundation of the holiness of the Jewish people. Man has the power to uproot this **impulse** from himself completely. In this lies our sanctity."

*Bris: P'gamo v'tikuno, Entry 11*: "*Ikar hachnaas ushviras col hataavos, bifrat **taavas niuf**, shezeh ha'ikar shetzarich l'shaver*"

*The Covenant, Entry 11*: The key to subduing and breaking your desires, and especially **sexual desire**, which is the main challenge, is to strive to gain mastery of the Holy Tongue.

*Bris: P'gamo v'tikuno, Entry 40:* "*Mi shemeshaver **taavah zos shel niuf**, azei b'kal yuchal l'shaver col hataavos, v'al kein hu tikun haclali.*"

*The Covenant, Entry 37 [40]* – (brackets added for clarififcation): "Once one breaks his **sexual desire**, he can easily break all his desires. This is why the *tikun* [rectification] for sexual impurity is called the *tikun klali* [all-encompassing rectification]."

[32] See, for example, our attempts below to accurately translate the terms "*tovaato b'peh*" (footnote to page 38 and endnote 125), "*sichah yeseirah/sichah kalah/sichah kalah yeseirah*" (pp. 72-83), "*bushah*" (pp. 187-188, footnote to p. 33, and endnote 417) and "*dvar ervah*" (endnote 698).

And see, for example, our attempt to accurately interpret Rabeinu Yonah's and Rabeinu Nissim's understanding of Maimonides' ruling in regard to anal sex/intra-anal ejaculation (below, endnote 484).

[33] Translation by Rabbi Aryeh Kaplan, *The Living Torah* (Moznaim, 1981), Introduction, page vi.

[34] In Talmudic times it was considered dangerous for a nursing mother to get pregnant within two years of her previous birth, for her milk flow might then be disrupted, putting her current infant in harm's way (See, for example, *Talmud, Tractate Yevamos 12b, 34b*). Perhaps Rabbi Caro, here, was meaning to say that a husband is obligated to fulfill his wife

sexually even at risk of impregnating her again within this two-year time frame. And further research into the matter is required.

[35] This belief is expressed in *Babylonian Talmud, Nidah 31a*. See also *Midrash Tanchuma, Shemos 1*, suggesting that Bat Sheva believed sexual intimacy with her husband, King David, during her pregnancy with Solomon would make their son comely and vibrant.

[36] Rabbi Moshe Isserles, in his glosses to Rabbi Caro's Code of Jewish Law, amends this sentence to read:

> And if his intention in having sex with her is to guard himself from temptation to sin, because he senses within himself such temptation, *for this, too, he is rewarded, but* it would have been better if he had ignored his sexual instincts and conquered them...

Rabbi Isserles is merely adding back in a phrase from Rabbi Caro's source, Rabbi Yaakov ben Asher's *Tur, Orach Chaim 240* and/or *Even Haezer 25:8-10*, which, in turn, are paraphrasing Raavad III's *Baalei HaNefesh, Shaar Hakedushah*. Why Rabbi Caro removed this (moderately sympathetic) phrase is unclear. Perhaps he had a different manuscript version of *Baalei HaNefesh* and/or *Tur*.

See also *Eshel Avraham* of Rabbi Avraham Dovid Wahrman of Buczacz to *Orach Chaim 240:1*.

[37] *Babylonian Talmud, Sukkah 52b; Sanhedrin 107a*.

Note that this teaching is taught on *Sukkah 52b* by Rabbi Yochanan bar Napacha, who, as we shall see and discuss at length below, himself rules that "Anything a husband craves to do with his wife sexually, he may do" – including any kind of (non-illicit) sex-talk during intercourse, gazing at or kissing the female genitals, and creative sex positions ("overturning the table").

Note also that Rabbi Yehoshuah Falk, in his *Prishah* commentary to *Tur, Even Haezer 25:8-10:23* applies this teaching specifically to restraining oneself from indulging the desire for *prostitutes*.

[38] Micah 6:8

[39] Exodus 20:17

[40] Presumably, this "incitement" is a reference to the deliberate bringing on of an erection, which some sages seem to have considered unfavorable (though not necessarily forbidden) as a sort of "gateway drug" that could lead to more serious sexual infractions. See *Nidah 13b*. And see our discussion below, Part Five, pp. 190.

[41] Leviticus 20:25

[42] An example of that which is not "forbidden," but only discouraged, as noted above, pp. 16-17.

[43] *Babylonian Talmud, Tractate Nedarim 20b*.

[44] The meaning of this choice of wording is unclear. What kind of "awe" would be caused by a demon? And the kind of "fear" the presence and forcefulness of such a terrifying creature would instill would hardly allow for one to achieve, or maintain, an erection.

Arguably, the expression is hyperbolic.

[45] *Babylonian Talmud, Kesubos 48a* tells us that if a man forces his wife to only have sex while clothed it is justifiable grounds for her to demand a divorce, for such a practice is

deemed alien to Judaism, a "practice of the Persians." However, *Babylonian Talmud, Brachos 8b* tells us that one Raban Gamliel personally preferred the "modest" sex practices of the Persians.

In light of the reference above, endnote 7, that the House of Raban Gamliel accepted stringencies upon itself that it did not expect of the common folk, it is possible that Rabbi Eliezer and Ima Shalom, Raban Gamliel of Yavneh's brother-in-law and sister, respectively, took upon themselves a hyper-modest approach to marital sexual intimacy as well.

See also Rabbi Avraham Hayarchi in his commentary to *Callah Rabti* (Toledano edition, end of page 32, top of page 33).

The following citation was kindly shared with me by Rabbi Chaim Rapoport of London, UK from an unpublished article of his:

תניא (יבמות לט, ב): "אבא שאול אומר, הכונס את יבמתו לשם נוי ולשום אישות ולשום דבר אחר, כאילו פוגע בערוה, וקרוב אני בעיני להיות הולד ממזר. וחכמים אומרים, יבמה יבא עליו מכל מקום". ואיתא בירושלמי (יבמות פי״א הי״א) "דרבי יוסי בן חלפתא ייבם את אשת אחיו חמש חרישות וחמש נטיעות נטע ודרך סדין בעלי״, ובספר התרומה הל׳ חליצה סי׳ קלג (הוי״ד בסמ״ג עשין נב): "ודרך סדין בעל, פירש יבמתו היתה ולא הי׳ רוצה ליהנות ממנה רק מעט ונתן סדין בינו לבינה רק נקב עשה בסדין דרך מקום ביאה והוליד ממנה חמשה בנים". ובשו״ת מהר״ם מרוטנבורג (חיי׳ד סי׳ תתסן): "ואפי׳ חסידים הראשונים דור התנאים כשהיו מיבמין היו בועלין דרך סדין כדמשמע בירושלמי רבי יוסי ברבי חלפתא הי׳ בועל יבמתו דרך סדין". ובשו״ת בנימין זאב (סי׳ עח באה״ד): "פירוש יבמתו היתה ולא רצה ליהנות ממנה רק מעט ונתן סדין בינו לבינה להפסיק רק נקב עשה בסדין דרך ביאה והוליד ממנה חמשה אנשים גדולים".

כל הנ״ל הוא לענין **יבום** דוקא.

אבל בבעלי הנפש להראב״ד שער הקדושה (הוי״ד בבי״י אוי״ח סי׳ רמ) כתב: "ודוגמת המעשה הזה בגמ׳ דבני מערבא ברבי יוסי בר חלפתא שכנס יבמתו חמש בעילות בעל ודרך סדין בעל, ואותו הענין לא הי׳ אלא כדי שלא תהא כוונתו אלא לשם מצוה בלבד". ובשו״ע (אוי״ח סי׳ רמ סי״ח) כתב: "ויי״מ מגלה טפח ומכסה טפח, שלא הי׳ ממרק האבר בשעת תשמיש כדי למעט הנאתו". ובביאור הגר״א שם כתב שמקורו הוא מיימ״ש בפ״י דיבמות בירושלמי' ר״י בן חלפתא כו' והביאו הגי״מ פכ״א, **ואף שיש לומר יבמה שאני כאבא שאול** [ראה מור וקציעה להיעב״ץ סי׳ רמ שם "כי דווקא ביבמה יש מקום לחסידות כזה לא זולתה"], **מכל מקום נכון ג״כ באשתו"**.

ובשו״ת אחיעזר (חלק ג סוי״ס כד) נראה שנקט שהסדין שימש כמו נרתק שהיי' כרוך על אבר המילה גם בשעת ביאתו אלא די״מיירי באופן שיכנוס הזרע והסדין הי' רק כדי למעט הנאתו דהרי נטע הי' ארזים והוליד בנים". וכי״מ ממיי״ש בסי' חידושי הגיי״ר זעליג ראובן בענגים (חי״ב סי' סז אות נ) ד״רבי יוסי בן חלפתא שבעל דרך סדין [עשה כן] כדי שלא לעבור על איסור קירוב בשר בטרם יקיים מצות יבום", עיי״ש.

[46] Note that Rabbi Caro, here, is restating interpretations listed by the medieval scholar, Rabbi Avraham ben David of Posquières, "Raavad III," in his *Baalei HaNefesh, Shaar Hakedushah* (pp. 176-177 in the Buchwald edition). But Raavad III, there, rejects the interpretation that Rabbi Eliezer was trying to minimize the pleasure of intercourse, for it runs contrary to the reason Rabbi Eliezer himself gave as reported by his own wife in the Talmudic account on *Nedarim 20b*. Rabbi Eliezer is reported, there, as expressly saying his concern was to avoid intentionally entertaining sexual fantasies of other women. He is not reported saying that he was trying to minimize sexual pleasure.

Rabeinu Asher, however, in his *Peirush HaRosh* to *Nedarim 20b*, does put forth an interpretation that Rabbi Eliezer was trying to minimize his pleasures of the flesh, and Rabeinu Asher's son, Rabbi Yaakov ben Asher, lists this interpretation in his *Arbaah Turim, Orach Chaim 240* and *Even Haezer 25*. This is presumably why Rabbi Caro lists it in his *Shulchan Aruch, Orach Chaim 240* as well. But then this interpetation would appear to run somewhat contrary to the spirit of both Rabbi Yaakov ben Asher's and Rabbi Caro's definition of the term "sex-related talk" (*mili d'tashmisha*) – which the Talmud says Rabbi Eliezer himself spoke with his wife during sex – as talk that is intended to increase the husband's sexual desire (see below, pp. 57-58, and endnotes thereon).

And see below, endnote 82.

46* See below, endnote 414*.

47 Amos 4:13

48 In modern slang, "doggystyle"

49 "*Lo yenavel piv b'divrei havai*."

See also *Shulchan Aruch, Even Haezer 23:7*, where the term "*divrei havai*" has nothing to do with sexual *talking*, but with marveling at the beauty of the naked body. See also the explanation of the term quoted in parentheses, there, in the 2008 Friedman edition of *Shulchan Aruch*.

Rabbi Caro's choice of the term "*divrei havai*" in *Shulchan Aruch, Even Haezer 25:2* and *23:7* was clearly borrowed from Maimonides' *Mishneh Torah, Deos 5:4* and *Isurei Biah 21:4*, respectively.

In translating Rabbi Caro's texts, here, and Maimonides' texts, below, we have chosen to translate "*divrei havai*" as "vain talk," connoting fixation on the beauty of the bodily form.

49* See below, endnote 414*.

50 Here is where Rabbi Isserles adds his important gloss-note, which we shall discuss next.

Note that Rabbi Isserles's gloss – a verbatim quote of Maimonides' ruling in *Mishneh Torah Sefer Kedushah, Isurei Biah 21:9* permitting sex "any time the husband wants" – was inserted immediately after Rabbi Caro's restrictions on *talk during sex*, not a mere paragraph later, after Rabbi Caro's discussion about minimizing the *frequency of sex*. This would imply that Rabbi Isserles may have understood Maimonides' intention in permitting sex "any time the husband wants" as (part of the context of the Sages' rejection of Rabbi Yochanan ben Dahavai's four cautions on *Nedarim 20ab*, which included a caution against "non-sex-related talk,") meaning that sexual intercourse is permitted no matter what conversation husband and wife may be having or may have had just prior. This would be supported by the fact that nowhere does Maimonides forbid "non-sex-related talk" during sex (and see our discussion below, pp. 76-77).

[But this assumes that Rabbi Isserles himself, rather than his publishers, chose the precise location of all his glosses. Did he?]

See also Rabbi Yisrael Alnaqua's interpretation of the Sages' ruling on *Nedarim 20ab*, "Anything a husband craves to do with his wife sexually, he may do." Rabbi Alnaqua writes that this includes "sex any time the husband wants." The fact that he would introduce "sex any time" into that particular discussion on *Nedarim 20b*, which is speaking about four specific behaviors – "overturning the table," gazing at or kissing the female genitals, and non-sex-related talk during sex – suggests that Rabbi Alnaqua, too, may have meant to say (or at least he understood Maimonides as meaning to say) that sex is permitted any time, no matter what conversation husband and wife may be having or may have had just prior.

In any case, Rabbi Eliyahu Kramer (the "Vilna Gaon – Genius of Vilna") in his *Biur HaGra* commentary to *Shulchan Aruch, Even Haezer 25:2* explains this to mean that a husband is permitted to have sex "any time – even in excess of the amount he is mandated to perform by Jewish law to satisfy his wife." But note that Rabbi Kramer derives this meaning from the Sages' analogy on *Nedarim 20b* of a husband's permission to eat his kosher meat in any culinary manner he prefers – an analogy which does not on the surface have any relevance to what Rabbi Kramer learns from it, for it came to explain that a husband and wife may enjoy each other sexually *in any manner* they crave, not *at any time* they crave (see below, pp. 34-35, 41-42, 45-46, 66 point 2).

A simpler interpretation might be that Maimonides was referring back to a statement he made in *Sefer Hamada, Deos 3:2*, that a husband should ideally not initiate sex just any time he desires pleasure (*col zman sheyisaveh*), but rather only (to fulfill his obligation to fulfill his wife sexually, or only) when he feels the therapeutic need for it or for the sake of procreation (*ele b'chol eit sheyeidah shehu tzarich l'hotzi shichvas zera, c'mo derech harefuos, oe l'kayem zera*). In *Isurei Biah 21:9*, Maimonides was perhaps then clarifying that (consensual) marital sex "any time" – i.e., even purely for the sake of the *husband's* sexual fulfillment – is still acceptable in the eyes of G-d from a baseline legal standpoint.

[51] Literally: "'Holy' shall be said of him" (Isaiah 4:3).

[52] See above endnote 50, and our discussion below, pp. 76-77.

[53] The title "*Tanna*" (plural: *Tannaim*) refers to a rabbinic scholar of the period roughly spanning 10-220 CE. The major center of Tannaitic learning was in the Land of Israel.

In contrast, the title "*Amora*" (plural: *Amoraim*) refers to a rabbinic scholar of the period roughly spanning 200-500 CE. Major centers of Amoraic learning existed both in the Land of Israel and in Babylonia.

[54] A Tannaitic teaching not included in the *Mishnah* of Rabbi Yehudah Hanasi.

[55] A 5th generation Tanna.

[56] A 4th generation Tanna.

[57] *Shita Mekubetzes, Nedarim 20a*, in the name of Re'em.

[58] According to *Tosfos Yeshanim*, even without "gazing."

[59] *Tosfos Rabeinu Peretz, Nedarim 20a*.

[60] See *Artscroll Talmud, Nedarim 20a*, footnote 32.

[61] An unsurprising prediction, considering that a child, and especially a son, generally observes and imitates his father's behavior.

Rabbi Achi's first warning, too, that habitual looking at other women will eventually lead to actual sin, is not necessarily a remarkable or mystical prediction, but rather an observation of behavioral science.

Raavad III, however, in *Baalei HaNefesh, Shaar Haprishah*, (pp. 6-7 in the Buchwald edition) insists that the result of rearing uncouth children, as predicted here, is an "act of Heaven" (*maaseh shamayim*).

*Tosfos* here, as well as Rabeinu Asher in *Tosfos HaRosh* and Meiri in *Beis Habechirah*, also seem to understand this as a supernatural punishment.

But note that Raavad III, ibid, interprets this "punishment" of rearing uncouth children as resulting even from gazing at one's own *pure* wife, whereas Rabeinu Asher and Meiri apply it only to gazing at one's own *impure* wife or *another forbidden woman*, pure or impure (see below, pp. 177-182, and endnote 660, for more on this point).

In that case, it is perhaps understandable why Rabeinu Asher and Meiri interpreted this as a divine "punishment" rather than a matter of simple behavioral science, for from a scientific perspective the negative impact upon the child should be the same whether he or she observes the father lasciviously gazing at their mother when she is pure or impure.

According to Raavad III, however, who suggests that one will rear uncouth children even for gazing at one's own pure wife (during non-sexual moments), the argument is ever more compelling that Rav Achi's warning was not about divine punishment, but behavioral science – at least if such gazing is done in the presence of one's children. Yet Raavad III himself categoricaly insists it to be "an act of Heaven."

And more research into the matter is required.

[62] A 3rd generation Babylonian Amora.

[63] *Dikdukei Sofrim, Nedarim 20a; Peirush HaRan.*

[64] A 2nd generation Israeli Amora. He was also the close colleague and brother-in-law of Rabbi Yochanan bar Napacha, who is quoted later on *Nedarim 20b*.

[65] Literally, "the place of filth" (*makom hatinofes*). And see *Dikdukei Sofrim Hashalem* (*makom hatoref*).

According to *Meiri* and *Shitah Mekubetzes* (possibly in the name of *Ritz*), this refers specifically to her buttocks, with the man "checking out" her backside from behind, "head-to-heel" (though, according to *Meiri*, the same caution would apply to gazing at her front genital area as well).

See also *Peirush R. Avraham min Hahar* to *Nedarim 20a*.

[66] Exodus 20:17

[67] Seemingly, this means to imply that he descends from the union of a Jewish woman and non-Jewish man.

According to *Shitah Mekubetzes*, however, this implies that he descends from converts. But why would the Talmud denigrate a convert for his lineage, especially when there is a biblical commandment to love the convert, and when so many great scholars and righteous men descended from converts, such as King David and Rabbi Akiva? The future Messiah, too, being from the House of King David, will descend from converts.

Indeed, it is none other than King David himself whom the midrash has invoking this teaching in order to reject the full Jewish status of the Gibeonites (*nesinim*). See sources below, endnote 704.

And note that Maimonides in his *Mishneh Torah, Sefer HaMada, Hilchos Deos 5:4*, says that if one "sanctifies" oneself during marital intimacy, one's children will have the (worthy) character trait of "shame" – thereby implying that the progeny of unsanctified sex may be devoid of this virtue even though they are of pure Jewish lineage. And see a similar implication at the end of his *Sefer Kedushah, Isurei Biah 21:12*.

[68] A 5th generation Tanna.

[69] According to the medieval Rabbi Yehudah bar Kalonymous of Speyer, Rabbi Yochanan ben Dahavai was known for his extreme piety (*chasid gadol*), which would perhaps also

imply a proclivity for sexual stringency. See *Erchei Tannaim v'Amoraim vol. 1, entry: Yochanan ben D'havai HaSheni*.

Rabbi Kalonymous also suggests there were actually two historical sages named "Yochanan ben Dahavai," one with mystical, one with pious, inclinations – both qualities of which would match the profile of any author of a teaching like the one of Rabbi Yochanan ben Dahavai in the name of the "ministering angels" on *Nedarim 20a*.

[70] The general consensus among the medieval commentaries appears to be that Rabbi Yochanan ben Dahavai was explaining the causes of congenital illnesses in children, not illnesses in adult couples themselves.

See also *Callah Rabti 1:11* and *1:13*, which specify that these afflictions were understood by Rabbi Yochanan ben Dahavai as affecting an unborn child – albeit only if the child is conceived during the same sexual encounter in which these behaviors are performed.

*Tosfos* to *Nedarim 20a* also comments that these were all meant to afflict the unborn child, not the couple themselves.

[The English edition of the *Artscroll Talmud*, however, in *Nedarim 20a*, footnote 44, suggests that according to Rabeinu Nissim in *Peirush HaRan*, here, it is not the offspring from such a union that allegedly become afflicted, but rather the parents themselves. Rabbi Yochanan ben Dahavai would then be warning about the causes of such physical degeneration in adults – namely, that such are forms of "punishment" for specific sexual behaviors between husband and wife that may have been performed any time over the course of their married life. But in reality, Rabeinu Nissim merely comments: "Because they changed the [natural work of the] leg, the leg is afflicted" – which can just as easily be interpreted as referring to the leg of the unborn child (G-d forbid). And Artscroll's suggested interpretation of *Peirush HaRan* would also render incomprehensible the Talmud's immediate challenge to Rabbi Yochanan ben Dahavai: "They asked Ima Shalom, 'How did your *children* turn out to be so beautiful...?'" If Rabbi Yochanan ben Dahavai had been referring to the husband and wife *themselves* being afflicted, then the question the Talmud poses from a discussion about Ima Shalom's *children* would be irrelevant.]

[70*] Ostensibly, "they" could also include the mother initiating "overturning the table" with her husband, gazing at or kissing her husband's genitals, or speaking to her husband during sex. However, for the purpose of our study to outline and analyze the rabbinic sources on the subject, we have presented the cautions of Rabbi Yochanan ben Dahavai as addressing the father specifically, for such is the context in which these cautions are generally discussed in rabbinic literature. See, for example, below, pp. 34-35, 41-42, 46, the ruling of the Sages in response to Rabbi Yochanan ben Dahavai, that "Anything a *man* craves to do with his wife sexually, he may do." See also below, pp. 45-46, Rava's interpretation of the "measure-for-measure" justice behind these cautions, all in the context of the *husband's* actions. And see below, endnotes 72, 75.

[71] There is debate among the medieval commentaries as to the definition of the term "overturning the table." See below, pp. 59-61.

[72] Literally: "Because they kiss that place" (*oso makom*).

This passage is generally interpreted by commentaries as referring to a husband kissing his wife's genitals – that is, oral sex performed by a husband on his wife, "cunnilingus."

We have therefore translated this passage on *Nedarim 20a*, as well as parallel passages in *Tractate Callah* and *Callah Rabti* (to be discussed below), and made reference to them throughout our study, as referring to the husband kissing "the female genitals" specifically.

Why, according to this prevalent manner of interpretation, Rabbi Yochanan ben Dahavai or his "ministering angels" would have found a husband giving his wife oral sex more objectionable than a wife giving it to her husband remains to be explored.

In any case, if the Talmudic sages, the Talmud's compilers-editors and/or the rabbinic commentaries did in fact understand this passage as including the male genitals, then much, if not all, of our discussion throughout this study regarding cunnilingus would arguably apply equally to the matter of a wife giving her husband oral sex – "fellatio."

But we discuss the matter of fellatio under the separate category of "intercourse between limbs" (see below, footnote to p. 103, as well as pp. 123-129 and endnotes 511-513 thereon).

And note that Maimonides, in his *Commentary to the Mishnah, Sanhedrin 7:4* (see below, p. 103), implies that he understood intercourse between limbs as being among the sexual behaviors the Sages on *Nedarim 20b* (to be quoted next in our study) came to permit in contrast to Rabbi Yochanan ben Dahavai – even though Rabbi Yochanan ben Dahavai himself made no mention of it specifically. It is therefore perhaps possible that Maimonides actually understood "kissing that place" as referring to either husband or wife kissing each other's genitals – which would include fellatio, a manner of intercourse between limbs.

Alternatively, Maimonides may have understood intercourse between limbs as being included in the term "overturning the table," as implied by the fact that in his *Commentary to the Mishnah, Sanhedrin 7:4*, he speaks of both anal intercourse and intercourse between limbs being included in "the response of one of the sages to a wife who asked him about this subject" (see below, p. 103) – that sage being either Rebbi or Rav, both of whom are quoted on *Nedarim 20b* as having responded to wives who sought their guidance specifically in regard to "overturning the table" within marriage.

**Added note to the third edition:** See Rabbi Eliezer Melamed's *Simchat Habayit v'Birchato* (second edition, 2015), bottom of page 63, asserting that there are no restrictions on a wife kissing her husband's genitals – though it is not specified if fellatio is permitted to the point of ejaculation. And see Rabbi Maor Kayam's *Harchavot l'Simchat Habayit v'Birchato* (2015), pages 183-184, discussing ejaculation between limbs for married couples.

[73] *Tosfos Yeshanim,* here, interprets "deaf" as deaf-mute. See also *Callah Rabti 1:13.*

[74] Only in regard to non-sex-related talk does Rabbi Yochanan ben Dahavai specify "during sex" – during intercourse.

Kissing the female genitals is not physically possible during actual intercourse, but gazing at them is. And the term "overturning the table" itself refers to a manner of intercourse.

[75] This passage is generally interpreted by commentaries as referring to a husband gazing at his wife's genitals.

We have therefore translated this passage on *Nedarim 20a*, as well as parallel passages in *Tractate Callah* and *Callah Rabti* (to be discussed below), and made reference to them throughout our study, as referring to the husband gazing at "the female genitals" specifically.

Why, according to this prevalent manner of interpretation, Rabbi Yochanan ben Dahavai or his "ministering angels" would have found a husband gazing at his wife's genitals more objectionable than a wife gazing at her husband's remains to be explored.

In any case, if the Talmudic sages, the Talmud's compilers-editors and/or the rabbinic commentaries did in fact understand this passage as including the male genitals, then much of our discussion throughout this study regarding a husband gazing at his wife's genitals would arguably apply equally to the matter of a wife gazing at her husband's.

[Parenthetically, in his commentary on the prayer book, *Mitas Hakesef*, chapter 7, section 2:2, Rabbi Yaakov Emden quotes the four cautions of Rabbi Yochanan ben Dahavai. On the caution against gazing at one's wife's genitals, Rabbi Emden suggests a loose scriptural support for it from the verse in Leviticus 20:17:

> "And *he* shall see *her* nakedness and *she* shall see *his* nakedness, and *they* will be cut off before the *eyes* of the children of their nation."

(Note that although a literal translation of the verse could loosely associate it with gazing at genitals, the actual context of the verse is referring to illicit sexual *intercourse* – the term "seeing nakedness" being a common biblical euphemism for intercourse. The verse is also speaking about a very specific case of incest. And it is clearly speaking about an adult man and woman, not their offspring. It is therefore not clear what relevance this verse actually has to the caution of Rabbi Yochanan ben Dahavai.)

See Rabbi Yehudah Leib Nachmanson's *Sheyekadesh Atzmo* (2015), Chapter 43, page 449, footnote 11, for opinions that differentiate between a husband gazing at his wife's genitals and a wife gazing at her husband's.

See also *Callah Rabti* 1:13, which explains in the name of the Amoraic sage, Rava, that the gravity of a husband gazing at his wife's vagina (during the same sexual encounter in which conception occurs) is on account of gazing "at that which is hidden from all" – which would not necessarily apply to a wife gazing at her husband's genitals. But as noted below, endnotes 158, 161, this passage in *Callah Rabti* fails to explain what is so objectionable about gazing "at that which is hidden from all" in the first place.]

**Added note to the third edition:** See also Rabbi Eliezer Melamed's *Simchat Habayit v'Birchato* (second edition, 2015), bottom of page 63, asserting that there are no restrictions on a wife gazing at her husband's genitals.

[76] A 3rd generation Tanna.

[77] Rabeinu Peretz understands the question to be: "How did your children all turn out to be unblemished – none are blind or lame?"

This interpretation requires further investigation, for it seems to assume that the majority of families in Talmudic times had a least one blind or lame child.

[78] See *Tractate Callah 22*, discussed below pp. 43, 49, 50-51, 58, that Rabbi Eliezer encouraged husbands to talk seductively to their wives during sex (*yefateh osah b'shaas tashmish*).

While *Callah Rabti* 2:11 asserts that this refers to seductive *actions*, not *talk*, it does so only on account of the caution of Rabbi Yochanan ben Dahavai against talk during sex. But *Nedarim 20b* maintains that even Rabbi Yochanan ben Dahavai himself would embrace "sex-related talk," of which "seductive talk" would arguably be a subcategory.

[And according to *Callah Rabti*, perhaps we should interpret Rabbi Eliezer's other actions described by his wife on *Nedarim 20b* – covering and uncovering hand's-breadths of her skin and thrusting 'like a demon' – as actions of seduction and heightened pleasure for her as well, not only as behaviors motivated by piety and/or fear. At the very least, they may have been meant to more speedily bring her to climax so that he himself could climax quickly (after her) and still avoid intentional fantasies of other women without denying his wife her sexual needs. And see endnote 80 below.]

[79] See above, pp. 23-24 and endnotes thereon, the interpretations of this behavior listed by Rabbi Yosef Caro in his *Shulchan Aruch* and their sources in medieval commentary.

[80] The *Mefaresh* commentary (see below, page 60), here, gives two interpretations of the phrase "compelled by a demon":

> He would thrust into her with force, as if a demon were pushing him.
>
> And some say he would cover himself completely [with a blanket] like someone afraid of a ghost [in the room].

Other medieval scholars, such as Raavad III, interpret Rabbi Eliezer's behavior as a means of speeding through the act of intercourse and ejaculating as fast as possible. Raavad III notes in *Baalei HaNefesh, Shaar Hakedushah* (p. 176 in the Buchwald edition) that this would imply that he never brought his wife to climax first, at least not on the nights they were trying to conceive, which creates a problem according to the Talmudic belief that one can only conceive male offspring if the mother climaxes first (*ishah mazraas techilah*). Raavad III offers his solution: if a husband's motives in rushing through sex are pure, then even if the wife is not satisfied first (and, we might add, potentially not satisfied at all), G-d still "rewards" the husband with "beautiful" children (which Raavad III implies will also be male).

It should be noted, however, that one medieval source can perhaps be read as offering an alternate interpretation of Rabbi Eliezer's motives, which also negates the notion that he ever tried to rush through intercourse at his wife's expense.

Rabbi Yitzchak Aboab, in his *Menoras Hamaor, Clal 6, Part 6, chapter 5* (page 390 in the Mosad HaRav Kook edition) writes:

> At the time of intimacy (*eis hachibur*), do not have sex just for your own pleasure, but for her pleasure as well, and like one who is fulfilling the obligation placed upon him by the commandment of the Torah to satisfy her sexual needs, like Rabbi Eliezer's wife described about him, that he was like one compelled by a demon.

His associating the focus of giving pleasure to one's wife with the focus of Rabbi Eliezer discharging his obligation "as if he were being compelled by a demon" suggests that Rabbi Aboab may have been leaving it open to interpretation that Rabbi Eliezer's "forceful intercourse" was with the intent of bringing his wife to faster, perhaps stronger, climax.

In that case, perhaps Rabbi Eliezer's customs to talk to her and to uncover one "fistful" of her flesh (at a time), were actually intended to tease and heighten her arousal, culminating in forceful thrusting during intercourse that would make her, as well as him – and her before him – climax quickly, thereby minimizing the risk of intentional illicit fantasies without compromising her sexual needs.

And see pages 43 and 49 above, that *Tractate Callah* and *Callah Rabti* report Rabbi Eliezer himself encouraging husbands to speak and/or act seductively with their wives during sex.

And see above, endnote 78.

[81] Arguably, Rabbi Eliezer's concern was not about fantasy thoughts that might naturally and uncontrollably pop into a spouse's head during sex, for to fear such uncontrollable thoughts would be to keep them at the forefront of one's mind. Rather, it seems Rabbi Eliezer's concern was that he might come to *willingly entertain* such thoughts – in his words: "So that I not come to *set my [mind's] eye* upon [fantasies of] another woman."

*Mishnas Rabbi Eliezer (ben Rabbi Yossi Haglili), Parshah 18* describes one of the nine flawed conditions of mind during sex (to be discussed below), *Bnei Irbuvya*, as "one who has sex with his own wife, and *he sets the intentions of his heart (mechaven libo)* upon another woman – even if she, too, is his wife."

Rabbi Yosef Caro, in his *Code of Jewish Law, Shulchan Aruch, Even Haezer, 25:10* words this most precisely:

> Do not have sex with your wife *in order to fantasize* of other women, not even another one of your own wives (*lo yeshamesh im ishto litein daato al acheres, afilu shteihen nashav*).

Apparently the issue here is about intentionally "living out a fantasy," not about thoughts that might naturally pop into one's mind against one's inner will or desire.

[But note Rabbi Caro's wording in his *Beis Yosef* to *Tur, Orach Chaim 240:Casav HaRaavad Yesh Meforshim Megaleh Tefach...* where he implies that Rabbi Eliezer was concerned about any thoughts of foreign women even popping into his head in passing (*v'col zeh c'dei shelo ticaneis alav shum machshavah acheres*). And this can be understood in different ways – especially in light of what we've said that intentionally trying to avoid uncontrollable thoughts is hardly effective in banishing them. At most one can only fight the will to entertain and/or enjoy them.

And while Rabbi Eliezer's custom to have sex only in the middle of night is understood as his effort to create an *environment* that would be free of *stimulations* that could cause even *unintentional* thoughts to arise, his manners of uncovering only a hand's-breadth of his wife's body and of thrusting "like a demon" during intercourse themselves suggest that the fear – that is, the actual concern – of illicit fantasies was, at least at times, *consciously* on his mind throughout the sexual act.]

This would also explain why it is not forbidden for divorcées to remarry, even though the Talmud takes it for granted that thoughts of their ex-spouses will inevitably haunt them in the bedroom (*Babylonian Talmud, Pesachim 112a*). And see below, endnote 128.

See also *Likutei HaPardes*, p. 7b in the Munkatch edition:

> If one has sex with his wife, *and he is haughty* and fantasizes in his heart of another woman (*v'gas hu v'libo mechashev b'ishah acheres*), or she of another man, and they conceive a child that night [during that sexual encounter], in the end that child will be afflicted three-fold: it will be mute, lame and deaf.

Without getting into the question of the unknown source of this three-fold caution, it is obvious that unintentional and/or uncontrollable thoughts are not manifestations of haughtiness.

[See also Rabbi Schneur Zalman of Liadi's *Tanya*, Chapter 12, where it is explained that for the average individual, "sinful" thoughts in general can be expected to arise in the mind or heart on their own; it is only for the person to banish them when they arise and not willfully entertain them.]

In any case, a detailed analysis of the Sages' concerns about sexual fantasies will be the subject of an essay in a future volume of this series.

[82] The avoidance of fantasies is the sole purpose stated by Rabbi Eliezer himself, as quoted by the Talmud. For this reason, Raavad III, in his *Baalei HaNefesh, Shaar Hakedushah* (pp. 176-177 in the Buchwald edition) rejects an interpretation already circulating in his own day that Rabbi Eliezer would not thrust his penis very much in order to "minimize sexual pleasure."

Rabbi Avraham Hayarchi, however, in his commentary to *Callah Rabti* (Toledano edition, page 32), in the midst of copious paraphrased quotes of Raavad III, writes:

> ...This was all so that the thought of another woman would not enter his mind during intercourse, and in order to shorten the intercourse; *he did all this so as not to derive pleasure from it (hayah hacol shelo yehaneh min hamaaseh)*.

Rabbi Avraham Hayarchi is the only medieval commentary I've seen who suggests Rabbi Eliezer was attempting to avoid *all* sexual pleasure – in what may possibly have been an innocent misquote of Raavad III.

*Shitah Mekubetzes* quotes in the name of Ritva that Rabbi Eliezer would uncover only a hand's-breadth of her genital area so as to *minimize* his pleasures of her flesh (*c'dei shelo yehaneh harbeh mimenah*).

Rabeinu Asher, in his *Peirush HaRosh* to *Nedarim 20b* puts forth a similar ascetic interpretation as to why he would uncover only a hand's-breadth of her flesh (*shelo yehaneh b'kiruv basar*), which is quoted by his son, Rabbi Yaakov ben Asher, in his *Tur, Orach Chaim 240* and *Even Haezer 25*, and, in turn, by Rabbi Yosef Caro, in his *Shulchan Aruch, Orach Chaim 240*.

But neither Ritva nor Rabeinu Asher suggest that Rabbi Eliezer would not thrust his penis during intercourse so as to avoid pleasure.

And Ritva, Rabeinu Asher, as well as Rabbi Avraham Hayarchi, offer alternate interpretations that have nothing at all to do with minimizing or avoiding sexual pleasure within marriage.

Finally, none of Rabbi Eliezer's behaviors in this regard are legally binding in any case. And, as we shall see below, Rabeinu Asher (and possibly even Ritva, as quoted in *Shitah Mekubetzes*; see below endnotes 224, 508) permits occasional intra-anal ejaculation to married couples, the sole halachic justification of which is that it serves to provide the husband sexual fulfillment within marriage.

[83] The meaning of the statement "tantamount to bastards" is somewhat problematic. It certainly has no ramifications in Jewish law, and even its spiritual implications are unclear.

There appear to be two general approaches:

One approach is that fantasizing about another woman makes it as if the husband has spiritually cohabited with her, leaving his children conceived during such fantasies spiritually blemished and prone to rebelliousness (see, for example, *Callah Rabti 1:16*; Commentary of Rabbi Avraham Hayarchi to *Callah Rabti*, Toledano edition, pp. 31, 33-36; *Shitah Mekubetzes, Nedarim 20b*).

A second approach is based upon the belief that what one envisions in one's mind during conception affects the physical form of the fetus. Thus, according to this belief, fixating on thoughts of another woman during conception may cause the baby to actually resemble her physically (see *Tosfos Yeshanim, Nedarim 20b*).

A future volume of this series will explore in-depth the belief of some of the sages that what one fixates one's mind upon during conception affects the spiritual and/or physical attributes of the child conceived. We will mention here only briefly some of the difficulties in the underpinnings of this belief as found in certain rabbinic literature:

In Chapter Four of the anonymous medieval work on "sanctified" sex, *Igeres Hakodesh* (attributed by some to Nachmanides), the author writes:

You must understand the great secret in that which the Sages said: "Fantasies of sin are stronger than the sin itself."

I will enlighten your eyes in matters concerning the fundamentals of the universe that are hidden in many inner chambers [of secrets].

Know that G-d, blessed be He . . . gave a power in the imagination of man such that man can procreate the likeness of that which he imagines. And we know this to be true even from the natural world.

When a man is intimate with his wife, if his imagination and thoughts are focused on wisdom and understanding and good and proper character traits, then that imagination in his thought has the power to cause the form of his sperm to develop later [in the form of his child] according to [the form of] his imagination at the time of conception. This is without doubt.

And this is the secret of (Genesis 30:37): "Jacob took a moist rod of poplar..." Then the flocks became heated by the rods... [i.e., the flocks bore spotted offspring because they somehow became aroused by looking at the spotted rods].

And our Sages said in *Babylonian Talmud, Tractate Brachos* [20a]: "Rabbi Yochanan would go and sit by the gates of the *mikveh*. He said: 'When the Jewish girls come up from the river, let them gaze upon me, so that they will have offspring beautiful like me.'"

Envision this picture: This righteous man made known that by a woman thinking about his beauty as she came out from her immersion to be intimate with her husband, the form [and/or quality] of the child they would conceive would be in the likeness of her imagination.

Thus, the imagination is a great factor, and one's fantasies and thoughts cause the fetus and its character traits to be as we've said.

Thus, the imagination and thoughts cause the fetus to be righteous or wicked...

Every man must clean his thoughts and his fantasies, and purify them during sex, and not think about sin or fornication, only about holy things. And he should think of pure righteous men, men of knowledge, intellect and wisdom, for these thoughts during sex will affect the sperm and cause it to form in the likeness of their form [and/or quality].

And the same goes for the thoughts of his wife...

Now, do not be flabbergasted about this, for this is simple natural law in the eyes of the wise men of science – that the quality of thought and fantasy that pass through the heart of man and wife during intercourse determines the quality of the form of the fetus, for good or bad.

And the Sages already brought the case of a [Roman] noblewoman (*matronisa*) who gave birth to a dark-skinned baby, while she and [her husband] the king were extremely white and fair. The king had mind to execute her, until a certain wise man came and said to him: "Maybe she fantasized during sex about a black man." They investigated and [indeed] found black images in the room in which he had sex with her, and she confessed that she would gaze at those images and fantasize about them during intercourse. [Compare to *Midrash Tanchuma, Naso 7-8*]. This is just like the rods [of Jacob's flock].

> And do not be flabbergasted, because even greater than this is known from science: If a person is bitten by a rabid dog, and he contracts the known disease from that bite, then due to the imagination of his mind, water cannot be brought close to him, because he immediately imagines it to be infested with rabid dogs. Even in his urine he sees tiny dogs. And if the urine is put through a strainer, he doesn't see anything in it; but if the urine is put in a glass vessel and left for an hour, he will see puppies.
>
> Due to the excessive fantasy and fear, he visualizes in the urine his fantasies and fears.
>
> Understand this greatly, and realize just how far the power of visualization and fantasy during sex goes.
>
> The bottom line: If a man visualizes good and pure things, that good visualization affects the sperm and the fetus will be formed in the likeness of that visualization and it will grow to be completely righteous…
>
> And if the man thinks something sinful and ugly, the fetus will be established on an evil and ugly foundation, and will grow to be wicked and disgusting…

These arguments of *Igeres Hakodesh* are repeated by later commentators, including medieval scholars such as Rabbi Yisrael Alnaqua (*Menoras Hamaor-Alnaqua, vol. 4, Perek Nisuei Ishah*, pp. 101-104) and Rabbi Yitzchak Aboab (*Menoras Hamaor-Aboab, Clal 6, Chelek 6, Perek 4, Siman 184*).

Rabbi Yaakov Emden, in his commentary to the prayer book, *Mitas Hakesef 6:8-11*, also quotes these ideas, ending off with an additional support:

> The Romans would take the captive Jewish children of Jerusalem and tie them to their bedposts so that they [the Romans] could gaze upon them during intercourse and conceive children beautiful like them. (*Babylonian Talmud, Gitin 58a*)

To spell out the obvious:

Whatever was going on with those spotted rods in the story of Jacob, it need not be assumed to have been scientific. If it were, we should be able to replicate it today. Note also Rashi's interpretation of Genesis 30:38, in the name of the Talmudic sage, Rabbi Oshiya: "The water [that the female livestock drank] transformed into sperm inside them, and they did not even need a male [to impregnante them]." Clearly, then, whatever was going on there, this rabbinic tradition openly admits it was not natural.

Rational readers will not rule out the possibility that the fair-skinned noblewoman actually *did* have sex with a dark-skinned man, or that she or her husband simply had some recessive dark genes.

The entire "proof" from rabies is questionable in light of modern scientific understandings of the disease, its causes and its symptoms.

And the ancient beliefs of pagan Romans can hardly be used to argue scientitic truths about reproductive science from a Torah standpoint.

See also the pseudo-midrash, *Braisa D'nidah* – of which numerous textual versions exist.

The following version is brought in the medieval work, *Sefer HaRokeach, Hilchos Nidah*, by Rabbi Elazar of Worms (c.1176–1238):

> Any woman who immerses [in the *mikveh* in order to be sexually intimate with her husband], and then she encounters a dog [on her way home, but rather than returning to immerse again she continues on] and has sex with her husband [that night], her child will be disgusting and have a face resembling a dog.

# ENDNOTES

If she encounters a donkey [on her way home, but continues on and has sex with her husband that night], her child will be foolish like the personality of a donkey.

If she encounters an ignoramous [on the way home, but continues on and has sex with her husband that night], her child will be an ignoramous...

... If she encounters a horse [on the way home], *she should continue on* and have sex [with her husband that night].

Let me teach you how to know which creature a woman encountered [on her way home from *mikveh*]:

Any woman whose son eats as he walks in the marketplace – she, his mother, encountered a dog.

If his saliva dribbles down upon his beard and his tongue prevents him from talking, his mother encountered a donkey.

And if there is no substance in his words, and he forgets his studies, his mother encountered an ignoramous.

But if her son is pleasant and well spoken, and he is able to study everything – she, his mother, encountered a horse. And such a son is studious, humble, and his words are well received.

And if one wrings his hands, one hand inside the other, and his tongue twists around, know that when his father and mother had sex [and conceived him], his father kissed his mother and gave her tongue [lit. his tongue went out of his mouth (*yatza leshono mipiv*)].

Another version is quoted in *Col Bo 145, Dinei Nidah m'Baal HaTerumah*:

Rabbi Chanina said: If a woman immerses [in the *mikveh*] and comes out and encounters a dog – if she is wise and there is fear of Heaven within her, she will not allow her husband to have sex with her that night, until she immerses again, so that her children will not grow up to be ugly and their faces doglike.

If she goes back [and immerses] and then encounters a donkey [on her way home], she has no permission to have sex with her husband until she immerses a third time, so that her children will not grow up to be foolish of heart, like a donkey.

If she goes back [and immerses] and then encounters an ignoramous [on her way home], it is forbidden for her to have sex with her husband that night, until she immerses a fourth time.

If she goes back [and immerses] and then encounters a horse [on her way home], she should go and have sex [with her husband].

Those described as having doglike faces are those who walk in the marketplace eating with their saliva dribbling down upon their beards, and their tongues do not allow them to speak. If you see such a person who exhibits such characteristics, know that after his mother immersed [in the *mikveh*] she encountered a dog and went on to have sex [with her husband that night].

Those described as being donkeylike are those whose hearts are foolish like a donkey, and they are unable to comprehend Torah, they are unkempt in public (*mechuarin b'halichasan*), and flies swarm around their faces. If you see such a person who exhibits such characteristics, know that after his mother immersed [in the *mikveh*] she encountered a donkey and went on to have sex [with her husband that night].

And those who speak and are unable to express themselves well, who learn Torah and forget their learning, and who walk in the marketplace and are the laughingstock even of the simple-folk – they are those whose mothers encountered an ignoramous. If you see such a person, know that after his mother immersed [in the *mikveh*] she encountered an ignoramous and went on to have sex [with her husband that night].

Take this rule in hand: warn the women that if they encounter any of these three [on their way home from *mikveh*] they should go back and immerse a second time [and a third time], up to four times.

Rabbi Chiya said: Happy is he, and happy is the one who gave birth to him, and happy are his mother and father – he whose mother encountered a horse [on her way home from *mikveh*]. The children of such mothers will grow up to be well-spoken, they will hear and understand, they will learn Torah and not forget their learning, and they will sleep little. And not only that, the awe of them shall be upon the simple-folk, and their words will be heeded. If you see such a person, know that after his mother immersed [in the *mikveh*] she encountered a horse [and went on to have sex with her husband that night].

If you see someone whose tongue twists around, and who wrings his hands, one hand inside the other, know that when his father and mother had sex [and conceived him], his father kissed his mother and saliva came out of his mouth.

A section of *Braisa D'Nidah* is also brought in *Shaarei Dura, Hilchos Nidah 23*, quoting from *Sefer Hamiktzo'os*:

> When a woman goes out from immersing [in the *mikveh*] she should arrange for her friend to encounter her, lest she encounter ... a pig or a dog or a donkey greeting her [as she leaves].
>
> For *Sefer Hamiktzo'os* writes: If she immersed and then encountered a dog or any impure creature, if the woman has fear of Heaven she will not have sex with her husband until she goes back and reimmerses, so that her children will not be ugly and doglike.
>
> Similarly, if she encountered a donkey she should immerse another time, so that her children will not be foolish of heart like a donkey.
>
> Similarly, if she encountered an ignoramous ...

*Sefer Hamiktzo'os*, as well as *Shaarei Dura* in its quotation of *Sefer Hamiktzo'os*, go on to relate that the wife of the High Priest Elisha once immersed ten times on the night she intended to be with her husband, because after each immersion she encountered an impure creature. In this merit, it is related, and as a result of her encountering an angel sent by G-d after the tenth immersion, she gave birth to the great and holy Rabbi Yishmael ben Elisha Cohen Gadol. Note, however, that in the story of Elisha's wife it is said that one of those impure creatures she encountered was a *horse*, and yet she went back to immerse in the *mikveh* – contrary to the instruction of *Braisah D'Nidah* that encountering a horse is a good thing.

Now, one might be inclined to say that there is no internal contradiction in the specific version of *Braisah D'Nidah* quoted by *Shaarei Durah* from *Sefer Hamiktzo'os*, because that version also makes no distinction between horses and dogs or donkeys in regard to reimmersion; and, according to *Shaarei Dura*, it actually extends its caution about reimmersion to one who encounters "*any* impure creature."

# ENDNOTES

But if we look into *Sefer Hamiktzo'os* itself, at least the critical edition put out by Rabbi Simcha Asaf (Mosad HaRav Kook, 1947), there is no caution, there, against encountering "any impure creature." Nevertheless, there is also no distinction made between horses and dogs or donkeys, and the story about Elisha's wife does have her reimmersing even after encountering a horse.

However, the version of *Braisa D'Nidah* recorded in *Likutei HaPardes*, pp. 5b-7b in the Munkatch edition, *does not* specifically identify a horse as one of the impure creatures Elisha's wife encountered after immersion, and it *does* go on to encourage a woman who encounters a horse on the way home from *mikveh* to go ahead and enjoy sexual intimacy, and conception of a child, with her husband.

In any case, it appears that *Shaarei Dura* understood *Braisa D'Nidah's* caution as being only to avoid encountering an impure creature as the *first* thing one sees after leaving the *mikveh*. That is presumably why it suggests a woman arrange for a female friend to greet her upon emerging from the *mikvah* – a role filled today by the *mikveh* lady. This is also how Rabbi Moshe Isserles in his gloss-note to *Shulchan Aruch, Yoreh Deah 198:48* presents the issue.

Now, I do recall seeing a discussion somewhere that some scholars believe this *Braisa D'Nidah* to be a forgery (and search the term "*niddah*" at www.jewishvirtuallibrary.org for a claim that some believe it to be the product of a heretical Jewish sect). But venerated sources do quote it, as seen above – three of which are cited by Rabbi Moshe Isserles in his said gloss-note to *Shulchan Aruch, Yoreh Deah 198:48* (those three being *Shaarei Dura*, *Rokeach* and *Col Bo*). Rabbi Shabsai Hacohen, in his *Sifsei Cohen (Shach)* commentary, there, also discusses them.

All to be explored further in a future volume of this series.

In the meantime, see Rabbi Chaim Meir Horowitz's critical study of *Braisa D'Nidah* in his *Tosefta Atikta-Kuntres Pischei Nidah* (Frankfurt, 1890) and Eden Deshe's *Yalkut Midrashim vol. 3* (Safed, 2005), pp. 203-226.

[Parenthetically, Rabbi Menachem M. Schneerson, the seventh rebbe of Chabad-Lubavitch, invokes Rabbi Isserles in *Shulchan Aruch, Yoreh Deah 198:48*, along with the above-mentioned *Shaarei Dura*, *Rokeach* and *Col Bo*, as the *halachic* support for his instruction not to unnecessarily expose children to images, illustrations or toys that are in the forms of non-kosher animals – for to do so, he warns, could have negative spiritual impacts upon a child (See *Likutei Sichos vol. 25*, p. 311, footnotes 8-10).

As one who dedicated twenty years of life to Rabbi Schneerson's teachings, nine of them devoted also to researching, translating and disseminating his talks to the world via film – including this very address in regard to "kosher toys" – I have enormous appreciation of, and respect for, his insight and scholarship.

Still, I must ask:

Are we obligated to believe that, historically or today, tragic developmental disabilities were/are caused by what a mother sees on her way home from *mikveh* and her reluctance to go back (in the middle of the night) to repeat the immersion process?

Has the actual full context of this *Braisa D'Nidah* been made sufficiently clear to those who are taught to follow, and promulgate, this (oftentimes impractical) instruction, along with the fact that important versions of *Braisa D'Nidah* make a clear distinction within the "non-kosher animal kingdom" itself between animals that are of noble character (e.g. horses) and lowly character (e.g. donkeys or dogs – and, arguably, even among dogs there are noble breeds)?

And has it been sufficiently considered that if the entire caution of *Braisa D'Nidah* only really applies to the *first* creature a woman sees after emerging from the *mikveh*, not to any other creature she might encounter thereafter (no matter how impure, not matter how lowly) on her way home to be intimate and conceive a child with her husband, then, arguably, the entire teaching has no definite relevance to any other time or circumstance of life, nor to children's toys, book illustrations or the like?

Note that Rabbi Schneerson does invoke some non-legal sources in support of his instruction as well, such as Rabbi Elazar of Worms' *Rokeach Hagadol, Hilchos Shavuos, Chapter 296*, where the custom is mentioned not to allow a child to see a dog on the morning of his very first day entering yeshivah; and Rabbi Tzvi Hirsch Kadainaver's *Kav Hayashar, Chapter 2*, where, in the midst a discussion about the positive and negative powers of sight in general, a caution is made not to habitually view non-kosher animals.

But in the case of the former source, Rabbi Eliezer of Worms (c.1176-1238) speaks of avoiding the child's sight of a dog specifically, not non-kosher animals in general, and only on his very first day of entry to yeshivah, never else. He also suggests a loose scriptural support for this custom from the verse in Exodus 34:3 cautioning the Jewish people not to allow their sheep or cattle – kosher animals – to graze facing Mount Sinai in lead up to Moses' ascension of the mountain to prepare and bring them the second set of Tablets of the Covenant.

And in the case of the latter source, I believe readers should at least be made aware of some of the other assertions made by Rabbi Tzvi Hirsch Kadainaver (17th century) in his greater discussion, there, about the spiritual "dangers" of seeing non-kosher animals. To list but two: In his attempt to argue just how "corrupting" the power of sight can be (*she'hare'iyah pogem umafgim*), he describes a bird whose vision is so piercing it literally cracks the shells of its eggs. And he associates the spiritual "peril" of gazing at non-kosher animals to *Talmud, Nedarim 20a's* caution against a husband gazing at his own impure wife's body. Without getting into the complexities of the *Talmud's* context there (for a discussion on that, see below, pp. 177-182), Rabbi Kadainaver himself asserts that if a husband gazes at his own impure wife's body it will literally draw her impurity into his eyeballs. Empirical evidence of this, Rabbi Kadainaver says, is that when a menstruating woman gazes into a mirror, permanent blood stains appear on the glass – proof of how profound the power of sight, and the power of her impurity, are. And see a similar statement made by the medieval Nachmanides in his *Peirush HaRamban* commentary on Leviticus 18:19; in his essay *Toras Hashem Temimah* (*Kisvei Ramban*, Mosad HaRav Kook, Jerusalem, 1963, p. 167), Nachamanides reveals his source for this belief: Aristotle.

For related comments by Nachmanides on the subject of menstrual impurity in general, see his *Peirush HaRamban* to Genesis 31:35 and Leviticus 12:4.]

[84] Actually, it is a matter of dispute among the medieval commentaries as to which part of Ima Shalom's testimony proved that talking during intercourse is okay.

One approach says it was her description of Rabbi Eliezer "speaking" to her during intercourse (*Beis Yosef, Shulchan Aruch, Even Haezer 25:2b:V'al yesaper ima lo b'shaas tashmish, v'lo kodem l'chen...*). Another says it was the fact that she asked him mid-intercourse to explain his behavior (*Peirush R. Avraham min Hahar, Nedarim 20b; Shitah Mekubetzes* to *Nedarim 20b* possibly in the name of Ritz; see also *Tosfos Yeshanim*, ibid). And yet another says it was the fact that Rabbi Eliezer actually responded to her question mid-intercourse (*Tosfos Rabeinu Peretz, Nedarim 20b; Re'em* quoted in *Shitah Mekubetzes* to *Nedarim 20b*).

But the latter two explanations are somewhat problematic, for:

# ENDNOTES

a) There is no indication at all that their conversation took place mid-sex.

b) It is unlikely that Ima Shalom would have questioned her husband's sexual performance mid-act.

c) Even if she did question him mid-act, it would have been highly innapropriate of him to respond (again, mid-act) that he was struggling not to fantasize of other women – and struggling so much that he resorted to what the average individual would consider (indeed, what his own wife seems to have at first considered) extreme behavior. [See the version of Ima Shalom's wording in *Tractate Callah 10* and *Callah Rabti 1:15*: "Why such extremes?" (*col cach lamah*).]

And even if Rabbi Eliezer had no qualms about confessing his human frailties to his wife, he presumably would have had enough decency to tell her *after* the act rather than while he was still inside her (or about to enter her) – especially considering that if thoughts of other women were his concern, speaking about the issue, and causing his wife to thereby think about it as well, would have been the worst way to banish such thoughts from the bedroom.

It is thus arguable that the first interpretation – the one supported by a straightforward reading of the text – is the correct one, that the fact that Ima Shalom described her husband as *initiating sex by talking to her*, and then *continuing to talk to her* "as he uncovered a hand's-breadth and covered over a hand's-breadth" – that is, during intercourse – proves that talk is permitted both during foreplay and intercourse, and thus Rabbi Yochanan ben Dahavai's caution against it was suspect. And so the compilers-editors of the Talmud offered their resolution: even Rabbi Yochanan ben Dahavai himself would accept sex-related talk (*mili d'tashmisha*) during sex, his caution was only against non-sex-related talk (*mili achronaisa*) – and Rabbi Eliezer only spoke the former.

[85] A 2nd generation Israeli Amora.

[86] The entire give-and-take, here, requires explanation, for Rabbi Yochanan ben Dahavai was not necessarily coming to "forbid" these four actions as much as to give "caution" about the physical repercussions caused by them. If his words are to be taken at face value, he was not arguing "Jewish law," but "medical wisdom" as he reported to have received from certain "ministering angels."

Rabbi Yochanan bar Napacha and the Sages, however, respond with legalities.

THE FOLLOWING IS MEANT ONLY AS A STARTING POINT FOR FURTHER RESEARCH AND DISCUSSION:

One would presume that if a certain sexual behavior causes medical harm to a fetus, then G-d would forbid its practice – just like He would forbid any other behavior that is medically dangerous to anyone's health (even if that behavior in-and-of-itself bears no intrinsic moral or spiritual deficiency). In that case, Rabbi Yochanan ben Dahavai's medical caution against the four sexual behaviors even within marriage could perhaps be understood as equivalent to his prohibition of them. And Rabbi Yochanan bar Napacha's and the Sages' opposition to him would mean they disputed and rejected the very facts of his science.

Indeed, next in the Talmudic discussion, on *Nedarim 20b*, a Babylonian sage of the late Talmudic period, Ameimar, explains that when Rabbi Yochanan ben Dahavai reported to speak in the name of "ministering angels," Rabbi Yochanan bar Napacha and the Sages understood him to be referring to other human rabbis (*rabanan*) who were "distinguished like ministering angels." The logic that compels him to conclude this is of the nature we just explained: if Rabbi Yochanan bar Napacha and the Sages understood Rabbi Yochanan ben Dahavai as in fact quoting actual ministering angels who knew the accurate science of fetal development, why would Rabbi Yochanan bar Napacha and the Sages not have acceded to these angels' cautions as a matter of Jewish law?

Ameimar's logic implies that if danger to the fetus had been proven – that is, if the "ministering angels," here, had in fact been actual spiritual beings with full access to the secrets of the universe revealed to them – then Rabbi Yochanan bar Napacha and the Sages would have most certainly agreed to prohibit the four behaviors medically cautioned against by Rabbi Yochanan ben Dahavai not only as a matter of health, but of law.

Now let us first clarify what is meant, here, by the "science" of fetal development.

When Ameimar speaks about actual ministering angels being proficient in the science of fetal development (*tzuras havlad*), he could be speaking about their knowledge of the *natural* and/or *supernatural* influences upon the formation of a child. These would potentially include physical causes, metaphysical causes, and spiritual causes resulting from matters of divine justice. But the ultimate *effect* of them all in the Talmud's discussion here is physical – that is, medical: congenital health or congenital illness.

Therefore, Ameimar's implication that actual ministering angels can be assumed to be proficient in the science of fetal development, whereas human rabbis – no matter how pious, no matter how learned – need not be assumed to be so proficient, could be referring to human rabbis' fallibility in any one of the above three categories: physical science, metaphysical science, or the "science" of divine justice.

[And see footnote to p. 35.]

But whatever the case may have been, Ameimar understood Rabbi Yochanan bar Napacha and the Sages as effectively saying that the earthly – medical – cautions warned by Rabbi Yochanan ben Dahavai and his masters, the *rabanan*, were invalid cautions.

Thus, it could perhaps be argued that there may be other Talmudic era cautions predicting physical or metaphysical or even spiritual rupercussions for certain behaviors that need not be feared *to the point of anxiety,* for the case of the Sages' (*chachamim's*) rejection of the Rabbis' (*rabanan's*) cautions on *Nedarim 20ab* is proof positive that the scholars of the Talmud did not necessarily possess perfect knowledge in any of these three areas, and therefore their cautions are not necessarily categorical and/or absolute, at least not in all times and places.

One could especially suggest to argue this in regard to Talmudic cautions for which there is no empirical evidence today – of which Rabbi Yochanan ben Dahavai's cautions are also apparent examples:

It is not unreasonable to presume that a vast number of people today do engage in the four sexual behaviors cautioned against by Rabbi Yochanan ben Dahavai, even on the nights they end up conceiving children. And yet the vast majority of children are, thank G-d, born unharmed. This, too, would perhaps suggest that (not only halachic law, but also) natural law and supernatural law do not support this teaching of the "ministering angels," whoever they might have been.

And according to any interpretation of Rabbi Yochanan ben Dahavai that he meant to say that the four congenital illnesses were the results of *divine justice*, rather than mere physical or metaphysical scientific cause-and-effect, it could be argued that if we now know based on empirical observation that these four behaviors do not, or no longer, cause such illnesses in children, this could be indication that according to the Sages they never were, and according to Rabbi Yochanan ben Dahavai they no longer are, worthy of such harsh punishment.

# ENDNOTES

To explain, drawing on a more recent case in point:

Rabbi Dovber Schneuri of Lubavitch (1773-1827), the second Rebbe of Chabad, writes in his Yiddish work on repentance, *Pokeach Ivrim*, Chapter 9, that "the only reason" four-fifths of babies born in his day were born chronically ill with a certain fatal disease was because their mothers were gazing at and flirting with other handsome men, and then having sexual dreams about them at night.

In his Hebrew translation of the work, the famous Chabad Chasid, Rabbi Shmuel Dovber of Borisov (1808-1889), who was nearly twenty years old when Rabbi Schneuri passed away, explained this passage as attributing not only the widespread congenital *illness*, but also the resulting *deaths*, of eighty percent of infants of the day to such causes.

[The fundamental message of the Yiddish and Hebrew versions, are, in fact, the same, for the cause of the widespread illness would have been the cause of the widespread mortality rates.

Note that the 1923 and 1924 editions of *Pokeach Ivrim* left out this passage. It was added back into the most recent edition of the work, *Maamarei Admor HaEmtzai, Kuntreisim* (Kehot Publication Society 1991), pp. 482 and 511.]

Looking back from today, it is not unreasonable to counter that any infant mortality rates of early 19th century White Russia had more to do with problems of hygiene and lack of proper medicine than with sexual flirtations and/or fantasies. The proof? People today in Western societies are flirting and sexually fantasizing more than ever before in history. Yet the infant mortality rates in western societies are also lower than ever before.

But even if one chooses to accept Rabbi Dovber's assertion, it could theoretically be argued that G-d no longer punishes such things so harshly (even if they remain utterly objectionable), because we are a spiritually orphaned generation that cannot be held so accountable; or because we are perhaps no longer "holy enough" to "merit" the punishment – along the lines of an explanation Rabbi Dovber's own father, Rabbi Schneur Zalman of Liadi, gives in his *Igeres HaTeshuvah, Chapters 4-6*, as to why people no longer routinely die by the ages of fifty or sixty for sins deserving the punishments of "excision" or death by the hand of Heaven, respectively (and a similar explanation has been given for why we no longer witness cases of the biblical "tzaraas" skin affliction). See also *Talmud, Sotah 47b*, that once adultery began to proliferate, the Sotah-waters no longer demonstrated their power. Credit goes to Rabbi Simcha Feuerman for bringing this source in *Sotah* to my attention on page 40 of his *Kuntres Es Lifrosh v'Es Le'ehov* (2016). And see the Steinsaltz Hebrew edition of the Talmud, *Sotah 47b, Iyunim: Misherabu Hamenaafin.*]

In any case, the notion that the Sages did not possess perfect physical or metaphysical scientific knowledge should not come as a surprise to the educated Talmudic Jew, for there are even more direct assertions of such made by none other than one who is quoted on *Nedarim 20b* among those who rejected the medical cautions of Rabbi Yochanan ben Dahavai's *rabanan*: the author of the Mishnah himself, Rabbi Yehudah Hanasi.

*Babylonian Talmud, Sanhedrin 91b* and *Breishis Rabah 34:12* both record two disputes between Rabbi Yehudah HaNasi and a Roman Emperor, one about when the living soul enters the body, the other about when the evil inclination enters the body – questions that are metaphysical and spiritual in nature and are fundamental not only to Jewish law, but to the mystical kabbalah. And yet, based on simple "logic" put forth by the non-Jewish king, Rabbi Yehudah HaNasi reevaluated his stance.

Even more so, in *Babylonian Talmud, Pesachim 94b*, Rabbi Yehudah HaNasi declares that the non-Jewish scholars' understanding of astronomy seemed more correct than that of the

Jewish Sages. See Rabbi Nathan Slifkin's erudite essay tracking the historical evolution of Jewish commentary on this Talmudic passage, demonstrating that it was never a universally accepted tenet in Judaism that the Talmudic Sages possessed perfect scientific knowledge. He has made this essay, *The Sun's Path at Night*, available online at: www.zootorah.com/RationalistJudaism/TheSunsPathAtNight.pdf.

See also Rabbi Slifkin's *Introduction* to his *Sacred Monsters* (Zoo Torah, 2007-2011) for a fundamental discussion on Talmudic-rabbinic science, and *Chapter 16*, there, *The Spontaneous Sweat Louse*, for a fascinating analysis of the Talmudic and medieval sages' belief in spontaneous generation and its ramifications in practical Jewish law.

As pertains to our subject, a fundamental question raised by all this is how Talmudic scholars generally determined what they considered to be "forbidden" or "inappropriate" in the marital bed. Did they deem certain positions or techniques forbidden purely on the basis of divine revelation/Torah exegesis or also based on scientific beliefs of the day about health and/or hygiene? If the latter, then new findings of modern science could ostensibly render certain marital sexual behaviors that were forbidden by the commentaries into permitted ones, and certain behaviors that were permitted by the commentaries into forbidden ones.

An example of the latter would be the expectation of some rabbinic commentaries that anal intercourse be followed immediately by intra-vaginal ejaculation (see below, page 120, authorities listed under "Anal Sex – without intra-anal ejaculation") – which modern science has revealed to be extremely dangerous to the health of the wife (certainly more empirically dangerous for her than any of the four behaviors cautioned against by Rabbi Yochanan ben Dahavai might be for an unborn child).

On the other hand, see below, pp. 45-47, an alternate version of this entire Talmudic discussion on *Nedarim 20ab* found in an early work of debated origin, *Callah Rabti 1:13-14*. *Callah Rabti* implies that the term "ministering angels" was in fact literal, and it asserts that the sages actually conceded to Rabbi Yochanan ben Dahavai that these four behaviors are dangerous to the fetus on health grounds – albeit only if they are performed during the same sexual encounter in which conception occurs. Still, according to *Callah Rabti* there, the Sages refused to forbid these four behaviors on legal grounds even when performed during the same sexual encounter in which conception occurs.

This, too, is highly revolutionary: If sexual behaviors considered by the Sages to be potentially harmful to a fetus cannot actually be "forbidden" on legal grounds, then, theoretically, we need not even assume Talmud-era understandings of the physical, the metaphysical and/or the spiritual to be fallible in order to *permit* from a halachic standpoint that which certain rabbis of the day warned against on medical grounds.

Alternatively, as a friend pointed out to me, according to *Callah Rabti*, the Sages themselves may have believed that although such behaviors could cause congenital illness if performed during the same sexual encounter in which conception occurs, the actual *risk* of them causing such is low. But Rabbi Yochanan ben Dahavai's wording according to *Callah Rabti* – "Why are there children who are lame... blind... mute... deaf...?" – implies that he believed these four behaviors to be the *main* causes of these four congenital illnesses. Consequently, if the Sages, according to *Callah Rabti*, conceded to Rabbi Yochanan ben Dahavai about their dangers, we would have to force a reading into *Callah Rabti's* version that while the Sages, too, may have believed these behaviors to be the *main* causes of these congenital diseases, they only considered them to be *remote* causes. And if we were to read the Sages' opinion in this way, then the explanation of Rava (quoted in *Callah Rabti*) about these illnesses resulting "measure-for-measure" from these behaviors would lose much significance as well.

But then Rava appears to understand these cautions as being about divine justice, "measure-for-measure," not about physical or metaphysical cause-and-effect. Yet according to this manner of understanding, the Sages's rejection of Rabbi Yochanan ben Dahavai's *prohibition* of them would perhaps force us to re-explore how the Talmudic era sages themselves viewed the falliblity of their own perceptions and/or calculations about divine justice. And the fact that, according to *Callah Rabti*, the Sages rejected Rabbi Yochanan ben Dahavai's *prohibition*, but *not* his *medical caution*, would call into question the notion that divine justice was at play at all – for what justice would need to be served against something that is permissible? And if this "measure-for-measure" justice was said to be meted out for behaviors that are permissible, but *unpious*, it remains to be satisfactorily justified why such harsh punishments, and in one's children no less, should be considered commensurate – "measure-for-measure"?

And see below, endnotes 158, 161.

[Note that while one might suggest that the congenital illnesses cautioned against by Rabbi Yochanan ben Dahavai on *Nedarim 20a* were referring to *spiritual* lameness, blindness, muteness and deafness (whatever that might mean), similar to the "congenital uncouthness" cautioned against by Rabbi Achi earlier on *Nedarim 20a* and the "congenital rebelliousness" cautioned against by Rabbi Levi later on *Nedarim 20b*, this does not appear to be how any of the medieval commentators understood Rabbi Yochanan ben Dahavai, nor how he was understood by the Amoraic sage, Ameimar, on *Nedarim 20b*, who, as stated, presents the matter as an issue of fetal development (*tzuras havlad*).]

[87] An obvious question begging to be asked in all this: What were Jews doing in their marital beds for two thousand years before Rabbi Yochanan ben Dahavai, his *"rabanan,"* the *"chachamim,"* Rebbi, Rav or Rabbi Yochanan bar Napacha walked the earth?

Perhaps new scientific beliefs in the world about the dangers of these sexual behaviors caused the matter to be reexamined in the rabbinic academies as well.

Or perhaps the matter was simply reexplored by the Tannaitic rabbis in their own day due to their understanding that the new Torah insight G-d reveals to the sages of the Sanhedrin in every generation in fact sanctions them to supersede the Torah exegesis of previous Sanhedrins even in certain areas of Jewish law (see Maimonides, *Mishneh Torah, Sefer Shoftim, Memrim 2:1* – to be explored further in volume two of this series).

[88] A 5th-6th generation Babylonian Amora.

[89] It remains to be explored who these angelic rabbis actually were, as well as the reason for the distinction in title between "sages" (*chachamim*) and "rabbis" (*rababan*).

[90] What is the meaning of "distinguished like ministering angels"?

    a) They were adorned in ritually-fringed robes, a sign in those days of a distinct level of piety. (*Mefaresh; Rabeinu Peretz*)

    *Maharsha, Nedarim 20b:V'lo sasuru acharei levavchem* explains further that the ritual fringes served as a reminder of sexual chastity in particular.

    b) The *rabanan* separated themselves from the common folk and did not mix among them. (*Peirush HaRan*)

    c) They are called 'angels' because they carry out the mission of G-d. Alternatively, they stand out in their extra-scrupulous observance of G-d's commandments. Alternatively, they wore white robes, giving them an angelic appearance. (*Shitah Mekubetzes*)

d) They were distinguished in Torah and *mitzvos*, and were separate and distinctly holy from the rest of the nation. (*Peirush HaRosh*)

e) Rabbi Yochanan ben Dahavai referred to his masters as "angels" for they were the "pure, holy ascetics who taught him the path of holiness," and because Moses, too, is sometimes referred to as an "angel" (Rabbi Avraham Hayarchi, *Commentary to Callah Rabti*, Toledano edition, page 28)

Note that the Talmud in numerous places stresses that one should not be a perfectionist and/or obsessive about Jewish ritual observance, because "Torah was not given to ministering angels." See *Babylonian Talmud, Brachos 25b, Yoma 30a, Kidushin 54a, Meilah 14b*. And see *Encyclopedia Talmudis vol. 34, Entry: Lo Nitnah Torah l'Malachei Hashares*. Note also that *Brachos 25b* has this principle being taught in the name of Rava – the same Rava quoted on *Sanhedrin 58b* permitting anal sex within marriage, and the same Rava quoted in *Callah Rabti 1:13* asserting that even Rabbi Yochanan ben Dahavai's "ministering angels" themselves did not consider the four sexual behaviors they cautioned against to be dangerous to a fetus unless performed during the same sexual encounter in which conception occurs.

[91] A 6th generation Tanna.

[92] Why did the women complain to the Sages?

a) They were upset at their husbands' actions and wanted either to divorce them or have them reprimanded. (*Shitah Mekubetzes*)

b) The husbands had performed anal sex with them and the wives were complaining that it was painful. (*Tosfos HaRosh, Nedarim 20b, Yevamos 34b; Rabeinu Asher, Yevamos 34b* – as preserved in *Hagahos HaBach* to *Rosh* and in *Yam Shel Shlomoh* to *Yevamos 34b; Mordechai Hilchos Nidah 731-732; Tosfos, Yevamos 34b; Tosfos, Sanhedrin 58b; Tosfos Yeshanim, Yevamos 34b*)

Note that especially in ancient times, without lubricant, anal sex could have been extremely painful for the wife, and particularly if she was not psychologically-emotionally-erotically in sync with her husband about it. Thus, according to this explanation, the Sages' permission for the husbands to continue engaging in anal sex despite the discomfort to their wives is perplexing.

Perhaps it could be explained, in line with the beliefs of the time that what one thought and felt during sex affected one's conceived or growing fetus, that the women were not coming to ask for the sages to put an end to their husband's sexual predilections, but rather to ease their fears that such discomfort during sex might have harmed their babies. Perhaps the Sages were simply easing their concerns, explaining that since anal sex is permitted by G-d's law in the context of marriage and with the wife's permission, no harm can come to their child on account of it despite any discomfort she might (willingly) endure in the course of pleasing her husband.

c) Her concern was whether or not "overturning the table" was forbidden. Thus, it must be referring to anal sex, because her-on-top is obviously permitted (sic). (*Rabeinu Yeruchem, Nesiv 32*)

d) The husbands performed rear-entry vaginal intercourse, and the women were comfortable with them doing so. But they wanted to know from the Sages if this was permissible by Jewish law. (*Raavad III, Baalei HaNefesh, Shaar Hakedushah*, pp. 179-180 in the Buchwald edition)

## ENDNOTES

See also endnotes 95 and 96 below, as well as page 192 below and endnotes thereon.

[93] Lit. "Rebbi answered her."

[94] Lit. "My daughter, Torah permits you to him."

Our looser translation factors in the reasoning behind why the Sages permitted a husband to do anything he craves sexually with his wife. See below, pp. 66-67.

[95] Rabbi Yehudah Hanasi's permissive stance, here, is highly significant, for he was also known as "Rabeinu Hakadosh – Our Holy Master," by virtue of his extreme sexual piety (*Talmud, Shabbos 118b* reports that he earned this title because he never in his whole adult life gazed at his own membrum, and he avoided even touching it). Thus, his ruling, here, implies that while an individual's personal proclivities may lean toward extra (or even extreme) piety, it is forbidden to force such piety upon others.

[Note that *Shitah Mekubetzes* to *Nedarim 20b* quotes an interpretation that Rabbi Yehudah Hanasi considered himself powerless to even chastise the husband for his sexual predilections (*hee haisah rotzeh l'hisgaresh mimenu oe sheyasruhu al cach, al cein amar lah: "HaTorah hitirasech loe b'chol inyan, ani eini yachol laasos loe shum davar"*).]

Rav, the other sage approached by the other wife in the other story recounted on *Nedarim 20b*, was also reportedly known for his extreme piety (see *Encyclopedia L'chachmei HaTalmud v'Hageonim*, Entry: *Rav*, p. 35, citing *Teshuvos Hageonim*; compare *Hagigah 5b*; and compare *Babylonian Talmud, Yoma 18b* and *Yevamos 37b* and the understanding of *Tosfos, Yevamos 37b:Yichuda b'alma havu meyachdi*).

Perhaps this might allow us to offer a new explanation as to why the wives had approached these two sages to begin with, and what we were meant to learn from their responses:

These two wives may have come seeking guidance on how to compel their own husbands to be more "refined" and "pious" – like the sages they, the wives, admired. That is, even though the women may have known their husbands' sexual predilections to be permissible, and even though the women may have been willing to tolerate such things or even enjoyed them, they still wanted their spouses to be more "holy."

The responses of Rabbi Yehudah Hanasi and Rav, then, may have been meant to guide the women not to be judgmental about their husband's natural inclinations, for G-d Himself does not judge them.

This would also perhaps explain Rabbi Yehudah Hanasi's concluding phrase, "And now my daughter, what can I do for you?" – implying *not* that he felt powerless to stop her husband from causing her physical pain, but that he felt powerless to forcefully deny a husband his simple, permissible, consensual marital sexual pleasures in life.

And see next endnote.

[96] Note the wording of *Tosfos Yeshanim, Nedarim 20b*: "Torah permits *him* to *you* – to do everything you want [with him]" (*HaTorah Hitiraso Lach – Laasos col retzonech*)

According to this, Rebbi was informing the wife that her husband was permitted to *her*, for *her* to do everything *she wanted* sexually.

This would suggest that the husband, in "overturning" his wife, was actually trying to please *her*, and the wife had come to the sage concerned that maybe she had been the cause of her husband transgressing the law because he had lovingly put her and her desires above G-d's.

[To be sure, the manuscript of *Tosfos Yeshanim* is unpunctuated, and therefore the Hebrew word *reish-tzadi-vov-nun-chof* could ostensibly be read either in the feminine form, "retzonech," or the masculine form, "retzonecha." But it would make no sense for *Tosfos Yeshanim* to have had Rebbi using the masculine form in addressing the wife standing before him.]

Alternatively, the unique wording could merely have been a typographical error. And more research into the matter is required.

[97] A 1st generation Babylonian Amora.

[98] Note that Rav, Rabbi Yochanan bar Napacha and Rabbi Shimon ben Lakish all studied under Rabbi Yehudah HaNasi. And Rabbi Yochanan bar Napacha and Rabbi Shimon ben Lakish were not only sparring partners, they were brothers-in-law. See *Encyclopedia L'chachmei HaTalmud v'Hagaonim*.

[99] Lit. "Rav answered."

[100] Lit. "How is it different than fish?"

[101] Raavad III has this teaching being taught in the name of an entirely different sage, Rabbi Natan (*Baalei HaNefesh, Shaar Hakedushah*, Buchwald edition, p. 175). So does *Mishnas Rabbi Eliezer (ben Rabbi Yossi Haglili), Parshah 18*.

[102] Numbers 15:39

[103] Note that the Hebrew terms for "prohibition" and "prohibited" are nowhere to be found in this Talmudic teaching here.

[104] As discussed above, endnote 81, the term "setting one's eyes (or heart or mind) upon another woman" arguably refers to intentional illicit fantasies, not thoughts that pop into one's mind beyond one's control and/or conscious desire.

[105] A 6th generation Babylonian Amora.

[106] Ezekiel 20:38

[107] Raavad III innovates that such parents themselves are also called by the verse "rebels and transgressors" (*Baalei HaNefesh, Shaar Hakedushah*, p. 178 in the Buchwald edition).

[108] That is, the wife consents to sex with her husband out of fear of his wrath if she were to speak her heart and say no [*Ran, Shitah Mekubetzes*, Ritz quoted in *Shitah Mekubetzes*, to *Nedarim 20b*].

Some say this is not to be read "*Bnei Eimah* – children conceived in a state of fear," but rather, "*Bnei Amah-Bnei Shifchah* – Children born of a slave girl." [See *Tractate Callah 1:10*; *Callah Rabti 1:16*; *Likutei HaPardes* (page 5b in the Munkatch edition), *Peirush HaRosh, Nedarim 20b*; *Tosfos Yeshanim, Nedarim 20b*; *Peirush R. Avraham min Hahar, Nedarim 20b*; *Tosfos Rabeinu Peretz, Nedarim 20b*; Ritz quoted in *Shitah Mekubetzes, Nedarim 20b*; *Chidushei HaMeiri* (and *Meiri, Beis Habechirah*), *Nedarim 20b* has this referring to a non-Jewish slave girl, even after she has converted to Judaism, on the assumption that she was accustomed to prostitution in her previous non-Jewish life.]

Ritz quoted in *Shitah Mekubetzes, Nedarim 20b*, mentions another textual version that has this referring to the "beautiful captive woman" (*yefas toar*), a woman captured at war, whom a soldier might decide to forcefully marry – an act which Torah permits, but severely denigrates as immoral. Ritz explains that because the soldier marries her only for her beauty, he will one day come to despise her, and thus it is a case of *Bnei Snuah* in potentia. And see below, endnote 384.

## ENDNOTES

[109] That is, a husband forcefully demands his wife have sex with him, even against her will [*Raavad III, Baalei HaNefesh, Shaar Hakedushah,* page 177 in the Buchwald edition; *Ran, Nedarim 20b; Ohel Moed, Shaar Isur v'Heter, Derech 11*].

[110] That is, a husband feels hatred toward his wife during intimacy [*Ohel Moed, Shaar Isur v'Heter, Derech 11; Peirush R. Avraham min Hahar Nedarim 20b* (and according to some, he hates her so much that he fantasizes of other women – *Mefaresh, Ran, Tosfos Rabeinu Peretz, Shitah Mekubetzes,* Ritz quoted in *Shitah Mekubetzes,* to *Nedarim 20b*).]

*Chidushei HaMeiri* (and *Meiri, Beis Habechirah), Nedarim 20b,* has this referring to a husband who finds his wife repulsive and therefore only has sex with her occasionally, thus treating her as if she weren't actually his wife.

Either way, this category would presumably also include a wife who is angered or repulsed by her husband.

[111] That is, the husband is in a state of excommunication by the rabbinic court [*Mefaresh, Ran, Chidushei HaMeiri* (and *Meiri, Beis HaBechirah), Peirush R. Avraham min Hahar, Tosfos Rabeinu Peretz, Talmidei Rabeinu Peretz, Shitah Mekubetzes* to *Nedarim 20b*]. *Peirush HaRosh* to *Nedarim 20b* says it applies if either husband or wife are excommunicated.

As commentaries note, there is a question brought in *Talmud, Moed Katan 15b,* if, according to the rabbis – the very ones who enact such excommunications in the first place – a person whom they've excommunicated is forbidden to have sex. But the Talmud, there, does not come to a definite conclusion. And certain medieval commentaries actually permit it (See Rabbi Yaakov ben Asher's *Tur, Even Haezer 334* and Rabbi Caro's *Beis Yosef* thereon. Note that Rabbi Caro, there, says Maimonides implies it is permitted in *Mishneh Torah, Sefer Hamada, Hilchos Talmud Torah 7.* But note also that in *Sefer Kedushah, Isurei Biah 21:12,* in discussing the nine-ten flawed conditions, Maimonides cautions against a married couple having sex whilst either one of them, husband or wife, is in excommunication).

See *Pesach Einaim* of Rabbi Chaim Yosef Dovid Azulai (Chida) to *Nedarim 20b,* where he quotes a commentary saying that according to those who permit sex during excommunication, the context of *Bnei Nidoi* as mentioned on *Nedarim 20b* must be referring only to a couple upon whom the rabbinic court *expressly added* a ban against sex. He also notes that Rabbi Yaakov ben Asher himself in *Tur, Orach Chaim 240* and *Even Haezer 25,* does list *Bnei Nidoi* as one of the nine-ten flawed conditions as an alternative to *Bnei Nidah.*

But note that *Tractate Callah 1:10, Callah Rabti 1:16, Likutei HaPardes* (page 5b in the Munkatch edition) and Ritz quoted in *Shitah Mekubetzes, Nedarim 20b,* count both *Bnei Nidoi* and *Bnei Nidah* among the nine-ten flawed conditions.

Finally, there is an approach that a caution against *Bnei Nidoi* would imply a caution as well against sex with a spouse who is in mourning or who is a *metzora*-leper [See, for example, Ritz quoted in *Shitah Mekubetzes, Nedarim 20b.*]

[112] That is, a husband has sex with his wife during her impure menstrual period. [*Raavad III, Baalei HaNefesh, Shaar Hakedushah,* page 177 in the Buchwald edition; *Ohel Moed, Shaar Isur v'Heter, Derech 11*].

*Tosfos HaShalem al HaTorah, Breishis 29:31:7* says that this refers not to sex during the actual menstrual period, but to sex on the day the wife expects her cycle, for the rabbis imposed a stricture upon husband and wife not to engage in sexual intercourse on that day. [See *Kovetz Meforshim* (Yerid Haseforim, 2003) *Leket Rishonim, Nedarim 20b,* page 63].

Note that *Tractate Callah 1:10, Callah Rabti 1:16, Likutei HaPardes* (page 5b in the Munkatch edition) and Ritz quoted in *Shitah Mekubetzes, Nedarim 20b*, count both *Bnei Nidoi* and *Bnei Nidah* among the nine-ten flawed conditions.

[113] That is, a husband thought he was having intercourse with a forbidden woman and it turned out to be his own wife. [*Mefaresh, Nedarim 20b*; Raavad III, *Baalei HaNefesh, Shaar Hakedushah*, page 177 in the Buchwald edition; *Chidushei HaMeiri* (and *Meiri, Beis HaBechirah*), *Nedarim 20b*; *Ohel Moed, Shaar Isur v'Heter, Derech 11*; *Peirush R. Avraham min Hahar*; *Shitah Mekubetzes, Nedarim 20b*; *Tosfos Yeshanim, Tosfos Rabeinu Peretz* and Ritz (quoted in *Shitah Mekubetzes*) to *Nedarim 20b* have it referring to a man fantasizing specifically of another married woman].

*Mefaresh*, Ran, *Peirush R. Avraham min Hahar* and *Peirush HaRosh* also offer a polygamous interpretation, that *Bnei Temurah* refers to a husband who expected one of his wives in bed, and then, after the fact, discovered it was a different one of his wives. Rabbi Avraham of Montpellier (*Peirush R. Avraham min Hahar*) may have considered this to be the more true interpretation of the two. Raavad III, however, rejects this interpretation, arguing that if this were the case, why should anyone be called "rebellious" or be punished for such an inadvertent mistake [*Baalei HaNefesh*, Buchwald edition, page 177].

Raavad III also questions the validity of this interpretation from the episode of the wedding night of Jacob and Leah, when Jacob thought he was in bed with Rachel. If, Raavad III's question goes, Jacob's eldest son, Reuben, was conceived that night, how is it that Reuben did not turn out to be rebellious?

Firstly, let us note that in the case of Jacob, the two sisters were not yet both his own wives, ostensibly making the act even more spiritually deficient.

Secondly, we do find that Reuben was rebellious later in the Bible, when he had sex with one of his father's concubines (Genesis 35:22, 49:4). Despite how some Jewish scholars have attempted to interpret this episode non-literally, the overriding rule of the sages themselves is that a biblical verse never loses its literal meaning. And if it were not meant literally at all, then the author of the Bible – G-d Himself – could ostensibly be accused of slander.

So Raavad III's question would appear to be a non-sequitur.

[Parenthetically, commentaries who say that Reuben must have been conceived on Jacob and Leah's wedding night, do so based on the verse in Genesis 49:4, where Jacob calls Reuben, "My firstborn, my strength, my first vigor." They explain that "first vigor" refers to Jacob's first ejaculation ever – implying that Reuben was conceived the first night Jacob was with Leah. But Jacob himself in that same verse goes on to speak of Reuben's later transgression – "You ascended upon your father's bed..." In that case, the verse itself could theoretically be interpreted as associating Reuben's rebellion with the deficient nature of Jacob's union with Leah on their wedding night, the night of Reuben's conception, when Jacob's thoughts were of another, of Rachel.]

These two points aside, we must note that Raavad III's first approach to resolving this question is that before the Giving of the Torah, the family of Abraham, Issac and Jacob "had not yet been *prohibited* in the details of the commandments" (*lo ne'esru b'dikdukei mitzvos*) – suggesting that sex under all these nine-ten flawed conditions is actually a legal prohibition. But nowhere does the Talmud on *Nedarim 20b*, *Tractate Callah* or *Callah Rabti* designate Rabbi Levi's intentions as such (though, of course, two of the nine, forced sex and sex during menstruation, are certainly forbidden from other sources in Torah; and see below, endnote 128).

# ENDNOTES

Raavad III's second approach to resolving this matter is that perhaps Reuben was not actually conceived on Jacob and Leah's wedding night.

[Ritz, quoted in *Shitah Mekubetzes* to *Nedarim 20b* offers the same two approaches as Raavad III.]

This answer brings us to two additional observations:

One, Raavad III clearly understood the designation, "rebels and transgressors," as not only referring to a husband and wife themselves, but also to their children (a point that will be of significance in our expanded treatment of the subject in a future volume of this series).

Two, it implies that Raavad III did believe in *Callah Rabti 1:13's* stipulation (in the name of Rava) that congenital illnesses only result from parents' deficient sexual behaviors during the same sexual encounter in which conception occurs. However, *Callah Rabti 1:13* said this in regard to Rabbi Yochanan ben Dahavai's cautions about physical congenital illnesses resulting from "overturning the table," non-sex-related talk during sex and gazing at or kissing the female genitals, not in regard to Rabbi Levi's cautions about psychological-emotional-spiritual effects resulting from the nine-ten flawed conditions. But Raavad III brings this stipulation *only* in regard to the latter. The fact that he does not mention it also in regard to Rabbi Yochanan ben Dahavai's physical cautions is perplexing – and, innocent as this omission may have been, it has possibly contributed to significant confusion and distress to married couples through the ages and until today (and see below, pp. 63-64, 162-163, 202-203).

Ritz, quoted in *Shitah Mekubetzes* to *Nedarim 20b* offers yet another interpretation of *Bnei Temurah*, involving a pre-existing biblical prohibition much more grave than anything else listed among the nine: wife-swapping.

One issue with this interpretation, at least according to *Tractate Callah* and *Callah Rabti*, is that offspring proven to have been conceived from such activity would be considered actual bastards in the eyes of Jewish law, whereas *Tractate Callah 1:10* and *Callah Rabti 1:16* both introduce their discussions of this topic stating: "Ten are like bastards, but are not actual bastards."

[114] That is, the wife tells her husband that she has no need for him to give her sex, and yet he has sex with her anyway. [Raavad III, *Baalei HaNefesh, Shaar Hakedushah*, page 177-178 in the Buchwald edition; Ritz, quoted in *Shitah Mekubetzes* to *Nedarim 20b* adds that such sex is tantamount to sex with a prostitute, even if the wife agrees to let him do it].

*Tosfos HaShalem al HaTorah, Breishis 29:31:7*, based on *Babylonian Talmud, Kesubos 72a*, says that this refers to a wife who rebels against the "manners" of the Jewish people (*das yehudis*), such as feeding her husband untithed produce or cursing his children in front him [quoted in *Kovetz Meforshim* (Yerid Haseforim, 2003), *Leket Rishonim, Nedarim 20b*, page 63. Note, however, that while *Kesubos 72a* categorizes a wife who curses her husband's children in front of him as transgressing the manners of the Jewish people (*das yehudis*), it categorizes a wife who feeds her husband untithed produce as transgressing the religion of Moses (*das Moshe*)].

Rabbi Yehoshuah Falk, in his *Prishah* commentary to *Tur, Even Haezer 25:8-10:29*, suggests that the wife, here, tells her husband that she has no desire for him to be her spouse, and that she no longer desires to remain his.

[115] That is, the husband and wife are constantly fighting day and night [Raavad III, *Baalei HaNefesh, Shaar Hakedushah*, page 177-178 in the Buchwald edition; Ritz quoted in *Shitah Mekubetzes* to *Nedarim 20b* – but Ritz says the couple do not actually "hate" each other, it's only that their sex is loveless].

Others interpret this as a case where husband and wife harbor hard feelings toward one another only *temporarily*, but such feelings happened to coincide with the act of intercourse [*Mefaresh, Ran, Peirush HaRosh, Peirush R' Avraham min Hahar* to *Nedarim 20b*.]

*Chidushei HaMeiri* (and *Meiri, Beis HaBechirah*) to *Nedarim 20b* has this referring specifically to a husband who hits and rapes his wife.

*Shitah Mekubetzes, Nedarim 20b* has this referring to a husband who rushes his wife to let him use her body for sex, without first arousing her to the mood.

Note that *Callah Rabti 1:16* has the letter "*mem*" standing not for "*Bnei Moredes*" or "*Bnei Merivah*," but for "*Bnei Mefutah* – Children conceived as a result of seduction." Or perhaps this category was meant to be counted in place of "*Bnei Anusah* – Children conceived in a state of force," which *Callah Rabti* does not count either (though *Likutei HaPardes,* page 5b in the Munkatch edition, does count both *Bnei Mefutah* and *Bnei Anusah*).

Others have the letter "*mem*" standing for "*Bnei Meshugaas*" – Children conceived by an insane woman" – the stated problem being that due to her deficient mental state she is unlikely to purify herself properly after her menstrual period [*Tosfos Yeshanim* and *Shitah Mekubetzes* to *Nedarim 20b. Shitah Mekubetzes* actually has "*Bnei Meshugah*" – Children of an insane man," though he also mentions the problem of an insane woman not purifying herself properly before sex]. *Chidushei HaMeiri* (and *Meiri, Beis HaBechirah*) to *Nedarim 20b*, however, argues that this is a textual error, probably originating in the pneumonic some Talmudic versions put forth to help students remember the list of the nine flawed conditions – A'S'N'T M'Sh'G'A'H.

[116] That is, the husband or wife are intoxicated during sex. [*Raavad III, Baalei HaNefesh, Shaar Hakedushah*, page 178 in the Buchwald edition; *Peirush HaRosh* to *Nedarim 20b; Chidushei HaMeiri* (and *Meiri, Beis HaBechirah*) to *Nedarim 20b; Ritz* quoted in *Shitah Mekubetzes, Nedarim 20b*, adds that the problem with this is that the sex is loveless and they aren't even aware of what they are doing, making it tantamount to prostitution (and see below, endnote 666)].

Versions of *Callah Rabti 1:16* have this referring specifically to an intoxicated wife.

*Ran* and *Peirush R' Avraham min Hahar* to *Nedarim 20b* have it referring specifically to an intoxicated husband.

*Tosfos Yeshanim* and *Shitah Mekubetzes* to *Nedarim 20b* apparently believed the problem with intoxication only to be that it might lead to sex during the wife's menstrual period.

In any case, later authorities explain that there is no problem if either spouse, or both together, are just a little tipsy. The problem is only if they have lost control of their senses (*nitbalbel daato*). See Rabbi Yosef Teomim, *Pri Megadim, Shulchan Aruch Orach Chaim,* 240:3:11 (quoted also in *Mishnah Berurah, Orach Chaim* 240:3:18).

*Tosfos HaShalem al HaTorah, Breishis* 29:31:7 quotes a variant textual version which has the letter "*Shin*" standing for "*Shotah* – Insane woman" rather than "*Shichrus* – Intoxication" [quoted in *Kovetz Meforshim* (Yerid Haseforim, 2003) *Leket Rishonim, Nedarim* 20b, page 63].

[117] That is, a husband has already made the final decision in his heart to divorce his wife, and yet he still has sex with her. [*Raavad III, Baalei HaNefesh, Shaar Hakedushah,* page 178 in the Buchwald edition; *Ran, Nedarim 20b*].

*Peirush HaRosh* says that such a state of heart is problematic even if he does not bear hatred toward her, because he will still be intentionally fantasizing about another woman. *Ohel*

*Moed, Shaar Isur v'Heter, Derech 11* and Ritz quoted in *Shitah Mekubetzes, Nedarim 20b* say this also.

But see *Chidushei HaMeiri* (and *Meiri, Beis HaBechirah*) to *Nedarim 20b*, who also says there is an issue here even if the husband does not hate his wife – though Meiri does not speak about the problem of illicit fantasies.

And *Peirush R' Avraham min Hahar* and *Tosfos Rabeinu Peretz* mention the problem of illicit fantasies, here, but don't address the possibility that despite his intention to divorce her, the husband might still actually love her.

*Shitah Mekubetzes* acknowledges that the husband, here, may not actually hate his wife, he may just want to leave her in order to marry a woman *with more money*.

[118] That is, a husband has sex with his wife in order to live out a sexual fantasy he has of another woman, even if that other woman is another one of his own wives [*Mishnas Rabbi Eliezer (ben Rabbi Yossi Haglili), Parshah 18*; Raavad III, *Baalei HaNefesh, Shaar Hakedushah*, page 178 in the Buchwald edition; *Chidushei HaMeiri* (and *Meiri, Beis HaBechirah*) to *Nedarim 20b* doesn't differentiate between fantasies of another one of one's own wives or of an entirely forbidden woman].

The *Mefaresh* commentary to *Nedarim 20b*, however, offers three entirely different interpretations, which it does not seem to restrict to the context of marriage:

a) A man had sex with one out of multiple women, but he doesn't know which one it was (*Peirush HaRosh* to *Nedarim 20b* quotes this interpretation too, but he has it referring to a husband who has multiple wives, and he does not know which wife he slept with).

b) A woman had sex with multiple men, and she doesn't know which one is the father of her child (*Ran* to *Nedarim 20b* offers this interpretation too).

c) A woman (*Mefaresh* does not mention if she was unmarried, a widow or a divorcée) had sex with a new man and found herself to be pregnant all within less than three months since having sex with her last man, thus calling the paternity of the child into question.

Ritz quoted in *Shitah Mekubetzes, Nedarim 20b*, echoes interpretations b) and c) of the *Mefaresh*.

*Tosfos Rabeinu Peretz* echoes interpretation c).

*Tosfos Yeshanim, Peirush R. Avraham min Hahar* and *Shitah Mekubetzes* offer interpretation c) as well, but they specify it as referring specifically to a widow or divorced woman who remarries and consummates the marriage within three months of losing or divorcing her previous husband.

[119] Some include, here, two alternates:

1) *Bnei Yesheinah* – Children conceived in a state of sleep. See *Tosfos, Nidah 12a*, that sex is permitted while one's wife is "half-asleep," but not while she is totally asleep and completely oblivious to what's going on.

2) *Haboel Arusaso b'beis Chamav* – One who has sex with his betrothed in the house of his future father-in-law.

[See *Tractate Callah 1:10; Callah Rabti 1:16*; commentary of Rabbi Avraham Hayarchi to *Callah Rabti* (page 3 in the Toledano edition).]

3) *Bnei Taharas Safek* – One who has sex with a woman whose state of menstrual purity is in question.

[See *Likutei HaPardes*, page 5b in the Munkatch edition.]

[120] A 2nd generation Israeli Amora.

[121] A 1st generation Israeli Amora.

*Babylonian Talmud, Eruvin 100b* has this teaching in the name of a different sage, Rabbi Yochanan. But both Talmudic tractates have alternate manuscript versions featuring the names of Rabbi Yonasan and Rabbi Yochanan interchangeably in connection with this teaching. [See *Dikdukei Sofrim, Eruvin 100b*; *Dikdukei Sofrim Hashalem, Nedarim 20b*.]

Rabbi Shmuel bar Nachmani was in fact a disciple of Rabbi Yonasan ben Elazar. And Rabbi Yonasan ben Elazer was a colleague of Rabbi Yochanan bar Napacha. [See *Encyclopedia L'chachmei HaTalmud*, Entries "Rabbi Yonasan ben Elazar" and "Rabbi Shmuel bar Nachmani."]

[122] Compare to *Eruvin 100b*: "Any woman who asks her husband for sex will bear children the likes of whom even the generation of Moses did not merit." Even more than *Nedarim 20b*, this is a clear praise of the wife for her solicitous behavior toward her husband.

[123] The Talmud on *Nedarim 20b*, in the course of Rabbi Shmuel bar Nachmani's teaching, mentions only the term "*tovaato*" – that is, she asks him for sex. But the Talmud on *Eruvin 100b* clarifies that the context of Rabbi Shmuel bar Nachmani's teaching was about a wife being "*toveia b'peh* – asking for sex **verbally**" – as the matriarch Leah ostensibly did when she asked her husband, Jacob, to come to her. It is also clear from the commentaries to *Nedarim 20b* that they understood "*tovaato*" to be equivalent to "*tovaato b'peh*."

It is related in Genesis that our forefather Jacob had four wives: Leah, Rachel, Bilhah and Zilpah. His favorite wife, Rachel, was barren for many years, while his lesser-favored wife, Leah, bore him many sons. Each wife had established nights on which they enjoyed their marital "right" to physical intimacy with their husband. But Rachel "sold" one of her nights to Leah, and thus Leah approached Jacob and informed him (Genesis 30:16): "You shall come to me tonight, for I have paid for [the rights to] you." Leah thus verbally demanded of Jacob that she be the one he come to that night – without any concern as to what Jacob's own wishes might have been. And behold, that night Leah conceived a son, Isachar, whose tribe hundreds of years later produced intellectual leaders.

[One translation of the Bible, the Gutnick Edition (Kol Menachem, 2003), renders Leah's wording to Jacob as, "You *can* come to me tonight…" This minimizes the forcefulness of her verbal expression. But see the *Artscoll Talmud, Eruvin 100b* and *Nedarim 20b*, footnote 40, both of which render Leah's wording as, "You *shall* come to me…"]

The compilers-editors of the Talmud on *Nedarim 20b* therefore challenge Rabbi Levi's designation of a wife who verbally asks her husband for sex as "brazen" (*chatzufah*), for we find even the matriarch Leah herself verbally demanding sex from her husband, Jacob, and, nevertheless, her descendants from that union turned out well.

[124] Rabbi Shmuel bar Nachmani goes on to explain that in Deuteronomy 1:13, Moses relates that soon after the Giving of the Torah he was unable to judge the entire people on his own, and he thus commanded the people to find others to help him, including "men of wisdom," who could comprehend the laws, and "men of understanding," who could derive new laws from the original ones (see Rashi, there). But two verses later, Moses goes on to retell only that he appointed "men of wisdom." Rabbi Shmuel bar Nachmani assumes from this that there must not have been any "men of understanding" in the entire generation of Moses.

Later in the Bible, however, in Chronicles I 12:33, there is a verse that speaks of the Tribe of Isachar during the days of King David as producing "men of understanding of the times." Rabbi Shmuel bar Nachmani thus makes a connection: The Bible tells us in Genesis that the original Isachar, the father of the tribe, was conceived the same night that his mother, Leah, demanded Jacob come to her for physical intimacy. Therefore, Rabbi Shmuel bar Nachmani concludes, the acumen that manifested in the Tribe of Isachar four hundreds years later must have been a result of Leah's verbal demand of her husband for physical intimacy.

Thus, the compilers-editors of the Talmud challenged Rabbi Levi: How can you say that a wife who asks for sex from her husband is considered "brazen," and that her "brazenness" will be inherited by her children, when Rabbi Shmuel bar Nachmani "proved" that Leah's demand for sex from Jacob resulted in her offspring being intellectual greats?

But this entire teaching of Rabbi Shmuel bar Nachmani, and the suggested challenge from it to the teaching of Rabbi Levi, is highly problematic, for:

a) Either the children of Isachar were already "men of understanding" in the generation of Moses himself, which was also the generation of the Giving of the Torah itself, for already then they were the offspring of Leah's union with Jacob, or the children of Isachar were *not* "men of understanding" even in the generation of Moses himself, even in the generation of the Giving of the Torah itself – and thus, if they possessed such lack of understanding just three-four generations after their matriarch, Leah, walked the earth, the fact that their tribesmen may have possessed deep "understanding" four hundreds years later can hardly be attributed to her behavior with Jacob on the night of Isachar's conception.

b) Nowhere did Rabbi Levi say that offspring of the nine-ten flawed conditions would be lacking in intelligence ("understanding"), but only that they would be lacking in spiritual refinement.

c) The fact that Isachar may have produced great Jewish scholars in his descendants in the time of King David, cannot override the fact that, according to Jewish tradition, in the generation of Moses itself the Tribe of Isachar took part in the sin of the Golden Calf – thus implying that they were no more spiritually superior than any of their brethren tribes at that time – save for the Tribe of Levi, which did not take part in the sin.

Additionally, we are not told that the original Isachar himself was any less guilty than his brothers in the selling of Joseph – which cannot be ignored just because his descendants centuries later stood out. Indeed, it is quite clear that the teaching of Rabbi Levi on *Nedarim 20b* is warning specifically about *the child who is conceived* in a state of one of the nine-ten flawed conditions – not to that child's descendants for all time after. In that case, how Isachar's own descendants turned out generations later is arguably irrelevant to Rabbi Levi's teaching – and it is on the surface surprising that the compilers-editors of *Nedarim 20b* brought it into the discussion in the first place.

d) According to Rashi on Deuteronomy 1:13, Moses was looking for "men of understanding" who could compare and derive Torah law, whereas according to Rashi on Chronicles I 12:33, the "understanding of the times" that manifested in the Tribe of Isachar during the reign of King David had to do with their understanding of political science and/or military strategy.

See, however, *Breishis Rabah 72:5*, which does interpret this verse as attesting to the Torah scholarship of the Tribe of Isachar.

e) Even in regard to the science of astronomy that the Tribe of Isachar is said to have at some point possessed, it is not clear if they actually derived the essential equations themselves or if they were merely entrusted with them by prophets who had recorded divine revelation (see Maimonides, *Mishneh Torah, Sefer Zmanim, Kidush Hachodesh 17:24*; and see below, endnote 846*).

[And see *Yalkut Shimoni, Korach 16:2*, that the 250 Jewish leaders (*nesi'ei ha'eidah*) who stood with Korach in rebellion against Moses – that is, in Moses' own generation – were from among the distinguished of the nation (*meyuchadin she'b'eidah*) and they knew how to calculate leap years and establish the months (*she'hayu yodin l'aber shanim v'likvoa chadashim*). Thus, if by "men of understanding" Moses had been referring to those possessing an understanding of astronomy, according to this passage in *Yalkut Shimoni* such understanding did exist already among others in his generation. But perhaps they all died out in the episode of Korach. And more research into the matter is required.]

[125] Most commentaries suggest that the conclusion of the Talmud's compilers-editors was that a wife should not initiate sex by talking sexy to her husband at all, or at least not use explicit, direct phrases like "let's have sex." See the following commentaries to *Nedarim 20b*: *Mefaresh, Ran, Peirush HaRosh, Piskei Riaz* (quoted in *Kovetz Shitos Kamai*), *Meiri-Beis Habechirah, Tosfos Rabeinu Peretz*. See also Raavad III in *Baalei HaNefesh, Shaar Hakedushah* (p. 178 in the Buchwald edition) and *Ohel Moed, Shaar Isur v'Heter, Derech 11*. See also *Eruvin 100b, Rabeinu Chananel*: *Meratzya artzuyei* and *Rashi*: *D'meratzya artzuyei kamei*. See also *Prishah* to *Tur, Orach Chaim 240:2-4:7* – but compare to *Prishah* to *Tur, Even Haezer 25:8-10:32*.

But, arguably, it is possible to read their conclusion another way: that Rabbi Levi was only denigrating a wife who knows that confident and/or aggressive sexual overtures make her husband uncomfortable, and she nevertheless torments him – brazenly (*chatzufah*); and that Rabbi Shmuel bar Nachmani was praising a wife who knows her husband will be pleased and/or aroused by such overtures, and it would thus be perfectly acceptable for her to playfully ask for/demand sex of him – for such would be loving, not brazen.

Such a reading would perhaps follow in the spirit of Rabbi Betzalel Ashkenazi's and Rabbi Avraham of Montpellier's comments on this Talmudic passage – as we shall now explain:

Considering that it must certainly be permitted for a wife to express her sexual desires and needs to her husband once they are actually in bed (as a matter of sex-related talk – *mili d'tashmisha*) without having to resort to "mime" or euphemism, it is difficult to accept that she is forbidden to express such desires to him verbally, lovingly, in order to arouse him to come to her bed in the first place. And in certain real-life scenarios between husband and wife, to insist on her doing otherwise may simply be unrealistic.

We would therefore argue that at issue here is not so much the wife's *wording* in expressing her sexual desires to her husband, but her *tone* in doing so – not only because this arguably makes more sense from the simple context of Leah's precedent and a simple reading of the Talmud's words, but because the term "*toveia*" in rabbinic literature is generally used in the context of someone who *forcefully demands* their legal rights from another. In the case at hand, Jewish law gives a wife three basic legal rights she can expect from her husband within marriage, one of them being "conjugal rights" – i.e. sexual fulfillment to the fullest extent of her husband's abilities.

# ENDNOTES

[And note the wording of Rabeinu Avigdor Tzarfati (13th century) in *Peirushim uPsakim al HaTorah, Parshas Mishpatim, Psak 76: Chayav adam l'ishto she'er, csus v'onah. V'im machal lo zeh . . . b'davar sheb'mamon tenao kayem, v'ein lah alav she'er csus. Aval onah, shehu davar sheb'gufo, tenao batel, v'yicholah* **litvoa** *mimenu din onasah.*]

Therefore, in the absence of any real evidence to the contrary in the original biblical account, the connotation and context of the "*chatzufah*," here, can arguably be understood as that of a wife who makes *a forceful verbal claim against her husband's will* for her legal right to enjoy sexual satisfaction from him.

[See also *The Artscroll Talmud, Nedarim 20b*, footnote 34: "She *brazenly demands* marital relations from her husband (Ran; see Ritz, cited by *Shitah Mekubetzes*)."

See also footnote 42 there: "When a wife conveys her needs in this pleasant, tactful manner (as opposed to making an *imperious demand*), she is clearly being considerate of her husband's needs as well. She wants to gladden him and promote his wellbeing (Tos. Yeshanim)."

Actually, earlier in footnote 42 it implies that the lesson to be learned from Leah is that a wife should not speak to her husband in sexual terms at all, but rather she should speak "euphemistically, in a manner that need not necessarily be interpreted as referring to cohabitation." But it then abruptly changes the message of the story into an objection against a wife making "imperious demands" for sex.]

This understanding is also supported by the fact that the teaching of Rabbi Shmuel bar Nachmani - as quoted in both *Eruvin 100b* and *Nedarim 20b* according to various manuscript versions - literally reads: "a wife who verbally asks for *the commandment (d'var mitzvah)* from her husband." While it can be argued that this is merely a "clean way" of saying "sex," there are certainly other terms the Talmudic sage could have used if he were *not* referring to a night on which the husband is also *obligated* by G-d's command to give his wife satisfaction.

[Consider, as one alternative option, the term found in *Tractate Callah 8*: "*Tovaata lamitah* – he asks that she come to bed," which implies no context of legal obligation of husband to wife or wife to husband.

Note also that Rabbi Yaakov Emden comments on an earlier discussion on *Eruvin 100b*, in regard to a husband not being allowed to force his wife to have sex, that this applies even on nights when he is technically *obligated* to give it to her (see *Shas Wagshal-Nehardea, Tractate Eruvin, Hagahos v'Chidushim, Eruvin 100b, Yaavetz*). The same restriction would therefore presumably apply to the wife, preventing her from forcefully demanding sex even on a night when her husband technically "owes" it to her by divine mandate].

Therefore, even in the concluding resolution of the compilers-editors of the Talmud on *Nedarim 20b*, "*d'meratzya artzuyei*," it is reasonable to suggest that they were still encouraging a wife to lovingly and playfully ask for/demand sex from her husband so long as she does so with good - not selfish - intentions, especially being that when all is said and done, it is difficult to deny that the matriarch Leah herself verbally "demanded" sex from Jacob, it is only that she did so for his sake as well - in the words of *Tosfos Yeshanim, Nedarim 20b, "D'artzei artzuyei"*:

> Her whole intention is not about satisfying her own sexual desires, but rather her intention is *also* to gladden and increase his wellbeing.

The clearest expression in the commentaries supporting this reading of the Talmud's conclusion is that of Rabbi Betzalel Ashkenazi in the closing paragraph of his *Shitah Mekubetzes* to this passage of *Nedarim 20b*:

"*D'meratzya artzuyei*" – She appeases him and shows him body language indicating her interest in sex (*m'fayasto umasberes lo panim l'tashmish*), as [our matriarch] Leah did.

But if she asks for sex with her mouth *with force* (*bachazakah*) and with *light-headedness* (*ub'kalus rosh*) and *with brazenness* (*v'azus panim*) and *she's demanding about it* (*u'makpedes b'chach*), she is like an adulteress, and the children [conceived of such a sexual encounter] will not be upright.

But to put him in the mood is perfectly fine (*aval meratzya artzuyei shapir dami*).

See also the medieval Rabbi Avraham of Montpellier (*Peirush R. Avraham min Hahar*) to *Nedarim 20b*:

"*D'meratzya artzuyei*" – Like [our matriarch] Leah. But to ask for sex from him with her mouth and *forcefully* and with *light-headedness*, this is like a prostitute.

And when Leah said, "You shall come to me [tonight]," she worded it [suggestively, not directly,] as if to say, "You will come to eat, and drink and sleep, [etcetera]…"

While both Rabbi Betzalel Ashkenazi's and Rabbi Avraham of Montpellier's interpretations of Leah's behavior imply that only "suggestive" verbalization is acceptable from a wife, not direct talk, such as "let's have sex," if a wife were to use the latter direct language to her husband lovingly and playfully, because she knows it will arouse him, then she can hardly be accused of demanding sex "with force, light-headedness, brazenness, and/or demandingness," in the manner of "an adulteress or prostitute." In other words, both rabbis speak, here, in extremes, and in so doing they arguably leave a wide range of agreeable verbal expression at a loving wife's disposal.

In any case, both Rabbis Betzalel Ashkenazi and Avraham of Montpellier make clear that *Nedarim 20b's negative* use of the term "*tovaato/tovaas b'peh*" was meant to refer to a wife who *forces* her husband to give her sex, not a wife who *lovingly* asks for or *playfully* demands sexual attention from her husband using her words.

But what of their categorization of "light-headedness" as a form of brazeness? Does that not imply that even according to them *Nedarim 20b* was discouraging a wife from speaking anything "sexy" – i.e., "light-headed" – to her husband, ever, at all?

Firstly, neither one says that a wife is considered brazen if she asks for sex "forcefully OR with lightheadedness," but rather if she asks for sex "forcefully AND with lightheadedness" – implying that lightheadedness *combined* with forcefulness is the way of an adulteress or prostitute, in contrast to playful forcefulness that is combined with respect, love and sensitivity to the other's limits. We thus need not assume that they objected to loving "light-headed" behavior or sexy talk (*kalus rosh* and/or *sichah kalah*) in-and-of-themselves, absent of any uncomfortable forcefulness, and expressed by a wife respectfully to her husband to share her mood for lovemaking.

In fact, Maimonides, in his *Mishneh Torah, Sefer Nashim, Ishus 14:5* – interpreting *Talmud, Kesubos 71b-72a* – speaks of both husband and wife verbalizing "words of joking and light-headedness" of a private sexual nature to one another, as if such words were natural and commonplace and permitted coming from either spouse (*mah she'amar lah oe mah she'amrah lo midivrei schok v'kalus rosh shemidaber adam im ishto al iskei tashmish*). Indeed, he only raises the issue there in order to object to a husband forcing his wife to repeat to others what she said to him.

[In *Ishus 15:18*, Maimonides implies four points that "the Sages instructed a wife": a) to be modest in her home (*shetihiyeh tznuah b'toch beisah*); b) not to be excessive in joking and light-headedness in front of her husband (*v'lo tarbeh b'schok v'kalus rosh bifnei baalah*); c) not to verbally ask for/demand sex (*v'lo titva tashmish hamitah b'peh*); d) not to be conversant about sex (*v'lo tihiyeh midaberes b'esek zeh*).

But only point c) is clearly in regard to the time of actual sexual intimacy – where, again, the concern is arguably about *forceful* demand, not *loving-playful* demand.

Point a) is about modesty in the home in general. Point b) is about avoiding general excessive joking and light-headedness – which even a husband is cautioned against by the Talmud on *Hagigah 5b*. And point d) can easily be read to mean that a wife should not be conversant about sex in general – but we need not assume from here that there would be anything objectionable in her talking sexy to her husband in lead up to sexual intimacy and during foreplay in a manner that is pleasing and/or arousing to him – just like on *Hagigah 5b* there is a textual version that accepts any sexy talk a husband might say to his wife in the lead up to intercourse, even if such talk is (partly) intended by the husband to increase his own sexual passion (as discussed below, pp. 79-80 in regard to the view of Rabbi Yaakov ben Asher; and see also below, pages 57-58).]

In fact, in the Talmud's conclusion on *Nedarim 20b*, it uses the phrase "*d'meratzya artzuyei*" – nearly identical to the phrase "*c'dei l'ratzuyah*" used on *Hagigah 5b* to describe the sexually-charged talk Rav spoke with his wife in order to arouse her to the mood (and which, according to some textual versions of the Talmud, there, is understood to be synonymous with "*sichah kalah* – light-headed talk"). See below, pp. 73-74.

Thus, Rabbi Betzalel Ashkenazi's and Rabbi Avraham of Montpellier's concern about a wife behaving with "light-headedness" (*kalus rosh*) with her husband as she "forcefully" demands him to give her sex, cannot be assumed to apply to loving sexy talk between spouses, even that which is initiated by the wife.

Additionally, as we discuss below, p. 76, the term "light-headedness" doesn't even necessarily refer to light-headed *talk*, but rather to light-headed *behavior* in the form of creative sexual positions/exploration – including "overturning the table" and gazing at or kissing the female genitals. In this light, the meaning of "forcefully and with light-headedness" could mean that she not only forces him to give her sex, but she forces him to engage in sexual behaviors that push him beyond his comfort zone.

Be all that as it may, even if Rabbis Betzalel Ashkenazi and Avraham of Montpellier, or any other commentator, did intend to discourage sexy talk of any kind initiated by a wife to her husband, even when spoken lovingly in order to make her mood known to him and/or to please/arouse him, it still remains to be explained (by them) why such "light-headed talk" (*sichah kalah*), even of a sexual nature, was perfectly encouraged for Rav to speak with his wife on *Hagigah 5b*.

Now, one might be inclined to cite *Babylonian Talmud, Eruvin 100b* to argue that Torah differentiates between the sexes in this regard, and that it does accept a husband's sexy talk to arouse his wife while it does not accept the same from a wife to arouse her husband.

Let us take a moment to explore this.

The compilers-editors of the Talmud on *Eruvin 100b*, like on *Nedarim 20b*, quote Rav Shmuel bar Nachmani, who invokes the story of Leah with Jacob to extol a wife who asks her husband for sex.

The compilers-editors of the Talmud then counter with a challenge:

> Is this so? – But Rav Yitzchak bar Avdimi said: "Ten curses were cast upon Eve [and all womankind, as a result of her part in the sin of eating of the Tree of Knowledge], as

it is written [Genesis 3:16], 'And G-d said to the woman . . . and your desire shall be for your husband . . . and he shall dominate you' – this teaches that a wife asks for sex with her heart, while a husband asks for sex with his mouth. And this is considered a fine trait of character among women."

[The compilers-editors of the Talmud resolve the challenge:] When do we say this [that a wife who verbally asks for sex from her husband is meritorious]? – Only when she is trying to be pleasing and/or arousing to him (*d'meratzya artzuyei kamei*).

This is how we would suggest translating the conclusion of the Talmudic passage.

[Note that even in reading the alleged curse, we would say that a husband is still expected to ask for sex only *lovingly*, as we would say the Talmud on *Nedarim 20b* concludes in regard to a wife. We do so because to understand it as giving a husband license to forcefully demand sex of his wife would go against the spirit of everything Jewish law says about a husband not being allowed to force his wife into sex at all, ever – as taught by *Nedarim 20b*, *Hagigah 5b* and earlier on the very same page of *Eruvin 100b*.

*Nedarim 20b*, too, never gives *a husband* license to be "*toveia b'peh*" in a manner of chutzpah.]

Rashi, however, interprets:

"And he shall dominate you" – for he dominates by explicitly stating the sexual desires of his heart, while a woman harbors [sexual desires] in her heart, but is embarrassed to reveal them verbally.

"*d'meratzya artzuyei*" – She shows him signs of affection [in order to reveal to him the sexual desires of her heart].

In other words, while *Nedarim 20b* was coming to say that a wife who is "*toveia b'peh*" demonstrates *chutzpah*, *Eruvin 100b*, according to Rashi, was coming only to say that a wife *by nature* will generally not be "*toveia b'peh*" because she is *embarrassed* to directly express her sexual desires.

According to this understanding, *Eruvin 100b* is not necessarily relevant to the discussion of *Hagigah 5b* at all, for, as explained by Rashi, the curse against Eve spoken of on *Eruvin 100b* was not that womankind would be *forbidden* or *discouraged* from directly (lovingly) expressing their sexual desires to their husbands, but rather that they would be *embarrassed* to do so.

Thus, as radical a suggestion as it may be, if we see sweeping changes in the world such that wives are no longer embarrassed to lovingly, vulnerably, directly express their sexual needs to their husbands, it is not necessarily a sign that women have become less refined or less "modest" or more "brazen," but rather that the primordial "curse" of sexual inhibition within marriage has run its course, and that it is coming, or has already come, to its end, at least in civilized societies – not the least because modern men, modern husbands, have become more sensitive and refined and less chauvinistic (i.e., less "dominating") and therefore they themselves strive to make their wives feel comfortable in expressing their sexual needs and desires.

# ENDNOTES

Secondly, it must be noted that *Eruvin 100b* itself mentions numerous other primordial "curses" that befell womankind as a result of Eve's sin (besides those that befell men as a result of Adam's sin), four of which – to name just a few, and in no particular order – are: a) that women urinate sitting down; b) that women are embarrassed to go outside in the street with their hair uncovered (see Rashi); c) that a woman's place is in the home (see Rashi); d) that a woman is like a "pillow" to her husband, for he comes on top of her during sexual intercourse (see Rashi).

The first of these four "curses," that women urinate sitting down, suggests that prior to the curse the female body was formed in way that did not require a sitting position during urination. We shall leave this point for further discussion another time – but let it be noted that it is clearly not about that which is "permitted" versus "forbidden," but, again, merely about the historical nature of things.

The second of these four "curses," that women would be "embarrassed" to leave their homes with their hair uncovered, certainly no longer applies to vast numbers of women across the globe, perhaps because the original "embarrassment" was really a concern about male aggression – "dominance" – which has largely subsided in modern times in civilized societies. [Still, for Jews, married women cover their hair not as a matter of embarrassment, but of modesty.]

The third of the four, that a woman's place is in the home, is certainly not a matter of legal obligation or prohibition – and, for better or for worse, it is fast becoming a thing of the past even in Ultra-Orthodox Jewish circles.

But most importantly, it is difficult to assert that the fourth "curse," that a woman would be like a "pillow" for her husband, was said in the realm of halachic "obligation" or "prohibition" as to which spouse must or must not be on top or bottom during intercourse, for numerous medieval and post-medieval authorities expressly permit sex with the wife on top (see below, p. 115) – and this in spite of *Callah Rabti 1:23*, which casts a moral judgment on the position, calling it "arrogant."

[Incidentally, *Tractate Callah* calling the wife-on-top position "arrogant" is not all that different from *Nedarim 20b* calling a wife's forceful verbal demand for sex "chutzpah" – for both are referring to a wife who is attempting to dominate her husband. Therefore, just as the former is permitted legally if the husband actually enjoys such "domination," the latter should arguably be legally permitted as well to a wife whose husband enjoys it.]

Therefore, when considered in the context of all these other curses, it does not appear that Rashi understood *Eruvin 100b* as "forbidding" a wife from speaking sexy talk with her husband in a loving manner. If anything, it appears he understood the Talmud as merely expressing what it believed to be the historical cause of women's sexual inhibitions in general, relative to men, and that it was possible, under the patriarchal societal conditions that prevailed through history as a result of Adam and Eve's sin, to actually view such female inhibition as a positive "modest" outcome ("and this is considered a fine trait of character among women"). But in no way would this imply that the Talmud, there, meant to make such verbal sexual inhibition "obligatory" upon a wife by law (and certainly not when her husband actually enjoys direct verbal overtures) – just like it in no way meant to "obligate" her by law to be "a pillow" under her husband during sex (and certainly not when her husband actually enjoys her being on top).

This understanding of the Talmud's intention is also reflected in the comments of Rabbi Menachem Meiri in his *Beis Hebechirah, Eruvin 100b*, who speaks only of how "praiseworthy" – not "obligatory" – "modesty" is for people in general, and especially for women.

This also appears to be the understanding of Rabbi Yeshayah of Trani II in his *Piskei Riaz to Eruvin, Chapter 10 (Halachah 4, Paragraph 9)*, where he states that it is a sign of "modesty" for a woman not to verbally ask her husband for sex. He calls it only "a sign of modesty," he doesn't use terms like "obligation" or "prohibition." [Note that Riaz, there, distinguishes between "*tovaas b'peh*" and verbal "*divrei ritzoi*," whereas Rashi distinguishes between "*tovaas b'peh*" and perhaps non-verbal "*inyonei chibah*" (signs of affection).]

See also Rabbi Moshe Stern, in his *Be'er Moshe vol. 3, Responsum 152:11-12*, pp. 203-204, who understood Riaz's precise wording to be intentionally avoiding the categorization of a wife's verbal sexual solicitation of her husband as a "prohibition."

Rabbi Stern goes on to say that there is actually a full-fledged argument between *Eruvin 100b* and *Nedarim 20b* – with the former legally permitting a wife's verbal request for sex and the latter forbidding it. He also makes the categorical statement that we rule according to *Nedarim 20b*. But this is arguably questionable, for nowhere on *Nedarim 20b* are any of the nine-ten flawed conditions (including a wife's verbal demand for sex) referred to as "prohibited." We are only taught, there, to avoid them (although at least two of them we know to be prohibited from other sources, and for entirely other reasons, those being *Bnei Nidah* and *Bnei Aimah-Anusah*). This is possibly why many medieval commentaries also refrain from categorizing the nine-ten flawed conditions as being *collectively* "forbidden" (see below, endnote 128).

[Note also that Rabbi Stern goes on to quote *Talmud Kesubos 72a* that a "loud woman" transgresses the "manners" of a Jewess and loses her right to her *kesubah* money should her husband divorce her due to her insolence. He brings various explanations of what the term "loud woman" means, all in the context of a woman quarreling with her husband over sex.

Behold: Rabbi Stern quotes the medieval interpretations of Rabbi Alfasi and Rabeinu Asher, quoted also by Rabbi Yosef Caro in his *Beis Yosef* to *Tur, Even Haezer 115*, that a "loud woman" refers to a wife who demands sex loudly enough for the neighbors to hear, which is considered "*chutzpah*" – the very same term used on *Nedarim 20b*, "*chatzufah*," to describe a wife who "asks for/demands sex with her mouth."

While *Kesubos 72a* seems to be more interested in the *volume* of the wife's voice, whereas *Nedarim 20b* seems to be more interested in her *tone* (as discussed above, this endnote), they can certainly be read as addressing one overlapping context: a wife who forcefully demands sex against her husband's will.

Rabbi Stern himself acknowledges this overlap, but he does not equate them due to other contextual differences between *Kesubos 72a* and *Nedarim 20b*. See there, *Be'er Moshe vol. 3, Responsum 152:12*, page 204.

Rabbi Avraham Dovid Wahrman of Buczacz, however, in his *Ezer Mekudash* to *Shulchan Aruch, Even Haezer 25:Hagaah*, does seem to equate them:

> She will not tell him that she wants her conjugal rights and that she does not forego them – for this is not the way of Jewish girls, because if a woman verbally asks for [read: demands] sex it is grounds for divorce (*mah she'ein kein lomar sherotzah kiyum onasah v'einah mocheles, ein zeh derech bnos am yisrael, caivan she'hatovaas b'peh misgareshes al yedei zeh*).

But *Tur* and *Shulchan Aruch, Even Haezer 115:4* say only that a woman who demands sex *loud enough for the neighbors to hear* can be compelled into divorce…

In any case, we will yet address more points about Rabbi Stern's presentation in a future volume of this series.]

But *Eruvin 100b*, at least according to Rashi's interpretation, appears to be merely explaining the historical cause of female sexual inhibition in general, it is not forbidding a woman to express herself if she feels comfortable doing so, and especially if her husband himself makes her feel so comfortable – and even more so, if he himself finds it pleasing and/or arousing. Thus, the same teaching on *Hagigah 5b* that allows a husband to initiate loving sexy talk with his wife in order to arouse her to the mood for lovemaking would arguably equally allow a wife to initiate loving sexy talk with her husband in order to arouse him.

[See also *Otzar Midrashim, vol. 1, Yetziras Havlad*, page 245:

> Even the light-headed talk *between a wife with her husband* (*afilu sichah kalah she'bein ishah l'baalah*) is recounted after death, as the verse [Amos 4:13] states…

According to this pseudo-midrash, the same permission on *Hagigah 5b* that justified Rav's talking sexy with his wife in spite of the verse in Amos, would also permit a wife to talk sexy with her husband.]

We thus strongly suggest that at issue in the episode of Leah and Jacob was not *what* she said, but *how* and *why* she said it. And we thus also strongly suggest that any loving, respectful wife who uses sexy, erotic talk in a loving, respectful manner with her husband, and even directly asks her husband to "come have sex," would be in perfect harmony with G-d's will, so long as she is not doing so to taunt him or purely for her own selfish desires, but rather because she knows her husband will also enjoy it and/or become aroused by it.

**Added note to the third edition:** See also Rabbi Eliezer Melamed's *Simchat Habayit v'Birchato* (second edition, 2015), p. 33, footnote 4.

[126] See above, endnote 69.

[127] Being that Rabbi Yehudah Hanasi and Rav were the master and elder colleague, respectively, of Rabbi Yochanan bar Napacha, it is possible they were the "Sages" whom Rabbi Yochanan bar Napacha was quoting in rejection of Rabbi Yochanan ben Dahavai.

Nevertheless, for the purpose of our study, we will list the Sages as an independent opinion, being that the Talmud itself does not ultimately identify them.

[Note also that Rabbi Yochanan bar Napacha considered Rav Cahana – a disciple of Rav, and the very one who confronted Rav from under the bed during Rav's performance of marital intimacy – as his own master (see *Babylonian Talmud, Brachos 62a* and the Steinsaltz Talmud edition's biographical margin notes, there.)]

[128] A dedicated chapter on the nine-ten flawed conditions will be featured in a future volume of this series.

In the meantime, an important question to touch upon is whether this teaching of Rabbi Levi was intended by him himself as a *ruling* about their *prohibition* or merely as a *caution* about their potential *danger*.

Clearly, two of the nine-ten conditions, forced sex and sex during menstruation, are forbidden. But for forced sex, *Bnei Aimah-Anusah*, there is an alternate version, *Bnei Amah*, that is, sex with a servant girl (see above, endnote 108) – about which, at least in ancient times, there presumably were spiritual concerns regarding the union and the future of the offspring even if she were not forced during conception. And for sex during menstruation, *Bnei Nidah*, there is an alternate version, *Bnei Nidoi*, sex during excommunication, the legal "prohibition" of which is not definitively determined (see above, endnote 111).

And even if any of the nine-ten flawed conditions were known to be forbidden from elsewhere, it would not have necessarily precluded Rabbi Levi from coming to add spiritual caution on top of legal prohibition.

In other words, for those of the nine-ten conditions that were already known to be forbidden, Rabbi Levi could have merely been coming to add additional warning about the spiritual repurcussions of their transgression. And for those that were not forbidden by any other source, it is possible Rabbi Levi was issuing caution about them too, without going so far as to suggest a full-fledged prohibition in their regard.

[Parenthetically, note that on *Nedarim 20a*, *Tosfos Yeshanim* explains what it believed to be Rav Yosef's logic in interpreting Rav Achi's caution against gazing at women's "heels" as referring to one's own impure menstruating wife. *Tosfos Yeshanim* explains that there would have been no need for Rav Achi to issue such a warning about gazing at other women, for we already know from the rabbinical interpretation of a verse reported in *Talmud, Tractate Avodah Zarah 20ab* not to gaze at women other than one's own wife. But this logic requires further investigation, for without getting into the question of whether Rav Achi himself were actually aware of, or even agreed with, the particular rabbinic interpretation reported on *Avodah Zarah 20ab*, the Talmud does feature passages that add caution to prohibition – including just a page later, on *Nedarim 20b*, where, according to many commentaries, including Raavad III, Rabbi Levi cautioned that children conceived in a state of menstruation – *Bnei Nidah* – could be born spiritually challenged, even though we already know from explicit biblical verses (not just rabbinical interpretations) that sex during menstruation is forbidden.]

Now, it is perhaps informative that *Talmud, Nedarim 20b, Tractate Callah 1:10, Callah Rabti 1:16*, Rabbi Yitzchak of Corbeil (*Sefer Mitzvos Katan, Positive Commandment 285*), Rabbi Elazar of Worms (*Rokeach, siman 317*), Meiri (*Beis Habechirah, Nedarim 20b*) and Rabbi Yitzchak Aboab (*Menoras Hamaor, Clal 6, Lisa Ishah, Part 5, B'derech Hachibur, Chapter 2*) all refrain from speaking in terms of "prohibition" when discussing the point of Rabbi Levi's teaching.

Raavad III in *Baalei HaNefesh, Shaar Hakedushah* is somewhat unclear, for he begins his discussion about Rabbi Levi's nine conditions (p. 175 in the Buchwald edition) describing only how they rob the act of marital intimacy of its goodness and reward, he does not simply call them "forbidden." But then later (p. 177 in the Buchwald edition), in discussing the episode of Leah's conception of Reuben on her wedding night, in which it is understood that Jacob's intentions were for another, for Rachel – an apparent condition of *Bnei Temurah* – Raavad III suggests that perhaps the Hebrews before the Giving of the Torah were not *"prohibited* in the minor details of the commandments" (*lo ne'esru b'dikdukei hamitzvos*). And in that same discussion he implies that the husband and wife who engage in sex under the nine flawed conditions are themselves called by the verse "rebels and sinners" (*mored u'posheia*). Some textual versions of *Baalei HaNefesh* have Raavad III reiterating this last assertion again later in his closing statements on the subject (p. 178 in the Buchwald edition) – but even there he does not issue a simple clear-cut prohibition. And more research into Raavad III's opinion is required.

[Also requiring research in conjunction with this is the difference in nuance between the different Hebrew terms for "sin" and/or "sinner" – such as *chet, avon, aveirah, mored, posheia, rasha* – and whether they all, always, in every context, connote the transgression of a full-fledged biblical or rabbinical legal prohibition. And see below, endnote 736*.]

In one place in his commentary to *Callah Rabti*, Rabbi Avraham Hayarchi calls the nine-ten conditions "forbidden" (Toledano edition, page 24), but in another place (page 40) he calls the avoidance of them an act of "sanctification."

[See also Rabbi Avraham Hayarchi's commentary to *Callah Rabti*, pp. 2-5, where he claims that children born of the nine-ten flawed conditions do not carry the "holiness of the Jewish people." Rabbi Avraham Hayarchi goes on to say much else throughout his commentary in regard to the nine-ten flawed conditions (see pp. 24, 33-40, 47-48) that we will explore in a future volume of this series. But note, again, that on page 24 he refers to the nine-ten flawed conditions as "forbidden intercourses," while on page 40 he implies that they are actually permitted by the letter of the law, it is only that one should "sanctify oneself during sex" and "abstain and separate oneself from that which is permitted." While it is perhaps possible to read his passage, there, as two separate sentences, with the principle of "sanctifying oneself during sex" applying to the nine-ten flawed conditions and the principle of "separating oneself from that which is permitted" applying to avoidance of sexual indulgence in general, the fact remains that he includes in the former principle sex performed standing, sitting or side-by-side – all three of which are legally permitted.]

*Tractate Callah* and *Callah Rabti* in fact derive their cautions against these flawed conditions directly from the story of Ima Shalom and Rabbi Eliezer – and thus the fact that Rabbi Eliezer's sexual extremes are not required by Jewish law perhaps implies that Rabbi Levi's intention in cautioning about the nine-ten flawed conditions was not originally about teaching a matter of law either, but a matter of additional non-legal caution (even though, as stated, we already know forced sex and sex during menstruation to be forbidden from other sources in Torah; and as mentioned, there are alternate textual versions that do not even include these two among the nine-ten).

Rather, it seems that Rabbi Levi's own point was to teach couples to avoid sex in a manner of *relationship flaw*, where the heart, mind and soul of husband and wife are not lovingly focused on one another. This, Rabbi Levi warned, could cause the heart and mind and soul of the child conceived that night to be improperly directed in kind, resulting in "rebellion" and "spiritual insensitivity/waywardness." But he was not necessarily revealing any new *legal* issue.

Rabbi Shmuel ben Meir (Rashbam, c.1085-c.1158), grandson of Rabbi Shlomoh Yitzchaki (Rashi, 1040-1105), in his commentary to *Pesachim 112a* also implies that Rabbi Levi's intention in cautioning about these flawed conditions was not about strict legal prohibition, for Rabbi Shmuel ben Meir includes under the category of *"Bnei Gerushas Halev"* two divorcées who marry each other and who cannot help but fantasize about their previous spouses during sex. Yet divorcées are certainly permitted by Jewish law to remarry and have children together.

*Talmud, Pesachim 112a* [with Rashi's and Rashbam's commentaries in brackets] reads:

> "Do not cook in the pot that your friend cooked in" – this refers to [a divorced man not marrying] a divorced woman while her husband is still alive, for the master said: 'when a divorced man marries a divorced woman, there are four minds in the marital bed [because during sex the remarried husband's heart is fantasizing about his ex-wife, and the remarried wife's heart is fantasizing about her ex-husband; and we learned that a husband should not have sex with his wife and set his fantasies on another woman, and that the children conceived during such a union will be tantamount to bastards, a case referred to in *Tractate Nedarim* as *"Bnei Grushas Halev." Rashbam*].
>
> And some say it refers even to [marrying] a widow, because not all 'fingers' [i.e. penises. *Rashi, Rashbam*] are alike [and the new husband's penis might not satisfy the widow the way her first husband's did. *Rashi, Rashbam*].

Now, why Rabbi Shmuel ben Meir categorizes the case of two remarried divorcées as *"Bnei Gerushas Halev"* rather than *"Bnei Irbuvya"* is perplexing. But the message is clear: Even though this is a case of illicit fantasizing cautioned against no less than three times on *Nedarim 20b* – by Rabbi Eliezer and Ima Shalom, by Rebbi and/or Rabbi Natan, and by Rabbi Levi (as one of the nine-ten flawed conditions), it is still perfectly allowed by Jewish law for a divorced man and divorced woman to marry each other and have children together.

[Parenthetically, Rabbi Yaakov Reischer (1661-1733), in his *Iyun Yaakov* commentary to *Ein Yaakov*, attempts to explain why the Talmud specifically cautions against marrying a divorced *woman*, rather than against marrying a divorced *man*.

He writes that in Talmudic times, a divorced woman was more likely to have been forcefully divorced by her husband. Therefore, in spite of the emotional trauma she experienced by his rejection, she may still have continued to harbor vestiges of unresolved love for him, the only man she ever knew sexually, and consequently she may have continued to fantasize about him even if she remarried. But the husband, who initiated the divorce, and who in Talmudic times possibly had other wives with whom he shared his heart, certainly did not love his ex-wife anymore, and therefore there was no concern that he might fantasize about her ever after. In modern times, however, when the wife cannot be forced into divorce due to the decree of Rabeinu Gershom, if and when a divorce does occur, both husband and wife are more likely to be equally "over" each other.

(*Iyun Yaakov* adds in his conclusion that today, a husband, too, can only marry one spouse at a time. But according to his use of this point earlier in regard to women in Talmudic times, this would be a reason for a husband today to continue to fantasize about his first wife, the only woman he was ever sexually intimate with until his first remarriage.)

This theory is problematic, for human nature is certainly complex enough such that even when spouses mutually agree to divorce they could still continue to harbor memories and fantasies of each other. The theory also goes against the simple context of the Talmud, which speaks in regard to *two* divorcées who remarry as *"four* minds in the bedroom" – which means the husband, too, even in Talmudic times, was assumed to still harbor sexual-emotional connections to his former wife. And Rashbam explicitly says so.]

Now, we do find Maimonides in his *Mishneh Torah* calling deliberate fantasizing of other women "rabbinically forbidden." And while he does not clearly repeat this legal term in listing any of the other flawed conditions, it is certainly implied [*Mishneh Torah, Deos 5:4, Isurei Biah 21:12-13*]. But one must wonder when and where he understood such a "rabbinic prohibition" to have been formally decreed, for the manner in which this ethical teaching is brought in the Talmud gives no indication that any rabbinic court or assembly ever gathered together to issue a formal ban on such practices (unless the compilers-editors of the Talmud themselves are to be considered such an assembly, as Maimonides himself perhaps implies in his *Introduction* to *Mishneh Torah* – to be explored further in a future essay).

Rabeinu Nissim to *Nedarim 20b* does not call them "forbidden," though he says they carry a "small transgression" (*ketzas aveirah*) – whatever that is intended to mean.

Rabbi Shmuel ben Meshulam Yerondi, in his *Ohel Moed* (*Shaar Isur v'Heter, Derech 11*), also uses the term "forbidden" only in reference to fantasizing of other women. But he does so only commenting on the teaching found earlier on *Nedarim 20b* about not "drinking from one cup and setting one's mind's eye upon another. In listing the nine flawed conditions he does not use the term "forbidden" at all (see *Kovetz Shitos Kamai, Nedarim 20b*, p. 190).

And Rabbi Yosef Caro in his *Shulchan Aruch* does not use the term "forbidden" in conjunction with *any* of them. See *Orach Chaim 240:2-3; Even Haezer 25:8-10*.

Rabbi Betzalel Ashkenazi in his *Shitah Mekubetzes, Nedarim 20b* writes:

> These are the nine flawed conditions through which it is rebellious (*mered*) and sinful (*pasha*) to come upon one's wife, contrary to religious norms (*shelo c'das*) and contrary to manners of refinement (*shelo derech tarbus*).

Like we noted in regard to Raavad III, above, this endnote, if Rabbi Betzalel Ashkenazi understood Rabbi Levi as meaning to categorize these as forbidden, all he had to do was use the term "*asur.*" The terms "rebellious" and "sinful" are merely borrowed from the verse in a manner of interpretation (– an interpretation which, Rabbi Levi himself presumably understood, is not literal to the simple reading or context of the actual verse).

But perhaps the original meaning in all this was that implied by the textual version mentioned by "Ritz," quoted in *Shitah Mekubetzes*, which has the first of these nine-ten flawed conditions referring to the "beautiful captive woman" (*yefas toar*), a woman captured in war, whom a soldier might decide to forcefully marry – an act which Torah permits, but severely denigrates as immoral.

Ritz himself emphasizes the possibility that because the soldier marries her only for her beauty he will one day come to despise her, and thus it is a case of *Bnei Snuah* in potentia. But it is reasonable to say that the categorization of the "beautiful captive woman" as one of the nine-ten flawed conditions – the first of them no less – goes much deeper:

*Talmud, Sanhedrin 107a* quotes a teaching of Rabbi Yehudah in the name of Rav – the same Rav discussed on *Hagigah 5b, Yoma 18b, Yevamos 37b* and in *Tosfos, Yevamos 37b: Yichuda b'alma havu meyachdi* – that Torah's juxtaposition of G-d's discussions about the "beautiful captive woman" and the "rebellious child" (*ben sorer umorer*) was meant to warn that if one were to behave immorally and take a captive woman as a wife, even though such union is permitted by the letter of the law, the offspring of such a union would likely be rebellious in nature.

It is perhaps implied, then, by the fact that none of the *Talmudic-era sources themselves* speak in terms of the nine-ten flawed conditions being "forbidden," but only in terms of their breeding "rebelliousness," that they were only coming to give caution that all nine-ten had equivalent moral status to that of sex with a captive woman and therefore they all could potentially have similar spiritual side effects upon children conceived in their wake.

And see below, endnote 384, in regard to the teaching found in the medieval *Igeres Hakodesh* about the beautiful captive woman and her offspring.

But all this raises another significant point:

According to Meiri on *Sanhedrin 107a*, the presumption that the offspring of a "beautiful captive woman" will turn out "rebellious" is not predicated upon a belief in some divine punishment against the father, but rather upon the recognition that the mother's *natural* child-rearing skills will likely draw upon her own non-Jewish upbringing.

In other words, it is not a question, here, of spiritual *nature*, but *nurture*.

Along this line of reasoning, then, if in ancient times the children born of the nine-ten flawed conditions displayed higher rates of "rebelliousness," it could – and arguably should – more reasonably be attributed to environmental factors in their upbringing, including toxic home environments and/or social stigmas, as well as genetic predispositions, such as:

*Bnei Aimah* – A child raised in a fearful environment.

*Bnei Anusah* – A child raised in an abusive environment – and a sexually abusive environment.

*Bnei Snuah* – A child raised in an environment of favoritism, or an environment of strife.

*Bnei Nidoi* – A child raised with a communal stigma.

*Bnei Nidah* – A child raised with a spiritual stigma; a child raised in a non-halachically-observant environment; a child raised in an environment without proper sexual boundaries/discipline.

*Bnei Temurah* – A child whose own father questions his or her paternity.

*Bnei Moredes* – A child raised in an environment of confusing religious identity.

*Bnei Merivah* – A child raised in an environment of strife, and possibly inheriting genes with a predisposition toward mental-emotional illness.

*Bnei Meshugaas* – A child raised in a dysfunctional and/or insane environment, and possibly inheriting genes with a predisposition toward mental-emotional illness.

*Bnei Shichrus* – A child raised in an alcoholic environment.

*Bnei Grushas Halev* – A child raised in a broken home; an unwanted child.

*Bnei Irbuvyah* – A child raised amidst sexual addiction.

*Bnei Chatzufah* – A child raised in a disrespectful environment.

[In this vein, reread *Callah Rabti 1:16* and the commentary of Rabbi Avraham Hayarchi to *Callah Rabti*, pp. 31, 33-37 in the Toledano edition. Note especially that *Callah Rabti 1:16* says that babies conceived by drunk parents will themselves be "like drunkards" (*c'ilu shikurin*), which Rabbi Avraham Hayarchi translates to mean "like fools" (*c'ilu shotim*). He also says they will be of weak constitution (*sheyihiyu bneihem chalashim v'ein bahem co-ach col cach*). It would be worth investigating if and how these "symptoms" correlate to what modern medicine has found to unfortunately manifest in babies born to alcoholic parents.]

Note that even if one chooses to believe that these nine-ten flawed conditions have some kind of mystical effect upon a child, one still cannot ignore the contribution of the genetic/environmental factors. It is thus somewhat surprising that the sage who cautioned about these nine-ten flawed conditions seems to have focused entirely on spiritual factors and not at all on natural factors – unless natural factors were in fact what he was alluding to all along. And further research into all this is required.

In any case, parents who would be concerned about the nine-ten flawed conditions would do well to be equally, if not more, concerned about the nurturing enviroment they provide their children.

[129] For a detailed discussion on the authorship of these two works, see the critical edition of *Mesechtos Callah* by M. Higger, New York, 1936, *Introduction to Tractate Callah*, Parts 3 and 6, and *Introduction to Callah Rabti*, Parts 4 and 8.

*Babylonian Talmud, Tractate Taanit 10b* mentions a "Tractate Callah," but the medieval commentaries disagree as to whether this was referring to a specific individual tract by that name (i.e., the "*Tractate Callah*" in our hands today or some other tract by a similar name) or in general to any of the tractates of Talmud chosen to be studied during the bi-annual communal "Callah Assembly" of Torah scholars in Talmudic times.

[See M. Higger, Ibid, *Introduction to Tractate Callah, Part 3,* and *Steinsaltz Talmud, Taanit 10b, Iyunim-Notes.*]

Note that the early medieval scholar, Rabbi Avaraham Hayarchi, author of *Sefer Hamanhig* and a one-time disciple of Raavad III of Posquières, states at the beginning of his commentary to *Tractate Callah* (Toledano edition, Tiberias 1906):

> I received from my masters in France that this is the '*Tractate Callah*' mentioned in the first chapter of *Babylonian Talmud, Tractate Taanis.*

Thus, it is possible that Raavad III, too, understood this work as having pre-dated the Talmud – and how this may have influenced his unusal interpretation of *Nedarim 20ab* would be worth exploration.

[See also *Igeres Rav Sherirah Gaon,* English edition by Rabbi Nosson Dovid Rabinowich, end of Chapter 5, p. 49, regarding the authority of *braisa*-literature whose authorship is unknown.]

[130] In exploring *Tractate Callah* and *Callah Rabti*, we will highlight key comments by the medieval scholar, Rabbi Avraham Hayarchi, in his *Commentary to Callah Rabti,* and by the post-medieval scholars, Rabbi Yaakov Neumberg, in his *Nachlas Yaakov,* and Rabbi Chaim Yosef Dovid Azulai (Chida), in his *Kisei Rachamaim.*

Two additional later commentaries have come to my attention, *Lechem Shearim* and *Mayan Ganim,* as well as a *Biur* compiled by Rabbi Chaim Kanievsky and his son-in-law. A proper review of these commentaries will have to wait for a future edition of this work.

[131] Translations of obscure medical terms in our section on *Tractate Callah* and *Callah Rabti* rely upon the Soncino Edition of *Minor Tractates* by Rabbi Dr. J. Rabinowitz, 1965.

[132] *Nedarim 20a* says only that this causes one's children to be "uncouth."

[133] None of the three reasons that follow are mentioned on *Nedarim 20ab.*

[134] This seems to be how *Callah Rabti 1:11* understood the context here. And it would be astonishing to blame the wife for congenital illnesses in their children on account of her not being in the mood for sex.

But then would it not be just as astonishing, if not more so, to suggest she should endure the challenge of giving birth to, and raising, handicapped children on account of her husband's behavior – and after submitting to his forceful demands (or, in even worse context, after suffering his violent rape – if such context were in fact included in the intentions of the sages here)?

Perhaps there was a different or deeper intent here. And the matter requires further investigation.

[135] The medieval scholar, Rabbi Avraham Hayarchi, in his commentary to *Callah Rabti* (Toledano edition, page 26) assumes there must be a sexual context to Rabbi Akiva's opinion. Thus, he explains this "unwarranted hatred" to mean either that husband and wife have sex while they still harbor hard feelings against one another from an earlier argument, or that husband and wife speak ill of others during sex, thereby transgressing the Talmud's teaching on *Nedarim 20ab* and *Hagigah 5b* not to engage in "excess talk" (*sicha yeseirah*) during sex.

[Actually, at this point in his commentary it is not clear if Rabbi Avraham Hayarchi is referring to the teaching on *Nedarim 20ab* or the teaching on *Hagigah 5b,* for only *Hagigah 5b* speaks of "excess talk" (*sicha yeseirah*) while *Nedarim 20b* speaks of "non-sex-related talk" (*mili achronaysa*). Speaking ill of others would fall under the latter category, not the former. And see our analysis of the distinctions between the two terms below, pp. 75-83.]

However, on the next page of his commentary (Toledano edition, page 27), Rabbi Avraham Hayarchi suggests that if husband and wife are speaking well of their friends, or about their friends' hardships, then this is permitted during sex according to the letter of the law – although, he says, it is not ideal, because it could still cause their children to be deaf (sic).

Rabbi Avraham Hayarchi then rejects this interpretation, due to the obvious question: If a couple should not talk about anything unrelated to their sex during intercourse, what difference should it make if they are speaking ill or well of others? They should not be talking about others at all!

He thus deduces that the correct interpretation must be that husband and wife are speaking about having sex in an unloving manner, with the husband making demands for sex against her will, and her subordinating herself to his desires without a full loving heart.

It is not clear why he didn't take Rabbi Akiva's words at face value: that baseless discord in the home in general, at any time, will affect the children's health negatively, perhaps even physically.

[136] Rabbi Yaakov Neumberg, in his *Nachlas Yaakov* commentary to *Tractate Callah*, understands this to mean that she tells him mid-intercourse that she is impure in order to torture him. He points to *Menoras Hamaor*, Chapter 179, as a supporting source.

[137] Exodus 20:17.

[137*] See above, endnote 70.

[138] Here, each of the various textual manuscript versions of *Tractate Callah* list only some of the four culinary variations listed on *Nedarim 20b* in regard to meat. Combined, however, the versions do include all of the four, and not only for meat, but also for fish (see M. Higger, *Mesechtos Callah*, p. 136).

Thus, Raavad II's interpretation in *Sefer HaEshkol* of the Sages' permissive ruling on *Nedarim 20b*, that the *four* culinary types were listed in order to permit all *four* of the behaviors cautioned against by Rabbi Yochanan ben Dahavai, could be applied to *Tractate Callah* as well (see below, page 66, point 2).

[139] In Aramaic: "*Achilu*." Compare to *Babylonian Talmud, Tractate Gitin 70a*: "*Avis*."

*Nachlas Yaakov* to *Tractate Callah* seems to understand "*achilu*" as a form of anxiety ("*eimah nofeles alav, v'hu milashon cheil ur'adah*").

See also Rabbi Yisrael Alnaqua's *Menoras Hamaor, vol. 4*, page 82: "Intercourse standing causes *achilu* – that is, body pain."

[140] In Aramaic: "*Dilria*." Compare to *Babylonian Talmud, Tractate Gitin 70a*: "*Dalaria*." And see the explanation of the term in the Steinsaltz edition of the Talmud.

See also Rabbi Yisrael Alnaqua's *Menoras Hamaor, vol. 4*, page 82: "Intercourse sitting causes *dalaria* – that is, madness (*shigaon*)."

[141] In Aramaic: "*Avis*." Compare to *Babylonian Talmud, Tractate Gitin 70a*: "*Dalaria*."

[142] Rabbi Yisrael Alnaqua, *Menoras Hamaor vol. 4*, p. 83, explains the "obstinacy" here:

> Both lying on their sides is obstinacy – that is, she doesn't want to listen to him to bother herself to be below him for sex, and he doesn't want her to be on top of him.

They are thus obstinate with each other until they reach a compromise and they both lie on their sides [for intercourse].

According to this manner of understanding, if a husband actually enjoys his wife being on top, or if both spouses actually enjoy intercourse side-by-side, there should presumably be nothing objectionable about it – even according to Rabbi Alnaqua.

[143] One textual variant reads here: "And whoever turns himself away from sin and seed [semen] was not ejaculated from him for no reason (*v'lo yatzas mimenu shichvas zera l'chinam*)..."

This is a unique twist of context, which is not implied at all, nor contextually supported, by the version of this teaching as appears on *Nedarim 20a*.

[144] What this verse has to do with a person who avoids sin is unclear.

[145] Note that verse 5 is speaking of the *youth* of the Children of Israel, whom Moses had bring sacrifices upon the altar, while verse 11 is speaking of the *nobles* of the Children of Israel.

In any case, it is not clear from the verses themselves what they have to do with the context of Rabbi Achi's teaching.

[146] Literally: "seduce her during sex."

Although "seduction" could technically refer to non-verbal behaviors, the simple connotation is that of seductive words. Even *Callah Rabti 2:11* seems to first assume this as the more likely meaning of the term.

In any case, our translation, here, follows that of the Soncino edition.

[147] *Nachlas Yaakov* to *Tractate Callah* gives a unique interpretation: that Rabbi Eliezer's concern, here, was to ensure that the *wife* does not fantasize of *other men*.

I, personally, have not found this explanation anywhere else.

[148] Ecclesiastes 8:5.

[149] See above, endnote 132.

[150] *Nedarim 20a* quotes this interpretation of Rav Achi's caution in the name of Rav Yosef (as pointed out also by Rabbi Baruch Toledano in his footnotes to the commentary of Rabbi Avraham Hayarchi on *Callah Rabti*, Toledano edition, page 26).

Historically speaking, *Callah Rabti's* version would perhaps be more compelling, for Rabbi Yochanan bar Napacha was a colleague of Rabbi Shimon ben Lakish in the Land of Israel, whereas Rav Yosef lived and taught a generation later in Babylonia.

It is also somewhat perplexing that Rav Yosef is quoted before Rabbi Shimon ben Lakish in the Talmudic version in *Nedarim 20a*, leaving room for the (possibly erroneous) impression that Rabbi Shimon ben Lakish was "interpreting" the interpretation of someone who lived and taught later and in a different land. Still, it is possible the compilers-editors of the Tamud ordered it this way because although they did not have an actual oral or written record of Rabbi Shimon ben Lakish stating clearly that he understood it as referring to an impure wife, they had a reason to believe he did, and since they did have such a record from Rav Yosef they placed the record of Rav Yosef's statement first to set the context for Rabbi Shimon ben Lakish – but this is a stretch. [Raavad III, however, does quote one interpretation of Rabbi Shimon ben Lakish that has him interpreting Rav Yosef in this way. See below, p. 179.]

In any case, even if we were to insert Rabbi Yochanan bar Napacha in place of Rav Yosef on *Nedarim 20a*, we already know from Rabbi Yochanan bar Napacha's ruling in the name of the Sages on the very next page, *Nedarim 20b*, that he rejects Rabbi Yochanan ben Dahavai's caution against gazing at one's own pure wife's (naked) genitals (during sexual intimacy). Rabbi Yochanan bar Napacha's (and the Sages') view would therefore be understood to be that it is inappropriate to gaze even at own's own wife's heel when she is menstrually impure, but when she is pure, and especially in private and during intimacy, it is permitted even to gaze at her naked genitals. And see below, pp. 180-182.

[151] Rabbi Shimon ben Lakish, as quoted on *Nedarim 20a*.

[152] Rabbi Avraham Hayarchi, in his commentary to *Callah Rabti* (Toledano edition, pp. 26-27) is unsure if this means to say that gazing at one's own wife's buttocks/genitals *on its own* causes *all four* illnesses – lameness, blindness, muteness, deafness. If not, he says, then it means to say that *according to Rabbi Eliezer* these four illnesses are caused by the nine-ten flawed conditions of mind or circumstance discussed later in *Callah Rabti 1:16*.

But *Callah Rabti 1:16* says nothing of these nine-ten flawed conditions causing such extreme physical harm to one's children.

*Talmud Nedarim 20b*, too, states only that the nine-ten flawed conditions result in the conception of children who will be spiritually rebellious, not physically ill.

[153] This version of the argument between Rabbi Yochanan and Rabbi Shimon ben Lakish appears to match Raavad III's first interpretation of the argument between Rav Yosef and Rabbi Shimon ben Lakish on *Nedarim 20a* (see below, p. 179).

And see next endnote.

[154] *Callah Rabti's* presentation of Rava's interpretation of Rabbi Achi appears to match that of Raavad III's second interpretation of Rabbi Shimon ben Lakish on *Nedarum 20a* (see below, p. 179).

And see previous endnote.

Note that Rava himself does not specify that the wife is pure, it is only implied by the response of his colleagues and/or disciples. Nor does Rava clarify whether he understood the context to be of gazing: a) at clothed or naked genitals; b) only in the presence of others or even in private; c) if in private, only during non-sexual moments or even during sexually intimate moments. But whatever his context may have been, his colleagues and/or disciples clearly considered his caution to be unreasonable/unrealistic.

[155] The question is rhetorical: How can one say that all the children of every husband who gazes at his pure wife's body will be physically ill, when we see that the reality is *not* that way – for we can assume that a great many husbands *do* gaze at their own pure wives' bodies, and yet the vast majority of children are born, thank G-d, with all their physical faculties intact?

The same challenge could be posed to Rabbi Yochanan ben Dahavai on *Nedarim 20a* and to many, if not all, other sages or Talmudic passages that warn of physical illnesses resulting from certain (seemingly harmless) sexual practices even within marriage: the vast majority of the world can be assumed to engage in them – in many, many cases even during the same sexual encounters in which conception occurs – and yet the vast majority of children are born healthy.

An equally perplexing question is this: If, as stated in the name of Rava, gazing at one's own pure wife's body is so "evil" so as to permanently disable one's unborn child, then such "punishment" should be meted out against the husband-father regardless of when he does the gazing; it should be immaterial whether or not conception occurs during that same sexual encounter or during another encounter before or after. We certainly have no reason to believe a husband would intentionally gaze at his wife's body on the night of conception in order to rebelliously taunt G-d – especially since no man knows for certain which night conception might occur. Similarly, when Rava is quoted later in *Callah Rabti 1:13* as saying that Rabbi Yochanan ben Dahavai's cautions against the four marital-sexual behaviors only applied to when a husband performs them during the same sexual encounter in which conception occurs, the logic in this remains to be explained. If such illnesses were meant to be understood as "punishments" for the husband's "inappropriate" behaviors, resulting from G-d's exacting and precise divine measure-for measure justice, then why should it matter at all in G-d's eyes *when* the behaviors occur? Rather, it would seem that Rabbi Yochanan ben Dahavai, according to Rava, thought that such behaviors and/or the mindsets engendered by them would physically and/or metaphysically bring about such illnesses as a matter of natural cause-and-effect only if performed during the same encounter in which conception occurs. But then Rava's wording in *Callah Rabti 1:13* about G-d's divine "measure for measure" justice leads one to believe that he understood Rabbi Yochanan ben Dahavai as viewing these illnesses as "punishments." And further investigation into the matter is required.

And see above, endnote 86.

[156] Here, too, perhaps this debate would support the notion that according to the belief of these sages it is not some heavenly decreed "punishment" that causes an illness in the fetus, but rather some physical and/or metaphysical cause-and-effect resulting from the mother's anxiety level, or the degree of the husband's degenerate mental/emotional state. Otherwise, why would it matter to these sages which stage of forcefullness they believed could cause the congenital repercussions?

And see previous endnote.

Alternatively, if we may be so bold, perhaps Rabbi Yehoshua meant to add that even if a wife agrees to sex at first but then changes her mind mid-intercourse, the husband has no right to continue no matter how far along or close to climax he may be – and if he does continue, G-d will take note and exact divine justice.

And see below, endnote 160.

[156*] See above, endnote 70.

[157] Rava, here, is explaining the reasoning behind Rabbi Yochanan ben Dahavai's 'ministering angels.' (See also Rabbi Avraham Hayarchi, in his commentary to *Callah Rabti*, Toledano edition, 1906, page 29.) But Rava soon qualifies that even Rabbi Yochanan ben Dahavai and his 'ministering angels' *themselves* were *only* medically concerned about these four behaviors *if they are performed during the same sexual encounter in which conception occurs*. Therefore later, when *Callah Rabti 1:14* says that the Sages (or as *Callah Rabti* calls them, the "*rabanan* – rabbis") rejected Rabbi Yochanan ben Dahavai and his 'ministering angels' only from a legal standpoint, not a medical one, the Sages, too, would still consider these behaviors to be completely safe if performed during a sexual encounter in which conception *does not* occur.

[158] While Rava is quoted here attempting to explain how these four sexual behaviors are similar *in form* to the illnesses the "ministering angels" reportedly said they cause, he never actually justifies how such horrific life-long manners of suffering are *proportionate* to such innocent, natural, widespread human sexual curiosity within the covenant of marriage.

And see below, endnote 161.

[159] Rava, here, does not define the term "overturning the table," although some versions of *Tractate Callah* describe it as rear-entry vaginal intercourse specifically. But it is none other than Rava himself who permits anal intercourse on *Sanhedrin 58b* (see below, pp. 84-87).

Anal intercourse is the most extreme – but also the most popular – definition of "overturning the table" among the medieval commentaries. And any permission of anal intercourse would logically imply permission of rear-entry vaginal intercourse as well. So why would Rava, here, be speaking so harshly against "overturning the table" of any kind, if he unreservedly permits anal intercourse on *Sanhedrin 58b*?

But perhaps Rava in *Sanhedrin* also meant to permit anal intercourse legally even while he considered it dangerous medically if performed during the same sexual encounter in which conception subsequently occurs. In any case, anal intercourse to the point of intra-anal ejaculation – which many commentaries understand Rava on *Sanhedrin 58b* to be permitting – would generally preclude any issue of conception (unless the husband goes on to ejaculate a second time, intra-vaginally, during the same intimate encounter). And see below, page 156 point 3.

[160] But again, why should the wife or child be made to suffer for all these four actions, which, it is implied by Rava's wording, were performed by the father and apparently against the mother's will?

And more research into the matter is required.

[161] Note that in none of these four explanations of "measure for measure justice" does Rava actually tell us what is *fundamentally wrong* with these four behaviors. He only tells us how the act and the resulting illness resemble each other *in form*.

Even when Rava tells us that the husband "abandoned the mouth to which kiss was given," or that he "gazed at that which is hidden from all," he does not tell us *why* abandoning the mouth or gazing at that which is hidden are so objectionable in the first place – and to such a degree that lifelong muteness or blindness, and in one's children no less, are proportionate to them.

[It is noteworthy that *Callah Rabti* does not fault the husband for his "sexual indulgence" or "objectification of his wife" by gazing at his wife's vagina, but rather faults him for the seemingly arbitrary fact that the place he gazes at is "hidden from all." If his fault were in the fact that his gazing is purely sexually motivated or is an insensitive act of objectifying his wife, then he should be faulted as well for gazing at her breasts – which many, if not most, husbands do also mainly out of sexual desire (and see below, pp. 54-56). Nevertheless, Rabbi Yochanan ben Dahavai and his "ministering angels" do not caution a husband against gazing at any other part of his wife's naked body.

Note also that Rabbi Avraham Hayarchi, in his commentary to *Callah Rabti* (Toledano edition, Tiberias 1906, page 30) attempts to explain how exalted is "the mouth to which kiss was given," for: a) the kiss of the mouth represents the deepest loving kiss; b) man speaks to G-d with the mouth; c) G-d kisses the righteous man on the lips to take his soul at death, as He did to Moses. Therefore, Rabbi Avraham Hayarchi implies, "abandoning" such lips, that have such human and G-dly potential, to kiss the vaginal lips instead, deserves lifelong muteness in one's children. But this justification, too, arguably falls short.]

[162] Literally: Why is a deaf person called a "*cheresh*"? Because he is [also] silent (*choresh*). As the verse says…

[163] Genesis 34:5.

## ENDNOTES

[164] Some, such as Rabbi Eliyahu de Vidas in *Reishis Chochmah* and Rabbi Elazar Azikri in *Sefer Charedim*, try to prove from this statement of Rava that "overturning the table" cannot possibly refer to anal sex, because anal sex does not result in conception. See below, page 156 point 3 and page 158 point 5, for responses to this argument.

[165] Rabbi Avraham Hayarchi here, (commentary to *Callah Rabti*, Toledano edition, page 29, and separately on page 30), maintains that the Sages permitted all four of the behaviors cautioned against by Rabbi Yochanan ben Dahavai – defying the interpretation of Raavad III (whom he quotes first, and who was a one-time teacher of his) that the Sages only permitted "overturning the table," and against his (Rabbi Avraham Hayarchi's) personal understanding of Rabbi Alfasi (that Rabbi Alfasi ruled like Rabbi Yochanan ben Dahavai; but see below, p. 65 and endnote 261 thereon).

However, he insists that "overturning the table" must not result in extra-vaginal ejaculation and therefore it must refer to a form of vaginal penetration – presumably rear-entry vaginal intercourse or her-on-top (though he could technically have also permitted anal intercourse without ejaculation, followed by vaginal intercourse with intra-vaginal ejaculation – like the first approach of Rabeinu Yitzchak of Dampierre (also a one-time teacher of his) in *Tosfos* to *Yevamos 34b* (see below, p. 91).

Regarding Rabbi Avraham Hayarchi's studies under both Raavad III of Posquières and Rabeinu Yitzchak of Dampierre, see Rabbi Hersh Goldwurm's *The Rishonim* (Artscroll, Mesorah Publications, 1982) page 171.

[166] *Callah Rabti*, here, has the "Rabbis" (*rabanan*) disagreeing with Rabbi Yochanan ben Dahavai, whereas according to *Nedarim 20b*, the "Rabbis" (*rabanan*) were the very source of Rabbi Yochanan ben Dahavai's teaching, which the "Sages" (*chachamim*) rejected.

[166*] *Callah Rabti* has Rabbi Yochanan ben Dahavai saying that "these" behaviors – in the plural – are forbidden (*asurim heim*), implying that it understood Rabbi Yochanan ben Dahavai as forbidding all four. The implication, then, is that according to *Callah Rabti* the Rabbis' *rejection* of any legal prohibition here was also in regard to all four.

See below, page 193, for an important possible implication of this point in regard to the opinion of Raavad III.

[167] Actually, nowhere on *Nedarim 20ab* or in *Tractate Callah 9* do we find Rabbi Yochanan ben Dahavai calling the four sexual behaviors he cautioned against, "forbidden." He only cautioned that they are medically harmful. But it is perhaps inferred from the Sages' (or Rabbis') response, worded in the form of legality, that Rabbi Yochanan ben Dahavai, too, was speaking in the context of law. And see above, endnote 86.

[167*] See above, endnote 166*.

[168] According to the Soncino translation of this passage, the Sages responded: "Seeing that you made your statement in the name of the ministering angels *it must be so*, but there is no actual prohibition against it."

This translation is problematic, for according to it, why does *Callah Rabti* go on to recount in the very next line that Rabbi Yochanan ben Dahavai demanded the Sages at least admit that these behaviors cause such illnesses? According to Soncino's translation, the Sages already did concede to Rabbi Yochanan ben Dahavai on this point.

Similarly, two lines later, *Callah Rabti* reads into the Sages' choice of expression ("If he wants...") that they must have admitted to Rabbi Yochanan ben Dahavai that while these behaviors are permitted, they are still dangerous. Again, according to the Soncino translation, such a reading into the Sages' expression would have been entirely unnecessary, for the Sages would have already admitted it to him outright.

[169] This version of the story is entirely irreconcilable with Ameimar's version on *Nedarim 20b*, where he has the term "ministering angels" referring to human rabbis (*rabanan*), because, according to Ameimar, if Rabbi Yochanan ben Dahavai had meant actual spiritual angels, the Sages would certainly have ruled the law in accordance with their medical opinion.

Rabbi Avraham Hayarchi in his commentary to *Callah Rabti* (Toledano edition, page 28 and page 29) suggests that *Callah Rabti*, too, understood the term "ministering angels" as a reference to rabbis (*rabanan*). But this is arguably unlikely being that *Callah Rabti* does not even hint to such a claim. And being that Ameimar's interpretation on *Nedarim 20b* (that the title "ministering angels" actually referred in this case to human rabbis) is highly unusual, we have no reason to believe *Callah Rabti* endorsed it without expressly saying so.

And this is besides the fact that *Callah Rabti* has the "*rabanan*" as the ones arguing with Rabbi Yochanan ben Dahavai, not as the ones who taught him his ideas in the first place. [Rabbi Avraham Hayarchi, on page 29 of his commentary, suggests an explanation that there were two sets of "*rabanan*" here, one comparable to 'ministering angels' and one not.].

And see next endnote.

[170] Rabbi Avraham Hayarchi suggests a re-writing of this entire back-and-forth discussion between the rabbis and Rabbi Yochanan ben Dahavai.

He starts with a premise and a problem that he feels necessitate such a re-writing: If the "ministering angels" (whom he says *Callah Rabti* understood to be a certain group of pious rabbis, not actual spiritual entities) cautioned against these four sexual behaviors based on the logic put forth a few paragraphs later, in the name of Rava, that the four illnesses result "measure for measure" from the sexual behaviors they say cause them, how, then, could the other set of rabbis (the ones not on the level of "ministering angels") not accept such logic? If divine "measure-for measure" justice is a fundamental principle in Torah, how, then, could any rabbi deny the logic of the "ministering angels" and defy their "prohibition" against these four sexual behaviors?

There are two responses to Rabbi Avraham Hayarchi's question:

Rabbi Yochanan ben Dahavai was a 5th Generation Israeli Tanna, and his teachers, the "ministering angels," if they were in fact human rabbis, were either his contemporaries or predecessors. Rava, on the other hand, was a 4th Generation Babylonian Amora. Thus, we have no reason to assume that the logic Rava is said to have offered hundreds of years later was actually that of Rabbi Yochanan ben Dahavai's "ministering angels" themselves. Such logic may very well have been Rava's own philosophical contribution to the discussion.

And even if the "ministering angels" *were* basing their own cautions on the premise of divine "measure-for-measure" justice, who is to say that the other set of rabbis agreed with their "comparative analysis" of behavior to illness in each of these four cases. It is not far-fetched to believe that many rabbis (even in Mishnaic-Talmudic times) felt that lameness, blindness, muteness or deafness (especially in one's children) were entirely disproportionate "measures" of punishment for such common, natural human behaviors within marriage. Therefore, nobody was necessarily arguing about the *principle* of "measure-for-measure" divine justice, but only about *if* and *how* it applies here.

But Rabbi Avraham Hayarchi, on pages 29-30 of his commentary, rewrites the entire passage.

# ENDNOTES

Here, again, is the simple reading of the relevant passage in *Calla Rabti 1:14*:

> But still, Rabbi Yochanan ben Dahavai was not speaking in his own name [*another version has: from his own reasoning*], [he was speaking in the name of the ministering angels], so why did the rabbis [*rabanan*] not concede to him?
>
> Because Rabbi Yochanan [ben Dahavai] said that these practices are 'forbidden.' The rabbis [therefore] said back to him, "It could be that you are speaking in the name of the ministering angels. But no 'prohibition' can be said to prohibit them."
>
> Rabbi Yochanan [ben Dahavai] said back, "But at least admit to me that it is because of these [practices that these illnesses occur].
>
> Know [that the rabbis must have admitted this to him], because [when] they responded [with the analogy of how a man likes to eat his kosher meat or fish,] they used the term "If he wants..." [– as if to say that it is not necessarily healthy for him to eat it prepared certain ways, but as long as it is kosher it is not 'forbidden' for him to do so "if he wants"].

Here is how Rabbi Avraham Hayarchi rewrites the passage:

> It appears in my eyes that this beginning should be read as a question, and this is its interpretation:
>
> Why did the rabbis not concede to Rabbi Yochanan [ben Dahavai]? Did Rabbi Yochanan [ben Dahavai] ever say that they [husband and wife] are 'forbidden' to have sex in such ways? No, he did not say that! He only said that through these four behaviors the children will become maimed, "measure-for-measure."
>
> Why, then, did the Sages (rabbis) rule that the law does not follow Rabbi Yochanan ben Dahavai, but rather a man may have sex with his wife any way he craves? Behold, even Rabbi Yochanan [ben Dahavai] himself did not *forbid* these four behaviors, and the husband is permitted to perform them.
>
> But [this is what actually happened:] the rabbis said back to him [to Rabbi Yochanan ben Dahavai]: We admit to you that children become maimed as a result of these four behaviors, "measure-for-measure." But tell us: what did the ministering angels tell you about these four behaviors – are they forbidden [according to the letter of the law] or permitted?
>
> Rabbi Yochanan [ben Dahavai] answered: If children become maimed through these four behaviors, then certainly they are forbidden by law, for if these behaviors were permitted, they would not harm children in this way.
>
> [But the Sages responded that one is allowed to do them 'if he wants.']

This reading is largely non-literal to the text, nor does it ultimately resolve the most important question: how could the rabbis permit by law something they allegedly believed to be of such definite harm to the health of children if performed during the same sexual encounter in which conception occurs?

The sage, Ameimar, however, on *Nedarim 20b*, has the Sages only permitting these four behaviors *because they did not believe them to cause these four illnesses*, even if performed during the same sexual encounter in which conception occurs.

[But see the M. Higger edition of *Callah Rabti 1:14*, page 184, footnote to lines 47-48.]

[171] The *Biur* commentary of Rabbi Chaim Kanievsky to *Callah Rabti* agrees with this reading of *Callah Rabti's* intent here.

But if this reading is true, then the meaning *Callah Rabti* injects, here, into the Sages' words is astonishing, for the analogy of permitting a person to eat kosher meat or fish however he "wants" regardless of the risk it might have on his own personal health is not in any way proportionate to the lesson being learned and applied from it, namely, the permission for a father and/or mother to risk lifelong debilitating suffering in their innocent unborn child in the form of blindness, lameness, muteness or deafness (G-d forbid), just because they "want" to do a certain sexual behavior.

Rather, *Nedarim 20b's* version is arguably more reasonable, that the Sages did not believe these behaviors to cause any such illnesses, even if performed during the same sexual encounter in which conception occurs, because they believed the "science" upon which the Rabbis (*rabanan*) based their cautions to be factually incorrect.

[172] A very curious back-and-forth debate indeed.

And see previous endnote.

[See also *Sanhedrin 100b*, which interprets a passage in the apocryphal *Book of Ben Sira* about how to properly eat a fish as euphemistically discouraging (though not forbidding) anal sex with one's own wife. See also below, endnote 509.]

[173] From the fact that *Callah Rabti* turns these into one question – as if to say: "How are your children so beautiful? What is the secret? How does he behave with you during sex?" – it implies that these disciples took it for granted that the sexual conduct of the parents is what determines the physical form of their child.

*Tractate Callah 9*, however, separates these questions into two: How are your children all so beautiful, *and* how does he behave with you during sex? Still, the fact that they asked the two questions in tandem suggests the same intention as that of *Callah Rabti*.

In any case, from Ima Shalom's response it seems that she at least took it for granted that the physical and/or spiritual beauty of her children derived from the sexual conduct of her husband.

[174] In this version she says that he "never spoke" – in the past tense.

[175] In Aramaic, "*Diria*." Compare to *Tractate Callah* above, endnote 140.

Compare also to *Babylonian Talmud, Tractate Gitin 70a*: "*Dalaria*."

Note that a warning that sex sitting down could cause diarrhea may not have been so much a caution about divine retribution, but rather a statement of belief that sex sitting down could physically irritate the bowels, at least temporarily.

See also Rabbi Avraham Hayarchi's unique interpretation of the word "*Diria*" here [page 50 in the Toledano edition of his commentary to *Callah Rabti*], that it connotes a diminishment of the man's sexual functions.

See also Rabbi Yisrael Alnaqua's *Menoras Hamaor, vol. 4*, page 82: "Intercourse sitting causes *dalaria* – that is, madness (*shigaon*)."

[176] Rabbi Avraham Hayarchi comments here (page 51 in the Toledano edition): "Arrogant – *and lewd*. So too, their children will be arrogant *and lewd*, measure for measure." He offers no source for this interpretation.

He goes on to explain that wife-on-top is inappropriate because the verse in Genesis suggests that the husband should "dominate" the wife (Genesis 3:16). Here, too, he offers no clear Talmudic source-precedent for this interpretation.

In any case, if the husband actually wants his wife to be on top, then it would in no way be a "threat" to his "dominance" and would presumably be perfectly acceptable even to Rabbi Avraham Hayarchi.

[177] Some versions have, here, in Aramaic, "*Diliriah*," which could mean diarrhea (see above, endnotes 140, 175).

But another version, here, has, in Hebrew, "*shema havlad hafchafchan*." Soncino translates this as, "feeble-mindedness." Marcus Jastrow translates "*hafchafchan*" as "fickle-minded."

[178] Compare to *Tractate Callah 15* above, page 42 and endnote 141: "Intercourse with him-on-bottom and her-on-top causes convulsions" – "*Avis*."

Compare also to *Babylonian Talmud, Tractate Gitin 70a*: "*Dalaria*."

[179] Alternatively, see above, endnote 142.

See also Rabbi Avraham Hayarchi's *Commentary to Callah Rabti* (page 50 in the Toledano edition):

> Because they perverted their ways (*me'akshim darcheihem*) out of their hatred and drunkenness, such that she refuses to accept his authority over her, so too, their child will not accept authority or rebuke, and will be obstinate (*ikesh*), not listening to his teachers and rebukers.

In any case, if husband and wife actually enjoy being side-by-side, there would be no "obstinacy" to speak of – which is presumably why the side-by-side position is permitted by law (see below, p. 116).

**Added note to the third edition:** See also Rabbi Maor Kayam's *Harchavot l'Simchat Habayit v'Birchato* (2015), page 188.

[180] This would imply, again, that Rava understood Rabbi Yochanan ben Dahavai's "ministering angels" as only warning against the four behaviors if they are performed during the same sexual encounter in which conception occurs. But if one's wife is already pregnant, post-menopause, or on (halachically-sanctioned) birth control – i.e., if she is not "fertile" – then there would presumably be no concern in performing these four behaviors.

[181] Rabbi Avraham Hayarchi in his *Commentary to Callah Rabti* (page 51 in the Toledano edition) interprets this analogy to mean that just like the farmer works the ground from above, and he does so thoroughly in the best way possible, for otherwise his efforts will not be met with success, so too the husband should be on top of the wife during sex, not her-on-top or side-by-side or sitting or standing – "for these are not the way of a field."

He adds that the nine-ten flawed conditions are also examples of bad "sowing," along with: a) not ejaculating strongly (though it is not clear how he expected a man to be able to control this), and b) coitus interuptus (the husband pulling out of the wife's vagina to ejaculate) followed by the husband immediately penetrating her again in order to finish satiating his sexual fulfillment (sic).

[182] Note that verse 5 is speaking about the *youth* of the Children of Israel, whom Moses had bring sacrifices upon the altar, while verse 11 is speaking about the *nobles* of the Children of Israel. In any case, on the surface it is not clear what these verses have to do with the context of Rabbi Achi's teaching.

[183] "*Banim*" – possibly referring to *male* offspring specifically.

Compare to *Tractate Callah 21* above, p. 43: "So that his offspring will become wealthy (alt. survive)."

[184] Ecclesiastes 8:5.

[185] *Talmud, Nedarim 20a* makes no distinction between a sexual encounter in which conception occurs versus a sexual encounter in which conception does not occur. It gives the impression that Rabbi Yochanan ben Dahavai's cautions were meant to apply to the offspring of a couple who engages in such behaviors at *any* time.

And *Nedarim 20b* gives the impression that the Sages rejected Rabbi Yochanan ben Dahavai's cautions about such behaviors *even* if they are performed during the same sexual encounter in which conception occurs.

[186] See below, pp. 57-58.

[187] See *Babylonian Talmud, Gitin 58a.* And see Rabbi Yehuda Henkin's *Bnei Banim vol. 4, 16:2,* p. 57, column 2, paragraph 2.

[188] See above, endnotes 158, 161.

Similarly, the comments of Rabeinu Nissim and *Tosfos* to *Nedarim 20a*, that according to Rabbi Yochanan ben Dahavai "overturning the table" results in lame children because the parents change their manner of sex in a way that requires unusual legwork, are merely explaining the "measure-for-measure" aspect of how the behavior and the punishment are similar in *form*, but not why "unusual legwork" might be objectionable in the first place – and to such a severe extent that it might be said to cause lameness, and in one's children no less.

[189] Raavad III, *Baalei HeNefesh, Shaar Hakedushah* (p. 179 in the Buchwald edition).

See below, endnote 664, for an explanation of our choice of translation of the phrase "*nahag bah minhag hefker*" as "He treats his wife without regard for her dignity."

[190] Implied by the comments of Rabeinu Nissim and *Tosfos* to *Nedarim 20a*, that according to Rabbi Yochanan ben Dahavai "overturning the table" results in lame children because the parents change their manner of sex in a way that requires unusual legwork.

And see above, endnote 188.

[191] *Peirush HaRosh, Nedarim 20a.*

[192] See above, endnote 189.

*Tosfos Yeshanim* to *Nedarim 20b* suggests that the reason Rabbi Eliezer uncovered only a small part of his wife's nether regions was so that he not come to gaze at her genitals (*megaleh tefach m'csus ishto, umechaseh oso tefach m'csus atzmo, cedei shelo yistakel b'ervah*). If, according to *Tosfos Yeshanim*, this, too, was done by Rabbi Eliezer out of a concern of avoiding intentional fantasies of other women, then perhaps it could be theorized to have been Rabbi Yochanan ben Dahavai's own concern about gazing at the female genitals as well (that is, his concern about gazing at them was that it might lead the husband to intentionally fantasize about other women). But the next entry in *Tosfos Yeshanim* suggests that it was *only* Rabbi Eliezer's *hasty rush through intercourse* that was done in order to avoid intentional illicit fantasies (*v'domeh alav c'mi shekafao shade – umemaher umisasek b'tashmish. . . umeshamesh meheirah shelo yitein einav b'ishah acheres*).

And see endnote 194, below.

[193] See above, endnote 189.

# ENDNOTES

Note also that cunnilingus is not usually about oral sex alone, but is generally followed by intercourse and the kissing of face and lips. In ancient times, then, when hygiene was not what it is today, the wife had additional reasons to be repelled by her husband going down on her – because he would then come back up to kiss her face.

Even today this can still be a concern for many women, but due to vast improvements in hygiene it no longer has to be.

[194] Raavad III, *Baalei HaNefesh, Shaar Hakedushah* (pp. 176 and 179 in the Buchwald edition); *Peirush R' Avraham Min Hahar, Nedarim 20b; Shita Mekubetzes* in the name of *Ritz, Nedarim 20a; Menoras Hamaor Alnaqua,* vol. 4, page 80; *Tosfos Yeshanim, Nedarim 20a; Tur Orach Chaim* 240:9, *Even Haezer* 250:2.

Now, in the case of Rabbi Eliezer and Ima Shalom brought in the Talmud on *Nedarim 20b* it is stated that Rabbi Eliezer's bedroom customs were intended to keep his mind free of intentional fantasies of other women. But here, too, the commentaries offer varying suggestions about which specific custom(s) it was that facilitated his purity of thought and how:

A) His reserving sex only for the middle of night

   a. When no voices could be heard from the street. (*Tosfos Yeshanim; Peirush R. Avraham min Hahar; Shitah Mekubetzes; Rabeinu Yehonoson miLunil* quoted in *Kovetz Shitos Kamai, Nedarim,* page 179)

   b. When memories of the faces of the previous day are not fixed in one's mind. (*Peirush R. Avraham min Hahar*)

   c. When memories of the voices of the women and men (sic) he heard the previous day are no longer fresh in his mind, and before he hears the voices of the next day. (Raavad III, *Baalei HaNefesh, Shaar Hakedushah,* page 176 in the Buchwald edition; Rabbi Avraham Hayarchi, commentary to *Callah Rabti,* Toledano edition, page 31, in the name of Raavad III)

   d. When memories of the women he saw that evening, and thoughts of the women he plans to see the next day, will not be fresh in his mind. (Rabbi Avraham Hayarchi, commentary to *Callah Rabti,* Toledano edition, page 31)

   e. When his lusts of the previous day are no longer fresh in his mind. (*Shita Mekubetzes*)

   f. Because, if done in the morning, he might carry memories of the sexual encounter into the next day and fantasize of other women he meets or continue to fantasize about his wife during the day (sic). (*Rabeinu Yehonoson miLunil* quoted in *Kovetz Shitos Kamai, Nedarim,* page 179)

B) His uncovering only one hand's-breadth of her body

   a. So that he would ONLY gaze at HER body and not end up seeing some other woman (*Tosfos Rabeinu Peretz*) [I presume that according to this the concern was that he might see another woman through the window]

   b. So that he would NOT gaze at her body and end up comparing her body to another woman's (*Shitah Mekubetzes,* quoting *Peirush*)

C) Penetrating "as if he were compelled by a demon"

    a. He would rush through intercourse before his attention would turn to fantasies of other women
       (*Tosfos Yeshanim*; *Shitah Mekubetzes* in name of Re'em)

Raavad III in *Baalei HaNefesh, Shaar Hakedushah* (pp. 176-177 in the Buchwald edition) writes that all three of Rabbi Eliezer's behaviors were meant to avoid his coming to entertain thoughts of other women.

BUT BEHOLD: Not a single medieval commentary *on the story* of Rabbi Eliezer claims that he himself *restricted speaking* with his wife *in order to avoid thinking of other women*. At most, the commentaries explain that this was *Rabbi Yochanan ben Dahavai's* concern about it. But in commenting in between the lines of *Ima Shalom's* account, the commentaries focus solely on the *time, manner and speed* of Rabbi Eliezer's sexual intimacy, they do not focus on his reasons for *speaking or not speaking* to her.

Even Ima Shalom herself does not appear to have been surprised or bothered by her husband's custom of speaking with her before and during intercourse. Her confusion was only about his manner of having sex in the middle of night, uncovering only one small part of her body, and penetrating her forcefully and/or hastily. Thus, Rabbi Eliezer's response about trying to avoid fantasies would have been in regard to (one or more of) those three behaviors alone.

In other words: A simple reading of the Talmudic discourse has the story of Ima Shalom brought not to explain why Rabbi Yochanan ben Dahavai was concerned about talk during sex, but only to prove that Rabbi Eliezer was *not* concerned about it. And even once the compilers-editors of the Talmud reconcile that Rabbi Eliezer himself only spoke sex-related talk during sex, there is no indication in the Talmud itself that his reason for avoiding non-sex-related talk had anything to do with trying to avoid fantasies of other women – for when Rabbi Eliezer expressed that concern to his wife, Ima Shalom, he was arguably only addressing her question about his timing, manner and/or speed of sexual intercourse. Yet the commentaries and halachic authorities go on to warn about non-sex-related talk during sex as a potential harbinger of illicit fantasy.

[195] Because he penetrates her while his mind is elsewhere. [Raavad III, *Baalei HaNefesh, Shaar Hekedushah*, Buchwald edition, page 179.]

Behold: Raavad III singles out "non-sex-related talk" alone as being tantamount to prostitution, because it lacks loving intention. This implies that Raavad III recognized that "overturning the table" and gazing at or kissing the female genitals do not necessarily display a lack of loving intent – even if they are a more crass expression of sexual passion – and therefore they also do not turn the act of marital intimacy into an act tantamount to prostitution.

[See also *Meiri, Beis Habechirah, Nedarim* 20a, acknowledging that a husband might gaze at his pure wife's genitals as an expression of her preciousness to him (*c'dei l'chavevah*).]

Speaking mundane chit-chat during intercourse, on the other hand, displays that one's mind is entirely elsewhere and disinterested in the act at hand. Only this, Raavad III implies, is tantamount to prostitution.

Raavad III even differentiates between one's mind being entirely absent during intercourse and one's mind straying to thoughts of other women (the concern of Rabbi Eliezer), and he defines only the former as making the act of marital intimacy tantamount to an act of prostitution [See *Baalei HaNefesh, Shaar Hekedushah*, page 179 in the Buchwald edition; and see below, page 172 and endnote 666]. This suggests that Raavad III recognized there can be love and passion for one's own wife even if, G-d forbid, one's mind strays to another woman – but not if one is entirely disinterested and/or psychologically-emotionally detached from her and/or the act of intimacy itself.

See also the *Mefaresh* to *Nedarim 20b*, interpreting the flawed condition of *Bnei Snuah*:

> "*Snuah*" – The husband sets his heart upon another woman during intercourse. And they said that it is not considered true intercourse *because he hates her so much*, rather it is tantamount to mere prostitution.

The *Mefaresh's* wording makes clear that it is not the illicit fantasy, but the profound hatred – that is, the lack of any loving intention – that makes the case of the *Bnei Snuah* tantamount to prostitution.

[But then note Rabbi Eliezer's statement as reported on *Nedarim 20b* that, in his estimation, intentional sexual fantasies would have made his children "tantamount to bastards" – implying that such fantasies *would* have made the marital sex act "tantamount to prostitution" even if it was not devoid of love. However, the child of a woman who is halachically categorized as a "prostitute" is not automatically halachically categorized as a "bastard." Therefore, a precise reading of Rabbi Eliezer's words perhaps reveals that he was not necessarily concerned so much about intentional sexual fantasies of other single women, or even of "prostitutes," but rather of other *married* women – for of the three, only illicit sex and conception with a *married* woman results in children who are definitely halachically categorized as "bastards." And more research into the matter is required. And see below, endnote 666.]

In any case, Raavad III, here, clearly understood illicit sexual fantasies as being problematic even if they are not devoid of loving intention for one's own spouse. It only appears that he did not necessarily deem them "tantamount to prostitution."

[196] *Tosfos Rabeinu Peretz, Nedarim 20b*, says Rabbi Eliezer would only have sex in the middle of night because "everyone is sleeping, and no one would hear." But it is not clear if Rabeinu Peretz meant no one would hear them "talking" or no one would hear their sounds of sex.

[197] *Tosfos, Nedarim 20a; Shitah Mekubetzes, Nedarim 20a*, in the name of Re'em.

Note that if these commentaries understood the Sages as rejecting all four of Rabbi Yochanan ben Dahavai's cautions, then they would also seemingly understand the Sages as allowing a married couple to be as loud as they want during the throes of passion.

[198] *Shitah Mekubetzes, Nedarim 20a*, in the name of Re'em.

[199] *Tosfos Yeshanim, Nedarim 20a*.

[200] And see Rabbi Yehudah the Pious, *Sefer Chasidim 509*, below, p. 107:

> In all such matters, it all follows the personal tastes of husband and wife. And if a man has found a *good wife* who is of same mind with him in these matters, to him applies the verse in Proverbs (18:22): "[He who has found a wife has found goodness,] and has elicited favor from the Lord," and the verse in Ecclesiastes (9:7): "[Go, eat your bread with joy and drink your wine with a merry heart, for] G-d has already approved your deeds."

[201] Pages 62-63.

[202] *Shitah Mekubetzes, Nedarim 20ab*.

Note, however, that Re'em, here, is merely explaining the objection of Rabbi Yochanan ben Dahavai in the name of the "ministering angels" to this behavior. Concerning the opinion of the Sages, who reject Rabbi Yochanan ben Dahavai and the "ministering angels," *Shitah Mekubetzes* quotes Re'em saying that according to the Sages, "A husband may do anything he craves sexually with his wife – *and there is no lack of holiness.*" See below, p. 68.

[203] In any case, if the couple engages in sexual intimacy in a place where they know they will not be heard, such concerns about modesty would presumably not even begin.

And see Rabbi Mordechai Tendler's *Mesores Moshe*, p. 407, paragraph 70, where he reports in the name of his grandfather, Rabbi Moshe Feinstein, that in today's houses, which are generally built so that one cannot hear normal sound levels through the walls (or floors or doors), it is unlikely that any such problem of modesty would be of concern.

Of course, in a house where one knows the walls or floors or doors to be "thin," one should be prudent.

[204] *Commentary to the Mishnah, Sanhedrin 7:4* and *Mishneh Torah, Sefer Kedushah, Isurei Biah 21:9*.

[205] *Beis Habechirah, Nedarim 20ab*.

[206] *Tosfos Yeshanim, Nedarim 20ab* implies that the reason the Sages rejected Rabbi Yochanan ben Dahavai was because they believed that the four behaviors he spoke against do not lack sanctity. Consequently, this also implies that *Tosfos Yeshanim* understood Rabbi Yochanan ben Dahavai's concerns about the four behaviors as stemming from a belief that they do lack general sanctity.

[207] Like *Tosfos Yeshanim*, Rabbi Eliezer of Metz (quoted in *Shitah Mekubetzes* to *Nedarim 20b*) implies that the Sages rejected Rabbi Yochanan ben Dahavai because they believed that the four behaviors he spoke against do not lack sanctity (see previous endnote).

Note also, as we've seen above, that Rabbi Eliezer of Metz says Rabbi Yochanan ben Dahavai's objection to non-sex-related talk was that it might cause a distraction and a diminishment of a couples' passion – which, Rabbi Eliezer of Metz says, would compromise sexual "sanctity."

[208] In this section we will be quoting definitions brought in post-medieval sources as well.

[209] Raavad III, *Baalei HaNefesh, Shaar Hakedushah* (Buchwald edition, p. 175, footnote 10\* *Shinuyei Mahaduros*); *Tur, Orach Chaim 240:10, Even Haezer 25:3*; *Shulchan Aruch, Orach Chaim 240:10, Even Haezer 25:2*.

[210] *Peirush HaRan, Nedarim 20b*: "Ha b'mili d'tashmish: shari kedei l'ratzosa."

[211] *Tosfos Yeshanim, Nedarim 20b; Peirush HaRosh, Nedarim 20b*; Rabbi Menachem Ibn Zerach, *Tzeidah Laderech, Maamar 3, Clal 4, Chapter 14* (See *Kovetz Shitos Kamai, Nedarim 20b*, page 188); *Shitah Mekubetzes, Nedarim 20b*, in the name of *Ritva*; *Tur, Even Haezer 25:3; Tur, Orach Chaim 240:9; Shulchan Aruch, Even Haezer 25:2*.

[212] *Tosfos Yeshanim, Nedarim 20b*:

> One should *certainly* speak sex-related talk (*vadai b'mili d'tashmish mesaprin*), because since it is about their sex he will fantasize about her [his wife] in his heart and have passion, and he will climax with joy, thus causing the children [conceived] to be beautiful.
>
> But mundane chit-chat (*mili d'alma*) one should not speak.

*Shitah Mekubetzes, Nedarim 20a*:

> Sex-related talk is *good* to speak (*mili d'tashmish tov lesaper*), because through this he will climax with joy, causing his children to be beautiful.

[213] Rabbi Mordechai Yoffe, in his *Levush, Orach Chaim 240:9*, says that the husband may speak words that will increase *her* passion so that she will climax first (though Rabbi Yoffe's stated objective in this is to conceive a male child – based on a belief put forth by *Babylonian Talmud, Shavuos 18b*; see below, endnote 355).

*Tzeidah Laderech, Maamar 3, Clal 4, Chapter 14* (quoted in *Kovetz Shitos Kamai, Nedarim 20b*, page 188) says that talk is permitted "to increase passion," without distinguishing between his or hers (*c'dei l'harbos taavah mutar b'osah shaah*).

In any case, this category would seem to include the wife allowing herself freedom to make vocal sounds if such will help her reach maximum climax. And the same would presumably go for the husband, especially in light of the sources referenced above, endnotes 211, 212.

[214] And see below, endnote 312.

[215] See Raavad III's *Baalei HaNefesh, Shaar Hakedushah* (pp. 175-177 in the Buchwald edition); *Tur, Orach Chaim 240* and *Even Haezer 25*; *Shulchan Aruch, Orach Chaim 240*.

See also *Peirush HaRan* to *Nedarim 20b*.

Raavad III actually implies that sex-related talk (*mili d'tashmisha*) is permitted even mid-intercourse, for he writes (p. 176 in the Buchwald edition):

> Do not think that non-sex-related talk is wrong only from the moment intercourse begins...

This implies that sex-related talk is permitted during intercourse, which is why one might think that the objection to non-sex-related talk begins only then. (In other words, if sex-related talk were already objectionable mid-intercourse, and non-sex-related talk is more stringent than it, then of course non-sex-related talk would be objectionable even from an earlier point in time).

Raavad III ultimately discourages non-sex-related talk even during foreplay, which might lead one to believe that, in the end, he embraces sex-related talk only during foreplay, and discourages both during actual intercourse. But if this were his intention, Raavad III certainly could – and presumable would – have made it clear, especially since he interprets the phrase "uncovering and covering a hand's-breadth" in the story of Rabbi Eliezer and Ima Shalom as referring to the act of actual intercourse, and he therefore has Ima Shalom stating clearly that her husband would speak to her during intercourse.

And note that Raavad III is only able to argue his point that non-sex-related talk is discouraged even during foreplay from entirely other Talmudic passages, *Eruvin 100b* and *Hagigah 5b*. This implies that he himself was aware that the simple context of *Nedarim 20ab* itself was about talk during actual sexual intercourse.

See also *Tur* and *Shulchan Aruch* to *Orach Chaim 240* and *Even Haezer 25*, both of which can be read, as well, as implying that sex-related talk is permitted even mid-intercourse.

And see below, pp. 79-81.

See also *Aruch Hashulchan, Orach Chaim 25:1*:

> Do not speak <u>non-sex-related</u> talk with her *during intercourse*, nor immediately beforehand (*al yespaer imah inyonim acherim b'shaas tashmish, v'lo kodem lachen*)...

*Aruch Hashulchan* does not caution against <u>sex-related</u> talk during intercourse.

²¹⁶ As far as how Raavad III categorized "seductive talk," see below, page 75.

²¹⁷ The idea that *Callah Rabti* might not have accepted, or been aware of, a Talmudic conclusion on *Nedarim 20b* should not come as too much surprise, considering that *Callah Rabti* did not either accept, or know, the conclusion of *Nedarim 20b* in the name of Ameimar that the "ministering angels" were actually human rabbis (not spiritual entities) whose knowledge about fetal development was fallible, and, therefore, whose cautions about congenital illness connected therewith were considered by the Sages to be invalid.

*Callah Rabti* seems to insist that the Sages admitted that the "ministering angels" were real spiritual entitites, and it definitely insists that while the Sages permitted all four of the behaviors cautioned against by Rabbi Yochanan ben Dahavai, they still believed such behaviors to be the cause of congenital illness if performed during the same sexual encounter in which conception occurs.

Considering the disputed origins of *Callah Rabti*, it is just possible that it was authored before the interpretation of Ameimar – a rather late Babylonian Amora – was taught.

See also *Kisei Rachamim* of Rabbi Chaim Yosef Dovid Azulai (Chida) to *Tractate Callah 3:1*, where he insists that *Tractate Callah* was compiled prior to the Talmud – though it is not clear if he understood *Callah Rabti* as predating the Talmud as well.

²¹⁸ Referred to in rabbinic literature as *"panim k'neged oref"* (face-to-back) or *"maaseh b'heimah"* (animal-style).

In modern slang: "doggystyle."

²¹⁸* According to those textual versions of *Tractate Callah* that interpret "overturning the table" as rear-entry vaginal intercourse specifically.

²¹⁹ Page 175 in the Buchwald edition.

²²⁰ Referred to in rabbinic literature as *"biah shelo k'darkah"* and usually translated as "unnatural intercourse."

²²¹ Quoted in *Kovetz Meforshim, Leket Rishonim* published by Yerid Haseforim, 2003.

²²² See *Kovetz Shitos Kamai, Sanhedrin vol. 2*, page 1081-1082.

²²³ Printed in the back of the Steinsaltz Talmud Hebrew edition and on the Talmud page of the Artscroll English edition.

²²³* Page 81. And see below, page 64 and endnote 252 thereon.

²²⁴ It is possible that *Shitah Mekubetzes* is quoting this in the name of Ritva.

²²⁵ See *Kovetz Shitos Kamai, Nedarim*, page 188. Rabbi Menachem Ibn Zerach rules according to the second approach of Rabeinu Yitzchak, implying that he accepts Rabeinu Yitzchak's interpretation of "overturning the table" as anal sex.

²²⁶ In rabbinic terminology: *"hee l'maalah, hu l'matah."*

²²⁷ Quoted by Rabbi Betzalel Ashkenazi in *Shitah Mekubetzes, Nedarim 20b*.

²²⁸ Quoted in *Kovetz Meforshim*, "Leket Rishonim," published by Yerid Haseforim, 2003.

²²⁹ In modern slang: "reverse cowgirl."

# ENDNOTES

[230] Rabeinu Peretz's precise wording, there, is: "They 'overturn' their table: face-to-back, because he is on bottom" (*Hofchin shulchanan: c'neged oref, d'ish l'matah*).

[230*] For more on the authorship of this commentary, see the Artscroll English edition of the Talmud, *Tractate Nedarim: General Introduction: Notes about our Commentary: A. Ran's Commentary*.

Credit goes to Rabbi Yossi Newfield for bringing the question of this authorship to my attention.

[231] In modern slang: "reverse cowgirl" – vaginal or anal.

[232] In contrast to face-to-face anal sex with the wife on her back facing her husband, in which case there is no "overturning the table."

[233] There is reason to say that this interpretation of the Talmud is the most likely, for if Rabbi Yochanan ben Dahavai on *Nedarim 20ab* were discussing anal sex alone, it is reasonable to believe he would have used the standard rabbinic term for it across the sea of Talmud, "unnatural intercourse" (*shelo cedarcah*); if he were discussing rear-entry vaginal intercourse alone, it is reasonable to believe he would have used either of the usual rabbinic terms for it, "face-to-back" (*panim k'neged oref*) or "animal-style" (*maaseh beheimah*); and if he were discussing wife-on-top alone, it is reasonable to believe he would have used the rabbinic term "him-on-bottom, her-on-top" (*hu l'matah, hee l'maalah*).

Rabbi Yochanan ben Dahavai's choice of a new euphemism, "overturning the table" (*hafichas shulchan*), which technically could include any of the above-mentioned positions, suggests he in fact meant to include them all, and whether performed one at a time or in combination.

[234] *Yad Malachi, Clalei Haposkim - Rashi, Clal 2* quotes opinions that say Rashi's commentary to the Talmud cannot to be used to interpret Jewish law. But *Yad Malachi*, there, also quotes opinions that say it can.

See also Rabbi Elazar Azikri in *Sefer Charedim*, Chapter 64 (discussed below, pp. 157-158 and endnote 615 thereon) who attempts to determine the halachic definition of "overturning the table" from these very same comments of Rashi to *Nedarim 20a*.

But then see *Yad Malachi, Clalei Haposkim - Rashi, Clal 6*, that the commentary on *Nedarim 20ab* traditionally attributed to Rashi was not actually penned by him. And see above, endnote 230*.

[234*] **Added note to the third edition:** See also Rabbi Eliyahu David Rabinowitz-Teomim's *Machshirei Mitzvah: "Lo Yarbeh Lo Nashim"* (Machon Ahavat Shalom).

[235] Albeck edition.

*Sefer HaEshkol* interprets the *four* culinary choices of how a man might like his meat or fish – compared on *Nedarim 20b* to how a man might like his sex – as coming to negate the *four* cautions of Rabbi Yochanan ben Dahavai.

[236] Toledano edition (Tiberias 1906), page 29 and page 30.

On pages 28-29, Rabbi Avraham Hayarchi first quotes the interpretation of Raavad III (a one-time teacher of his), that the Sages on *Nedarim 20b* permitted *only one* out of the four, namely, "overturning the table." But he immediately goes on to *reject* Raavad III's interpretation in favor of his own, that the Sages permitted "everything."

Later, on page 31, however, he paraphrases Raavad III's statement that the punishment in this world for "non-sex-related talk" during sex is that one's children will be deaf. Thus, the same enigma that applies to Raavad III's view (discussed next in our study, page 63) would appear to apply to Rabbi Avraham Hayarchi's in an even greater way, for the latter states clearly that the Sages *permitted all four* behaviors between husband and wife, which would include any kind of talk during sex.

But Rabbi Avraham Hayarchi was writing this in a commentary on *Callah Rabti*, and, unlike *Nedarim 20b*, *Callah Rabti* understands the Sages as legally permitting all four behaviors cautioned against by Rabbi Yochanan ben Dahavai, while also still believing all four of them to be medically dangerous if performed during the same sexual encounter in which conception occurs. Therefore, according to *Callah Rabti*, which Rabbi Avraham Hayarchi is interpreting here, non-sex-related talk during sex, gazing at or kissing the female genitals, and even "overturning the table" could all still cause congenital illness if performed during the same sexual encounter in which conception occurs.

We could therefore say that this was, perhaps, the context Rabbi Avraham Hayarchi was referring to when he said (that the Sages permitted all four behaviors, but) that non-sex-related talk during sex still causes deafness – he was referring specifically to non-sex-related talk spoken *during the same sexual encounter in which conception occurs*, relying upon *Callah Rabti* (not *Nedarim 20ab*) as his source.

Raavad III, however, appears to concede that the Sages rejected Rabbi Yochanan ben Dahavai's cautions about "overturning the table" both halchically and medically – which suggests *Callah Rabti* was not the main source he was relying upon.

[Rabbi Avraham Hayarchi, at the top of page 37 of his commentary, argues that Raavad III did believe that "overturning the table" could cause congenital lameness if it is done without the wife's permission. But Raavad III in *Baalei HaNefesh* does not spell this out clearly. And the bottom line is that Raavad III certainly does not predict congenital lameness for "overturning the table" at any time if performed with the wife's permission, while Rabbi Avraham Hayarchi – based on *Callah Rabti* – would presumably predict such even if performed with the wife's permission if it happens to be during the same sexual encounter in which conception occurs.]

[237] Rabbi Yitzchak of Corbeil in his *Sefer Mitzvos Katan* states clearly and unequivocally that all four are permitted, even according to those (like *Callah Rabti*) who believe they might still cause illnesses. And, he writes, if one chooses to avoid them out of concerns about congenital illnesses it is only a measure of added piety (*midas chasidus*).

[238] It is not clear what Rabbi Alnaqua meant with the phrase "sex any time" in reference to the Sage's rejection of Rabbi Yochanan ben Dahavai's four cautions on *Nedarim 20ab*. Perhaps he meant it to refer to non-sex-related talk, meaning: "any time – even immediately after or during non-sex-related discussion."

The phrase "sex any time" is clearly borrowed from Maimonides' wording in *Mishneh Torah, Sefer Kedushah, Isurei Biah 21:9*. Considering that Maimonides does not bring restrictions on "non-sex-related talk" during sex (only on "excess lightheaded talk" or "vain talk" – as a matter of piety, not law – in *Deos 5:4*; see below pp. 76-77), and considering that many commentaries take it for granted that Maimonides himself understood the Sages on *Nedarim 20b* as rejecting all four of Rabbi Yochanan ben Dahavai's cautions, including his caution against non-sex-related talk during sex, we can thus suggest that Maimonides' own intention with the phrase "sex any time" may have been to permit sex not only at times other than when it is specifically mandated by Jewish law for the husband to please his wife, but also to permit sex regardless of what conversation the couple may be having or may have had just prior.

Or it could be a reference to the point about Rabbi Eliezer's custom to have sex only in the middle of night to avoid hearing voices from the street and the risk of intentional illicit fantasies, which is followed in the order of the Talmudic discourse on *Nedarim 20b* by Rabbi Yochanan's and the Sages' rejection of Rabbi Yochanan ben Dahavai's cautions.

Or it could be referring to (consensual) sex that is purely for the sake of the husband's sexual fulfillment, contrary to the ideal pious intention of intercourse as discussed by Maimonides himself in *Sefer Hamada, Deos 3:2*, where he also says that ideally a man does not initiate sex just "any time" he has the compulsion (*lo yivol ele c'dei l'havros gufo u'c'dei l'kayem es hazera. L'fichach eino boel col zman sheyisaveh ele col eis sheyeida shehu tzarich lehotzi shichvas zera c'mo derech harefuos oe lekayem es hazera*).

See also *Sefer Hamada, Deos 5:4*, "A man's wife is permitted to him any time" (*ishto shel'adam muteres lo tamid*).

And see above, endnote 50.

[239] Page 81.

[240] *Baalei HaNefesh, Shaar Hakedushah*, page 179 in the Buchwald edition.

[241] Quoted also in *Kovetz Shitos Kamai, Nedarim,* page 190.

[242] *Baalei HaNefesh, Shaar Hakedushah*, page 179 in the Buchwald edition.

[243] *Baalei HaNefesh, Shaar Hakedushah*, page 176 in the Buchwald edition.

[244] The phrase "what is his punishment?" is found in only one manuscript version of *Baalei HaNefesh* (see Buchwald edition, *Shinuyei Nuschaos*, p. 251). But even without it, the connotation of the passage remains the same.

Rabbi Avraham Hayarchi in his *Commentary to Callah Rabti*, page 31 (Toledano edition) does bring this phrase.

And see next endnote.

[245] The phrase "And what is his punishment in this world?" is found in only one manuscript version of *Baalei HaNefesh* (see Buchwald edition, *Shinuyei Nuschaos*, p. 251). But even without it, the connotation of the passage remains the same.

Rabbi Avraham Hayarchi in his *Commentary to Callah Rabti*, page 31 (Toledano edition) does bring this phrase.

And see previous endnote.

[246] *Orach Chaim 240:4*. In *Even Haezer 25:2*, however, the author of *Levush* rules the letter of the law according to Maimonides (and Rabbi Isserles), who understood the Sages as embracing all four of these behaviors both halachically and medically.

And see below, endnote 640.

[247] *Shaar Beis Hanashim, Clal 128:7*. And see below, p. 162.

[248] *Orach Chaim 240:4*. And see below, pp. 162-163.

[249] *Orach Chaim 240:4:40*. And see below, p. 163.

[250] *Baalei HaNefesh, Shaar Hakedushah*, Buchwald edition, page 177.

[251] Rabbi Yehuda Henkin agrees that Rabbi Avraham of Montpellier probably meant to permit kissing the female genitals along with the other three behaviors even though he did

not enumerate it specifically. See *Bnei Banim vol. 4, Responsum 16:3*, p. 58, left column, end of paragraph 2.

See also Rabbi Avraham de Boton's assertion in his *Lechem Mishneh* commentary to *Mishneh Torah, Sefer Hamada, Deos 5:4*, that although Maimonides in *Isurei Biah 21:9* only identified two of the four behaviors cautioned against by Rabbi Yochanan ben Dahavai – anal sex ("overturning the table") and kissing the female genitals – as being permitted, it is obvious that he meant the other two – gazing at the female genitals and non-sex-related talk during sex – to be permitted as well.

[252] See Rabbi Alnaqua's *Menoras Hamaor, vol. 4, Perek Nisuei Ishah*, pp. 72-80.

Also of significant note, there, is the fact that Rabbi Alnaqua quotes extensively from the opinion of Raavad III as stated in *Baalei HaNefesh, Shaar Hakedushah*, but when he comes to explain what the Sages permitted against Rabbi Yochanan ben Dahavai, he specifically includes kissing the female genitals, which Raavad III, in *Baalei HaNefesh, Shaar Hakedushah*, claims to still be forbidden.

Rabbi Alnaqua also argues, in explaining the view of Rabbi Yochanan ben Dahavai, that the term "overturning the table" means anal sex, contrary to Raavad III's implication that it means only rear-entry vaginal intercourse.

[253] Below, Part Five.

[254] The author of *Halachos Gedolos* simply quotes the teaching of Rabbi Yochanan ben Dahavai followed by the ruling of the Sages against him – indicating that he took the Sages' words at face value that they were rejecting all four of Rabbi Yochanan ben Dahavai's cautions according to the letter of the law.

[255] Maimonides, there, in relating the argument between Rabbi Yochanan ben Dahavai and the Sages on *Nedarim 20ab*, expressly states that the Sages permitted "overturning the table," kissing the female genitals and "other forms of [sexual] lightheadedness."

See below, pp. 103-104.

[256] It is implied by Maimonides' rulings in his *Commentary to the Mishnah* and *Mishneh Torah* that he understood the Sages as permitting all four of the behaviors Rabbi Yochanan ben Dahavai had cautioned against – which would include gazing at the female genitals and non-sex-related talk during sex.

It is evident that this is how both Rabbi Yosef Caro and Rabbi Yoel Sirkis understood Maimonides – from Rabbi Caro's words in his *Beis Yosef* (*Tur, Even Haezer 25:2; 25:8-10*) and from Rabbi Sirkis's words in his *Bayis Chadash* (*Tur, Even Haezer 25:2*).

See also Rabbi Yehoshua Falk's *Prishah* commentary to *Tur, Even Haezer 25:8-10:35*.

And this is how *Lechem Mishneh* (*Sefer Hamada, Deos 5:4*), *Biur HaGra* (*Shulchan Aruch, Even Haezer 25:2*), *Atzei Arazim* (*Even Haezer 25*) and *Ikvei HaBayis–Rosh Pinah* (*Shulchan Aruch, Even Haezer 25:1*) all understood Maimonides' view.

[Note that in his *Commentary to the Mishnah*, Maimonides mentions both her-on-top and anal intercourse as being permitted sex positions within marriage. In his *Mishneh Torah*, however, Maimonides does not mention the her-on-top position, only anal intercourse. Perhaps he felt that stating his permission for anal intercourse – the most-strictly-dealt-with position in halachah – would make it obvious to the reader that all other sex positions within marriage are legally acceptable before G-d as well.]

[257] Hurwitz edition, 1928.

ENDNOTES

Credit goes to the author of *Dvar Seser* for bringing this source to my attention on page 43 of his 2013 edition.

[258] Page 375 in the Mosad HaRav Kook edition.

Like the author of *Halachos Gedolos*, Rabbi Aboab does not single out a specific number of Rabbi Yochanan ben Dahavai's cautions that Rabbi Yochanan bar Napacha and the Sages meant to reject. He simply states that they rejected Rabbi Yochanan ben Dahavai – implying that they did so categorically.

[259] Meiri mentions "'overturning the table' and all other light-headedness (*kalus rosh*) and foolishness (*hedyotos*)," which he says the Sages' permit – even though one should *strive* for sanctity in them as well.

Meiri certainly does not specify that any of the four behaviors were excluded from the Sages' permissive legal ruling.

[259*] Such as: Rabbi Aharon Hacohen of Lunil, *Orchos Chaim, Hilchos Kesubos Siman 7*; *Col Bo, Hilchos Ishus, Siman 75*; Rabeinu Yaakov of London, *Etz Chaim, Hilchos Piryah Vrivyah, Chapter 3*; Rabbi Menachem Ibn Zerach, *Tzeidah Laderech, Maamar 3, Clal 4, Chapter 14*.

[260] This is besides the fact that Rabbi Alfasi generally leaves out laws that are irrelevant during the time of exile. See *Yad Malachi, Clalei Haposkim - Geonim, Clal 7*.

[261] See also Rabbi Moshe Stern's responsum in *Be'er Moshe vol. 3, Responsum 152*, Part 10, pp. 202-203, where he understands Rabbi Alfasi as permitting all four of the behaviors cautioned against by Rabbi Yochanan ben Dahavai.

However, an early medieval scholar, Rabbi Avraham Hayarchi, in his commentary to *Callah Rabti* (Toledano edition, page 29) suggests the exact opposite. He says that because Rabbi Alfasi omitted the view of (Rabbi Yochanan bar Napacha, the Sages, Rav and) Rabbi Yehudah HaNasi, who permitted "overturning the table," Rabbi Alfasi must have ruled the letter of the law according to Rabbi Yochanan ben Dahavai in regard to all four behaviors – an even more stringent view than that of Raavad III (who at least admitted that the Sages permitted "overturning the table").

What Rabbi Avraham Hayarchi does not mention is that while Rabbi Alfasi does omit the view of (Rabbi Yochanan bar Napacha, the Sages, Rav and) Rabbi Yehudah Hanasi, he also omits the view of Rabbi Yochanan ben Dahavai. Perhaps Rabbi Avraham Hayarchi had a different manuscript version of Rabbi Alfasi. But according to the version available to us today, the correct deduction is arguably that Rabbi Alfasi considered the entire discussion about marital sex positions and technique on *Nedarim 20ab* to be a matter of extra-halachic piety, and therefore he cannot be assumed to have legally forbade any of the four behaviors – just like his later halachic admirer, Maimonides, did not forbid them.

In any case, the principle that Rabbi Alfasi's omission of a Talmudic passage is tantamount to his rejection of it as a legally binding one is at least born out by Rabbi Avraham Hayarchi's comment on this very Talmudic piece.

[Parenthetically, Rabbi Avraham Hayarchi, there, seems to be transposing the Talmud's quotations of Rabbi Yehudah Hanasi and Rav, placing Rav's words – comparing a husband's predilections for how he likes his sex to how he likes his fish – in the mouth of Rabbi Yehudah HaNasi.]

[262] See *Yad Malachi, Clalei Haposkim - Geonim, Clal 29, 32*.

[263] See, for example, Maimonides, *Commentary to the Mishnah, Sanhedrin 7:4*; *Sefer Chasidim 380, 509*; Rokeach, *Hilchos Chasidus* (quoted in *Kovetz Shitos Kamai, Nedarim 20b*, page 186); Meiri, *Beis Habechirah, Nedarim 20b*.

[264] Through marriage. Or, perhaps, through a halachically-established *pilegesh* relationship – a concept to be explored in a future volume of this series.

[265] *Sefer HaEshkol, Hilchos Tznius* (Albeck edition).

[266] See *Peirush HaRan, Peirush R' Avraham min Hahar* and *Shitah Mekubetzes* (possibly in the name of Ritz) to *Nedarim 20b*.

Note that, technically speaking, this particular reasoning would only explain why sexual exploration is permitted between husband and wife *within marriage*, the subject of the verse in Deuteronomy 24:1. It would not, however, necessarily justify such exploration within a halachically-established *pilegesh* relationship – a relationship that is, according to some commentaries, fundamentally defined by a *lack* of "acquisition" on the man's part.

[267] See *Sifra-Toras Cohanim, Leviticus 20:13*; *Babylonian Talmud, Tractate Kesubos 46a*; *Mishneh Torah, Sefer Kedushah, Isurei Biah 3:15*.

[268] *Tosfos Yeshanim, Yevamos 34b*; Rabbi Netanel ben Yeshaya of Yemen, *Maor Ha'afelah, Parshas Acharei Mos*, p. 347, and *Parshas Kedoshim*, p. 362 (published from manuscript for the first time in 1957 by Rabbi Yosef Kapach).

This approach is also brought – though not in the name of these medieval sources – in various post-medieval commentaries, such as *Maharsha* to *Nedarim 20b*, Rabbi Moshe of Trani's *Kiryas Sefer, Isurei Biah 21*, and *Meromei Sadeh* of Rabbi Naftali Tzvi Yehudah Berlin (Netziv) to *Sanhedrin 58b*. See also Rabbi Berlin's *Meishiv Davar vol. 1, Responsum 88*.

See also *Shas Wagshal-Nehardea, Tractate Yevamos, Hagahos v'Chidushim, Yevamos 34b*, "R'aMa", Rabbi Elazar Moshe Horowitz (1817-1890), Chief Rabbi of Pinsk.

See also Rabbi Avraham Dovid Wahrman of Buczacz's *Ezer Mekudash* to *Shulchan Aruch, Even Haezer 25:2:Beis Shmuel*, where he writes an even stronger variation of this approach, and not only in regard to anal intercourse, but in regard to intra-anal ejaculation:

> . . . But in regard to one-time intra-anal ejaculation, since it [anal sex] counts [as "intercourse"] in regard to liability, as is known, it also counts as [fulfilling the commandment in regard to] satisfying one's wife sexually, which is why it [intra-anal ejaculation] is permitted randomly [in the heat of passion].
>
> (*mah she'ein kein paam achas shelo cedarcah, caivan shehu bichlal biah l'chiyuvim, c'yadua, hava leih gam kein b'geder onah, ul'zeh hitiru b'akrai*)

But see *Ezer Mekudash* to *Even Haezer 76:1:Chayiv B'onah*.

[Note that throughout his analysis of *Even Haezer 25*, Rabbi Avraham Dovid speaks of those who permit "one-time intra-anal ejaculation" – that is "only once in a lifetime" (*paam achas*). But see his comment regarding *Sefer Charedim* in his analysis of *Even Haezer 25:2:Hagaah*, where he says that he does not know where this notion of permitting intra-anal ejaculation "only once in a lifetime" comes from, for Rabeinu Yitzchak, Rabeinu Asher, *Tur* and *Beis Yosef* all speak of permitting it "randomly, in the heat of passion" (*b'akrai*) with no stipulation of it being permitted only once in a lifetime.

And while one of Rabeinu Asher's disciples, Rabeinu Yeruchem (*Nesiv 23*), does use the term "*paam achas*" in discussing the permission of intra-anal ejaculation within marriage, as does *Tosfos Talmid Rabeinu Tam* (manuscript to Genesis 38:9, quoted in *Kovetz Meforshim, Nedarim 20, Leket Rishonim* by Yerid Haseforim, 2003; see above endnote 221; and compare to *Tosfos Hashalem al HaTorah, Vayeshev 38:9:11:V'shicheis Artzah*, p.66), it is clear from both of them that they did not mean to permit intra-anal ejaculation only once in a lifetime, but rather once in a while.

See also Rabbi Yehuda Henkin in his *Bnei Banim*, vol. 4, end of *Responsum 18:1*, pp. 64-65, who says that Rabeinu Yeruchem's use of the term "*paam achas*" could mean once between each menstrual cycle.

And see below, endnote 613.]

[See also *Nedarim 51a, Peirush Rabeinu Nissim*: "*Toeh atah bah,*" that G-d's objection to homosexual anal intercourse is that the penetrator "chooses male intercourse over the *places* of intercourse of a woman" (*shemeiniach mishkevei ishah v'holech etzel zachar*) – implying that anal intercourse is acceptable within heterosexual marriage. Credit goes to Rabbi Yossi Newfield for bringing this source to my attention.]

[269] The question of whether a woman experiences pleasure from anal intercourse is pertinent here. While modern science certainly considers this possible, especially when done considerately and with proper lubrication, halachah appears to have had differing views on the matter going back to ancient times.

For preliminary references of sources to explore, see *Sanhedrin 58b: Peirush Rashi:"Shelo cedarcah;" Gilyon Hashas; Hagahos Maharam Ranshburg*. See also Rabbi Reuven Margolis, *Mekor Chesed* commentary to *Sefer Chasidim 509*, footnote 12.

See also Rabbi Yitzchak Lampronti's *Pachad Yitzchak, Entry: Beilah Shelo Cedarcah*, and his reference, there, to Rabbi Shlomoh Algazi's *Gufei Halachos, Ois 153*.

Most pertinent is the rhetorical question recorded in the name of one sage and reported in *Babylonian Talmud, Kidushin 22b*:

> Who is to say that man and woman do not both experience pleasure from anal sex? (*man leima lan d'lav hanaah is l'hu l'tarvaihu*)

See also the commentary of Rabbi Yeshayah of Trani I (*Tosfos Rid*), quoted by Rabbi Chaim Yosef David Azulai (Chida) in his biblical anthology, *Pnei David, Parshas Vayishlach*, Section 1, that Torah recognizes both vaginal and anal intercourse as being pleasurable to a woman when done lovingly and with her consent, and both as painful if done against her will. [Credit goes to the author of the humorously titled booklet, *Rabbi, My Husband wants Anal Sex*, for bringing this comment of Rabbi Yeshayah of Trani I to my attention on pages 17-18 of his 2015 work.]

**Added note to the third edition:** See also *Shaalos uTeshuvos Torah Lishmah, Responsum 299* (credit goes to Rabbi Yossi Newfield for bringing this source in *Torah Lishmah* to my attention). And see Rabbi Maor Kayam's *Harchavot l'Simchat Habayit v'Birchato* (2015), pp. 181-183.

[270] Rabbi Eliezer of Metz, Re'em, is quoted in *Shitah Mekubetzes, Nedarim 20b*.

[271] Note that we do not know with certainty which of Rabbi Yochanan ben Dahavi's four cautions *Tosfos Yeshanim* and Rabbi Eliezer of Metz each understood the Sages (and Rabbi Yehudah HaNasi, Rav and Rabbi Yochanan bar Napacha) as coming to permit. But see above, pp. 62-65, that virtually all medieval writers (at least those whose writings have come down to us) appear to have understood the Sages as coming to permit all four.

And *Tosfos Yeshanim* interprets "overturning the table" to mean anal sex. Thus, if *Tosfos Yeshanim* considered anal sex – the most-strictly-dealt-with sexual position in halachah – to be lacking no holiness, it presumably considered no other sex position to be lacking in holiness either.

What is more, being that most medieval commentaries who permitted anal sex to couples also permitted occasional intra-anal ejaculation, it can reasonably be believed that *Tosfos Yeshanim* meant to permit such as well (especially in the absence of any qualifying statement in *Tosfos Yeshanim* to the contrary; and it is arguable that "*stam biah*" implies intercourse to the point of climax, as suggested by the comments of Rabeinu Asher preserved in *Hagahos Habach* to *Rosh, Yevamos 34b*, in *Yam Shel Shlomoh* to *Yevamos 34b*, and in *Beis Yosef* to *Tur, Orach 240:2-4:4*; see also below, endnote 616, the opening excerpts of Rabbi Elazar Azikri's interpretation of *Sanhedrin 58b*, where he, too, notes that "*stam biah*" generally implies ejaculation) – and still there would be "no lack of holiness."

Taking the implication of *Tosfos Yeshanim's* and Rabbi Eliezer of Metz's comments further, the meaning of the Sages' comparison of individual sexual predilections to individual culinary predilections perhaps becomes even more clear and more down-to-earth – meaning to say that just like the way a person instinctually craves his or her meat or fish to be prepared is a natural individual preference for which he or she need not feel guilty or ashamed or unholy or perverse, because it is simply part of his or her natural makeup and part of who they are as G-d made them (through nature and/or nurture), so, too, there is nothing shameful, unholy or perverse about the sexual techniques and positions one is curious about, enjoys or prefers within the context of a loving and respectful halachically-established relationship.

That being said, sexual fetishes that physically harm or psychologically/emotionally damage either partner would obviously not be acceptable in G-d's eyes. And even where both partners enjoy, or at least agree to, such fetishes it is unlikely that *Tosfos Yeshanim* or Rabbi Eliezer of Metz, or G-d Himself, would consider them holy or healthy. Rather, in such cases we would recommend a mental health professional be consulted.

Light nipping, light biting or light scratching, if found erotic, would not seem to be problematic.

[The topic of sex toys will be addressed in a future volume of this series.]

[272] A 3rd Generation Israeli Amora.

[273] A 3rd-4th Generation Babylonian Amora.

[274] Amos 4:13.

[275] A 1st Generation Babylonian Amora. This is the same Rav quoted on *Nedarim 20b* permitting "overturning the table."

*Callah Rabti 3:1* (M. Higger edition) has this teaching quoted in the name of Rabbi Yehoshua ben Levi, a contemporary of Rav.

[276] As noted, we are given no clear indication that Rav himself actually applied his own statement to the verse quoted by Rav Illa. Rather, the compilers-editors of the Talmud, whoever they were, may have suggested this connection. Still, Rav's teaching in-and-of-itself requires explanation. And so the Talmud goes on to challenge, and clarify, it.

[277] This retort of Rav Cahana is not generally found in manuscript versions of *Hagigah 5b*, though it is found in a parallel telling of the story in *Tractate Brachos 62a*.

See also *Dikdukei Sofrim, Hagigah 5b*, footnote 20.

278 *Dikdukei Sofrim, Hagigah 5b.*

279 *Dikdukei Sofrim,* Ibid.

280 *Peirush R' Avraham min Hahar, Hagigah 5b* - though in actuality, he is only interpreting the word "talk - *sichah,*" there, he does not speak of "*excess* talk - *sichah yeseirah.*"

281 See, for example, *Tur* and *Shulchan Aruch - Orach Chaim 240* and *Even Haezer 25.*

282 Note that if Rabeinu Chananel were in fact *not* limiting this teaching to a sexual context, but rather explaining that Rav cautioned against "excess light-headed talk" with one's wife in general at any time, unless for the sake of her (or his) emotional need, then the question the Talmud brings next about Rav's excessive light-headed talk in bed could have really been asked about excessive light-headed talk during any activity of life at any time of the day.

The Talmud's answer, then, that "excess light-headed talk" is acceptable before intercourse in order to facilitate the mood (*tzarich leratzuya*), could perhaps be extended to a husband joking with his wife in a light-headed manner (perhaps even in a sexual manner) at any time of day that his wife might require a mood lift.

And note *Maharsha* to *Hagigah 5b,* who interprets Rav's teaching about "excess talk between husband and wife" to mean "*trivial* talk (*sichah shel mah*) between husband and wife."

283 See above, footnote to page 32, for an explanation of this translation choice of the phrase "*al tarbeh sichah im ha'ishah.*"

284 Although the term "excess talk" is not actually mentioned in the episode of Rav Cahana, the fact that the Talmudic compilers-editors brought the episode of Rav Cahana as a contradiction to Rav's teaching against "excess talk," proves that they themselves understood whatever talk Rav was speaking with his wife in bed (to which Rav Cahana expressed astonishment about its extremes) to be equivalent to, or at least included in, the "excess talk" mentioned in the prior teaching quoted in Rav's own name.

285 Rabbi Yaakov Emden, in an addendum to *Mor uKetziah 240,* page 283 in the 1996 Machon Yerushalayim edition, takes it as a given that "light-headed talk" (*sichah kallah*) refers to "vulgar talk and foolishness" (*nivul peh v'letzanus*), and that Rav was only speaking with his wife words of affection to appease and arouse her to the mood and awaken her desire (*divrei cheivah l'faisah ul'ratzosah, gam l'orer taavasah*) - which he had to do in excess because of the unfortunately difficult nature of his relationship with her.

And see below, endnote 316.

It is not clear what Rabbi Emden means in his distinguishing between words that are meant to arouse a woman to the mood (*l'ratzosah*) and words that are meant to awaken her desire (*l'orer taavasah*), nor where he draws the line between "vulgar talk and foolishness" versus "words of affection" that are erotic enough to fan the flames of female passion. It is also not clear why any amount of *asexual affectionate* talk would have shocked Rav Cahana.

286 For additional Talmudic-era sources that discuss "vulgar talk," see Mosad HaRav Kook's *Otzar HaAgadah vol. 2, Entry: Nivul Peh.*

287 Rabbi Yisrael Alnaqua, in his *Menoras Hamaor vol. 4, Perek Nisuei Isha,* page 80, says that "vulgar talk" is forbidden "even" during sexual intercourse (*asur lenavel piv afilu b'shaas tashmish*). But he does not define, there, what constitutes "vulgar talk."

288 See *Mishneh Torah, Sefer Kedushah, Isurei Biah 21:24.*

[289] The summary of this analysis will also be repeated below in Part Five, pp. 175-176.

[290] Note that in the following analysis about talk during sex, I have intentionally omitted relevant passages from the anonymous medieval work on sexual piety, *Igeres Hakodesh, Chapter 6, Part 5* (attributed by some to Nachmanides).

While the anonymous author's presentation, there, is quite interesting, it mixes in much that is unrelated to, and does not help clarify, the discussions of *Nedarim 20ab* versus *Hagigah 5b*, and it raises points that can only be fully understood in the context of earlier discussions in that same work.

A full review of this *Igeres Hakodesh* will feature in a future volume of this series.

[291] *Baalei HaNefesh, Shaar Hakedushah*, pp. 175-176 in the Buchwald edition.

[292] See above, endnote 215.

[293] See *Baalei HaNefesh, Shaar Hakedushah*, Buchwald edition, page 175 and footnote 10* thereon.

[294] As mentioned above, p. 43, *Tractate Callah 22* implies that Rabbi Eliezer would permit, and even encourage, "seductive talk," even mid-intercourse (*b'shaas tashmish*). Raavad III, however, who discusses seductive talk as one definition of "mood-related talk," would seem to permit it only during foreplay, and only if "necessary" to arouse her to the mood for sex.

[And see *Shevet Musar*, beginning of Chapter 16, by Rabbi Eliyahu Hacohen (c.1659-1729)]

But note also that Raavad III quotes the teaching of *Callah Rabti 22* again later in his work, on page 181 of the Buchwald edition, where the context has nothing to do with a husband having to arouse his wife to sex (and where there does not appear to be any doubt as to the authenticity of the passage resulting from textual variations of *Baalei HaNefesh*).

[295] Although the phrase *"tisyashvu nafsham"* might simply be translated as "their souls become *settled*," I would suggest that perhaps "their souls become *aligned*" more accurately conveys the intention here, as well as the reality of the experience of sexual intimacy (which is not always performed in a "settled" state – though perhaps in the case of a Torah scholar the presumption is that it generally is). And note that the Hebrew word *"yishuv"* itself can connote not just "settling," but also "settlement" – as in agreement, alignment.

[296] Note that alternate versions of *Mishneh Torah* have this passage referring only to the settling of *her* or *his* soul. But the most authoritative manuscript of *Sefer Hamada* in our hands today has it in the plural: "their souls." See *Rambam Meduyak, Sefer Hamada*, Mahadurat Sheilat, 2004.

And see *Mishneh Torah, Sefer Nashim, Ishus 14:5*, where Maimonides implies that it is natural, and permissible, for both husband and wife to speak words of arousal to each other during intimacy – it is only problematic for one spouse to force the other to reveal to others what words of such nature were spoken between them.

[297] See also *Mishneh Torah, Sefer Nashim, Ishus 15:17*:

> And he should not force her, penetrating her against her will, but rather with her agreement, and through words and joy (*umitoch sichah v'simchah*).

[298] Rabbi Yosef Caro in his *Kesef Mishneh* to *Sefer Hamada, Deos 5:4*, suggests that Maimonides' instruction to "talk and joke a little" derives from *Hagigah 5b* – thereby implying that it is only permitted if necessary to arouse the wife to the mood for sex.

# ENDNOTES

This, however, does not fit into Maimonide's wording, which states clearly that the purpose of such "talk and joking" is to settle *both* their souls, not just the wife's, and which implies that it should *always* be done, not just when "needed." Nor does it fit into the clear context of *Hagigah 5b*, which permits not "a little," but *a lot* of talking and joking if need be to arouse the wife to the mood (which negates Rabbi Caro's suggestion even according to the version that has Maimonides speaking only of settling *her* soul).

See also *Lechem Mishneh* to *Sefer HaMada, Deos 5:4*.

And see *Arbaah Turei Even* quoted in the *Sefer Halikutim* supplementary section to the Shabsi Frankel edition of Maimonides' *Mishneh Torah, Sefer Hamada, Deos 5:4*.

[299] See above, pp. 57-58 and endnotes 212-213 thereon.

[300] *Lechem Mishneh, Deos 5:4*, notes that when Maimonides, there, discourages certain marital sex behaviors *for Torah scholars*, he did *not* mean to suggest that such behaviors were *all* perfectly permitted for laymen, because *some* of them – such as when husband and/or wife are intoxicated or when the wife is forced against her will – Maimonides discourages, or even forbids, even for laymen in *Isurei Biah 21*.

On the matter of avoiding "light-headedness," however, even in *Isurei Biah 21:9* Maimonides writes for the layman that it is a matter of *voluntary piety*, not binding law.

And he does not discuss restrictions on talk during sex for laymen at all in *Isurei Biah 21*.

[301] See *Arbaah Turei Even* quoted in the *Sefer Halikutim* supplementary section to the Shabsi Frankel edition of Maimonides' *Mishneh Torah, Sefer Hamada, Deos 5:4*.

[302] Rabbi Avraham de Boton actually does not reference the discouragement of "vain talk" as evidence of Maimonides incorporating the discussion of *Hagigah 5b*. Rather, he references only Maimonides' encouragement of "speaking and joking a little to settle [align – see above, endnote 295] their souls."

This is somewhat perplexing, for earlier in his commentary, Rabbi Avraham de Boton suggests that the reason the compilers-editors of *Nedarim 20b* did not choose "mood-related talk" (*c'dei l'ratzosa*, the context of *Hagigah 5b*) as the context of Rabbi Eliezer's talk during sex was because Ima Shalom described him as *always* speaking to her before sex, and the compilers-editors probably found it unlikely that Rabbi Eliezer would have *always* needed to arouse his wife to the mood for sex through words. But at the end of his commentary, Rabbi Avraham de Boton suggests that Maimonides' encouragement for a husband to *always* "talk and laugh a little to settle [align] their souls" was a reference to *Hagigah 5b's* teaching about "mood-related talk," in which case Rabbi Avraham de Boton would now be saying that such talk perhaps *is* always needed!

Rather, we would suggest (as we inserted parenthetically into our presentation of Rabbi Avraham's own words) that Maimonides' reference to *Hagigah 5b* was his discouragement (though not prohibition) of "vain talk." And his encouragement of "talking and laughing to settle [align] their souls" was a reference to *Tractate Callah 22's* teaching in the name of Rabbi Eliezer himself, that a husband should always talk "seductively" to his wife.

And if this "seductive talk" were in fact the kind of talk Ima Shalom herself was describing, then it would explain why Rabbi Eliezer made it a part of his regular customs of intimacy – and it would mean that Maimonides did in fact make veiled reference to the "sex-related talk" of *Nedarim 20b*, which he equated with "seductive talk."

See also above, pp. 57-58 and endnotes 212-213 thereon, that some commentaries define "sex-related talk" as talk that is meant to increase sexual passion, and that some even say such talk is *good* to talk with one's spouse – that is, presumably, *always*.

And further research into the matter is required.

[303] See *Kovetz Shitos Kamai, Nedarim 20*, page 180.

[304] Rabbi Yaakov Emden says the same. See *Shas Wagshal-Nehardea, Tractate Nedarim, Hagahos v'Chidushim, Nedarim 20b*, first entry for *Yaavetz*.

[305] Although the terms "*kalus rosh*" and "*sichah kalah*" (the latter of which some sources equate with the "*sicha yeseirah*" of *Hagigah 5b*) are related, Meiri's use of the former term when commenting on the context of *Nedarim 20b* was not necessarily intended to include the context of *Hagigah 5b* (as we noted above, p. 76, in regard to Maimonides' use of the term "*kalus rosh*" in reference to sexual *positions*, not sexual *talk*).

[However, Rashi to *Talmud Berachos 62a* does use the term "*kalus rosh*" to describe Rav's behavior/talk, in a separate telling of the episode described on *Hagigah 5b*.]

In any case, even if Meiri to *Nedarim 20b* did have Rav's behavior in mind, it would have been only to *permit* his behavior according to the letter of the law, not to forbid it – which would be in line with Meiri's comments on *Hagigah 5ab*.

[306] And it is apparent that Meiri extends this extra-halachic categorization of the Talmudic discussion not only into the teaching of Rav on *Hagigah 5b*, but even after.

[307] See below, p. 187.

[308] See *Tractate Brachos 62a*, Rashi: *D'sach v'tzachak*.

[309] See also *Lechem Mishneh* to *Mishneh Torah, Sefer Hamada, Deos 5:4* in regard to Rabbi Yaakov ben Asher's presentation in *Tur*.

[310] Rabbi Yehoshuah Falk in his *Drishah* commentary to *Tur, Orach Chaim 240:10:20* also quotes a currently non-extant version of *Brachos 62a* that has Rav talking with his wife in order to increase *his own* sexual passion.

[311] It is, in fact, the Talmudic manuscript version that has the phrase "*sichah kalah*," not the version that has "*sichah yeseirah*," which also includes this second, lesser-known approach of the Talmud permitting any "excess-lightheaded talk" during foreplay (see *Dikdukei Sofrim, Hagigah 5b*, footnotes 6 and 30). And from his wording in *Tur, Orach Chaim 240*, Rabbi Yaakov ben Asher seems to have had the "*sichah kalah*" text-version of the Talmud.

[312] Again, evidence to support this comes from Ima Shalom's own account on *Nedarim 20b*, where she reports that, "as he spoke, he would uncover a hand's-breadth and cover over a hand's-breadth," – i.e., he would continue to speak to her during intercourse.

Rabbi Yaakov ben Asher quotes Ima Shalom both in *Even Haezer 25:3* and in *Orach Chaim 240:7-8*.

Rabbi Yoel Sirkis, *Bayis Chadash, Even Haezer 25:3:4*, relies on one textual version of *Tur*, there, (*peirush mesaper – tashmish*) against another (*peirush mesaper – b'shaas tashmish*) to argue that Rabbi Yaakov ben Asher himself did not believe Ima Shalom meant her husband would actually speak to her verbally during intercourse.

But Rabbi Yaakov's uncontested wording in *Tur, Orach Chaim 240:7-8* (*peirush mesaper – al iskei tashmish*) calls Rabbi Sirkis' argument into question.

[And see Rabbi Yosef Caro, in his *Beis Yosef, Even Haezer 25:2b:V'al yesaper imah,* who states clearly that when Ima Shalom described her husband as speaking to her "as he uncovered a hand's-breadth and covered over a hand's-breadth," she was referring to him literally speaking to her verbally during intercourse.]

That being said, the fact that Rabbi Yaakov ben Asher discusses "talk intended to intensify sexual arousal" as an example of *Rav's* behavior in talking with his own wife *before* intercourse, and in tandem with "talk that is required to appease one's wife" *before* intercourse, leaves open the possibility that even "talk intended to intensify arousal" was acceptable to him *only before* intercourse. But such would still contradict the simple reading of *Nedarim 20b,* which has *the Sages* permitting according to the letter of the law even "non-sex-related talk" even during intercourse, and which has even Rabbi Yochanan ben Dahavai himself permitting "sex-related talk" even during intercourse (*b'shaas tashmish*).

[313] *Tur, Orach Chaim 240:5, Even Haezer* end of *25:10.*

[314] Perhaps Rabbi Caro did so based on Maimonides' wording in *Isurei Biah 21:9:* "*midas chasidus shelo yakel adam es rosho lekach.*"

[315] Page 57.

[316] See *Babylonian Talmud, Shas Wagshal-Nehardea, Tractate Nedarim, Hagahos v'Chidushim, Nedarim 20b, Yaavetz.*

And see also above, endnote 285.

[317] *Babylonian Talmud, Sanhedrin 58b* does not give us enough information to know which Rabbi Elazar this was, nor when he lived. All we can say for certain is that he lived contemporaneously with, or after, this Rabbi Chanina, whose exact identity is also unclear.

Note, however, that *Jerusalem Talmud, Kidushin 1:1* and *Breishis Rabah 18:5* mention two other sages, a Rabbi Shmuel and a Rabbi Abahu, alongside a Rabbi Elazar, who all quoted a similar teaching in the name of a Rabbi Chanina. It is thus possible these were all 3rd-4th generation Amoraic contemporaries.

For an analysis of the important discrepancies in Rabbi Chanina's teaching as reported by *Babylonian Talmud, Sanhedrin 58b* compared to *Jerusalem Talmud, Kidushin 1:1* and *Breishis Rabah 18:5,* see below, endnotes 325, 344.

[318] See previous endnote.

[319] Genesis 2:24

[320] See *Rashi:Shelo Cedarcah,* that an integral part of "clinging" is plain and simple sexual pleasure between husband and wife – and in the case of anal sex it is debatable whether the wife experiences sufficient pleasure to foster "clinging."

[321] The 4th generation Babylonian Amora, quoted also in *Callah Rabti 1:13* (see above, pp. 45-46).

[322] See our analysis below, p. 86 point 1, that even according to the textual versions that read "not liable," here, the meaning is understood to be equivalent to "permitted."

[323] See above, endnotes 317, 321.

[324] Medieval commentaries, such as R' Meir Abulafia (*Yad Ramah*), Rabeinu Nissim of Gerona (*Chidushei HaRan*) and Rabeinu Yonah of Gerona (*Chidushei Rabeinu Yonah*) already point out that while Torah law for non-Jews is more lax than for Jews in terms of *what* behaviors are forbidden, and *with whom* such behaviors are forbidden, it can be more severe in terms of the *legal repercussions* of transgression.

But for this very reason, these commentaries insist that Rava, here, was not speaking about the severity of *punishment*, only the severity of *prohibition* – i.e., that there is never a sexual behavior that is *forbidden* to a non-Jew that is not also *forbidden even in some small way* to a Jew. Therefore, they explain, Rava obviously took it as a given that anal sex is *permitted* to Jews.

See also the post-medieval commentary, *Sanhedri Gedolah*.

[*Yeshuos Yaakov* to *Shulchan Aruch, Orach Chaim 240:5:4* seems to have been unaware of *Yad Ramah, Chidushei HaRan* or *Chidushei Rabeinu Yonah* here.]

As for why Rava would have taken it as a given that anal sex is permitted, it could have been based on his knowledge of earlier halachic discussions on the subject, such as those reported on *Nedarim 20b* in the names of his scholarly forebears, the Sages, Rebbi, Rav and Rabbi Yochanan bar Napacha in regard to "overturning the table;" or on the fact that the verses in Leviticus 18:22 and 20:13 speak in the plural of a woman's "places of intercourse" (see above, p. 66 point 4); or on the fact that anal sex is considered a valid form of consummating marriage between husband and wife – and therefore it is obviously permitted at the most basic legal level (see *Kidushin 9b; Mishneh Torah, Sefer Nashim, Ishus 3:5*).

[325] Rava is portrayed by some (such as Rabbi Elazar Azikri in his *Sefer Charedim, Chapter 64*) as "rewriting," or "restoring," the teaching of Rabbi Elazar in the name of Rabbi Chanina. But nowhere does Rava say anything of the sort. He merely offers a different interpretation of the verse's phrase, "and he shall cling to his wife."

In fact, it is difficult to believe that Rabbi Chanina's teaching as quoted by Rabbi Elazar was incorrectly reported, for we have two other sages on record, in *Jerusalem Talmud, Kidushin 1:1* and in *Breishis Rabah 18:5*, repeating nearly the exact same teaching in the name of Rabbi Chanina (see above, endnote 317).

Could all three sages be wrong?

[Note, though, that *Sanhedrin 58b* has Rabbi Chanina focusing in on the phrase of the verse, "and he shall cling to his wife," while *Jerusalem Talmud, Kidushin 1:1* and *Breishis Rabah 18:5* focus in on the phrase "and they shall become one flesh." See our analysis of this point below, endnote 344.]

It is therefore quite possible, and arguably more probable, that Rava was simply arguing with Rabbi Chanina's teaching entirely and offering his own personal interpretation of what the biblical phrase "and he shall cling to his wife" was meant by G-d to teach – namely, a (merciful) leniency in regard to adulterous anal sex for non-Jews.

[326] Two pages back in the Talmudic discussion, on *Sanhedrin 57b*, an argument is recorded between Rabbi Meir and the Sages regarding sexual prohibitions for non-Jews.

Rabbi Meir states that non-Jews are only prohibited against types of sexual relations for which a Jewish court would punish a Jew. But any sexual behavior for which a Jewish court would not punish a Jew – even if it carries a punishment by the hand of Heaven (such as excision of the soul) – is not forbidden to a non-Jew.

# ENDNOTES

The Sages, however, argue with Rabbi Meir. They maintain that non-Jews are in fact forbidden from engaging in numerous sexual behaviors for which a Jew is only punished by the hand of Heaven (see *Peirush Rashi,* there, for examples).

Thus, ostensibly, Rava's choice of wording according to the Vilna edition of the Talmud, that a Jew is "not liable" for anal sex, could potentially have meant only that anal sex is not "punishable" for a Jew in the human court, but that it is still forbidden and punishable for a Jew in the Heavenly court.

But if that were the case, then Rava's full argument would make no sense, for his full argument reads: "Is there ever something for which a Jew is not liable *and a non-Jew is liable?*" As stated above, the Sages DO believe that a non-Jew can be punished by the human court for sexual behaviors that a Jew is punished for only by the hand of Heaven. Thus, according to the Sages, if Jewish couples *were* liable for anal sex in the court of Heaven, then non-Jewish couples *could* be liable for it in the court of man. Why, then, did the compilers-editors of the Talmud accept Rava's argument?

It is thus very strongly implied that the compilers-editors of the Talmud understood Rava as saying that anal sex is perfectly permitted to Jewish couples, even in the eyes of the court of Heaven, and therefore it is also perfectly permitted to non-Jewish couples, both in the court of Heaven and of man.

[327] Although the subsequent teaching on the Talmudic page, there – also in the name of Rabbi Chanina, though not reported by Rabbi Elazar – is understood by some medieval scholars, like Meiri (*Beis Habechirah, Sanhedrin 58b*) and Maimonides (*Mishneh Torah, Sefer Shoftim, Melachim 10:6;* and see *Kesef Mishneh,* there), as referring to a penalty by the hand of Heaven, this is not the simple context of the biblical case under discussion there, in which an Egyptian beating a Jew was actually put to death by Moses – as already pointed out by another medieval authority, Rabeinu Nissim of Gerona (*Chidushei HaRan, Sanhedrin 58b*).

[See *Maharsha,* there, who attempts to reconcile Maimonides.]

Thus, Meiri's and Maimonides' interpretations about this subsequent Talmudic passage – while they may be theoretically valid – cannot be used to definitively prove the context of the preceding teaching (about anal sex for non-Jews) as being anything other than a debate about punishment meted out by the human court.

See also the tradition reported in *Shemos Rabah 1:28,* that this Egyptian had actually raped the Jew's wife and was subsequently beating him with intentions to kill. In that case, there is even more reason to argue that the Egyptian was deserving of death by the hand of an earthly court. And an in-depth analysis of that entire episode will feature in a future essay.

[328] See the following commentaries to *Sanhedrin 58b*: *Tosfos; Leket Chidushei HaRid,* printed in the collection, *Sanhedri Gedola,* by Rabbi Yaakov Lifschitz; *Kuntres Harayos L'Riaz; Chidushei Rabeinu Yonah; HaAgudah; Chidushei HaRan; Maharsha.* See also *Yad Ramah.*

See also *Tosfos* to *Yevamos 34b;* Rabeinu Asher to *Yevamos 34b,* preserved in *Hagahos HaBach* to *Rosh* and in *Yam Shel Shlomoh* to *Yevamos 34b; Tosfos HaRosh* to *Yevamos 34b* and *Nedarim 20ab;* and other medieval commentaries to those two Talmudic passages.

And while the author of *Sanhedri Ketanah, Sanhedrin 58b,* creatively defends the Talmud's use of the terms "not liable" and "liable" instead of "permitted" and forbidden," he still states clearly that he understood the Talmud's intention to be the equivalent of "permitted" and "forbidden." See there at length.

The only two (relatively late) commentaries I have come across who argue otherwise are Rabbi Elazar Azikri in his *Sefer Charedim, Chapter 64*, and Rabbi Yaakov Meshulam Orenstein in his *Yeshuos Yaakov* commentary to *Shulchan Aruch, Orach Chaim 240:5:4* (the latter of whom mentions and endorses the former, but only in one respect). But Rabbi Azikri reinterprets the Talmudic discussion in an attempt to prove his *preconceived notion* that anal sex of any kind is forbidden (see below, page 87 and endnotes 333, 616). And Rabbi Orenstein does not attempt to read the passage as forbidding anal *penetration*, but only *intra-anal ejaculation* – and only according to the textual version that reads "not liable" and "liable."

Note also that Rabbi Orenstein references another place in his writings ("novellae-responsa") where he says he discusses this passage from *Sanhedrin 58* at length, though I have personally not as of yet found it. He certainly wasn't referring to his commentary on *Shulchan Aruch, Even Haezer 25:2:2*, where he does bring the combined teachings of *Sanhedrin 58b, Nedarim 20b* and *Yevamos 34b* – as understood and reconciled by Rabeinu Yitzchak in *Tosfos* to *Yevamos 34b* and by *Tosfos* to *Sanhedrin 58b* – as sources to legally permit intra-anal ejaculation performed solely for sexual fulfillment between husband and wife (even though he ends off, there, advising *spiritually* that "in our generations one should be strict in all these matters and the likes of them").

See also Rabbi Yaakov Emden's *Hagahos Yaavetz* to *Sanhedrin 58b*, where he chooses to side with the first approach of Rabeinu Yitzchak and permit only anal penetration without intra-anal ejaculation, even while he quotes the wording of *Sanhedrin 58b* to read that anal sex for a Jewish couple is "permissible" [See *Shas Wagshal-Nehardea, Tractate Sanhedrin, Hagahos v'Chidushim, Sanhedrin 58b* and *59b*].

[329] Though Rabbi Elazar Azikri, in his *Sefer Charedim, Chapter 64*, does attempt to dispute this, as will be discussed in the next point.

[330] The only commentary I have found to even note Raavad III's silence on *Mishneh Torah, Isurei Biah 21:9* is *Yad Aharon, Even Haezer vol. 2, 25:1* (at the end).

Note that Raavad III is also silent, there, about Maimonides' permission for cunnilingus, suggesting that he ultimately conceded to Maimonides in regard to that as well – at least according to the letter of the law.

[**Added note to the third edition:** See also *Yabia Omer vol. 7, Even Haezer 8:4*, where Rabbi Ovadia Yosef (1920-2013) cites numerous rabbinic authorities who suggest that whenever Raavad III is silent on a ruling of Maimonides in *Mishneh Torah*, the implication is that Raavad III agreed with Maimonides on the matter. Credit goes to Rabbi Yossi Newfield for bringing this responsum of Rabbi Ovadiah Yosef to my attention.]

[331] Raavad III's silence on *Mishneh Torah, Sefer Kedushah, Isurei Biah 21:9* could perhaps also be on account of the Talmud's ruling on *Kidushin 9b* that anal intercourse is a valid form of consummating marriage. And see *Mishneh Torah, Sefer Nashim, Ishus 3:5*.

And see above, endnote 324.

[332] Rabbi Spira does not explain what he found problematic with Rabbi Azikri's interpretation, but we will identify some possible difficulties with it below, endnote 616.

[333] See also below, endnote 616, for why understanding the difficulties in Rabbi Azikri's interpretation is so important.

[334] See above, pp. 59-61.

[335] A few important points to clarify in regard to the episode of Er, Onan and Tamar:

# ENDNOTES

1. The concept of the levirate marriage is that a Jewish man may not marry his brother's widow unless the brother died childless – in which case it is considered worthy for a surviving brother to marry the widow and bear a child who will carry on the deceased brother's name.

2. The "sin" that Onan is generally said to have been accused of, here, is that of "wasting seed in vain" – a complex and highly misunderstood concept that shall be explored in depth in volume two of this series. And see above, footnote to page 3.

3. It is generally taught based on this biblical passage that masturbation is a grave sin, even though it is not explicitly prohibited anywhere in the Bible. However, it is clear from the context of these verses that Onan did not masturbate, but rather in the course of normal sexual intercourse with his wife he would consistently take measures to avoid pregnancy, seeing to it that his seed never did go into the place of conception. And so the Talmud on *Yevamos 34b* discusses what was Onan's (and Er's) precise crude form of birth control: would he perform vaginal intercourse culminating in coitus interuptus or would he perform anal intercourse culminating in intra-anal ejaculation?

   *Yevamos 34b* says he performed anal sex. *Breishis Rabah 85:5* says he performed coitus interruptus.

   Thus, all the early and later texts (including *Talmud, Nidah 13ab* and the *Book of Zohar*) that point to the episode of Er and Onan as "proof" of the "severity" of masturbation require serious reevalution.

   [See *Atzei Arazim, Even Haezer 23:1*, quoted also in *Otzar Haposkim, Even Haezer 23*, page 180 (90b), that the implication from the story of Er and Onan that "wasting seed in vain" is a most severe sin is only in regard to coitus interruptus for the sake of intentional unsanctioned birth control, not self-masturbation for the sake of pleasure. Note, however, that the author of *Atzei Arazim*, there, is actually attempting to relegate the *Zohar's* harsh condemnations of "wasting seed in vain" to a context of coitus interruptus – even though the *Zohar* itself does clearly include masturbation in its harsh condemnations (see below, p. 143). Still, the author of *Atzei Arazim* is objectively correct in relegating the "wasting seed in vain" of Er and Onan to the context of intentional unsanctioned birth control.]

   See also the brilliant point made by Rabbi Dr. David Feldman in his 1968 work, *Marital Relations, Birth Control and Abortion in Jewish Law* (later renamed *Birth Control in Jewish Law*), pp. 151-152, that the entire justification for a man to marry his brother's childless widow – which is otherwise an incestuous relationship punishable by spiritual excision at the hand of Heaven – is in order to bear her a child. Therefore, Onan's utter refusal to get Tamar pregnant caused his relationship with her to revert back to one of an essentially incestuous nature, in this case punishable by death at the hand of Heaven.

   [Only because of the reality that some Ultra-Orthodox readers will deem it important, I will note that while Rabbi Feldman was Orthodox-ordained, he later associated with the Union for Traditional Judaism, formerly a branch of the Conservative Movement. Still, I believe it is possible to quote what I believe to be a worthy point from a scholarly study without endorsing the entire study itself or its author's entire world outlook. I am personally of the belief that one should accept the truth from whoever speaks it – be they Orthodox or non-Orthodox,

Jew or gentile, believer or heathen. And see the end of Maimonides' preface to his *Introduction to Ethics of the Fathers, Shmoneh Perakim*. And there is certainly much more to be said on the subject, but here is not the place for it.]

[Along this line of reasoning, note that even after Onan had married Tamar and was engaging in sexual relations with her, verse 9 continues to stress that she was "his brother's wife."]

Rabbi Avraham Dovid Wahrman of Buczacz, in his *Birchas David* commentary to Genesis, *Parshas Vayeshev*, Lemberg edition, p. 128b, does not say this exactly, but says something similar: that Er and Onan, by refusing to allow Tamar to become pregnant, caused their marriage to her to become retroactively annulled. Therefore, we can deduce, in the case of Onan, the annulment of his levirate marriage would have caused his relationship with Tamar to revert back to one of an incestuous nature.

[But see *Encyclopedia Talmudis*, vol. 21, Entry Yibum, footnotes 9-10.]

And in the case of both brothers – even Er, whose marriage was not levirate – it could be argued that the severity of their sin was not (only) on account of constant, intentional unsanctioned birth control, but on account of abusing their wife, using her purely for sexual gratification and depriving her of the ability to become a mother. And see *Talmud, Kesubos 72a*, the opinion of Shmuel as reported by Rabbi Yehudah, that if a man insists his wife perpetually expel his seed after intercourse in order to avoid ever becoming pregnant it is grounds for her to demand a divorce.

And more research into the matter is required.

See also *Tosfos Hashalem al HaTorah, Vayeshev*, p. 65, that in the case of Onan, the real reason he did not want to give his brother a child was because he wanted a piece of the property left by his brother's demise, which he would have lost if he gave his brother an "heir." This approach, too, supports the notion that there was much more to the "sin" of Onan than "wasting seed."

4. According to rabbinic tradition, Er and Onan were under the age of thirteen when they died – that is, below the age of liability either in the human or Heavenly court. Therefore, Rabbi Moshe Feinstein argues in one responsum that whatever lesson there is to learn from their deaths, it is NOT that "wasting seed in vain" is an act that Jewish law finds worthy of death by the hand of Heaven *across the board*. Rather, Rabbi Feinstein says, all we can learn from their story is that *sometimes* G-d *might* take a person's life for it *for reasons known only to Him*. See *Igros Moshe, Orach Chaim 4, Responsum 116*, pp. 207-208.

Rabbi Feinstein also asserts, there, that this *must* have been the meaning of Rabbi Yochanan bar Napacha's statement on *Nidah 13a* that "wasting seed in vain" is "deserving of death" by the hand of Heaven. And he maintains that this was also the understanding of Maimonides, Rabbi Yaakov ben Asher and Rabbi Yosef Caro in their respective codes of Jewish law. And see below, pp. 139-140.

Perhaps, then, in the case of Er and Onan, G-d in His wisdom had some reason for a line of progeny to issue specifically from the union of Tamar and the House of Judah, and when He observed Er frustrating that plan, He resorted to tragic drastic measures to free her from her marital bond to Er so that she would be free to marry Onan. But when that too failed, he again freed Tamar and realized His plan through Judah's own union with her.

And see Rabbi Avraham Dovid Wahrman of Buczacz, in his *Birchas David* commentary to Genesis, *Parshas Vayeshev*, Lemberg edition, p. 128b, who implies that G-d may have perceived in the hearts of Er and Onan that they intended to *never* get Tamar pregnant. A similar notion was put forth by Rabbi Yeshaya of Trani I, that G-d foresaw that Er and Onen would "continue to sin" – i.e., continue to avoid pregnancy – into adulthood (*Tosfos Hashalem al HaTorah, Vayeshev*, pp. 63-64). Rabbi Yosef Bechor Shor, as well, in his Bible commentary (quoted also in *Tosfos Hashalem al HaTorah, Vayeshev*, pp. 63, 65), comes close to this idea, saying that perhaps Er never wanted to deal with the challenges of childrearing (*tzaar gidul banim*); and Onan, too, knowing that the child of his union with Tamar would not be considered his in the eyes of the community, did not want to deal with raising such a child.

[Parenthetically, it is reported in *Talmud, Brachos 10a* that G-d caused the righteous king Hezekiah to fall deathly ill because he refused to procreate. When the prophet Isaiah explained the cause of his illness to him, Hezekiah responded that he did not want to bring a child into the world because he knew through prophecy that his progeny would be wicked.

Isaiah famously responded, "Why do you meddle with the hidden design of the Holy One, Blessed be He? That which you have been commanded is for you to do, and that which the Holy One, Blessed be He, deems appropriate is for Him to do."

Hezekiah thus agreed to have a child. And indeed, his son, Manasseh, grew to be wicked (see Kings II 21:1-18) – though according to rabbinic tradition he repented before he died (see sources referenced in Yishai Chasidah's *Ishei Hatanach-Encyclopedia of Biblical Personalities*, Entry: Manasseh son of Hezekiah, English edition by Shaar Press, 1994).

Behold: According to a reported family tree, the great Rabbi Yehudah Loew, the "Maharal" of Prague, descended from King David specifically through the line of Manasseh. If this family tree is in fact authentic, it would mean that Manasseh was also the progenitor of many other great Jewish leaders who themselves descended from Loew, including the rebbes of Chabad. See the family tree printed in *Daas Doros*, Feldheim 2005, pp. 105-106.]

See also Rabeinu Avigdor Tzarfati (13th century), *Peirushim uPsakim al HaTorah, Parshas Vayeshev*, Psak 30, that although Er and Onan were only eight or nine years old at the time, when it comes to punishment "by the hand of heaven" perhaps G-d overlooks biological age if a child's intellectual/emotional maturity is that of at least a twenty year old. See also *Tosfos Hashalem al HaTorah, Vayeshev*, p. 63-64, for additional medieval commentaries suggesting this principle. But if this is true, then it is all the more questionable if the entire episode of Er and Onan has any practical relevance to the average adolescent of today.

[336] The same Rabbi Eliezer quoted above on *Nedarim 20b*, and also on *Nidah 13a*.

[337] See *Igros Moshe, Even Haezer vol. 1, Responsum 63*, pp. 154-157, for an explanation of Rabbi Eliezer's opinion, here, versus that of the Sages.

See also below, p. 138-140.

[338] A 4th generation Babylonian Amora, who was also a colleague of Rava – the same Rava who expressly permitted anal sex, as reported on *Sanhedrin 58b*.

See *Encylopedia L'chachmei HaTalmud v'Hageonim*, Entry: *Nachman bar Yitzchak*.

[339] According to the commentary of Rabbi Shlomoh Yitzchaki's (Rashi's) son-in-law, Rabbi Yehudah ben Noson (Rivan, 11th-12th century), here, it may have been the custom back then to actually refer to such a child as the son of the deceased brother. For example, if Onan had sired a son named Levi, the community would have referred to him as "Levi son of Er," not "Levi son of Onan."

In that case, one must wonder what Onan's grave sin here was, for what normal person would want their child – their first born, no less – to be thought of as the child of another man?! And further research into the matter is required.

[340] A leading Tosafist and contemporary of Raavad III and Maimonides.

[341] See also *Shas Wagshal-Nehardea, Tractate Yevamos, Hagahos v'Chidushim, Yevamos 34b, "R'aMa"*, Rabbi Elazar Moshe Horowitz (1817-1890), Chief Rabbi of Pinsk.

**Added note to the third edition:** For another, post-medieval, approach to resolving *Yevamos 34b* with *Sanhedrin 58b* and *Nedarim 20ab*, see *Aruch Lenair, Yevamos 34b, "Tosfos: V'lo."* Credit goes to Rabbi Yossi Newfield for bringing this source in *Aruch Lenair* to my attention.

[342] See, for example, *Tosfos, Sanhedrin 59b:V'ha piryah v'rivyah*.

[See also *Mishnas Rabbi Eliezer (ben Rebbi Yossi Haglili)*, end of *Parshah 18*.]

[343] The question of whether this same logic should permit self-masturbation for a married man – and even more so, for an adolescent, an unmarried man, or even a homosexual – is an entirely separate topic with other halachic factors to consider. To be addressed in volume two of this series. And see above, footnote to page 3.

[344] Rabeinu Yitzchak's revolutionary approach, here, can arguably resolve another contradictory Talmudic-era teaching on the subject:

We discussed, above, the Talmudic discourse in *Babylonian Talmud, Sanhedrin 58b*:

> Rabbi Elazar said in the name of Rabbi Chanina:
>
>> If a non-Jewish man has anal sex with his own wife, he is liable – for G-d states [in regard to man]: "And he shall cling [to his wife]," which implies that he should not engage in anal sex with her [for it does not create a bond of "clinging."]
>
> Rava responded:
>
>> Is there ever a case where a Jew is not liable and a non-Jew is? [Meaning to say, if a Jewish man is permitted to have anal sex with his own wife, why can't a non-Jewish man?]
>
> Rather, Rava explained [the verse in Genesis as teaching a different law]:
>
>> If a non-Jewish man has anal sex with another [non-Jewish] man's wife, he is exempt from liability. Why? Because the prohibition against [non-Jewish] adultery learned from that verse in Genesis only applies where there is a bond of "clinging," which is not the case with anal sex.

[See above, footnote to page 84, that it is not clear at all that the Talmud meant to actually "permit" adulterous anal sex to non-Jews.]

But there is another version of this teaching of Rabbi Chanina, taught in not one, but two, other Talmudic-era sources, and in the name of not one, not two, but three, sages – Rabbi Elazar himself included.

*Jerusalem Talmud, Kidushin 1:1* and *Breishis Rabah 18:5* report:

> Rabbi Shmuel, Rabbi Abahu and Rabbi Elazar taught in the name of Rabbi Chanina:
>
> A non-Jew who has anal sex with his wife is liable for death.
>
> How was this teaching derived?
>
> [It was derived from the verse in Genesis:] "And he shall cling to his wife and become one flesh" – [as if to say, he should cling to her only] in the place that enables them to become one flesh [that is, in the vagina, where conception of a child is enabled].

According to the *Jerusalem Talmud* and *Breishis Rabah*, then, Rabbi Chanina's teaching, derived from the verse in Genesis, was in fact left as an open prohibition against anal sex for non-Jews, even within marriage.

But if we wanted to attempt to reconcile the two versions – that of *Babylonian Talmud, Sanhedrin 58b* with that of *Jerusalem Talmud, Kidushin 1:1* and *Breishis Rabah 18:5* – Rabeinu Yitzchak's approach to reconciling *Yevamos 34b* with *Nedarim 20b* and *Sanhedrin 58b* offers a solution, for his explanation that *Yevamos 34b* was speaking only against constant intra-anal ejaculation that is intended as unsanctioned birth control could be applied to *Jerusalem Talmud Kidushin 1:1* and *Breishis Rabah 18:5*, and Rava on *Sanhedrin 58b* could be said only to be permitting occasional intra-anal ejaculation for the sake of the husband's pleasure.

This would in fact fit quite neatly into the wording of *Sanhedrin 58b* compared to *Jerusalem Talmud, Kidushin 1:1* and *Breishis Rabah 18:5*:

*Sanhedrin 58b*, which ultimately permits anal sex, focuses in the verse on the phrase "*v'Davek b'Ishto* – *And he shall cling to his wife*," which is about the sense of clinging and bonding the couple fosters through the pleasure of penetration and climax – even if no conception occurs (for not every couple merits to have children, though they, too, certainly experience "clinging" through sexual intercourse; similarly, not every act of intercourse results in conception, yet every act of intercourse is intended by G-d to increase the bond, the "clinging," of every husband and wife).

[See Rashi, *Sanhedrin 58b:Shelo Cedarcah*, who makes clear that an integral part of '*dveikus*-clinging" is the pleasure of sex – which is why anal intercourse is questionable in this regard, for it is unclear how much pleasure the woman actually enjoys from it.

Nevertheless, Rava himself, there, takes it as a given that anal sex is permitted, implying also that he assumed a woman can – and does – experience pleasure and "clinging" from it when done lovingly and consensually. And see above, endnote 269.]

The *Jerusalem Talmud* and *Breishis Rabah*, however, which appear to forbid anal sex, both focus in the verse on the phrase "*v'hayu l'basar echad* – *And they shall become one flesh*," which is about the additional oneness forged between husband and wife through the conception of a child – which requires intra-vaginal ejaculation.

Thus, being that *Sanhedrin 58b* is concerned about sexual pleasure, "clinging," not conception of children, once the phrase "and he shall cling to his wife" is rejected as precluding anal sex for a married couple, Jewish or not, there is no other verse to prohibit it, and anal sex is therefore permitted – and even, occasionally, to the point of intra-anal ejaculation, when done for the sake of marital sexual pleasure. [See also *Sanhedri Gedolah* to *Sanhedrin 58b*].

The *Jerusalem Talmud* and *Breishis Rabah*, on the other hand, are concerned with the conception of children. Thus, they, too, arguably only meant to forbid intra-anal ejaculation which is performed *constantly* and *intentionally* for the sake of unsanctioned birth control, but not to forbid anal penetration in-and-of itself nor even *occasional* intra-anal ejaculation for the husband's (or couple's) sexual fulfillment – neither of which, in the greater scheme of things, frustrate the process of procreation, of "becoming one flesh."

So we see that the same approach Rabeinu Yitzchak offers to reconcile *Yevamos 34b* with *Sanhedrin 58b* and *Nedarim 20b* can be used to reconcile *Jerusalem Talmud, Kidushin 1:1* and *Breishis Rabah 18:5* with *Babylonian Talmud, Sanhedrin 58b*.

[See also *Torah Shleimah, Genesis 2:24, #298 and #300*, and footnotes thereon.]

[345] This, despite the notion brought in *Yad Malachi, Clalei Haposkim – Rashi, Clal 24*, that the first of two answers suggested by *Tosfos* is generally the main answer. In any case, *Yad Malachi*, there, brings dissenting opinions that *Tosfos'* second answer is always the main one.

[346] See *Biur HaGra, Shulchan Aruch, Even Haezer 25:2:18:Col hamekadesh*.

[347] There are a number of biblical verses – Leviticus 11:44, 19:2, 20:7, 20:26 – that share a similarly, yet vaguely, worded command to "be holy, because G-d is holy."

None of these four verses have overt sexual contexts. But because of their similar wording and the fact that they all share close proximity to other biblical discussions about sex, some Talmudic/medieval sources interpret them to be hinting to some form of "sexual sanctification."

But only one of the verses, Leviticus 11:44, is brought by the Talmudic literature to teach about sanctifying oneself during *marital* sex. The other three are understood to be hinting to abstinence from *illicit* sex.

Leviticus 11:44 is actually speaking about the kosher dietary laws, and specifically about abstaining from eating insects or other creepy-crawlers. But because it is situated in the Bible in close proximity to the laws of childbirth, and more specifically, the laws of birth of a male child, the Talmud on *Shavuos 18b* suggests that "sanctification" during marital intimacy can result in male offspring.

The other three verses, Leviticus 19:2, 20:7 and 20:26 are situated in close proximity to two major biblical discussions about incest, adultery, menstrual impurity, homosexuality and bestiality. Therefore, whatever sexual connotation and "sanctification" the rabbinical writings may read into them, they arguably have little, if anything, to do with *marital* lovemaking.

[Raavad III, in his *Baalei HaNefesh, Shaar Hakedusha* (page 170 in the Buchwald edition), does invoke Leviticus 20:7 along with 11:44 to argue that the double wording, "*Sanctify yourself and you will be holy*," comes to instruct not only abstinence from illicit sexual *action*, but also abstinence from illicit sexual *thought* – which he applies even to marital intimacy of husband and wife.

Raavad III also quotes the verse in Ezekiel 14:5 that suggests sinful thought is equivalent to sinful action, in an attempt to lend support to his thesis. (The 1992 Buchwald edition of *Baalei HaNefesh*, p. 170, inadvertently references Ezra 14:5.)

He then goes on to say that such exalted sanctity of both action and thought can only be attained if a person deliberately forbids for himself that which is sexually *permitted* even with his own wife (Raavad III, there, addresses the husband in the marriage, but his words could perhaps be understood as addressing the wife as well).

Now, why Raavad III chose to invoke these two verses specifically, out of the four, remains to be explored. What is important to note, however, is that the simple context of the verse in Leviticus 20:7 is referring to abstinence from idol worship. And the verse in Ezekiel 14:5, which compares sinful thought to sinful action, is referring to thoughts of idol worship, as well.

Rabbi Avraham Hayarchi, a one-time disciple of Raavad III, in his *Commentary to Callah Rabti* (page 41, Toledano edition), already calls Raavad III to task for invoking the verse in Ezekiel 14:5, being that sexual thought and idolatrous thought certainly cannot be compared. He therefore offers an alternate explanation that illicit sexual thought may require atonement even though it is not considered an action. See there.

Note, however, that in *Sefer Hamanhig, Hilchos Prishus uKedushah*, Rabbi Avraham Hayarchi does seem to extend the verse in Leviticus 20:7 to warn even against unfavorable sexual encounters with one's own wife, namely, the nine-ten flawed conditions discussed on *Nedarim 20b* (see above, pp. 37-38). But, notably, he does not extend the verse to speak against the four behaviors cautioned against by Rabbi Yochanan ben Dahavai on *Nedarim 20a* – "overturning the table," non-sex-related talk during sex, and gazing at or kissing the female genitals – presumably because the Sages ultimately permitted them.]

In any case, a complete analysis of these four verses and their various rabbinical interpretations is beyond the scope of this work and will be covered in a future volume of this series.

[348] The latter concept, that of "sanctifying oneself in that which is permitted," would seem to be a category that includes only pious stringencies a person accepts upon him or herself voluntarily, beyond the letter of the law.

However, according to one view in the Talmud – namely, Rava, as quoted in *Babylonian Talmud, Yevamos 20a* – this category can also include official rabbinic prohibitions designed to impose certain standards of piety upon the masses.

[Parenthetically, this is the same Rava who legally permits anal sex on *Sanhedrin 58b*, and whom most medieval commentaries understand as permitting even occasional intra-anal ejaculation for the sake of a husband's (or couple's) sexual fulfillment. See above, pp. 84-87.

And it is the same Rava who is quoted in *Callah Rabti 1:13-14* limiting the medical cautions of Rabbi Yochanan ben Dahavai against the four sexual behaviors only to when they are performed during the same sexual encounter in which conception occurs, never else. See above, pp. 45-46.]

But only that which the Talmud or medieval commentaries clearly designate as rabbinic "law" can be assumed to be "obligatory" in their eyes. In the realm of "sanctified sex," however, fairly little is clearly designated as "forbidden" and it is therefore debatable how much is "legally" binding (as we shall see in the present section of our study).

See also Rabbi Yitzchak Lampronti's *Pachad Yitzchak, Entry: Kadesh Atzmecha Bemutar Lach*, that this principle is not meant to categorically forbid that which G-d Himself permits, it is only meant to *discourage over-indulgence*.

[And even in regard to those pious strictures that the rabbis instituted as official universal rabbinic ban, if it happens that in later generations certain bans begin to turn people away from Judaism, the Sanhedrin is perhaps expected by G-d to lift them at least temporarily – for the ultimate goal of it all is not the wielding or defense of rabbinic authority, but the organized facilitation of the creation's closeness to its Creator. And in some cases, where it turns out even many years later that the majority of the people were never actually able to practically implement the ban, then the ban can – and presumably should – be revoked even by a Sanhedrin that is lesser in "size and/or wisdom" than the original one that instituted it (see *Mishneh Torah, Sefer Shoftim, Memrim 2:4, 2:6, 2:7, 2:9* – to be explored further in volume two of this series).]

[349] See, however, *Yevamos 20b* about this verse.

[350] *Peirush Rashi* to *Shavuos 18b*.

See also *Peirush Rashi* to *Nidah 71a: Vikadesh atzmo*.

[351] See also *Mordechai, Shavuos, 731-732*, who defines "sanctifying oneself during sex" as "modesty." But he immediately follows this by proving that anal sex and her-on-top are permitted by the letter of the law, for the Sages on *Nedarim 20b* rule that a husband may do anything he craves sexually with his wife.

See also *Tosfos* to *Nidah 17a*, which describes the strictures of Rabbi Yochanan ben Dahavai on *Nedarim 20a* as matters of "modesty." In that case, *Tosfos* would also seem to understand the Sages, Rebbi, Rav and Rabbi Yochanan bar Napacha on *Nedarim 20b* as rejecting the issue of "modesty" as a *legal* concern in regard to non-sex-related talk during sex, "overturning the table" and gazing at or kissing the female genitals.

See also Maimonides in his *Commentary to the Mishnah, Sanhedrin 7:4*, where he permits, upon the Sage's authority, all four sexual behaviors cautioned against by Rabbi Yochanan ben Dahavai on *Nedarim 20a*, even though he says that "*modest* pious ones distance themselves from all these animalistic behaviors, they denigrate these behaviors, and they denigrate those who *fixate* all their thoughts and yearnings upon them" – a possible reference to what is now recognized as "sexual addiction."

[Maimonides makes a similar statement in *Mishneh Torah, Sefer Kedushah, Isurei Biah 21:9*, though he does not use the word "modesty" there.]

[352] See the Steinsaltz Edition of the Talmud, *Shavuos 18b, Iyunim*, in the name of "*Rid*."

**Added note to the third edition:** See also Rabbi Eliezer Melamed's *Simchat Habayit v'Birchato* (second edition, 2015), p. 49, footnote 13, quoting a similar interpretation in the name of Rabeinu Bachya (1255-1340).

[353] See also *Teshuvos Hageonim*, quoted in *Kovetz Shitos Kamai, Shavuos 18b*, page 112, which brings three of Rabbi Alfasi's examples.

See also Rabbi Avraham Hayarchi, *Sefer Hamanhig, Din Yoledes*, who quotes Rabbi Alfasi's five examples (also quoted in *Kovetz Shitos Kamai, Shavuos 18b*, bottom of page 91, top of page 92).

[354] Note that there are numerous interpretations of what Rabbi Eliezer's behaviors actually were (see above, pp. 23-24), and Rabbi Alfasi does not tell us how he himself understood them.

# ENDNOTES

[355] The purpose of giving one's wife her climax first is discussed in the Talmud purely as a means of bearing male offspring. However, the Talmud offers mixed messages as to whether the expectation of male offspring as a result of the wife climaxing first is a matter of reproductive "science" or Heavenly reward.

*Babylonian Talmud, Tractate Nidah 71a* states clearly that this is a matter of reward, presumably for the husband having put his wife's sexual needs ahead of his own. See also *Shavuos 18b*, implying the same.

But the *Babylonian Talmud* in *Brachos 60a*, *Nidah 25b* and *Nidah 28a* treats it as a matter of definitive reproductive science, that if the wife climaxes first the child is sure to be male, and if the husband climaxes first the child is sure to be female.

*Nidah 31ab* discusses the matter vaguely, and could be interpreted either way.

The anonymous author of the medieval *Igeres Hakodesh*, in Chapter 3, explains this teaching kabbalistically, based upon the "scientific" approach (end of page 200 in the Buchwald edition of *Baalei HaNefesh*).

For an interesting perspective on the "scientific" approach, see Yehudah Levi, *The Science in Torah*, Feldheim 2004, pp. 13-16.

[Parenthetically, let us note how the Talmud derives that a wife climaxing first results in male offspring:

Leviticus 12:2 states: "When a woman conceives (*lit.* gives seed – *ki tazria*) and gives birth to a male child..."

Employing a hyper-literal reading of this verse, the Talmud in *Brachos 60a* derives that if the mother "gives seed" first – that is, if she climaxes before her husband – then the child conceived will be male. But if the husband climaxes first, the child conceived will be female.

According to the Talmud, then, the verse could – should – really be read: "If a woman had a climax first and she therefore gave birth to a male child..."

In any case, the simple context of the verse is obviously addressing not climax, but *conception* – and of both male and female offspring: "When a woman *conceives* and gives birth to a male...(Leviticus 12:2) And if she gives birth to a female...(Leviticus 12:5)."]

**Added note to the third edition:** See also Rabbi Maor Kayam's *Harchavot l'Simchat Habayit v'Birchato* (2015), pp. 49-55.

[356] Rabbi Yehudah Leib Nachmanson, in his *Sheyekadesh Atzmo* (2015), page 380, says 9-12 minutes.

[357] See also *Rabeinu Yehonasan Milunil, Hilchos Nidah* (quoted in *Kovetz Shitos Kamai, Nedarim 20b*, page 179), who offers "modesty" and "not fantasizing of other women" as *alternate* interpretations of 'sanctifying oneself during marital sex."

However, *Peirush Rabeinu Yitzchak Karkosha, Shavuos* (quoted in *Kovetz Shitos Kamai, Nedarim 20b*, page 182), implies that both these definitions of "sanctifying oneself during marital sex" complement each other.

[358] See *Baalei HaNefesh, Shaar Hakedushah* (p. 176 in the Buchwald edition) that Raavad III took it as a given that Rabbi Eliezer was more concerned about his purity of thought than about giving his wife her climax first (which very well may have meant risking not giving her a climax at all). Nevertheless, Raavad III believed that G-d would have still rewarded Rabbi Eliezer with male offspring on account of what Rabbi Eliezer believed to be good intentions.

358* The most direct statement I have seen attesting to the non-legal nature of Rabbi Eliezer's personal behavior is that of Rabbi Yaakov Emden in his marginal notes to *Talmud, Brachos 62a*, commenting on Rav's sexual play with his own wife, as reported on *Hagigah 5b*:

> We see from here [i.e. Rav's sexual play] that Rabbi Eliezer's custom to reveal only one hands-breadth [of his wife's body] at a time, etc., and to perform intercourse as if he were being pressured by a demon, was an added measure [of piety] (*milsa yeseirta avid*), and it is not what is normal for most people – not even for great people like Rav (*v'einah midas col adam, afilu hagadol c'Rav*).

See *Shas Wagshal-Nehardea, Tractate Brachos, Hagahos v'Chidushim, Brachos 62a, Yaavetz*. Credit goes to Rabbi Simcha Feuerman for bringing this source to my attention on page 50 of his *Kuntres Es Lifrosh v'Es Le'ehov* (2016).

359 Note that the content of the discussion of Rabbi Yochanan and Rabbi Shimon ben Lakish on *Nidah 16b* is actually about daytime *conception*, not daytime *sex*.

359* See below, endnote 365.

360 See *Talmud, Chulin 91a*, and the medieval commentaries thereon (many of them quoted in *Kovetz Shitos Kamai*) that in the context of another restriction, the justification for which we are also told is that "the Jews are holy" (*yisrael kedoshim*), the implication is that it was never originally "forbidden" – not biblically (that is, not by G-d) nor even rabbinically – but at some point in time the Jewish people collectively found it innapropriate.

And see Rabbi Yehuda Henkin's *Bnei Banim vol. 4, Responsum 17*, end of *Section 2*, page 61.

[But see *Tosfos, Shabbos 86a:Yisrael Kedoshim Heim*. And contrast *Tosfos* to *Rashi: D'kaamar Rav Huna* and *Talmid Chacham*. See also the (curious) wording of Maimonides' *Mishneh Torah, Isurei Biah 21:10*: "It is <u>forbidden</u> (*asur*) for an Israelite (*yisraeli*) to have sex during the day, for it is impudent (*she'azus panim hee loe*)." Contrast this to Maimonides' *Introduction to Ethics of the Fathers, Shmoneh Perakim, Chapter Four* (Hebrew translation by Rabbi Yosef Kapach): "Our elders created boundaries in order to minimize sexual behavior, and they <u>warned</u> (*hizhiru*) against sex during the day, as we explained in [*Commentary to the Mishnah,*] *Sanhedrin* [*7:4*]." And in his *Commentary to the Mishnah, Sanhedrin 7:4*, Maimonides writes only that the sages: "<u>abhorred</u> sex during the day" (*umetaavim es hatashmish bayom* - Hebrew translation by Rabbi Yosef Kapach).]

361 *Shabbos 86a*. But see *Tosfos*, there, *Yisrael Kedoshim Heim*.

362 Consider also *Meiri, Beis Habechirah, Shavuos 18b*:

> It is appropriate (*raoi*) for a person to sanctify himself during sex and to behave with extra modesty, both in terms of the time for sex – only to engage in sex at times *when everyone is asleep, [that is,] not during the daytime at all and not at the beginning or end of night* – and in terms of the quality and form of the behaviors (*b'eichus ha'inyanim utechunasam*).

[**Added note to the third edition:** See also the statement of Rabbi Yosef Messas in his *Mayim Chaim, Responsum 97*, supporting the notion that the original warnings of the Sages against sex in a lit room were made at a time when it was customary for multiple families to live under the same roof, and out of a concern that there was a high risk of being caught in the act.]

In any case, this posited approach would perhaps explain why this sense of "holiness" described by the *Talmud* is said only in regard to precluding sex by day, it is not said in regard to precluding sex by night to candlelight.

But this would not appear to be how the sage, Rava, understood this teaching of Rav Huna, for in all three places in the *Talmud* where Rav Huna's teaching is quoted it is immediately followed by Rava's qualification that sex by day is permitted in a darkened room or under the covers. If the concern about sex during the day were in fact about the increased possibility of being caught in the act, it should presumably have made no difference to Rava if the room were darkened or if husband and wife were covered by a blanket.

But even this is not necessarily so clear cut, for perhaps Rava did understand the concern about holiness as being about getting caught – and nevertheless he permitted marital sex during the day in a darkened room or under the covers because when all is said and done there always remains the possibility of a couple being seen or heard even at night, when sex is certainly permitted to them, and therefore sex during the day in a darkened room or under the covers (that is, in a somewhat equivalent setting to the darkness of night) should have at least been no worse.

A more extreme reinterpretation might be that Rava himself never originally came to qualify the concern of Rav Huna about holiness, but only to qualify the concern of his colleague, Abayei, about hygiene (see below, endnote 365). Perhaps it was only the later compilers-editors of the Talmud who applied Rava's statement to Rav Huna's concern as well.

Similarly, even though the compilers-editors of *Nidah 17a* go on to equate sex by day in the daylight with sex by night to candlelight, it is not clear that they did so on account of Rav Huna's concern about holiness, they may have done so only on account of Abayei's concern about hygiene.

And much more research into the matter is required.

[363] *Rabeinu Yehonasan Milunil, Hilchos Nidah*, quoted in *Kovetz Shitos Kamai, Nedarim 20b*, page 180.

But then would such husbands refrain from ever gazing upon their wives' faces at all, even in regular daily daytime life?

Did this mean to say that such husbands only did not wish to see their wives' facial expressions during the throes of sexual ecstasy?

[364] *Peirush Rabeinu Yitzchak Karkosha, Shavuos*, quoted in *Kovetz Shitos Kamai, Nedarim 20b*, page 182.

[365] Considering the poor state of nutrition and/or medicine in ancient times, as well as the poor conditions of hygiene and the crude cosmetics available, this last issue need not necessarily be of any concern to one living in a modern western society.

And see Rabbi Yitzchak Abadi, *Or Yitzchak, vol. 2, Orach Chaim, Responsum 95, Part 1*, p. 62, reporting in the name of Rabbi Moshe Feinstein that the sole concern here is about hygiene (*hacavanah al min lichluch ucayotzei bazeh shenimtza alehah shelo b'cavanah b'oeso zman*). See also Rabbi Yosef Messas, *Mayim Chaim, Responsum 97*, implying the same.

Note also that if we understand the concern of Abayei on *Nidah 17a* as being about hygiene, any such problem that might arise would be *temporary*, for matters of hygiene, especially today, are easily remedied and need not be recurring.

If, however, one were to read Abayei's concern as being about a husband's reaction to his wife's permanent bodily features, then his explanation of Rav Chisda's concern about a husband's ability to "love his wife like himself" might be understood as having been about a husband's *lifelong* attraction to his wife. But this manner of reading Abayei would also arguably be unrealistic – for it is unreasonable to believe that a husband will never notice his wife's nakedness and bodily imperfections throughout their entire marriage, even during non-sexual moments.

[As for why the concern is not mentioned that a wife might find her husband's hygiene (or bodily imperfections) unappealing, perhaps it is because such lack of attraction (on occasion) would not necessarily be detected by the husband, whereas the husband's lack of attraction, resulting in the diminishment of his active passion and/or his loss of erection, would be obvious to the wife.]

And more research into the matter is required.

[366] *Rabeinu Yehonasan Milunil, Hilchos Nidah*, quoted in *Kovetz Shitos Kamai, Nedarim 20b*, page 180.

*Peirush Rabeinu Yitzchak Karkosha, Shavuos*, quoted in *Kovetz Shitos Kamai, Nedarim 20b*, page 182.

[367] Which allegedly could, in turn, spiritually harm the child conceived from that sexual encounter. See *Nedarim 20b*, the nine-ten flawed conditions of mind or circumstance during sex (discussed above, pp. 37-38).

[368] *Rabeinu Yehonasan Milunil, Hilchos Nidah*, quoted in *Kovetz Shitos Kamai, Nedarim 20b*, page 180.

[369] Note that in regard to sex during the day, the terminology of the Talmud's teaching in *Nidah 17a* is that *sexual intercourse (tashmish)* uncovered in a lit room is problematic. But then perhaps manual or oral stimulation of one's spouse's genitals even naked and uncovered in a lit room during the day (so long as any subsequent intercourse is done in a darkened room; or, for a Torah scholar, so long as any subsequent intercourse is done with husband and wife appropriately covered) would be permitted – at least from husband to wife, and according to some we shall see below, even from wife to husband. And see below, *Appendices: Sex Above the Covers* and endnote 845 thereon.

But then the notion that the men wanted to avoid the sight of their wives' nakedness at all (as a concern about holiness, not hygiene) would seem to negate this.

See also Rashi to *Shavuos 86a*, who suggests that the men not wanting to have sex during the day on account of sensibilities of holiness was motivated by their sense of *modesty*, which made them feel it innapropriate to "gaze." Rashi does not specify what exactly they did not want to gaze at, and due to this lack of specificity it is possible he meant to say they felt it unbecoming to gaze at their wives' naked bodies in general. But legally speaking, even gazing at one's (pure) wife's genitals is permitted according to many, and perhaps even a majority, of medieval writers on account of the Sages' ruling on *Nedarim 20b* (see below, p. 113). This would then call into question whether this stringency not to have sex during the day was ever – or is now, after the Sages' ruling on *Nedarim 20b* – *legally binding* upon all couples. To that point, the fourth generation Amoraic sage, Rava, seems to have taken it as a given that sex during the day is forbidden unless it is done in a darkened room (see *Kesubos 65b* and *Nidah 17a*). But perhaps Rava himself did not think the reason behind this stipulation to be specifically about the avoidance of gazing at nakedness or the female genitals – which he knew to be permitted by the Sages (and see above, endnote 362).

# ENDNOTES

At the very least, note Rashi's implication that rabbinical discussions about a husband "gazing" at his wife's nakedness are about gazing in a lit up room, and specifically during sexual activity, presumably foreplay. Indeed, what "gazing" could there really be in the dark? This, then, perhaps supports yet further the argument that when the Sages on *Nedarim 20b* legally permitted a husband to gaze at his own wife's genitals during sexual intimacy, the permission included naked foreplay uncovered by a blanket in a lit up room.

In any case, according to the logic of Abayei's explanation of Rav Chisda, that the concern about sex during the day was that the husband might find something unhygienic on his wife's body (see above, endnote 365), become turned off sexually and cause her to become self-conscious, one could perhaps argue that this concern was only in regard to actual intercourse, where the husband's loss of erection would certainly be noticed by the wife and not only deny her her sexual fulfillment, but affect her self-image. In terms of a husband's oral or manual sexual stimulation of his wife, however, without intercourse, even if the husband would have found something unappealing on her body on that occasion, so long as he kept his temporary feelings to himself, his lack or loss of sexual arousal would not have been evident to her and would in no way have compromised her pleasure, climax or self image. And if afterwards she noticed and inquired why he wasn't erect, a husband could have always attributed it to tiredness, mundane distraction or some other excuse – even while insisting that he enjoyed pleasuring her. And the same is true for husbands and wives today.

Another distinction that could be made between actual intercourse and oral or manual sexual stimulation in the daylight is the issue of illicit fantasies: If the husband were to have gone on to attempt actual intercourse after being repulsed by something unhygienic, he may have been tempted to focus on illicit fantasies to divert his attention and/or maintain his erection. This, too, would not have been so much of a concern where the husband limited his performance to oral or manual stimulation of his wife. And so, too, today.

In fact, according to this last suggested approach, Rav Huna's concern about holiness could also be resolved, for if the concern about holiness, too, is that the husband might come to deliberately fantasize about other women *during intercourse* (especially if conception might occur and thereby ostensibly spiritually harm the child on account of it being one of the nine-ten flawed conditions), then, as explained, this concern need not be a worry if the husband limits his performance to oral or manual stimulation. Behold: this would perhaps explain why when explaining Rabbi Alfasi's example about sex during the day not being in line with the *holiness* of the Jewish people, commentaries explain that the concern about lack of *holiness* is that the husband might notice something unhygenic on the wife's body and perform *intercourse* without love and/or with deliberate illicit fantasy (see above, endnotes 366, 367, 368 – in the words of Rabeinu Yitzchak of Carcassonne (*Peirush Rabeinu Yitzchak Karkosha*): *shelo yiru b'nishoseihem davar megunah v'yisa'enah b'shaas tashmish*; and in the words of Rabeinu Yehonasan Milunil: *shelo yiru b'nishoseihem davar megunah v'yisa'enah b'shaas tashmish, v'lo yihiyeh libo alehah ele achar ishah acheres yafeh mimenah*).

And much more research into the matter is required.

And see in the body of our study, here, the footnote to page 96 for a relevant ruling of Rabbi Yosef Messas.

[**Added note to the third edition:** See also the final paragraph of Rabbi Baruch Halevi Epstein's *Torah Temimah, Vayikra 19:123*.]

[370] See *Shabbos 86a, Kesubos 65b, Nidah 17a*. For a brief summary of halachic opinions on the matter, see the Steinsaltz edition of the Talmud, *Tractate Nidah 16b, Orach Halachah*. And see below, endnotes 833, 845.

Note that although on *Nidah 17a* and *Shabbos 86a*, Rava permits covered sexual intercourse during the day in a lit room that cannot be darkened *only to a Torah scholar* (*talmid chochom*), Rabbi Eliyahu Spira, in his *Elyah Rabah* commentary to *Levush, Orach Chaim 240:11:17* points out that the way Rava's ruling is quoted on *Kesubos 65b* implies that it extends also to laymen and their wives.

**Added note to the third edition:** And see Rabbi Yisrael Meir Kagen's *Mishnah Berurah-Shaar Hatziyun 240:28*, noting that the wording of Rabbi Avraham Danizg in *Chochmas Adam* implies that this ruling of Rava applies equally to all couples in any circumstance where delaying marital sex could lead to illicit sexual outlets. Rabbi Kagen does not specify where in *Chochmas Adam* this is implied, but it appears he was referring to *Chochmas Adam, Shaar Beis HaNashim, Clal 128:9*, where Rabbi Danizg discusses the subject without any distinction between scholar and non-scholar. [Credit goes to the 2016 English translaton of *Darchei Taharah Hashalem*, Chapter 22, Passage 29, page 323, footnote 201, for bringing this source in *Shaar Hatziyun* to my attention. It is also referenced in the corresponding chapter and passage in the 2011 Hebrew edition, page 276, footnote 66.]

[371] Rabbi Yitzchak Abadi, *Or Yitzchak, vol. 2, Orach Chaim, Responsum 95, Part 1*, p. 62, reporting in the name of Rabbi Moshe Feinstein that even for intercourse in a lit room during the day, a Torah scholar need only cover the actual genitals and their immediate surrounding bodily areas (*tzarich rak lechasos makom ha'ervah v'hakarov l'zeh*).

[372] Note that Rabbi Yitzchak of Corbeil in his *Sefer Mitzvos Katan, Positive Commandment 285*, calls it a practice of piety (*midas chasidus*) not to engage in sexual behaviors that are believed to be a congenital risk to one's child, even though such behaviors are permissible by law (though he is speaking, there, in reference to the nine-ten flawed conditions and the four behaviors cautioned against by Rabbi Yochanan ben Dahavai, not to sex performed immediately after using the latrine).

[373] For evidence that the Sages' statements on science and health were (at least sometimes) based on the limited scientific perceptions of their times, see *Talmud, Tractate Yoma 83b-84a*, where two viewpoints are offered in regard to the cause of rabies in dogs: witchcraft (*cishuf*) or evil spirit possession (*ruach raah*).

See also Julius Pruss's *Biblical and Talmudic Medicine, Chapter III, Part II, Demons as a Cause of Illness* (page 139 in the 1993 Jason Aronson edition, translated by Dr. Fred Rosner) and Rabbi Yehudah Levi's *The Science in Torah: The Scientific Knowledge of the Talmudic Sages, Chapter 10, Evil Spirits and Demons*, pp. 128-130 (Feldheim 2004).

And see above, endnote 86, and below, *Appendices: A Word about Rabbinic Fallibility*.

[374] Albek edition.

[375] The compilers-editors of *Talmud, Nidah 17a* equate sex at night in the candlelight to sex during the day in the daylight (*hameshamesh mitaso l'or haner . . . meshamshin mitoseihem bayom . . .*). But some later commentaries suggest a halachic distinction between the two.

To be discussed in a future volume of this series.

And see endnotes 371, 845.

[376] See below, *Appendices: Sex Above the Covers*.

[377] *Commentary to Callah Rabti*, Toledano edition, page 40.

See also *Sefer Hamanhig, Hilchos Nidah Dinei Yoledes, siman 120*, where Rabbi Avraham Hayarchi quotes the five examples of "sanctified sex" given by Rabbi Alfasi.

See also *Sefer Hamanhig, Hilchos Prishus uKedushah*, where Rabbi Avraham Hayarchi mentions the nine-ten flawed conditions listed on *Nedarim 20b*, as well as the example of Rabbi Eliezer and his wife, Ima Shalom.

[378] *Commentary to Callah Rabti*, ibid.

[379] The work was first attributed to Nachmanides less than a century after his death, by Rabbi Yisrael Alnaqua in his *Menoras Hamaor*. To the best of my knowledge, its authorship was first questioned by Rabbi Chaim Dov Shevel in his scholarly compilation of Nachmanides' works, *Kisvei Ramban* (Mosad HaRav Kook, 1963), pp. 315-319.

Rabbi Shevel's arguments against accepting Nachmanides as its author are compelling. Rabbi Efraim Ariel Buchwald, who included *Igeres Hakodesh* in his edition of Raavad III's *Baalei HaNefesh*, raises additional evidence that could perhaps support Rabbi Shevel (see there, page 194).

Still, evidence points to a kabbalistic author or group of authors.

[380] See the author's opening remarks to the work, and his entire Chapter One.

[381] See the author's closing remarks to the work.

[382] *Igeres Hakodesh*, Chapter Four (pp. 202-203 in the Buchwald edition). See also *Igeres Hakodesh*, Chapter Three.

Rabbi Yisrael Alnaqua presents this teaching – with slight variation in wording – in his *Menoras Hamaor, vol. 4, Perek Nisuei Ishah, HaShaar Hagimmel*, pp. 100-101.

[383] *Igeres Hakodesh*, Chapter Five (pp. 203-204 in the Buchwald edition of *Baalei HaNefesh*).

Actually, based on the surrounding discussion in *Igeres Hakodesh*, there, the author may have even meant that thoughts about righteous men will not only affect the spiritual *quality* of the child conceived, it will also cause that child to *physically resemble* the righteous man or men the husband and wife are thinking about.

[Parenthetically, one must wonder whether it would be encouraged for a husband to also focus on thoughts of other righteous *women*. If not, then why would it be acceptable to encourage a wife to focus on thoughts of other righteous men? And the very notion that during sexual intercourse and climax a husband is ideally to focus on thoughts of men, and perhaps a wife is ideally to focus on thoughts of women, is questionable on many levels.]

[384] Both of these examples are arguably highly questionable from a scientific standpoint, as are other statements put forth as fact in this medieval *Igeres Hakodesh*. A full review of the work will be included in a future volume of this series.

This mystical *Igeres Hakodesh* is invoked by some in the Chasidic-Charedi community as proof of a down-to-earth kabbalistic approach to sex. They base this assertion on the opening section of Chapter Two of the work, where the author argues that sexual intercourse is not intrinsically "disgusting" in the eyes of the Creator, but rather G-d sees sex as "holy and clean when done according to that which is appropriate and in the time that is appropriate and with the intention that is appropriate."

Less talked about, however, is how the author of the work goes on to define "appropriate" and how he goes on to describe the physical and spiritual repercussions of that which he deems "innapropriate."

As stated, a full review and analysis of the work will feature in a future volume of this series. In the meantime, let us note:

In Chapter Five of the work (p. 204 in the Buchwald edition), the author asserts in the name of *Talmud, Kidushin 70a* that whoever marries a woman for her beauty will bear untoward children.

He then continues:

> And the great secret in this is that if a man marries a [Jewish] woman for her beauty, their union is not for the sake of heaven, because he fantasizes about the shape of her body, focusing on her bodily attributes rather than on pure elevated thoughts. And the child conceived from such fantasizing is considered a stranger [to G-d], and it is of him that the verse [in Hosea 5] speaks, "They bore strange children" – and G-d wants no part in him . . .

> . . . And I have come to alert you to a fundamental principle: know that this is why the biblical section of the "wayward rebellious son" (*ben sorer umoreh*) was juxtaposed to the section of the "beautiful captive woman" (*yefas toar*) – to make known that from a captive woman no righteous person will come out. [Rather, as implied by *Talmud, Sanhedrin 107a*,] due to the fact that the original intention [of the father in marrying her] was purely for her beauty and illicit sex (*she'ein hacavanah rak l'yofi v'zimah*), therefore, from [him and] her will issue rebellious, wayward children (*banim sorerim umordim*), worthy of the four capital punishments of the court . . .

> . . . And the same goes for what we have said [earlier] in this chapter in regard to the intention of sexual union [between husband and wife] and the quality of thought and fantasy.

Now, we've aleady noted above, in the second half of endnote 128, that when *Sanhedrin 107a* predicts that the children of a "beautiful captive woman" will turn out "rebellious," it is not necessarily attributing this to the *father's lust*, but to the *mother's natural child-rearing skills* (which would obviously draw upon what she experienced and observed growing up in a non-Jewish home and living in a non-Jewish culture).

But even if it were referring to the husband's lust, it cannot be ignored that the lust of a man who rapes a captive woman (even just one time – see *Mishneh Torah, Sefer Shoftim, Hilchos Melachim 8:2*) – a woman who just lost her tribe, and probably her husband and other family members, at war – followed by his forcibly converting and marrying her "all for the sake of lust," is in no way similar to an average normal husband who marries his wife in a loving manner with her heartfelt consent, and who, to his wife's delight, finds her body enticing.

Are such a normal husband's intentions entirely pure? Perhaps not.

Are such a normal husband's intentions worthy of his bearing a rebellious child of whom G-d wants no part and who will be so evil as to be worthy of gruesome capital punishment? Certainly not!

And as far as the interpretation of *Kidushin 70a* is concerned, there is a fundamental difficulty: according to the simple text, and clear context, of that Talmudic passage, it has nothing to do with marrying a woman *for her looks*, but marrying her *for her money*.

# ENDNOTES

[Even if the author of *Igeres Hakodesh* did not mean to caution that such extreme repurcussions result from a loving husband finding his wife's body attractive, but only that they result when a man *originally marries* his wife *solely* for her looks or her money – without any interest *whatsoever* in her personality, her values, her dreams, or their compatibility – the point still cannot be ignored that any rebelliousness that might later manifest in his children would arguably be the result (not of the technicality of his original lust, but) of their growing up in a home with parents who are in a loveless marriage.]

[385] See above, p. 68.

[386] *Mishneh Torah, Sefer Hamada, Deos 5:4.*

[387] *Mishneh Torah, Sefer Kedushah, Isurei Biah 21:11.*

[388] See, for example, *Shulchan Aruch, Orach 240:1* (quoted above, p. 22).

[389] *Eruvin 100b.*

[390] *Mishneh Torah, Sefer Hamada, Deos 5:4; Sefer Kedushah, Isurei Biah 21:10.*

In *Isurei Biah*, Maimonides does not offer a reason for this prescription. In *Deos*, he says it is so that one is neither overstuffed from dinner nor famished for breakfast, and one's food has properly digested.

[391] *Mishneh Torah, Sefer Hamada, Deos 3:2*

[392] See, however, *Mishneh Torah, Sefer Kedushah, Isurei Biah 21:9*, where Maimonides rules the letter of the law that a couple may have sex "any time he [i.e., the couple] wants."

And see above, footnote to page 29, for limitations on the term "any time" that even Maimonides himself obviously believed in.

[393] See, for example, *Babylonian Talmud, Bechoros 44b*, where it is reported in the name of Rabbi Shimon ben Lakish (Reish Lakish) that ejaculation can at times be essential to a man's health.

[394] *Commentary to the Mishnah, Sanhedrin 7:4.*

[395] *Baalei HaNefesh, Shaar Hakedushah*, Buchwald edition, pp. 173-175.

[396] Though one must wonder how a person can succeed in keeping illicit sexual thoughts out of his or her mind if his or her entire intention in having sex is in order to avoid them.

In any case, curious as it may be that Raavad III does not specify "love" or "bonding" or "vulnerability" with one's wife – i.e., psychological-emotional *dveikus* – among his list of virtuous intentions, Maimonides (just quoted above) doesn't list them clearly either.

[397] See above, pp. 54-56.

[398] *Mishneh Torah, Sefer Hamada, Deos 5:4.*

[399] It would seem to be of unanimous halachic opinion that abstinence from sex on the day the wife expects her menses is obligatory.

As already touched upon, sex in a bright room during the day or at night with the lights on are more complex topics and there are in fact scenarios where these are permitted. To be discussed at length in a future volume of this series. And see above, pp. 95-96 and endnote 371 thereon, and below, endnote 845.

[400] *Babylonian Talmud, Makos 11a* and *Sukkah 53b.*

[401] See Maimonides' words toward the beginning of *Sanhedrin 7:4*:

> I shall now discuss general principles on the topic of illicit sexuality.
>
> Even though they are scattered throughout the Mishnah, and we've already explained each of their principles in each of their individual places, I shall compile them all here in one place for those seeking a clarified view of them.
>
> And I will mention also topics that were not elucidated in the Mishnah, so that the subject shall be made complete.

[402] At least among those whose writings have come down to us.

See above, pages 62-65 and below, Part Three.

[403] English translation based upon Rabbi Yosef Kapach's Hebrew translation of Maimonides' original Arabic manuscript.

[404] Referring to Rabbi Yehudah Hanasi, "Rebbi," and/or his disciple, Rabbi Abba Arikha, "Rav," as related on *Nedarim 20b*.

[405] Referring to Rabbi Yochanan ben Dahavai, as related on *Nedarim 20a*.

[406] Literally, "*mishkav hapuch*," which Maimonides defines earlier in his chapter, there, as "him-on-bottom, her-on-top."

[407] Rabbi Yochanan bar Napacha in the name of the Sages, as related on *Nedarim 20b*.

[408] It should be noted that while the human male's arousal may dissipate after one climax, the female's arousal might not. Similarly, in Jewish law the purpose of a required minimum of sexual activity between spouses is for the sake of the wife's sexual fulfillment – having nothing to do with procreation and everything to do with her pleasure and/or physical-psychological-emotional wellbeing.

Why some elements in rabbinic teaching seem to regard sexual fulfillment as less necessary for a man and his wellbeing than for a woman is one of the great mysteries. To be explored further in a future volume of this series.

An alternate explanation of why G-d created the nature of male sexual arousal to dissipate after ejaculation could arguably be that this is a naturally built in limitation mechanism to prevent a man from becoming obsessed with and addicted to sexual activity and spending his every waking hour engaged in it. But this need not imply that G-d expects a husband – even a pious one – to minimize his enjoyment of marital sex or to completely curb his interest in sexual exploration with his own loving wife.

[Parenthetically, the Bible itself implies that sex is not just about procreation, but rather it is also, and firstly, about "*davek*-clinging" – which, according to at least one medieval commentator, includes connection and intimacy fostered by mutual sexual pleasure (see *Sanhedrin 58b, Rashi: Shelo Cedarcah*). Perhaps this is another reason why sex between husband and wife is not only permitted, but required, even when conception is not possible.

As for the concern that anal sex does not create "clinging" because it does not provide pleasure to the wife, even this is a matter of debate among the sources (see above, endnote 269). And the fact is that anal sex (and even intra-anal ejaculation) IS permitted to married couples by many sources in Jewish law – as is intercourse between limbs and, as we shall see according to some sources, even ejaculation between limbs, the latter of which also brings many women erotic pleasure and a sense of "bonding" between spouses. If, according to these sources, such behaviors ran contrary to "intimacy" for all couples, then they presumably would never have allowed them for anybody. Rather, these sources appear to have recognized that for some (read: many) couples such behaviors can, and do, foster deeper closeness, vulnerability and love – "clinging." And even those sources who forbid intra-anal ejaculation and/or ejaculation between limbs do not do so under the concern that it frustrates marital bonding, but on the technicality that it might be considered "wasting seed."

Note also that some women may find intercourse and/or ejaculation between limbs to be more pleasurable and bonding – or at the very least, more comfortable – than anal intercourse and/or intra-anal ejaculation. Thus, for such women, if the latter is permissible as far as *davek*-clinging" is concerned, as implied by the opinion of Rava on *Sanhedrin 58b*, it is arguable *a fortiori* that the former should be permissible as well. And more research into the matter is required.

**Added note to the third edition:** See also *Shaalos uTeshuvos Torah Lishmah, Responsum 299*. Credit goes to Rabbi Yossi Newfield for bringing this source in *Torah Lishmah* to my attention.]

In any case, Maimonides is not speaking here against a husband's avoidance of all marital sexual *pleasure*, he is merely speaking against a pious husband's avoidance of *fixation* on it.

[409] Our translation of Maimonides' use of the term *"prishus"* as "moderation," rather than "abstention," is based upon his own explanation of the term's meaning in his *Introduction to Ethics of the Fathers (Shmoneh Perakim)*, beginning of Chapter 4.

The word *"haflagah"* generally means "exaggeration," which in this context would seem to connote "extreme moderation."

[410] See above, footnote to page 29 and endnotes 50, 238, for a clarification of the meaning of "any time."

[411] The implication of this textual version would be that a husband is allowed to perform anal *penetration* or *penetration* between limbs, but not *ejaculation* – for any ejaculation would have to be intra-vaginal.

But see our discussion below, pages 119 and 123, about the contested origin of this caveat in Maimonides' text.

[It would also presumably be incomprehensible to many Chasidic-Charedi readers to attribute to Maimonides, a renowned Torah scholar and physician, any instruction to penetrate anally and immediately thereafter ejaculate intra-vaginally, an unhygenic act that could cause severe bodily harm to the woman – unless, of course, the Chasidic-Charedi reader is prepared to admit that Maimonides' own medical knowledge, even as related to a ruling in Torah, could have been limited according to the science of his times.

Rabbi Moshe Feinstein, in *Igros Moshe, Even Haezer, vol. 4, Responsum 66*, page 136, seems to read Maimonides in *Isurei Biah 21:9* as permitting anal sex without expecting any eventual ejaculation on the man's part at all, not even intra-vaginal ejaculation – even though, as Rabbi Feinstein himself admits, "we do not know of such a thing" as a man who is capable of withstanding the urge to ejaculate during anal sex. Rabbi Feinstein appears to deduce from this that if it is permitted for a man to intentionally bring himself to erection for the purpose of anal sex with his wife, because he is confident that he will not ejaculate whatsoever during the sexual encounter, then general acts of affection with one's wife which one is confident will not lead to ejaculation – even if they lead to erection – should be permitted as well.

But even if one accepts it as fact that Maimonides himself wrote the caveat against "wasting seed in vain" in regard to marital anal sex, a simple reading of such a ruling would imply that the husband would be expected to penetrate anally and immediately thereafter ejaculate intra-vaginally – not to not ejaculate at all.]

[412] As we shall discuss in Part Four, Maimonides' ruling in *Mishneh Torah, Isurei Biah 21:9* was the obvious source of Rabbi Moshe Isserles's ruling in *Shulchan Aruch, Even Haezer 25:2*, quoted above, p. 29.

[413] See above, footnote to page 29 and endnotes 50, 238, for a clarification of the meaning of "any time."

[414] According to most commentaries, Rabbi Eliezer reserved sex with his wife for the middle of night so as to minimize the chances of thoughts of other women entering his mind, which could lead to his intentionally entertaining such thoughts during intercourse (see above, endnote 194).

Maimonides, however, implies that Rabbi Eliezer's preference for sex in the middle of night had to do with concerns about digestion. The further implication, then, is that Rabbi Eliezer's concern about illicit fantasies was the motivation only behind his custom to uncover small parts of his wife's body and/or to penetrate "as if forced by a demon" (however Maimonides himself might have interpreted this latter phrase).

[414*] Maimonides presents this teaching in the names of "sages." *Hagigah 5b* presents it in the name of *one* sage, Rav.

[415] See above, endnote 300.

[416] See above, endnote 295.

[417] Literally, "*b'bushah*," often translated (regardless of context) as "with shame."

The fact that Maimonides contrasts "*bushah*" with "*azut* – brazenness" supports the argument that this is not about acting with embarrassment of sexuality or nakedness or the like, but rather with sensitivity and respect.

And see above, footnote to page 33, and below, Part Five, p. 187-188, for further explanation of our choice of translation here.

[Note also the statement of Aristotle in his *Nichomachean Ethics, Book 3, Chapter 6* (translation by W.D. Ross, http://classics.mit.edu/Aristotle/nicomachaen.3.iii.html):

> To fear some things is even right and noble, and it is base not to fear them - e.g. *disgrace*; he who fears this is good and *modest*, and he who does not is *shameless*.

Maimonides quotes from Aristotle's *Ethics, Book 3* in a later work of his, *Guide for the Perplexed*. It is thus noteworthy that Aristotle, too, compares one who is "modest" (i.e., one who possesses a sense of "shame") to one who fears disgrace (i.e., one who possesses a sense of dignity), and he compares one who is "shameless" to one who cares not about "disgrace" (i.e., one who lacks a sense of dignity).]

The continuing search for the most accurate translation of the term "*bushah*" will be the subject of a dedicated essay in a future volume of this series.

[418] See previous endnote.

[419] I emphasize that these sources constitute Maimonides' *legal-halachic* perspective on sex, because in the *philosophical* work authored by him later in life, *Moreh HaNevuchim, Guide for the Perplexed*, Maimonides makes some statements about sex that are far more extreme than anything found in his earlier halachic works.

To be sure, even in his *Mishneh Torah* and *Commentary to the Mishnah* we find Maimonides discouraging fixation on, and addiction to, sex. But at the end of the day, he codified a liberal Jewish legal baseline approach for couples within marriage. In his *Guide for the Perplexed*, however, Maimonides' philosophical statements are almost exclusively about the dangers of sex as an impediment to moral, spiritual and/or intellectual development.

Delving into Maimonides' philosophical beliefs is beyond the scope of this work, and will be the subject of a dedicated essay in a future volume of this series. But those who would like to explore some of his philosophical statements in the meantime can find them in his *Guide for the Perplexed, Part 2, Chapter 36* and *Part 3, Chapters 8, 33, 35, 37, 49* and *52*.

See also Dr. Avraham Grossman's *Vehu Yimshol Bach* (Zalman Shazar Center for Jewish History, Jerusalem, 2011), Chapter Three on Maimonides, painting a rather critical philosophical view of sex in general.

[Dr. Grossman portrays other medieval Jewish scholars as sharing a similarly critical philosophical outlook toward sex. To what extent these medieval Jewish scholars' criticisms of sex were colored by societal conditions of their times, by illicit sexual behaviors among medieval Jews, and/or by Greek/Catholic philosophies is beyond the scope of our present study. As stated in our introduction, more on the overall evolution of Judaism's philosophical attitudes toward sex will be addressed in a future volume of this series.]

For now, let us suffice with a few brief observations about Maimonides' discussions on sex in his *Guide for the Perplexed*, as points to consider for further future discussion (Hebrew transliterations according to the translation of Rabbi Yosef Kapach):

1. Maimonides speaks in extremes, describing those who are focused *entirely* on G-d and truth versus those who focus *entirely* on food, drink, sex and foolishness, invoking also in the same discussion King Solomon's Proverbs, which he says was composed entirely to exhort against *alcoholism* and *prostitution*. [Part 3, Chapter 8]

   To be sure, Maimonides himself must have recognized that there is a huge spectrum of human maturity and development in between these extremes, during which a person might be drawn after both the spiritual and the erotic, and especially within the covenant of a loving, committed, devoted marriage. Indeed, today this arguably constitutes the majority of intelligent, educated, civilized people – from adolescents to adults to elders.

2. As he writes in his introductions to Parts 1 and 3 of the work, Maimonides authored his *Guide for the Perplexed* (hereafter, the "*Guide*") for elevated, intellectual Torah scholars, unlike his *Commentary to the Mishnah* and *Mishneh Torah*, which were written with the masses in mind – in his own words regarding the latter toward the end of his *Introduction* to *Mishneh Torah*: "for young and old alike" (*lakatan v'lagadol*).

   Therefore, if Maimonides *had* wanted to communicate such harsh statements about sex to the masses, and if he did consider them to be psychologically-emotionally-physically-spiritually healthy for them, he could have – and presumably would have – included them in his *Mishneh Torah* in any of his many revisions of the work. Yet he did not.

3. With all the references cited above to discussions in his *Guide* against sexual excess, nowhere in these discussions have I found him to speak against creative sexual positions or techniques between loving husband and wife within marriage.

The only comment I have found as of yet that does make reference to the discussion of *Nedarim 20ab* is where Maimonides mentions that "our famous sages (*chachameinu hamefursamim*) would 'uncover a hand's-breadth and cover over a hand's-breadth' of their wives bodies" [Part 3, Chapter 52]. But he does not call this an obligation.

4. More than once he asserts that the pleasure of touch – including sex – are man's "disgrace" (*cherpah*).

But in the first instance of his designation of touch as such, he explains why: because it is the only sense of pleasure among the five senses that man shares equally on the same base level with animals. And he designates it so based on the teachings of the Greek philosopher, Aristotle – hardly a source acceptable to the average Chasidic-Charedi Jew. [See *Guide for the Perplexed*, Part 2, Chapter 36; Part 3, Chapters 8 and 49]

In Part 3, Chapter 8, in the context of this assertion in the name of Aristotle, Maimonides goes so far as to say that ideally a person should be discomfited by having to enjoy the pleasure of touch (*l'hitztayer ba'asiyaso*) – a statement that is problematic not only from a psychological point of view, but even, arguably, from a Torah viewpoint, especially when it comes to the enjoyment of marital sex.

Behold: G-d's original instruction, and blessing, to man was that he and his wife would "cling to one another and become one flesh." According to Rashi in *Babylonian Talmud, Sanhedrin 58b: Shelo Cedarcah*, an integral part of such clinging is the couple's mutual enjoyment of the physical pleasure of sexual contact.

What is more, a reader of Maimonides' words might not be left with a clear understanding of Aristotle's own context in his *Nichomachean Ethics, Book 3, Chapters 10-13*. Consequently, he or she may walk away with a somewhat exaggerated impression of Aristotle's own message.

See the English edition of Aristotle's *Ethics* by W.D. Ross, available online at http://classics.mit.edu/Aristotle/nicomachaen.3.iii.html).

Book 3 is wholy devoted to discussions about man's voluntary versus involuntary nature. Chapters 10-12 in particular speak about the ills of excess self-indulgence, and how it leads its victims to obsess about and compulsively seek pleasures of touch (food and drink and sex). But Aristotle stresses that the temperate man does not abstain from such pleasures, he merely does not compulsively seek them, especially when they are unhealthy.

In the conclusion of his discussion, Aristotle even admits that: "For the self-indulgent man . . . the particular acts are voluntary (for he does them with craving and desire), *but the whole state is less so; for no one craves to be self-indulgent*."

# ENDNOTES

Thus, what Aristotle arguably spoke of in the context of obsessions, compulsions and/or addictions, Maimonides could potentially be misread, or misinterpreted, as turning into an asexual, or even anti-sexual, Jewish psychology.

[Aristotles' own context is perhaps more clearly reflected in a different passage of Maimonides, in his *Introduction to Ethics of the Fathers, Shmoneh Perakim, Chapter Five* (page 256, column two, in the Kapach edition), where Maimonides writes that if a person eats purely out of desire and a sense of taste, *without regard for the fact that the desired food could potentially harm him, sicken him, or even kill him*, then he is acting no better than an animal; and that if a person has sex every single time he desires it, *without thought about how it could potentially harm him or what purpose there is in it*, then he, too, is acting no better than an animal.]

Finally, note that according to the W.D. Ross translation, nowhere in Book 3 of his *Ethics* does Aristotle refer to the sense of touch as a "disgrace." He speaks of "disgrace" only in discussing the traits of courage versus cowardice. And see above, endnote 417.

5. He states that it is forbidden to talk of sex or make mention of it for any reason (*aval hatashmish eini tzarich lomar boe nosef al mah she'amarti b'peirush Avos mimah sheba b'toraseinu hachachamah hatehorah mitiuv davar zeh v'isur hazcaraso oe hasicha boe clal, v'loe b'shum sibah*). [Part 3, Chapter 8]

This could only be referring to *illicit* sexual talk (*nivlos hapeh*), which he in fact refers to later in the same chapter, but not to a husband's loving (non-illicit) "sexy talk" with his own wife, which is permitted according to *Hagigah 5b* and according to many commentaries' understanding of *Nedarim 20b* (see above, pp. 57-58) – and which Maimonides himself does not forbid in *Mishneh Torah, Deos 5:4-5* or *Isurei Biah 21*.

[At one point, in Part 3, Chapter 49, Maimonides seems to be attempting to prove from the biblical story of Judah and Tamar (Genesis 38) that "any talk about sex" is "shameful."

How?

In the story, there, Judah sleeps with Tamar thinking her to be a prostitute. Because he has no money on him at the time, he offers her his personal signet ring, staff and cloak as collateral until he would send her a calf as payment. But when he later sends her the calf with one of his servants, Tamar is nowhere to be found, and the servant's attempts questioning the townsfolk as to her whereabouts turn out futile. Thus, Judah instructs the servant not to go out seeking her again, "lest we be made a mockery" (*pen nihiyeh lavuz*) [Genesis 38:23].

Maimonides argues that before the Giving of the Torah prostitution and marriage were morally equivalent in the eyes of the masses, and therefore there should have been no shame in seeking out a harlot to pay her her dues – even if it meant going from townsperson to townsperson asking after her. Therefore, Maimonides concludes, Judah must have been concerned about becoming a "mockery" only because any talk of sex in-and-of-itself – even of permissible sex – is shameful and should be kept quiet and hidden (*shekol inyonei hamishgal, v'afilu hamutar meihem, cherpah lanu l'daber bo, v'raoi lishtok mimenu u'l'hastiro*).

But Maimonides' deduction is arguably difficult, for a simple reading of the verse and its greater context does make it appear to be about shame deriving from the prostitution factor, not from the act of "talking about sex" in general – and that is how other medieval commentaries understood it.

[See, for example, *Rashi, Rashbam, Even Ezra, Radak, Sforno* to Genesis 38:22-23; See also *Peirush HaRokeach al HaTorah, Breishis* (Klugman 2001), p. 268, paragraph 23.

Note also that while prostitution may have been accepted as a practice, a) it may still have been denigrated as a matter of public discussion; b) it may have only been so acceptable as a practice for *unmarried* men; c) it may have only been expected among non-Jews of other non-Jews, but not of the family of Jacob; d) Judah himself may have felt it his duty to uphold his father's good name and/or his own as a Jew (a Hebrew).

(Parenthetically, see Rabbi Yosef Kapach's Hebrew translation of the Arabic Bible commentary of Rabbi Saadiah Gaon (referenced in the Mosad HaRav Kook *Toras Chaim* Bible seres), which interprets the word *"lavuz"* in the verse as *"lacherphah"* – the same Hebrew term Rabbi Kapach uses in translating Maimonides' description of the pleasure of touch in the *Guide*. But Rabbi Saadiah Gaon interprets the verse differently than others, saying that Judah commanded his servant to go out yet again to find Tamar, lest they be disgraced in the eyes of the people for not making good on their promise to repay her.)]

In any case, loving "sexy talk" between husband and wife *IS* kept quiet and hidden – *between husband and wife*.

More significantly, in Part 3, Chapter 8, Maimonides writes:

> On the matter of [talking about] sex, I have nothing to add to what I already stated in my commentary to *Ethics of the Fathers* in regard to what is brought in our wise, pure Torah about the abomination of such, and the prohibition (sic) of mentioning it or speaking about it at all, not for any reason.

But turning to his commentary on *Ethics of the Fathers* we do not actually find a categorical prohibiton against loving, respectful (non-illicit) sexual talk between husband and wife.

In his newly-translated and annotated edition of the *Guide*, Maimonidean scholar Rabbi Yosef Kapach points us, here, to *Chapter 1, Mishnah 5* of *Ethics of the Fathers*. But in *Chapter 1, Mishnah 5*, Maimonides does not say it is forbidden to talk about sex. Rather, in explaining the teaching of the *Mishnah*, there, that "A husband should not unlimit conversation even with his own wife (*al tarbeh sichah im ha'ishah . . . u'b'ishto amru*), Maimonides puts forth the assertion that most talk between man and wife is about sex, and therefore it is forbidden to **unlimit** the amount of such talk even within marriage, for the constant arousal of sexual desire will serve as an impediment to character development (*yadua shehasichah im hanashim b'rov hu b'inyonei hamishgal, mipnei zeh amar sheharbos hasichah imahen asur ci hu gorem raah l'atzmo, rachmana l'tzlan, sheyikneh pchisus midos l'nafsho v'hu rov hataavah*). Nowhere in his commentary to that Mishnah does Maimonides forbid **all** sexy talk between a couple within marriage.

# ENDNOTES

Perhaps Maimonides was actually referencing his commentary on *Ethics of the Fathers 1:16*, where he enumerates five categories of talk – as Rabbi Eliyahu Touger translates them in his English edition of the work: a) what we are commanded to speak; b) what we are forbidden to speak; c) speech that should be eschewed; d) speech that is desirable; e) speech that is left to our discretion.

In describing talk that is forbidden (type b), Maimonides includes "vulgar talk" (*nivlus hapeh*), which, as explained above, pp. 73-74, presumably refers to *illicit* sexual discussion specifically. See also our footnote to page 74, that although Maimonides in *Mishneh Torah, Deos 5:4* discourages a pious Torah scholar from "making his mouth vulgar with vain talk," the definition of "vain talk" is not necessarily equivalent to full-fledged "vulgar talk;" and whatever the case may be, in *Deos 5:4* Maimonides does not actually *forbid* "vain talk," he only discourages it, and only in the context of his instructions to Torah scholars, not laymen.

In describing talk that should be eschewed (type c), Maimonides mentions "talk that has no beneficial purpose" (*sichah she'ein boe to'eles*), which (according to the Hebrew translation of Rabbi Yosef Kapach) he says the sages would call "empty talk" (*sichah beteilah*). And he goes on to mention that the sage, Rav, was said to have never spoken an empty word in his life. Maimonides mentions this report about Rav as well in his *Mishneh Torah, Sefer Hamada, Deos 2:4* – a report which Rabbi Yosef Caro in his *Kesef Mishnah* commentary, there, points out has no known source. Perhaps Maimonides deduced this himself from the discussion on *Hagigah 5b* regarding Rav and his caution against "excess lightheaded talk" – which, it is noteworthy, Rabbi Yaakov ben Asher in his *Tur* translates as "empty talk" (see above, page 79). But even if *Hagigah 5b* were Maimonides' source for this, neither in *Mishneh Torah, Deos 2:4* (nor in *Deos 5:4*) nor in his commentary on *Ethics of the Fathers 1:16* does he *forbid* such "empty talk." And it is just as likely that the talk permitted by *Hagigah 5b* – that is, arousing (non-illicit) marital-sexual talk between spouses, at least from husband to wife, and possibly even from wife to husband (see above, endnote 125) – would fall under the category of speech that is left to our discretion (type e), which Maimonides says includes talk that is necessary to fulfill all of a man's (and woman's) physical (and presumably also psychological-emotional) needs.

Finally, whatever Maimonides might have meant to imply in his *Guide*, he certainly would not deny that we find the sage, Rav Chisda, speaking to his daughters and educating them on how to sexually tease and excite their husbands (*Shabbos 140b*); we find Rav speaking excessively sexy with his own wife in order to arouse her to the mood for sex (*Hagigah 5b*); and we find Rabbi Eliezer encouraging husbands to speak seductively to their wives during intercourse (*Tractate Callah 22*).

This is all besides the fact that the Talmud, and even the Bible itself, G-d's own Word, are full of sexual imagery, both negative and positive. And while this last point is better left as a separate topic for another time, it is yet further compelling evidence that the matter of Torah's – G-d's – opinion on "sexy talk" is not as black and white as Maimonides' words in his *Guide for the Perplexed* – read in a vacuum – might imply.

6. Maimonides generally speaks against excess in food, drink and sex in tandem.

   Therefore, if one recognizes that extremes in avoiding pleasure in food and drink are not healthy to the average individual – at least not today – then how much more so must one recognize the harm in sexual extremism – at least today.

Behold: Chasidic-Charedi rabbis are known to invoke the notion that "nature has changed" in order to reconcile certain scientific or medical statements found in the Talmud or early medieval commentaries that are not supported by modern empirical science. In that case, the fact that any medieval scholar, including Maimonides himself, might have made such harsh statements about physical pleasure of any kind should arguably be fundamentally reevaluated today if modern medicine and psychology have provided ample evidence of the damaging psychological-emotional-physical effects of such attitudes.

And see below, *Appendix: A Word about Rabbinic Fallibility.*

7. In Part 3, Chapter 35, he offers a more measured statement, reminiscent of his wording in *Commentary to the Mishnah*, that one "should not fixate on sex in the manner of fools" (*lo laasos es hadavar tachlis c'maaseh hasichlim*) – possibly a reference to what is today recognized as "sexual addiction."

   If we were to read the rest of his statements in the *Guide* in this spirit, then we could perhaps understand that Maimonides was never coming to deny the reality of the need for sexual satisfaction and fulfillment in normal, healthy human beings within an appropriate healthy, loving, devoted marriage relationship, but only to gravely warn against the sexual drive's potential to develop into a psychologically-emotionally-intellectually-spiritually crippling and enslaving addiction.

   In fact, Maimonides finishes his sentence there, in Chapter 35, that one "should not fixate on sex in the manner of fools – as we explained in our commentary to *Ethics of the Fathers*."

   In his newly-translated and annotated edition of the *Guide*, Maimonidean scholar Rabbi Yosef Kapach points us to Maimonides' *Introduction to Ethics of the Fathers (Shmoneh Perakim)*, Chapter 4.

   In Chapter 4 of his *Introduction*, Maimonides argues emphatically that the path toward G-d is one of balance, not extremism – not even extremism in the direction of "pious" asceticsm and/or avoidance of pleasure. He explains that finding, and then maintaining one's course upon, this G-dly balanced middle path is an individual life-long journey for each and every person, and that it requires adjustment from time to time and from stage to stage, and sometimes even from day to day. And in offering examples of such adjustment, he says that a person who (was raised or) became accustomed to denying himself pleasure may have to *overindulge* in pleasure for a while in order to come back to center (a very relevant prescription for many Chasidic-Charedi men and women today).

   He goes on to say that one should not deny oneself permissible sex in healthy moderation. And when he mentions that the Sages instituted fences around the law to help people maintain sexual balance, he refers back to a mention he makes in his *Commentary to the Mishnah, Sanhedrin 7:4* about the rabbinic restriction against sex in the daylight – the same *Commentary to the Mishnah, Sanhedrin 7:4* where he also permits all sexual techniques and positions between husband and wife, including non-sex-related talk during intercourse, "overturning the table," and gazing at or kissing the female genitals.

   We have thus come full circle: In regard to sexual pleasure in general, Maimonides in his *Guide for the Perplexed, Part 3, Chapter 35* references a much more balanced, healthy discussion about sex for the masses in his *Introduction to Ethics of the Fathers*, where he, in turn, references his presentation in his

# ENDNOTES

> *Commentary to the Mishnah, Sanhedrin 7:4*, where he distinguishes between philosophy and law, and ultimately permits a husband and wife to enjoy complete sexual vulnerability and fulfillment with one another within marriage, and which served as the clear basis for his liberal, permissive ruling in *Mishneh Torah, Sefer Kedushah, Isurei Biah 21:9*.

See also Chapters 2 and 3 of the medical *Treatise on Cohabitation*, attributed to Maimonides, in regard to achieving and maintaining strong male sexual functioning (English translation by Dr. Fred Rosner, The Maimonides Research Institute, 1984):

> Chapter 2: ... Happiness, delight, laughter, rest and sleep that is not excessive are of value in this matter. And the opposite of these is extremely detrimental: that is, mourning, sorrow, anxiety, fasting, weariness, toil and wakefulness – all these markedly abolish erection and diminish sperm. And similarly, excessive mention of the subject of intercourse, and discussions thereof, and praising it, are among the things that are helpful (for coitus), whereas directing one's thoughts far therefrom causes the penis to shrink and weaken its activity.
>
> In addition, the engagement in coitus for lust is among the things that strengthen the penis and aid in increasing sexual intercourse, whereas engagement therein without lust weakens the penis, causes it to shrivel up and diminishes the desire (for coitus). All the more so if one combines with this the elimination of thoughts (of intercourse) and the abstention from the act itself, since this is the first thing that the abstainers practice to save themselves from licentiousness.
>
> Chapter 3: And it is known that this activity is not purely a natural function; that is, erection is not similar to nutritional or growth activities in which emotions play no part. Rather it is also an emotional process controlled by the psyche. As a result, various emotions can be greatly detrimental or beneficial (for coitus): i.e., sorrow, anxiety and mourning, or the repulsiveness of the woman with whom one intends to have sexual intercourse, are among the things that markedly weaken coitus. The converse emotions incite one thereto and produce a powerful stimulation.
>
> [Credit goes to Rabbi Yehoishophot Oliver for reminding me of this source.]

Now, granted this treatise appears to have been written to a non-Jewish nobleman either suffering sexual dysfunction or seeking sexual excesses, the latter being what Maimonides was apparently coming to denigrate in his *Guide for the Perplexed*, as explained above, and hence its moral-philosophical value to Jews is undetermined. But it cannot be denied that its author recognized that *asexuality* in thought, speech and action (without even getting into sexual anxiety) is highly detrimental to normal, healthy sexual functioning.

Thus, if we are to accept this treatise as coming from the pen of Maimonides, it further adds to the complexity of what his personal prescription for normal, healthy, as well as spiritual, sexuality within marriage might have been.

Finally, see Maimonides' *Mishneh Torah, Sefer Zmanim, Hilchos Shabbos 30:14*: "Marital sex is among the [holy] pleasures of the Sabbath" (see also Rabbi Yosef Caro's *Shulchan Aruch, Orach Chaim, 280*). [Credit goes to a friend for bringing these sources in *Mishneh Torah, Hilchos Shabbos* and *Shulchan Aruch, Orach Chaim 280* to my attention.]

To summarize then: While it is certainly *curious* that Maimonides expressed such a harsh philosophical stance in his *Guide for the Perplexed*, written for men of spiritual-intellectual height, there is no denying the fact that he took a milder philosophical approach in his

*Introduction to Ethics of the Fathers*, and a liberal legal-halachic approach to the enjoyment of marital sex for the masses in his *Commentary to the Mishnah* and *Mishneh Torah*.

And let each individual couple mutually decide for themselves what level of spiritual-intellectual height they are at or ready to strive for. But let it certainly *never* be at the expense of vulnerability and bonding and harmony and sexual fulfillment of loving husband and wife.

[420] See above, endnote 256.

[421] See below, p. 113.

[422] See above, pp. 69-74, 81-83.

[423] I say that *perhaps* Maimonides was again including "vain talk" in his statement in *Deos* 5:5, because by this point in his discussion Maimonides has introduced elements of the nine-ten flawed conditions, including intoxicated sex, sex while one spouse is asleep, and forced sex. It would therefore appear that when he goes on to caution that the behaviors of "those who walk in darkness" could result in spiritually insensitive children, he was referring solely to those behaviors that are among the nine flawed conditions – which the Talmud on *Nedarim 20b* clearly cautions could have negative spiritual impacts upon children conceived in their wake.

As to why Maimonides only lists these three out of the nine, this remains to be explored. In *Isurei Biah 21:12-13* he actually lists more than nine – and he does not include, there, sex while one spouse is asleep.

[If Maimonides were including "vain talk" again in *Deos 5:5*, as a category of "non-mood-related talk," we would have another issue to address, for nowhere does *Hagigah 5b* predict that such talk will result in spiritually uncouth children. It cautions only that one might be called to justify it on Judgement Day. Only *Nedarim 20b* implies that spiritual challenges in children may result from a father having intentionally fantasized of other women when they were conceived – a belief that Ima Shalom reported on *Nedarim 20b* in the name of her husband, Rabbi Eliezer, and which the compilers-editors of the Talmud, there, associate with the issue of "non-sex-related talk." Thus, if Maimonides were referring again to "vain talk" in *Deos 5:5*, and cautioning that it could result in uncouth children, it could perhaps be said that he did in fact equate the non-sex-related talk of *Nedarim 20b* with the non-mood-related talk of *Hagigah 5b*, and therefore "vain talk" would be a subcategory of both. But this would be highly forced into Maimonides' words.

And more research into the matter is required.]

[424] Whereas Raavad III might still predict congenital deafness resulting from non-sex-related/non-mood-related talk. See above, p. 63.

[425] Founder of a mystical group of Torah scholars in medieval Germany, known as "The Pious of Germany" (*Chasidei Ashkenaz*).

Rabbi Elazar of Worms (1176-1238), author of *Sefer HaRokeach*, was a chief disciple of his.

[426] On *Nedarim 20b*.

[427] See also *Sefer Chasidim 380*:

> ...And the verse permits a wife to her husband any time he wishes to have sexual pleasure from her [with her permission], so that he will not set his eye upon [i.e., intentionally fantasize of] another woman.
>
> And a husband should behave as described in *Tractate Callah*...

See also the words of Rabbi Yehudah the Pious's disciple, Rabbi Elazar of Worms, in his *Sefer HaRokeach, Hilchos Chasidus* (quoted in *Kovetz Shitos Kamai, Shabbos 118b*, page 602):

> Anything a husband craves to do with his wife sexually he may do, so that he does not set his eyes upon [i.e., intentionally fantasize of] another woman. Nevertheless, [ideally] he should be face-to-face with her so that she derives pleasure…"

Note that Rabbi Yehudah the Pious and Rabbi Elazar Rokeach, master and disciple, are cautious in their respective permissive rulings regarding sex with the wife on top (Rabbi Yehudah the Pious) and face-to-back (Rabbi Elazar Rokeach) *only* because they assumed these would not satisfy the wife's need for sexual fulfillment. But in the case of a wife who actually enjoys, or prefers, these positions, and with her husband's wholehearted agreement, Rabbi Yehudah the Pious and Rabbi Elazar Rokeach would presumably each have no objection to the specific position they each addressed.

[428] See *Peirush Kadmon* to *Sefer Chasidim 509* (in the *Otzar Haposkim* edition), that although Rabbi Yehudah the Pious left out the first phrase of the verse, he obviously understood it to be implied (presumably as evident from his previous point about "finding a good wife").

[429] Note that while the mystic-ascetic Rabbi Yehudah the Pious invokes this verse to assert the goodness, and the Creator's own approval, of a husband and wife who see eye-to-eye in matters of sexual exploration, Raavad III, also a mystic, interprets the verse in a negative light. See the Buchwald edition of *Baalei HaNefesh, Shaar Hakedushah*, page 171.

[430] See our analyses above, pp. 57-58 and 71-83.

[431] See above, pp. 57-58, and endnotes thereon.

Regarding "vulgar talk" – which is not mere "sexy talk," but talk of an *illicit* nature – see above, pp. 73-74.

[432] See above, pp. 75, 79-81 and endnotes thereon.

[433] See above, pp. 62, 65, 76-77.

Note that Rabbi Yochanan ben Dahavai's own caution was against non-sex-related talk *during intercourse* (*b'shaas tashmish* – and see above, footnote to p. 24). Thus, those who reject all four of Rabbi Yochanan ben Dahavai's cautions would presumably permit any kind of talk both during foreplay and intercourse.

[434] For additional sources that imply they understood the Sages on *Nedarim 20b* as rejecting all four of Rabbi Yochanan ben Dahavai's cautions – though they do not necessarily spell it out clearly – see above pp. 64-65.

[434*] As seen above, pp. 62-63, Raavad III interprets the Sages on *Nedarim 20b* as coming to permit only one of the four behaviors cautioned against by Rabbi Yochanan ben Dahavai, namely, "overturning the table." But see below, pp. 172, 174, 192, that part of his argument in insisting this is that the compilers-editors of the Talmud, there, only go on to report actual case precedents of sages permitting that one behavior. *Tractate Callah*, however, does not report these case precedents, and thus they cannot be invoked as indication that *Tractate Callah* meant only to permit that one behavior. A straightforward reading of *Tractate Callah* has the Sages permitting all four behaviors – and this appears to be how the author(s) of *Callah Rabti* also understood it (see above, p. 46 and endnotes 166*, 167*).

[435] While *Callah Rabti 1:13-14* has the Sages permitting any kind of talk during sexual intercourse by the letter of the law, it still has them believing such talk could cause

congenital deafness if spoken during the same sexual encounter in which conception occurs. But during a sexual encounter in which conception will not occur, it would be both permitted and perfectly safe according to *Callah Rabti*.

Accordingly, when *Callah Rabti 2:11* says, on account of Rabbi Yochanan ben Dahavai's teaching, that Rabbi Eliezer could not possibly have encouraged a husband to talk seductively with his wife *in order to succeed in conceiving children*, it is possibly not because it believed such talk to be forbidden by the Sages or Rabbi Eliezer, but because it believed that even they thought such talk could be dangerous to a child *if performed during the same sexual encounter in which conception occurs*. And see above, pp. 51, 58.

[436] Albeck edition.

[437] See above, endnote 256.

In his *Commentary to the Mishnah, Sanhedrin 7:4*, Maimonides also says simply that the Sages rejected the view of Rabbi Yochanan ben Dahavai and that the law follows the Sages – implying that this is the case even in regard to non-sex-related talk during sex.

[438] See above, endnote 236.

[439] Rabbi Yitzchak of Corbeil expressly permits all four behaviors cautioned against by Rabbi Yochanan ben Dahavai, but he still mentions that they could all cause congenital illness. If so, he would be endorsing the view of *Callah Rabti 1:13-14*. But then even he would have to admit that these behaviors are only dangerous to a fetus if they are performed during the same sexual encounter in which conception occurs – never else.

[440] See above, pp. 64-65, 76-77 and endnote 251.

[441] See above, pp. 78-79.

[441*] See above, pages 62-65, and our discussion, here, throughout Part Three.

[441**] See above, endnote 434*.

[442] While *Callah Rabti 1:13-14* has the Sages permitting gazing at the female genitals by the letter of the law, it still has them believing that it could cause congenital blindness if done during the same sexual encounter in which conception occurs. But during a sexual encounter in which conception will not occur, it would be both permitted and perfectly safe according to *Callah Rabti*.

[443] Albeck edition

[444] See above, endnote 256.

[445] See above, endnote 439.

[445*] 2015 edition, pp. 62-64, and footnotes thereon.

[446] See above, pp. 62-63.

[447] *Baalei HaNefesh, Shaar Hakedushah,* Buchwald edition, page 179. And see below, pp. 171-174, 177-192, our analysis of Raavad III's views on this matter.

[447*] See above, endnote 434*.

[448] While *Callah Rabti 1:13-14* has the Sages permitting kissing the female genitals by the letter of the law, it still has them believing that it could cause congenital muteness if done during the same sexual encounter in which conception occurs. But during a sexual

encounter in which conception will not occur, it would be both permitted and perfectly safe according to *Callah Rabti*.

[449] Albeck edition.

[450] Page 81.

[451] See above, endnote 439.

[452] See *Kovetz Shitos Kamai, Nedarim*, page 183.

[453] See *Kovetz Shitos Kamai, Nedarim*, page 188.

[454] See *Kovetz Shitos Kamai, Nedarim*, page 187.

[455] See *Kovetz Shitos Kamai, Nedarim*, page 183.

[456] Rabbi Shmuel ben Uri Shraga Feivush (1640-1700), in his *Beis Shmuel* commentary to *Shulchan Aruch, Even Haezer 25:2*, is understood by some as claiming that Rabbi Isserles meant to permit a husband to kiss any part of his wife's body *except* her genitals. However, Rabbi Feivush may not have actually been *interpreting* Rabbi Isserles at all, but merely offering his own personal opinion on the matter. See our discussion on this below, pp. 167-168.

[457] And see below, endnote 640.

[458] And see below, endnote 641.

[458*] 2015 edition, pp. 62-64, and footnotes thereon.

[459] See our analysis of *Tur* below, pp. 136-137 and endnote 549 thereon.

[460] *Babylonian Talmud, Tractate Gitin 70a; Tractate Callah 15; Callah Rabti 1:23; Tur, Even Haezer 25:2; Be'er Heitev, Shulchan Aruch, Orach Chaim 240:5:15*.

The only medieval authority I have found to use the term "forbidden" (*asur*) in relation to the her-on-top position, and possibly the side-by-side position, is Rabbi Yisrael Alnaqua in his *Menoras Hamaor, vol. 4, Perek Nisuei Ishah*, page 83. But he points to *Tractate Callah* as his source – which does not use such strong terminology.

*Tractate Callah* calls the wife-on-top position "arrogant." Arguably, then, if the husband enjoys his wife on top, there is nothing arrogant or otherwise objectionable about it.

[461] See above, pp. 60-61.

[462] Quoted in *Kovetz Meforshim, "Leket Rishonim,"* published by Yerid Haseforim, 2003.

[463] As Rabbi Yehudah the Pious himself makes clear, this stipulation was based on the assumption that a woman does not fully enjoy sex when she is (forced to be) on top. The implication, however, is that if a wife wants to be on top, and her husband is agreeable or even enjoys it, then even on the night of her *mikveh* immersion there would be no legal or moral objection to it, not even from Rabbi Yehudah the Pious himself.

[464] On *Nedarim 20a*, Rabeinu Peretz describes the position of "overturning the table" as "face to back, because the man is on bottom" – in other words, the wife is on top and facing away from her husband (with her back to him). See also above, p. 60.

[464*] This reference to Rashi presumably refers to the *Mefaresh* commentary on *Nedarim 20ab*. See above, page 60.

[465] In *Even Haezer* 25:10, Rabbi Epstein defines Rabbi Yochanan ben Dahavai's term, "overturning the table," as "her-on-top, him-on-bottom." Then, in *25:11*, he rules the letter of the law according to the Sages (who reject the cautions of Rabbi Yochanan ben Dahavai), that "Anything a man craves to do with his wife sexually he may do." Thus, according to Rabbi Epstein, "her-on-top, him-on-bottom" would be permitted.

[465*] 2015 edition, p. 61.

[466] Toledano edition (Tiberias 1906), page 29.

[467] And see above, endnote 176.

[468] *Tractate Callah 15; Callah Rabti 1:23.*

Certain sources refer to the side-by-side position as "obstinate." Arguably, however, if husband and wife both enjoy side-by-side intercourse, there would be nothing obstinate or otherwise objectionable about it.

And see above, endnote 179.

[469] *Babylonian Talmud, Tractate Gitin 70a; Tractate Callah 13, 15; Callah Rabti 1:23.*

See also *Likutei HaPardes*, page 4b in the Munkatch edition, in regard to standing.

[470] Maimonides, *Mishneh Torah, Sefer Hamada, Deos 4:19; Tur, Orach Chaim 240:15, Even Haezer 25:2; Shulchan Aruch, Orach Chaim 240:15.*

Regarding the view of Rabbi Yisrael Alnaqua, see above, endnote 460.

For a discussion about performing these positions, and others, naked and without any covers on, see *Appendices: Sex Above the Covers.*

[471] *Babylonian Talmud, Kesubos 60b.*

See also *Likutei HaPardes*, p. 4b in the Munkatch edition, which mentions it as a health issue, but not about the baby's neck specifically.

[472] In modern slang: "doggystyle."

[473] According to those textual versions of *Tractate Callah* that interpret "overturning the table" as rear-entry vaginal intercourse specifically.

[474] See previous endnote.

[475] While *Callah Rabti 1:13-14* has the Sages permitting "overturning the table" by the letter of the law, it still has them believing that it could cause congenital lameness if done during the same sexual encounter in which conception occurs. But during a sexual encounter in which conception will not occur, it would be both permitted and perfectly safe according to *Callah Rabti*.

[476] It goes without saying, but Raavad III does stipulate that this position is only permitted with the wife's consent (see page 179 in the Buchwald edition of *Baalei HaNefesh*). The same stipulation would be assumed to apply to any other "non-missionary" position according to any other opinion – as implied by *Talmud, Nedarim 20b*, which warns either spouse from ever coercing the other in matters of sex (see above, pp. 37-38, footnote to page 38, and endnote 125; see also *Eruvin 100b*, referenced in endnote 125). And see Rabbi Yehudah HaChasid's statement on the matter in *Sefer Chasidim 509*, quoted above, page 107.

[477] In the name of Raavad III's *Baalei HaNefesh, Shaar Hakedushah.*

## ENDNOTES

⁴⁷⁸ According to *Sefer HaAgur*, rear-entry vaginal intercourse is permitted only once in a while, randomly in the heat of passion (see also Rabbi Yehoshua Falk's interpretation of Raavad III in his *Prishah* commentary to *Tur, Orach Chaim 240:2-4:9* and Rabbi Yaakov Emden's *Commentary to the Siddur, Mitas Hakesef,* chapter 7, section 2:2).

The application of this limitation on frequency to rear-entry *vaginal* intercourse is highly questionable, for it is a limitation applied by all other commentaries only in regard to intra-anal ejaculation, where there is the concern of it being abused as an intentional and constant means of unsanctioned birth control (which is never a concern in regard to rear-entry vaginal intercourse).

And see below, page 166, and endnotes 606* and 607*, for a further point in this regard.

And see endnote 647.

⁴⁷⁸* This reference to Rashi presumably refers to the *Mefaresh* commentary on *Nedarim 20ab*. See above, page 60.

⁴⁷⁸** But see below, pp. 153-156.

⁴⁷⁸*** 2015 edition, p. 61.

⁴⁷⁹ Toledano edition (Tiberias 1906), page 29.

⁴⁸⁰ See above, pp. 89-90 and endnote 335.

⁴⁸¹ For a lengthy discussion on this point, see Rabbi Yehuda Henkin's *Bnei Banim vol. 4, Responsum 18.*

This important textual variation is noted in the margin of the Shabsi Frankel edition of *Mishneh Torah,* and the entire phrase in question has been deleted from the Mechon-Mamre.org and Kapach editions.

⁴⁸² There is a famous essay by Rabbi Menachem M. Schneerson (1992-1994) discussing the fact that in the 20ᵗʰ century unprecedented access to library collections and comparative manuscript analysis has proven beyond reasonable doubt that certain rulings disseminated for centuries in Maimonides' name, and upon which other medieval and post-medieval halachic authorities based their own rulings, were in fact erroneous or that Maimonides had ultimately changed his mind about them. (*Toras Menachem, Hadranim al HaRambam v'HaShas,* Kehot Publication Society, 1992, pp. 268-273)

This phenomenon especially came to light with the publication of Yemenite manuscripts of Maimonides' *Mishneh Torah*. The Yemenite community traditionally followed the rulings of Maimonides in practice, and they are custodians of some of the most reliable versions of his works, having sent messengers to Egypt during Maimonides' own lifetime to update the copies from which they derived sacred instruction for daily living.

Rabbi Schneerson asks the obvious: If it is true that Maimonides himself changed his mind about certain rulings, or that certain rulings spread in his name were erroneous textual corruptions to begin with, shouldn't the rulings of later authorities which were based upon them be revised today – including those codified by Rabbi Yosef Caro in *Shulchan Aruch*?

Rabbi Schneerson answers no, and for four reasons:

1. Even if a certain authority ruled according to the incorrect version of *Mishneh Torah* that happened to be in his possession, that authority "many times" (*al col panim b'riboi paamim*) did not rule according to Maimonides blindly, but rather came to the same conclusion as the version of Maimonides' opinion he had access to based upon his own investigation of the sources. Therefore, even if he would

have subsequently found out that Maimonides had changed his mind on the matter, it in no way proves that he himself would have changed his mind in kind.

2. The fact that Maimonides later changed his mind doesn't mean his original ruling had no basis in Torah. His original viewpoint must have also been well grounded.

3. True, there is a concept brought in Jewish law that if we know a certain later halachic authority did not have access to a certain earlier halachic source, we cannot assume he would *not* have ruled according to it had he known of its existence. But still: a) a double negative does not equal a positive – not having proof that he would *not* have accepted it, is not proof that he in fact would have; b) the commentaries who speak of such cases have generally only been prepared to revise widely-established rulings under three conditions: 1. There is another authority of equal standing who already ruled in kind; 2. Only in matters of biblical law; 3. Only to make observance of the law more stringent, not more lenient.

4. Although Rabbi Yosef Caro writes in his introduction to *Beis Yosef* that in determining his practical rulings of law in that work he relied heavily upon three great medieval scholars, Rabbi Yitzchak Alfasi, Maimonides and Rabeinu Asher, and that in cases where two out of three of them ruled a certain way he himself would rule accordingly, the truth is that he always ruled the law according to how *he* saw fit – and if it happened that two out of three of the above scholars ruled in a manner that Rabbi Caro himself originally did not agree with, in most such cases (*b'ruba d'ruba*) Rabbi Caro simply delved deeper into the law until he *convinced* himself to see it their way.

While such arguments can certainly be invoked to justify defending the status quo, one must also consider whether such an approach, in all cases, puts sufficient concern upon individuals' psychological-emotional-physical balance and wellbeing alongside concerns about maintaining religious organization.

In addition, Maimonides himself certainly *was* concerned that Jewish law be determined only by the most up-to-date version of his *Mishneh Torah* (see Rabbi Yitzchak Sheilat's Introduction to *Rambam Meduyak, Sefer Hamada*, Mahadurat Sheilat, 2004). In some cases, the incorrect versions that were disseminated really did have no basis in Jewish law (see Yohai Makbili's Introduction to *Mishneh Torah*, Mifal Mishneh Torah, 2009) And Rabbi Schneerson himself does not deny that halachic authorities through the ages may have simply relied on Maimonides' opinion despite what they themselves might have thought on a given matter, he says only that in "many cases" they probably did not do so (see above, point 1).

As pertains to our present case, Maimonides' view on intra-anal ejaculation for married couples (and, as we shall discuss next, ejaculation between limbs for married couples), the fact that certain later authorities quote *verbatim*, or practically verbatim, the stringent ruling disseminated in Maimonides' name, makes it hard to believe that the weight of his authority was not a determining factor in their own decisions to rule stringently on the matter.

But even if the Orthodox rabbinate were to officially and universally change the wording of *Mishneh Torah, Sefer Kedushah, Isurei Biah 21:9* to exclude the questionable restrictive phrase, this would not constitute any actual "contradiction" between Maimonides' ruling and Rabbi Caro's, for, as we shall discuss below (Part Four, pp. 148-149), Rabbi Caro does not actually "forbid" anal sex or intra-anal ejaculation (or intercourse/ejaculation between limbs) anywhere in his *Shulchan Aruch* or *Beis Yosef*.

And even if one chooses to believe that Rabbi Caro himself did forbid intra-anal ejaculation and/or ejaculation between limbs, still, Rabbi Moshe Isserles and numerous venerable post-medieval/post-*Shulchan Aruch* authorities permit intra-anal ejaculation to married couples, and at least one, Rabbi Yeshoshuah Falk, insists that Rabeinu Yitzchak permitted ejaculation between limbs to married couples as well (see below, pp. 124-125, 164-165).

[482*] See also below, end of endnote 484, point 3.

[483] See also Rabbi Yehuda Henkin, *Bnei Banim*, vol. 4, Responsum 18:5.

[484] One could argue that this, in fact, is how Rabeinu Yonah (*Chidushei Rabeinu Yonah*) and Rabeinu Nissim (*Chidushei HaRan*) to *Sanhedrin 58b* understood Maimonides' intention with this restrictive phrase.

In Rabeinu Yonah's words:

> Rabbi Moshe [Maimonides], of blessed memory, writes: "A man's wife is permitted [to him]. Therefore, anything a man craves to do with his wife [sexually], he may do at any time he wants: he may kiss any part of her body he wants, and he may penetrate her between limbs, etcetera, so long as he does not ejaculate, etcetera (*ubilvad shelo yotzi shichvas zera v'chulhu*) . . .
>
> . . . But there is no contradiction [from *Yevamos 34b* to *Sanhedrin 58b* and *Nedarim 20b*], for there [in the case of the anal sex of Er and Onan reported on *Yevamos 34b*] they were not punished because of the anal *penetration*, but because they would "*destroy* their seed."
>
> But if a man penetrates his wife [anally] *for the sake of his pleasure*, and he does not "destroy his seed," there is no prohibition.
>
> And so did the Rabbi [Moshe Maimonides], of blessed memory, write.

Although Rabeinu Yonah's wording is unclear, for he appears to be mixing the two approaches of Rabeinu Yitzchak together, the fact that he adds in the factor of *pleasure* as a reason to permit anal sex, rather than simply stating the *lack of ejaculation* as the reason to permit it, suggests that the categorization of a seminal ejaculation as "destruction" of seed is determined by the man's intention – i.e., it is determined by whether his intention is for unsanctioned birth control or for sexual fulfillment (as stated by Rabeinu Yitzchak in his second approach, by Rabbi Yeshayah of Trani I, by Rabeinu Asher, and by others).

[Note that in his paraphrase of Maimonides' restrictive version, Rabeinu Yonah words the concluding phrase: ". . . so long as he does not **ejaculate, etcetera** (*ubilvad shelo yotzi shichvas zera v'chulhu*)." The prevalent wording of this phrase, however, is: ". . . so long as he does not **"ejaculate in vain"** (*ubilvad shelo yotzi shichvas zera levatalah*). It thus appears that in Rabeinu Yonah's paraphrase, "etcetera" (*v'chulhu*) substitutes for, "in vain" (*levatalah*).]

Such an interpretation of Maimonides' restrictive phrase is perhaps slightly more clear in the wording of Rabeinu Nissim:

There are those who answer [the contradiction between *Yevamos 34b* and *Sanhedrin 58b/Nedarim 20b,* explaining] that even though it is forbidden [to ejaculate intra-anally], the [anal] penetration in-and-of-itself is not illicit and is not a forbidden penetration. And the issue of "destroying seed" is a separate prohibition. So [on *Nedarim 20b,*] when he [Rebbi] said [to the wife who informed him that her husband had performed anal sex with her, that] "Torah permits you to him," he meant that it is not an illicit penetration, but only an issue of "destruction of seed." And if the husband "destroys his seed" [while penetrating his wife anally] the wife is not held accountable.

And the Tosafists, of blessed memory, said that it [anal sex] is completely permitted in all cases that his intention is not the "destruction of seed" and he does not ejaculate "for waste" (*shehu heter gamur b'chol makom she'eino mechavein l'hashchatas zera, v'lo yotziuhu l'vatalah*). And these are the words of Maimonides, of blessed memory, in *Isurei Biah 21.*

Rabeinu Nissim first presents in the name of anonymous commentators the equivalent of Rabeinu Yitzchak's first approach, that anal sex is permitted only without ejaculation. He then quotes *Tosfos* as a *second* approach, that anal sex is permitted so long as the husband's *intention* is not to "destroy seed" *and thus his ejaculation is not considered to be "for waste."* And he equates this *second* approach with Maimonides' ruling in *Isurei Biah 21:9.*

This implies that Rabeinu Nissim understood Maimonides as ruling in line with the second approach of Rabeinu Yitzchak, permitting intra-anal ejaculation so long as it is for the sake of the husband's pleasure – in which case it is categorized neither as "destruction" nor as "waste."

[Note that while it is perhaps possible to read Rabeinu Nissim on *Sanhedrin 58b* as quoting *Tosfos in support* of "those" who permit only anal penetration without intra-anal ejaculation, it would be a somewhat unusual way of reading the flow of his words. In any case, as we shall see below (this endnote), Rabbi Chaim Yosef Dovid Azulai (Chida) did not read him this way.

Also, it is arguable that by "*Tosfos,*" Rabeinu Nissim (on *Sanhedrin 58b*) was referencing not *Tosfos* on *Yevamos 34b,* but *Tosfos* on *Sanhedrin 58b,* which offers only one approach – in line with the *second* approach of Rabeinu Yitzchak. That is, if Rabeinu Nissim had been referencing *Tosfos* on *Yevamos 34b,* then he presumably would not have quoted it as a *separate* approach from the one he presented first in the name of anonymous commentators – for *Tosfos* on *Yevamos 34b* in fact offers *both* approaches (in the name of Rabeinu Yitzchak). And if Rabeinu Nissim were referencing *Tosfos* on *Sanhedrin 58b,* he clearly would have been invoking an opinion that permits occasional intra-anal ejaculation within marriage – and equating it with the opinion of Maimonides in *Mishneh Torah.*]

This would in fact be in line with Rabeinu Nissim's commentary to *Nedarim 20b,* where he says that the reason the Sages' ruled that "Anything a husband craves to do with his wife sexually, he may do," is because through marriage, he "acquires" the right to enjoy her body (with her permission) in any way he pleases. As Rabbi Moshe Feinstein explains – specifically in regard to Rabeinu Yitzchak's *second* approach – this "right" includes the husband's enjoyment of "intra-anal ejaculation" for the sake of pleasure, which Rabbi Feinstein says cannot be categorized as "wasted" seed, for it is not ejaculated for "no reason." (See below, pp. 140-141).

# ENDNOTES

Now, unlike Rabeinu Yonah, Rabeinu Nissim to *Sanhedrin 58b* does not actually quote the text of Maimonides' ruling, so we do not know from there whether his manuscript of *Mishneh Torah* included the restrictive phrase against "wasting seed" at the end of *Isurei Biah 21:9* or not. We do know, however, from his commentary to *Nedarim 20b: HaTorah Hitirasecha* that his manuscript of *Mishneh Torah did* include this phrase – and, nevertheless, he still implies in his commentary to *Sanhedrin 58b* that Maimonides permits intra-anal ejaculation for the sake of sexual fulfillment within marriage, because such is not *defined* as "destruction" or "waste."

Thus, a combination of Rabeinu Nissim's comments to *Sanhedrin 58b* and *Nedarim 20b* would yield an interpretation of the restrictively-phrased version of Maimonides' ruling in *Isurei Biah 21:9* that renders it equivalent to the second approach of Rabeinu Yitzchak – permitting intra-anal ejaculation on occasion for the sake of a husband's sexual fulfillment within marriage.

[And see below, endnotes 492, 493, in regard to Rabeinu Nissim, and endnote 494 in regard to Rabeinu Yonah.]

Behold: Rabbi Chaim Yosef David Azulai (Chida), in his *Birchei Yosef* commentary to *Shulchan Aruch, Orach Chaim 240:5*, writes clearly:

> And it is implied from the wording of Rabeinu Nissim [in his commentary to *Sanhedrin 58*] that according to *Tosfos and Maimonides* it is permitted even to ejaculate [intra-anally].
>
> And this is also implied somewhat from the wording of Rabeinu Yonah in his commentary to *Sanhedrin*.

[**Added note to the third edition:** See also *Yabia Omer vol. 8, Even Haezer 21:2*, where Rabbi Ovadia Yosef (1920-2013) appears to understand Rabeinu Nissim as equating Maimonide's ruling in *Mishneh Torah, Isurei Biah 21:9* with the *second* approach of Rabeinu Yitzchak cited in *Tosfos* to *Yevamos 34b*. Credit goes to Rabbi Yossi Newfield for bringing this responsum of Rabbi Ovadiah Yosef to my attention.]

[See also the *Birur* commentary in the *Halachah Berurah* edition of the Talmud to *Yevamos 34b*, which agrees that Rabeinu Nissim equated Maimonides' view with that of Rabeinu Yitzchak's second approach in *Tosfos*, permitting intra-anal ejaculation within marriage so long as the husband's intention is occasional sexual fulfillment, not constant birth control.

Note, however, that the *Birur* commentary appears to make three assertions that could be argued otherwise:

1. It states that Rabeinu Yitzchak's second approach in *Tosfos* to *Yevamos 34b* did not make a distinction about a husband's *intention* in intra-anal ejaculation, but only about a husband's *frequency* of it. Rather, the *Birur* commentary suggests, Rabeinu Nissim was the first to report *Tosfos* as making a distinction about intention.

    But it is in fact clear in the wording of Rabeinu Yitzchak's second approach as reported in *Tosfos* to *Yevamos 34b* that a distinction is made between intentions of birth control versus intentions of sexual fulfillment.

2. It suggests that Rabeinu Nissim's manuscript of Maimonides' *Mishneh Torah, Isurei Biah 21:9* did not include the restrictive phrase against "wasting seed in vain."

But we know from Rabeinu Nissim's commentary to *Nedarim 20b* that he was in possession of a manuscript of *Mishneh Torah* that included this phrase (though it is possible he possessed multiple manuscript versions of *Mishneh Torah*).

3. In regard to the comments of *Hagahos Maimonios* to *Mishneh Torah, Isurei Biah 21:9*, the *Birur* commentary suggests that the author of *Hagahos Maimonios* understood Maimonides as permitting only anal *penetration* without ejaculation – and even that, only on *occasion*.

But as discussed above, p. 119, the author of *Hagahos Maimonios* clearly understood Maimonides as permitting *intra-anal ejaculation* on *occasion* – and this, most likely, because *his* manuscript of *Mishneh Torah* did not include the restrictive phrase against "wasting seed in vain."]

485 Concerning the notion brought in *Yad Malachi, Clalei Haposkim – Rambam, Clal 37*, that Maimonides customarily relies on that which he writes later in the same chapter to clarify that which he writes earlier, and why this notion cannot be applied here, see Rabbi Yehuda Henkin, *Bnei Banim, vol. 4, Responsum 18:6*.

As for the argument that perhaps Maimonides did not bring prohibitions against intra-anal ejaculation or ejaculation between limbs later in law *21:18* because he had in fact already stated their prohibition on the grounds of "wasting seed in vain" in law *21:9*, it is true that this could be argued. But we are not noting Maimonides' silence about them in *21:18* as "proof" that he never mentioned a caution against "wasting seed in vain" in *21:9*; rather we are suggesting that if Maimonides in fact did not intend to assert a prohibition against them in *21:9*, following the second approach of Rabeinu Yitzchak, then the fact that he did not include a prohibition against them in *21:18* either is consistent with Rabeinu Yitzchak's second approach as well.

486 Rabbi Avraham of Montpellier (*Peirush R' Avraham min Hahar*) argues that since Rabbi Yochanan bar Napacha on *Nedarim 20b*, who permits "overturning the table," is the same Rabbi Yochanan who condemns "wasting seed in vain" on *Nidah 13a*, he must have permitted anal intercourse even to married couples only without intra-anal ejaculation. Rabbi Avraham of Montpellier concludes quoting (the questionable manuscript version of) Maimonides' *Mishneh Torah, Isurei Biah 21:9* in support of this.

And see our response to this argument below, pp. 138-142.

487 See *Kovetz Shitos Kamai, Nedarim*, page 183.

488 See *Kovetz Shitos Kamai, Nedarim*, page 183.

489 See *Shas Wagshal-Nehardea, Tractate Sanhedrin, Hagahos v'Chidushim, Sanhedrin 58b* and *59b*.

490 The following opinions either do not mention a restriction on intra-anal ejaculation or ejaculation between limbs, or they can be read to differentiate between anal intercourse and intercourse between limbs, forbidding ejaculation only in the case of the latter.

In the case of Maimonides, we have already explained the difficulties in determining his precise intentions, which is why he is included in this category.

And see the endnotes upon Rabeinu Yonah and Rabeinu Nissim (endnotes 484, 492, 494) explaining why they have been included in this category as well.

491 See above, pp. 60-61 and endnotes thereon.

⁴⁹² At first glance, Rabeinu Nissim in his *Peirush HaRan* appears to equate Maimonides' opinion in *Isurei Biah 21:9* with the first approach of Rabeinu Yitzchok in *Tosfos*, namely that anal sex is permitted only without intra-anal ejaculation.

But in light of our analysis above, endnote 484, we have listed him among those whose opinion on the matter of intra-anal ejaculation remains unclear.

⁴⁹³ See above, endnote 484.

⁴⁹⁴ At first glance, Rabeinu Yonah appears to equate Maimonides' opinion in *Isurei Biah 21:9* with the first approach of Rabeinu Yitzchok in *Tosfos*, namely that anal sex is permitted only without ejaculation.

But in light of our analysis above, endnote 484, we have listed him among those whose opinion on the matter of intra-anal ejaculation remains unclear.

Note also that Rabeinu Yonah in *Sefer Hayirah* (page 17 in the Mesivta Publication Society edition, and in other editions) writes about sex in general only that, "One should be *as careful as he is able (yizaher kefi yecholto)* not to waste seed."

⁴⁹⁵ See *Kovetz Shitos Kamai, Nedarim,* page 187.

⁴⁹⁶ Page 347 in the Kapach edition.

⁴⁹⁷ Page 362 in the Kapach edition.

⁴⁹⁸ See above, endnote 439.

⁴⁹⁹ Pages 8-9. And see below, our study, pp. 125-127.

⁴⁹⁹* Page 81. And see above, page 64 and endnote 252 thereon.

⁵⁰⁰ See also the commentary of a certain *R"I* to *Sheiltot D'Rav Hai Gaon, Ki Teitzei,* page 42 of the Sura-Yeshiva University edition by Rabbi Shmuel Kalman Mirsky. This *R"I* quotes the words of *Tosfos Rid* practically verbatim, though it is not clear who this author was or when and where he lived.

⁵⁰¹ See *Kovetz Shitos Kamai, Sanhedrin* vol. 2, pp. 1081-1082.

⁵⁰² Printed in the back of the Steinsaltz Talmud Hebrew edition and on the Talmud page of the Artscroll English edition.

⁵⁰³ Note that the wording of Rabeinu Asher as quoted in *Hagahos Habach* to *Rosh* and in *Yam Shel Shlomoh* is identical to his wording in *Tosfos HaRosh* to *Yevamos 34b*. But the version of *Hagahos Habach* and *Yam Shel Shlomoh* (and *Beis Yosef*) concludes with an additional passage: a clear ruling endorsing the second approach of Rabeinu Yitzchak, which permits occasional intra-anal ejaculation for the sake of a husband's sexual fulfillment within marriage.

Although *Tosfos HaRosh* to *Yevamos 34b* is missing this "final ruling," *Tosfos HaRosh* to *Nedarim 20a* does corroborate it, by virtue of the fact that Rabeinu Asher, there, offers *only* the logic of the second approach of Rabeinu Yitzchak to reconcile *Yevamos 34b* with *Nedarim 20ab* and *Sanhedrin 58b*. He doesn't offer the logic of Rabeinu Yitzchak's first approach (permitting only anal penetration without intra-anal ejaculation) at all.

[Note that Rabbi Yoel Sirkis in his *Bayis Chadash* commentary to *Tur, Even Haezer 25:2:2:V'R"I Pireish d'afilu...* cites Rabeinu Asher's comments on *Yevamos 34b*, and suggests that Rabeinu Asher not only limited intra-anal ejaculation to "occasion," but that he limited anal penetration without ejaculation to "occasion" as well. He bases this deduction on a minor linguistic difference between Rabeinu Asher's wording and that of Rabeinu Yitzchak in *Tosfos* to *Yevamos 34b*. And he then goes on to attempt to read this meaning into Rabeinu Yitzchak's words as well.

But if Rabbi Sirkis had seen Rabeinu Asher's comments in *Tosfos HaRosh* to *Nedarim 20b*, where the wording in question is almost identical to that of Rabeinu Yitzchak's, it is unlikely Rabbi Sirkis would have read such an interpretation into either Rabeinu Asher's or Rabeinu Yitzchak's words on *Yevamos 34b* (for it is clear that he only attempted to read it into Rabeinu Yitzchak's words after establishing it upon Rabeinu Asher's slightly more supportive wording in *Yevamos*).

And the meaning Rabbi Sirkis attempts to read into Rabbi Yaakov ben Asher's words, there, is arguably questionable as well. See there.]

504 Quoted in *Kovetz Meforshim*, "Leket Rishonim," published by Yerid Haseforim, 2003.

Note that this *Talmid Rabeinu Tam* does not clearly specify the context of intra-anal ejaculation. But from his contrast of "occasional" anal sex, which he permits, with the "constant" anal sex of Er and Onan, which he forbids, it appears obvious that he was coming to permit occasional intra-anal ejaculation.

And see above, endnote 478.

505 See *Kovetz Shitos Kamai, Nedarim 20*, page 188.

505* See Rabbi Moshe Feinstein, *Igros Moshe, Even Haezer 1, Responsum 63*, end of p. 156, top of page 163. And see below, pp. 136-137 and footnote 549 thereon.

**Added note to the third edition:** See also Rabbi Yosef Yuspa Hahn Nordlinger (d. 1637), *Yosef Ometz 192*. Credit goes to Rabbi Yossi Newfield for bringing this source in *Yosef Ometz* to my attention.

506 Rabbi Heller references Rabeinu Asher's ruling permitting occasional intra-anal ejaculation within marriage as if it were practical law.

See also Rabbi Moshe Feinstein in his *Igros Moshe, Even Haezer 1, Responsum 63*, page 157, top of column 1, where he takes it as a given that Rabbi Heller ruled according to Rabeinu Asher in *Lechem (Divrei) Chamudos*.

507 Referenced in *Pischei Teshuvah* to *Shulchan Aruch, Even Haezer 25:2*.

508 Rabbi Betzalel Ashkenazi may be quoting this in the name of *Ritva*.

In any case, he does not word it as Rabeinu Yitzchak and most others do, that intra-anal ejaculation must be performed only "randomly" in the heat of passion (*b'akrai*), but rather he says it should be only "from time-to-time" (*l'pa'amim*). The two wordings, however, are equivalent in meaning: it should be only occasional.

509 See our discussion on Rabbi Caro's halachic and kabbalistic cautions, below, pp. 148-149, based on *Ezer Mekudash* of Rabbi Avraham Dovid Wahrman of Buczacz and *Igros Moshe* of Rabbi Moshe Feinstein.

In regard to Rabbi Feinstein himself, his own personal baseline halachic view on the matter is unclear.

In a responsum dated 1935, published in his *Igros Moshe, Even Haezer vol. 1, Responsum 63*, Rabbi Feinstein is well aware of, and explains at length, Rabeinu Yitzchak's permission of anal sex even with intra-anal ejaculation, and he lists other medieval and post-medieval opinions who agreed with Rabeinu Yitzchak's permission of it. Yet at one point he still calls it "one of the most severe of severe prohibitions" (*isur chamur shebachamurim*. See page 157, column 2, in the responsum there).

However, if one reads the surrounding context of that sentence, it is not at all clear that Rabbi Feinstein was categorically forbidding it by the letter of the law, but rather acknowledging how severe the issue can be in an *unsanctioned* form and/or how extremely polar-opposite the approaches to it can be in halachic literature.

In the following responsum in that volume, dated 1958, Rabbi Feinstein expresses his personal repulsion for intra-anal ejaculation, calling a husband's desire for it "evil and disgusting" (*taavaso haraah v'hamichueres*). Nevertheless, he stops short of calling it "forbidden." (*Igros Moshe, Even Haezer, vol. 1, Responsum 64*, page 164. And see Maimonides' distinction between that which is "distasteful" (*megunah*) and that which is "forbidden," quoted in our study, above, pp. 103-104).

But in a responsum dated 1971, printed in *Igros Moshe, Even Haezer 3, Responsum 28*, page 452, Rabbi Feinstein states that anal sex (to the point of climax) cannot count for a man fulfilling his obligation to satisfy his wife's sexual needs, "because it is forbidden" (*ub'shelo cedarcah barur sheleca b'zeh mitzvas onah, d'ha hu davar ha'asur*). [See above, endnote 268, the view of Rabbi Avraham Dovid Wahrman of Buczacz in this regard.]

The 1971 responsum goes on to innovate that even according Rabeinu Yitzchak, intra-anal ejaculation is not just "permitted, but not holy," it is "permitted, but *less than* not holy."

[Rabbi Feinstein's logic for this is that in *Shulchan Aruch, Even Haezer 25:2*, after discussing Rabeinu Yitzchak's permission of intra-anal ejaculation for couples, Rabbi Isserles writes:

> And even though all these things are permitted, *whoever sanctifies himself in that which is permitted shall be called 'holy.'*

Rabbi Feinstein points to *Biur Hagra*, there, which references the concept of "sanctifying oneself in that which is permitted" on *Babylonian Talmud, Yevamos 20a*. The sage, Rava, on *Yevamos 20a* states that one who upholds the secondary categories of incest that are *legally forbidden by the rabbis* as a safeguard against cases of biblically prohibited incest is considered to have "sanctified himself in that which is *permitted* to him" – even though the secondary categories of incest are *not* actually *permitted* to anyone, because the rabbis *legally forbade* them. And Rava says that one who does *not* uphold such commands of the rabbis is not just called "not holy," he is called "wicked."

Rabbi Feinstein is thus suggesting – albeit not in so many words – that *Biur Hagra* understood Rabbi Isserles as understanding Rabeinu Yitzchak as believing that a husband who performs occasional intra-anal ejaculation with his own wife for the sake of sexual fulfillment within marriage is not only "not holy," but "wicked."

But then Rabbi Feinstein concedes that *Biur Hagra* also references *Shavuos 18b*, where the concept of "sanctification of sex" is brought also in regard to *voluntary* acts of sanctification. This negates Rabbi Feinstein's earlier argument, especially considering that Rabbi Isserles himself states clearly that "all these things are *permitted*," which means that Rabbi Isserles's case (of what he believed to be a biblically and rabbinically *permitted* form of intercourse) is not entirely comparable to Rava's case on *Yevamos 20a* (of rabbinically *forbidden* forms of intercourse). Thus, to take Rava's use of the term "wicked" in regard to one who transgresses a rabbinic *prohibition* and to put it in the mouth of Rabbi Isserles (or Rabeinu Yitzchak) in regard to one who performs what they believed to be the *permissible* act of marital intra-anal ejaculation is arguably difficult to justify.

(Note also that Rabbi Isserles's wording, "whoever sanctifies himself in that which is permitted *shall be called holy (kadosh yomar lo)*," can be read as incorporating the implied view of Abayei on *Yevamos 20a*, that one who upholds the words of the sages "is called holy (*nikra kadosh*)," but one who does not uphold them is *not* necessarily called "wicked.")

Nevertheless, Rabbi Feinstein concludes that Rabbi Isserles believed occasional marital intra-anal ejaculation to be "less than not holy."]

Now, while the 1935 and 1971 responsa are both clearly referring to intra-anal *ejaculation* specifically, not just anal *penetration* in-and-of-itself, and while there are certainly medieval commentaries, including even Maimonides, who suggest that anal sex (and other sexual positions, as well as oral sex) are not necessarily "holy" (see Maimonides' *Mishneh Torah, Isurei Biah 21:9*; and see his *Commentary to the Mishnah, Sanhedrin 7:4* where he calls them "animalistic behaviors" (*dvarim bahami'im*) and where he says that the Sages denigrate (*meganim*) those who *fixate all their thoughts and yearnings* upon them), it cannot go unmentioned that calling anal sex of any kind between husband and wife "disgusting" or "evil" or "wicked" or "less than holy" or "less than not holy" does fly in the face of at least one medieval source – namely, *Tosfos Yeshanim* to *Nedarim 20a*, which interprets "overturning the table" as anal intercourse, and which comments on the ruling of the Sages' there: "Anything a husband craves to do with his wife sexually, he may do – *and there is no lack of holiness.*" [See above, page 68. *Shitah Mekubetzes* quotes the same comment in the name of Rabbi Eliezer of Metz, but it is not clear if Rabbi Eliezer of Metz, too, interpreted the term "overturning the table" as anal intercourse.]

While it is possible *Tosfos Yeshanim* were referring only to anal *penetration* without ejaculation, it is arguably unlikely, considering that it did not specify so, and considering that the majority of other medieval commentaries who interpret "overturning the table" as anal sex believed it to mean anal intercourse even to the point of the husband's climax (compare above, pp. 120-122).

And while *Babylonian Talmud, Sanhedrin 100b* implies that anal sex is not "befitting" (Rashi – *eino hagun*), or that one should not do so because it leads to "wasting seed in vain" (*Yad Ramah*), it is quoting a homiletical interpretation of a passage in the obscure and controversial *Book of Ben Sira*. In any case, nowhere does *Sanhedrin 100b* call anal sex "forbidden," "disgusting" or "evil." And even its assertion about polite and/or respectable and/or befitting behavior would have little, if any, relevance to spouses who both actually enjoy anal sex.

See also Rabbi Yeshayah of Trani II, in his *Kuntres Harayos L'Riaz, Sanhedrin 58b: Amar Rava mi ica midi* (published by Rabbi Yaakov Lifshitz in *Sanhedri Gedolah*, Mechon Fishel 1972), that even if the *Book of Ben Sira* were cautioning against "wasting seed in vain" through anal sex, it does not actually forbid it.

[Parenthetically, in his 1971 responsum Rabbi Feinstein could not possibly have been calling anal *penetration* in-and-of-itself "forbidden," for it is none other than Rava himself – the same Rava he invokes, there, from *Yevamos 20a* calling one who transgresses the instructions of the rabbis, "wicked" – who unequivocally permits anal sex on *Sanhedrin 58b* (which at the very least includes anal penetration). Not only that, but anal intercourse is considered a valid form of consummating marriage (*Babylonian Talmud, Kidushin 9b*; *Mishneh Torah, Sefer Nashim, Ishus 3:5*). Rather, when Rabbi Feinstein calls anal sex "forbidden," there, he was clearly referring to intra-anal ejaculation, as evident from the entire context of the discussion about a husband's obligation to satisfy his wife's sexual needs, a critical component of which, some opinions tell us, is the wife's need to feel her husband ejaculate inside her, and as evident from the fact that Rabbi Feinstein immediately contrasts his statement about "anal sex" being "prohibited" with Rabeinu Yitzchak's permission of *intra-anal ejaculation.*]

In any case, in light of all the above, Rabbi Feinstein's personal opinion in regard to the legal permissibility of occasional intra-anal ejaculation for couples as a matter of sexual fulfillment within marriage requires further investigation.

[510] See below, pp. 164-165 and endnotes 523, 638.

[511] Rashi, *Yevamos 55b: Derech Evarim.*

Regarding Maimonides' definition of the term, see above, footnote to page 103.

And see below, endnote 513.

See also Rabbi Yitzchak Ratzabi, *Shulchan Aruch Hamekutzar, Even Haezer vol. 1,* supplement to Yoreh Deah, Siman 153, footnote 40, pp. 54-55. And see below, endnote 806.

The following citation was kindly shared with me by Rabbi Chaim Rapoport of London, UK from an unpublished article of his:

ראה רש"י סנהדרין סו, ב על 'מעשה חידודים', והיינו 'דרך אברים' (וכמ"ש התוס' יבמות סוד"ה לאחר, בשם רש"י, וכ"כ ברש"י שעל הרי"ף שבת לט, ב. וראה גם מאירי סנהדרין שם) דהיינו ששעושים כמין ינקבי בין עגבותיו (שו"ת גאונים קדמונים סי' קי, [וע"ש שכתב שי"אי אפשר לברר הדבר לגמרי מפני שהוא גנאי"]. ונראה שזוהי כוונת פי' המלבי"ם בבאור המלות למשלי ה, יט שכתב לבאר הפסוק ידדי' ירווך בכל עתי שהכוונה לדדים שלמטה, וכ"כ שם בפי' ליחזקאל כג, ג, והיינו העגבות שנראות כדדים) או בין דדי' (רש"י יבמות שם, ואולי זוהי כוונת הגמ' בכתובות לו, ב ש"מיעך לה **בין** דדיה"), דהיינו שמיעך אברו יבין' דדי') **או בין אצילי ידי'** (ספר הערוך ערך הרדוס) או בין ירכותיו (**שו"ת תורה לשמה סי' רצט**) או בין אצבעות ידי' (המאוחדות ומקובצות יחדיו כאגרוף, אלא ששמשארת מקום מרווח ביניהם כדי כניסת האבר) או בכפיפת זרועה (וכמו"ש ר' תנחום הירושלמי (מחכמי מצרים לאחר תקופת הרמב"ם) בספר המדריך המספיק ערך דרכון, לבאר ענין דרך אברים, בזה"ל: היינו שפועל את התשמיש בחלק מן האברים השקועים, כמו: בית השחי [דהיינו בחור שבין אצילי ידי'], ודיבוק הירכים [בין עגבותיו] או הברך [בין ירכותיי], או כפיפת הזרוע, **או בתוך ידה**, וכדומה מאלו הדברים הבזויים והמזוהמים, עכ"ל, וכל שכן בפיה.

[512] Fellatio. Or in modern slang: a "blowjob."

[513] In modern slang: a "handjob."

See *Sefer Hamaspik* of Rabbi Tanchum Hayerushalmi (14th century), pp. 102-103 in the Toledano edition, *Entry: Darchon*, where Rabbi Tanchum includes in his definition of "intercourse between limbs" penile stimulation against the woman's hand.

Rabbi Tanchum does not call intercourse between limbs "forbidden," though he does degrade it.

[Note that Rabbi Tanchum goes on to say: "In our entry on '*Hordos*' we shall recall that these are among the customs of sinners and hedonists."

But when we turn to the entry on "*Hordos*," we are told about a man who was so perverse that after repeatedly failing to seduce a woman he was infatuated with, he actually dug up her corpse after she died to have sex with it – and, by the way, he also used to engage in intercourse between limbs.

It is therefore implied by the greater context that the "sinners" Rabbi Tanchum was referring to were not having "intercourse between limbs" with their own wives, but with other women (i.e., "adultery by hand or foot" – see above, footnote to page 103). And see footnote 94 in the Toledano edition, that Rabbi Tanchum's attribution of the act of "intercourse between limbs" to Hordos is highly problematic.]

[514] See Rabbi Yehuda Henkin's *Bnei Banim, vol. 4, Responsum 18:3*, where he quotes the opinion of his grandfather, Rabbi Yosef Eliyahu Henkin, that oral intercourse is not considered "intercourse." From the context there, however, it seems that his intention is merely to emphasize that the general legal term "intercourse" applies only to vaginal or anal penetration, and therefore adulterous oral intercourse does not carry the same legal ramifications as adulterous vaginal or anal intercourse. To my understanding, he is not denying that oral intercourse is halachically designated as "intercourse between limbs."

[515] For a lengthy discussion on this, and about ejaculation between one's wife's limbs, see Rabbi Yehuda Henkin's *Bnei Banim vol. 4, Responsum 18*.

[516] See also Rabbi Yehuda Henkin, *Bnei Banim, vol. 4, Responsum 18:5-6*.

[516*] See above, endnote 127.

[517] See also Rabbi Yehoshua Falk, in his *Drishah* commentary to *Tur, Even Haezer 25:2:5-6*, where he states clearly his understanding that Maimonides' source for permitting intercourse between limbs was the ruling of the Sages on *Nedarim 20b*.

But Rabbi Falk, there, is commenting on Rabbi Yaakov ben Asher's version of *Mishneh Torah*, which has Maimonides permitting intercourse between limbs only without ejaculation.

Nevertheless, Rabbi Falk goes on to explain that Rabeinu Yitzchak learns from the Sages' ruling on *Nedarim 20b* that both intra-anal ejaculation and ejaculation between limbs are permitted to married couples on occasion.

[518] As for the Talmud on *Nidah 13b* suggesting that intercourse between limbs was a sin, or *the* sin, of the Generation of the Flood, that, too, would be referring to *constant* extra-vaginal ejaculation for the sake of unsanctioned birth control, not occasional ejaculation between limbs for the sake of the husband's (or couple's) sexual bonding and/or fulfillment. And this is obviously how Rabbi Yehoshuah Falk understood Rabeinu Yitzchak's opinion on the matter, as he explains in his *Drishah* commentary to *Tur, Even Haezer 23:1:1* and *25:2:5-6*.

Now, the notion that the Generation of the Flood was destroyed for "wasting seed in vain" is generally invoked to admonish against masturbation – based on statements found in *Talmud, Nidah 13a*, in *Callah Rabti 2:8*, and in numerous places in the *Zohar*.

But this is arguably highly questionable.

A complete survey of the midrashic sources shows that the Generation of the Flood was reportedly liable for a great diversity of practices, including, but not limited to:

1. Idolatry (*Breishis Rabah 28:9, 31:6; Midrash Agadah, Parshas Noach 6:11; Midrash HaGadol, Noach 6:11; Tanna Devei Eliyahu Zuta, ch. 10; Midrash Lekach Tov, Noach 6:12, 6:13*)

2. Murder (*Breishis Rabah 31:6; Midrash Agadah, Parshas Noach 6:11; Midrash HaGadol, Noach 6:11; Tanna Devei Eliyahu Zuta, ch. 10; Pirkei D'Rabbi Eliezer, ch. 22; Midrash Lekach Tov, Noach 6:13*)

3. Theft (*Sanhedrin 108a; Breishis Rabah 31:1, 31:2, 31:3, 31:4, 31:5; Midrash Agadah, Parshas Noach 6:11; Midrash Tanchuma, Noach 4; Midrash HaGadol, Introduction to Parshas Noach; Midrash HaGadol, Noach 6:11; Tanna Devei*

# ENDNOTES

      *Eliyahu Zuta, ch. 10; Pirkei D'Rabbi Eliezer, ch. 22; Midrash Lekach Tov, Breishis 6:5; Midrash Lekach Tov, Noach 6:13)*

4. Magic (*Midrash Tanchuma, Breishis 12; Midrash HaGadol, Breishis 6:5*)

5. Adultery – initiated by both men and women, and including kidnap, rape, spouse-swapping, nudism and incest (*Sanhedrin 108a; Breishis Rabah 26:5, 26:7, 31:1, 31:2, 31:6; Midrash Agadah, Parshas Breishis 6:2, Midrash Agadah, Parshas Noach 6:11, 7:4; Midrash Tanchuma, Breishis 12; Midrash Tanchuma, Noach 12; Pirkei Drabbi Eliezer, chapter 22, chapter 24; Sifri, Behaalotecha 86; Sifri Zuta, Behaalosecha, 11:4 (Torah Shleimah, Breishis page 369); "Midrash" quoted in Torah Shleimah page 371, on verse 6:2, entry 13; Midrash HaGadol, Breishis 6:2, 6:4, 6:5, Introduction to Parshas Noach, 6:11, 6:17; Tanna Devei Eliyahu Zuta, ch. 10; "Midrashic manuscript" quoted in Torah Shleimah pg. 396 #144; "Midrash Yilamdenu" quoted in Torah Shleimah pg. 398 #149; Midrash Lekach Tov, Breishis 6:2, Midrash Lekach Tov, Noach 6:12, 6:13*)

6. Homosexuality (*Breishis Rabah 26:5; Midrash HaGadol, Noach 6:11; Midrash Lekach Tov, Breishis 6:2. Breishis Rabah*, ibid, may be speaking specifically about homosexual *marriage*. See its commentaries there. And see *Talmud, Chulin 92ab*.)

7. Bestiality (*Sanhedrin 108a; Breishis Rabah 26:5; Midrash Agadah, Parshas Noach 6:12; Midrash Tanchuma, Noach 5; Midrash Tanchuma, Noach 12; Midrash HaGadol, Noach 6:11, 6:13; Midrash Lekach Tov, Breishis 6:2. Breishis Rabah*, ibid, may be speaking specifically about *marriage* to animals. See its commentaries there.)

Thus, according to rabbinic tradition destruction was decreed upon that generation for much graver infractions than masturbation.

And although midrashim do throw into the mix a "sin" of "wasting seed in vain," the context of this was arguably not masturbation, but, like the case of Er and Onan, a matter of constant, intentional, unsanctioned birth control.

According to the tradition of the Tannaitic sage, Rabbi Levi, as quoted in *Pirkei D'Rabbi Eliezer, Chapter 22, Breishis Rabsi* to *Genesis 6:12* and *Midrash HaGadol, Genesis 6:12*, Noah had warned the generation to mend their ways lest G-d punish them and force them to witness the annihilation of their children. The people thus brazenly responded that they would simply no longer have children. And ever after, whenever they would have sex, the husbands would pull out of their wives and spill their seed to the ground – that is, they would perform *constant coitus interruptus with the specific intention of perpetual birth control*. Perhaps, with same intention, they would also perform *constant* intra-anal ejaculation or ejaculation between limbs or even masturbation – but all as a means to satisfy themselves sexually *without ever having to bear children*.

[The fact that *Pirkei D'Rabbi Eliezer* reports this is especially significant, considering that it is, according to some, the earliest extant work of Tannaitic literature, and that its authorship is attributed by some to (the school of) Rabbi Eliezer ben Hyrcanus – the same Rabbi Eliezer reported on *Babylonian Talmud, Nidah 13a* arguing to the Sages that grasping hold of one's own shaft during urination is tantamount to causing a flood upon the earth because it might cause sexual arousal and thus lead to "wasted seed" through masturbation and ejaculation (or perhaps even through resultant involuntary seminal emission of pre-ejaculate – to be discussed in volume two of this series; and see below, endnotes 593, 816). If, at the time of this argument to the Sages, Rabbi Eliezer himself was already aware of the historical tradition that the sin of the Generation of the Flood in regard to "wasting seed in vain" had nothing to do with masturbation, but with constant unsanctioned birth control, then perhaps we can understand his concern about masturbation as a legal safeguard, a "fence," around the actual problematic behavior, unsanctioned birth control. And in that case, his argument that one should not even grasp hold of the shaft while urinating would perhaps be legally considered a "fence around a fence."

Alternatively, being that this tradition is quoted in both *Pirkei D'Rabbi Eliezer* and in *Breishis Rabsi* in the name of the Tannaitic sage, Rabbi Levi, who lived and taught three generations after Rabbi Eliezer ben Hyrcanus, it is possible that this tradition was added into *Pirkei D'Rabbi Eliezer* at a later date and was in fact unknown to Rabbi Eliezer himself.

For more on the authorship of *Pirkei D'Rabbi Eliezer* according to rabbinic sources, see the *Kuntres Hamevo* in the 2006 Zichron Aharon edition of *Pirkei D'Rabbi Eliezer*.]

*Meam Loez, Genesis 6:1* has a different twist on this narrative, saying that the people's manner of avoiding pregnancy was through constant homosexuality and/or bestiality.

*Callah Rabti 2:7* (M. Higger edition) offers another interpretation: Astrologers had told the generation that it was written in the stars that mankind would exist upon the earth for at least 6,000 years. Because of this belief, the people decided not to have any more children, thinking that this would force G-d to allow them to live for all 6,000 years and enable them to enjoy all the benefits of creation for themselves. And so they began to engage in perpetual coitus interruptus.

[Note that this specific passage of *Callah Rabti 2:7* implies that the problem with such behavior was that the adults of the generation inflated their own place in the history of the world – the fact that seed was being "wasted" appears to be of secondary concern. And even when the author of the passage goes on to equate their actions with those of Er and Onan, the implication remains that Er and Onan's sin, too, was the inflation of their own self worth.]

In any case, if the generation as a whole were in fact practicing permanent birth control, and thus actually (intentionally or unintentionally) threatening the very survival of the human race, this might shed a new light on the notion that the Generation of the Flood "sealed its fate" in the Creator's mind on account of their "wasting seed in vain."

[Note also that the collective interpretations of *Pirkei D'Rabbi Eliezer*, *Breishis Rabsi*, *Midrash HaGadol* and *Callah Rabti* appear to address the two main concerns expressed to this day by those who intentionally choose to never have children: fear of seeing their children suffer and/or fear of diminishing their own enjoyment of life – though in the case of *Pirkei D'Rabbi Eliezer*, *Breishis Rabsi*, and *Midrash HaGadol*, it is implied that the potential suffering of the children could have been avoided by the repentance of the parents (and perhaps the same applies today to some extent, if the adults of society would actively and collectively repair the ills of society), and in the case of *Callah Rabti*, it appears to have been talking at a time when G-d wished to see the world become populated, per His original blessing and command to Adam and Eve: "be fruitful and multiply and fill the earth and conquer it," whereas today it is perhaps arguable that mankind as a whole has fulfilled this commandment sufficiently, such that not every couple need attempt to bear children – to be discussed further in Volume Two of this series. And see above, pp. 91-92, that according to some sources, only those who are halachicaly obligated to procreate are prohibited against "wasting seed."]

Even *Avos D'Rabbi Noson, Chapter 32*, which reports the people of the Generation of the Flood mourning, "Woe is to us for we annihilated our seed," has an alternate version of the text, which reads, "Woe is to us for we annihilated our seed *from the earth*" (though even the first version is not clearly referring to "wasting seed in vain").

And although the Babylonian Talmud in three places – *Rosh Hashanah 12a, Sanhedrin 108b* and *Zevachim 113b* – suggests that the generation was punished with "hot, thick water" measure-for-measure for their transgressions through "hot, thick semen," there is no proof that this reference was about masturbation or extra-vaginal ejaculation in particular, for there were enough *other* forms of sexual behavior going on – involving "hot, thick semen" – for which this punishment might have been said to be justified "measure for measure." And see *Avnei Nezer, Even Haezer, Hilchos Ishus 79:7*, which supports this logic. See also the concluding passage of *Tosfos Hashalem al HaTorah, Noach 6:13:6:Ci Malah Haaretz Chamas*, p. 205, implying that the "hot, thick water" was a punishment for illicit sexuality in general (*znus*).

What is more, Genesis 6:1-2 relates:

> 1. And it came to pass, as man began to increase upon the face of the earth, and daughters were born to them, 2. that the *bnei elohim* saw the daughters of man, that they were beautiful, and they took for themselves wives from whomever they so chose.

*Breishis Rabah 26:4* explains:

> "To increase upon the face of the earth" – that is, they would spill their seed upon trees and stones, and because they were steeped in prostitution, therefore G-d ensured that more girls would be born to them [than boys].

Rabbi Ze'ev Wolf Einhorn of Grodno/Vilna (d. 1862), in his *Maharzu* commentary to *Midrash Rabah*, does not ask, but by implication addresses, the obvious: What does men "wasting seed" – whether through masturbation, coitus interruptus or in the course of prostitution – have to do with G-d causing there to be an increase in the birth rate of females?

Rabbi Einhorn explains:

> Through the sin of Adam, their [mankind's] sexual desire became increased, as stated in *Breishis Rabah 23:5*. It was overwhelming in their bodies, and [in order to release the excess sexual energy] they would destroy their seed [that is, they would masturbate] upon the ground, upon trees and stones.

> And to rectify this, G-d gave them a surplus of females. But they sinned even with these, taking wives from whomever they so chose – stealing wives from one another.

The implication of this is that G-d did not punish men for masturbating, nor did He even hold it against them or expect them to abstain from it. On the contrary, He understood and empathized with them, and attempted to give them a constructive outlet (in that society, and in that time, through polygamy).

The authors of the *Eitz Yosef* and *Eshed Hanechalim* commentaries to *Breishis Rabah* offer similar interpretations.

[Note that a post-medieval authority, Rabbi Avraham Dovid Wahrman of Buczacz, in his *Ezer Mekudash* commentary to *Shulchan Aruch, Even Haezer 23, 25* and *76*, and in his *Mili D'Chasidusa* commentary to *Sefer Chasidim 176*, theorizes that the severity spoken of by *Talmud, Nidah 13ab* against "wasting seed" through masturbation only applied in earlier generations when a man could marry more than one wife and thus he always had a constructive outlet for his sexual energy, even when one wife was menstrually impure. But today, Rabbi Avraham Dovid argues, after the decree of Rabeinu Gershom prohibiting

Jewish polygamy, and with Jews living in non-Jewish lands that prohibit polygamy even for non-Jews, and with cases where young men and women are forced to delay marriage simply because they cannot afford to establish a home (*c'she'einam yecholim l'hashvos es atzmam b'nedunia - Ezer Mekudash, Even Haezer 25:2:Beis Shmuel:2*), the severity spoken of by the Talmud against "wasting seed" through masturbation does not apply on the same level.

In one place, Rabbi Avraham Dovid actually concedes that it is difficult to argue a logical distinction between intra-anal ejaculation for a husband's pleasure and self-masturbation for pleasure – and that if the former is permitted, one at least cannot be blamed for making the "mistake" of thinking the latter to be permitted as well.

In any case, Rabbi Avraham Dovid's comments on the above three sources are developed in three separate contexts: masturbation as a sexual outlet, masturbation as a means of avoiding worse sexual behaviors (such as adultery), and masturbation as a means of checking male potency. I have merely attempted, here, to summarize some key points he raises in these three contexts combined. But in all three, Rabbi Avraham Dovid stops short of unreservedly permitting masturbation.]

Thus, all the early and later texts (including *Talmud, Nidah 13ab*, *Callah Rabti*, the *Book of Zohar*, etcetera) that point to the Generation of the Flood as "proof" of the "severity" of masturbation require serious reevaluation. At the very least, people should know that there appears to exist an alternate midrashic view, that whatever "wasting seed in vain" that generation may have been punished for, it had nothing at all to do with masturbation in-and-of-itself as a part of innocent psychological-emotional-physical development or sexual/stress relief.

[Relevant to this entire discussion is a principle that we do not generally derive Jewish law from midrashic works, at least not when a midrashic version of things contradicts a Talmudic version. For sources on this topic, see *Encyclopedia Talmudis, vol. 1, Entry: Agadah, Section 4: Ein Lomdin Me'Agadah*; *Sdei Chemed, vol. 1*, pp. 40 (subsections 95-97) and 51 (subsection 150); Rabbi Ovadia Yosef, *Yabia Omer vol. 8, Even Haezer 21:2* (credit goes to Rabbi Yossi Newfield for bringing this source in *Yabia Omer* to my attention). The basis and parameters of this principle, and if or how it applies to the present discussion about "wasting seed in vain," shall be explored in volume two of this series. One point we shall consider is whether the midrashic versions we have discussed are truly contradictory to *all* related discussions in the Talmud – and if we can find even a single Talmudic version that is in congruence with them, then it can perhaps be argued that it is a matter of dispute within the Talmud itself. To this point, note that our entire discussion in this endnote was sparked by the passage in *Talmud, Nidah 13b* which speaks of (constant) intercourse between limbs, not masturbation, as the sin of the Generation of the Flood. Note also that as discussed above, this endnote, *Pirkei D'Rabbi Eliezer 22* (considered by some a Tannaitic source) as well as *Callah Rabti 2:7* both already describe the "wasting of seed" of the Generation of the Flood in the context of coitus interruptus for the sake of constant intentional unsanctioned birth control.

And the Talmud itself, in *Yevamos 34b*, describes the "wasting of seed" of Er and Onan in the context of anal sex, while *Breishis Rabah 85:5* describes it in the context of coitus interruptus – both, again, for the sake of constant intentional unsanctioned birth control. This is especially pertinent, being that the entire premise that the Generation of the Flood "wasted seed in vain" is generally assumed to be derived from a textual equivalence between Genesis 6:11-12 (*"vatishaches"-"nishchasah"-"hishchis,"* in the episode of the flood) and Genesis 38:9 (*"shicheis,"* in the episode of Er and Onan). It is thus arguably implicit that the context of "wasting seed in vain" in both episodes was the same. [See also Rabbi Menachem Kasher, *Torah Shleimah vol. 1*, Genesis 6:12, entry and footnote 150; *Tosfos Hashalem al*

*HaTorah, Noach 6:11:2:Vatishaches Haaretz*, p. 202, *Vayeshev 38:9:13:V'shicheis Artzah*, p. 66.]

In regard to questionable representations about the episode of Er and Onan itself and its relevance to the issue of masturbation, see above, endnote 335.

And see *Atzei Arazim, Even Haezer 23:1*, quoted also in *Otzar Haposkim, Even Haezer 23*, page 180 (90b), that the implication from the story of Er and Onan that "wasting seed in vain" is a most severe sin is only in regard to coitus interuptus for the sake of intentional unsanctioned birth control, not self-masturbation for the sake of pleasure. Note, however, that the author of *Atzei Arazim*, there, is actually attempting to relegate the *Zohar's* harsh condemnations of "wasting seed in vain" to a context of coitus interruptus – even though the *Zohar* itself does clearly include masturbation in its harsh condemnations (see below, p. 143). Still, the author of *Atzei Arazim* is objectively correct in relegating the "wasting seed in vain" of Er and Onan to the context of intentional unsanctioned birth control.]

The wider topic of "wasting seed in vain" and masturbation (including the related matters of involuntary emission of pre-ejaculate and nocturnal emissions), all the beliefs and threats said about them in the rabbinic texts, the various rabbinic derivations (*asmachtos*) upon which they are based, and the innumerable questions that must be raised about them all from halachic, midrashic and scientific perspectives, will be the dedicated subject of volume two of this series. And see above, footnote to page 3, and below, endnote 524.

But getting back to the issue of ejaculation between limbs specifically, if ejaculation between limbs were in fact considered by G-d to be a sin of the Generation of the Flood, as *Nidah 13b* suggests, we can reasonably say that it was all in the context of *constant* and *intentional* unsanctioned birth control, not in the context of occasional sexual fulfillment between loving husband and wife.

And this would also be the explanation of the passages found in *Pirkei Rabeinu Hakadosh 5:2* (see *Yalkut Midrashim vol. 1*, Eden Deshe, 2009) and *Halachos Gedolos* (Rome edition, page 588), which state that anal sex is a cause of flood in the world – they would be referring only to intra-anal ejaculation as a constant, intentional means of unsanctioned birth control. (Note also that *Pirkei Rabeinu Hakadosh* may only be speaking about anal sex with one's *menstruating* wife.)

See also end of *Levush, Orach Chaim 240:4*, which implies that *constant* intra-anal ejaculation would be tantamount to the sin of the Generation of Flood, whereas *occasional* intra-anal ejaculation would not. The same line of reasoning would therefore arguably apply to constant versus occasional ejaculation between limbs.

[Note that *Eliyahu Rabah*, middle of Chapter 18, tells a story about an entire yeshivah of 18-20 year old rabbinical students supposedly wiped out by G-d because they "would do ugly, innapropriate, corrupt things with one another, and they would 'waste seed in vain.'" But a careful reading between the lines of the story suggests that there was something much more heinous going on, involving the sexual molestation of young children. And more on this in volume two of this series.]

[519] *Tur, Even Haezer 23:1:1* and *25:2:5-6*.

In *Tur, Even Haezer 25:2*, Rabbi Yaakov ben Asher quotes the opinion of Maimonides (that he had access to) followed by the opinion of Rabeinu Yitzchak:

> A man's wife is permitted to him. Therefore, anything a man craves to do with his wife sexually, he may do: He may have intercourse with her whenever he wants, and kiss any part of her body he wants, and he may have intercourse with her vaginally, anally or between limbs, as long as he does not waste seed in vain.

> And Rabeinu Yitzchak explains that anal intercourse is permitted even to the point of [intra-anal] ejaculation, as long as one does not make a habit of it constantly, but only does it "randomly" [in the heat of passion] out of a desire to have anal sex with his wife. But it is forbidden to do constantly.

Commenting on various phrases of Rabbi Yaakov ben Asher's passage (underlined below), Rabbi Falk writes in footnotes 5 and 6:

> Or between limbs – He [Maimonides] learns this [permission for intercourse between limbs] from the end of chapter 2 of *Nedarim* [*20a*]:
>
> > Rabbi Yochanan ben Dahavai said, "Why are some lame, etcetera"...
>
> > Rabbi Yochanan [bar Napacha] said, "That is the view of Rabbi Yochanan ben Dahavai, but the Sages said the law does not follow Rabbi Yochanan ben Dahavai, rather anything a husband craves to do with his wife sexually, he may do."
>
> As long as he does not waste seed in vain – [Maimonides makes this stipulation] because we learn in *Nidah 13a*:
>
> > Rabbi Yochanan said, "One who wastes his seed in vain deserves death [by the hand of Heaven]."
>
> And we learn that anal intercourse was the sin of Er and Onan [and Maimonides understood their sin to be intra-anal ejaculation as opposed to anal penetration in-and-of-itself, without ejaculation].
>
> But Rabeinu Yitzchak explains that the Sages' ruling [on *Nedarim 20b*] that 'anything a husband craves to do with his wife sexually, he may do,' implies that even [if he performs anal intercourse] to the point of ejaculation [*lit.* to the point of "wasting seed in vain"] there is nothing wrong with it, as long as it is not constant as was the case with Er and Onan, where it was their specific intention [to destroy their seed as a means of constant unsanctioned birth control.]
>
> And Rabeinu Asher writes the same [as Rabeinu Yitzchak].
>
> [Here Rabbi Falk quotes a halachic caution – but not prohibiton – of Rabbi Yosef Caro against "wasting seed in vain," to be discussed below, pp. 138-149]
>
> And Rabeinu Yitzchak explains that anal intercourse is permitted even to the point of [intra-anal] ejaculation – The logic of Rabeinu Yitzchak is as we've explained.
>
> And from here we can deduce that any form of intercourse that is not in the usual manner of nature [i.e., that is not vaginal], is included in the term [that is generally used for anal intercourse,] "*shelo cedarcah*" [which translates literally as "*unnatural intercourse*"], for Rabeinu Yitzchak [himself] would agree that intercourse between limbs is also permitted, and he understood it to be included in the term "unnatural intercourse."

Two chapters earlier, in *Tur, Even Haezer 23:1*, Rabbi Yaakov ben Asher quotes Maimonides ruling from *Isurei Biah 21:18*:

> It is forbidden to waste seed in vain. Therefore, a person should not perform coitus interruptus.

Rabbi Falk comments in footnote 1:

## ENDNOTES

<u>It is forbidden to waste seed in vain, etcetera</u> – It is obvious that Rabeinu Yitzchak agrees with this. For even though our master [Rabbi Yaakov ben Asher] quotes in his [Rabeinu Yitzchak's] name at the beginning of chapter 25 that it is permitted to have intercourse with one's wife even anally and even between limbs and even to the point of ejaculation, it is different, there, for [in those two cases] the ejaculation [*lit.* the 'wasting of seed in vain'] occurs as a natural consequence of the intercourse and he has no specific intention to 'waste seed in vain' [that is, he has no specific intention for unsanctioned birth control]. In the case of coitus interruptus, however, it is obvious that his intention is to 'waste seed in vain' [for the sake of (unsanctioned) birth control].

[520] *Drishah* to *Tur, Even Haezer 23:1:1*.

[521] According to Rabbi Moshe Feinstein, Rabbi Yaakov ben Asher actually rules according to Rabeinu Yitzchak in regard to intra-anal ejaculation – as Rabbi Yaakov's father, Rabeinu Asher, did before him (see *Igros Moshe, Even Haezer 1, Responsum 63*, page 156, bottom of column 2 and page 163, top of column 1; and see above, endnote 505*, reference to *Yosef Ometz*).

Therefore, if Rabbi Yaakov ben Asher ruled the law permitting intra-anal ejaculation, and he in fact understood this as including ejaculation between limbs as well, then we would have Rabbi Yaakov ben Asher himself permitting the latter.

And further research into the matter is required.

[522] Just as in *Tur, Orach Chaim 240:2-4:9* Rabbi Falk interprets Raavad III's understanding of the term "overturning the table" as meaning *occasional* rear-entry vaginal intercourse, but Rabbi Falk does not indicate in any way that he himself ruled according to Raavad III.

And see above, endnote 478.

[523] See below, pp. 138-149, in regard to Rabbi Yosef Caro's halachic caution in *Beis Yosef* to *Tur, Even Haezer 25* and his kabbalistic caution in *Bedek Habayis* there.

Rabbi Falk's master, Rabbi Moshe Isserles, clearly permits intra-anal-ejaculation within marriage for the sake of sexual fulfillment – even though Rabbi Isserles himself certainly saw the halachic caution of Rabbi Caro in *Beis Yosef*.

Rabbi Isserles presumably did not see Rabbi Caro's kabbalistic caution in *Bedek Habayis*, it having been published only after Rabbi Isserles's death. Rabbi Falk, on the other hand, was alive when *Bedek Habayis* was printed. But if Rabbi Falk saw this kabbalistic caution of Rabbi Caro in *Bedek Habayis*, he certainly does not mention it in his *Drishah* commentary.

We therefore have no reason to believe that as a matter of baseline practical law Rabbi Falk ever contradicted his master's – and Rabeinu Yitzchak's – permissive view in regard to intra-anal ejaculation for the sake of sexual fulfillment within marriage. And, as discussed, he went on to extend Rabeinu Yitzchak's view – upon which the view of his master, Rabbi Isserles, was based – to include permission for ejaculation between limbs (for the sake of sexual fulfillment within marriage) as well. See above, endnote 519, and below, pp. 124-125, 164-165. And see below, endnote 638.

See also the author of *Rosh Pinah–Ikvei Habayis, Shulchan Aruch, Even Haezer 25:2:3*, who quotes and clarifies Rabbi Falk's view of Rabeinu Yitzchak's opinion as stated in *Drishah*, though it is not clear if he himself is actually endorsing it.

[524] See *Encyclopedia Talmudis vol. 34, Entry: Lo Tinaf*, footnotes 95-96, that some latter-day authorities claim the act of masturbating itself is problematic even without ejaculation – for

in regard to masturbation there are two concerns expressed in rabbinic writing: one that it involves "wasting seed in vain," the other that it is a form of pseudo-adultery of which the act of "penetration" in and of itself is a concern.

[And note that *Callah Rabti 2:6* (M. Higger edition) describes one who masturbates as both "penetrator and penetratee" – though the concern expressed about this in that particular passage of *Callah Rabti* is that the person "arouses the evil inclination upon himself," it does not say that there is any literal connection to the commandment of "*lo tinaf.*" And the meaning of "evil inclination," there, remains to be determined – perhaps it refers to intentional arousing of the inclination for sake of illicit fantasy, not to masturbation that results from the body's natural inclination (and need) for regular orgasm and/or ejaculation.]

To be addressed at length in volume two of this series. And see above, footnote to page 3.

In the meantime, note that *Babylonian Talmud, Nidah 13ab* cites a number of biblical verses that certain sages interpreted as hinting to the evils of "wasting seed in vain" – interpretations that could perhaps potentially be superseded by reinterpretations of a future Sanhedrin (see *Mishneh Torah, Sefer Shoftim, Memrim 2:1* – to be explored further in volume two of this series). These interpretations, which are generally invoked by later rabbinic texts to caution against masturbation specifically, are cited alongside other rabbinical statements about "wasting seed in vain" – in the following order, and with the following suggested possible responses, **for further research and discussion**:

1. "If one grasps hold of his shaft during urination it is tantamount to bringing flood upon the earth."

See above, endnote 518, the debatable basis of this assertion. And see below, endnote 818.

2. <u>Genesis 38:10</u>: "And what he [Onan] did was evil in the eyes of G-d, and He put him to death also."

As explained above, endnote 335, the Bible does not tell us that Onan or his elder brother, Er, "wasted seed" through masturbation. It tells us only that they spilled their seed to the ground in the course of regular marital sex, through constant coitus interuptus and/or intra-anal ejaculation with the express intention of *perpetual* unsanctioned birth control.

And see there, in endnote 335, other elements of "evil" that can be said to have been at play.

3. <u>Isaiah 57:5</u>: "Those who became warmed by the wood of the elm trees, under every leafy tree; the slaughterers of children in the valleys, under the clefts of rocks." This refers to some manner of sexual activity ("they became warmed"), perhaps even orgies, performed in association with idol worship ("under every leafy tree"), the practice of which, the verse tells us, sometimes included human sacrifice (see Rashi on Isaiah 57:5; Rashi on Jeremiah 7:31; Deuteronomy 12:2, employing the same phrase, "under every leafy tree," in relation to Canaanite idolatry, and 12:31 in relation to Canaanite human sacrifice; Kings I 14:23, with the phrase "under every leafy tree" in relation to Canaanite idolatry and leading into verse 24 about prostitution; Kings I 15:12, speaking of idolatry and prostitution (*kedeshim*) in tandem. Kings II 23:6-7, possibly associating the idol worship of Asherah with prostitution (*kedeshos*); Jeremiah 3:6, with the phrase "under every leafy tree" in relation to Canaanite idolatry – in this case euphemistically referred to as adultery – and again in 3:13; Hosea 4:12-14, with the same term "elm tree" in relation to places dedicated for idolatrous sacrifice, and speaking of men secluding themselves with prostitutes (*zonos*) and sacrificing alongside prostitutes (*kedeshos*)).

One or two sages quoted on *Nidah 13a* interpret the phrase "slaughterers of children" as a hint that "wasting seed" is tantamount to murder (presumably on account of its juxtaposition to the phrase "they became warmed," which is understood here to connote sexual arousal). Another sage interprets the juxtaposition of the phrases "they became warmed" and "under every leafy tree" as hinting that "wasting seed" is tantamount to idolatry.

But whatever "wasting of seed" such murderous idolatrous practices involved, we have no reason to believe it involved masturbation specifically. It just as likely, if not more likely, involved adulterous vaginal intercourse culminating in extra-vaginal ejaculation (coitus interruptus, to avoid pregnancy), or adulterous anal intercourse and intra-anal ejaculation, or adulterous intercourse and ejaculation between limbs (and see above, footnote to page 103).

See *Mishnas Rabbi Eliezer (ben Rabbi Yossi Haglili)*, end of *Parshah 18*, invoking the verse in Isaiah 57:5 in relation to homosexual activity specifically, and not mentioning it at all in its subsequent discussion, there, about masturbation.

And see above, footnote to p. 144, that the comparison of masturbation to any of the three cardinal sins is hyperbolic.

4. "One who deliberately brings himself to erection is, or should be, excommunicated; and/or he is considered a transgressor, for such is the craft of the evil inclination – today it tells a person to do one thing, the next day it tells him to do another thing, and the third day it tells him to go serve idols – and he will serve them."

See below, endnote 718, that this arguably refers only to *compulsive* masturbation – i.e., a form of sexual addiction. And see below, this endnote, point 9.

[Note also that the comment that one who deliberately brings himself to erection is, or should be, excommunicated, is quoted in the name of Rav – the same Rav discussed on *Hagigah 5b, Shabbos 152a, Yoma 18b, Yevamos 37b*, and in *Tosfos, Yevamos 37b:Yichuda b'alma havu meyachdi*.]

5. Psalms 5:5: "For You are not a G-d Who desires wickedness, no evil sojourns with You." One sage draws a connection between the use of the word "evil" in this verse and the appearance of the same word in the verse cited above, this endnote, point 2, regarding Onan, and concludes that anyone who deliberately brings himself to sexual thought will not be welcomed into the domain of the Holy One, blessed be He.

Quite aside from the fact that the word "evil" can have myriad meanings, the account recorded in Genesis 38 does not suggest at all that Onan actively brought himself to sexual thought. Whatever his transgression was, a simple reading of the verses implies that it was done in the course of regular marital sex with his wife.

[Parenthetically, it would not be surprising if many innocent readers have walked away from this passage on *Nidah 13b* with the impression that sexual thought itself is "evil" – yet another psychologically-emotionally-physically-spiritually damaging impression. The same impression could be derived from another teaching found in the Talmud in *Tractate Avodah Zarah 20b*. We shall reexplore and clarify both these passages further in volume two of this series. In the meantime, note that *Talmud, Brachos 57a* suggests that wet dreams involving fantasies of incest and adultery are actually signs of psychological-emotional maturing. Perhaps this was originally said specifically in reference to adolescents during puberty. But clearly, the Talmudic sages' views about sexual thought were complex.]

6. Isaiah 1:15: "Your hands are full of bloods (*damim*)." One sage interprets the plural form of "bloods" as speaking not only about actual murder, but hinting also to "those who commit adultery with their hands" – presumably self-masturbation – and who therefore "waste" ("murder") their own seed ("blood").

But the fact remains that this verse has no implied sexual context at all. And it is debatable if the plural form of "bloods" truly does require any unusual explanation or justification.

And see above, footnote to p. 144, that the comparison of masturbation to any of the three cardinal sins is hyperbolic.

And see next point.

7. Exodus 20:13: "Do not commit adultery" – one of the Ten Commandments. The verse is interpreted: "There should not be adultery amongst you, whether by hand or by leg" (*bein b'yad, bein b'regel*). The common assumption is that the sage was speaking against masturbation – as *Tosfos* comments: "He rubs his membrum against hand or leg."

But *Tosfos* does not actually specify *whose* hand or leg. It can thus very well have been referring to the hand or leg of a forbidden woman – certainly a soft form of "adultery."

*Tosfos Chachmei Angliah* in fact interprets "leg," here, as "fooling around with [forbidden] women" (*she'sochakin im nashim derech niuf*) – presumably including adulterous intercourse between limbs.

According to another medieval commentator, albeit in a different context, there is precedent in the Talmud itself to understand the term "leg" as a euphemism for actual vaginal intercourse (see *Babylonian Talmud, Eruvin 100b, Rashi: B'raglaim*).

It is therefore perhaps possible to understand this sage's interpretation as speaking not about self-masturbation, but about adulterous sexual behavior between two people whether it involves actual intercourse or is limited to sexual touching – "soft adultery."

[Some point to the fact that while Exodus 20:13 speaks against "adultery," it does not actually mention "adultery *with a woman*." Therefore, they argue, G-d meant to include "solo-adultery" – i.e., masturbation – in the Ten Commandments. But it is equally reasonable, or perhaps more reasonable, to say that this commandment was simply spoken generally and succinctly, just like its neighboring commandments against murder and theft. And there is strong basis to say that the Hebrew term for adultery – *niuf* – by definition always means the illicit act of a man and (married) woman together (see *Torah Shleimah, Yisro, Exodus 20:13, Sections 341-342* and footnotes thereon, pp. 104-105).

But even accepting the view of those who understand the term "*niuf*" in this verse as referring to *any* illicit union, the simple context is arguably between *two* living beings. At the very least, according to this latter approach, the original logic for including masturbation within the verse would become all the more tenuous, for then it would be obvious why G-d did not specify "Do not commit adultery *with a woman*" – because the commandment, according to this approach, encompasses also illicit unions of men with *men*, and men or women with *animals*. One would therefore be forced to derive masturbation's status as a form of "adultery" from an entirely separate source.

For further research, see *Encyclopedia Talmudis vol. 34, Entry: Lo Tinaf, footnotes 30-39, 83-93*).]

[An additional note: The wording of the sage's interpretation, "'Do not commit adultery' – there should not be adultery amongst you, **whether** by hand or by leg (*bein b'yad, bein b'regel*)," is also perhaps curious, for, read literally, it implies that the base commandment, "Do not commit adultery," encompasses *only* that which is performed "by hand or by leg," not that which is done "by intercourse." This would of course be preposterous. But if the wording of the interpretation were, "Do not commit adultery . . . *even* by hand or by leg" (*afilu b'yad, afilu b'regel*), adultery "by intercourse" would have at least been intrinsically implied. Perhaps, then, the sage's choice of wording, "*whether* by hand or by leg," lends further support to the possibility that he used the term "leg" as a euphemism for illicit intercourse (full-fledged adultery) and the term "hand" in reference to illicit sexual touching between two people (soft adultery), and therefore male self-masturbation was not necessarily part of his discussion at all. And more research into the matter is required.]

And see above, footnote to p. 144, that the comparison of masturbation to any of the three cardinal sins is hyperbolic.

8. *Nidah 13b* goes on to state that, "Intercourse between limbs was the sin of the Generation of the Flood."

See endnote 518 above, addressing this statement at length.

9. Finally, *Nidah 13b* concludes discussing the "curse" mentioned in the Mishnah that the hand of a man who constantly checks his penis for unusual impure secretions should be cut off. The Talmud goes on to imply that the curse extends also to one who touches his penis in general – even where such might be necessary to alleviate some sort of ailment.

But see *Tosfos* to *Sanhedrin 58b* that this refers specifically to one who touches his penis *constantly* – perhaps *compulsively*. Thus, the context of *Nidah 13b* in this regard, as well as that of the Mishnah itself, may also perhaps be understood as referring only to compulsive touching or checking. And it is possible that not every ancient sage was aware that compulsions, or addictions, are beyond normal human control and may be the symptoms of factors or traumas which no manner of threat or curse will cure. In any case, like we said above (in points 3, 6 and 7) in regard to the comparison of masturbation to the three cardinal sins, this "curse" that the hand be cut off is arguably hyperbolic.

As a final note: even if some of the arguments above will not be found to stand up to standard rabbinical rules of debate, the fact remains that we are being asked by the rabbinic sources to perform no small stretch of the intellect in order to find the semblance of a basis for considering masturbation a sin at all, let alone (one of) the greatest. And see above, footnote to page 3 and cross-references there.

[525] *Drishah* to *Tur, Even Haezer 23:1:1; Rosh Pinah–Ikvei Habayis* to *Shulchan Aruch, Even Haezer, 25:2:3.*

[525*] See also below, endnote 553, discussing the statement of Rabbi Avraham Dovid Wahrman of Buczacz in his *Ezer Mekudash, Shulchan Aruch, Even Haezer 23:2*, that according to those who permit intra-anal ejaculation within marriage it is difficult to argue a distinction between it and masturbation (i.e., if the former is permitted for the sake of a man's pleasure [within marriage], then simple logic dictates that the latter should be permitted as well). In Rabbi Avraham Dovid's words: *Gam l'hamatirim shelo cedarcah paam achas, rachok l'chalek bein shelo cedarcah l'b'yad.*

While Rabbi Avraham Dovid does not go on to outright permit male masturbation, the logic of his argument could potentially be used to support the permission of occasional ejaculation between limbs for married couples.

[526] See the introductions of the publishers to his commentaries on Exodus, Leviticus, Deuteronomy and Job.

[527] Rabbi Moshe Feinstein argues that intra-anal ejaculation was permitted by Rabeinu Yitzchak and other medieval scholars because it is not considered "wasted seed" if it is done for the husband's sexual fulfillment (see above, pp. 140-141). Rabeinu Meyuchas, however, appears to be saying that it *is* considered "wasting seed" no matter who derives pleasure from it, and that it is therefore only ideally acceptable if the *wife* is deriving pleasure.

[Note also that on page 15 of his Genesis commentary, Rabeinu Meyuchas writes that the phrase in the verse "and they shall become one flesh" teaches that a non-Jewish husband is liable for anal sex with his own wife – in line with *Jerusalem Talmud, Kidushin 1:1* and *Breishis Rabah 18:5*, but contrary to the definitive ruling of *Babylonian Talmud, Sanhedrin 58b*. And see above, endnote 344.]

[528] See above, endnote 484, for evidence that Rabeinu Yonah and Rabeinu Nissim understood Maimonides' restrictive wording in this very way in regard to anal intercourse.

And Rabeinu Yonah quotes Maimonides as speaking also about intercourse between limbs.

[529] See the Shabsi Frankel edition of *Mishneh Torah, Sefer Kedushah*, in the *Yalkut Shinuyei Nuschaos* section in the back of the book, *Isurei Biah 21:9*.

[530] See *Kovetz Shitos Kamai, Nedarim*, page 187.

[531] See *Kovetz Shitos Kamai, Nedarim*, page 183.

[532] See *Kovetz Shitos Kamai, Nedarim*, page 183.

[533] Rabbi Henkin does discuss the fact that most manuscripts of *Mishneh Torah* do not include the restrictive caveat in *Isurei Biah 21:9* against intra-anal ejaculation and ejaculation between limbs within marriage. But he concludes that being that Maimonides' view is ultimately not definitively determined, and being that Rabbi Yehoshuah Falk is a (virtually) lone opinion, one should avoid ejaculation between limbs. Still, he acknowledges, if a husband *inadvertently* ejaculates between his wife's limbs there is nothing for the couple to be anxious about. And see below, endnote 764.

[Note that in section 18:3 of the responsum, Rabbi Henkin argues that intra-anal ejaculation and ejaculation between limbs are not to be fundamentally equated, for anal sex legally constitutes full-fledged "intercourse," on account of the verses in Leviticus 18:22 and 20:13 which speak of a woman's "places" of intercourse (see above, page 66, point 4), whereas Jewish law does not consider intercourse between limbs as constituting full-fledged "intercourse" (and see above, endnote 514).

But this argument can be countered by the fact that we are not discussing what legally constitutes *penetration*, but rather what constitutes *permissible extra-vaginal ejaculation*, and therefore there IS reason to equate intra-anal ejaculation and ejaculation between limbs that are done for the sake of sexual fulfillment within marriage rather than for constant intentional unsanctioned birth control.

This would explain why, when discussing the permissibility of intra-anal ejaculation, Rabeinu Yitzchak and other medieval commentaries do not invoke the verses in Leviticus at all, but only the logic that such ejaculation is for the sake of sexual fulfillment within marriage. It would also explain why Maimonides equates anal intercourse and intercourse between limbs in his *Commentary to the Mishnah, Sanhedrin 7:4* and *Mishneh Torah, Isurei Biah 21:9* – particularly if he is understood as having meant to permit both to the point of ejaculation. It would justify Rabbi Yehoshuah Falk's equation of intra-anal ejaculation and ejaculation between limbs in interpreting Rabeinu Yitzchak's opinion as quoted in *Tur, Even Haezer 25:2*. And it would clarify Rabbi Yechiel Michel Epstein's manner of presentation of Rabeinu Yitzchak's opinion in *Aruch Hashulchan, Even Haezer 25:11*, where he appears to apply Rabeinu Yitzchak's permission for extra-vaginal ejaculation to both intra-anal ejaculation and ejaculation between limbs equally.

See also below, endnote 553, discussing the statement of Rabbi Avraham Dovid Wahrman of Buczacz in his *Ezer Mekudash, Shulchan Aruch, Even Haezer 23:2*, that according to those who permit intra-anal ejaculation within marriage it is difficult to argue a distinction between it and masturbation (i.e., if the former is permitted for the sake of a man's pleasure [within marriage], then simple logic dictates that the latter should be permitted as well). In Rabbi Avraham Dovid's words: *Gam l'hamatirim shelo cedarcah paam achas, rachok l'chalek bein shelo cedarcah l'b'yad.* While Rabbi Avraham Dovid does not go on to outright permit male masturbation, the logic of his argument could be said to support even more so the permission of occasional ejaculation between limbs for married couples.]

[534] The following opinions either do not mention a definite restriction on ejaculation between limbs, or they can perhaps be read as differentiating between intra-anal ejaculation and ejaculation between limbs, permitting only the former.

In the case of Maimonides, we have already explained the difficulties in determining his precise intentions (above, pp. 123-124, 128), which is why he is included in this category.

In regard to Rabbis Yaakov ben Asher, Moshe Isserles, and Mordechai Yoffe, as discussed above, page 125, they first present the view of Maimonides as being that intra-anal ejaculation and ejaculation between limbs are both forbidden. But then they present the view of Rabeinu Yitzchak that intra-anal ejaculation is permitted – which would arguably imply that ejaculation between limbs is permitted as well (see above, pp. 124-125 and endnote 520 thereon, and above, endnote 533). But being that these three authorities do not explain this outright, they are included in this category as being "undetermined" in regard to ejaculation between limbs.

See also *Rabeinu Yonah, Sanhedrin 58b:Mi ika midi d'yisrael lo mechayev v'goy mechayev,* and endnotes 484, 528, above.

[535] Pages 8-9.

[536] Rabeinu Meyuchas does not address the question of cunnilingus. But considering that he quotes the Sages' blanket permissive ruling as reported on *Nedarim 20b* without excluding from it any of the four behaviors cautioned against by Rabbi Yochanan ben Dahavai, it is reasonable to believe that he understood the Sages as permitting all four of them, including the kissing of the female genitals.

Regarding the view of Rabbi Yaakov ben Asher in his *Tur* about cunnilingus, see below, pp. 136-137 and endnote 549 thereon.

As for Rabbi Yehoshua Falk (*Drishah*), he does not issue a "ruling" about cunnilingus in his commentary, though he does make a point of mentioning Maimonides' permission of it, later, in *Even Haezer 25:8-10:35,* in contrast to Raavad III's view of it quoted by *Tur,* there, from *Baalei HaNefesh Shaar Hakedushah.* In his *Prishah* commentary to *Tur, Orach Chaim 240:2-4:10,* Rabbi Falk notes Raavad III's assertion that cunnilingus is "evil and forbidden." But in both places, Rabbi Falk appears to be assuming the role of interpreter, not halachic decisor. And with the lack of any clear evidence to the contrary, it is not unreasonable to believe he would have upheld the view of his master, Rabbi Moshe Isserles, permitting it (in *Shulchan Aruch, Even Haezer 25:2*).

[537] In modern slang: the "69" position.

[538] See below, *Appendices: Jewish "Family Purity" and Marital Intimacy Guide Reviews.*

As far as what Chasidic-Charedi premarriage teachers are divulging to young grooms and brides, I cannot claim to have done an exhaustive survey in wide-ranging communities. I do know of teachers out there who are striving to provide a more balanced presentation of the sources. But in conversation with people I continue to hear things being taught that are not only most strict or threatening, but also most bizarre.

As it is not my intention to embarrass any individual or community, I shall refrain from recording specifics here. But these conversations only convinced me ever more that come what may, and regardless of any potential backlash, what Judaism really says about passion in the marital bed had to be made accessible.

[538*] See also below, endnote 748.

[539] See Dr. Avraham Grossman, *Vehu Yimshol Bach* (Zalman Shazar Center for Jewish History, Jerusalem, 2011).

And see above, endnote 419.

[540] At least among those whose works have reached us.

[541] It is not our purpose, here, to explore in-depth the complex question of the *Zohar's* authenticity or on what halachic grounds there might be an obligation to accept upon oneself its authority. Such will be explored in volume two of this series.

[542] A point to explore: If the *Zohar* was originally circulated by Rabbi Moshe de Leon as individual pamphlets for individual collectors, and, presumably, such pamphlets were then copied further by others to enable wider circulation, then by what means and criteria did later copyists and publishers collect and authenticate these pamphlets for print?

[543] See the passage quoted by Rabbi Elazar Azikri at the beginning of his *Sefer Charedim*, Chapter 64, from "*Heichalos Hatumah, Heichal Hanikra Shachas.*"

Rabbi Eliyahu de Vidas in his *Reishis Chochmah, Shaar Hakedushah* 17:22 appears to make veiled reference to this passage as well (see footnote 78 in the 1984 Waldman edition).

[544] See Rabbi Caro's own introduction to *Beis Yosef*, describing its purpose as he intended it.

[545] See Rabbi Caro's own introduction to *Shulchan Aruch*, describing its purpose as he intended it.

[546] See Rabbi Yehoshua Falk's introduction to his *Drishah* commentary on the *Tur*. He writes that neither Rabbi Caro nor Rabbi Isserles ever intended for anyone to rule out of the *Shulchan Aruch* without first studying the *Tur* in-depth with their respective *Beis Yosef* and *Darchei Moshe* commentaries. And, Rabbi Falk writes, those who do rule out of the *Shulchan Aruch* without this in-depth preparation are "destroyers of the Jewish people."

See also *Yad Malachi, Clalei Haposkim, HaShulchan Aruch v'HaRema 1*.

See also Rabbi Moshe Walter's, *The Making of a Halachic Decision* (Menucha Publishers 2013), Chapter 4.

[547] *Ohel Moed, Shaar Isur V'heter, Derech 11, Nesiv 2*.

See *Kovetz Shitos Kamai, Nedarim 20b*, p. 190.

[548] See, for example, Rabbi Yisrael Alnaqua in his *Menoras Hamaor, Perek Nisuei Ishah*, pp. 72-80 (discussed above, endnote 252), who quotes copiously of Raavad III's interpretation of *Nedarim 20b* in *Baalei HaNefesh, Shaar Hakedushah*, but does not actually rule like Raavad III's views, there, in regard to kissing the female genitals and anal sex.

[549] Rabbi Moshe Isserles, in his *Darchei Moshe* commentary to *Tur, Even Haezer 25:2*, asserts that although Rabbi Yaakov ben Asher quotes Maimonides' permission for cunnilingus, there, he does not actually rule like Maimonides to permit it – the proof being that in *Orach Chaim 240*, Rabbi Yaakov ben Asher only brings Raavad III's opinion

# ENDNOTES

forbidding it, and that in *Even Haezer 25* he quotes Raavad III's prohibition of it at the end of the discussion, as if it were Rabbi Yaakov ben Asher's own final word.

[Rabbi Yosef Caro, in his *Beis Yosef* commentary to *Tur, Even Haezer 25:2*, also notes Rabbi Yaakov ben Asher's citations of Raavad III in this regard, but he does not assert clearly that Rabbi Yaakov ben Asher actually ruled according to Raavad III.

And Rabbi Caro's comments in his *Beis Yosef* to *Tur, Orach Chaim 240* only reference additional points made by Raavad III in *Baalei HaNefesh, Shaar Hakedushah*, they do not assert anything in regard to Rabbi Yaakov ben Asher's own final legal opinion on the matter of cunnilingus one way or the other.]

However, this "proof" is somewhat surprising, at least coming from Rabbi Moshe Isserles himself, for he, too, in his glosses to *Shulchan Aruch*, only brings Maimonides' permission of cunnilingus in *Even Haezer 25*, not in *Orach Chaim 240*, yet it is unequivocally clear from his wording in *Even Haezer* ("...And even though all these things are permitted...") that he rules according to Maimonides.

Rabbi Isserles's disciple, Rabbi Mordechai Yoffe, in his *Levush*, as well as Rabbi Yechiel Michel Epstein, in his *Aruch Hashulchan*, also bring Maimonides' permission of cunnilingus only in *Even Haezer 25*, not in *Orach Chaim 240*. In *Orach Chaim 240*, they both quote only Raavad III's prohibition of it, though it is clear from their wordings in *Even Haezer* that they, too, both ruled the letter of the law according to Maimonides.

Thus, if Rabbi Isserles, and others, felt it sufficient to quote their permissive rulings in only one place, in *Even Haezer 25*, why can't we believe Rabbi Yaakov ben Asher felt it sufficient to do the same? We thus simply cannot be so certain that Rabbi Yaakov ben Asher categorically rejected Maimonides' opinion on cunnilingus just because he quoted it in only one place.

And the fact that Rabbi Yaakov ben Asher quoted Raavad III after Maimonides in *Even Haezer 25* is also no conclusive proof, for, as noted in regard to "overturning the table," while in *Even Haezer 25* he quoted Raavad III's interpretation of the term (that it refers only to rear-entry vaginal intercourse) after Maimonides' and Rabeinu Yitzchak's (that it refers even to anal intercourse and intra-anal ejaculation, respectively), in *Orach Chaim 240* he quoted Rabeinu Yitzchak's interpretation *after* Raavad III's. And Rabbi Moshe Feinstein asserts that Rabbi Yaakov ben Asher ruled according to Rabeinu Yitzchak, permitting not only anal intercourse, but also intra-anal ejaculation (see *Igros Moshe, Even Haezer 1, Responsum 63*, end of p. 156, top of page 163).

[Rabbi Elazar Azikri, in his *Sefer Charedim, Chapter 64*, argues that Rabbi Yaakov ben Asher ruled like Raavad III forbidding anal sex, because in *Tur, Even Haezer 25* he quoted Raavad III's opinion last. But Rabbi Azikri does not address the fact that in *Tur, Orach Chaim 240*, the opinion of Rabeinu Yitzchak permitting anal sex – and intra-anal ejaculation – was quoted by Rabbi Yaakov ben Asher last (after Raavad III's).

Compare also *Elyah Rabah, Levush 240:4:10* to *Sefer Charedim, Chapter 64*. See also *Igros Moshe, Even Haezer vol. 1, Responsum 63*, end of page 156, top of page 163.

Rabbi Chaim Yosef Dovid Azulai (Chida), in his *Kisei Rachamim*, "*Tosfos*" commentary to *Tractate Callah 2:5*, suggests that Rabbi Yaakov ben Asher in *Tur* permitted anal intercourse, but only without intra-anal ejaculation. There is, however, no clear basis to such a claim according to any reading of *Tur*, for Rabbi Yaakov ben Asher quotes Rabeinu Yitzchak's permission of intra-anal ejaculation both in *Even Haezer 25* and in *Orach Chaim 240*, and in the latter place he quotes Rabeinu Yitzchak as the final opinion in his presentation, while he brings Maimonides' view permitting anal sex (allegedly) only *without* intra-anal ejaculation only in *Even Haezer*, not in *Orach Chaim*. Thus, it is difficult to accept that Rabbi Yaakov ben Asher in *Tur* endorsed Maimonides' view about intra-anal ejaculation over Rabeinu Yitzchak's.]

It is therefore very difficult to argue *definitively* that Rabbi Yaakov ben Asher, in his *Tur*, "forbade" cunnilingus based on inexplicable discrepancies between *Orach Chaim* and *Even Haezer* – discrepancies that are perpetuated by subsequent codifiers like Rabbis Isserles, Yoffe and Epstein, all of whom still clearly *permit* cunnilingus.

[See also *Yad Malachi, Clalei HaPoskim, Baal HaTurim, Clal 7-11* in regard to the *Tur's* quoting of Maimonides in general, and *Clal 32* in regard to his quoting of Rabeinu Yitzchak.]

550 It is unclear what Rabbi Caro meant to refer to with the phrase, "and the like." Perhaps he meant to hint to ejaculation between limbs. And see below, top of page 149.

551 See above, endnote 486.

552 Pages 118-120, 123-124, 128.

553 See, however, Rabbi Avraham Dovid Wahrman of Buczacz in his *Ezer Mekudash, Shulchan Aruch, Even Haezer 23:2*, where he writes that according to those who permit intra-anal ejaculation within marriage it is difficult to argue a distinction between it and masturbation (i.e., if the former is permitted for the sake of a man's pleasure [within marriage], then simple logic dictates that the latter should be permitted as well). In Rabbi Avraham Dovid's words: *Gam l'hamatirim shelo cedarcah paam achas, rachok l'chalek bein shelo cedarcah l'b'yad.*

Still, Rabbi Avraham Dovid does not outright permit masturbation.

[Note that although Rabbi Avraham Dovid speaks in *Even Haezer 23*, and elsewhere in *Even Haezer 25*, of those who permit intra-anal ejaculation "once" (*paam achas*), he also writes in his comments to *Even Haezer 25:2:Hagaah* that there is actually no source for such a restriction of "once," only a restriction of "occasionally." And see above, endnote 268, and below, endnote 613.]

An in-depth study on the rabbinical approach to masturbation will be the subject of volume two of this series. And see above, footnote to page 3.

554 *Igros Moshe, Even Haezer 1, Responsum 63*, page 154. And see next endnote.

[Rabbi Yaakov Shlomoh Holzberg, in his *Pri Shlomoh* commentary to *Yevamos 34b*, references a responsum in which he says he offers numerous approaches to resolve the contradiction between Rabbi Eliezer's teaching on *Nidah 13a* and his teaching on *Yevamos 34b*.]

555 *Igros Moshe, Even Haezer 1, Responsum 63*, pp. 156-157.

See also Rabbi Eliezer Melamed's *Simchat Habayit v'Birchato* (second edition, 2015), page 61, end of footnote 19, and Rabbi Maor Kayam's *Harchavot l'Simchat Habayit v'Birchato*, pp. 178-179, quoting a similar explanation from Rabbi Avraham Yitzchak Kook, of blessed memory, in *Ezras Cohen 35* and *37*.

556 See above, pp. 66-67.

557 *Igros Moshe, Orach Chaim 4, Responsum 116*, pp. 207-208.

And see above, endnote 335.

## ENDNOTES

[557*] Note also that some manuscripts of *Nidah 13a* do not even have Rabbi Yochanan's name associated at all with the teaching that "wasting seed in vain" could warrant death by the hand of Heaven. See the Hebrew edition of *The Steinsaltz Talmud, Nidah 13a, Girsaos.*]

[558] Rabbi Falk, there, still refers to intra-anal ejaculation (and, by extension, ejaculation between limbs) performed for the sake of sexual fulfillment within marriage as "wasting seed in vain" (*motzi shichvas zera levatalah*), he just says that "there is nothing wrong with it" (*leis lan bah*). Others, however, say that such intra-anal ejaculation does not fall under the category of "wasting seed" to begin with, as we shall explain next.

[558*] Regarding this notion of "acquisition," see above, page 66, point 3.

[559] Note that Rabeinu Nissim, himself, on *Nedarim 20b*, references the textual version of Maimonides' *Mishneh Torah, Isurei Biah 21:9* that permits anal sex only "without wasting seed." But he does not clearly *rule* the law, there, like Maimonides. Or he can perhaps be read as understanding the *definition* of "wasting seed" in this context as only that which is ejaculated intra-anally as a menas of (constant and) intentional unsanctioned birth control (see above, endnotes 484, 492).

[560] *Tosfos Rid* to *Tractate Yevamos* was published from manuscript only in the 20th century.

Note, however, that Rabbi Yeshayah of Trani I's commentary seems to have been known and circulating in earlier times, as his comments to *Yevamos 12b* are quoted practically verbatim in the commentary of *R"I* to *Sheiltot D'Rav Hai Gaon, Ki Teitzei*, p. 42 of the Sura-Yeshiva University edition by Rabbi Shmuel Kalman Mirsky.

[It is not clear from the Sura-Yeshiva University edition who this *R"I* was or when and where he lived – though it is interesting that he shared the same acronym as Rabbi Yeshayah of Trani I.]

And while Rabbi Yeshayah of Trani I's general view in regard to intra-anal ejaculation was reported as well by his grandson, Rabbi Yeshayah of Trani II, in his *Kuntres Harayos L'Riaz, Sanhedrin 58b* (published by Rabbi Yaakov Lifshitz in *Sanhedri Gedolah*, Mechon Fishel 1972), the grandson did not enumerate this specific point that such ejaculation is not categorized as "wasting seed."

[561] Rabbi Menachem Mendel (1789-1866) was a grandson and the foremost expositor of the legal teachings of Rabbi Schneur Zalman of Liadi (1745-1812).

Rabbi Menachem Mendel's assertion, that according to Rabeinu Yitzchak and Rabeinu Asher (and thus, by association, also according to their halachic supporters) intra-anal ejaculation for the sake of a married couple's sexual fulfillment does not fall under the category of "wasting seed," is extremely significant, as it would acknowledge that according to *them*, the harsh teachings against "wasting seed" found in Rabbi Schneur Zalman's *Tanya*, in the writings of Rabbi Chaim Vital in the name of Rabbi Yitzchak Luria (the Arizal), among the kabbalists in general, in the *Zohar*, and even in the Talmud itself (*Nidah 13ab*), would not apply in any way whatsoever to occasional intra-anal ejaculation for married couples.

[And, we might add, if occasional intra-anal ejaculation for married couples and occasional ejaculation between limbs for married couples are to be equated according to Rabeinu Yitzchak, as Rabbi Yehoshua Falk says they are to be, then ejaculation between limbs should not either fall under the category of "wasting seed" according to Rabeinu Yitzchak. But Rabbi Menachem Mendel himself does not address ejaculation between limbs in his discussion.]

And see below, endnote 633.

[562] Another Talmudic-era phrase, the meaning of which is, for all intents and purposes, equivalent to that of "wasting seed in vain." It is used in rabbinic literature to refer to masturbation or coitus interruptus.

[563] *Vayeshev, paragraphs 182-183* in the *Sulam* edition of the *Zohar*.

[564] *Vayechi, paragraphs 191-194* in the *Sulam* edition of the *Zohar*.

[565] The *Zohar* in *Vayechi*, there, actually goes much farther, stating that all other sinners eventually "rise" – presumably from Purgatory, or perhaps with the Resurrection – while masturbators never do. And even more so: for all other sins there is repentance, while for masturbation there is not.

[See also Rabbi Eliyahu de Vidas's *Reishis Chochmah, Shaar Hakedushah 17:11-13*.]

This latter teaching of the *Zohar* apparently caused much consternation when it began to circulate, presumably ever more so after it was published in print for the first time in 1558 and became available to the masses. Some commentators went to great lengths to come up with complex reinterpretations of what it could possibly mean. See, for example, Rabbi Eliyahu de Vidas (1518-1592) in his *Reishis Chochmah, Shaar Hakedushah 17:13-23* and the majority of Rabbi Schneur Zalman of Liadi's *Igeres Hateshuvah* (chapters 4 through 10) explaining *Reishis Chochmah*.

[See also the letter attributed to Rabbi Schneur Zalman of Liadi, written to Rabbi Levi Yitzchak of Berditchev, discussing how to counsel a certain individual dealing with unresolved sexual anxieties apparently relating to masturbation (*Meah Shearim, Letter #8*, pp. 5-6 in the 2005 Kehot Publication Society edition; the letter is also printed in the Kehot Publication Society Chabad prayer book, *Tehilat Hashem*, pp. 329-330 in the old edition, pp. 568-569 in the new).]

See also Rabbi Yeshayah Horowitz (c.1565-1630) in his *Shnei Luchos Habris, Shaar Haosios, Ois Kuf, Kedushas Hazivug*, paragraphs 12-36.

Rabbi Horowitz, in paragraph 15, hints to a prevailing problem that people who were hearing about this teaching of the *Zohar* were giving up on Judaism altogether, believing themselves to be beyond spiritual repair. Rabbi Eliyahu Hacohen (c.1659-1729) in his *Midrash Talpios, Anaf Zera L'vatalah* (page 198, column 2, in the 1875 Warsaw edition) implies this as well.

And see Rabbi Yaakov Emden in his *Mitpachat Sofrim*, pp. 21-22 in the Lvov edition, where he lists this teaching among those he believed could not possibly have issued from the mouth or pen of Rabbi Shimon ben Yochai himself or his disciples. See also the end of Chapter One, there, bottom of page 6, where Rabbi Emden asserts that the aramaic style of *Zohar, Parshas Vayechi* is particularly suspect.

An alternate teaching in the *Zohar* has also been pointed to, in the portion of *Noach* (paragraph 57 in the *Sulam* edition), which says that "wasting seed in vain" can be forgiven, but "only through extreme repentance" (*bar b'teshuvah sagi* – which the *Sulam* translates as: *chutz b'teshuvah rabah*). Rabbi Elazar Azikri (1533-1600) may have been referring to this passage at the end of his *Sefer Charedim, Chapter 64*, where he writes that according to Rabbi Shimon ben Yochai – i.e., the *Zohar* – the sin of wasting seed in vain "has no remedy, other than great and constant repentance" (*she'ein l'avon zeh terufah im loe b'teshuvah gedolah tadirah*).

Finally, in regard to the notion of "losing one's portion in the World to Come" – a separate future study shall explore wider rabbinic expressions about reward and punishment and perfectionism and repentance. But let it be made known to readers here and now that even if one accepts the validity of the idea that some sins could cause one to forfeit his or her portion in the World to Come, Rabbi Eliyahu Hacohen (c.1659-1729) cites two medieval scholars, Rabeinu Bachya ben Asher (1255-1340) and Rabbi Menachem Recanati (c.1250-c.1310), who insist that even those who do not merit a personal, individual portion in the World to Come shall certainly share a collective portion of reward and eternal happiness (see *Midrash Talpios, Anaf Chelek L'olam Haba*, page 216a in the 1875 Warsaw edition – cited by Rabbi Menachem Mendel Schneerson in his *Igros Kodesh vol. 2*, page 73, footnote 15\*; and see Rabbi Schneerson's lengthy analytical studies about the World to Come and the Resurrection in his *Igros Kodesh vol. 1*, Letter 85, pp. 141-153 and *Igros Kodesh vol. 2*, Letter 200, pp. 65-77).

**[Added note to the third edition:** See also *Yabia Omer, vol. 6, Yoreh Deah 36*, where Rabbi Ovadiah Yosef quotes this notion from *Midrash Talpios, Anaf Chelek L'olam Haba*, as well. Credit goes to Rabbi Dr. Marc Shapiro for bringing this source in *Yabia Omer* to my attention.

See also Rabbi Moshe Chaim Luzzato (1707-1746), *Derech Hashem 2:3:8*, that those who are unworthy of the World to Come in their own right may come to merit a place in it by virtue of their association with the righteous (pp. 118-121 in the English edition of *Derech Hashem, The Way of G-d*, by Rabbi Aryeh Kaplan). It is, however, unclear if Rabbi Luzzato meant to suggest that association with the righteous in-and-of-itself makes one worthy of the World to Come, or only that such association can, in turn, help lead one to the path of righteousness as well.

See also Rabbi Nissan Dovid Dubov, *To Live and Live Again* (Sichos in English, 1995), p. 55, footnote 187, presenting a theory by Rabbi Yitzchak Abravanel which potentially implies that all Jews and non-Jews of all generations, righteous and non-righteous alike, shall rise in the Resurrection (i.e., the World to Come), perceive the truth of G-d, and serve Him together as one.

See also Rabbi Dr. Marc Shapiro's *Changing the Immutable: How Orthodox Judaism Rewrites its History* (The Littman Library of Jewish Civilization, 2015), chapter 8, page 242, footnote 15: "Rabbi Simeon ben Tsemah Duran notes that the Sages exaggerated when describing sins that cause a person to lose his share in the world to come. See *Ohev Mishpat*, ch. 10." See there as well for further references by Shapiro to rabbinic discussions about the Sages' exaggerations, including the acknowledgment by Rabbi Yitzchak ben Sheshes (1326-1408) that the Sages' exaggerated when describing the severity of certain sins, as a means of deterrence (*Shaalos uTeshuvos Rivash, Responsum 171*).]

And let any mere mortal – short of a living prophet – stop pretending to know who will go where and who will get what. Let the Divine Judge of all things and of all hearts decide this on His own. In the end, it is only His opinion that will matter – not a rabbi's and not one's own.

[566] And therefore we arguably have the moral obligation to reconsider Rabbi Caro's words for the sake of couples' marital harmony and individuals' psychological-emotional-physical-spiritual-sexual balance and wellbeing.

And see above, endnote 482.

[567] The obvious question is therefore the reverse: why should self-masturbation, if done only occasionally and/or purely for the sake of pleasure (especially by a single unmarried male, or by a homosexual) be worse than, or even equal to, constant extra-vaginal ejaculation or coitus interruptus done for the sake of unsanctioned birth control?

[568] *Erech Shai* to *Shulchan Aruch, Even Haezer 25*, quoted also verbatim in *Erech Shai* to *Talmud, Tractate Yevamos 34b*.

In Rabbi Tabak's own words there: *"D'b'Zohar Vayechi muchach d'chomer hagadol rak b'mis-chavein l'hashchis zara b'riknei oe ragil b'cach, v'gam dayek d'oseh byadoi."*

[See also *Erech Shai* to *Shulchan Aruch, Even Haezer 23*.]

Rabbi Tabak also gives a fascinating explanation as to why intra-anal ejaculation done with one's wife for the sake of sexual fulfillment within marriage should be halachically permissible: The rule is that in a case where, a) one does not have the intention to sin, and, b) it is also doubtful if there is a sin in the first place, the action in question is permitted.

As Rabbi Tabak applies the rule here: The fundamental halachic issue with "wasting seed" has to do with unsanctioned birth control. But scientifically speaking, not every ejaculation into one's wife's womb will result in conception. Therefore, in each occasional time that a husband ejaculates outside his wife's womb (i.e., intra-anally) in the course of sexual fulfillment, there is no *definite* "sin" of unsanctioned birth control involved, for we have no way of knowing if conception would have resulted from that specific ejaculation. And so long as his intention in doing so is about pleasure with his wife, not unsanctioned birth control, there is no *intention* to sin either.

Therefore, Rabbi Tabak explains, the problem only arises if a husband, a) ejaculates outside his wife's womb (i.e., intra-anally) *constantly*, in which case Jewish law assumes that conception is *most likely* being frustrated because of his actions, or, b) if his actual *intention* is unsanctioned birth control.

[Note that Rabbi Tabak concludes his analysis of *Even Haezer 25:2* saying that such an innovative reconciliation "is certainly not the approach of the extra-halachic pious to the matter, especially since some do say that it *is* a severe sin." But he is not questioning the veracity of his Talmudic reconciliation of the *Zohar* and Rabeinu Yitzchak's second approach. Rather, he is merely pointing out that it would not be a reconciliation endorsed by those inclined to extra-halachic piety (*"mishnas chasidim"* – possibly, in the context of Rabbi Tabak's times, a reference to those of the latter-day Chasidic Movement) or by those *who take it as a given* that intra-anal ejaculation is a "great sin" – meaning, those who endorse the *first* approach of Rabeinu Yitzchak (which permits only anal penetration without intra-anal ejaculation), to whom his entire reconciliation would be irrelevant. (In Rabbi Tabak's own words: *Aval vadai lav mishnas chasidim hu, ubifrat sheyesh omrim d'isur chamur hu*.)

*Otzar Haposkim, Even Haezer 25:2:10*, page 241 (1982 edition) references this explanation of Rabbi Tabak in *Erech Shai*, but without presenting the main body of his argument reconciling the *Zohar* and Rabeinu Yitzchak's second approach. Instead, it focuses only on Rabbi Tabak's concluding observation in regard to the "extra-halachic pious" and those who inherently reject Rabeinu Yitzchak's second approach. See also Rabbi Moshe Stern's *Be'er Moshe, Responsum 153*, page 208.]

[569] Note that this isolated excerpt of *Erech Shai* comes close to implying that masturbation, too, could perhaps only be so severely problematic according to the *Zohar* if done constantly in order to enjoy sexual gratification *without ever having to bear children*. But this might not have been Rabbi Tabak's own actual intention.

More on this in volume two of this series. And see above, footnote to page 3.

[570] See above, endnote 546.

## ENDNOTES

⁵⁷¹ I've included *Bedek Habayis*, here, only in parentheses, for, as we discuss below in the next section, it is not entirely clear if Rabbi Caro wrote this particular caution into *Bedek Habayis* prior to his writing of *Shulchan Aruch, Orach Chaim 240* and *Even Haezer 25*.

⁵⁷¹* Though, granted, Raavad III is also silent in his glosses to *Mishneh Torah, Isurei Biah 21:9* in regard to Maimonides' permission of cunnilingus, yet Rabbi Caro does go on to prohibit it based on Raavad III's *Baalei HaNefesh, Shaar Hakedushah*.
And see above, endnote 330, the added note to the third edition.

⁵⁷² *Igros Moshe, Even Haezer vol. 1, Responsum 63*, end of page 155, and page 156 middle of column two.

[**Added note to the third edition:** See also *Yabia Omer vol. 8, Even Haezer 21:2*, where Rabbi Ovadia Yosef (1920-2013) parenthetically references these cautions of Rabbi Yosef Caro in *Beis Yosef* and *Bedek Habayis*, and then, somewhat mysteriously, points the reader's attention to this same general section in *Igros Moshe*. Credit goes to Rabbi Yossi Newfield for bringing this responsum of Rabbi Ovadiah Yosef to my attention.]

⁵⁷³ *Ezer Mekudash* to *Even Haezer, 25:2:Hagaah*.

⁵⁷³* Even in *Shulchan Aruch, Even Haezer 23*, where Rabbi Caro addresses the concept of "wasting seed in vain," he does not list intra-anal ejaculation or ejaculation between limbs as examples of "wasting seed in vain" between husband and wife. He speaks, there, only against coitus interruptus (and male self-masturbation).

⁵⁷⁴ Compare to *Otzar Haposkim, Even Haezer 25:2*, page 240, "*Daas Ha'achronim Lahalachah*."

⁵⁷⁵ *Gur Aryeh* to *Even Haezer 25:2* quotes only Rabbi Caro's kabbalistic caution.

⁵⁷⁶ Rabbi Falk, there, can be understood simply as quoting Rabbi Caro's *Beis Yosef* to show that not all opinions who might intellectualy understand or accept Rabeinu Yitzchak's second interpretation of *Yevamos 34b* necessarily *encourage* intra-anal ejaculation. But there is no proof that Rabbi Falk personally meant to rule the letter of the law according to Rabbi Caro's caution – especially being that Rabbi Falk's own master, Rabbi Moshe Isserles, certainly knew of this caution in *Beis Yosef* and nevertheless legally permitted occasional intra-anal ejaculation within marriage, and considering that even Rabbi Caro himself did not express an actual legal prohibition against it.

⁵⁷⁷ Rabbi Caro died in 1575.

⁵⁷⁸ In the second edition of *Bedek Habayis*, published a year later in 1606, the editors changed the wording to read:

> . . . The editors rushed to put out the second edition, *and numerous other editions*, before my manuscript reached them.

This is strange wording indeed, for it is unlikely that *numerous* editions would have left the printer's hand before *one* updated manuscript by the author managed to reach them.

⁵⁷⁹ *Orach Chaim, Yoreh Deah* and *Even Haezer* were already out before the *Zohar* was first published in print in 1558.

⁵⁸⁰ *Sarei Ha'elef vol. 2* (second edition, 1979), Part 6, *Sifrei Haposkim*, 101, p. 379.

⁵⁸¹ Online catalogue of the Central Library of Agudas Chasidei Chabad, New York.

[582] See the publisher's introduction to the Friedman edition of *Shulchan Aruch* (1994), p. 20.

[583] See *Yad Malachi, Clalei Haposkim, HaShulchan Aruch v'HaRema 14*, that the *Shulchan Aruch* was probably written after *Bedek Habayis*, because there are places in *Shulchan Aruch* that are clearly worded in line with corrections Rabbi Caro made in *Bedek Habayis*. But while this may be evidence that *some* glosses of *Bedek Habayis* predated the completion of *Shulchan Aruch*, it in no way proves that *all* of them did.

[584] Such as the works of Rabeinu Asher, Rabeinu Yeruchem, Rabbi Yitzchak of Corbeil (*Sefer Mitzvos Katan*), Rabbi Mordechai ben Hillel (*Mordechai*), Rabeinu Nissim, Rabbi Aharon Hacohen of Lunil (*Orchos Chaim*), as well as *Hagahos Maimonios* – all of which Rabbi Caro himself says he made use of in composing his *Beis Yosef* commentary. See Rabbi Caro's own introduction to *Beis Yosef*. He also mentions, there, that he had access to *Col Bo*.

All of these medieval works permit anal intercourse, and some permit even occasional intra-anal ejaculation, within marriage.

[585] While it is not widely known or at least not widely discussed (or perhaps simply not widely accepted) among Chasidic-Charedi circles, there is one rabbinic source that suggests Rabbi Caro's *Shulchan Aruch* is prone to innacuracies, while another reports a rumor that Rabbi Caro didn't actually write the *Shulchan Aruch* himself, but delegated its composition to his students, possibly accounting for discrepancies between it and his *Beis Yosef* commentary. See *Yad Malachi, Clalei Haposkim, HaShulchan Aruch v'HaRema 2*.

[586] Rabbi Caro could not necessarily have foreseen in his own day that study of his *Shulchan Aruch* amongst the masses would eventually eclipse, and take precedence over, study of his *Beis Yosef-Bedek Habayis*.

[Parenthetically, it could be argued that even if Rabbi Caro did foresee such a trend, he may have deliberately left certain halachic behaviors out of his *Shulchan Aruch* because of what he considered to be deteriorating spiritual conditions of his times – conditions that he may have felt would have been exacerbated by indulgence in permitted sexual exploration even within marriage. Thus, the argument would go, in times – like ours – when the opposite appears to be true, when restrictions on sexual vulnerability and exploration within marriage are causing people to give up on, or lose trust in, Torah, Rabbi Caro would have perhaps taught a more balanced version to the masses. But one who would argue this would also apparently have to concede that Rabbi Caro's *Shulchan Aruch* is not – and was never intended to be – timeless.]

[587] "Anything a husband craves to do with his wife sexually, he may do" (*Nedarim 20b*).

[588] "A man's wife is permitted to him…" (*Mishneh Torah, Isurei Biah 21:9; Deos 5:4*).

[589] See *Shulchan Aruch, Orach Chaim 240:1*, where Rabbi Caro cuts a husband no slack for having sexual needs of his own. Rabbi Isserles, however, in a gloss-note, there, offers a thread of understanding for the husband's needs.

And see above, endnote 36.

[590] Rabbi Luria, who died at age 38, only led the Safed mystics for roughly two years. His voluminous teachings, however, were recorded by his chief disciple, Rabbi Chaim Vital, and fundamentally changed the world of Jewish mystical thought ever after.

## ENDNOTES

[591] *Pri Etz Chaim, Shaar Krias Shema al Hamitah, Perek 11* (page 341 in the Brandwein edition); *Likutei Torah-Taamei Hamitzvos, Parshas Noach* (page 43 in the Brandwein edition).

But see Rabbi Yosef Yafah, *Ashreichem Yisrael* (Mayan HaTorah, 2013), page 254, footnote 89, referencing various rabbinic responsa that pre-ejaculate leaving the head of the penis during foreplay is "uncontrollable" (*onais*) and therefore one cannot be held liable for it in the eyes of Heaven. Specifically, he references *Pri Hasadeh, Responsum 77; Mahari Asad, Responsum 238; Imrei Aish, Responsum 69; Imrei Binah vol. 4, Responsum 8; Chashev HaEfod vol. 1, Responsum 60*.

See also *Olas Yitzchak vol. 2, Responsum 242*.

[592] *Shaar Hamitzvos, Parshas Noach* (pp. 9-10 in the Brandwein edition); *Shaar Hakavanos, Inyan Drushei Halailah, Drush 7* (page 364 in volume one of the Brandwein edition).

But see *Ben Ish Chai, Shanah 2, Vayeira 25*, that the drips of semen that are expelled after ejaculation has subsided are "uncontrollable" (*onais*) and therefore one cannot be held liable for them in the eyes of Heaven.

[593] The Brandwein edition of *Shaar Hamitzvos, Parshas Noach*, page 10, points us three pages earlier, to *Parshas Breishis*, page 7, where Rabbi Vital foreshadows his caution against "wasting seed" through the (uncontrollable) drips of sexual fluid that emerge from the penis even after climax has subsided. A gloss-note, there, by Rabbi Vital's son, Rabbi Shmuel, attempts to source "this stringency" (*hachumra hazos*) in the Talmudic passage in *Talmud, Nidah 71a*, which says that a man will merit male offspring by "waiting on the belly of his wife until she climaxes first."

[Credit goes to Rabbi Yehudah Leib Nachmanson's *Sheyekadesh Atzmo* (2015), Chapter 18, footnote 1, for bringing this gloss-note of Rabbi Shmuel Vital to my attention.]

Rabbi Shmuel's explanation, however, is problematic, for that Talmudic passage in *Nidah* is referring to a husband waiting upon his wife's belly *before* either he or she climaxes, whereas his father, Rabbi Chaim, is referring to a husband waiting upon his wife's belly *after* he has climaxed.

Regarding pre-ejaculate before intercourse, perhaps Rabbis Luria and Vital understood the caution of Rabbi Eliezer found in *Talmud, Nidah 13a*, about not grasping hold of one's own shaft during urination lest it lead to sexual arousal and "wasted seed," as referring not (only) to a concern about it leading to actual masturbation, but even to a concern about it leading to pre-ejaculate dribbling from the penis. To be discussed further in volume two of this series. And see below, endnote 816. And see above, endnote, 591.

[594] *Shaar Ruach Hakodesh, Tikun 27*.

A SENSITIVE POINT TO CONSIDER FOR FURTHER RESEARCH AND DISCUSSION, WHICH OUR CHILDREN'S PSYCHOLOGICAL-EMOTIONAL-PHYSICAL-SPIRITUAL BALANCE CANNOT ALLOW US TO IGNORE:

Note that all these teachings about the severity of "wasting seed in vain" are quoted by the same Rabbi Chaim Vital who states that one should ideally not kill one's own lice (following the example of Rabbi Yitzchak Luria himself) because they are spontaneously generated from human sweat and are thus, in a sense, part of man. See *Shaar Hamitzvos, Parshas Noach*.

If this great kabbalist could be mistaken about such a physical biological fact, is it not possible he, or his master, Rabbi Luria, could have been mistaken about the nature of metaphysical reality, including the supposedly grave metaphysical, or even spiritual, repercussions of "wasting seed in vain"?

[On our use of the terms "metaphysical" and "spiritual," see above, footnote to page 35 and endnote 86.]

The same could be asked, of course, about the Talmudic sages themselves, who believed in certain scientific notions prevalent in their times that we now know to be empirically unfounded. On this topic, see above, endnotes 13, 86, and below, *Appendices: A Word about Rabbinic Fallibility*.

And further investigation into the matter is required. But such discussion can no longer be ignored.

[595] Introduction of Rabbi Chaim Vital to *Eitz Chaim, Sur Mera #7* (page 23 in the Brandwein edition). Rabbi Vital lists this among ten behaviors he says the righteous seeking kabbalistic truth must "avoid to the ultimate extreme" (*l'hisrachek b'tachlis harichuk*).

And see above, endnotes 46, 82.

Although Rabbi Vital is addressing "the righteous," here, the fact that he even suggests Judaism idealizes sex without pleasure is already potentially damaging to innocent minds.

This "anti-pleasure" approach to sex apparently deeply influenced the latter-day 18th century Chasidic movement as well.

This Chasidism, it was/is explained, came to reveal how, according to the deepest mysteries of Torah and kabbalah, G-dliness can be found even in, and specifically in, the physical, and to show even the simplest Jew how to elevate the mundane within himself and in the world around him rather than attempt to escape from or break it.

Such notions were not necessarily new in Jewish thought, for already in medieval times Maimonides wrote at length about how the path of Torah is the "middle path" according to which man should not go to spiritual extremes, but should rather utilize the physical world and all its pleasures, including food, drink and sex, in healthy moderation and for G-dly purpose (See *Mishneh Torah, Sefer Hamada, Deos 3:2; Introduction to Ethics of the Fathers-Shmoneh Perakim, Chapters 4-5*). Chasidism's revolution in this area was perhaps that it attempted to balance psychologically-emotionally-physically grounded living within the framework of a Jewish mysticism that had until then been prone to extreme ascetisim.

[**Added note to the third edition:** See also the final chapter of *Mesilas Yesharim*, chapter 26, and especially its concluding passages, where Rabbi Moshe Chaim Luzzato (1707-1746) describes the path of *"kedushah"* and *"chasidus"* in a manner that appears to parallel certain principles taught by Rabbi Yisrael Baal Shem Tov. Credit goes to Rabbi Simcha Feuerman for bringing this source in *Mesilas Yesharim* to my attention. Rabbi Feuerman also made me aware that there may be a fundamental difference between the approach of Maimonides and that of Chasidism, for Maimonides appears to have taught that man's ultimate elevation only comes by *transcending* the physical, while certain mystics and Chasidic masters imply that man's ultimate elevation is only *through* the physical.]

# ENDNOTES

To what extent the Chasidic movement succeeded in providing such groundedness, how its degree of success may have changed over time, and how it even defined such success – originally and today – shall be the topics of a future study. There is certainly little doubt that in many respects it vastly improved the spiritual lives of masses of Jews over the last two to three hundred years. Some would perhaps even say that it saved Orthodox Judaism in the 20th century. But as pertains to our present discussion, we ask: were the original Chasidic masters themselves really seeking to sanctify sex without stripping it of its physical garb? And if they were, did they succeed in doing so?

*PLEASE NOTE THAT THE FOLLOWING DISCUSSION, WHILE IT IS SENSITIVE, IS NOT MEANT IN ANY WAY TO DISHONOR THE MEMBERS OR LEADERS OF ANY CHASIDIC COMMUNITY – PAST, PRESENT OR FUTURE. I PERSONALLY OWE A TREMENDOUS AMOUNT OF MY OWN SPIRITUAL DEVELOPMENT OVER THE PAST TWO DECADES TO CHASIDIC TEACHING. BUT, AS ONE WHO HAS LIVED AND BREATHED THAT LIFE, I BELIEVE IT IS CRITICAL TO RAISE THE FOLLOWING POINTS IN THE HOPE THAT CERTAIN STATEMENTS IN ITS LITERATURE WILL BE REEXAMINED BY CHASIDIC LEADERS TOGETHER WITH MENTAL HEALTH PROFESSIONALS, SO THAT THE MEMBERS OF THE WIDER CHASIDIC COMMUNITY MAY BE SPARED SEXUAL ANXIETIES AND RELATED SUFFERING:*

One of the fascinating facts about the early leaders of the Chasidic movement is that many, if not most, of them were reared in the severely ascetic, self-mortifying kabbalistic milieu of the day, largely a result of the newly promulgated teachings of Rabbi Yitzchak Luria, and their "conversion" to such a radically positive philosophy as we are told Rabbi Yisrael Baal Shem Tov came to reveal would, arguably, have required nothing short of a psychological, emotional, even neurological, rebirth.

So how successful were the original Chasidic masters in shedding the ascetic tendencies so deeply ingrained in their psyches?

The answer is: we do not have the ability to truly know, for no matter what their books may say, or what their followers' stories may tell us, they reveal only what they want us to know.

But we must somehow attempt to comprehend the fact that the practitioners of Chasidism, an approach to living that we are told was originally intended to marry the physical and the spiritual in perfect loving union, are today those in the religious Jewish community whose physical and spiritual sensibilities are perhaps most divorced from one another – especially in the realm of sex.

This topic shall be explored at greater length in a future dedicated essay, *Chasidism and the Joy of Sex – Mixed Messages.*

In the meantime, see Rabbi Elimelech of Lizhensk, *Noam Elimelech, Parshas Breishis*:

> The way of the true *tzadik* [holy man] is that he has no sexual thought or fantasy or desire, even for his own wife.
>
> And even when he has sex with his wife, he must be thinking about the supernal spiritual realms and not be conscious at all that he is with his wife.

One must wonder, in fact, how such a man is supposed to fulfill his halachic obligation to satisfy his wife sexually, or, for that matter, even maintain an erection, if he is expected to force his thoughts so far away elsewhere.

Such was the question addressed by a certain Rabbi Zechariah Mendel, in a letter he composed upon the instruction of Rabbi Elimelech of Lizhensk himself. (See the letter printed in the back of *Noam Elimelesh* already in the 1788 Lvov edition, and the publisher's forward to it. See also, on the topic, Rabbi Eliyahu de Vidas's *Reishis Chochmah, Shaar Hakedushah* 16:13-19).

In the course of a lengthy response to a detractor of Chasidism, in which he describes a utopian Chasidic society of spiritual purity and brotherly love, Rabbi Zechariah Mendel interjects the following in a description of its leaders' superhuman perfection:

> They sanctify themselves to such an extent that the physical impulse for pleasure dissipates from them completely, and they have no drive or sensual passion for any of this world's pleasures.
>
> And now that I've touched upon this quality, I will recall . . . what I once heard from one of the great among them, an interpretation on the verse [in Leviticus 23:3-4], "If you walk in My statutes... I will give you your rain in its [beneficial] time." Rashi [on the words of the verse, "in its beneficial time"] comments [based on *Babylonian Talmud, Taanis 32a*]: "On the Sabbath [or Festival] night [when one does not have to travel]."
>
> The interpretation: A person must attach himself to the service of G-d, Blessed be He, with so much constant purity of mind, until he reaches this level that all sensual passion has dissipated from his body completely, and he has no drive for the pleasures of this world, whether for food or drink or sex or any other human pleasure, such as honor or the like.
>
> But if he is on such a level, he is unable to fulfill the commandment placed upon him by Torah to give his wife regular sexual satisfaction [because he cannot achieve an erection]?
>
> The answer is that G-d, Who is good, in His great mercifulness, has mercy upon such a person who is on such a level, and G-d provides him at the moment he really needs it the physical impulse and drive for the duration of that time alone, so that he may fulfill the commandment. And afterwards, he returns to his previous state which he was at before and he continues without any sensual passion or drive for physical pleasure, as he had caused within himself through his pure actions and holy thoughts.
>
> And according to this, the meaning of the verse is self-understood:
>
> "If you will walk in My statutes" – this refers to what I described before, that the righteous *tzadik* goes with thoughts of G-d, Blessed be He, constantly, without pause, until he reaches this level that the physical drive for pleasure dissipates from him, as described above.
>
> "And I will give you your rain in its [beneficial] time" – G-d, Blessed be He, promises that He will give him a new "physicality" ["*gashmius*," sharing the same Hebrew root as "*geshem* – rain"] at the time it is needed to fulfill the biblical commandment to give one's wife sexual satisfaction.
>
> And this is why Rashi comments, "On the Sabbath night" – [for the Sabbath night is] the mandated time for Torah scholars to satisfy their wives.
>
> On your life, is there sweeter [Torah teaching] than this?!

To mitigate the fallout of such teachings, some will point to an interpretation reported in the name of Rabbi Elimelech of Lizhensk's most famous disciple, Rabbi Yaakov Yitzchak Horowitz, the "Seer" of Lublin (1745-1815), who had yet spent time in the court of Rabbi Elimelech's own master, Rabbi Dovber of Mezritch (the "Maggid of Mezritch," second leader of the collective Chasidic Movement).

It is reported that Rabbi Yaakov Yitzchak interpreted the above prescription of Rabbi Chaim Vital about "sanctification" of sex – i.e., that the man should avoid any sense of enjoyment in it at all – as applying only to the time of foreplay, or perhaps immediately before sexual contact commences, but certainly not to intercourse itself, for, as Rabbi Yaakov Yitzchak reportedly conceded, it is impossible not to experience pleasure during intercourse.

Rabbi Yaakov Yitzchak's proof that pleasure during sex cannot be a hindrance to sexual sanctity is from a comment in *Midrash Socher Tov*, that King David's father, Jesse, reportedly had sex (at least once) purely for his own pleasure, and it is also reported among the sages that Jesse was one of the few men in history whose death was not caused by sin.

Now, let it be stated from the outset that it is unclear how Rabbi Yaakov Yitzchak's interpretation actually resolves anything, for if one is expected to repress enjoyment of the sensual pleasures of foreplay, or if one is at least expected to truly and successfully force all thoughts of sex and sexual pleasure out of the mind and emotions immediately prior to physical contact, then a) we have still perpetuated an approach to sex that views sexual pleasure as evil; and b) how will this same person reasonably be able to build up the physical heat and passion to achieve or maintain erection?

Be that as it may, this teaching of Rabbi Yaakov Yitzchak is cited in two early Chasidic sources: *Sur Mera*, by Rabbi Tzvi Hirsch of Ziditchev (1763-1831), a disciple of Rabbi Yaakov Yitzchak, and *Derech Pikudecha*, by Rabbi Tzvi Elimelech Shapiro of Dinov (1783-1841), also a disciple Rabbi Yaakov Yitzchak, a close colleague of Rabbi Tzvi Hirsch, and a great-nephew of Rabbi Elimelech of Lizhensk.

[Actually, Rabbi Tzvi Elimelech in his *Derech Pekudecha* is merely quoting and analyzing the report of his colleague, Rabbi Tzvi Hirsch; and Rabbi Tzvi Hirsh's report in *Sur Mera* is accompanied in the 1997 edition by marginal notes of Rabbi Tzvi Elimelech.

Credit goes to Rabbi Dr. Louis Jacobs (1920-2006) for bringing this source in *Sur Mera* to my attention, in the chapter on sex in his book, *What Does Judaism Say About...?* (Ktav, 1973).]

Rabbi Tzvi Hirsch, in *Sur Mera* (pp. 36-37 in the 1997 edition), endorses Rabbi Yaakov Yitzchak's interpretation, bringing in support of it a comment of their own teacher, Rabbi Elimelech of Lizhensk, who cites in his *Noam Elimelech, Parshas Vayishlach* an explanation among the Jewish legal commentaries that the reason no ritual blessing was instituted for sex is because it's impossible to have sex without a little "evil inclination" mixed in.

[Alternatively, it is possible Rabbi Tzvi Hirsch meant to say that Rabbi Yaakov Yitzchak himself brought *Noam Elimelech, Parshas Vayishlach* in support of his own interpretation. In any case, why the pleasure of sex should be deemed less "rectifiable" than other physical pleasures, such as food, remains to be explored.]

Now, it cannot go without immediate mention that this teaching of Rabbi Elimelech in *Parshas Vayishlach* would appear to soften the teaching of his we saw above, this endnote, in *Parshas Breishis*, about the proper mindset of a righteous *tzadik* during sex. HOWEVER, it does not *resolve* the teaching in *Parshas Breishis*, it merely creates a tension that is arguably irreconcilable and could arguably lead to neurotic tendencies among innocent readers. And the very fact that the teaching in *Parshas Vayishlach* categorizes sexual pleasure as a matter of the "evil inclination," and so much so that it is not even worthy of a blessing, itself has – not empathetic, but – extremely negative implications.

In any case, Rabbi Tzvi Hirsch himself goes on to write that he encourages his own students to personally thank G-d for the joy of sex, but he immediately adds:

> However, *as much as is possible for each individual to avoid sensing sexual pleasure, he should avoid it* (*amnam, mah sheb'yecholes ha'adam l'harchik atzmo min hanaah, b'vadai yarchik*).
>
> As I heard in the name of the holy rabbi, our master, Rabbi Dov Ber [the Maggid of Mezritch], that when [it is related in *Talmud, Kesubos 104a* that] Rabeinu Hakadosh [Rabbi Yehudah Hanasi, "Rebbi," author of the Mishnah – the same Rebbi who permitted "overturning the table" on *Nedarim 20b*] testified [to G-d on his deathbed], 'I did not derive pleasure even from my little finger,' he was referring to sanctity in sex – as the Sages say elsewhere [*Talmud, Pesachim 112a*] "Not all 'fingers' [i.e., penises] are alike."

We will yet see another teaching of Rabbi Dovber, below, that is perhaps in line with the spirit of this one cited by Rabbi Tzvi Hirsch.

[Note that Maimonides in two places, in his *Introduction to Ethics of the Fathers, Shmoneh Perakim, Chapter Four* (p. 253, top of column two, in the Kapach edition) and in his commentary on *Ethics of the Fathers 5:13* (p. 301, second half of column one, in the Kapach edition) does speak about the virtue of *avoiding sensual pleasure* in general – but he says to do so *only slightly*, and in both places he is speaking in the context of those who are *psychologically-emotionally-physically mature and prepared* to strive for elevations of the spirit.

In his words (transliteration according to the Hebrew translation of Rabbi Yosef Kapach):

<u>Introduction to Ethics of the Fathers, Chapter Four</u>: loe hayu **hachasidim** maamidin techunos nafsham b'tchunas hamemutzaas beshaveh, ele hayu notim netiyah me'atah clapei ha'yitur oe ha'chisur derech siyag, c'lomar she'heim notim derech mashal min haprishus clapei he'eder ha'hergesh b'hanaos **me'at**.

<u>Commentary to Ethics of the Fathers 5:13</u>: hacharigah min haprishus **me'at** l'tzad he'eder hahergesh **zehu min haraoi l'shleimim . . . nikra chasid**).]

Moving on to Rabbi Tzvi Elimelech's treatment of the subject, both in his glosses to *Sur Mera* and in his *Derech Pikudecha* (*Mitzvah 1, Pru u'Rvu, Chelek Hadibur*, paragraphs 5-6, pp. 35-36 in the 1914 Lemberg edition), he deflates Rabbi Yaakov Yitzchak's proof from *Midrash Socher Tov* in regard to Jesse.

In footnote 43 to *Sur Mera*, he also implies that his master, Rabbi Yaakov Yitzchak, may have forced his interpretation of *Midrash Socher Tov* in order to find merit for the common-folk.

And in *Derech Pikudecha*, paragraph 5, he ends off that:

Whatever the case may be, *from a halachic perspective* there is no reason to hold back from fulfilling the commandment [to give one's wife sexual satisfaction] just because one truly enjoys sex – *only from a pious perspective*, and we will explain this further to come, with G-d's help (*yihiyeh eich sheyihiyeh, al pi hadin ein zeh ikuv l'maaseh hamitzvah im b'emes neheneh mei'ha'maaseh, rak hu mimili d'chasidi, v'yevuar ode l'kaman im yirtyzeh Hashem*).

Note that Rabbi Tzvi Elimelech's use of the term "*mili d'chasidi*" may or may not have been referring to the teachings of the latter-day "Chasidic Movement" specifically. And it is unclear which exact later part of his lengthy presentation he was pointing the reader to for further clarification. But whatever part it was, this passage says what it says and leaves its readers with a distinct impression.

In any case, he goes on in *Derech Pikudecha*, paragraph 6, and in footnote 44 to *Sur Mera*, to discuss the question of why no blessing was instituted for the joy of sex. In the course of that discussion, he admits that he had never come across any halachic authority that gives the explanation cited by Rabbi Elimelech of Lizhensk in *Noam Elimelech, Parshas Vayishlach*, though he equally admits that this is not proof against it, and he is prepared to rely upon Rabbi Elimelech's saintly authority and knowledge.

Rabbi Tzvi Elimelech concludes his discussion in *Derech Pikudecha*, reiterating Rabbi Tzvi Hirsch's encouragement that, in the absence of an officially-established ritual blessing, one should still thank G-d in his or her own personal way for the joy of sex.

Here ends our analysis of the teachings of Rabbi Elimelech of Lizhensk in *Noam Elimelech* and the teaching reported in the name of his disciple, Rabbi Yaakov Yitzchak of Lublin, in *Sur Mera* and *Derech Pikudecha*.

See also Rabbi Menachem Mendel of Chabad-Lubavitch (*Tzemach Tzedek*, 1789-1866), *Derech Mitzvosecha*, end of chapter "*Masa HaAron b'Kesef*":

> [The *tzadik's*] involvement in that which is necessary for the world's existence and for the existence of his own body and the bodies of his family members *should only be by force, without pleasure in it* (*b'hechrech, bilti oneg b'zeh*), only because he is forced to maintain his body and the bodies of his family members according to Torah obligation so that he may achieve the ultimate true goal, service of G-d and comprehension of Him through Torah and its commandments, to which his face gazes and stares and longs and pines.
>
> *And this is what the Sages spoke of* [on Nedarim 20b, describing Rabbi Eliezer as having sex] *"as if he were forced by a demon."*

[Parenthetically, two separate friends of mine, in two separate post-high school Chabad yeshivahs, expressed to me that according to the *Book of Tanya* of Rabbi Schneur Zalman of Liadi (1745-1812) – founder of the Chabad-Lubavitch Chasidic movement and grandfather of Rabbi Menachem Mendel (*Tzemach Tzedek*) – a husband is not supposed to enjoy sex. When I've shared this with others, the response has been that these students did not properly understand the *Tanya's* message in regard to the enjoyment of physical pleasure. Perhaps. But this passage by Rabbi Schneur Zalman's grandson suggests they may have been subject to what is often a confusing and contradictory message in Chabad Chasidic teaching (and in the teachings of other Chasidic groups) about physical pleasure in general. And see our forthcoming study, *Chasidism and Physical Pleasure – Mixed Messages*. And see our next points below.]

See also, in related spirit, *Or HaEmes* p. 14 (7b) and *Tzavaas HaRivash*, chapter 101, in the name of Rabbi Dovber of Mezritch (d.1772). Text below in parentheses appears only in *Or Haemes* or denotes original Hebrew wording; brackets added for clarification:

> During sex, a person must be as non-existent. And this is the meaning of [the Talmudic passage in *Nidah 17a*]: "Rabah would chase away the flies" – that is, he didn't consider himself even as significant as a fly.
>
> (Regard oneself as no more than a craftsman's tool. When a craftsman hits the rock with a hammer, this happens because of *his* desire, not because of the hammer's desire to hit the rock – for if it were the latter, the hammer would be independent of the craftsman...
>
> Then all of a man's limbs are but tools:
>
> He needs to eat to feed his body, he doesn't eat to indulge his desires (*v'lo yochal l'shem taavosav*).
>
> Similarly, he needs to preserve the species into the next generation, which is impossible without [sex between] male and female. And he views her [his wife] and himself as but tools, not that they are having sex for their own desires.
>
> And he will not love anything but G-d and His commandments. Thus,) he will love his wife like he loves his *tefilin* [phylacteries], which he loves only for the sake of observing G-d's commandment.
>
> And he will not fantasize about her (*v'lo yeharher acharehah*), for the matter is no different than the analogy of one who is traveling to [market on] marketday, and he cannot do so without a horse. Would he therefore come to love the horse(s)? Is there anything more foolish than this?! (Rather, he is disgusted by them – *v'yima'es osam*.)
>
> Likewise, in this world a man needs a wife for the service of the Creator in order to merit the World to Come. Thus, could anything be more foolish than to forsake his (holy) affairs to fantasize about her? Rather, he is disgusted by her (*v'yima'es osah*).

While this teaching reported in the name of Rabbi Dovber does not address the question of *enjoying* the *pleasure* of sex in particular, it is possible that the attitude it expresses influenced the attitudes of his disciples, including that of Rabbi Elimelech of Lizhensk, discussed above (this endnote).

Now, in his *Igeret Hakodesh 25*, Rabbi Schneur Zalman of Liadi asserts that the general wording of the teachings in *Tzavaas Harivash* cannot be relied upon as being precise, for they were in many cases recorded second-hand and translated into Hebrew from Yiddish. But in the case of the specific teaching quoted above in the name of Rabbi Dovber, the main body of its text is corroborated nearly word for word in *Or Haemes* of Rabbi Levi Yitzchak of Berditchev, and the latter includes an entire preface not found in *Tzavaas Harivash*.

Nevertheless, we must still give Rabbi Dovber the benefit of the doubt that his words may not have been recorded and/or reported accurately or within their full original context.

That being said, Rabbi Schneur Zalman himself does speak about the virtue of a man training himself to be disgusted by the thought of a woman's body, in a nuanced discussion in his *Book of Tanya* about what differentiates a *tzadik*, a "righteous" person, from a *benoni*, an "intermediate" person – i.e., one who is neither righteous nor sinful.

As stated, the discussion is nuanced. But if we must summarize in a general way:

# ENDNOTES

Rabbi Schneur Zalman explains that there is a fundamental change in the psychological-emotional-spiritual makeup of a person whom G-d chooses to elevate to the level of *tzadik*, whereby his inclination for the physical is literally transformed into pure good. One manifestation of this, Rabbi Schneur Zalman tells us, is that he becomes disgusted by physical desires that *completely lack* G-dly intent. See, for example, *Tanya, Chapter 10*:

> He is therefore called a "*tzadik* who is completely good" ... He is very much disgusted by the commoners' pursuit of the pleasures of this [physical] world for the sake of satiating the body's desires ***alone***, without intention for the service of G-d.

The *benoni*, on the other hand, has his natural inborn inclinations for the physical. He is therefore not disgusted by base physical desire, nor is he expected to be. But when he does experience base desire, he does not *entertain* it in thought, and he certainly does not speak about it or act upon it. If he were to do so, Rabbi Schneur Zalman says, he would descend into the category of *rasha* – wicked – until he repents. Rather, when the *benoni* enjoys the physical in thought, speech or action, he does so, like the *tzadik*, with at least some conscious G-dly intent.

[Let it be stressed again that this summary does not do justice to Rabbi Schneur Zalman's lengthy analysis in *Tanya* defining the psychological-emotional-spiritual natures of the *tzadik*, *benoni* and *rasha*. Those interested in understanding his thesis in greater depth may find what they are looking for in *Shiurim B'Sefer HaTanya-Lessons in Tanya*, published by Kehot Publication Society. The original Yiddish edition was authored by Rabbi Joseph Weinberg and edited by Rabbi Menachem Mendel Scheerson, the seventh rebbe of Chabad-Lubavitch.]

Still, Rabbi Schneur Zalman adds, even the *benoni* should *attempt to train himself* to be disgusted by base physical desire – in his words (*Tanya, Chapter 14*):

> Not every person merits to be transformed [by G-d] into a *tzadik*, and it is not even within [the natural spiritual makeup of] a person to choose to find true pleasure in G-d alone and to be truly disgusted by evil ...
>
> Nevertheless, he must set aside times to train himself to become disgusted by evil – for example, [implementing] the advise of our sages, of blessed memory (*atzas chachmeinu zal*), [to focus on the thought that] "A woman's intestines are a vessel full of feces [and the mouth of her womb is full of blood]."

Rabbi Schneur Zalman's intention, here, is not necessarily that a man train himself to be disgusted by sex in-and-of-itself. It is reasonable to believe that his message was that if a man approaches sex purely as a base physical desire to be indulged, then he should at least ***sensitize*** himself to the true purpose of sex – to cleave to one's wife and become one with her – by remembering that if sex is purely about focus on the physical body, it "logically" leads to disgust.

Therefore, perhaps Rabbi Schneur Zalman's master, Rabbi Dovber, had a similar intention in his analogy about the horses cited above from *Or HaEmes* and *Tzavaas HaRivash*.

[Two points, however, worth mentioning for further research and discussion:

Firstly, even along the lines of Rabbi Schneur Zalman's reasoning, it could be argued that so long as the average husband's sexual behaviors are not *solely* motivated by erotic desire, but *also at least a little bit* by more altruistic intentions, he need not be ***anxious*** about his human imperfections (– of course, a person's goal in life in general should be to grow, but the growth that is to be strived for is growth that is healthy, functioning and stable; spiritual striving that results in poor self-image, physical or spiritual, or, within marriage, lack of harmony in the marital relationship or in the home and family life in general, is neither ideal nor meritorious, which is why we are stressing this point). We've already seen above, page 99, the lists of worthy sexual intentions provided by Maimonides and by Raavad III. Add to them the intention of the verse itself in Genesis 2:24 to cleave to one's spouse – psychologically, emotionally and physically, including through simple mutual sexual pleasure (see *Sanhedrin 58b*, Rashi: *Shelo Cedarcah*) – and the average husband and wife have plenty of intentions at their disposal to *complement*, not *replace*, their erotic desires and pleasures and to elevate their sex life without resorting to physical or spiritual extremes. And see above, pp. 93-107.

We should also be reminded that from a *halachic* perspective, the very justification for anal sex within marriage, or at least intra-anal ejaculation, is that it is for the sake of a husband's sexual fulfillment (as discussed, above, pp. 91-92, 118-122) – but being that such is obviously to be done only with the wife's permission, it presumably also becomes a form of bonding, of cleaving (see above, endnotes 344, 408). At the very least, it may be a way for the husband to avoid illicit fantasies (see above, p. 107 and endnote thereon). It therefore also can be said to involve elements of holiness.

And see above, p. 68 and endnote 271 thereon, that according to *Tosfos Yeshanim* on *Nedarim 20b*, the Sages, there, not only permitted anal sex within marriage, they believed that in performing anal sex (with one's wife's permission) "there is no lack of holiness."

And even in regard to a *tzadik*, there is a teaching in the name of Rabbi Schneur Zalman's same master, Rabbi Dovber, that sometimes the body of a *tzadik* can have a mind of its own (see *Tehilim Ohel Yosef Yitzchak, Kovetz Michtavim*, p. 197: "*gam guf kadosh basar hu*"). Perhaps this principle would apply also in the realm of sexual eroticism.

And further research into the matter is required.

Secondly, there is yet another fundamental issue to address in all this – namely, that the source of this "advice of the Sages" mentioned by Rabbi Schneur Zalman remains to be verified.

The authoritative commentary on Rabbi Schneur Zalman's work mentioned above, *Shiurim B'Sefer HaTanya-Lessons in Tanya*, references *Babylonian Talmud, Shabbos 152a*. But there, we do not find *advice* by any sage that a man should ever train himself to be disgusted in any way by the female body. Perhaps Rabbi Schneur Zalman was referencing the interpretation of a commentary.

[**Added note to the third edition:** Rabbi Schneur Zalman may have been drawing upon one manuscript version of a passage in Raavad III's *Baalei HaNefesh*, quoted on page 174 of the Buchwald edition of *Baalei HaNefesh*. Credit goes to Rabbi Simcha Feuerman for bringing this source to my attention on page 43 of his *Kuntres Es Lifrosh v'Es Le'ehov* (2016). See also page 12 of Rabbi Feuerman's work, where he addresses the potential danger to marital harmony by a husband's misinterpretation and/or misapplication of such a notion.]

The relevant passage on *Shabbos 152a* reads:

# ENDNOTES

[What is the meaning of the phrase in Ecclesiastes 12:5,] "And the desire fails" – this refers to the sexual impulse.

Rav Cahana was once reciting verses before [his master], Rav. When he came to this [phrase in this] verse, Rav sighed. He [Rav Cahana] later said: "We can deduce from this that Rav's sexual impulse had dissipated."

Rav Cahana taught: "'He commanded, and it [His command] stands' (Psalms 33:9) – this refers to [man's attraction to] woman . . ."

It was taught: A woman's intestines are a vessel full of feces, and the mouth of her womb is full of blood, and yet all run after her.

See the commentary of Rashi, there (*Zu Ishah*), where he combines the last two points of the Talmudic discussion, and explains that if not for the decree of G-d, the Almighty King, that man be attracted to woman, man would not, based on his own powers of *intellect*, find it worthy to be attracted to her. See also the medieval commentary, *Nimukei Yosef*, there.

But we do not find a *recommendation* by any sage on *Shabbos 152a* that it is holy, or healthy, for a man to attempt to think of women in an unattractive manner – let alone to think in such a way about one's own wife. Rather, we find the sage, Rav, reportedly sighing that he had lost his sexual impulse; we find Rav Cahana stating that the sexual impulse exists, and exists in full force, by G-d's own decree; and we find a passage attesting to, and perhaps even marveling at, the power of this divine decree, such that intellectualizing the sexual impulse in order to break it is utterly futile. In other words, the Talmud appears to be saying that G-d *wants* a man to be *uncontrollably* sexually attracted to his own wife.

(See also, in regard to Rav, *Hagigah 5b*, *Shabbos 152a*, *Yoma 18b*, *Yevamos 37b*, and *Tosfos*, *Yevamos 37b:Yichuda b'alma havu meyachdi*.

And note that in discussing the intellect's inability to break the natural sexual urge G-d Himself fashioned, the passage attests to the futility in attempting to think of a woman as either "a vessel full of feces" or "a mouth full of blood" – perhaps alluding to the unbreakable nature of the male desire for either anal intercourse or vaginal intercourse, respectively.)

As for why the uncontrollable urge for sex might be considered so necessary if it ostensibly reduces man as an intellectual being, in addition to the fact that this urge is critical for the perpetuation of the human species, two succinct passages in *Midrash Rabah*, both commenting on the very same verse in Ecclesiastes as *Talmud, Shabbos 152a*, might shed further light on the matter:

*Vayikrah Rabah 18:1*: "And the desire fails" – this refers to the sexual impulse, **which fosters peace between husband and wife.**

*Koheles Rabah 12:1:5*: "And the desire fails" – this refers to the sexual impulse, **which fosters peace between husband and wife**, and then dissipates . . .

See also *Shabbos 152a, Nimukei Yosef*: "*Meisim Shalom Babayis – taavas tashmish.*"

See also *Shabbos 152a, Peirush Rashi*: "*Meisim Shalom Babayis – ever tashmish.*" Credit goes to Rabbi Simcha Feuerman for bringing this source to my attention on page 32 of his *Kuntres Es Lifrosh v'Es Le'ehov* (2016).

See also *Breishis Rabah 9:7*.

And further research into the matter is required.]

Moving on in our discussion, see also Rabbi Daniel Frisch's *Kedushah uTznius* (1994), page 81, section 13, quoting *Ateres Yeshuah* in the name of a Rebbe of Radomsk

> "Send away the mother [bird], and [only then] the children [the eggs] take for yourself" [Deuteronomy 22:7].
>
> The verse is instructing us that one needs to sanctify oneself very much during sex, so that thoughts of one's wife – the "mother" – should not arise in one's mind at all, but only [thoughts of] the perpetuation of the [human] species, to bear "children."
>
> And this is the interpretation of the verse: 'Send away the mother [bird]' – that is, banish from yourself all thoughts [during sex] of the mother; only 'the children take for yourself' – for your intention should be [only] to bear children.

See also *Kuntres Divrei Tznius* (printed in the back of Rabbi Frisch's *Kedushah u'Tznius*), page 17 section 9, a speech of a Toldos Aaron rebbe to young married men instructing them about sanctification in marital intimacy:

> I heard from Rabbi Asher Zelig Margolis, that he heard from his teacher, the holy rabbi of Barnov, who was very close to the holy rabbi [Rabbi Chaim] of Sanz, that once he came very late at night and he peeked through the keyhole of the door of the holy rabbi. He saw a candle lit on the table, and the holy rabbi of Sanz was holding his holy hand above the flame, burning his hands at the wrists (*makom hadofek*), and blood was running from his hands.
>
> The rabbi of Barnov shuddered, unsure whether to open the door to enter to make him stop, because if he entered perhaps the holy rabbi would be upset at him. He decided: "Come what may upon me, I must enter" – and he opened the door and entered.
>
> As soon as the holy rabbi saw him, he hid his hand inside the other, as if nothing had occured, and greeted him with a happy countenance: "Welcome, grandson of the holy rabbi of Ropshitz!"
>
> And he spoke to him with love and friendship, as if nothing had occurred.
>
> And the rabbi of Barnov concluded that afterwards it became known to him that every time it was his [Rabbi Chaim of Sanz's] wife's *mikveh* night, he would do this [burn his hands].
>
> Let us imagine how much pain a person experiences in burning his hand through fire or boiling water. He endures great suffering and must involve himself in its healing to quiet the suffering and heal the pains. How much more so to burn oneself at the wrist, and to the point of bleeding. And all this the holy rabbi of Sanz did in order to turn his holy intentions from that thing, and so that no physical sensations should enter his intentions.
>
> And who can compare himself to the holy rabbi of Sanz, but still we see from this how early righteous *tzadikim* took measures so that thoughts of [sexual pleasure] would not enter their hearts at all.
>
> And well known is the great and awesome holiness of the holy Rabbi Avraham Hamalach (1739-1776), son of the holy Rabbi Dovber, that in his entire life he fulfilled the commandment [to have sex with his wife] only twice. And on the wedding night he cried out, so difficult was it for him to lower himself to the physical. And his cry caused his wife to faint. And the holy rabbi bore two supernally holy sons.

After his death, he came [in a dream] to appease his widow for not treating her in the way of the world.

We see from all this how the early righteous *tzadikim* behaved in holiness and purity, and merited through their holiness and self-sacrifice to draw down holy souls [into their children] who radiated holiness and purity to the entire generation.

Notice how even after Rabbi Avaham Hamalach is said to have apologized to his wife for his behavior, his behavior itself is still praised by the speaker!

And despite the qualification that these were acts of righteous *tzadikim*, it is arguable that the extollation of such acts is itself damaging to innocent, and especially young, minds.

But even if these stories never actually occured, and even if few ever heard of them, and even if we could force softer meaning into all the teachings of all the Chasidic masters cited above, the existence of such stories and teachings cannot be ignored, nor can their implication, namely, that there is evidence of an anti-sex, anti-pleasure mentality and consciousness going back to the earliest Chasidic masters that would possibly best explain the extremist mindest that continues to prevail in many parts of the Chasidic world to this day.

And see Professor Benjamin Brown's 2013 study, *Kedushah: The Sexual Abstinence of Married Men in Gur, Slonim and Toledot Aaron.*

[It has been argued to me that we simply do not understand the original context or tone of such stories or teachings – that "That's not what they meant!" Perhaps. But this argument does not change the damaging impact such stories or teachings may have had upon the collective Chasidic psyche over many generations.

For an acknowledgment by a venerable Chasidic rabbi about the confusion and anxiety caused to many in the realm of marital sexuality by (a widespread misunderstanding of) the teachings of Chasidism, see the letter of Rabbi Avraham Shimon Engel-Horowitz of Zelichov (1886-1943), a pre-war Rosh Yeshivah of the Chabad Yeshivas Tomchei Temimim in Warsaw, and later Mashgiach Ruchni of Yeshivas Chachmei Lublin, printed in *Naharei Eish, Letter 50* (credit goes to Rabbi Chaim Rapoport of London, UK for bringing this source to my attention; translation is my own):

> In regard to marital sex (*inyonei ishus*), I know with certainty that many souls have sunk, fallen, broken and been ensnared by what they've seen in [holy] books, and from what they've heard, without comprehending the nuance of the subject. They are of the impression that if a Jewish man is not pure like an angel then there is nothing that can remedy him or he has no worth at all. Such impressions have caused many to fall into despair [of attaining holiness] and nihilism. For some, the despair has even led them to forsake that which is [actually] permitted and to fall into the forbidden, Heaven forfend. It anguishes me greatly, this that they are stringent on account of exaggerations, thus causing what has been caused – and G-d, blessed be He, knows the truth.
>
> And so I write to you what is clear to me was the approach of the Tannaim and Amoraim – as one who investigates properly will discover: Certainly a person must guard his thoughts very, very much, not to dwell on sex, etcetera. And so must he also remove from his ruminations (*raayonav*) even [thoughts of] his own wife, may she be well. His focus and his heart should be pure, [engrossed] in Torah and service of G-d.
>
> However, if after all attempts to guard himself his mind remains firmly fixated on [his wife,] his portion gifted to him by G-d, blessed be He, let him rejoice in line with the

law of our holy Torah. But in all the various permitted behaviors try to keep dignity, humility and modesty in mind . . .

And give thanks and blessing [to the Creator] for the pleasure that He grants you, which is [granted to you] in an honorable and holy context. And the increased vibrance one feels through this pleasure should bring one to safeguard one's Torah with subservience before G-d . . .

Here it is in the original Hebrew:

ואודות ענייני אישות, מפני שידעתי בבירור שהרבה נפשות נשתקעו בזה, נפלו ונשברו נוקשו ונלכדו ממה שראו בספרים ומן מה ששמעו ולא הבינו העניין לאשורו, כי חשבו שבאם אין האדם מישראל נקי כמלאך שוב אין לו תקנה או אינו שוה כלום, ומזה הרבה נפלו ליאוש ושממון, גם לאיזה מהם היאוש הוליך אותם הלאה לפרוש מן ההיתר ונפלו באיסור רח"ל. צר לי מאד על מה שהחמירו בגוזמאות וגרמו מה שגרמו, והשי"ת יודע האמת.

והנני כותב לך מה שברור אצלי שזאת דעת התנאים ואמוראים, דוק ותשכח. בודאי האדם צריך לשמור מחשבתו מאד לבלי להרהר משום עניין אישות וכו', וכן צריך לסלק מרעיוניו אפי' את זוגתו תחי', ויהי דעתו ולבו נקי בתורה ועבודה, אולם אחרי כל שמירה אם מחשבתו חזקה עליו לחלקו אשר נתן לו השי"ת, ישמח כדת תוה"ק, אבל בכל מיני היתר יש לזכור בושה ענוה וצניעות, וידע, כי זוגתו היא בתו של אברהם אבינו, והוא מן בני אבות הקדושים, ובורא כל הנשמות הבאים וזווגם יחד. ישום אל לבו כי כל ההנאות של יופי ועדינות, הכל חיות אלקי שנשתלשל אלפי אלפים מדריגות עד עוה"ז הגשמי וכו', ויתן שבח וברכה על הנאה הנתונה לו בכבוד ובמצוה, והחיות שנסתתף בו ע"י ההנאה תביאנו לקיום תורתך בהכנעה לפניך יתברך, ואל תביאנו לידי רחבות וגבהות הלב בעסקו בדברי חול, ויעמוק במחשבות טובות כפי כוחו.

ואם זוגתו יש לה מעט הבנה, נכון לדבר עמה מעט בנחת להבינה כי הקב"ה יצר אותנו יש מאין למען נדבק יחד באהבה מפני שמשורש אנו אחד וכו', וכמו"כ דברים טובים ונעימים המשמחים הלב ונפש. ובזה תתקדש ההנאה והההרגש לצאת מעט מתאות בשרי אל תאות זוג מישראל וכו'. המבין יבין שזה הדרך של חכמינו זי"ל, והבחינה לזה אם אינו שקוע בהנאה שטף תאוה אח"כ, ואם הוא בנקיות המחשבה כל היום זאת סימן כי נתעלתה גם ההנאה לקדושה.

גם לידע כי גוף בת ישראל העושה כמה מצוות שומרת שבת קודש ומתענת ביוה"כ וגם בזה העניין עצמו מזדככת בטבילה וטבילה, ובזה מתקשר לחיות אלקית ששם גוף טהור הזה ביפיפתו ועדינותו, ויודה להשי"ת בהכנעה ובושה וכו'. וידורו באהבה ושמחה בחלקם אשר נתן להם השי"ת, ויששו עליהם באהבתם זה לזה באמת, ויעמידו בנים כשרים נאמנים לאלקי ישראל.

For an acknowledgment by an early Chasidic master already in the third generation of the movement about the prevalence of depression and other mental illnesses manifesting among those seeking righteous elevation in general without proper maturity, preparation and/or guidance, see *Ohev Yisrael, Likutim, Parshas Vayikra*, by Rabbi Avraham Yehoshua Heschel of Apta (1748-1825).]

A future study in this series will explore if there exists any evidence that sexually ascetic figures throughout Jewish history may have been, to varying degrees, asexual.

[596] Rabbi Hersh Goldwurm, *The Early Acharonim* (Artscroll, Mesorah Publications 1989).

[597] See there, end of paragraph 1.

In many Chasidic-Charedi bookstores, I've seen *Reishis Chochmah, Shaar Hakedushah* stocked on the shelves alongside modern-day "family purity" and marital intimacy guides, suggesting that it is popular, or even recommended, reading for Chasidic-Charedi couples.

[598] *Reishis Chochmah, Shaar Hakedushah* 16:1.

⁵⁹⁹ Page 65 above, and endnote 258 thereon.

⁶⁰⁰ In any case, I suspect that many, if not most, young Chasidic-Charedi readers of *Reishis Chochmah*, here, do not go so far as to check up Rabbi Aboab's actual words. Instead, I suspect many rely on what they are taught by their pre-marriage teachers or on what they find in pious family purity/marital intimacy guides and/or *Shulchan Aruch, Orach Chaim 240*.

⁶⁰¹ *Reishis Chochmah, Shaar Hakedushah 16:28*.

⁶⁰² *Reishis Chochmah, Shaar Hakedushah 16:29-30*.

⁶⁰²* This reference to Rashi presumably refers to the *Mefaresh* commentary on *Nedarim 20ab*. See above, page 60, and endnote 230* thereon.

⁶⁰³ In reality, it is *Callah Rabti 1:13-14* that insists Rabbi Yochanan ben Dahavai's cautions were referring only to behaviors performed during the same sexual encounter in which conception occurs. *Nedarim 20ab* itself makes no such qualification.

That being said, Ameimar on *Nedarim 20b* does say that the "ministering angels'" superior knowledge would have been in the realm of the science of *fetal development* – so clearly Ameimar himself understood Rabbi Yochanan ben Dahavai's concerns on *Nedarim 20a* as relating to *congenital* illnesses that could result in the children of those who perform such sexual behaviors. It is only unclear if Ameimar understood his concerns as being limited to performance of such behaviors during the same sexual encounter in which conception occurs or as applying also to performance of such behaviors even prior to conception or any time after conception throughout pregnancy.

⁶⁰⁴ See *Pischei Teshuvah, Shulchan Aruch, Even Haezer 25:2* referencing *Panim Meiros vol. 2, Responsum 158*, whose author proves that any attempt to translate *"shelo cedarcah"* as anything other than anal intercourse is futile.

⁶⁰⁵ *Yad Aharon, Even Haezer 25:1* also makes note of Rabbi Eliyahu de Vidas's mistaken presentation of Rabeinu Asher.

⁶⁰⁶ Perhaps Rabbi Eliyahu de Vidas read this meaning into the *Mefaresh's* use of the term *"shelo cedarcah,"* because the *Mefaresh* also uses the term *"panim c'neged oref,"* which, *on its own*, usually does refer in rabbinic writing to rear-entry vaginal intercourse.

And perhaps he read this meaning into Rabeinu Asher's use of the term *"shelo cedarcah,"* because Rabeinu Asher emphasizes the discomfort the husband causes his wife *upon her knees*, and Rabbi Eliyahu may have assumed that if he had been referring to anal intercourse, he would have instead emphasized the (potentially much greater) pain of the penetration itself.

But whatever Rabbi Eliyahu's understanding might have been, it does not change the fact that his interpretation of the *Mefaresh* can be challenged. And the wider evidence all but proves that his interpretation of Rabeinu Asher is, with all due respect, incorrect, for in *Tosfos HaRosh* to both *Nedarim 20b* and *Yevamos 34b*, Rabeinu Asher himself makes perfectly clear that his use of the term *"shelo cedarcah"* was meant as referring to anal sex and that he understood the term "overturning the table" as referring to *"shelo cedarcah."*

⁶⁰⁶* Indeed, in both places Rabeinu Asher's interest is to reconcile the context of *Nedarim 20ab*, about "overturning the table," with the context of *Yevamos 34b*, about the "sin" of Er and Onan. Therefore, to argue that Rabeinu Asher intended the term *"shelo cedarcah"* to be understood as rear-entry vaginal intercourse would be to equally imply that he intended the

"sin" of Er and Onan to be understood as rear-entry vaginal intercourse – an extremely difficult notion.

And see below, endnote 607*.

⁶⁰⁷ True, we have demonstrated that Raavad III may still have permitted anal sex, as suggested by the silence we find in his glosses to *Mishneh Torah, Isurei Biah 21:9*. But Rabbi Eliyahu himself does not seem to be aware of this point.

And Raavad III's silence, there, would appear to be due to the clear and unequivocal ruling of the Talmud on *Sanhedrin 58b* permitting anal sex (*shelo cedarcah*), not to the definition of the ambiguous term "overturning the table" (*hafichas shulchan*) on *Nedarim 20ab* – the latter apparently being Rabbi Eliyahu's sole concern here.

⁶⁰⁷* Additionally, in the same way we explained above, endnote 606*, in regard to Rabeinu Asher, Rabeinu Yitzchak's interest in *Tosfos* to *Yevamos 34b* is to reconcile the context of *Nedarim 20ab*, about "overturning the table," with the context of *Yevamos 34b*, about the "sin" of Er and Onan. Therefore, to argue that Rabeinu Yitzchak intended the term "*shelo cedarcah*" to be understood as rear-entry vaginal intercourse would be to equally imply that he intended the "sin" of Er and Onan to be understood as rear-entry vaginal intercourse – an extremely difficult notion.

⁶⁰⁸ Not to be confused with the work by the same title by Rabbi Yitzchak Aboab. Rabbi Alnaqua's work was actually the inspiration for Rabbi Aboab's.

See Rabbi Alnaqua's *Menoras Hamaor*, volume 4, *Perek Nisuei Ishah*, page 81.

⁶⁰⁹ See the Shabsi Frankel edition of *Mishneh Torah, Sefer Kedushah*, in the *Yalkut Shinuyei Nuschaos* section in the back of the book, *Isurei Biah 21:9*.

It states there that in the 1574-1576 Venice edition of *Mishneh Torah* – printed in the lifetime of Rabbi Eliyahu de Vidas himself, and just three to five years prior to the first printing of his *Reishis Chochmah*, also in Venice – the Christian censors had removed Maimonides' entire passage, "And he may penetrate her vaginally or anally or between limbs."

It is thus not only possible, but probable, that Rabbi Eliyahu de Vidas had seen this version of Maimonides' ruling. He may have even assumed this "modern edition" to be more accurate than earlier editions of *Mishneh Torah* which did include the passage. Still, the fact that Maimonides' full ruling had already been quoted in other well-circulated authoritative books, including the *Tur*, leaves Rabbi Eliyahu's presentation of Maimonides problematic.

*Yad Aharon, Even Haezer 25:1* also notes Rabbi Eliyahu's mistaken understanding of Maimonides.

[As to how Rabbi Eliyahu would have known about Maimonides' (alleged) wording against "wasting seed in vain" in *Isurei Biah 21:9* if he had the 1574-1576 censored edition of *Mishneh Torah*, the censors of that edition did not remove that phrase.]

⁶¹⁰ See above, pp. 118-120, 123-124, 128.

⁶¹¹ See *Reishis Chochmah, Shaar Hakedushah 17:22*, where Rabbi Eliyahu de Vidas appears to make veiled reference to the same passage in *Zohar* that Rabbi Elazar Azikri openly references in *Sefer Charedim, Chapter 64*, which specifically speaks against "wasting seed in vain" through anal sex (see footnote 78 in the 1984 Waldman edition of *Reishis Chochmah*).

And see our response to Rabbi Azikri about this point, below, p. 157 point 1.

⁶¹² *Elyah Rabah* to *Levush, Orach Chaim 240:4:10*.

[613] Rabbi Azikri argues that because Maimonides permits anal sex only without intra-anal ejaculation, and because Rabeinu Asher only permits intra-anal ejaculation "once in a lifetime" (*paam achas*), and because Rabbi Yaakov ben Asher in his *Tur, Even Haezer 25* quotes Raavad III's interpretation of the term "overturning the table" last (after Rabeinu Yitzchak's), namely that the term refers to rear-entry vaginal intercourse, it must therefore be that couples who engage in anal sex of any kind deserve the special place in Purgatory described by the *Zohar* for those who "waste seed . . . through anal sex."

Rabbi Azikri also seems to invoke the teaching in *Zohar, Parshas Noach* (paragraph 57 in the Sulam edition) that "wasting seed in vain" can only be rectified through "great repentance."

There are three fundamental difficulties in Rabbi Azikri's argument, the last two of which *Elyah Rabah* to *Levush, Orach Chaim 240:10:4* already points out:

1. Maimonidean scholars today reject the authenticity of the phrase in *Mishneh Torah, Sefer Kedushah, Isurei Biah 21:9* restricting intra-anal ejaculation or ejaculation between limbs for married couples (see above, pp. 118-120, 123-124, 128).

   [And even if we were to accept its authenticity, the *definition* of "wasting seed in vain" in this context (as Maimonides himself may have intended it) could perhaps be understood as *constant* intra-anal ejaculation or *constant* ejaculation between limbs for the sake of *intentional* and *unsanctioned* birth control, not *occasional* intra-anal ejaculation or *occasional* ejaculation between limbs for the sake of *sexual fulfillment* within marriage (see above, pp. 119-120, 128 and endnote 484 in regard to how Rabeinu Yonah and Rabeinu Nissim understood the restrictive version of *Isurei Biah 21:9*).]

2. Nowhere does Rabeinu Asher ever stipulate that intra-anal ejaculation is permitted only once in a lifetime. On the contrary, it is obvious from Rabeinu Asher in three separate places – *Tosfos HaRosh* to *Nedarim 20b*, *Tosfos HaRosh* to *Yevamos 34b*, and *Rabeinu Asher (Rosh)* as quoted in *Hagahos Habach* to *Rosh, Yevamos 34b*, in *Yam Shel Shlomoh* to *Yevamos 34b*, and in *Beis Yosef* to *Tur, Orach 240:2-4:4* – that it is permitted many times, so long as it is not habitual to the point of betraying obvious intentions of unsanctioned birth control.

   [It is interesting to note that one of Rabeinu Asher's disciples, Rabeinu Yeruchem, in *Rabeinu Yeruchem, Nesiv 23*, does use the term "*paam achas*" in discussing the permission for intra-anal ejaculation within marriage, as does *Tosfos Talmid Rabeinu Tam* (manuscript to Genesis 38:9, quoted in *Kovetz Meforshim, Nedarim 20, Leket Rishonim* by Yerid Haseforim, 2003; see above endnote 221; and compare to *Tosfos Hashalem al HaTorah, Vayeshev 38:9:11:V'shicheis Artzah*, p.66). But it is clear from both of them that they did not mean to permit intra-anal ejaculation only *once in a lifetime*, but rather *once in a while*.

   And see Rabbi Yehuda Henkin, in his *Bnei Banim*, vol. 4, end of *Responsum 18:1*, pp. 64-65, who says that Rabeinu Yeruchem's use of the term "*paam achas*" could mean once between each menstrual cycle. And see above, endnote 268.

   See also *Birchei Yosef* of Rabbi Chaim Yosef Dovid Azulai (Chida) to *Orach Chaim 240:5*, who quotes Rabeinu Yeruchem's use of the term "*paam achas*," but concludes that this was not the intention of Rabeinu Yitzchak in *Tosfos*. And as we know, Rabeinu Asher echoes Rabeinu Yitzchak.

# HALACHIC POSITIONS

Rabbi Azulai, there, also mentions *Elyah Rabah's* objections to *Sefer Charedim*. And Rabbi Azulai himself accuses the author of *Sefer Charedim* of "great, great exaggeration" (*higzim meod meod*) in his treatment of the topic of anal sex. Rabbi Azulai levels the same accusation in his *Pesach Einaim* to *Yevamos 34b*.]

3. Although in *Tur, Even Haezer 25*, Rabbi Yaakov ben Asher does bring Raavad III's interpretation of "overturning the table" last, *after* Rabeinu Yitzchak's, in *Orach Chaim 240* he does the opposite, quoting Rabeinu Yitzchak last, *after* Raavad III (which is why other halachic authorities come to the exact opposite conclusion as Rabbi Azikri, understanding Rabbi Yaakov ben Asher in *Tur* as ruling according to Rabeinu Yitzchak, permitting anal sex even with intra-anal ejaculation (see Rabbi Moshe Feinstein, *Igros Moshe, Even Haezer 1, Responsum 63*, end of p. 156, top of page 163).

Behold: By the very manner in which Rabbi Azikri builds his argument, he implicitly admits that if Maimonides *had* permitted intra-anal ejaculation – which we now have every reason to believe he *did*, and if Rabeinu Asher *had* permitted intra-anal ejaculation more than once in a lifetime – which Rabeinu Asher in fact *does*, and if Rabbi Yaakov ben Asher in *Tur had* brought Rabeinu Yitzchak after Raavad III – which Rabbi Yaakov ben Asher *does do* in *Tur, Orach Chaim 240*, then he (Rabbi Azikri) could never have made the claim that anal sex or occasional intra-anal ejaculation performed for sexual fulfillment within marriage are included in the "special place in Purgatory" described in the *Zohar*.

Therefore, the *Zohar's* condemnation of intra-anal ejaculation within marriage, if such was actually the author(s) of the *Zohar's* original intent, could be said to be relevant **only** to *constant* intra-anal ejaculation performed for the sake of *intentional* and *unsanctioned* birth control.

And note again that if *occasional* intra-anal ejaculation between husband and wife for the sake of *sexual fulfillment* within marriage is *not* to be included in the *Zohar's* condemnations, then occasional ejaculation between limbs between husband and wife for the sake of sexual fulfillment within marriage could arguably *not* be included in the *Zohar's* condemnations as well (at least according to the logic Rabbi Yehoshua Falk applied to the view of Rabeinu Yitzchak – see above, pp. 124-125).

See also our discussion of *Erech Shai* to *Even Haezer 25:2*, above, pp. 144-145 and endnotes thereon, in relation to other, much harsher, passages in the *Zohar* about "wasting seed in vain," albeit in the context of masturbation, and why they have no bearing on the permissibility of anal sex and intra-anal ejaculation between loving husband and wife for sexual fulfillment within marriage.

[614] Rabbi Azikri quotes Rabeinu Asher as permitting intra-anal ejaculation "only once in a whole lifetime" (*paam achas b'chol yamav*). On this, see previous endnote, point 2.

[615] Rabbi Azikri presents the *Mefaresh* as defining the term "overturning the table" *exclusively* as "her-on-top."

But see above, pp. 60-61, that the *Mefaresh* in no way limits the meaning of the term to her-on-top; it clearly speaks of anal sex (*shelo cedarcah*) as another valid interpretation.

[615*] Though I personally have not seen such alternate versions reported.

[616] Understanding the possible difficulties in Rabbi Azikri's argument is critical, for, as we shall see next in our study, it is arguably largely due to Rabbi Yeshayah Horowitz's endorsement of Rabbi Azikri's approach (in Rabbi Yeshayah's own legal-moral-mystical work, *Shnei Luchos Habris*) that anal sex within marriage for couples' sexual fulfillment has been villified in, or censored from, later Chasidic-Charedi publications on "family purity"

and marital intimacy. Another consequence has arguably been that no room was ever allowed among Chasidic-Charedi rabbinic circles for mature discussion to develop about permitting ejaculation between limbs when done between husband and wife purely for the sake of loving bonding and sexual fulfillment (not as a means of constant and intentional unsanctioned birth control).

We will only translate, here, Rabbi Azikri's main points. The sections in ellipses the interested reader can seek further on his or her own in the original Hebrew, but they are not germane to the key points of, and possible difficulties in, Rabbi Azikri's argument. Brackets are added for clarification and elucidation.

Rabbi Azikri writes in his *Sefer Charedim, Chapter 64, The Severity of the Sin of Anal Sex*:

> The main proof of the commentaries who permit anal sex is from *Sanhedrin 58b*, "Rabbi Elazer said..."
>
> But the view of Raavad III is that this is no proof, because according to them, one can counter with another question: Why did Rava assume in the first place that Rabbi Chanina was referring to a type of anal sex that a Jew is not liable for? Perhaps Rabbi Elazar [in the name of Rabbi Chanina] was referring to intra-anal ejaculation, which is the simple meaning of "[anal] intercourse" [unless otherwise specified (*b'hotzaas zera kaamar, c'stam biah*), and thus Rabbi Elazar was speaking of a case of anal sex which is forbidden even for Jews according to the first approach of Rabeinu Yitzchak]. Or perhaps Rabbi Elazar was speaking about habitual intra-anal ejaculation [for the sake of unsanctioned birth control, which is forbidden even for Jews] according to the second approach [of Rabeinu Yitzchak].
>
> [If Rabbi Elazar were in fact referring to either one of these two types of anal sex, each forbidden according to their respective approaches of Rabeinu Yitzchak] then Rava would have had no question [about a Jewish husband being exempt for anal sex with his wife, because Rabbi Elazar would have in fact been referring to a type of anal sex for which *both Jewish and non-Jewish husbands* are liable]!
>
> This would have certainly been a preferable way [for Rava] to reconcile [the teaching of Rabbi Chanina,] rather than [Rava] rewriting the teaching as reported in the name of Rabbi Elazar [in the name of Rabbi Chanina] ...
>
> Rather, in order to reconcile all this, we are forced to say – and even these commentaries [who use *Sanhedrin 58b* as their source to forbid anal sex only if there is intra-anal ejaculation, or only if such intra-anal ejaculation is habitual as a means of unsanctioned birth control] are forced to say – that Rava [understood that Rabbi Elazar was not referring to either of these two cases, and Rava] worded his question in response to Rabbi Elazer's own precise choice of wording: [That is,] being that Rabbi Elazar chose to speak specifically about a *non-Jewish* husband [having "forbidden" anal sex with his wife, when he could have just as easily discussed a *Jewish* husband having "forbidden" anal sex with his wife due to intra-anal ejaculation according to Rabeinu Yitzchak's first approach, or due to *habitual* intra-anal ejaculation according to Rabeinu Yitzchak's second approach] it suggests that he [Rabbi Elazar, in the name of Rabbi Chanina] was [intentionally] *excluding* a Jewish husband [from liability in the scenario he was discussing].

[Rava recognized] that if Rabbi Elazar had in fact been referring to a case of intra-anal ejaculation [which is forbidden according to the first approach of Rabeinu Yitzchak] or habitual intra-anal ejaculation [for the sake of unsanctioned birth control, which is forbidden according to the second approach of Rabeinu Yitzchak, there would have been no reason for Rabbi Elazer to exclude a Jewish husband from the scenario, for] Jewish couples, too, would be liable [for punishment by the hand of Heaven]. Therefore, [Rava understood in regard to Rabbi Elazar's teaching that] it must have been taught only in the context of *no habitual or even occasional* intra-anal ejaculation at all.

Thus, Rava protested: [If Rabbi Elazar were merely referring to anal *penetration* alone without any intra-anal ejaculation at all], how could he make the non-Jew[ish husband with his wife] liable [for anal penetration alone] while a Jew[ish husband with his wife] is exempt for it?! Rather, [Rava concluded,] in actuality, Rabbi Elazar must certainly have been teaching [only] a leniency [for non-Jews], that a non-Jewish man who performs anal *penetration* with another married non-Jewish woman is exempt, whereas a Jewish man would be liable [even just for *penetration* with another man's wife, even without intra-anal ejaculation].

But now that we've established this, we can say further that there is in fact no proof from here [Sanhedrin 58b] to permit anal sex at all [even where there is only *penetration* and no intra-anal ejaculation at all], in line with the [simple reading of the] Talmudic passage in *Yevamos* [34b] which says that anal sex was the sin of Er and Onan – without qualification [whether or not they performed intra-anal ejaculation] . . .

. . . And there is [still] no contradiction [to *Yevamos 34b*] from the Talmudic passage we have been discussing [on *Sanhedrin 58b*], for Rava made his comment on the teaching [reported in the name] of Rabbi Elazar [in the name of Rabbi Chanina] only in order to prove how innacurate it was from every angle, and to clarify that it could not have been the actual original teaching of Rabbi Elazar [in the name of Rabbi Chanina], for [Rava understood that] the truth of the matter is that both a Jewish husband and a non-Jewish husband *are* both liable for death [at least by the hand of Heaven even for anal *penetration* alone, even without intra-anal ejaculation, even with their own wives], for it [anal penetration in-and-of-itself] was the sin of Er and Onan, to which the verse explicitly ascribed [their] death [by the hand of Heaven]. Therefore, it must have been that the one who reported this teaching in the name of Rabbi Elazar misquoted what was originally a leniency [for a non-Jewish man who has adulterous anal sex with another married non-Jewish woman] as a stringency [for a non-Jewish man who has anal sex with his own wife] . . .

. . . And the meaning of Rava's challenge [to the teaching reported in the name of Rabbi Elazar in the name of Rabbi Chanina] was this: Is there ever a case where a Jew is exempt and a non-Jew is liable? [Of course there is not!] Rather both of them [both Jewish and non-Jewish husbands] are certainly equally liable [for any form of anal penetration within marriage]. And there was never a need for Rabbi Elazar to teach us this [prohibition against anal penetration within marriage], for it's something that every school child already knows (*d'zil kri bei rav hu*)!

Obviously, then, he [Rabbi Elazar in the name of Rabbi Chanina] came only to teach a different law, a lenieny [to exonerate a non-Jewish man who performs adulterous anal sex with another married non-Jewish woman].

Some difficulties with this interpretation:

# ENDNOTES

Firstly, the medieval scholars approach the Tamudic discussion on *Sanhedrin 58b* with an open mind, letting *it* speak to *them*, and thus they innovatively derive from it (in the course of reconciling it with *Yevamos 34b*) that intra-anal ejaculation could be permitted between husband and wife under certain circumstances. Rabbi Azikri, however, approaches the Talmudic passage with a *pre-conceived notion* that he *projects* onto it, and thus he makes the statement that Rava could not possibly have meant to permit anal sex of any kind *for it's something every school child already knows is forbidden.*

In other words, the difference in interpretation between all the medieval commentaries versus the post-medieval Rabbi Azikri boils down to what they believed Rava's preconceived notion to be about anal sex. The medieval commentaries, based on a simple reading of Rava's own words in the Talmudic text, all understood his preconceived notion to be that anal sex is permitted for Jewish married couples – and therefore he was also stating his belief that anal sex must be permitted for non-Jewish couples as well. Rabbi Azikri, however, takes it as a given that Rava must have understood anal sex to be categorically forbidden, even for Jewish couples, because "everybody knows that."

Consequently, when Rabbi Azikri points out that according to the conclusion of Rava in the Talmudic discourse, Rabbi Elazar and Rabbi Chanina never spoke about anal sex *within marriage* to begin with, but rather only about *adulterous* anal sex, and therefore nothing can be learned from their teaching in regard to *permitting* anal sex for *married couples*, Jewish or not, his brilliant point is irrelevant to the medieval commentaries' approach – for according to the medieval commentaries, the original "proof" that anal sex is permitted for both Jewish and non-Jewish married couples was not from Rabbi Elazar's or Rabbi Chanina's teaching (indeed, the original teaching quoted in their names *forbade* anal sex for non-Jewish couples), but rather from the fact that *Rava* expressed it *as a given, as his own preconceived notion*, that anal sex IS permitted to Jewish couples, and that therefore it must be permitted to non-Jewish couples as well.

As the medieval commentaries read it, nowhere in the Talmudic discussion does Rava change his mind about this preconceived notion permitting anal sex to married Jewish couples, and Rava's rewriting of, or argument against, Rabbi Elazar's and Rabbi Chanina's teaching does not in any way impact it. According to the medieval commentaries, Rava obviously believed anal sex to be permitted for Jewish couples before he ever heard Rabbi Elazar's or Rabbi Chanina's teaching, and thus even if he can be read as "correcting" the record of what they taught from a context of marriage to a context of adultery, we have no indication that it changed *Rava's own pre-conceived views* on the matter of anal sex within marriage.

In simpler words: even if Rabbi Elazar and Rabbi Chanina had never taught anything at all about anal sex, it would have had no bearing on Rava's completely independent preconceived notion that anal sex is permissible to Jewish married couples, and therefore to non-Jewish married couples as well.

As for where Rava might have gleaned this preconceived notion, perhaps he understood it from the ruling of his rabbinic predecessors, the Sages, Rebbi, Rav and Rabbi Yochanan bar Napacha, as reported on *Nedarim 20b*; or perhaps it was from the fact that anal sex is considered by Jewish law to be a valid form of consummating marriage – the very first and most essential "clinging" of husband and wife together – and therefore it is unlikely that it is forbidden at the most basic legal level or that a couple who performs it consensually, Jewish or non-Jewish, would be "liable" in any way either in the court of man or Heaven (and see above, endnotes 324, 331, and below, end of endnote 509).

In any case, Rabbi Azikri's assumption that Rava was *rewriting* the teaching of Rabbi Elazar in the name of Rabbi Chanina, and thus robbing it *at its core* of any context about anal sex within marriage, is itself debatable. It is equally, if not more, likely that Rava was merely offering his own personal interpretation of the biblical verse (see above, endnote 325).

Finally, according to Rabbi Azikri's conclusion, Rava understood Rabbi Elazar in the name of Rabbi Chanina as considering both Jewish and non-Jewish men liable for anal sex of any kind with their own wives within marriage, but as exonerating a non-Jewish man for adulterous anal penetration with another married non-Jewish woman. The rational mind cannot tolerate this.

[**Added note to the third edition:** Of related interest, here, may be *Aruch Lenair, Yevamos 34b, "Tosfos: V'lo."* Credit goes to Rabbi Yossi Newfield for bringing this source in *Aruch Lenair* to my attention.]

[617] Rabbi Hersh Goldwurm, *The Rishonim* (Artscroll, Mesorah Publications, 1982), pp. 134-135.

[618] See below, p. 166, that the 1594 Venice edition of Rabbi Isserles's glosses to the *Code of Jewish Law* included an erroneous note in the margin claiming he did not permit anal sex, only rear-entry vaginal intercourse.

It is possible that Rabbi Azikri had access only to this edition, which was printed toward the end of his lifetime (he passed away in 1600, and his *Sefer Charedim* was published in 1601).

[619] Page 156.

[620] *Elyah Rabah* to *Levush, Orach Chaim* 240:4:10.

[621] See *Yad Aharon, Even Haezer* vol. 2, 25:1 (toward the end).

See also Rabbi Chaim Yosef Dovid Azulai (Chida), in his *Birchei Yosef* to *Shulchan Aruch, Orach Chaim* 240:5 and in his *Pesach Eianim* to *Yevamos 34b*, where he accuses Rabbi Azikri of "great, great exaggeration" (*higzim meod meod*) in his treatment of the topic of anal sex, including the manner in which he presented this story of Rabbi Caro's judgment against this husband.

[622] *Shnei Luchos Habris, Shaar Haosios, "Kuf", Kedushas Hazivug*, paragraphs 41-48.

[623] He introduces paragraph 77 saying: "As far as the baseline laws are concerned…" (*l'inyan hadinim*).

[624] *Shnei Luchos Habris, Shaar Haosios, "Kuf", Kedushas Hazivug*, paragraph 77.

Rabbi Horowitz actually references *Reishis Chochmah*, Chapter <u>17</u>, but it is obvious from the context that he meant to reference *Chapter 16*. Not only does Chapter 16 discuss marital intimacy, whereas Chapter 17 speaks about masturbation, it is also clear from Rabbi Horowitz's own words:

> In regard to the intentions and secrets [of marital intimacy], one must know, study and implement [the teachings of] that book which is small in quantity but great in quality, authored by the man of G-d, Nachmanides, called *Igeres Hakodesh*. And his words are quoted also in *Menoras Hamaor*, in *Sefer HaMusar*, and in *Reishis Chochmah, Chapter 17* (sic), *Shaar Hakedushah*.

Rabbi Eliyahu de Vidas, in *Reishis Chochmah, Shaar Hakedushah*, quotes *Igeres Hakodesh* in Chapter 16, not 17.

# ENDNOTES

Perhaps Rabbi Horowitz's edition of *Reishis Chochmah* had different chapter breaks, which could be confirmed by researching the various printings of the work. Or perhaps this was a mere typographical error on the part of the author or a publisher.

[Regarding the authorship of *Igeres Hakodesh*, see above, endnote 379.]

[625] That is – Rabbi Azikri, who, in his own understanding, was upholding the view of Raavad III, a contemporary of Maimonides and Rabeinu Yitzchak. See above, endnote 616.

[626] Note that in his attempt, there, to forbid intra-anal ejaculation, the author of *Be'er HaGolah* – like the authors of *Reishis Chochmah* and *Sefer Charedim* before him – quotes his sources innacurately. In his case, he is quoting father and son, Rabeinu Asher and Rabbi Yaakov ben Asher, claiming that Rabeinu Asher in *Yevamos* rejected the view of Rabeinu Yitzchak, and that Rabbi Yaakov ben Asher in *Tur, Orach Chaim 240*, did so as well.

See also Rabbi Moshe Feinstein in his *Igros Moshe, Even Haezer 1, Responsum 63*, end of page 156, where he calls out *Be'er Hagolah's* misquote of Rabeinu Asher.

And see above, pp. 136-137, regarding the view of Rabbi Yaakov ben Asher in his *Tur* – and particularly in his *Orach Chaim 240*.

[627] See page 65 above, and endnote 258 thereon.

And being that Rabbi Aboab himself never defines the term "overturning the table," we need not assume he understood it to mean anal sex, and thus he would not necessarily clash with Rabbi Horowitz in this regard either.

Rabbi Eliyahu de Vidas, who directly endorses Rabbi Aboab, certainly tried to argue that the term meant only rear-entry vaginal intercourse. See above, pp. 153-156.

[628] See above, endnote 549. In any case, Rabbi Isserles himself went on to *permit* kissing the female genitals in his glosses to *Shulchan Aruch, Even Haezer 25:2*.

[629] Before his coming to the ways of Chasidism, Rabbi Schneur Zalman of Liadi (1745-1812), founder of the Chabad branch of the Chasidic Movement and author of the *Book of Tanya*, was reportedly an enthusiast of, and mentor to others in, Rabbi Horowitz's teachings.

Rabbi Yosef Yitzchak Schneersohn, the sixth Chabad-Lubavitch Rebbe, related this on numerous occasions, calling Rabbi Schneur Zalman a "Shelah Jew," a nickname he said Rabbi Schneur Zalman called himself at times even in discussion with his own son and grandson – meaning, even after he was thoroughly entrenched in Chasidic philosophy and lifestyle (see *Sefer Hasichos 5706-5710*, Kehot Publication Society, 2001, pp. 99, 103, 111, 123, 197, 219, 255, 316).

See also Rabbi Yosef Weinberg's *Shiurim B'Sefer HaTanya, Lessons in Tanya*, commentary upon the Tanya's Title Page, that according to Chabad tradition, Rabbi Schneur Zalman's *Tanya* itself was fundamentally based off of Rabbi Horowitz's writings. Rabbi Weinberg's commentary was edited by Rabbi Menachem Mendel Schneerson, the seventh rebbe of Chabad-Lubavitch.

[630] *Mitas Hakesef*, chapter 7, section 2:2.

[631] *Pachad Yitzchak*, Entry: *Arbaah devarim amru li malachei hashares*.

[632] *Sefer HaAgur, Hilchos Tefilas Arvis, 336*.

⁶³³ The *Shulchan Aruch* (*Harav*) of Rabbi Schneur Zalman of Liadi (1745-1812) does not include the sections in *Orach Chaim* or *Even Haezer* on the laws of sex, as they were apparently destroyed in a fire in which the majority of the work was reportedly lost.

However, we can perhaps deduce from passages in his *Book of Tanya* that speak of lack of sanctification during sex resulting in *spiritually - not physically* - challenged children, that he, like Maimonides and most medieval authorities, understood the Sages on *Nedarim 20b* as rejecting Rabbi Yochanan ben Dahavai's cautions not only halachically, but also medically (See, for example, *Tanya*, end of Chapter 2).

Still, it would be unclear how he would have defined the term "overturning the table."

[Note also that being the Talmudist-halachist he was, it is possible that in all his negative *kabbalistic* discussions in *Tanya* about "wasting seed in vain" he did not mean to include intra-anal ejaculation or ejaculation between limbs performed occasionally between husband and wife for the sake of sexual fulfillment within marriage. As a Talmudist-halachist, not just a kabbalist, it is quite possible he was speaking only against male self-masturbation and, for married couples, coitus interruptus or constant intra-anal ejaculation (or constant ejaculation between limbs) performed for the sake of unsanctioned birth control.

Although he was also a staunch supporter of Rabbi Yeshayah Horowitz's teachings (see above endnote 629), which means it is quite possible that he *legally* forbade any intra-anal ejaculation (and ejaculation between limbs) for married couples, as Rabbi Horowitz did, it is still possible that in light of the halachic debate on these matters he may not have meant to include them in his harsh *kabbalistic* statements in *Tanya*.

And more research into the matter is required.]

⁶³⁴ Even if Rabbi Danzig were basing himself on *Callah Rabti*, it would mean that he was giving precedence to the ruling of *Callah Rabti* over that of the Talmud - which is itself problematic.

And see *Igeres Rav Sherirah Gaon*, English edition by Rabbi Nosson Dovid Rabinowich, end of Chapter 5, p. 49, regarding the authority of *braisa*-literature whose authorship is unknown.

⁶³⁵ I was gratified to find another recent author, Rabbi Rafael Shlanger, raise a partly similar point in a footnote to his *Mishkan Yisrael* (2010), Part 2, p. 49.

⁶³⁶ Even if Rabbi Kagan were basing himself on *Callah Rabti*, it would mean that he was giving precedence to the ruling of *Callah Rabti* over that of the Talmud - which is itself problematic.

And see *Igeres Rav Sherirah Gaon*, English edition by Rabbi Nosson Dovid Rabinowich, end of Chapter 5, p. 49, regarding the authority of *braisa*-literature whose authorship is unknown.

⁶³⁷ See also above, pp. 62-65.

⁶³⁸ *Shulchan Aruch, Even Haezer* 25:2.

Rabbi Isserles passed away in 1572, the same year Rabbi Yitzchak Luria passed away and thus well before the publication of Rabbi Luria's teachings, and over thirty years before Rabbi Caro's *Bedek Habayis* was printed, in 1605. *Reishis Chochmah* and *Sefer Charedim* were likewise printed after Rabbi Isserles's death, in 1579 and 1601, respectively. Thus, he could not have known the strong stance they collectively took against "wasting seed in vain" and/or even occasional intra-anal ejaculation for married couples (see also *Yad*

*Malachi, Clalei Haposkim, Baal HaTurim 39,* in the name of *Beis Shmuel,* that Rabbi Isserles never saw Rabbi Caro's *Bedek Habayis*).

Nevertheless, Rabbi Isserles certainly saw the earlier-printed halachic caution in Rabbi Caro's *Beis Yosef* commentary to *Tur, Even Haezer 25:2* (printed between 1522 and 1547), where Rabbi Caro writes that "one who is conscientious of his soul will distance himself from it [occasional intra-anal ejaculation] and the like." Still, Rabbi Isserles went on to permit occasional intra-anal ejaculation to married couples in his glosses to Rabbi Caro's *Shulchan Aruch, Even Haezer 25:2.*

Rabbi Isserles's disciple, Rabbi Yehoshua Falk, who died in 1614, and whose *Drishah* commentary to *Even Haezer* was printed posthumously in 1635-1638, possibly knew of Rabbi Caro's view in *Bedek Habayis,* along with the views of Rabbi Eliyahu de Vidas in *Reishis Chochmah* and Rabbi Elazar Azikri in *Sefer Charedim.* But if he did, it did not lead him to overtly reject the permissive, liberal approach of his master, which was, in turn, based on the opinion of Rabeinu Yitzchak – the latter of whose opinion Rabbi Falk went on to expand as permitting occasional ejaculation between limbs to married couples as well (see above pp. 124-125 and endnote 523).

[639] Rabbi Avraham Dovid Wahrman of Buczacz notes that Rabbi Isserles himself implies that he ruled the letter of the law according to Maimonides' permission of cunnilingus, anal intercourse and intercourse between limbs, as well as according to Rabeinu Yitzchak's permission of occasional intra-anal ejaculation – for after quoting both the views of Maimonides and Rabeinu Yitzchak in his gloss-note to *Even Haezer 25:2,* Rabbi Isserles concludes:

> And *even though all these things are permitted,* whoever sanctifies himself in that which is permitted shall be called 'holy.'

[640] *Levush, Even Haezer 25:2.*

Rabbi Yoffe rules leniently in *Levush, Even Haezer 25:2,* even though in *Levush, Orach Chaim 240:4* he paraphrases Raavad III's wording in *Baalei HaNefesh, Shaar Hakedushah* forbidding gazing at or kissing the female genitals. But even in *Orach Chaim 240:4* he permits intra-anal ejaculation – which Raavad III himself, in *Baalei HaNefesh, Shaar Hakedushah,* has until now generally been understood to forbid (see below, endnote 649).

[Rabbi Yoffe also mentions in *Orach Chaim 240:4* the danger of gazing at or kissing the female genitals causing blindness or muteness, respectively – which Raavad III himself does not enumerate. And see above, p. 63.]

[641] *Aruch Hashulchan, Even Haezer 25:11.*

Rabbi Epstein rules leniently in *Even Haezer 25:11,* even though in *Aruch Hashulchan, Orach Chaim 240:10* he quotes only Raavad III's prohibition in *Baalei HaNefesh, Shaar Hakedushah* against gazing at or kissing the female genitals.

And it is implied in Rabbi Epstein's own wording that his ruling in *Even Haezer* constituted his view on the baseline letter of the law, for he states, there, that when all is said and done we rule according to the Sages on *Nedarim 20b* that "Anything a husband craves to do with his wife sexually, he may do" (*kaima lan d'col mah sherotzeh adam la'asos b'ishto oseh*), including kissing the female genitals and anal intercourse – both of which Raavad III in *Baalei HaNefesh, Shaar Hakedushah* has until now generally been understood to forbid (see below, endnote 649).

[642] *Yam Shel Shlomoh, Yevamos 34b.*

[643] *Lechem Chamudos, Tractate Nidah*, Chapter 2, Comment 10.

[644] Literally: "'Holy' shall be said of him" (Isaiah 4:3).

[645] See *Shulchan Aruch*, Friedman edition, 2008, *Even Haezer 25:2, Shinuyei Nuschaos*.

[Perhaps this marginal note was inspired by Rabbi Eliyahu de Vidas's *Reishis Chochmah, Shaar Hakedushah 16:29-30*, discussed above, pp. 153-156.]

[645*] The Bible tells us that the sin of Onan involved *deliberate* and constant unsanctioned birth control, and the Talmud maintains that this was the sin of Onan's elder brother, Er, as well (see above, pp. 89-92). There are two traditions in Talmudic-era literature as to which specific crude form of birth control they employed – coitus interruptus (*Breishis Rabah 85:5*) or intra-anal ejaculation (*Yevamos 34b*). But there is no rabbinic tradition that they employed rear-entry vaginal intercourse – and for obvious reason: rear-entry vaginal intercourse does not prevent pregnancy.

Although one post-medieval source, Rabbi Mordechai Yoffe in *Levush, Even Haezer 23:5*, suggests that rear-entry vaginal intercourse does not result in conception, he is taken to task for this statement by Rabbi Eliyahu Spira in his *Elyah Rabah* commentary to *Levush* (see *Elyah Rabah, Orach Chaim 240:5:12*; note also that Rabbi Yoffe made his statement in the context of a case in which he believed that due to a particular woman's medical condition she could not conceive even through front-entry vaginal intercourse).

Even Rabbi Eliyahu de Vidas (see above, pp. 153-156) and Rabbi Elazar Azikri (see above, pp. 157-158) took it for granted that rear-entry vaginal intercourse results in conception – and they therefore both permitted it.

Additionally, if the sin of Er and Onan involved *deliberate* constant unsanctioned birth control, they must have believed that their actions were effective in preventing pregnancy. It is unlikely, then, that they would have engaged in rear-entry vaginal intercourse, after observing animals procreate in such a manner.

In any case, the fact is that rear-entry vaginal intercourse *does* result in conception. Therefore, barring any infertility issues the rabbinic sources do not inform us about, the fact that Er and Onan succeeded in avoiding conception suggests that their crude form of birth control was not rear-entry vaginal intercourse, but coitus interruptus and/or intra-anal ejaculation.

And see above, endnotes 606* and 607*. And see below, endnote 647.

Note also Rabbi Isserles's gloss-note to *Shulchan Aruch, Even Haezer 20:1*, where his use of the term "*shelo cedarcah*" is obviously in reference to anal intercourse.

[646] *Gur Aryeh*.

[647] *Panim Meiros vol. 2, Responsum 158*. Rabbi Eisenstadt definitively argues that "*shelo cedarcah*" always means anal sex, and that it is simply not possible to force any other meaning into Rabbi Isserles's words.

See also *Yeshuos Yaakov* to *Shulchan Aruch, Even Haezer 25:2:2*, who references *Panim Meiros* approvingly.

*Yad Aharon, Even Haezer vol. 2, 25:1* tries to prove that "*shelo cedarcah*" can sometimes mean rear-entry vaginal intercourse or her-on-top, because that is the definition that Raavad III, and perhaps Rashi, presumably referring to the *Mefaresh* (see above, page 60), give the term on *Nedarim 20ab*. But *Yad Aharon's* argument is difficult, for nowhere, there, are Raavad III or the *Mefaresh* defining the very common and contextually-precise

Talmudic-rabbinic term "*shelo cedarcah*," but rather they are defining the very rare and contextually-vague euphemism "*hafichas shulchan*" – "overturning the table."

See also *Birchei Yosef* of Rabbi Chaim Yosef Dovid Azulai (Chida), *Orach Chaim 240:5*, where he calls *Yad Aharon's* arguments "forced."

And even if there are to be found isolated cases where an individual commentary uses the term "*shelo cedarcah*" in the context of rear-entry vaginal intercourse, this is in no way typical, and such must be made obvious by the *author himself* in the context of his discussion – it can never be *assumed by the reader* to be the author's intention.

See, for example, *Levush, Even Haezer 23:5*, where R' Mordechai Yoffe makes use of the term "*shelo cedarcah*" in discussing a husband who engages in rear-entry vaginal intercourse with his wife due to pain she experiences when he is on top. Rabbi Yom Tov Lipman Heller, in his *Lechem Chamudos, Tractate Nidah, Chapter 2, Comment 10* clarifies for his readers that Rabbi Yoffe's use of the term "*shelo cedarcah*" in reference to "rear-entry vaginal intercourse" was imprecise, and that Rabbi Yoffe could only have justified such use as a borrowed term (*b'derech hashaalah*) or because he had specified the (unusual) context of his use of it (*b'derech shituf*) and therefore he never intended his readers to define it as such across rabbinic literature.

Rabbi Heller's assertion is supported by the fact that Rabbi Yoffe himself, in *Levush, Even Haezer 20:1*, states clearly that the definition of the term "*shelo cedarcah*" is anal intercourse. And even in *Levush, Even Haezer 23:5*, before employing the term "natural intercourse" (*derech col haaretz*) in reference to a husband performing front-entry vaginal intercourse rather than rear-entry vaginal intercourse, Rabbi Yoffe first employs the same term, "natural intercourse" (*derech col haaretz*), to describe a husband ejaculating intra-vaginally rather than performing coitus interruptus. Are we then to argue that one is always free to translate the term "*shelo cedarcah*" as coitus interruptus?

[Compare also Rabbi Yoffe's presentation in *Levush, Even Haezer 23:5* to his presentation in *Even Haezer 25:2*, where he uses the same term "*shelo cedarcah*" (without any specification of context) in apparent reference to anal sex, quoting from Maimonides and Rabbi Isserles. (Indeed, if he *had* understood Rabbi Isserles's ruling permitting "*shelo cedarcah*" (even to the point of ejaculation) as referring only to rear-entry vaginal intercourse, we would again be forced to raise all the difficulties we have discussed in the body of our study (page 166) in regard to the anonymous marginal note printed in certain Venice editions of *Shulchan Aruch*. Only it would be much harder to understand how such difficulties would have escaped Rabbi Yoffe, whereas an anonymous marginal note could have been authored by anyone. It is therefore reasonable to believe that Rabbi Yoffe in *Even Haezer 25* did intend to use the term "*shelo cedarcah*" according to its simple meaning of anal intercourse.)

But because in *Levush, Even Haezer 23:5*, Rabbi Yoffe suggests that rear-entry vaginal intercourse cannot result in conception, his intention in using the term "*shelo cedarcah*" in *Levush, Orach Chaim 240:4* becomes somewhat unclear. A simple reading of *Levush, Orach Chaim 240:4*, however, would seem to be referring to anal sex – and that is how Rabbi Eliyahu Spira, author of the *Elyah Rabah* commentary to *Levush*, understood it in his comments in *Orach Chaim 240:4:10*.

See also Rabbi Spira's comment in *Orach Chaim 240:5:12*, where he calls Rabbi Yoffe to task for suggesting that rear-entry vaginal intercourse cannot result in conception. And see above, endnote 645*.]

And note that if by the 16th century the term "*shelo cedarcah*" was widely understood by the rabbinic world as referring equally, or exclusively, to rear-entry vaginal intercourse, then why did Rabbi Elazar Azikri make no mention of it in his *Sefer Charedim, Chapter 64*? Defining "*shelo cedarcah*" as rear-entry vaginal intercourse would have spared him his entire reinterpretation of *Sanhedrin 58b* (see above, pp. 157-158 and endnote 616). Clearly, Rabbi Azikri took it as a given that "*shelo cedarcah*" means anal sex. He only argued that the vague and rare term found on *Nedarim 20ab*, "*hafichas shulchan*," referred exclusively to a manner of vaginal intercourse (i.e., rear-entry vaginal intercourse and/or wife-on-top).

Rabbi Azikri's contemporary and colleague in 16th century Safed, Rabbi Eliyahu de Vidas, did attempt to read Rabeinu Asher's and the Mefaresh's use of the term, "*shelo cedarcah*," as referring to rear-entry vaginal intercourse – and we have already addressed the fundamental problems with such a reading (see above, page 153-156).

The bottom line principle is this: To interpret the term "*shelo cedarcah*" as rear-entry vaginal intercourse is extremely problematic and highly unusual. Rather, the definition of the term "*shelo cedarcah*" is *always assumed* to be anal intercourse *unless otherwise specified*.

And those latter-day "family purity" or marital intimacy guides that present the term as referring to rear-entry vaginal intercourse appear to be basing themselves on an anonymous marginal note printed in some Venice editions of *Shulchan Aruch, Even Haezer 25*, an atypical usage of the term by Rabbi Mordechai Yoffe in *Levush, Even Haezer 23:5*, a problematic reading of the words of Rabeinu Asher and the Mefaresh by Rabbi Eliyahu de Vidas, and/or a blurring of the lines between the clear and common term, "*shelo cedarcah*," and the vague and rare term, "*hafichas shulchan*."

[648] See *Shulchan Aruch*, Friedman edition, 2008, *Even Haezer 25:2, Shinuyei Nuschaos*.

[649] Although we've noted above, p. 87, that there is reason to believe Raavad III legally permitted anal sex on account of *Sanhedrin 58b*, which is possibly why he did not argue with Maimonides' permission of it in *Mishneh Torah, Isurei Biah 21:9*, this is a logical deduction that is not found expressed in any rabbinic commentaries, and it is unlikely that the author of *Beis Shmuel* himself had this line of reasoning in mind. It is more likely he assumed Raavad III to forbid anal sex categorically – and yet Rabbi Isserles allowed it.

[650] See above, endnote 256.

*Otzar Haposkim, Even Haezer 25:2:6* quotes an interpretation by the author of *Pnei Moshe*, which attempts to justify *Beis Shmuel's* comment. His argument is that perhaps Rabbi Yaakov ben Asher *himself* understood Maimonides as forbidding the kissing of the female genitals. And since Rabbi Isserles is actually quoting Rabbi Yaakov ben Asher's citation of Maimonides, he, too, did not mean to permit kissing the female genitals.

The difficulties in this argument:

    a)   His proof that Rabbi Yaakov ben Asher understood Maimonides in this way is that later on at the end of *Even Haezer 25*, when quoting Raavad III who forbids kissing the female genitals, Rabbi Yaakov ben Asher does not specifically point out that this opposes the view of Maimonides, which he quotes at the beginning of the chapter.

        Besides for the tenuous strength of an argument based on what Rabbi Yaakov ben Asher *doesn't* say, it cannot be ignored that Rabbi Yaakov ben Asher does not either point out, there, at the end of the chapter, that Raavad III's interpretation of "overturning the table" as rear-entry vaginal intercourse opposes the view of Rabeinu Yitzchak, who interprets it as anal intercourse even with intra-anal ejaculation, and whom he also quotes at the beginning of the chapter in tandem with the view of Maimonides permitting kissing the female genitals. (Although

    *Tur* also quotes Maimonides, there, permitting anal penetration, it is not certain that Maimonides defined the term "overturning the table" itself as anal sex. It is possible he translated it to mean "wife-on-top" – and *in addition* to this he *also* permitted anal intercourse (and intercourse between limbs). See above, page 61).

b)    Even indulging *Pnei Moshe's* interpretation, that it can be argued that *perhaps* Rabbi Yaakov ben Asher understood Maimonides as forbidding the kissing of the female genitals, we would have no reason to assume that Rabbi Isserles understood Rabbi Yaakov ben Asher in this way. A simple reading of the *Tur's* text betrays no such interpretation, and we would have no reason to believe that Rabbi Isserles himself read it any other way.

c)    But most importantly: Rabbi Isserles himself, in his *Darchei Moshe* commentary to *Tur, Even Haezer 25:2*, makes it clear that *he* understood Rabbi Yaakov ben Asher *as ruling against Maimonides' permission of kissing the female genitals*. (See above, endnote 549).

    Clearly, then, Rabbi Isserles *did* understand Rabbi Yaakov ben Asher as believing that Maimonides permitted kissing the female genitals. Thus, the entire premise of *Pnei Moshe's* justification of *Beis Shmuel* falls away completely.

d)    Finally, the author of *Pnei Moshe* attempts to bring support for his argument, saying that the author of *Hagahos Maimonios*, in his comments to *Mishneh Torah, Isurei Biah 21:9*, equated Maimonides' view with that of Raavad III in *Baalei HaNefesh, Shaar Hakedushah*, where the latter forbade kissing the actual female genitals.

    But such a reading of *Hagahos Maimonios* is questionable. A simple reading has its author *contrasting* Maimonides' and Raavad III's interpretations of *Nedarim 20b*.

    And behold, the very next comment in *Hagahos Maimonios*, there, acknowledges that Maimonides was permitting anal intercourse – which Raavad III in *Baalei HaNefesh, Shaar Hakedushah*, appears to forbid.

[651] *Tur, Even Haezer 25:2.*

[652] *Mishneh Torah, Sefer HaMada, Deos 5:4.*

[653] *Shulchan Aruch, Even Haezer 25:2.*

[654] *Beis Yosef, Tur, Even Haezer 25:2, 25:8-10*

[655] *Darchei Moshe, Tur, Even Haezer 25:2.*

[656] *Shulchan Aruch, Even Haezer 25:1.*

[657] *Shulchan Aruch, Even Haezer 25.*

[658] See also Rabbi Shmuel Dovid HaLevi Movshovitz's, *Sdeh Eliyahu Biur HaGra HaShalem al HaShas, Nedarim 20b*, footnote to page 85.

See also Rabbi Moshe Stern's *Be'er Moshe vol. 3, Responsum 152*, Part 10, Page 203.

[659] In this regard, note the cautionary words of another early post-medieval authority, Rabbi Aharon Shmuel Kaidanover, "Maharshak" (1614-1676), as excerpted in Rabbi Hersh Goldwurm's *The Early Acharonim* (Artscroll, Mesorah Publications 1989), page 186:

Rabbi Aharon Shmuel . . . looked with dismay at the prevailing trend to accept without reservation the opinions of such contemporary *Shulchan Aruch* commentaries as the *Shach* and *Taz*.

In a responsum to Rabbi Shmuel ben Dovid HaLevi (*Teshuvos Nachalas Shivah 50*), he chides the latter for not having *Beis Yosef's Tur* commentary and relying instead on *Shach* and *Taz*.

He declares, rather frankly, "Your Honor has concentrated on the works of the post-medieval authorities – the works of the *Shach* and *Taz*. As for me, I am opposed to this and occupy myself with the study of the early *poskim* and the Talmud . . . for the post-medieval authorities confuse one's logic and memory . . . Your Honor should sell their works and buy [instead] the *Arbaah Turim* with *Beis Yosef*."

In another responsum, he tells his correspondent, "First I must inform Your Honor that it is not my custom to study the works of the post-medieval authorities, especially those written in our generation . . . I have no regard for their conclusions, except where they have arrived at the truth."

[660] As mentioned earlier, p. 136, *Ohel Moed* is the only medieval text *clearly* ruling like Raavad III, that the Sages came only to permit "overturning the table," whereas gazing at or kissing the female genitals, and non-sex-related talk during sex, they still forbade and possibly considered dangerous (See *Ohel Moed, Shaar Isur v'Heter, Derech 11*, printed in *Kovetz Shitos Kamai, Nedarim 20b*, p. 190). Even still, it is not clear that the author of *Ohel Moed* defined "overturning the table" in the same restrictive manner as Raavad III did (i.e., rear-entry vaginal intercourse as opposed to anal intercourse).

As far as other medieval sources that might be invoked as lending support to Raavad III's approach – such as Rabbis Yaakov ben Asher, Elazar of Worms, Yaakov ben Yehudah Landau, Yisrael Alnaqua and Avraham Hayarchi:

Although Rabbi Moshe Isserles, in his *Darchei Moshe* commentary to *Tur*, asserts that Rabbi Yaakov ben Asher rules like Raavad III to forbid gazing at or kissing the female genitals, Rabbi Yaakov ben Asher in *Tur* is actually arguably ambiguous on these points. See above, pp. 136-137 and endnote 549.

[Parenthetically, in regard to gazing at the female genitals specifically, we've discussed that it is not entirely clear if Raavad III himself believed it to result in congenital blindness (see above, p. 63).

But Rabbi Yaakov ben Asher's father, Rabeinu Asher, in *Tosfos HaRosh*, commenting on the earlier teaching of Rav Yosef on *Nedarim 20a* (who was, in turn, commenting on Rav Achi's caution that gazing at a forbidden woman's "heel" will result in lewd children) says that gazing at one's own *pure* wife's body "results in blindness, but not lewdness [for the latter is only caused by gazing at (the bodies of forbidden women or at) the body of one's own *impure* wife]."

It is not clear if Rabeinu Asher was ruling that even according to the Sages gazing at one's own pure wife's genitals causes congenital blindness, or if he was just pointing out the difference between Rav Achi's caution and the caution of Rabbi Yochanan ben Dahavai – the latter of which Rabeinu Asher knew the Sages to ultimately reject.

Either way, the implication of this comment is astonishing, for it suggests that *blindness* in one's children for gazing at one's own *pure* wife's body *in private during intimacy* (the simple context of Rabbi Yochanan ben Dahavai's teaching) is *less harsh* a punishment than *lewdness* in one's children for gazing at one's own *impure* wife's body (the context of Rabbi Achi's teaching as interpreted by Rabbi Yosef). Logic dictates that if the discussion, there, is

## ENDNOTES

to be understood as speaking about gazing at the "heel" of one's own wife, then gazing when she is *impure* is *worse* than gazing when she is *pure*. And how much more so if the context of Rav Achi's teaching is to be understood as warning about gazing at *other* forbidden women!

Rabbi Chaim Yosef Dovid Azulai (Chida), in his *Kisei Rachamim*, *"Tosfos"* commentary to Tractate Callah 2:5, apparently understood blindness to be a worse punishment than lewdness:

> In *Nedarim 20* it says that one who gazes at the heel of a (forbidden) woman will have lewd children, *nothing more*.

But we have still not resolved the implication that gazing at a forbidden woman (or one's own impure wife) would then be said, *according to Rabbi Yochanan ben Dahavai*, to carry *less* harsh a punishment than gazing at one's own pure wife in privacy during intimacy.

Perhaps Rav Achi's teaching was speaking only of a *clothed* forbidden woman or impure wife, while Rabbi Yochanan ben Dahavai was clearly speaking of a *naked* pure wife. Thus, the harshness of the latter caution may have been, in Rabbi Yochanan ben Dahavai's own mind, on account of the nakedness factor.

Alternatively, it is possible that Rabbi Yochanan ben Dahavai himself was entirely unaware of the teaching of Rav Achi, and that if he had known of it he would never have accepted the harshness of the caution told to him by the "ministering angels" in regard to gazing at one's own pure wife.

Or, possibly, Rabbi Yochanan ben Dahavai would have disagreed with Rav Achi, and believed that gazing at a forbidden woman, or even one's own impure wife, in fact would have had a much worse effect on one's children than lewdness. Along this line of reasoning, note that *Tractate Callah 8* and *Callah Rabti 1:11* do say that gazing at a forbidden woman's "heel" will cause congenital birth defects – and one version of *Callah Rabti* has Rabbi Yochanan bar Napacha himself agreeing to this in regard to gazing at the *heel* of one's own *impure* wife, and it has Rabbi Shimon ben Lakish agreeing, but only in regard to gazing at one's impure wife's *genitals* (see above, p. 44).

*Mesechtos Derech Eretz-Perek Arayos 13* and *Mesechtos Zeiros-Mesechta Arayos 22* also both caution that gazing at the heels of forbidden women can cause congenital illness – in the name of "the Sages" (*chachamim* – see below, pp. 183-185; and see below, endnotes 691, 696). However, in neither of these two places is it specified that such caution extended to a husband gazing at his own wife, and thus we certainly have no reason to believe that it applied to a husband gazing at his own wife when she is pure and during marital intimacy.

But whatever the case might have been, both according to *Talmud, Nedarim 20b* and *Callah Rabti 1:13-14*, the Sages ultimately legally rejected Rabbi Yochanan ben Dahavai's caution against gazing at one's own pure wife's naked genitals, and to varying degrees they rejected his medical caution about it as well (as discussed at length above – and see pp. 50-51, 196-197, for a synopsis). And, as stated, there is no proof from Rabeinu Asher's comment on *Nedarim 20a* that he believed otherwise. His comment, therefore, cannot be invoked to shed definitive light on how his son, Rabbi Yaakov ben Asher, ruled legally in his *Tur* in regard to gazing at one's own pure wife's genitals. Rabbi Yaakov ben Asher certainly does not quote his father as forbidding it.]

Rabbi Elazar of Worms, in his *Rokeach, Hilchos Chasidus*, (quoted in *Kovetz Shitas Kamai, Nedarim 20b*, page 186) encourages couples to have sex only face-to-face, but he seems to understand the Sages on *Nedarim 20b* as permitting all four behaviors according to the letter of the law.

And Rabbi Yaakov ben Yehudah Landau, in his *Sefer HaAgur*, who we saw above (p. 117 and endnote 478 thereon) permits only rear-entry vaginal intercourse (as Raavad III appears to in *Baalei HaNefesh, Shaar Hakedushah*), is silent on the topics of talk during sex and the gazing at or kissing of the female genitals.

See above, p. 64 and endnote 252 thereon, for Rabbi Yisrael Alnaqua's views relative to Raavad III's.

See above, endnote 236, for Rabbi Avraham Hayarchi's views relative to Raavad III's.

[661] *Baalei HaNefesh, Shaar Hakedushah*, p. 179 in the Buchwald edition.

[662] But see above, pp. 63-64.

[663] See below, page 181 and endnote 683 thereon.

[664] The phrase "*nahag bah minhag hefker*" does not lend itself easily to translation.

The legal concept of "*hefker*" in Jewish law refers to an ownerless object.

The ethical concept of "*minhag hefker*" refers to one who acts without regard for authority – in other words, he considers *himself* "ownerless" and free to act with abandon.

In this context, then, Raavad III's message appears to be that the husband treats his wife without consideration for her authority over her own body – that is, without regard for her sensitivities, without regard for her dignity.

And see above, pp. 54-55.

An alternate translation in similar spirit might read: he treats her like an object.

[665] See previous endnote.

[666] Earlier (pp. 177-178 in the Buchwald editon of *Baalei HaNefesh, Shaar Hakedushah*), in discussing the nine flawed conditions of mind or circumstance during sex, Raavad III says that five of them, *Bnei Snuah* (hatred), *Bnei Moredes* (rebelliousness), *Bnei Merivah* (strife) *Bnei Shichrus* (intoxication) and *Bnei Chatzufah* (arrogance) are "tantamount to prostitution," because they are devoid of the loving intention of a married couple.

He does not describe *Bnei Irbuvyah* (intentional illicit sexual fantasy) as being tantamount to prostitution, presumably because a spouse suffering some form of sexual addiction might compulsively fantasize about another person while in his or her heart they harbor deep love and passion for their own spouse (and how much more so when such fantasies are entirely unintentional and merely pop into one's head in passing, against one's inner will).

Thus, according to Raavad III, it does not appear to be the expression or indulgence of "base animal sexual instinct" that makes something "tantamount to prostitution," but rather "lack of any loving passion."

Here as well, in regard to Rabbi Yochanan ben Dahavai's opinion of non-sex-related talk during sex, Raavad III maintains this same distinction: he says that it degrades the sex act EITHER because it leads to intentional fantasies of other women OR because it makes the act tantamount to prostitution due to the absence of loving interest/intent.

[This would also perhaps explain why Raavad III does not insist that Rabbi Yochanan ben Dahavai deemed "overturning the table" and gazing at or kissing the female genitals to be "tantamount to prostitution" – even though they are all expressions of base animal instinct, and much more so than non-sex-related talk during sex. To the male psyche, none of these three behaviors are necessarily contradictions to loving intention and passion for one's wife. Granted, they are not necessarily the way many females express or experience passion and bonding, but in the male nature as G-d created it, gazing at or kissing the female genitals, or engaging in creative sexual positions, can actually enhance the sense of love and passion and bonding. And when done in a loving manner, these behaviors are certainly not abusive. Therefore, the concern in their regard is only that they might be done without respect and sensitivity for how the wife, the female, experiences love and connection – i.e., the concern is that they might be done without her consent (see above, endnote 664).]

See, as well, the *Mefaresh* (and Ran) to *Nedarim 20b*, explaining that in the case of "*Bnei Snuah*" the husband's hatred for his wife makes the act tantamount to prostitution. Although the *Mefaresh* also discusses the issue of illicit fantasy there, it is not the fantasy, but the hatred, the utter lack of any loving intention, that makes the marital act tantamount to prostitution.

A careful reading of the *Mefaresh* makes this clear:

> "*Snuah*" – The husband sets his heart upon another woman during intercourse. And they said that it is not considered true intercourse *because he hates her so much*, rather it is tantamount to mere prostitution.

The *Mefaresh* compares the case of "*Snuah*" to prostitution because they both share the common denominator of utter lack of love – not because of the *resulting symptom* of illicit fantasy.

It is also informative that out of all the nine-ten flawed conditions, the *Mefaresh* only describes *Bnei Snuah* (hatred) and *Bnei Shichrus* (intoxication) as tantamount to prostitution. And in regard to the latter, too, the *Mefaresh* elaborates a similar reasoning:

> It is not proper intercourse [of marriage], but rather like intercourse of prostitution, *because the entire intention is just sex.*

Obviously, the *Mefaresh* is not condemning intoxicated sex because of its base animalistic nature, for there is undoubtedly animalistic passion involved in rear-entry vaginal intercourse, anal intercourse, and intercourse with the wife on top – all of which the *Mefaresh* has the Sages permitting (based on its interpretation of "overturning the table" on *Nedarim 20a*). But along with those three behaviors there is also generally loving/bonding intention. The *Mefaresh* is only condemning intoxicated sex because it involves no loving/bonding intention at all.

See also above, endnote 116, that according to Ritz, as quoted in *Shitah Mekubetzes, Nedarim 20b*, the problem with intoxicated sex is that it is loveless and the couple isn't even aware of what they are doing, making it tantamount to prostitution.

To summarize: According to a precise reading of the *Mefaresh* and Raavad III, it would seem that it is not erotic sexual desire or even illicit sexual fantasy that make marital sex "tantamount to prostitution," but only complete lack of loving/bonding interest/intention.

[But then note Rabbi Eliezer's statement as reported on *Nedarim 20b* that, in his estimation, intentional sexual fantasies would have made his children "tantamount to bastards" – implying that such fantasies *would* have made the marital sex act "tantamount to prostitution" even if it was not devoid of love.

However, the child of a woman who is halachically categorized as a "prostitute" is not automatically halachically categorized as a "bastard." Therefore, a precise reading of Rabbi Eliezer's words perhaps reveals that he was not necessarily concerned so much about intentional sexual fantasies of other single women, or even of "prostitutes," but rather of other *married* women – for of the three, only illicit sex and conception with a *married* woman results in children who are definitely halachically categorized as "bastards."

And more research into the matter is required. And see above, endnote 195.]

In any case, Raavad III, as well as the *Mefaresh*, clearly understood illicit sexual fantasies as being problematic even if they are *not* devoid of loving intention for one's own spouse. It only appears that they would not necessarily deem them "tantamount to prostitution."

[Parenthetically, one must wonder whether an opposite pious extreme that is focused entirely on G-d/G-dliness, and devoid of loving interest/intention toward one's spouse, should be extolled. And see above, endnote 595.]

[667] Although Raavad III, here, only mentions the wife who approached Rav, later on the same page (page 179 in the Buchwald edition of *Baalei HaNefesh*) he mentions also the wife who approached Rebbi.

Perhaps he originally only mentioned the episode of Rav, because the wording of Rav's response was closer in kind to the actual ruling of the Sages quoted earlier on the Talmudic page of *Nedarim 20b*.

[668] Actually, Raavad III, here, changes the wording of the teaching as it appears on *Nedarim 20a* and in *Tractate Derech Eretz-Perek Arayos 13*, both of which read: "One who has a sense of shame does not *readily* sin."

Raavad III implies that such a person does not sin *at all*.

[668*] The same Rav who permits "overturning the table" on *Nedarim 20b*, and who invokes, there, the ruling of the Sages that "[Anything a man craves to do with his wife sexually, he may do...for] it is no more objectionable [in G-d's eyes] than [how he likes his kosher] fish. See above, pp. 34-36.

[669] Raavad III seems to be interpreting the word "legs," here, as a euphemism for the genitals or sexual intercourse. See also Rashi to *Eruvin 100b: B'raglaim*.

The Talmud in *Eruvin 100b* applies this verse to a husband who forces his wife to have sex – though on the surface it remains somewhat unclear what relevance the verse actually has to the matter.

Be that as it may, perhaps the Talmud's intention was that when the Bible refers to sex as "*daas* – knowledge," it is only when sex is done in a manner that fosters deeper identification and oneness with one's spouse – which is obviously not the case when one spouse is forced.

The *Artscroll Talmud, Eruvin 100b* renders the word "*daas*" in this context as "consent."

[670] Pages 72-83.

[671] If Rabbi Yochanan ben Dahavai's own objection to non-sex-related talk during sex was that it might lead to intentional illicit sexual fantasies of other people, then one simple logical explanation for why the Sages might have rejected Rabbi Yochanan ben Dahavai's caution in this regard is that they simply considered it unlikely that general non-sex-related talk would actually spark such fantasies.

Or perhaps they recognized that fantasies about other people during sex are such a common occurrence among normal husbands and wives, even those in happy loving marriages, that there is no reason to restrict talk during sex out of a concern that it might contribute to such fantasies in some remote way.

[And perhaps on the contrary: consciously restricting talk in order to avoid fantasies only keeps the fear of fantasies at the forefront of the mind – perhaps another reason why Rabbi Eliezer's other customary behaviors, done out of conscious intention to avoid illicit fantasies, were never established as binding law.]

[672] Granted, as discussed earlier, p. 75, Raavad III himself equates "non-sex-related talk" with "excess light-headed talk." But we are not necessarily forced to accept Raavad III's equation of the two – not only because other medieval commentators do not do so, but also because such an equation of the two is not absolutely forced by logic.

[673] See above, pp. 76-77.

[674] See *Yad Malachi, Clalei HaReish, Clal 556, 557, 558*.

[675] See above, pp. 69-71.

[676] See Meiri, *Beis Habechirah, Nedarim 20a*, who discusses the teaching about the virtues of "shamefacedness" in connection with the teaching there *before* it, not the one after it.

*Biur HaGra* to *Shulchan Aruch, Orach Chaim 240:4:11*, says clearly that the teaching about "shamefacedness" was intentionally brought on *Nedarim 20a* "immediately after" the teaching of Rabbi Achi.

[677] See also our explanatory endnotes on this Talmudic passage, above, pp. 32-33.

[677*] The logic that Rabbi Achi was referring *only* to one's own wife is that there would have been no need for him to have warned against gazing at other women, for such should have already been obvious. See *Tosfos Yeshanim, Nedarim 20a*. But there are difficulties in this argument – to be discussed in a future essay. And see above, endnote 128, first brackets.

[678] According to Meiri, *Beis Habechirah, Nedarim 20a*, the caution of Rabbi Achi (and Rav Yosef and Rabbi Shimon ben Lakish) had nothing to do with gazing at one's own pure wife, at least not in private and certainly not during physical intimacy [brackets added for clarification]:

> Whoever gazes at the heel of a woman, if it is his own wife, *not* during her menstrual period, and as an expression of her preciousness [to him] (*uc'dei l'chavevah*), it is permitted.
>
> And not just [to gaze at] the heel, but even [to gaze at] that which is vertically opposite the heel, meaning, her buttocks (*agvosehah*), because she is dressed and walking.
>
> And even [to gaze at] her front [genital area] – for it only used the term "opposite the heel" because the *commonplace scenario* is of a woman who is walking [outside] and a man (*adam*) is *checking her out from behind* (*mipnei shestam hadvarim ne'emrah b'ishah shemehaleches lah v'adam tzofeh lah mei'achurehah*)
>
> And if his wife is impure, this is [all] forbidden.

Rabbi Avraham of Montpellier (*Peirush R. Avraham min Hahar*), and Ritz quoted in *Shita Mekubetzes*, also state clearly that if Rabbi Achi's caution were in fact against gazing at one's own menstruating wife's genitals, then it would not apply at all when she is pure.

And Rabbi Avraham of Montpellier (in the name of "Rabeinu Shlomoh," perhaps referring to Rabeinu Shlomoh of Montpellier, died c.1240) and Ritz also both say that, according to Rabbi Shimon ben Lakish, Rabbi Achi was mainly speaking about the scenario of a man gazing at a woman's buttocks.

[678*] See also *Tosfos Yeshanim, Nedarim 20a*, whose explanation of this caution supports this notion.

[679] Buchwald edition, *Shaar Haprishah*, p. 6-7.

As we shall now explain, it is perhaps implied by Raavad III's wording in *Shaar Hakedushah* (p. 179 in the Buchwald edition) that in *Shaar Haprishah* he meant to say that Rabbi Shimon ben Lakish was cautioning against gazing at one's own pure wife's genitals during *non-sexual* moments.

[680] This interpretation of Rabbi Shimon ben Lakish accords with one version of *Callah Rabti 1:11*, which has Rabbi Yochanan bar Napacha and Rabbi Shimon ben Lakish warning a husband against gazing at his own *impure* wife (see above, p. 44).

[681] Why there is a presumed "prohibition," here, is unclear. The fact that one particular sage cautioned about possible spiritual repercussions resulting in one's children from a certain kind of behavior, should not necessarily translate into a binding legal prohibition.

This is a general issue concerning interpretation of the Talmud that we shall address in a future study.

[682] Rabbi Yosef Caro quotes these last two lines of *Shaar Haprishah* in his *Beis Yosef* commentary to *Orach Chaim 240:2-4:4* in conjunction with Raavad III's statement about gazing at or kissing the female genitals in *Shaar Hakedushah*. We shall now explore in what ways Raavad III's context in *Shaar Haprishah* might possibly be said to be similar and/or dissimilar from his context in *Shaar Hakedushah*.

[683] Raavad III does not spell out this first interpretation of "gazing during intercourse," but it is implied by the fact that he offers "gazing during foreplay" as a *second* interpretation ("*v'yesh meforshim* – and *others* explain this to mean..." – see above, page 172).

He also implies that he was not oblivious to the practice of gazing at the female genitals during actual intercourse, for he writes in regard to the second interpretation that in that case the husband makes things modest so that gazing during intercourse will not be possible.

In addition, although according these "*others*'" interpretation, Raavad III describes the fathers as gazing at the mothers' genitals "at the time they *wish* to have intercourse" (*b'shaah sheheim rotzim leshamesh... samuch l'tashmish*), implying that they gaze during *foreplay*, in *prelude* to actual intercourse, he almost immediately goes on to contrast gazing at the female genitals during non-sexual moments with gazing at them "during intercourse" (*b'shaas tashmish*). While it is possible that Raavad III was stretching the meaning of "*b'shaas tashmish*" in this one case to include foreplay, it is equally possible that he had all along understood the *simple* meaning of Rabbi Yochanan ben Dahavai's case of gazing at the female genitals as referring to gazing during *intercourse*, and that the interpretation that they gaze during *foreplay* was already an additional interpretation.

[Note also the Buchwald edition of *Baalei HaNefesh, Shaar Hakedushah, Shinuyei Nuschaos*, p. 251, that later in the discussion, when Raavad III is insisting that gazing at the female genitals is still forbidden by the Sages despite their rejection of Rabbi Yochanan ben Dahavai, one manuscript version reads: "And so, too, one who gazes during *intercourse* (*v'chein hamistakel b'shaas hatashmish*)..." It is, however, possible that this, too, is loosely referring to sexual moments in general, including the time of *foreplay*.]

Alternatively, Raavad III perhaps assumed the simple context of Rabbi Yochanan ben Dahavai's caution against gazing as referring to gazing during non-sexual moments. And he began his comment with the phrase "And others interpret..." to contrast this simple assumption with the interpretation of "others" that it referred to gazing during sexual moments – but only during foreplay, not during actual intercourse.

[Finally, note that it is the amoraic sage, Rava, as quoted in *Callah Rabti 1:13*, who asserts that Rabbi Yochanan ben Dahavai himself only cautioned against congenital blindness resulting from gazing that is *immediately followed* by intercourse and conception (see above, p. 46). It is also Rava, as quoted on *Nidah 17a*, who permits sexual intercourse to all couples during the day if the room is made darkened, and who permits sexual intercourse during the day to Torah scholars and their wives even if the room cannot practically be made darkened, so long as they cover themselves appropriately (see above, p. 96). In that case, it is possible that Raavad III, here, was combining these two statements of Rava, when he stated (see above, page 172): "And others explain this to mean that they gaze *when they want to have sex*, even though during actual intercourse the husband makes things modest – that is, *by day he darkens things by covering themselves with his robes*, or by night he puts out the candle…"

But this would then raise three points for further clarification: a) Rava on *Nidah 17a* is generally understood by rabbinic sources as permitting only a Torah scholar and his wife to cover themselves in a lit room during the day for intercourse, whereas he is generally understood as requiring a non-scholar and his wife to darken the whole room. Raavad III, however, speaks here as if it is sufficient for *any couple* to darken things with a mere covering in a lit room during the day; b) pursuant to point a), if Raavad III were referring specifically to a Torah scholar in this scenario, then we either have confirmation that it is not beyond a Torah scholar to crave to gaze at his own wife's genitals, or it is perhaps possible to argue that when Raavad III goes on to say that (according to Rabbi Yochanan ben Dahavai) even if the husband does make things darkened, he has still "degraded himself," such criticism may have only been addressed toward a Torah scholar, not a layman, of whom no greater refinement is necessarily expected; c) when Raavad III goes on to say, in the context of discussing Rabbi Yochanan ben Dahavai's opinion, that gazing during non-sexual moments is worse than gazing during sexual moments, this would appear on the surface to contradict Rava's assertion (as reported in *Callah Rabti 1:13*) that Rabbi Yochanan ben Dahavai himself only gave caution against congenital blindness when such gazing is *immediately followed* by intercourse and conception. Thus, we may be forced to interpret Raavad III's elaboration, here, as referring to gazing during non-sexual moments *that still leads to immediate intercourse and conception*, and what makes it "worse" is the fact that such gazing turns a non-sexual moment into a sexual one, and then, in turn, leads to intercourse and conception. The question then would be: what is so evil about turning a non-sexual moment into a sexual one? And see below pp. 190-191.]

[684] Raavad III suggests that Rabbi Yochanan ben Dahavai was possibly referring to gazing at the female genitals during *non*-sexual moments.

But all the other three behaviors Rabbi Yochanan ben Dahavai mentioned were in relation to foreplay or sexual intercourse.

[And see *Callah Rabti 1:13*, where Rava insists that Rabbi Yochanan ben Dahavai was only cautioning against gazing that is immediately followed by sexual intercourse and conception. Still, Rava could ostensibly have been referring to gazing during non-sexual moments in a manner that causes the moment to turn sexual, and then, in turn, leads to intercourse and conception.]

[684*] Still, according to Rava's interpretation of Rabbi Yochanan ben Dahavai, as quoted in *Callah Rabti 1:13*, if Rabbi Yochanan ben Dahavai were in fact cautioning against a husband gazing during non-sexual moments, his caution about it causing congenital blindness would have only been meant to apply if such gazing turned the non-sexual

moment into a sexual one, and, in turn, led to immediate intercourse and conception (see above, page 46, and the concluding brackets of endnote 683).

[685] See *Yad Malachi*, *"Clalei HaReish,"* Clal 568.

[686] According to one version of *Callah Rabti 1:11*, Rabbi Yochanan bar Napacha issued a caution that gazing at one's own impure wife's normally-covered skin, even her heel, causes congenital illness (see above, p. 44). But there is no reason to believe he meant to extend that caution to gazing at one's own *pure* wife's body (and certainly no reason to believe he would have extended it into moments of physical intimacy).

Only Rava, there, seems to apply such a caution to gazing at one's own *pure* wife's body, and even during physical intimacy – but only if done during the same sexual encounter in which conception occurs. During any other time of life, or during a sexual encounter in which conception will certainly not occur, such gazing at one's own pure wife's body parts would be perfectly safe even according to Rava.

And see *Callah Rabti 1:13*, where Rava says that this is the view even of Rabbi Yochanan ben Dahavai himself in regard to the "dangers" of the four behaviors he cautioned against – that they are all only dangerous if performed during the same sexual encounter in which conception occurs.

[687] In Raavad III's own words: ". . . *And how much more so* is it treating a wife without regard for her dignity if he gazes there *at times other than during sex*, which also means the husband voluntarily arouses his evil urge, as we discussed in *Shaar Haprishah*."

[688] Obviously, the Sages and Rabbi Yochanan bar Napacha could not have known that one day in the future the compilers-editors of the Talmud would choose to juxtapose the teaching about "shame" and "shamefacedness" to the caution of Rabbi Achi, Rav Yosef and Rabbi Shimon ben Lakish. The point, however, is that these compilers-editors, in choosing such juxtaposition, injected a certain meaning into the teaching about "shame" and "shamefacedness" – which Raavad III interprets according to Rabbi Shimon ben Lakish as including denigration of a husband gazing at his own pure wife's genitals during non-sexual moments. We are therefore arguing that it cannot be assumed that the Sages and Rabbi Yochanan bar Napacha themselves would have agreed with this interpretation of the teaching about "shame" and "shamefacedness," at least not in regard to a husband lovingly gazing at his own (pure) wife's genitals *during intimacy*, considering that by their own words as reported on *Nedarim 20b* they rejected Rabbi Yochanan ben Dahavai's caution in regard to this very context (and see above, endnote 660, paragraphs 12-14, and below, endnote 696).

[689] Although Maimonides, who did understand the Sages as rejecting all four of Rabbi Yochanan ben Dahavai's cautions, does mention in *Sefer Hamada, Deos 5:4* that a Torah scholar should have sex with "shame" (*b'bushah*), we've already discussed above (footnote to page 33 and endnote 417) that the intention of this appears to be about *sensitivity* and *dignity*, not embarrassment.

And see our discussion below, p. 187-188, further exploring the definition of "shame" within marital intimacy.

In any case, Maimonides does not make this an obligation upon all couples, but an *ideal* that he encourages in the context of his instruction to pious Torah scholars. Thus, to the concept of "shame," too, Maimonides appears to apply the principle he set forth in his *Commentary to the Mishnah, Sanhedrin 7:4* that there is a critical difference between that which is ideal and that which is permitted or forbidden.

[Rabbi Yosef Caro in *Kesef Mishneh* to *Mishneh Torah, Sefer Hamada, Deos 5:4*, implies that Maimonides acquiesced to Raavad III according to the spirit of the law, encouraging a Torah scholar to behave like Rabbi Eliezer as described on *Nedarim 20a*. But Rabbi Caro derives this from Maimonides' instruction that sexual intercourse should be performed with "*bushah* – shame, not *azus* – arrogance" which, again, we have argued means only that he should penetrate her with sensitivity and diginity, not that he should engage in extreme pietistic behaviors, as did Rabbi Eliezer. And if Maimonides did mean to endorse Rabbi Eliezer's behavior, he certainly could have – and presumably would have – been a lot more, or even just a little more, direct about it.]

[690] *Peirush HaRokeach al HaTorah* (Klugman, 2001), p. 83.

Credit goes to the author of the humorously titled, *Rabbi, My Husband wants a Blowjob* (2015) and *Rabbi, My Husband wants Anal Sex* (2015), for bringing this source in *Peirush HaRokeach* to my attention on pages 12 of both works.

[691] Although in Talmudic-era literature the title "Sages-*Chachamim*" can apparently refer to different groups of rabbis living at different times and in different geographic locations, the fact that both *Tractate Derech Eretz-Perek Aryos* and *Mesechtos Zeiros-Mesechta Arayos* put the teaching cautioning against gazing at a forbidden woman's "heel" in the mouth of a collective rabbinic view of "Sages-*Chachamim*," implies that it was also in perfect alignment with the collective rabbinic view quoted on *Nedarim 20b*, also in the name of "Sages-*Chachamim*," which at face value *legally permits* a husband to lovingly gaze at his own pure wife's naked genitals during sexual intimacy.

[692] A 3rd Generation Israeli Amora.

[693] A 1st Generation Israeli Amora.

[694] A 4th Generation Tanna.

[695] Note that whichever textual version one chooses here, one is not necessarily forced by reason to accept that the earlier reference to "*the* woman" was referring to one's own wife, for why should conversation of a man with his own wife – whether initiated by her or by him – be *assumed* to generally have "adulterous" intentions?

Neither are we necessarily forced by reason to unquestioningly accept those commentaries who connect the version of this caution on *Nedarim 20a* with the passage in *Ethics of the Fathers 1:5*, the latter of which reads:

> Yosi ben Yochanan of Jerusalem, said, ". . . Do not unlimit conversation with the woman.
>
> [By '*the*' woman,] they were referring to one's own wife, so how much more so [should one refrain from unlimiting conversation with] the wife of another man.
>
> Based on this, the Sages (*chachamim*) said, "Whoever unlimits conversation with the woman does himself bad (*gorem raah l'atzmo*), and he neglects Torah study, and he ultimately inherits Purgatory.

*Avos D'Rabbi Nosson 7:2-3*, a work predating the medieval commentaries, gives a clear example of "unlimitting conversation" with one's own wife and the kind of bad it could do the husband: If he confesses to her that his friends disrespected him, this, in turn, could diminish his respect in her eyes.

So despite what some commentaries might have later tried to read into it, in no way are we necessarily forced to read *Ethics of the Fathers 1:5* as discouraging unlimited conversation with one's own wife *out of a concern that it will lead to "adultery."* And therefore, in no way are we forced to accept that the caution against unlimiting conversation with "the woman" on *Nedarim 20a* had anything to do with conversation with one's own wife.

[Even Maimonides, who in his commentary to *Ethics of the Fathers 1:5* explains that the concern about excess talk with women, there, is sexual in nature, does not assert that excess talk with one's own wife is likely to lead to all out adultery.]

And more research into the matter is required.

696 This caution about congenital physical illness resulting from gazing at forbidden women's "heels" accords with *Tractate Callah 8* and *Callah Rabti 1:11* (see above, pages 41 and 44 respectively). The same caution in *Mesechtos Zeiros-Tractate Arayos*, to be discussed next in our study, accords with them as well.

*Nedarim 20a's* version, however, has Rabbi Achi cautioning only that such lewd behavior might, in turn, cause one's children to be lewd.

And note that these two versions in *Mesechtos Derech Eretz* and *Mesechtos Zeiros* quote the caution in the name of "the Sages" (*chachamim*) - while, according to *Nedarim 20b*, "the Sages" (*chachamim*) considered gazing at one's own *pure* wife's naked genitals during sexual intimacy to be both legally permitted and medically safe.

[And see above, endnote 691.]

And according to *Callah Rabti 1:13-14*, the Rabbis (*rabanan*) considered gazing at one's own *pure* wife's naked genitals during sexual intimacy to always be legally permitted and to only be medically dangerous if performed during the same sexual encounter in which conception occurs.

In any case, *Tractate Callah 7-8* has this caution of the Sages against gazing at heels said by them in conjunction with another caution of theirs against touching even the little finger of a woman. The simple context of the caution against touching the little finger appears to have been in regard to touching a woman other than one's own wife – which implies that their caution against gazing at "heels" was also said in regard to other such women.

697 Note the explanation of the medieval commentator, *Rashi*, on the verse:

> <u>The recognition of their faces</u>: They are recognizable by the boldness of their faces.
>
> <u>Like Sodom they told, they did not deny</u>: They committed [sins] publicly."

Again, the context of this lack of "shamefacedness" is about *public* indecency. Thus, in the context on *Nedarim 20a* of Rav Achi's (and here, the Sages',) teaching, the caution against lack of "shamefacedness" would fittingly be against a man "checking out" other women in public, not against a husband gazing at (or kissing) his own pure wife's genitals, lovingly, in private, during sexual intimacy.

698 The term "*dvar ervah*," which we have translated here as "illicit sexuality," is actually a difficult one to translate accurately, and it could mean different things to different commentaries in different contexts.

The Soncino edition of *Tractate Derech Eretz Rabah*, p. 536, translates the term "*dvar ervah*" as "a naked part of the body." Perhaps they understood it to be reminiscent of Rabbi Yochanan ben Dahavai's teaching on *Nedarim 20a*, cautioning against gazing at one's own pure wife's naked genitals even during sexual intimacy.

But although the term "*ervah*" can technically refer to the genitals, such a translation in this context is questionable, for in many biblical and rabbinical discussions – the entire *Perek*

# ENDNOTES

*Arayos* included – the term *"ervah"* (the singular form of *'arayos'*) translates broadly as "illicit sexual relationships" or specifically as "illicit sexual intercourse."

And it speaks here not of *"ervah"* but of *"dvar ervah"* – "a *thing* of *ervah.*"

So even if the word *"ervah,"* here, were meant to refer to genitals, or nakedness in general, we'd have no reason to believe the teaching was speaking about a husband gazing at his own pure wife's nakedness, or a wife gazing at her own husband's, but rather only about a man or woman gazing at the nakedness of someone who is forbidden to them.

[*Midrash HaGadol, Vayera 18:1* (page 285 in the Mosad HaRav Kook edition) does record this teaching of Rabbi Miasha as applying the verse in Isaiah 33:15 to "Whoever beholds a *dvar ervah in a woman* and averts his eyes from her..." This would imply a woman's nakedness in general.

But again, there is no reason to believe that this would refer to one's own wife. The simple context of such "nakedness" would be speaking only of a forbidden woman – and halachically speaking, if she were married, the term *ervah* could refer even to so much as part of her uncovered hair.

And see on the same page of *Midrash HaGadol*, there, that it applies the same verse in Isaiah to Abraham not having gazed at the beauty of his own wife, Sarah – in a description of Abraham's extreme piety, not baseline Jewish law.

See also *Babylonian Talmud, Makos 24a*, which applies the verse to one who avoids gazing at women as they wash clothes in the river – also in a context of the nakedness of women forbidden to the viewer. See also the concluding passage of *Midrash Tehilim-Socher Tov 17:14.*]

See also the version of *Mesechtos Zeiros-Mesechta Arayos*, quoted next in our study, which has Rabbi Achi warning a man not to gaze at other women lest he "come to *dvar ervah*" (*shelo tavo l'dvar ervah*). It would be somewhat absurd to translate the phrase there as "nakedness." It clearly refers to illicit sexuality.

See also *Talmud, Pesachim 113b*, which reports that G-d despises a person who comes as a lone witness to testify having caught someone in *"dvar ervah"* (*haro'eh dvar ervah bachaveiro umeiyid bo yechidi*). Again, the context is about a sexual indiscretion.

But then see the words of Rabeinu Yonah in *Sefer Hayirah* (quoted in *Kovetz Shitos Kamai, Makos 24a*):

> If you encounter something sexual (*dvar ervah*), *like a woman* – whether Jewish or non-Jewish, married or single, adult or child – close your eyes or turn aside so that you will not see her...
>
> And similarly, if you encounter a male and female pig [alt. a male and female dog] or any other animals copulating, do not stare at them.

While this teaching of Rabeinu Yonah could be read as an extreme approach to separation of the sexes, perhaps he meant only to explain that the term *"dvar ervah"* encompasses anything that an individual personally finds arousing to the point of illicit thought – no matter who, or what, it might be, or in what context one encounters it, naked or clothed (and see *Talmud, Avodah Zarah 20ab*).

Thus, coalescing all these variations in context, Rabbi Miasha's teaching could be said to encompass one who chances upon: a) any sight he or she personally finds sexually arousing to the point of illicit thought; b) the sight of illicit nakedness (not the nakedness of one's own spouse); c) the sight of an unmarried couple engaging in illicit behavior; d) the sight of a married couple engaged in permissible sexual behavior which is still illicit for a bystander to watch.

In light of all the above, we have chosen, here, a broad translation of the term *"dvar ervah,"* as "illicit sexuality."

[699] Note the reverse in order of the teaching here, whereby the caution against gazing at the "heel" of a woman is brought *in continuation* of the teaching about "shamefacedness." This lends further support to the argument that the teaching extolling "shame" and "shamefacedness" on *Nedarim 20a* was brought only in conjunction with the teaching of Rav Achi (about gazing at a forbidden woman's "heel"), not the teaching of Rabbi Yochanan ben Dahavai.

[700] See also *Pesikta Rabti, 24:2*.

[701] See *Mishnas Rabbi Eliezer (ben Rabbi Yossi Gaglili)* toward the end of *Parshah 18*: "One who feasts his eyes upon a married woman (*eishes ish*) is called an adulterer."

[702] It can be strongly argued that Rabbi Miasha's teaching was brought by the compilers-editors of *Vayikra Rabah* in direct relation to the teaching of the paragraph before it, about "committing adultery with one's eyes."

*Chidushei HaRadal* to *Vayikra Rabah 23:13*, in fact, says this outright.

In that case, the compilers-editors of *Vayikra Rabah* themselves may have understood the teaching of Rabbi Miasha as referring only to one who observes, and turns away from, *illicit* sexuality, but not to a husband and wife who lovingly gaze at, and "feast their eyes upon," each other's nakedness.

*Peirush Maharzu*, there, states clearly that this reward Rabbi Miasha speaks about, of meriting to receive the Divine Presence, is on account of the person abstaining from *illicit* sex (*poreish me'arayos*). Once again, this would have nothing to do with the behaviors of husband and wife during marital intimacy.

[703] The verse itself certainly has no sexual context. And the only medieval commentary I have found who attempts to define the context of this "shame" or "shamefacedness" in relation to the revelation at Sinai gives it no sexual connotation either. See Rabeinu Avigdor Tzarfati (13th century), *Peirushim uPsakim al HaTorah, Parshas Yisro, Psak 72*, (quoted in *Kovetz Shitos Kamai, Nedarim 20a*).

See also *Biur Hagra* to *Shulchan Aruch, Orach Chaim 1:1:Hagaah:10*, which points to *Nedarim 20a* as the source for general "shame" before G-d in an entirely non-sexual context.

[704] See *Mechilta, Exodus 20:17; Mechilta D'Rashbi, Exodus 20:17; Jerusalem Talmud, Kidushin, Chapter 4, 42b; Babylonian Talmud, Yevamos 79a; Bamidbar Rabah 8:4; Midrash Tehilim-Socher Tov, 1:10, 17:14; Agadas Midrash Shmuel, Parshah 28; Yalkut Shimoni, Torah, 301, Exodus 20:17*.

*Yalkut Shimoni, Prophets-Writings 276, Jeremiah 6:15*, speaks of shame about committing "abominations" – though even if the term "abominations" were meant to include sexual sins, it would refer only to those of an *illicit* nature, as it does in other places in the Bible, but not to sexual exploration between husband and wife, within marriage, in private, during intimacy.

[705] For other examples, see *Otzar HaAgadah*, entry: "*Bushah*" (Mosad Harav Kook).

[706] For a kabbalistic discussion about "shame," marriage and illicit sexuality, see *Tikunei Zohar 58* (bottom of page 183, top of page 184, in the Mosad HaRav Kook edition) and Rabbi Reuven Margolis's *Nitzutzei Zohar* thereon.

[707] The term "*am haaretz*" is generally used to describe a person ignorant of Torah.

But see the "*Iyunim*" section in the Steinsaltz Talmud Hebrew edition, *Pesachim 49b*, entry: "*Am Haaretz*," that according to commentaries the numerous harsh comments quoted from various sages, there, in reference to the "*am haaretz*" were referring to one who is not only most ignorant, but also most uncouth. And in this context, the Talmud quotes the assumption that such an uncouth person also lacks basic shame. In that case, uncouthness and lack of shame may have been characteristics the Talmudic compilers-editors assumed to go hand-in-hand.

This would further support our understanding that on *Nedarim 20a* the Talmudic compilers-editors brought the teaching extolling a sense of shame specifically in conjunction with the teaching *before* it, of Rav Achi's caution to fathers not to act on their uncouthness so as to spare their children from developing similar spiritual challenges in their own adulthood.

[708] Lit. "penetrates her." But the clear connotation is that the husband rapes his own wife.

See for example, *Tosfos* there:

> Rabeinu Tam explained: [Just like the lion] tears and eats and does not wait for it [its prey] to die, the uncouth ignoramus does not wait for his wife to be agreeable [to sex].

[709] A study on ancient and modern rabbinical acknowledgement of, and advice on, domestic abuse – including analysis of their perceptions of its causes, the extent to which their advice and/or perceptions may have been influenced by cultural conditions of their times, and the insight that could be contributed to the discussion by the findings of modern psychology – would be a critical study indeed.

[710] Footnote to page 33 and endnote 417.

[711] See above, page 178 and endnote 678 thereon.

[712] See above, endnote 664.

[713] *Mishnah, Kesubos 40a; Mishnah, Bava Kama 83b.*

[714] Page 107.

[715] See above, pp. 56, 94, 97-98, 100.

[716] This is the understanding of all the medieval commentaries I have found on *Makos 24a* and *Sukkah 49b*.

See *Otzar Mefarshei HaTalmud* and *Rivan* (quoted in the Steinsaltz Talmud "*Iyunim*") to *Makos 24a*.

See *Otzar Mefarshei HaTalmud, Otzar Hageonim, Rashi* and *Meiri, Beis Habechirah* to *Sukkah 49b*.

Even Rashi to *Sukkah 49b* – who mentions something about not behaving at a party in a "light-headed" manner – does not sexualize the teaching.

And see Meiri, *Beis Habechirah, Sukkah 49b*, who brings the discussion of "appropriate partying" back into context as a matter of avoiding *ostentation*.

See also the biblical commentaries of Rabbi Saadiah Gaon, Rabbi Yeshayah of Trani I, Rashi, Ibn Ezra, Radak, *Metzudas David* and *Metzudas Tzion* to Micah 6:8.

See also the commentary of Rabbi Eliezer of Beaugency (*Peirush Rabbi Eliezer Mibalganzi*, 12th century) to Micah 6:8, p. 168, footnote 1, that the translation of "*tznius*" in this verse might just be "simplicity."

See also the commentaries of *Abravanel* and *Malbim* on the verse, which interpret it to also include simplicity in matters of faith.

[717] Note that the full Talmudic discussion on *Sukkah 49b* reads as follows (in this case, following the Soncino Translation):

> The School of R. Anan taught: It is written [Song of Songs 7:2], "The roundings of thy thighs [are like Jewels]."
>
> Why are the words of the Torah compared to the thigh? To teach you that just as the thigh is hidden, so should the words of the Torah be hidden – and this is the import of what R. Eleazar said:
>
>> "What is the implication of the text, "It hath been told thee, O man, what is good, and what the Lord doth require of thee: Only to do justly, and to love mercy, and to walk humbly with thy G-d?"
>>
>> 'To do justly' means [to act in accordance with] justice;
>>
>> 'to love mercy' refers to acts of loving kindness
>>
>> 'and to walk humbly with thy G-d' refers to attending to funerals and dowering a bride for her wedding.
>
> Now can we not make a deduction *a fortiori*: If in matters which are normally performed publicly the Torah enjoins 'to walk humbly', how much more so in matters that are normally done privately?

As stated in the previous endnote, the commentaries understand the Talmud's message, here, of "walking humbly/modestly" before G-d, as a lesson not to be ostentacious even in that which is not normally done in the public eye (such as in one's Torah study or charity-giving. *Meiri*). The lesson has no sexual connotation at all.

But note that not even the beginning of the teaching, which mentions that "the thigh is normally covered," can be used to support Raavad III's argument against a husband gazing at his own pure wife's genitals during physical intimacy. The context of that statement is merely that just like people's thighs *in general* are not revealed to all, so, too, one's Torah study should not be flaunted. But certainly a person's Torah study is revealed to those most close to his or her heart and soul, and, therefore, to take the analogy to its reverse logical conclusion, a person's thighs may be revealed to his or her own soulmate – one's own spouse – especially during intimacy.

In any case, Raavad III does not even quote the verse from Song of Songs (about the hiddeness of thighs) to prove his point, so we need not accept such an argument on Raavad III's behalf if he himself could have easily chosen to argue it from the very same Talmudic page, yet he did not.

[718] In fact, the concept of "*maksheh atzmo ladaas*" seems to be referring only to some sort of sexual compulsion, for the Talmud's rationale there that "this is the craft of the evil inclination – today it tells you to do one thing, tomorrow it tells you to do another thing, and then next day it tells you to go serve idols," is brought elsewhere in the *Talmud* to

describe what are arguably compulsive behaviors, such as ripping apart one's clothes in a fit of rage, destroying one's property in a fit of rage, throwing away one's money in a fit of rage, or pulling out one's hair in a fit of rage. See *Talmud, Shabbos 105b; Tosefta, Bava Kama 9:31; Avos D'Rabbi Noson 3:2.*

In that case, the original teaching about "one who deliberately brings himself to erection" may have only been referring to a *compulsive* masturbator – an addict, for whom the urge to constantly masturbate interferes with his basic daily living and function, as well as his daily Jewish commitments and general spiritual maturing and development.

[719] Buchwald edition, p. 175.

[720] Actually, Raavad III, here (p. 179 in the Buchwald edition), refers back to his discussion about "inciting the evil urge" in *Shaar Haprishah* (p. 7, ibid). But in *Shaar Haprishah*, there, he merely points the reader forward to his explanation in *Shaar Hakedushah* (p. 175, ibid).

[721] Top of page 179 in the Buchwald edition.

[722] *Makos 16b.*

[723] *Shabbos 90b* – in an episode involving Rav himself.

[724] The only possible explanation I can think of is that Raavad III was comparing the vagina to the cupping horn, for it becomes a "vessel to collect blood" each month during menstruation; and he was comparing the presence of pubic lice during cunnilingus to the passing of an insect over one's lips. If so, we could easily understand why other medieval commentaries might have rejected these comparisons: It is quite natural for a human male to be orally attracted to the genital region of his wife, while at the same time to be repelled by the very thought of drinking out of her medical instruments (similar, perhaps, in modern times, to how the average husband is orally attracted to kissing his wife's mouth, but repelled by the thought of using her toothbrush); and the issue of pubic lice is easily remedied by cleansing or shaving the area.

And once we've broached the topic of female genital shaving, lest any Ultra-Orthodox Chasidic-Charedi man be embarrassed to reveal to his wife that he would enjoy her genitals to be smooth, or lest any Ultra-Orthodox Chasidic-Charedi woman think her husband perverse in feeling or expressing himself so, let it be known that none other than the sage, Rava, was of the opinion that Torah – G-d – considers hairless female genitals in adult women to be more beautiful, and that such was the original genetic predisposition of Jewish women. See *Babylonian Talmud, Sanhedrin 21a*. [And lest it be argued that this teaching of Rava was meant metaphorically, note that *Tosfos* to *Gitin 6b* understood it literally. Credit goes to my friend, Yisroel Freeman, for bringing this source in *Gitin* to my attention. See also *Talmud, Kesubos 71b, Rashi: B'dvarim she'beino l'beinah:* "*Sam hameisir es hasaar.*" Credit goes to Tzvi Adams for bringing this source in *Kesubos* to my attention.]

[725] In volume 4 of Feldheim's English translation of Rabbi Yaakov Emden's commentary to the prayer-book, *Siddur Yaavetz Beis Yaakov*, in *Mitas Hakesef*, chapter 7, section 2:2, p. 134, the translator presents Rabbi Emden as quoting Raavad III to say: "With regard to the other matters, our Sages did not differ with Rabbi Yochanan ben Dahavai. *For they state* (sic) that a man who kisses a woman's genitals violates the prohibition against making oneself loathsome…"

Rabbi Emden's actual words in the Hebrew carry no such meaning. And not even Raavad III claimed that the Sages themselves verbalized a direct connection between cunnilingus and cupping horns/insects.

[726] And even that which the Talmud spoke against in this regard is arguably subject to change based on widespread societal changes in human sensibilities and/or hygienic conditions.

For one example, *Babylonian Talmud, Tractate Shabbos 90b*, prohibits the eating of kosher fish raw on the grounds that is disgusting – "*bal teshaktzu*" (See also *Encyclopedia Talmudis, vol. 3, "Bal Teshaktzu", footnote 16; Rema* to *Shulchan Aruch, Yoreh Deah 13:1*). Yet raw sushi has become one of the most popular kosher cuisines of the 21st century.

[727] See *Encyclopedia Talmudis vol. 3, Entry: "Bal Teshaktzu,"* footnotes 31-33.

And see *Dvar Seser* (2013), *Siman* 7, page 46, quoting additional support to this line of reasoning.

**[Added note to the third edition:** See also Rabbi Maor Kayam's *Harchavot l'Simchat Habayit v'Birchato* (2015), pp. 190-196.]

Obviously, a great number of spouses find oral contact with, and/or oral stimulation of, each other's genitals extremely enjoyable, especially as a means of pleasuring, becoming vulnerable with, and bonding to, each other.

And even when there are genital odors that might make them feel repelled by oral sex, such odors can generally be remedied through hygienic methods. Therefore, it is not necessarily the genitals themselves that they are "disgusted" by, but the dirt or sweat or (stagnant) sexual fluids. It is thus arguably comparable to eating with sweaty hands or off a dirty plate, both of which are rabbinically forbidden because of "*bal teshaktzu*" (*Mishneh Torah, Sefer Kedushah, Maachalos Asuros 17:30*; *Encyclopedia Talmudis vol. 3, Entry: "Bal Teshaktzu,"* footnote 21) – and both of which are easily remedied by simple washing and proper hygiene. There, too, it is not the hands or the plate that make one feel "disgusted," but the sweat or dirt upon them.

[See Rabbi Yehudah Leib Nachmanson's *Sheyekadesh Atzmo* (2015), Chapter 44, footnote 16, for a theory that genitals are intrinsically equivalent to bedpans, and clean genitals to "clean" bedpans. It would, however, be extremely difficult to argue that common human nature actually equates the two – a point Rabbi Nachmanson himself grants in his conclusion. And see *Encyclopedia Talmudis, vol. 3, Entry Bal Teshaktzu*, footnote 37, for an approach that even a bedpan may be used for eating after thorough scrubbing.

Note also that Rabbi Schneur Zalman of Liadi implies in his second edition of *Shulchan Aruch HaRav, Orach Chaim 3:9*, that the average individual in the late 1700s/early 1800s who was not "obsessive" about cleanliness (*istenis*) would wipe away their feces with their bare hands. Are we to believe, then, that it was irrevocably forbidden for them to eat with their fingers?]

But if a certain individual spouse *always* feels repulsed by performing oral sex, for that individual it would appear to in fact be a case of "*bal teshaktzu*" (as logic dictates based on *Encyclopedia Talmudis*, ibid, footnote 33).

Concerning oral contact with the sexual fluids themselves, male or female, which does make some people uncomfortable, if a particular husband or wife finds such oral contact erotic or pleasurable, as many do, then it arguably cannot be intrinsically forbidden upon the grounds of "*bal teshaktzu*." The only genital fluid expressly forbidden on the grounds of "*bal teshaktzu*" is urine (see *Encyclopedia Talmudis*, ibid, footnote 20).

[See Rabbi Yehudah Leib Nachmanson's, *Sheyekadesh Atzmo* (2015), Chapter 44, footnote 16, for a theory that semen should be considered problematic vis-a-vis "*bal teshaktzu*," because Jewish law also considers "putrid secretions" (*leichah sruchah*), such as pus, to be "disgusting," and semen is sometimes referred to in rabbinic writing as "a putrid drop" (*tipah seruchah*). But this comparison is debatable – especially considering that actual human nature differentiates between the two. In any case, the term "putrid drop" arguably refers only to actual ejaculate, not pre-ejaculate.]

[As for the question if male or female sexual fluids are "kosher" to ingest, it is beyond the scope of the present study to delve deeply into or analyze the sources on this subject. As preliminary research for future discussion, see **collectively**, Encyclopedia Talmudis vol. 1, Entry: "Adam – Human," footnotes 42-43; Encyclopedia Talmudis vol. 3, Entry: Bal Teshaktzu, footnote 20; Encyclopedia Talmudis vol. 23, Entry: "Yotzei Min Hatamei – Secretions of Impure Creatures," footnotes 340, 345, 383-390, 397, 403-407, 525-527, 1021.

Note also that it could perhaps be argued, at least in regard to female sexual fluids, that just as there is certainly no issue in "swallowing" one's spouse's saliva in the course of kissing, for if there were such an issue halachah would have told us so, so too, there should be no reason to assume there is any issue with swallowing sexual fluids that naturally collect at the opening of the female sex organ during sexual excitement according to those who permit kissing the female genitals – for if there were an issue, the Talmud would have told us.

[And see above, endnote 72, that Maimonides' implies that intercourse between limbs – which would encompass fellatio – was included in the Sages' permissive ruling on *Nedarim 20b*, without qualification about swallowing male sexual fluids either. And more research into the strength of this point is required.]

In fact, we find similar logic employed (in regard to a different marital-sexual behavior) in at least one commentary commenting on the very page of *Nedarim 20b*, and in regard to the very ruling of the Sages there:

Rabeinu Asher, as quoted in *Hagahos Habach* to *Rosh, Yevamos 34b*, in *Yam Shel Shlomoh* to *Yevamos 34b*, and in *Beis Yosef* to *Tur, Orach Chaim 240:2-4:V'haTosfos pirshu*, argues that occasional intra-anal ejaculation must be permitted for married couples, because if it weren't, then Rebbi and/or Rav should have clearly said so to the wives who informed them that their husbands wanted anal sex. The fact that they did not warn the wives about intra-anal ejaculation proves, according to this quotation in the name of Rabeinu Asher, that it is permitted.

Along this line of reasoning, then, it could perhaps be argued that the fact that the Sages on *Nedarim 20b* permitted kissing the female genitals without clarifying that ingesting female sexual fluids is problematic implies that there is no "kosher" issue to be concerned about.

A separate issue that is often taught to be categorically forbidden – at least rabbinically, not biblically – is for a husband to suck milk directly from his wife's breast. But see *Encyclopedia Talmudis vol. 15*, entry "*Chalav* – Milk," footnotes 133-134.

And I reiterate that further research is required in all of this before any practical conclusions may be derived.]

[728] *Encyclopedia Talmudis vol. 3*, Entry: "*Bal Teshaktzu*," footnote 36.

[729] And see our discussion below, pp. 193-194.

[730] *Rabeinu Yeruchem, Nesiv 32*; *Mordechai, Hilchos Nidah 731-732*; *Tosfos, Yevamos 34b*; *Tosfos, Sanhedrin 58b*; *Rabeinu Asher* as quoted by *Hagahos HaBach* to *Rosh, Yevamos 34b* and *Yam Shel Shlomoh* to *Yevamos 34b*; *Tosfos HaRosh, Nedarim 20b*.

But see above, endnote 92.

[731] Though it could ostensibly refer to rear-entry vaginal intercourse, for which the wife must turn over and position herself "uncomfortably" upon her knees.

[See, for example, Rabeinu Asher's *Peirush HaRosh* to *Nedarim 20a*, where he writes that "overturning the table" causes the woman "inconvenience upon her knees" (*shematriach osah al arkevosehah*), which could apply to rear-entry vaginal intercourse – although Rabeinu Asher himself applies it, there, to anal intercourse.]

But the only commentary I have found to raise this point is *Yad Aharon, Even Haezer vol. 2, 25:1*.

The commentaries' silence about this possibility is especially curious in light of the fact that anal sex can be performed with the wife lying flat, with no "leg work" at all on her part, while rear-entry vaginal intercourse is generally practical only with the wife ("inconvenienced") on all fours.

[732] Of course, Raavad III himself interprets "overturning the table" as referring to rear-entry vaginal, not anal, intercourse. Thus, he argues that the women were turning to the sages not to complain about the discomfort of the position (though in our previous endnote we saw Rabeinu Asher speaking of discomfort caused to a wife even by her being "inconvenienced" upon her knees – which could, in fact, apply to rear-entry vaginal intercourse), but to question its permissibility according to Jewish law. In that case, the fact that the other three behaviors cause no discomfort would not necessarily have precluded wives from seeking counsel about their permissibility.

But then this logic itself could be used as a counterargument to Raavad III: the fact that no stories were passed down of women asking about the permissibility of non-sex-related talk during sex, or about gazing at or kissing the female genitals, could be evidence that everyone knew these all to be allowed, so nobody ever had to ask.

In any case, Raavad III's attempt to bolster his interpretation of *Nedarim 20b* not by what the Talmud says, but by what it doesn't say, is arguably somewhat tenuous.

And see above, endnote 95, for another suggested interpretation of what the wives were actually concerned about.

[732*] This is all besides the simple possibility that there were in fact practical case precedents in which such behaviors were explicitly permitted, but, for whatever reason, such cases were never recorded and/or transmitted and/or included in the Talmud – another reason why attempting to bolster an argument based not upon what the Talmud says, but upon what it doesn't say, is arguably tenuous. And see above, pp. 10-11, and endnotes thereon.

[733] See, for example, the ends of pages 170 and 182, in the Buchwald edition.

[734] Buchwald edition, p. 178.

See also Rabbi Rafael Shlanger, *Mishkan Yisrael* (2010) *Part 2*, p. 47.

[735] Buchwald edition, p. 179.

[736] See above, p. 46 and endnote 166* thereon.

[736*] See *Sdei Chemed, vol. 9, Clalei Haposkim 16:12*, p. 188, for a discussion about whether the term "*asur*" can sometimes be understood as speaking in the realm of *piety* rather than the realm of *legal* prohibition (*midas chasidus*).

Credit goes to Rabbi Chaim Rapoport of London, UK for bringing this source in *Sdei Chemed* to my attention.

# ENDNOTES

**Added note to the third edition:** See also Rabbi Baruch Halevi Epstein's *Torah Temimah, Vayikra 19:123*. Credit goes to Rabbis Eliezer Melamed and Maor Kayam for bringing this source to my attention in their *Harchavot l'Simchat Habayit v'Birchato* (2015), page 162.

[737] The enormity of Raavad III's silence on Maimonides' ruling, there, is also noted by Rabbi Aharon Alfandri in *Yad Aharon, Even Haezer vol. 2, 25:1* (at the very end) - though Rabbi Alfandri notes only Raavad III's silence about Maimonides' permission of anal intercourse, not his silence about Maimonides' permission of cunnilingus.

[738] Though it is a stretch, perhaps in *Baalei HaNefesh, Shaar Hakedushah*, Raavad III was merely insisting that the *translation* of the obscure term, "overturning the table," was rear-entry vaginal intercourse, not anal intercourse, and therefore anal intercourse was simply not part of the discussion on *Nedarim 20ab*. But he may not have had any intention, there, of legally *forbidding* anal sex, on account of *Sanhedrin 58b*. Thus, there would be no contradiction to resolve between his interpretation of *Nedarim 20ab* in *Baalei HaNefesh, Shaar Hakedushah* and his silence in *Mishneh Torah, Isurei Biah 21:9*.

[739] Page 169 in the Buchwald edition of *Baalei HaNefesh, Shaar Hakedushah*.

[740] Albeck edition.

[741] Many of whom quote Maimonides' ruling in *Mishneh Torah, Isurei Biah 21:9* verbatim, or practically verbatim, and thus can perhaps be assumed to also follow his understanding of the Sages' ruling on *Nedarim 20b*.

**Added note to the third edition:** See also Rabbi Eliezer Melamed's *Simchat Habayit v'Birchato* (second edition, 2015), top of page 63, asserting as well that this is the view of most medieval writers (*l'daas rubam hamachria shel harishonim, daato shel Rabbi Yochanan ben Dahavai nidchasah v'halachah c'daas chachamim she'ein badavar lo issur v'lo sacanah*).

[742] See above, pp. 33-35, 39, 50-51, 62-67.

None of the medieval commentaries who understand the Sages on *Nedarim 20b* as rejecting all four of Rabbi Yochanan ben Dahavai's cautions halachically, warn of their causing physical illnesses either (save for Rabbi Yitzchak of Corbeil in his *Sefer Mitzvos Katan, Positive Commandment 285*, who, in actuality, seems to have been basing his ruling on *Callah Rabti 1:13-14*, not *Nedarim 20ab*).

[743] See above, p. 62-64. Raavad III is unclear, for in regard to the nine-ten flawed conditions he suggests that they only cause spiritual repurcussions in one's children if they coincide with the same sexual encounter in which conception occurs (*Baalei HaNefesh, Shaar Hakedushah,* Buchwald edition, p. 177). But he makes no such distinction in regard to the physical illnesses predicted by Rabbi Yochanan ben Dahavi as resulting from the four sexual behaviors he cautioned against. And see above, endnote 113.

[744] See above, p. 87 and endnote 330 thereon, and p. 191.

While it would not necessarily prove anything definitive one way or the other, it would be of interest which of Raavad III's two works - his *Baalei HaNefesh* or his glosses to *Mishneh Torah* - was composed first and which was composed second. But even if his *Baalei HaNefesh* were composed second, representing his more mature understanding of Torah wisdom, the fact that he did not go on to add a new annotation to Maimonides' *Isurei Biah 21:9* would perhaps be significant.

[745] See above, p. 136, 173.

⁷⁴⁶ See above, pp. 41-42.

⁷⁴⁶* See above, pp. 45-47, 50-51.

⁷⁴⁷ See above, pages 62-65, and the entire discussion in Part Three.

⁷⁴⁸ See above, pp. 120-122.

Rabbi Naftali Tzvi Yehudah Berlin (*Netziv*, 1816-1893), in his *Meishiv Davar vol. 1, Responsum 88* (bottom of page 156, top of page 157) asserts that, "Most halachic authorities (*rov poskim*) do not endorse Rabeinu Yitzchak in regard to anal sex [i.e., occasional intra-anal ejaculation within marriage]."

Perhaps the 19th century Rabbi Berlin did not have access to all the medieval commentaries we have access to today, but the fact of the matter is that the majority of those we now have who weigh in on the question of intra-anal ejaculation *do endorse* Rabeinu Yitzchak's permission of it for married couples.

And, as discussed, while many post-medieval authorities we have discussed quote Rabbi Caro's legal and/or kabbalistic cautions against it, not one of them – and not even Rabbi Caro himself – categorically "forbids" it (see above, pp. 148-149).

Thus, while it is possible that there may be a "majority" of post-medieval authorities who do not "categorically endorse" Rabeinu Yitzchak, there is certainly no "majority" of post-medieval authorities who "categorically reject" him either – all while there IS a majority of medieval scholars who do categorically endorse him.

And this is without even getting back into the questions we've raised above about the sources and/or reasonings upon which those who reject, or caution against, Rabeinu Yitzchak's permissive approach are based (see above, Part Four).

⁷⁴⁹ See above, p. 124-125, 164-165.

⁷⁵⁰ See above, p. 125-127.

⁷⁵¹ See above, p. 118-120.

⁷⁵¹* See above, pp. 123-124, 128.

⁷⁵² Rabbi Isserles actually writes "And there are *those* who are lenient…" – in the plural. He is thus possibly referencing not only Rabeinu Yitzchak in *Tosfos* to *Yevamos 34b*, but also *Tosfos* to *Sanhedrin 58b* and/or Rabeinu Asher to *Yevamos 34b* and *Nedarim 20b*, among other medieval commentaries who endorsed, or independently echoed, Rabeinu Yitzchak's second approach.

⁷⁵³ See above, pp. 164-165.

⁷⁵⁴ See above, pp. 86-87.

⁷⁵⁵ See the Shabsi Frankel edition of *Mishneh Torah, Sefer Kedushah*, in the *Yalkut Shinuyei Nuschaos* section in the back of the book, *Isurei Biah 21:9*.

⁷⁵⁶ See above, pp. 138-142, 148-149.

⁷⁵⁷ See above, pp. 143-145, 148-149.

⁷⁵⁸ See above, pp. 153-158.

⁷⁵⁹ See above, pp. 159-160.

⁷⁶⁰ See above, p. 166.

# ENDNOTES

[761] See above, pp. 124-125 and endnote 519 thereon.

[762] See the Shabsi Frankel edition of *Mishneh Torah, Sefer Kedushah*, in the *Yalkut Shinuyei Nuschaos* section in the back of the book, *Isurei Biah 21:9*.

[763] See above, p. 166.

[764] Rabbi Yehuda Henkin, in his *Bnei Banim, volume 4, Responsum 18*, deals with the permissibility of anal intercourse and intercourse between limbs, including whether both are permitted to the point of ejaculation.

[While I cannot recall with certainty, this responsum of Rabbi Henkin's may have been where I first learned that modern-day Maimonidean scholars have called into question the caveat mentioned in *Mishneh Torah, Isurei Biah 21:9* against such ejaculation.]

The responsum is groundbreaking, and, in my humble opinion, should be mandatory reading for every Chasidic-Charedi adult.

Rabbi Henkin only categorically permits intercourse between limbs *without* ejaculation. But he does conclude that if a husband *inadvertently* ejaculates between his wife's limbs there is nothing for the couple to be anxious about. And see above, endnote 533.

[There are those who might argue against permitting occasional ejaculation between limbs within marriage on the grounds that Rabbi Falk, in his *Drishah* commentary, is the only authority to expressly insist that Rabeinu Yitzchak permits it. But as discussed, it is arguable that a mature halachic dialogue about the permissibility of occasional ejaculation between limbs within marriage was precluded from ever developing amongst post-medieval scholars due to numerous negative (and arguably tenuous) rabbinic forces against permitting even occasional intra-anal ejaculation. In light of all this, it is arguably time to reopen the file on categorically permitting occasional ejaculation between limbs within marriage, without allowing the dearth of prior halachic discussion to be an admissible counter-argument.

Behold: Even Raavad III was originally a lone voice among medieval rabbinic writers in his interpretation of *Nedarim 20ab* – yet subsequently his voice was made dominant (see above, pages 62-65 and the entire discussions in Part Three and Part Four). And see *Encyclopedia Talmudis, vol. 9, Entry: Halachah C'Basrai, 2. B'Poskim*.]

[765] See above, pp. 170-194. And see above, endnote 330, the added note to the third edition.

[766] See above, pp. 136-137 and endnote 549 thereon.

[767] See above, pp. 132-137, 146-147, 150-151.

[768] See above, pp. 167-168.

[769] See above, pp. 162-163.

[770] See *Encyclopedia Talmudis, vol. 9, Entry: Halachah C'Basrai, 2. B'Poskim*.

[771] For a discussion on whether areas of Jewish law that were eventually categorized as matters of "*Orach Chaim*" ever required rabbinical ordination in order to rule upon them, and whether areas that were eventually categorized as matters of "*Even Haezer*" still do, see Rabbi Moshe Walter's *The Making of a Halachic Decision*, Chapter 9, pp. 115-116.

Everything we've discussed in this study in regard to marital sexual law would be categorized as matters of *Orach Chaim, Chapter 240*. And even that which was included only in *Even Haezer, Chapter 25*, does not relate to the complex laws of the marriage or divorce ceremonies (*tiv gitin v'kidushin*).

[772] *Babylonian Talmud, Makos 11a* and *Sukkah 53b*.

[773] See above, pp. 143-145. See also pp. 118-129, 138-142.

[774] One sexual behavior involving extra-vaginal ejaculation that we have not explored in-depth in this book, even in the context of marital intimacy of husband of wife, is male self-masturbation.

The rabbinical approach to masturbation will be the topic of volume two of this series. And see above, footnote to page 3.

[775] *Ufakadata Navecha*, p. 37, footnote 2.

I subsequently realized that Rabbi Moshe Stern, in his *Be'er Moshe vol. 3, 152:14*, pp. 205-206, also discusses this passage of *Lechem Mishneh* at length, and also rejects it.

And see also Rabbi Yitzchak Abadi, *Or Yitzchak, vol. 2, Orach Chaim, Responsum 95*, Part 4, pp. 64-65.

[776] Page 200, *siman 33*.

[777] See also Rabbi Moshe Stern's *Be'er Moshe vol. 3, Responsum 152*, p. 204; Rabbi B. Fink's *Ufakadata Navecha*, p. 37, footnote 2.

And the difficulty in this passage of *Taharas Yisrael* was brought to wider public attention by Rabbi Dr. Marc Shapiro on his Seforim Blog, at http://seforim.blogspot.com/2014/08/the-pew-report-and-orthodox-community.html. See footnote 35, there, for additional important discussion.

**Added note to the third edition:** I subsequently found that Rabbi Yehudah Leib Nachmanson provides an exhaustive presentation about the topic of vaginal massage within marriage in his 2015 work, *Sheyekadesh Atzmo*, Chapter 44, Sections 3 and 4 and footnotes thereon. See also Rabbi Maor Kayam's *Harchavot l'Simchat Habayit v'Birchato* (2015), pp. 60-62.

[778] Rabbi Yehudah the Pious perhaps implies in *Sefer Chasidim 509* that G-d Himself expects that the average man's inability to express his sexual needs with his own wife will likely lead him to *at least fantasize* about expressing them with other women.

[779] For one latter-day rabbinic author's acknowledgment of such damage, see the introduction of Rabbi B. Fink to his Hebrew work on Jewish marital sexual law, *Ufakadata Navechah*, 2000-2006-2010 (translation is our own):

> I saw many anthologies on this topic, and they all, as one, lump together without clarification all matters relating to this commandment, without distinguishing them according to their individual categories. They mix biblical obligations, rabbinic obligations, customs and stringencies as if they were all on the same level.
>
> And many Jewish homes – on account of our sins – have been destroyed because of this (*v'harbeh batim – ba'avonoseinu harabim – nechrivu mishum zeh*), for they did not know how to distinguish between that which is obligation versus that which is [merely] idealistic behavior (*hanhagah tovah*) and stringency (*chumra*), such that where the latter two lead to marital discord and strife one should not insist on upholding them.
>
> And because stringencies have been presented together with biblical obligations, there are many who have decided for themselves that they simply could not live up to them, and they abandoned even that which they are obligated according to the law in *Shulchan Aruch*, according to the letter of the law.

See also Rabbi Yitzchak Abadi, *Or Yitzchak, vol. 2, Orach Chaim, Responsum 95*, end of Part 3, p. 64.

[780] See pages 200, sections 32-35; page 201, section 36.

[781] See Chapters 2 and 14.

[782] See pages 122-127.

[783] See Chapter 12.

[784] See pages 179, 180, 187, 188, 194.

[785] A work of extraordinarily puritanical nature, including much that could arguably put a marriage today at risk.

A few examples:

<u>Page 130</u> – instructs not to kiss anywhere but the lips and face.

<u>Page 178</u> – warns a husband not to gaze at his wife while she's sleeping, even when she is pure, because it might sexually arouse him.

<u>Pages 179-180</u> – encourages a husband not to walk next to, or behind, his wife on the street, and not to talk to her in the market.

And see the contents of the footnotes there.

<u>Pages 185-188</u> – encourages a husband not to gaze at his wife's normally covered body parts in general, so as not to become sexually aroused and possibly masturbate.

On page 187, paragraph 40, he encourages not to gaze at her body even immediately prior to intercourse, lest drips of "impurity" [semen] emerge from his penis before penetration.

<u>On Pages 236-253</u> – quotes a discourse from "one of the important rabbis of our generation."

Two excerpts:

> <u>Page 241</u> – Other than what's necessary to fulfill your obligation to satisfy her during sex, do not engage in any hugging or kissing of your wife at all.
>
> Be careful from touching or rubbing against her body for pleasure, never gaze at her normally covered body parts, and be extremely careful not to think about her in a sexual way.
>
> <u>Page 248</u> – If you feel that your wife's conversation with you is hurting you spiritually, the sound advice is to reveal to her the depths of your heart with sincerity, and say to her, pleasantly, the following:
>
>> "Know that the purpose of life is not about the pursuit of love and our desires to have pleasure from one another. Rather, the purpose of life is to serve G-d.
>>
>> And know that the extensive conversation is hurting me, and it is also not pleasing to G-d, blessed be He. And it would be better if you heard my voice of Torah as I study – and that way you have a share in my study.
>>
>> And your merit is great in that you help me to serve G-d, blessed be He. And it is known that which the Sages of blessed memory said, that the main merit of the wife is that she saves her husband from sin and sinful thought."

Therefore, if there is anything that causes you to have sexual thoughts, you need to ask of her, and explain to her:

> "This is one of your main purposes in this world, to guard me from [sexual] sin and assist me in serving G-d, blessed be He – like the verse says, 'I will make for him a helpmate.'
>
> And in this merit, G-d will help that our home will be of good name and beauty, as G-d wants.
>
> Amen."

And see above, endnote 595.

[786] See Chapters 31 and 32. In an earlier Hebrew edition of the work, *Toras Hamishpachah* (1972), see Chapter 12.

[787] An excellent work on marital intimacy for Chasidic-Charedi readers, it does not actually address sexual positions or technique.

[788] See above, endnote 25.

[789] See page 137.

[790] See pages 37-39.

[791] See pages 95, 104, 107, 108-109

[792] See Chapter 2.

[793] See page 121.

[794] See page 184.

[795] See pages 1007, 1012-1013, 1016.

[796] See pages 261, 266.

[797] See pages 24-25, 45.

[798] See pages 375-376.

[799] This compendium curiosly omits *Shulchan Aruch, Even Haezer 25*.

See also page 70, footnote 40, where the quotation of *Sefer Chasidim 509* is cut short.

[800] See pages 47, 49.

[801] See pages 260, 269-270, 278-279.

It must be pointed out that on page 270, a footnote suggests that Maimonides (Rambam) himself did not permit cunnilingus. This is simply untrue and should be fixed. Perhaps the printers meant to write "Rabbi Moshe Isserles" (Rema) – though we personally would believe this, too, to be erroneous (see our discussion above, pp. 167-168).

**Added note to the third edition:** In January 2016, an English translation of *Darchei Taharah Hashalem* was published. See Part Three, and pages 313-315 in particular. Note that the claim that Maimonides forbade cunnilingus is perpetuated in the footnote to page 315.

[802] Credit goes to Orthodox sex therapist Talli Rosenbaum for bringing this source to my attention.

Its author has made it available at: http://www.files.org.il/BRPortalStorage/a/79/28/48-1Dk33JHjhg.pdf

[803] See pages 252, 254, 255.

[804] See page 95.

[805] See Chapters 6, 34, 41, 43, 44, 46, 47.

[806] It must be pointed out that in footnote 56 (top of page 365), the author writes that Maimonides, in his *Commentary to the Mishnah, Yevamos 6:1* and *Sanhedrin 7:4*, defined the term "intercourse between limbs" (*derech evarim*) only as partial penetration of the penile head (glans penis) into the vagina.

According to this, Maimonides would not necessarily permit a wife's oral or manual stimulation of her husband's penis, nor his thrusting against any other outside part of her body, and certainly not to the point of ejaculation – even according to the textual version of *Mishneh Torah, Isurei Biah 21:9* which does *not* caution against "wasting seed in vain."

But see our discussion about this above, footnote to page 103.

[807] Credit goes to Rabbi Chaim Rapoport of London, UK for bringing this source to my attention.

This responsum of Rabbi Abadi was brought to wider public attention by Rabbi Dr. Marc Shapiro on his Seforim Blog, at http://seforim.blogspot.com/2010/06/some-more-assorted-comments-part-1.html and at http://seforim.blogspot.com/2014/08/the-pew-report-and-orthodox-community.html.

[808] See above, bottom of page 96.

[809] *Likutei HaPardes*, p. 4b in the Munkatch edition.

[810] Rabbi Shaul Wagshal, *Taharas Am Yisroel*, 2002, p. 20.

[811] See above, pp. 59-61, 118-122.

[812] See above, pp. 59, 117.

[813] See above, pp. 60-61, 115.

[814] See above, pp. 60-61.

[815] See above, p. 116.

[816] Because he might sexually arouse himself, potentially leading to masturbation and "wasting seed in vain."

[Alternatively, Rabbi Eliezer may have been concerned that even minor sexual arousal, without actual masturbation, could lead to pre-ejaculate dripping from the body – which he may have considered tantamount to actual semen. And see above, endnote 593. See also endnote 591.]

Regarding the parameters of, and potential problems with, this entire notion, see below, endnote 818. And a critical discussion about it will be included in volume two of this series.

See also above, endnotes 335, 518. And see above, footnote to page 3.

[817] See above, pp. 103-104.

## HALACHIC POSITIONS

[818] I am perfectly aware that one of the four behaviors Rabbi Shimon ben Yochai listed, namely, not grasping hold of the shaft during urination, is categorized in subsequent halachic literature as a legal "prohibition," albeit a rabbinic one. But the categorization of it as such is not on account of Rabbi Shimon ben Yochai's teaching on *Nidah 17a*, but on account of Rabbi Eliezer's teaching on *Nidah 13a*.

[Note that Rabbi Shimon ben Yochai was a chief disciple of Rabbi Akiva, who was, in turn, a chief disciple of Rabbi Eliezer. Therefore, the fact that Rabbi Shimon tells us only that G-d "abhors" one who grasps hold of the shaft during urination, not that G-d "forbids" it, is extremely significant evidence that even Rabbi Eliezer himself, as reported on *Babylonian Talmud, Nidah 13a*, perhaps never came to "forbid" it for the masses – but rather only to strongly discourage it for his pious colleagues, the Sages.

Behold: Rabbi Eliezer, too, never actually calls grasping hold of the shaft during urination "forbidden." He only says that it "is tantamount to bringing flood upon the earth" (but see above, endnote 518). And when he responds to the Sages that, "It is better to have one's child's lineage called into question than to make oneself wicked before G-d even for a single moment," it is possible that he was not calling grasping hold of the shaft during urination "wicked," but rather he was calling wasting seed in vain "wicked" – and he was asserting that he personally believed one should go to all pious, voluntary extremes to avoid the test of masturbation.]

[Parenthetically, the notion that Rabbi Eliezer never repeated a single word of Torah he did not hear from his own masters requires clarification. Are we meant to believe that in all his disputes throughout the Talmud he never argued anything with the powers of his own intellect? *Igeres Rav Sherirah Gaon* implies that he did not (see the 1988 English edition by Rabbi Nosson Dovid Rabinowich, Chapter 3, page 29, "He never said anything that he had not heard from his teacher" (*shelo amar davar shelo shamo mipi rabo l'olam*)). But in Rabbi Eliezer's discussions with other sages there certainly arose questions that required newly-formulated responses?

Perhaps the meaning of this notion was merely that he never erroneously attributed any teaching to his masters, or that he never put words in their mouths – that is, when he would specifically invoke his masters' teachings, he would transmit them with absolute precision. See, for example, *Ethics of the Fathers 2:10*, and Maimonides' commentary thereon, that Rabbi Yochanan ben Zakai praised Rabbi Eliezer for his impeccable *memory*. And further research into the matter is required.]

In any case, let it be noted that *Talmud, Nidah 13a* and later halachic literature do permit grasping hold of the shaft during urination if due to the immediately-surrounding environment one is unlikely to get caught up in sexual fixations or if one is married. They also say it does not apply to holding the corona, glans penis or scrotum in order to direct the flow of urine. And it does not apply to holding the shaft through a piece of cloth.

See also *Or Zarua, Hilchos Baal Keri 121*, which implies that Rabbi Eliezer was only speaking against grasping hold of the shaft during urination if there are *three conditions combined*: The person is unmarried or his wife is in a faraway place AND there is nothing in the immediate environment that would distract him from sexual arousal AND he is holding the shaft to direct the flow of urine, not the corona, glans penis or scrotum. But if even one of these three conditions is not applicable, it would apparently be perfectly allowed for the man – married or single – to urinate holding his shaft normally and without second thought.

The author of *Or Zarua* also says, there, that every person can evaluate for himself what would be considered "distracting."

[Some commentaries find reason for concern even here, claiming that nowadays we are not "expert" to distinguish that which is distracting enough against sexual arousal (see, for example, *M'aseif l'Chol Hamachanos, Orach Chaim 3:14:35* and the entire treatment of the subject in *Otzar Haposkim, Even Haezer 23:4*). But to such manner of concern there can be no end... And where there is doubt concerning a rabbinic law, there is precedent to be lenient... And if we are to say that we are no longer expert in this, then perhaps we should equally argue that we are no longer expert in being able to determine the difference between involuntary versus voluntary sexual arousal to the point of erection (*maksheh atzmo ladaas*) – another topic of *Nidah 13ab* – and there should thus no longer be any concern at all about the latter. (And see above, endnote 718, that this latter concept may have originally been said only in regard to *compulsive* masturbation.)]

Even so, this stricture arguably remains psychologically-emotionally damaging to young (and adult) minds, and is fundamentally difficult to understand in light of what we've discussed above, endnote 518.

But more about it in volume two of this series.

[819] *Babylonian Talmud, Kesubos 48a.*

[820] For a brief discussion on the origins of the *Book of Ben Sira*, and the Sages' apparent attitude toward it, see *Steinsaltz Talmud, Nidah 16b, Hachaim.*

[821] See *Steinsaltz Talmud, Nidah 16b, Iyunim*, for various explanations as to what Rabbi Shimon ben Yochai allegedly meant to say, here, in regard to G-d "abhorring," and he himself "not loving," these four behaviors.

[822] The *Talmud*, on *Pesachim 112b*, has Rabbi Shimon ben Yochai's master, Rabbi Akiva, instructing his own son, Rabbi Yehoshua, not to enter anyone's home unannounced, even his own.

Rabbi Akivah does not go so far as to say that G-d would "hate" it if one did so. But it is not unreasonable to believe that his teaching was the source of Rabbi Shimon's.

[823] Note Rashi's commentary to Genesis 3:1, which implies that it was not Adam and Eve's naked uncovered sex in-and-of-itself that brought about negative consequences, but their naked uncovered sex *in front of other intelligent creatures.*

Note also that the two versions of Rabbi Shimon ben Yochai's teaching *combined* would have G-d abhorring "naked uncovered sex in front of others."

[824] I was gratified to discover that Rabbi Yehuda Henkin, as well, did not find any mention of it in any of these three codes of law. See *Bnei Banim vol. 4, Responsum 17:5*, page 63, column 2, paragraph 3.

[825] *Menoras Hamaor, vol. 4, Perek Nisuei Ishah,* page 86. But see three pages earlier there, page 83, where Rabbi Alnaqua also categorizes sex with the wife on top as "forbidden" (*asur*), based on *Tractate Callah*. Arguably, his categorization of these two behaviors as "forbidden" is not supported by any other medieval commentary we have discussed, nor, in regard to the wife on top, by the contexts of the discussions about it in *Talmud, Tractate Gitin 70a, Tractate Callah 15* or *Callah Rabti 1:23* (see above, pp. 42, 48, 51).

And see above, endnote 736*.

[826] Albeck edition.

[827] Page 4b in the Munkatch edition.

[828] *Reishis Chochmah, Shaar Hakedushah 16:33.*

[829] *Reishis Chochmah, Shaar Hakedushah 16:23.*

[830] See Rabbi Emden's *Mitas Hakesef, Chapter 7, Section 3:3-10.*

[831] See above, endnote 810.

[832] See above, endnote 409, for an explanation of our translation of the term *"prishus,"* here, as "moderation."

[833] Rabbi Henkin's *Responsum 17,* there, deals with sex in a bright room during the day or with the lights on at night – topics we shall address in depth in a future volume of this series.

In the meantime, see his footnote to page 61, where Rabbi Henkin makes an important ***theoretical*** point:

According to one Talmudic sage quoted on *Nidah 17a,* Abayei, explaining the teaching of an earlier sage, Rav Chisda, the problem with sex in the presence of a strong lightsource is that the husband might notice something he finds unattractive on his wife's body and lose his sexual arousal in the moment (and we would posit that the sage's main concern was that the wife would then suffer humiliation, not to mention doubt about his love and/or her own beauty).

Thus, Rabbi Henkin argues, if that is truly what the *main* halachic concern is about, then for a couple who has already had sex in the light and who knows without a doubt that they will find the sight of each other's naked bodies pleasing and arousing, the case could ***theoretically*** be made that the teaching about not having sex during the daytime in the daylight or at night with the lights on would not apply.

[And, if we may be so bold, we might tentatively argue further that even if a couple has never yet had sex in the light, but they have compelling reason to believe it will not pose any problem to their intimacy, or that it will in fact enhance it, it would be unreasonable to disallow it on account of Abayei's concern.]

Rabbi Henkin also makes the point that the actual sight of seeing oneself having intercourse with one's spouse does not seem to be believed by Abayei as being intrinsically revolting, for Abayei does not say that the problem would be seeing the "revolting act of intercourse," but only that the husband might find something unattractive on the body.

Note, however, that according to the explanation quoted above, endnote 365, in the name of Rabbi Moshe Feinstein, the concern here is that the husband might find something *unhygenic* on the body – in other words, he might *unexpectedly* find something that is *temporarily* unattractive. In that case, the concern might still be said to stand even if the couple has enjoyed positive sexual intimacy in the light in the past. But even this concern is arguably ever more remote in modern times, considering the infinite improvements in sanitary conditions enabled by indoor plumbing, the ease and immediacy by which thorough cleanlinees can be achieved in the home, and the widespread availability of quality cosmetics (and, if need be, effective medicines).

[834] *Mishneh Torah, Sefer Kedushah, Isurei Biah 21:24.*

[835] *Even Haezer 23:7.*

[836] Note that the fact that Rabbi Yossi's avoidance of gazing at his own penis is considered to be an act of extreme piety, not baseline obligatory law, could perhaps lend further support to the argument that the avoidance of gazing at one's spouse's genitals is not a binding legal "prohibition" either, but only a matter of piety.

# ENDNOTES

[837] *Mishneh Torah, Sefer HaMada, Deos 5:6.*

[838] *Orach Chaim 2:1.*

[839] *Orach Chaim 2:1.*

[840] Above, pp. 16-17.

[841] *Mahadurah Kama, Orach Chaim 2:1.*

[842] *Mahadura Basra, Orach Chaim 2:1-2*

[843] Credit goes to a friend for bringing this source to my attention.

[844] See Rabbi Yehuda Henkin's *Bnei Banim, vol. 4, Responsum 17, Section 5.*

[845] See Rabbi Yitzchak Abadi, *Or Yitzchak, vol. 2, Orach Chaim, Responsum 95, Part 1,* p. 62, reporting in the name of Rabbi Moshe Feinstein that even for intercourse in a lit room during the day a Torah scholar need only cover the actual genitals and their immediate surrounding bodily areas (*tzarich rak lechasos makom ha'ervah v'hakarov l'zeh*).

See above, endnote 833.

And see Rabbi Yehudah Henkin's *Bnei Banim, vol. 4, Responsum 17,* and the beginning of Section 3 in particular. At the very least, Rabbi Henkin says there, *foreplay* may be performed in a perfectly lit room, only actual intercourse is in question (...*v'zehu b'shaas tashmish, mah she'ein cein b'shaas chibuk v'nishuk likras tashmish yecholim l'hadlik es haner c'ragil*).

Note that Rabbi Henkin at the beginning of Section 3 of his responsum is not addressing whether such foreplay in a lit room may be done *naked and uncovered by a blanket*. But there is nothing in his later discussion restricting naked and uncovered *intercourse* in a lit room that would seem to restrict naked and uncovered *foreplay* in a lit room – **at least not that I am aware of**. And see above, endnote 369.

Thus, if we may be so bold, perhaps we may infer that those who permit cunnilingus could permit it even in a lit room as a manner of foreplay, and even naked and uncovered by a blanket.

As to whether intercourse between limbs, which includes fellatio, would be halachically closer in this regard to foreplay or to actual vaginal/anal intercourse, this remains to be explored. And even if it is to be considered closer to foreplay, it is possible that *ejaculation* between limbs (according to those who permit it within marriage in a darkened room) would still be considered closer to actual intercourse. And further research into the matter is required.

And see our footnote to page 221 for a relevant ruling of Rabbi Yosef Messas.

[846] *www.zootorah.com/RationalistJudaism/TheSunsPathAtNight.pdf*

And see above, endnotes 13, 86.

[846*] There is a rabbinic tradition that at some point in history the prophets entrusted scholars of the Tribe of Isachar with equations that enabled them to author works to accurately predict the appearance of the new moon (see *Mishneh Torah, Sefer Zmanim, Kidush Hachodesh 17:24*). But if these equations were in fact revealed by divine revelation, then it is possible, and perhaps even likely, that they traced back to what Moses himself was taught by G-d on how to fulfill the commandment of "Sanctifying the New Month." And see above, endnote 124 point e).

Regarding the *Sefer Refuos–Book of Remedies*, reportedly hidden by King Hezekiah (see *Talmud, Brachos 10b* and *Pesachim 56a*), there is great debate as to who its author even was, and if it contained natural or supernatural remedies. For a synopsis of the views on this, see Dr. Fred Rosner, *Medicine in the Bible and the Talmud* (Ktav, 1995), pp. 81-85.

[847] In the words of Isaiah 11:9, describing the Messianic Age: "And the knowledge of G-d shall fill the earth, as water covers the sea."

And see *Mishneh Torah, Sefer Shoftim, Melachim 12:5*.

[848] See *Vayikra Rabah 13:3* and *Yalkut Shimoni, Isaiah 429*.

See also *Koheles Rabah 11:1:8*.

And see Rabbi Menachem Mendel Schneerson's *Sefer Hasichos 5751 vol. 2, Address of Second Day Shavuos, B'inyan Torah Chadashah Me'iti Teitzei*.

# GLOSSARY OF KEY HALACHIC TERMS

*B'shaas Tashmish; B'shaas Maaseh* – During sex, including during intercourse (see page 24n)

*Tzarich L'ratzuyah; C'dei L'ratzosa* ("In order to appease/arouse her") – Talk intended by a husband to arouse his wife to sexual intimacy (see pages 69-71)

*Derech Evarim* ("Intercourse between Limbs") – Non-penetrative sex, including outercourse and a wife's manual or oral stimulation of her husband's sex organs (see pages 103n, 123; endnotes 511, 512, 513)

*Hafichas Shulchan* ("Overturning the Table") – A euphemism referring to an unspecified non-"missionary" position of intercourse, variously interpreted as rear-entry vaginal intercourse, anal intercourse, wife-on-top, or a combination of positions (see pages 59-61)

*Hashchatas Zera* ("Destruction of Seed") – Extra-vaginal ejaculation in a context not permitted by Jewish law (see pages 3n, 91-92)

*Hee L'maalah, Hu L'matah* ("Her on top, him on bottom") – Intercourse with the wife on top

*Hotzaas Zera* ("Releasing Seed") - Ejaculation

*Hotzaas Zera Levatalah* ("Releasing Seed in Vain," "Wasting Seed in Vain") – Extra-vaginal ejaculation in a context not permitted by Jewish law (see pages 3n, 91-92)

*Maaseh Beheimah* ("Animal-style") – Rear-entry vaginal intercourse

*Mili Achronaisa* ("Other discussion") – Non-sex-related talk during foreplay and/or intercourse (see page 34)

*Mili D'tashmisha* ("Discussion about sex") – Sex-related talk during foreplay and/or intercourse (see pages 34, 57-58)

*Menashek; Menashkim* ("Kiss") – A husband's kissing of his wife's genitals (see pages 33-34; endnote 72)

*Meratzya Artzuyei* ("She appeases/arouses him") – Talk and/or actions intended by a wife to arouse her husband to sexual intimacy (see pages 37-38; endnote 125)

*Mistakel; Mistaklim* ("Gaze") – A husband's gazing at his wife's genitals (see page 34; endnote 75)

*Oso Makom* ("That place") – The vagina

*Panim C'neged Oref* ("Face-to-back") – Rear-entry vaginal intercourse

*Shelo Cedarcah* ("Unnatural intercourse") – Anal intercourse (see pages 118, 166; endnote 647)

*Tashmish* – Sex, including intercourse (see page 24n)

# SUBJECT INDEX

*endnotes ("endn.") listed in italics*

## A

Addiction: 98, 100, 104n, 190, *endn. 128, 351, 419, 524, 666*

Anal Sex
  as a form of marital bonding: *endn. 408*
  as a permitted form of penetration: 86-87, *endn. 268, 324, 331*
  correct definition of "*shelo cedarcah*": 166, *endn. 606\*, 607\*, 647*
  inordinate discussion about: 16
  if anal intercourse with wife permitted, then, logically, rear-entry vaginal intercourse permitted as well: 117
  pain vs. pleasure: *endn. 269, 408*
  post-medieval vilification of: 132-163
  to the point of intra-anal ejaculation: 89-92, 118-122, 196-203

Aristotle: *endn. 83, 417, 419*

Asexuality: *endn. 419, 595*

## B

*Bal teshaktzu* (see: Vagina)

Bastard (tantamount to): *endn. 83*

Bestiality: *endn. 518*

Birth Control (see: Wasting Seed)

Blanket (intercourse without; see: Nakedness)

"Blowjob" (see: Intercourse between Limbs)

Bonding (see: Clinging)

Book of Remedies: *endn. 846\**

Brazenness: *endn. 417*

Breast
  husband ingesting milk from wife's: *endn. 727*
  husband touching wife's: 208

Breechcloth (wearing during intercourse): 24

## C

Censorship
  of *Mishneh Torah*: 128, 156, 200-201, *endn. 609*
  of R. Moshe Isserles: 166
  of permissive rabbinical views from post-medieval and latter-day halachic works: 1-7, 210-212, 150-151, 161-168, 202-203

Chasidism (and sex): *endn. 595*

Climax(es)
  ancient beliefs about effect on sex of child conceived: 93, *endn. 355*
  giving wife hers first: 94-95, 100
  multiple: 98

Clinging (Bonding, *Davek-Devek*): *endn. 344, 408*

Congenital Conditions (ancient beliefs about; see also: Rabbinic Fallibility):
  arrogance: *endn. 176*
  blindness, Lameness, Muteness, deafness: 33-34, 41, 44-47, *endn. 81, 660*
  crooked posture: 48
  demonic damage: 96-97
  developmental disabilities: *endn. 83*
  Divine justice: 45-46, 54-56, *endn. 61, 86, 155, 158, 161, 170, 176, 188*
  physical traits: *endn. 83*

444

rebelliousness and/or spiritual insensitivity (see also: Nine-Ten Flawed Conditions): 37, 97-98, *endn. 83, 128*

uncouthness, lewdness: 32, 50, 98, 177-180, 183, *endn. 61, 86, 132, 423, 660, 696, 707*

Cunnilingus (see: Vagina)

## D

Demon(s)

ancient belief in: *endn. 373*

intercourse as if pressured by: 23-24, 34, 42, 47, *endn. 44* (hyperbole), *78* (reinterpretation as manner of seduction), *80* (reinterpretation as manner of seduction), *358\** (not a matter of legal obligation), *595* (Chasidic interpretation)

of the latrine: 94, 96-97

Destruction of Seed (see: Wasting Seed)

Dignity (vs. "shame"): 33n, 187-188, *endn. 417*

Domination: *endn. 125, 176, 179*

*Dor Hamabul* (see: Generation of the Flood)

## E

Ejaculation between Limbs (see: Intercourse between Limbs)

Er (see: Onan)

Euphemism

as cause of confusion and marital discord: 16

"leg": *endn. 524*

"overturning the table" (definition of): 59-61, *endn. 233*

Evil Urge (inciting the): 190

Excommunication: *endn. 111* (as one of the Nine-Ten Flawed Conditions)

## F

Fantasy (see also: Imagination)

about one's own wife: *endn. 212*

ancient beliefs about effect on child conceived: 32, 34, 37, 42, *endn. 83, 86, 384*

chasidic teachings about: *endn. 595*

R. Eliezer's methods of avoidance: *endn. 194*

forbidden or discouraged: *endn. 128*

intentional vs. unintentional: 34, *endn. 81, 104, 110, 117, 118*

non-sex-related talk as potential cause of: 55, *endn. 194*

not necessarily tantamount to prostitution: *endn. 195, 666*

possible difference between fantasy during intercourse vs. during oral sex: 96, *endn. 369*

possible implications of Sages' ruling in relation to: *endn. 671*

sexual exploration permitted within marriage in order to avoid illicit fantasies: 107, 127-128, *endn. 427, 778*

wet dreams as sign of psychological-emotional maturing: *endn. 524*

Fellatio (see: Penis)

Foreplay (see: Vagina, Penis)

## G

Generation (changing needs of): 1-7, 127-128

Generation of the Flood (precise context of their "wasting seed"): *endn. 518, 524, 818*

Genitals (see: Vagina; Penis)

## H

"Handjob" (see: Intercourse between Limbs)

Hezekiah: *endn. 335*

Holiness (see: Sanctification)

Homosexuality: *endn. 268, 343, 347, 518, 524, 567*

Hygiene: 95-96, 100, 221n, *endn. 86, 193, 362, 365, 369, 726, 727*

I

Ima Shalom: 34, 42 47, 51, 57-58, 65, 77, *endn. 45, 69, 84, 173, 194*

Imagination (see also: Fantasy): *endn. 83*

Intention (during intercourse): 99

Intercourse (see: Sex; Positions)

Intercourse between Limbs
   as a form of marital bonding: *endn. 408*
   definition of: 103n, 123, *endn. 511, 513*
   to the point of extra-vaginal ejaculation (Ejaculation between Limbs): 123-129

Intoxication: 37, *endn. 116*

Isachar, Tribe of: 38, *endn. 123, 124, 846\**

K

Kissing (See: Vagina, Penis)

M

Manasseh: *endn. 335*

Maternal Impression (see: Fantasy, Ancient beliefs about effect on child conceived)

Mental Illness: *endn. 595* (in early Chasidic movement)

Masturbation (See: Penis; Wasting Seed)

Menstruation: 22n, 29n, 32-33, 37, 41, 97, 177, 179-180, 183, *endn. 83* (ancient beliefs about), 347, 678

Messianic Age: 225, *endn. 848*

Moderation: 104 (of the pious), *endn. 409, 419*

Modesty: 22-25, 94, 98, 100, 104, 149n, 164, 189, 194, 217-221, *endn. 125, 203, 351, 357, 362, 369*

Munbaz, King: *endn. 26*

N

Nakedness (during intercourse; without blanket): 95-96, 97, 100, 213-221, *endn. 369, 417, 698, 833, 845*

Nine-Ten Flawed Conditions
   definitions of: 37, *endn. 109-119, 125*
   forbidden or discouraged: *endn. 128*
   nature vs. nurture: *endn. 128*

Nudity (see: Nakedness)

O

Onan: 89-92, 118, 124, 126, 139-141, 166, *endn. 335, 339, 484, 504, 518, 524, 606\*, 607\*, 616, 645\**

Oral Sex (see: Vagina; Penis)

Orgasm (see: Climax)

Outercourse (see: Intercourse between Limbs)

"Overturning the Table"
   definition of: 59-61, *endn. 233*
   permission of: 62-66, 115-122, 196-203

P

Paternal Impression (see: Fantasy, Ancient beliefs about effect on child conceived)

Piety (cannot be forced upon spouse): 101, *endn. 95*

Positions (of Sex)

  Anal Intercourse (see also: Anal Sex): 118-122

  "Animal-style" (Face-to-back, rear-entry vaginal intercourse): 117

  "Missionary": 16

  On the floor: 116

  Outercourse (see also: Intercourse between Limbs) 123-129

  "Reverse Cowgirl": 60, *endn. 229, 230*

  Side by side: 116

  Sitting: 116

  "Sixty-Nine:" 129, *endn. 537*

  Standing: 116

  Wife on top: 115

Penis (see also: Wasting Seed)

  deliberate erection: 23, 190, *endn. 40, 524, 718* (compulsive masturbation), *818*

  grasping shaft during urination: 214-215, *endn. 518, 524, 818*

  factors (physical/emotional) that promote potency: *endn. 419*

  ingesting sexual fluids of: *endn. 727*

  piety as impediment to erection: *endn. 44, 595*

  wife gazing at husband's: *endn. 75*

  wife kissing husband's (fellatio): *endn. 72*

Persians (sexual customs of): 220, *endn. 45*

Procreation (see also: Wasting Seed): 91-92

Prophets: 10-11 (lost discussions about sex), 224-225 (fallibility of)

Prostitution (tantamount to): 55-56, 172, *endn. 195, 616*

Proverbs (*Book of Proverbs* composed to exhort against alcoholism and prostitution): *endn. 419 (point 1)*

Puberty: 5-6, 15, 104n, *endn. 524* (wet dreams as sign of psychological-emotional maturing)

Pubic shaving: *endn. 724*

R

Rabbinic Fallibility: 39, 50, 222-225, *endn. 86, 373, 419, 594*

S

Sanctification: 68, 93-101, 102-106 (Maimonides), 193-194 (Raavad III), *endn. 26, 347* (biblical verses), *348, 509, 595* (Chasidic teachings)

Sanhedrin

  fallibility of: 223n

  mistakenly believed/believe their decree was/is within the ability of the majority of the people: *endn. 348*

  power to reinterpret Jewish law in each generation: 2n, 224, *endn. 87*

Sex (see also: Positions)

  in a lit room (during the day and/or night): 95-96, *endn. 369, 833, 845*

  initiating (Husband or wife): 37-38, 38n, *endn. 125*

  limited frequency (as a matter of piety): 22, 28, 98, 105

  naked without a blanket covering: 213-221, *endn. 845*

  oral sex (see: Vagina; Penis)

  unlimited frequency (as a matter of law): 29, 105

  while spouse is asleep: *endn. 119*

Sexism: 12, 17

Sexual Exploration (within marriage)

husband and wife in agreement about: 107

need to reclaim as permissible/holy: 1-7, 127, *endn. 10*

no lack in holiness: 68

reasons for objections to: 54-56

reasons for permission of: 67-67

Sadomasochism: *endn. 271*

Seduction:

husband of wife: 43, 49, 51, 58, 75, *endn. 78, 80*

wife of husband: 38, *endn. 125*

Shame (Shamefacedness):

context of teaching extolling shame: 177-186

definition of "shame": 33n, 187-188

*Shelo Cedarcah* (see also: Anal Sex)

correct definition of: 166, *endn. 606\*, 607\*, 647*

*Sefer Refuos* (see: *Book of Remedies*)

"Sixty-Nine" (see: Positions)

T

Talk

during foreplay/intercourse: 55-56, 57-58, 69-83, 111-112, 196-203

sexual humor between spouses: 73, 82

sexy talk, vulgar talk, vain talk: 73-74, *endn. 419*

wife initiating sex verbally: 38, *endn. 125*

Talmud

basis for legal authority of: 10, *endn. 20*

identity of its compilers-editors: 10, *endn. 19*

lost discussions about sex: 10-11

Teenagers: 5-6, *endn. 8*

*Tesha Midos* (see: Nine-Ten Flawed Conditions)

Toys

kosher animal toys: *endn. 83*

sex toys: *endn. 271*

Translation

responsibility of translator: 18

use of explicit terminology: 16-17

V

Vagina

husband gazing at wife's: 33-35, 41-42, 45-47, 54-56, 62-68, 106, 113, 196-203

husband kissing wife's (cunnilingus): 33-35, 41-42, 45-47, 54-56, 62-68, 103-106, 114, 196-203

husband touching wife's: 208-209

if husband's kissing of wife's permitted, then, logically, husband's gazing at wife's permitted as well: 113

ingesting sexual fluids of: *endn. 727*

W

Wasting Seed: 91-92, 118-122, 123-129, 132-168, 134n, 144n, 190, *endn. 335, 343, 518, 524, 553, 563, 564, 565, 567, 569, 591-593, 594, 633, 718, 818*

Wet Dreams (as sign of psychological-emotional maturing): *endn. 524*

World to Come: *endn. 565* (Every human being has a place in)

Y

*Yefas toar: endn. 108, 128, 383*

# BIBLICAL SOURCES

Genesis
  1:28: 126
  2:24: 84, 153, *endn. 319, 344, 527, 595*
  2:25: 182
  3:1: *endn. 823*
  3:16: *endn. 125, 176*
  6:1: *endn. 518*
  6:12: *endn. 518*
  30:16: 38, *endn. 123*
  30:37: *endn. 83*
  31:35: *endn. 83*
  34:5: *endn. 163*
  35:22: *endn. 113*
  38:1-10: 89n, *endn. 518, 524*
  38:23: *endn. 419*
  49:4: *endn. 113*

Exodus
  20:13: *endn. 524*
  20:17: *endn. 39, 66, 137*
  24:5: 42, 48
  24:11: 43, 49
  34:3: *endn. 83*

Leviticus
  11:44: 93, *endn. 347*
  19:2: *endn. 347*
  12:1: 93
  12:2: *endn. 355*
  12:4: *endn. 83*
  12:5: *endn. 355*
  18:19: *endn. 83*
  18:22: 66, *endn. 324, 533*
  20:7: *endn. 347*
  20:13: 66, *endn. 324, 533*
  20:17: *endn. 75*
  20:25: *endn. 41*
  20:26: *endn. 347*
  23:3-4: *endn. 595*

Numbers
  30:2: 224n
  15:39: 36, *endn. 102*

Deuteronomy
  1:13: *endn. 124*
  12:2: *endn. 524*
  12:31: *endn. 524*
  22:7: *endn. 595*
  24:1: 66, 140, *endn. 266*

Kings I
  14:23: *endn. 524*
  15:12: *endn. 524*

Kings II
  21:1-18: *endn. 335*
  23:6-7: *endn. 524*

Isaiah
- 1:15: *endn. 524*
- 3:9: 184, 185
- 4:3: *endn. 51, 644*
- 11:9: *endn. 847*
- 33:15-17: 184, 185, 186, *endn. 698*
- 57:5: *endn. 524*
- 9:1: 205
- 57:5: *endn. 524*

Jeremiah
- 3:6: *endn. 524*
- 6:15: *endn. 704*
- 7:31: *endn. 524*

Ezekiel
- 14:5: *endn. 347*
- 20:38: 37, *endn. 106, 107, 113, 128*

Hosea
- 5: *endn. 384*
- 14:12-14: *endn. 524*

Amos
- 4:13: 25, 69, 76, *endn. 47, 125, 274*

Jonah
- 2:11: *endn. 29*

Micah
- 6:8: 189, *endn. 38, 716*

Psalms
- 5:5: *endn. 524*
- 19:13: 210
- 33:9: *endn. 595*

Proverbs
- 18:22: 107, 188, *endn. 200*
- 19:2: 173

Song of Songs
- 7:2: *endn. 717*

Ecclesiastes
- 8:5: *endn. 148, 184*
- 9:7: 107, 188, *endn. 200*
- 12:5: *endn. 595*

Chronicles I
- 12:33: *endn. 124*

# TALMUDIC SOURCES

*Avodah Zarah 20ab*: endn. 128, 524, 698

*Avos (Ethics of the Fathers)*: 32n, 73, 82, endn. 695, 818

*Bava Kama 83b*: endn. 713

*Bechoros 8a*: endn. 29

*Bechoros 44b*: endn. 393

*Beitzah 21b*: endn. 7

*Brachos 8b*: endn. 45

*Brachos 10a*: endn. 335

*Brachos 10b*: endn. 846*

*Brachos 20a*: endn. 83

*Brachos 25b*: endn. 90

*Brachos 57a*: endn. 524

*Brachos 60a*: endn. 355

*Brachos 62a*: endn. 127, 277, 308, 310, 358*

*Chulin 91a*: endn. 360

*Chulin 92ab*: endn. 518

*Eruvin 13b*: endn. 15

*Eruvin 100b*: endn. 30*, 121, 122, 123, 125, 215, 389, 476, 524, 669

*Gitin 6b*: endn. 724

*Gitin 58a*: endn. 83, 187

*Gitin 70a*: 51, endn. 139, 140, 141, 175, 178, 460, 825

*Hagigah 5b (fundamental references only)*: 69-83, 111-112

*Hagigah 11b*: endn. 11

*Kesubos 8b*: 73-74

*Kesubos 40a*: endn. 713

*Kesubos 48a*: 220, endn. 45, 819

*Kesubos 65b*: 95, endn. 360, 370

*Kesubos 71b*: endn. 724

*Kesubos 72a*: endn. 114, 125, 335

*Kidushin 54a*: endn. 90

*Kidushin 70a*: endn. 384

*Kidushin 1:1 (Jerusalem Talmud)*: endn. 317, 325, 344, 527

*Kidushin 4:1 (Jerusalem Talmud, 42b)*: endn. 704

*Makos 11a*: endn. 400, 772

*Makos 16b*: 173, endn. 722

*Makos 24a*: endn. 698, 716

*Meilah 14b*: endn. 90

*Moed Katan 15b*: endn. 111

*Nedarim 20ab (fundamental references only)*: 32-68, 81-83, 86-87, 91-92, 111-129, 138-145, 170-194, 196-203

*Nedarim 51a*: endn. 268

*Nidah 13ab*: 138-140, 143-145, 190, endn. 40, 335, 486, 518, 519, 524, 554, 557*, 561, 593, 818

*Nidah 16b*: 95-96, 214, endn. 359, 370, 820, 821

*Nidah 17a*: 56, 95-96, 215, endn. 18, 26, 351, 362, 365, 369, 370, 375, 595, 683, 818, 833

*Nidah 31a*: endn. 35, 355

*Nidah 31b*: endn. 29, 355

*Nidah 71a*: 93, endn. 350, 355, 593

*Pesachim 49b*: 187, endn. 707

*Pesachim 56a*: endn. 846*

*Pesachim 94b*: endn. 86

*Pesachim 112a*: endn. 81, 128, 595

*Pesachim 112b*: endn. 822

Pesachim 113b: 215, endn. 698

Rosh Hashanah 12a: endn. 518

Sanhedrin 57b: endn. 326

Sanhedrin 58b (*fundamental references only*): 84-88, 91-92, 118-122, 123-129, 138-145, endn. 325, 327, 328, 344, 408, 484, 509, 607, 616, 649

Sanhedrin 91b: endn. 86

Sanhedrin 107a: endn. 37, 128, 384

Sanhedrin 108a: endn. 518

Sukkah 49b: 189, endn. 716, 717

Sukkah 52b: endn. 37

Sukkah 53b: endn. 400, 772

Shabbos 33b: 73-74

Shabbos 86a: 95, endn. 360, 361, 370

Shabbos 90b: 173, 191, endn. 723, 726

Shabbos 44: 221

Shabbos 105b: endn. 718

Shabbos 118b: 218-220, endn. 7, 95, 427,

Shabbos 140b: 208, endn. 419

Shabbos 152a: endn. 524, 595,

Shavuos 18b: 65, 93, 98, endn. 347, 355

Shavuos 86a: endn. 369

Sotah 47b: endn. 86

Taanit 10b: endn. 129

Yevamos 12b: 141

Yevamos 20a: endn. 348, 349, 509

Yevamos 34b (*fundamental references only*): 89-92, 118-122, 123-129, 138-145, endn. 335, 518, 554, 568,

Yevamos 37b: endn. 95, 128, 524, 595

Yevamos 55b: endn. 511

Yevamos 79a: endn. 704

Yoma 18b: endn. 95, 524, 595

Yoma 30a: endn. 90

Yoma 83b: endn. 373

Yoma 84a: endn. 373

Zevachim 96b: 223n

Zevachim 113b: endn. 518

\*\*\*\*

Tosefta: endn. 718

Tractate Callah (M. Higger edition): 15, 37n, 40, 41-43, 50-51, 58, 59, 65, 72, 75, 76, 80, 82, 86, 112, 113, 114, 116, 117, 162, 197, endn. 72, 75, 78, 80, 84, 108, 112, 113, 119, 125, 128, 129, 130, 131, 138, 139, 147, 159, 167, 173, 175, 178, 183, 217 (if preceded the Talmud), 218\*, 294, 302, 419, 427, 434\*, 460, 468, 469, 473, 549, 660, 696, 825

Callah Rabti (M. Higger edition): 15, 40, 44-49, 50-51, 54, 58, 64, 65, 86, 112, 113, 114, 116, 117, 162-163, 193, 197, 202-203, endn. 14, 70, 72, 73, 75, 78, 80, 83, 84, 86, 90, 108, 111, 112, 113, 115, 116, 119, 125, 128, 129, 130, 131, 134, 135, 146, 150, 152, 154, 155, 157, 161, 165, 166, 166\*, 168, 169, 170, 171, 173, 175, 179, 181, 194, 217, 236, 237, 244, 245, 275, 294, 321, 348, 434\*, 435, 439, 442, 448, 460, 468, 469, 475, 518, 524, 603, 634, 636, 660, 680, 683, 684, 684\*, 686, 696, 742, 825

## MIDRASHIC SOURCES

Avos D'Rabbi Noson: 32n, 82, endn. 518, 695, 718

Bamidbar Rabah: endn. 704

Ben Sira: 214-215, endn. 172, 509, 820

Braisah D'Nidah: endn. 83

Breishis Rabah: endn. 29, 86, 124, 317, 325, 335, 344, 518, 527, 595, 645*

Breishis Rabsi: endn. 518

Chupat Eliyahu: endn. 29

Derech Eretz Rabah: endn. 698

Koheles Rabah: endn. 595, 848

Lekach Tov: endn. 518

Mechilta: endn. 704

Mechilta D'Rashbi: endn. 704

Mesechtos Derech Eretz (M. Higger edition): 183-184, endn. 660, 668, 691, 696

Mesechtos Zeiros (M. Higger edition): 183, 185, endn. 660, 691, 696, 698

Midrash Agadah: endn. 518

Midrash HaGadol: endn. 518, 698

Midrash Shmuel: endn. 704

Midrash Tehilim-Socher Tov: endn. 595, 698, 704

Mishnas R. Eliezer ben R. Yossi Haglili: endn. 81, 101, 118, 342, 524, 701

Otzar HaAgadah: endn. 286, 705

Otzar Midrashim: endn. 125

Pirkei D'Rabbi Eliezer: endn. 518

Pirkei Rabeinu Hakadosh: endn. 29, 518

Vayikra Rabah: 183, 186, 213-216, endn. 595, 702, 848

Sifra-Toras Cohanim: endn. 267

Sifri: 224n, endn. 518

Sifri Zuta: endn. 518

Tanchuma: 205, endn. 35, 83, 518

Tanna Devei Eliyahu Rabah: endn. 518

Tanna Devei Eliyahu Zuta: endn. 518

Torah Shleimah: endn. 344, 518, 524,

Yalkut Midrashim: endn. 29, 83, 518

Yalkut Shimoni: endn. 124, 704, 848

Yilamdenu: endn. 518

Zohar: 132-134, 134n, 143-145, 150-151, 153-156, 157-158, 161, 170, 200-201, 203, 217, endn. 335, 517, 561, 563, 564, 565, 568, 569, 579, 611, 613, 706

# POST-TALMUDIC TO PRESENT-DAY SOURCES
(*see also pp. 211-212, 226-231*)

## A

Abadi, R. Yitzchak (*Ohr Yitzchak*): endn. *365, 371, 775, 779, 807, 845*

Adams, Tzvi: endn. *724*

R. Aharon Hacohen of Lunil (*Orchos Chaim*): 114, 120, 129, endn. *194, 259\*, 357, 363, 366, 368, 369, 584*

R. Alexander Suslin Hakohen (*HaAgudah*): 60, 115, 121, 122, endn. *328*

Alfandri, R. Aharon (*Yad Aharon*): 158, endn. *330, 605, 609, 621, 647, 731, 737*

Algazi, R. Shlomoh (*Gufei Halachos*): endn. *269*

Altschuler, R. David (*Metzudas David, Metzudas Tzion*): endn. *716*

*Artscroll Edition of the Talmud*: 18, endn. *8, 11, 60, 70, 125, 223, 230\*, 502, 669*

Asaf, R. Simcha: endn. *83*

R. Asher ben Yechiel (*Rabeinu Asher, Rosh*): 59, 117, 119, 121, 136, 138, 140, 141, 142, 153-156, 157, 164, 200, 213, endn. *22, 26, 46, 61, 82, 92, 125, 268, 271, 328, 482, 484, 503, 506, 519, 521, 561, 584, 605, 606, 606\*, 607\*, 613, 614, 626, 647, 660, 727, 730, 731, 732, 752*

Ashkenazi, R. Betzalel (*Shitah Mekubetzes*): 55, 60, 62, 81, 98, 112, 113, 115, 122, endn. *57, 65, 67, 82, 83, 84, 90, 92, 95, 108, 110, 111, 112, 113, 114, 115, 116, 117, 118, 125, 128, 194, 197, 198, 202, 207, 211, 212, 224, 227, 266, 270, 509, 666, 678*

Ashkenazi, R. Yehudah (*Be'er Heitev*): 122, 149, 167, endn. *460*

*Ateres Yeshuah*: endn. *595*

R. Avigdor of France (*Rabeinu Avigdor Tzarfati, Peirushim uPsakim al HaTorah*): endn. *125, 335, 703*

R. Avraham ben Dovid, (*Raavad III, Baalei HaNefesh*): 55-56, 59, 62-64, 75, 77, 80, 87, 99, 111, 113, 117, 133 (virtually alone among extant medieval writings in his interpretation of *Nedarim 20ab*), 136-137, 146-147, 154, 155, 157, 160, 161, 162-163, 167, 170-194, 196-197, 199, 200, 202-203, 213, endn. *2, 10, 22, 26, 30\*, 36, 46, 61, 80, 82, 92, 101, 107, 109, 112, 113, 114, 115, 116, 117, 118, 125, 128, 129, 150, 153, 154, 165, 166\*, 189, 194, 195, 209, 215, 216, 236, 240, 242, 243, 244, 245, 250, 252, 261, 291, 293, 294, 330, 331, 340, 347, 358, 379, 395, 396, 424, 429, 434\*, 447, 476, 477, 478, 522, 536, 548, 549, 571\*, 595, 607, 613, 625, 640, 641, 647, 649, 650, 660, 661, 664, 666, 667, 668, 669, 672, 679, 682, 683, 684, 687, 688, 689, 717, 720, 724, 725, 732, 737, 738, 739, 743, 744, 764* (virtually alone among extant medieval writings in his interpretation of *Nedarim 20ab*)

R. Avraham ben Meir Ibn Ezra (*Ibn Ezra*): endn. *716*

R. Avraham ben Yitzchak (*Raavad II, Sefer HaEshkol – Albeck edition*): 62, 97, 112, 113, 114, 194, 216, endn. *138, 235, 265*

R. Avraham ben Yitzchak of Montepellier (*Peirush R. Avraham min Hahar*): 59, 60, 62, 112, 113, 117, 120, 138, endn. *65, 109, 113, 115, 116, 117, 118, 125, 251, 266, 486, 678*

R. Avraham Hayarchi (*Commentary to Callah Rabti*): 62, 97, 112, 115, 117, *endn. 45, 82, 83, 90, 119, 128, 129, 130, 135, 150, 152, 157, 161, 165, 169, 170, 175, 176, 179, 181, 194, 236, 244, 245, 261, 347, 353, 377, 660*

R. Avraham de Boton (*Lechem Mishneh*): 76, 77, 167, 208, *endn. 251, 256, 298, 300, 302, 309, 775*

R. Avraham "HaMalach": *endn. 595*

R. Avraham Yehoshua Heschel of Apta (*Oheiv Yisrael*): *endn. 595*

Azikri, R. Elazar (*Sefer Charedim*): 87, 115, 117, 157-158, 159-160, 161, 201, *endn. 164, 234, 268, 271, 325, 328, 329, 332, 333, 543, 549, 565, 611, 613, 614, 615, 616* (interpretation of *Sanhedrin 58b*), *618, 621, 625, 638, 645\*, 647*

Azulai, R. Chaim Yosef David (*Chida, Kisei Rachamim, Birchei Yosef, Pesach Einaim, Pnei David*): 115, 208, 216, *endn. 111, 130, 217, 269, 484, 549, 613, 621, 647, 660*

## B

Bergman, R. Meir Tzvi: *endn. 15*

Berlin, R. Naftali Tzvi Yehudah (*Netziv, Meromei Sadeh, Meishiv Davar*): *endn. 268, 748*

Berlin, R. Noach Chaim Tzvi (*Atzei Arazim*): 167, *endn. 256, 335, 518*

Boteach, R. Shmuel (*Kosher Sex*): 12, *endn. 25*

Brandeis, R. Shmaryahu (*Rosh Pinah-Ikvei Habayis*): 167, *endn. 256, 523, 525*

Brown, Dr. Benjamin: *endn. 595*

## C

Caro, R. Yosef (*Kesef Mishneh, Beis Yosef, Bedek Habayis, Shulchan Aruch*): 15, 22-30, 57, 80, 111, 122, 124-125, 129, 132-151, 157-158, 161-165, 170, 190n, 199, 200, 202, 216, 218, *endn. 26, 34, 36, 46, 49, 50, 79, 81, 82, 84, 111, 125, 128, 209, 211, 215, 256, 281, 298, 312, 314, 335, 388, 419, 460, 470, 482, 509, 519, 523, 544, 545, 546, 549, 550, 566, 571, 571\*, 572, 573\*, 575, 576, 577, 578, 582, 583, 584, 585, 586, 589, 600, 621, 638, 645, 682, 689, 748*

R. Chananel (*Rabeinu Chananel*): 73, *endn. 125, 282*

*Chashev HaEfod: endn. 591*

*Col Bo*: 114, 120, 128, *endn. 83, 259\*, 584*

## D

R. David Kimchi (*Radak*): *endn. 419, 716*

Danzig, R. Avraham (*Chochmas Adam*): 63, 161, 162, 203, *endn. 370*

*Dikdukei Sofrim*: *endn. 63, 121, 277, 278, 279, 311*

*Dikdukei Sofrim Hashalem*: *endn. 65, 121*

R. Dovber of Mezritch (*Maggid of Mezritch, Or HaEmes*): *endn. 595*

Dubov, R. Nissan Dovid (*To Live and Live Again*): *endn. 565*

*Dvar Seser*: Preface, 210, *endn. 12, 257, 727*

## E

Einhorn, R. Ze'ev Wolf of Grodno/Vilna (*Maharzu*): *endn. 518, 702*

Eisenstadt, R. Avraham Tzvi Hirsch (*Pischei Teshuvah*): 166, *endn. 507, 604*

Eisenstadt, R. Meir (*Panim Meiros*): 122, 166, *endn. 604, 647*

R. Elazar of Worms (*Sefer HaRokeach, Peirush HaRokeach al HaTorah*): 182, *endn. 7, 83, 128, 425, 427, 660*

R. Eliezer of Beaugency (*Peirush R. Eliezer Mibalganzi*): *endn. 716*

R. Eliezer of Metz (*Re'em, Sefer Yeraim*): 55, 56, 68, 98, 107, *endn. 1, 57, 84, 194, 197, 198, 202, 207, 270, 271, 509*

R. Eliyahu de Vidas (*Reishis Chochmah*): 117, 134n, 153-156, 157-158, 159-160, 161, 201, 216, *endn. 164, 543, 565, 595, 597, 598, 600, 601, 602, 605, 606, 607, 609, 611, 624, 626, 627, 638, 645, 645\*, 647, 828, 829*

R. Eliyahu Hacohen (*Midrash Talpios*): *endn. 565*

R. Eliyahu Mizrachi (*Re'em*): 126

Eliyahu, R. Mordechai (*Darchei Taharah*): 211, *endn. 784, 801*

R. Elimelech of Lizhensk (*Noam Elimelech*): *endn. 595*

Emden, R. Yaakov (*Siddur Yaavetz, Mitas Hakesef, Mitpachat Sofrim, Hagahos al HaShas*): 81, 120, 161, 216, *endn. 75, 83, 125, 285, 304, 316, 328, 358\** (R. Eliezer's personal customs in the bedroom are non-obligatory), *478, 565, 725, 830*

Encyclopedia of Biblical Personalities (*Ishei HaTanach*): *endn. 335*

Encyclopedia L'Chachmei HaTalmud: *endn. 95, 98, 121, 338*

Encyclopedia Talmudis: 3n, *endn. 90, 335, 518, 524, 726, 727, 728, 764, 770*

Engel-Horowitz, R. Avraham Shimon of Zelichov (*Naharei Eish*): *endn. 595*

Epstein, R. Dr. Louis: 212

Epstein, R. Yechiel Michel (*Aruch Hashulchan*): 114, 115, 122, 125, 129, 149, 164-165, 198, 199, 201, *endn. 215, 465, 533, 549, 641*

Even-Shoshan, R.: 211, *endn. 269, 690*

F

Falk, R. Yehoshua (*Drishah, Prishah*): 122, 124-125, 129, 140, 143-144, 144n, 149, 164-165, 198, 201-203, *endn. 37, 114, 256, 310, 478, 482, 517, 518, 519, 520, 522, 523, 525, 533, 536, 546, 558, 561, 576, 613, 638, 764*

Feinstein, R. Moshe (*Igros Moshe*): 8-9, 139-141, 148, 220-221, *endn. 11, 203, 335, 337, 365, 371, 411, 484, 505\*, 506, 509, 521, 527, 549, 554, 555, 557, 572, 613, 626, 833, 845*

Feldman, R. Dr. David: 212, *endn. 335*

Feldman, R. Dr. Emanuel (*Jewish Law and The New Reproductive Technologies*): 3n

Feuerman, R. Simcha (*Es Lifrosh, Es Le'ehov*): Preface, 225n, *endn. 86, 358\*, 595*

Finzi, R. Gur Aryeh HaLevi (*Gur Aryeh*): 122, *endn. 575, 646*

Frankel (R' Shabsi) edition of *Mishneh Torah*: *endn. 298, 301, 481, 529, 609, 755, 762*

Freeman, Yisroel: *endn. 724*

Frisch, R. Daniel (*Kedushah uTznius*): *endn. 595, 785*

G

Ganzfried, R. Shlomoh (*Kitzur Shulchan Aruch*): 115, 161-163, 203

Gold, R. Yechiel Michel (*M'aseif l'Chol Hamachanos*): *endn.* 818

Goldwurm, R. Hersh: *endn.* 165, 596

Grossman, Dr. Avraham (*Vehu Yimshal Bach*): *endn.* 419, 539

# H

Hahn, R. Yosef Yuspa Nordlinger (*Yosef Ometz*): *endn.* 505*

*Halachah Berurah*: *endn.* 484

Halberstam, R. Chaim of Sanz (*Divrei Chaim*): *endn.* 595

Havlin, R. Dr. Shlomoh Zalman: *endn.* 15, 19, 20, 23

Heller, R. Yom Tov Lipman (*Lechem Chamudos*): 115, 122, 164-165, 199, *endn.* 506, 643, 647

Henkin, R. Yehuda (*Bnei Banim*): Preface, 129, 210, 217, *endn. 187, 251, 268, 360, 481, 483, 485, 514, 515, 516, 533, 613, 764, 824, 833, 844, 845*

Henkin, R. Yosef Eliyahu: *endn.* 514

Higger, Dr. Michael: 40, 183

Holzberg, R. Yaakov Shlomoh (*Pri Shlomoh*): *endn.* 554

Horowitz, R. Chaim Meir: *endn.* 83

Horowitz, R. Elazar Moshe (Chief Rabbi of Pinsk): *endn.* 268, 341

Horowitz, R. Yaakov Yitzchak (*Chozeh-Seer of Lublin*): *endn.* 595

Horowitz, R. Yeshayah (*Shnei Luchos Habris*): 159-160, 161, 201, *endn. 565, 616, 622, 624, 627, 629* (influence upon Chabad Chasidic teaching), *633*

# I

*Igeres Hakodesh* (medieval): *endn. 83, 290, 379* (authorship of), *383, 384*

*Imrei Aish*: *endn.* 591

*Imrei Binah*: *endn.* 591

Isserles, R. Moshe (*Rema*): 27, 29-30, 114, 122, 124-125, 129, 149, 156, 158, 160, 163, 164-165 (and other permissive post-medieval/post-*Shulchan Aruch* authorities), 166-168 (censorship and misrepresentations of), 170, 199-202, *endn. 4, 36, 50, 83, 246, 412, 456, 482, 509, 523, 534, 536, 546, 549, 576, 589, 618, 628, 638, 639, 645*, 647, 649, 650, 660, 726, 752, 801*

*Iyun Yaakov*: *endn.* 128

# J

Jacobs, R. Dr. Louis: 212, *endn.* 595

# K

Kagan, R. Yisrael Meir (*Mishnah Berurah-Biur Halachah*): 15, 63, 161-163, 203, 217, *endn 116, 370*

Kaidanover, R. Aharon Shmuel (*Maharshak*): *endn.* 659

Kanievsky, R. Shmaryahu Yosef Chaim (*Biur to Callah Rabti*): *endn.* 130, 171

Kanievsky, R. Yisrael Yaakov (*Steipler Gaon; Karyana d'Igarta*): 104n

Kantor, R. Mattis: *endn.* 19

Kapach, R. Yosef: 103n, *endn. 268, 360, 403, 419, 481, 496, 497, 595*

Kaplan, R. Aryeh: *endn.* 33

Kaplan, Dr. Lawrence: 223n

Katz, R. Tzvi Hakohen (*Nachlas Tzvi*): 159

Kayam, R. Maor (*Harchavot l'Simchat Habayot v'Birchato*): Preface, 96n, 122n, 129n, 210n, 221n, *endn. 72, 179, 269, 355, 555, 727, 736*, 777*

Kook, R. Avraham Yitzchak (*Ezras Cohen, Shmoneh Kovtzim*): 122n, 224n, *endn. 555*

*Kovetz Meforshim* (*Yerid Haseforim*): *endn. 112, 114, 116, 221, 228, 268, 462, 504, 613*

*Kovetz Shitos Kamai*: *endn. 7, 125, 128, 194, 211, 213, 222, 225, 241, 263, 303, 353, 357, 360, 363, 364, 366, 368, 427, 452-455, 487-488, 495, 501, 505, 530-532, 547, 660, 698, 703*

Kramer, R. Eliyahu (*Vilna Gaon, Biur HaGra*): 167, 189, *endn. 50, 256, 346, 509, 676, 703*

## L

*Ladaat Le'ehov*: Preface

Lampronti, R. Yitzchak (*Pachad Yitzchak*): 117, 161, *endn. 269, 348, 631*

*Lechem Shearim*: *endn. 130*

R. Levi ben Gershon (*Ralbag*): 224n-225n

Levi, R. Yehudah (*The Science in Torah*): 222, *endn. 355, 373*

R. Levi Yitzchak of Berditchev (*Or HaEmes*): *endn. 565, 595*

*Likutei HaPardes*: 827, *endn. 81, 83, 108, 111, 112, 115, 119, 469, 471, 809*

Loew, R. Yehudah (*Maharal, Nesivos Olam*):

   Better to study and rule Jewish law from Talmud rather than from codifications: 204

   Family Tree: *endn. 335*

Luria, R. David (*Radal*): *endn. 702*

Luria, R. Shlomoh (*Yam Shel Shlomoh*): 59, 121, 122, 124, 164-165, 199, *endn. 22, 92, 271, 328, 503, 613, 642, 727, 730*

Luria, R. Yitzchak (*Kisvei HaArizal*): 152, 201, *endn. 561, 590, 593, 594, 595, 638*

Luzzato, R. Moshe Chaim (*Ramchal, Derech Hashem*): *endn. 565, 595*

## M

Maimonides (see: R. Moshe ben Maimon)

*Mahari Asad*: *endn. 591*

R. Malachi ben Yaakov Hacohen (*Yad Malachi*): *endn. 30, 234, 260, 262, 345, 485, 546, 549, 583, 585, 638, 674, 685*

Makbili, R. Yohai (*Mifal Mishneh Torah*): *endn. 482*

Margolis, R. Reuven (*Mekor Chesed, Nitzutzei Ohr*): *endn. 269, 706*

*Mayim Ganim*: *endn. 130*

*Medicine in the Bible and the Talmud*: 846*

Medini, R. Chaim Chizkiyahu (*Sdei Chemed*): *endn. 518, 736**

*Mefaresh*: 60-61, 115, 120, 153-155, 157, 213, *endn. 80, 90, 110, 111, 113, 115, 118, 125, 195, 464*, 478*, 602*, 606, 615, 647, 666*

R. Meir Abulafia (*Yad Ramah*): 84n, *endn. 324, 328, 509*

R. Meir Hacohen of Rothenburg (*Hagahos Maimonios*): 119, *endn. 484, 584, 650*

R. Meir Leibush (*Malbim*): *endn. 716*

Melamed, R. Eliezer (*Simchat Habayit v'Birchato*): Preface, 74n, 96n, 113, 113n, 114, 115, 117, 122n, 129n, 149n, 210n, 221n, *endn. 72, 75, 125, 352, 555, 736*, 741*

R. Menachem Hameiri (*Beis HaBechirah*): 56, 65, 78-79, 98, 112, 121, 178, *endn. 61, 65, 108, 110, 111, 113, 115, 116, 117, 118, 125, 128, 195, 259, 263, 305, 306, 327, 362, 676, 678, 716, 717*

R. Menachem Ibn Zerach (*Tzeidah Laderech*): 60, 114, 122, *endn. 211, 213, 225, 259\**

*Mesores Moshe*: *endn. 203*

Messas, R. Yosef (*Mayim Chaim*): 96n, 122n, 221n, *endn. 362, 365, 369, 845*

Messner, R. Henoch (*Contraception in Contemporary Orthodox Judaism*): 91n, 118n

Meyer, R. Gedalia (*Contraception in Contemporary Orthodox Judaism*): 91n, 118n

R. Meyuchas ben Eliyahu (*Peirush Rabeinu Meyuchas*): 121, 125-129, 198, 202, *endn. 527, 536*

*Midrash Talpios*: *endn. 565*

*Mitpachat Sofrim*: *endn. 565*

R. Mordechai ben Hillel Hakohen (*Mordechai*): 60, 115, 119, 122, *endn. 92, 351, 584, 730*

R. Moshe ben Maimon (Maimonides, *Peirush Hamishnayos-Commentary to the Mishnah, Mishneh Torah, Moreh HaNevuchim-Guide for the Perplexed, Treatise on Cohabitation*):

   censorship of *Mishneh Torah*: 128, 156, 200-201, *endn. 609*

   *Commentary on Ethics of the Fathers*: 206n, *endn. 335, 360, 409, 419, 595, 818*

   *Guide for the Perplexed*: *endn. 3, 417, 419*

   *Hilchos Memrim*: 2n, 224, *endn. 87, 348, 524,*

   *Mishneh Torah, Isurei Biah 21:9* as understood by Rabeinu Yonah and Rabeinu Nissim: *endn. 484*

   quoting Aristotle: *endn. 417, 419*

   *Treatise on Cohabitation*: *endn. 419*

   two versions of *Mishneh Torah Isurei Biah 21:9*: 118-120, 123-124

   collective references: 2n, 18, 56, 60, 61, 65, 74, 76-77, 80, 81, 84n, 87, 98-99, 102, 103-106, 107, 112-120, 123-129, 132, 135-140, 146-147, 150-151, 154-156, 159-160, 161, 164-165, 166-168, 170, 175, 180, 191, 193, 196-203, 206n, 214, 216, 217, 218, 224, 224n, *endn. 3, 8, 16, 19, 32, 49, 50, 67, 72, 87, 111, 124, 125, 128, 204, 238, 246, 251, 255, 256, 261, 263, 267, 288, 296, 297, 298, 300, 301, 302, 305, 314, 324, 327, 330, 331, 335, 340, 348, 351, 360, 384, 386, 387, 390, 391, 392, 396, 398, 401, 403, 406, 408, 409, 411, 412, 414, 414\*, 417, 419, 423, 437, 470, 481, 482, 484, 485, 486, 490, 492, 494, 509, 511, 517, 519, 524, 528, 529, 533, 534, 536, 549, 559, 571\*, 588, 595, 609, 613, 625, 633, 639, 647, 649, 650, 652, 689, 695, 727, 737, 741, 755, 762, 764, 801, 806, 818, 834, 837, 846\*, 847*

R. Moshe ben Nachman (Nachmanides): *endn. 83*

R. Moshe de Leon (first to circulate copies of the *Zohar*): 134, *endn. 542*

R. Moshe of Trani (*Kiryas Sefer*): 120, *endn. 268*

R. Moshe Leima (*Chelkas Mechokek*): 122, 149

Movshovitz, R. Shmuel David HaLevi (*Sdeh Eliyahu*): *endn. 658*

## N

Nachmanson, R. Yehudah Leib *Sheyekadesh Atzmo*: 211, *endn. 75, 356, 593, 727, 777*

R. Netanel ben Yeshaya of Yemen (*Maor Ha'afelah*): 121, *endn 268*

Newfield, R. Yossi: *endn. 230\*, 268, 269, 330, 341, 408, 484, 505\*, 518, 572, 616*

R. Nissim ben Reuven of Gerona (*Rabeinu Nissim, Ran*): 59, 78, 120, 140, *endn. 32, 70, 116, 118, 128, 188, 190, 215, 268, 324, 327, 484, 490, 492, 528, 559, 584, 613*

## O

*Olas Yitzchak*: *endn. 591*

Oliver, R. Yehoishophot: *endn. 419*

*Or HaEmes*: *endn. 595*

Orenstein, R. Yaakov Meshulam (*Yeshuos Yaakov*): 120, 122, *endn. 324, 328, 647*

*Otzar Hageonim*: *endn. 716*

*Otzar Haposkim*: 3n, *endn. 335, 518, 568, 574, 650, 818*

*Otzar Mefarshei Hatalmud*: *endn. 716*

R. Ovadiah ben Avraham Bartenura (*Peirush R. Ovadia Bartenura*): 73

## P

*Peirush HaRokeach al Hatorah*: 182, *endn. 419, 690*

R. Peretz ben Eliyahu of Corbeil (*Rabeinu Peretz*): 60, 115, 213, *endn. 59, 77, 84, 90, 108, 110, 111, 113, 117, 118, 125, 194, 196, 230, 464*

*Pnei David*: *endn. 269*

*Pnei Moshe*: *endn. 650*

*Pokeach Ivrim*: *endn. 86*

*Pri Hasadeh*: *endn. 591*

Pruss, Julius (*Biblical and Talmudic Medicine*): *endn. 373*

## R

Rabinovich, R. Nosson David: *endn. 19*

*Rambam Meduyak*: *endn. 296, 482*

Rapoport, R. Chaim (*Judaism and Homosexuality*): 230, *endn. 45, 511, 595, 736\*, 807*

Ratzabi, R. Yitzchak (*Shulchan Aruch Hamekutzar*): *endn. 511*

Reischer, R. Yaakov (*Iyun Yaakov*): *endn. 128*

Ribner, R. Dr. David (*The Newlywed's Guide to Physical Intimacy*): 12

*Ritz* (quoted in *Shitah Mekubetzes*): *endn. 65, 84, 108, 110, 111, 112, 113, 114, 115, 116, 117, 118, 125, 128, 194, 266, 666, 678*

Rivkash, R. Moshe (*Be'er Hagolah*): 159, 167, *endn. 626*

Rokeach, R. Elazar of Amsterdam (*Arbaah Turei Even*): *endn. 298, 301*

Rosenbaum, Talli: 3n, 12, *endn. 12, 802*

Rosenfeld, Dr. Jennie (*The Newlywed's Guide to Physical Intimacy*): 12

Rosner, Dr. Fred: *endn. 373, 419, 846\**

## S

R. Saadiah Gaon (*Arabic Commentary on the Bible*): *endn. 419, 716*

*Sarei Ha'elef*: *endn. 580*

Schneersohn, R. Menachem Mendel (*Tzemach Tzedek, Derech Mitzvosecha*): 142, *endn. 561, 595*

Schneersohn, R. Yosef Yitzchak (*Sefer HaSichos, Igros Kodesh*): *endn. 595, 629*

Schneerson, R. Menachem Mendel (*Likutei Sichos, Igros Kodesh, Teshuvos uBiurim, Hadranim al HaRambam*): endn. 27, 83, 482, 565, 629, 848

R. Schneur Zalman of Liadi (*Shulchan Aruch HaRav*): 218-220, endn. 15, 81, 86, 561, 565, 595, 629, 633, 727

Schneuri, R. Dovber (*Pokeach Ivrim*): endn. 86

Schonbuch, R. Daniel (*Understanding and Treating Issues in Marital Intimacy*): 12

*Sefer Chasidim*: 107, 115, 117, endn. 11, 200, 427, 778

*Sefer Hamiktzo'os*: endn. 83

Shapiro, R. Dr. Marc: 96n, 144n, endn. 565, 777, 807

Shapiro, R. Tzvi Elimelech of Dinov (*Derech Pikudecha*): endn. 595

Sheilat, R. Yitzchak: endn. 482

*Sheiltot D'Rav Hai Gaon*: endn. 500, 560

R. Sherira Gaon (*Igeres Rav Sherira Gaon*): endn. 19, 129, 634, 635, 818

Shevel, R. Chaim Dov (*Kisvei Ramban*): endn. 379

*Shevet Mussar*: endn. 294

R. Shimon ben Tzemach Duran (*Ohev Mishpat*): endn. 565

Shlanger, R. Rafael (*Mishkan Yisrael*): 211, endn. 635, 734

Rabeinu Shlomoh: endn. 678

R. Shlomoh Yitzchaki (*Rashi*): 60, 73, 84n, 94, 115, 117, 153, 157, 208, 218, 224n, endn. 29, 83, 124, 125, 128, 234, 269, 305, 308, 320, 326, 344, 350, 360, 369, 408, 419, 464*, 478*, 509, 511, 524, 595, 602*, 647, 669, 697, 716, 724, 823

R. Shmuel ben Meir (*Rashbam*): endn. 128

R. Shmuel ben Meshulam Yerondi (*Ohel Moed*): 62, 64, 136, endn. 109, 110, 112, 113, 117, 125, 128, 547, 660

R. Shmuel Feivush (*Beis Shmuel*): 167-168, 202, endn. 5, 456, 638, 649, 650

R. Simchah ben Shmuel of Vitri (*Machzor Vitri*): 65

Sirkis, R. Yoel (*Bayis Chadash, Bach*): 167, endn. 256, 312, 503

Slifkin, R. Dr. Natan: 222, endn. 86

Sofer, R. Moshe (*Chasam Sofer*): endn. 26

Sofer, R. Yaakov Chaim (*Kaf Hachaim*): 64, 161, 163, 203

*Soncino Edition of the Talmud*: 18, endn. 8, 131, 146, 168, 177, 698, 717

Spira, R. Eliyahu (*Elyah Rabah*): 87, 122, 142, 157, 158, endn. 332, 370, 549, 612, 613, 616, 620, 645*, 647

Steinsaltz, R. Adin – (*Steinsaltz Edition of the Talmud, Simple Words*): 12, 18, endn. 8, 11, 86, 127, 129, 140, 223, 352, 370, 502, 557*, 707, 716, 820, 821

Stern, R. Moshe (*Be'er Moshe*): endn. 125, 261, 568, 658, 775, 777

T

Tabak, R. Shlomoh Yehudah (*Erech Shai*): 144-145, endn. 568, 569, 613

*Taharas Am Yisroel*: endn. 810

*Taharas Yisrael*: 208-209

*Talmid Rabeinu Tam*: 59, 60, 115, 121, endn. 268, 504, 613

*Talmidei Rabeinu Peretz*: 60, 115, 121

*Tanya*: endn. 81, 561, 595, 629, 633

Tauger, R. Eliyahu (*Mishneh Torah: A new translation with commentary and notes*): 212, endn. 419

Teomim, R. Yosef (*Pri Megadim*): 220, endn. 116

Teshuvos Hageonim: endn. 95, 353

R. Tanchum Hayerushalmi (*Sefer Hamaspik*): endn. 513

Torah Lishmah: endn. 269

Torah Temimah: endn. 369, 736*

Tosfos: 56, 59, 91-92, 118-121, 198, 215-216

Tosfos Chachmei Angliah: endn. 524

Tosfos Hashalem: endn. 112, 114, 116, 268, 335, 518, 613

Tosfos Yeshanim: 56, 59, 60, 68, 115, 120, 121, 141, endn. 96, 128, 271, 509, 595

Treibitz, R. Dr. Meir: endn. 19

Tzavaas HaRivash: endn. 595

R. Tzvi Hirsch of Ziditchev (*Sur Mera*): endn. 595

U

Ufakadata Navecha: 208, endn. 775, 777, 779

V

Vital, R. Chaim: 152 (on sanctification of marital sex), endn. 561, 590, 593, 594 (belief about spontaneous generation of lice), 595 (on sanctification of marital sex)

Vital, R. Shmuel: endn. 593

W

Wahrman, R. Avraham Dovid of Buczacz (*Eshel Avraham, Ezer Mekudash, Mili d'Chasidusa, Birchas David*): 32n, 148 (*Beis Yosef* implies occasional intra-anal ejaculation is permitted within marriage by the letter of the law), endn. 36, 125, 268, 335, 509, 518, 525*, 533, 553, 639, 573

Walters, R. Moshe (*The Making of a Halachic Decision*): 14n, endn. 546, 771

Wasserman, R. Elchanan Bunim (*Kovetz Shiurim*): endn. 20

Weiss-Halivni, R. Dr. David: endn. 19

Winkler, R. Gershon: 212

Wolowelsky, R. Dr. Joel B. (*Jewish Law and The New Reproductive Technologies*): 3n

Y

R. Yaakov ben Asher (*Arbaah Turim, Tur*): 59, 63, 77, 79-80, 111, 114, 122, 124-125, 129, 135-137, 138, 139, 141-142, 147, 159, 160, 164, 170, 200-202, 216, endn. 26, 36, 46, 82, 111, 125, 194, 209, 211, 215, 268, 281, 309, 311, 312, 313, 335, 419, 459, 470, 503, 517, 519, 521, 533, 534, 536, 546, 549, 609, 613, 626, 650, 660

R. Yaakov ben Meir (*Rabeinu Tam*): endn. 708

R. Yaakov ben Yehudah Landau (*HaAgur*): 59, 117, endn. 161, 478, 632, 660

Yafeh, R. Yosef (*Ashreichem Yisrael*): 211

R. Yehudah the Pious (*R. Yehudah Hachasid, Sefer Chasidim*): 107, 117, 188, endn. 200, 425, 427, 428, 429, 463, 778

R. Yehudah bar Kalonymous of Speyer (*Erchei Tannaim v'Amoriam*): endn. 69

R. Yeruchem ben Meshulam (*Rabeinu Yeruchem*): 60, 115, 209, endn. 92, 268, 584, 613, 730

R. Yeshayah of Trani I (*Rid*): 59, 94, 119, 121, 124, 141, 144, 198, endn. 269, 484, 560, 716

R. Yeshayah of Trani II (*Riaz*): 59, 121, 198, endn. 125, 509, 560

R. Yisrael Alnaqua (*Menoras Hamaor*): 60, 62, 64, 114, 121, 156, 216, endn. 50, 83, 139, 140, 142, 175, 194, 238, 252, 287, 379, 382, 460, 470, 548, 608, 660, 825

R. Yisrael Baal Shem Tov: endn. 595

R. Yitzchak of Dampierre (*Rabeinu Yitzchak, Ri, Tosfos*): 59, 91-92, 118-119, 121, 123-125, 129, 132, 136-151, 155-156, 157-158, 159, 161, 164-165, 166, 170, 193, 198-203, endn. 165, 225, 268, 328, 344, 482, 484, 485, 492, 494, 503, 508, 509, 517, 518, 519, 521, 523, 527, 533, 534, 549, 561, 568, 576, 607*, 613, 616, 625, 626, 638, 639, 650, 748, 752, 764

R. Yitzchak Aboab (*Menoras Hamaor*): 65, 153, 160, endn. 80, 83, 128, 136, 258, 600, 608, 624, 627

R. Yitzchak Alfasi (*Rif*): 65, 94-97, endn. 125, 165, 260, 261, 353, 354, 369, 377, 482,

R. Yitzchak of Carcassonne (*Peirush R. Yitzchak Karkosha al HaRif*): endn. 357, 364, 366, 369

R. Yitzchak ben Moshe of Vienna (*Or Zarua*): endn. 818

R. Yitzchak ben Sheshes (*Rivash*): 144n, endn. 565

R. Yitzchak ben Yehudah Abravanel: endn. 565, 716

R. Yitzchak ben Yosef of Corbeil (*Sefer Mitzvot Katan*): 60, 62, 112, 113, 114, 121, 202-203, endn. 128, 237, 372, 439, 584, 742

Yoffe, R. Mordechai (*Levush*): 63, 114, 122, 125, 129, 164-165, 199, endn. 213, 246, 518, 534, 549, 640, 645*, 647

R. Yom Tov ibn Asevilli (*Ritva*): 60, 115, endn. 82, 211, 224, 508

R. Yonah ben Avraham of Gerona (*Rabeinu Yonah, Sefer Hayirah*): 59, 78, 120, endn. 32, 324, 328, 484, 490, 494, 528, 534, 613, 698

R. Yosef Bechor Shor of Orleans (*Peirush al HaTorah*): endn. 335

R. Yosef Chaim (*Ben Ish Chai*): endn. 592, (269)

Yosef, R. Ovadia (*Yabia Omer*): endn. 330, 484, 565, 572

Z

R. Zerachiah Halevi of Gerona (*Hasagos al Baalei HaNefesh*): 193-194

## About the Author

Yaakov Shapiro grew up in Conservative, Modern Orthodox, Lithuanian-Charedi and Chabad-Chasidic Jewish schools, earning rabbinical ordination in the latter.

A nine-year researcher, translator, writer and filmmaker for Chabad-Lubavitch's media wing, he is currently spending his days in the world of business. But he continues to spend the nights researching and writing on areas of Jewish belief that can, and have, put sincere students of Torah at risk – psychologically, emotionally, physically, and therefore spiritually – with the confident belief that exhaustive source-textual analysis and reexamined translation will uncover a balanced, humane understanding of the Creator's plan for Its creation.

www.ingramcontent.com/pod-product-compliance
Lightning Source LLC
Chambersburg PA
CBHW061923220426
43662CB00012B/1789